FAR EASTERN TOUR

Far Eastern Tour
The Canadian Infantry in Korea, 1950–1953

BRENT BYRON WATSON

McGill-Queen's University Press
Montreal & Kingston · London · Ithaca

© McGill-Queen's University Press 2002
ISBN 0-7735-2372-3

Legal deposit third quarter 2002
Bibliothèque nationale du Québec

Printed in Canada on acid-free paper.

This book has been published with the help of a grant from the Humanities and Social Sciences Federation of Canada, using funds provided by the Social Sciences and Humanities Research Council of Canada.

McGill-Queen's University Press acknowledges the financial support of the Government of Canada through the Book Publishing Industry Development Program (BPIDP) for its publishing activities. We also acknowledge the support of the Canada Council for the Arts for our publishing program.

National Library of Canada Cataloguing in Publication Data

Watson, Brent Byron, 1970–
    Far Eastern tour: the Canadian infantry in Korea, 1950–1953 / Brent Byron Watson.
    Includes bibliographical references and index.
    ISBN 0-7735-2372-3
    1. Korean War, 1950–1953 – Participation, Canadian. 2. Canada. Canadian Army – History – Korean War, 1950–1953. 3. Soldiers – Canada – History – 20th century. I. Title.
DS919.2.W37 2002   951.904'2   C2002-901520-0

Typeset in Sabon 10.5/13
by Caractéra inc., Quebec City

Contents

Abbreviations vii
Preface: Return to Korea ix
Acknowledgments xv

Introduction: Bums from the Slums 3

1 Slit-Trench Attitude 18
2 A Lot of Good Men Died 32
3 Domain of the Golden Dragon 47
4 Rice Burners and KATCOMS 62
5 Keeping the Gunners in Good Training 77
6 Pucker Factor 93
7 Butcher's Bill 108
8 Permanent Souvenirs 125
9 Forgotten People 142
10 Rum and Coke 157

Conclusion: Kap'yong Couldn't Have Been Much of a Battle 175

Notes 181
Bibliography 219
Index 229

Abbreviations

BCIB	British Commonwealth Infantry Brigade
CAORT	Canadian Army Operational Research Team
CASF	Canadian Army Special Force
CCF	Communist Chinese Forces
CCP	Casualty Clearing Post
CIB	Canadian Infantry Brigade
CO	commanding officer
DEA	Department of External Affairs
DGMS	Directorate General, Medical Services
DGMT	Directorate General of Military Training
DHH	Directorate of History and Heritage
DND	Department of National Defence
DOW	died of wounds
DRBD	Defence Research Board
FDS	Field Dressing Station
GSW	gunshot wound
KATCOM	Korean Augmentation Troops, Commonwealth
KATUSA	Korean Augmentation Troops, U.S. Army
KIA	killed in action
KSC	Korean Service Corps
LDSH	Lord Strathcona's Horse
LMG	light machine gun
MLR	Main Line of Resistance
MMG	medium machine gun
MO	medical officer
NCO	non-commissioned officer
NA	National Archives of Canada

NATO	North Atlantic Treaty Organization
NSU	non-specific urethritis
POW	prisoner of war
PRO	Public Record Office
PPCLI	Princess Patricia's Canadian Light Infantry
QMG	quarter-master general
R&R	rest and recreation
RAP	Regimental Aid Post
RCAMC	Royal Canadian Army Medical Corps
RCE	Royal Canadian Engineers
RCHA	Royal Canadian Horse Artillery
RCR	Royal Canadian Regiment
ROK	Republic of Korea
R22eR	Royal 22e Régiment
SAW	section automatic weapon
SIW	self-inflicted wound
SMG	submachine gun
WD	War Diary
WIA	wounded in action
WO	War Office

PREFACE

Return to Korea

Five decades after the signing of the ceasefire agreement at Panmunjom, the experiences of the Canadian infantry in the Korean War remain forgotten. Although there are numerous popular accounts of the Canadian Army in Korea, we still know little about the realities and practical details of the infantry's wartime experiences. This is a serious gap in Canadian military historiography. An in-depth study of soldiers' experiences expands our understanding of the conflict and furnishes the Canadian military with an institutional memory of its first major United Nations operation. As recent events have shown, the military ignores history at its peril. Somalia was not the first time the Canadians ran into difficulties in an unfamiliar operational environment. Many of the problems experienced by the Airborne Regiment were encountered by the soldiers of the 25th Canadian Infantry Brigade in Korea four decades earlier. A study of these problems provides the military with the analytical perspective it needs to understand its own recent history.

The Korean War remains the largest Canadian military operation of the post-1945 era. Although small by First and Second World War standards, the army's contribution of the 25th Canadian Infantry Brigade Group was by no means insignificant. Only the South Koreans, Americans, and British fielded larger contingents. The combat strength of the 25th Brigade lay in its three infantry battalions, drawn from the Royal Canadian Regiment, the Princess Patricia's Canadian Light Infantry, and the Royal 22e Régiment. Together, these units accounted for approximately two-thirds of the 25th Brigade's total manpower.

The terrain and limited nature of combat operations in Korea resulted in the infantry doing almost all the fighting. Tanks were important early in the war, but by the time the first Canadians took to the field they were primarily used as mobile artillery platforms. The static phase of the fighting also saw the artillery and engineers restricted to combat support missions. Rarely did soldiers from these arms engage the enemy in close combat. To speak of the 25th Brigade in the context of the Korean War is, then, to speak of the men in the three infantry battalions. Korea was the infantry's war, and a study of these battalions' experiences captures the essence of the larger Canadian involvement.

Some indication of how difficult the infantry's Far Eastern tours actually were can be found in the recently declassified Central Registry files at the National Archives of Canada. Unavailable to earlier researchers, these files suggest an army that was poorly prepared for service in Korea. Being official headquarters documents, however, the Central Registry holdings yield few clues about the repercussions on the common soldier of this unpreparedness. For this, I was compelled to look elsewhere.

In the summer of 1996 I had the opportunity to attend the Korean Veterans Association's conference in Calgary, Alberta. Through a series of historical questionnaires and interviews, the personal experiences of Korean veterans were brought to life. To actually hear these men talk about friends who were killed because a Sten gun jammed, or who returned to Canada as alcoholics after their Far Eastern tours, had a profound effect on me. For three days I listened to their stories, often late into the night. I became utterly convinced that something had gone terribly wrong in the ranks of the Canadian infantry in Korea and that these men had endured a needlessly difficult and uncomfortable ordeal.

With this hypothesis in mind, I travelled to the Republic of Korea in the fall of 1997. Unlike the soldiers of the 25th Brigade, I arrived by jumbo jet, not troopship. I had also acquired a reasonable knowledge of the Korean culture, geography, and climate, and could even speak a few words of the language. More importantly perhaps, I also had the benefit of proper medical preparations. Nevertheless, I experienced severe culture shock after my arrival as I adjusted to the sights, sounds, and smells of this fascinating yet completely foreign country. I can only imagine what Canadian soldiers must have thought as they stumbled down the gangplank into wartorn Pusan without being properly indoctrinated. And despite bed nets and copious amounts of insect repellent, I still managed to get eaten alive by aggressive mosquitoes during my first few nights in Korea. But unlike the soldiers of the 25th Brigade, my physician had prescribed me an effective malarial suppressant.

My first few days in Korea were spent in Seoul conducting research at the Eighth U.S. Army Historical Office. Located in the Yongsan Garrison, the office rarely sees researchers. This is a shame because it contains some incredibly useful material, especially on operational research. My time at Yongsan also allowed me to experience American army hospitality firsthand.

After gorging myself on T-bone steaks, potato salad, and ice-cold Coca-Colas, all courtesy of the Eighth U.S. Army, I boarded a rickety train for the Kap'yong River Valley in the rugged Korean interior. My objective was to visit Hill 677 where the Princess Patricias had made their famous stand during the battle of the Kap'yong River in April 1951.

Arriving in the sleepy little town of Kap'yong without a clue of where the battlefield was, I pulled out my compass and a wrinkled map photocopied from the Canadian official history and estimated that it was about seven kilometres to the north. With no public transportation to be found, I set out on foot but was lucky enough to be offered a ride in the back of a small farm truck. Reaching the tiny village of Naech'on, I walked along the Kap'yong River until I came to a small apple orchard flanked by large rice paddies. Sure enough, amongst the apple trees, I found the granite monument commemorating the battle of Kap'yong. In the background stood Hill 677. There were more trees on the hill than at the time of the battle, but its distinctive shape was clearly visible. Also visible above the monument was a massive spider's web. Veterans had warned me about the huge spiders, but I never expected them to be *that* big.

The next day I climbed to the top of Hill 677. Equipped with only a camera and a large stick given to me by my Korean hosts to ward off wild pigs, I made the difficult climb in just over two hours. Being in reasonable shape, I was amazed at the difficulty of the trek. I counted myself fortunate in not having to carry fifty pounds of equipment (more than twenty-two kilograms) as the Patricias had done.

After Kap'yong, I returned to Seoul, where I met the Canadian Forces attaché, Colonel Keith Eddy. He kindly agreed to escort me to the area along the Imjin River, where the rear echelons of the 25th Brigade had been located. From my earlier research, it was apparent that life on the banks of the Imjin had not changed all that much since the war. Most of the civilian population were poor farmers, and many of the roads just dirt tracks. It was hot, dusty, and smelly, and as I surveyed the scenes around me I was struck by a sudden feeling of homesickness. For people accustomed to the North American lifestyle, this was a very difficult place to spend a year. In fact, the American army considers nearby Camp Casey, the operational base of the 2nd U.S. Infantry Division, a "hardship" posting. Yet I could not help but feel that compared to the combat soldiers of the 25th Canadian Infantry Brigade, this current generation of fighting men had it easy. Nevertheless, every American soldier I spoke with could not wait for the day when his Far Eastern tour would be over. Moreover, despite being within artillery range of North Korea, Camp Casey has, among other things, a Burger King, a Baskin and Robbins, a bowling alley, a huge swimming pool, baseball diamonds, a large Post Exchange, video rental stores, a library, a theatre, a bookstore, a golf course, and several canteens. Canadian infantrymen in Korea could not even count on regular mail service, let alone a Whopper Burger!

Korea left an indelible imprint on me, as is reflected in the pages that follow. Having said this, the exhilaration of travelling around Korea, of interviewing veterans, and of accessing recently declassified documents did not necessarily translate into a painless writing process. As I went through the chapters, I was troubled by what seemed at times to be an endless catalogue of criticisms. From documenting the mind-numbing routine of life in the front line to lambasting medical authorities for their lack of foresight, I have very little to say that can be construed as "positive." This bothered me, for I have always believed it far easier to criticize than to offer constructive solutions, especially in today's politically correct social milieu. I therefore consoled myself with the notion that the ultimate legacy of the infantry's experiences in Korea lies in the lessons they have to offer. This, I believe, is *Far Eastern Tour*'s most important contribution.

This year marks the fifty-second anniversary of the outbreak of the Korean War. Barring any major changes in the international security scene, the men who fought in Korea will soon be this country's largest group of surviving war veterans. The media and general public are bound to pick up on this, leading to a profusion of popular commemorations of the war in both film and print. By showing that Korea was not Canada's last "good fight," this book reminds people that war is a terrible thing. All too often the public views war through the antiseptic lens of a high-tech gun camera – not from the perspective of the lowly combat soldier on the ground, who must actually do the fighting and dying. As the great French military theorist Ardant du Picq argued, the soldier is the first weapon of battle; study him, for it is he who brings reality to it. Whether this book succeeds in bringing reality to the experiences of the Canadian infantry in Korea, I leave for the reader to decide.

Brent Watson
Vernon, British Columbia

Acknowledgments

Many people assisted me in researching and writing this book. My warmest appreciation goes to the Korean veterans who answered my lengthy questionnaires and granted me interviews, often at short notice. Without the benefit of the insights offered by these men, this book would not have been possible.

Special thanks to Professors David Zimmerman, Patricia Roy, Ian MacPherson, James Boutilier, David Bercuson, and Chris Madsen. I would also like to thank Dr Stephen Harris for his unwavering support over the years. Colonel Keith Eddy and family deserve special mention for providing a cheery home environment during my stay in Seoul and for arranging my visit to the DMZ.

A big thanks to all my friends and family – you know who you are. Finally, a very special thanks to my wife Jennifer, to whom this book is dedicated, for enduring my frequent bouts of grumpiness and my many long absences.

Research for this book was funded by doctoral fellowships from the Department of National Defence and the Social Sciences and Humanities Research Council of Canada.

FAR EASTERN TOUR

INTRODUCTION

Bums from the Slums

On 8 August 1950 a full-page recruiting advertisement in the nation's major newspapers announced: "The Canadian Army Wants Men Now ... to meet aggression in accordance with the United Nations Charter." Preference would be given to veterans of the Second World War, and the term of enlistment was for eighteen months – "longer if required due to an emergency action taken by Canada pursuant to an International Agreement."

So began recruitment of the Canadian Army Special Force (CASF), the army's contribution to the war in Korea. Canada's navy and air force had quickly been committed to the fighting following the outbreak of hostilities on the Korean peninsula six weeks earlier, but the dilapidated state of Canada's postwar army precluded an immediate ground response. In the years following the Second World War, the Liberal government of Mackenzie King had slashed the defence budget from its wartime peak of $4.2 billion in 1943 to only $196 million in 1947.[1] Cold War tensions and Canada's entry into the North Atlantic Treaty Organization (NATO) in 1949 saw a slight increase, but most of the money went to the Royal Canadian Air Force.

The Canadian Army of 1950 was, then, only a shadow of its Second World War self. In 1945 the Canadian Army had over half a million men under arms, but by the outbreak of the Korean War this figure had plummeted to a measly 25,000, less than 7,000 of whom belonged to the combat trades.[2] This skeleton of a force was responsible for the defence of the entire Canadian land mass and, in the event of an overseas war, the mobilization of the militia. In other words, postwar Canadian defence policy was predicated on the assumption that any future conflict would be a replay of the last, with up to a year's time to recruit, train, equip, and deploy an expeditionary force for overseas – that is, European – service. North Atlantic men, Canadian politicians and senior defence planners never seriously considered military intervention outside Europe. That was where Canadian interests lay and where any threat from the emerging Communist bloc would have to be contained. The short-sightedness of this thinking became painfully apparent on 25 June 1950 when the North Korean People's Army crossed the 38th parallel into the Republic of South Korea, precipitating the Korean War.

In response to the invasion, American President Harry Truman asked for a special meeting of the United Nations Security Council. Because the Soviet Union was then boycotting the council over the U.N.'s refusal to recognize China's new Communist government, the United States was able to use its considerable influence to get easy passage of a resolution calling for the "immediate cessation of hostilities" and "the withdrawal of the North Korean forces to the [38th] parallel."[3] When news of the invasion reached Ottawa, the general reaction was one of astonishment. The secretary of state for external affairs, Lester B. Pearson, was "caught completely off-guard by the North Korean aggression and by the United States response to it."[4]

When it became apparent that the North Koreans did not intend to comply with the 25 June resolution, the Security Council passed a second resolution calling on member nations to provide "such assistance to the Republic of Korea as may be necessary to repel armed attack and to restore peace and security in the area."[5] Canadian Prime Minister Louis St Laurent quickly responded to the UN resolution by ordering three Tribal-class destroyers from Canada's Pacific naval base at Esquimalt to the Far East.

Contemporary media coverage suggests that most Canadians strongly favoured going to war in Korea.[6] Indeed, the editor of the *Globe and Mail* suggested that Canada's initial contribution of three destroyers was not enough.[7] The sense of obligation was strong. The *Winnipeg Free Press* commended the prime minister for answering the United Nations' call to arms: "There are, it is obvious, very few who would suggest Canada sell out responsibilities to the U.N., welch on its pledges and seek to let others carry the burden of preserving peace. That Mr. St. Laurent made clear Canada would not do. This nation will do its part as an honourable member of the U.N."[8] Similarly, the Halifax *Chronicle Herald* praised the St Laurent government for taking a stand against Communist aggression and safeguarding "our freedom and freedom elsewhere."[9] From this perspective, it is necessary to briefly examine the reasons behind Canada's decision to go to war.

Perhaps most important was Canada's firm support for the U.N. Charter. Canada had played a central role in the creation of the United Nations in June 1945. Under St Laurent, support for the international organization became a pillar of Canadian foreign policy. The prime minister made this very clear in his statement to the House of Commons on 30 June: "Our responsibility in [Korea] arises entirely from our membership in the United Nations ... Any participation by Canada in carrying out the [Security Council] resolution ... would not be participation in war against any state. It would be our part in collective police action under the control and authority of the United Nations for the purpose of restoring peace."[10]

The other reason for Canadian participation was to counter what the government perceived to be Soviet expansionism. In the years after the Second World War, the Soviet Union gradually became the great adversary of the Western democracies. Indeed, the two sides almost went to war in 1948 when the Soviet Union – upset by the British and American amalgamation of occupation zones in Germany into Bizonia and the consequent breakdown of diplomatic relations – blockaded the Western allies in Berlin. The following year, as an iron curtain descended over Eastern Europe, Canada, the United States, and Western European nations formed NATO. The Cold War then began in full force.

Within this bipolar context, Western governments largely viewed North Korea's invasion of South Korea as an act of Soviet-sponsored aggression. In the House of Commons, George Drew blamed the Soviet Union for the outbreak of war and warned that if the Soviets were not stopped in Korea, Europe itself would become the Kremlin's next target.[11] Many political leaders in the Western democracies shared Drew's point of view. The "real target [of the attack] was seen as NATO," and as a founding member of the alliance, Canada "felt obliged to respond one way or another."[12]

Canada's press also suspected Soviet complicity. The *Vancouver Sun* claimed that "Korea alerted us to what Russia threatened."[13] To the *Globe and Mail*, it was clearly "Soviet Communist imperialism that [was] waging war on the Republic of South Korea."[14]

And according to the editor of the *Montreal Star*, "the Russians [were] merely carrying on a half a century old campaign to lay [their] hands on the Korean peninsula."[15]

On 7 July 1950 the U.N. Security Council passed a third resolution, which called on all contributing members to place their forces under a unified U.N. command and asked the United States to choose its commanding general. That same day, Ottawa committed the Royal Canadian Air Force to the war by ordering the 426th (Transport) Squadron to begin operations as part of the U.N.'s Korean airlift.

For the next month, the principal question confronting the Canadian government was whether or not to commit ground forces to the fighting in Korea. During the first two weeks of July, St Laurent and the Department of National Defence discussed the feasibility of sending an army contingent to Korea. On 19 July the prime minister announced that the Liberal Cabinet had decided that the dispatch of Canadian Army units to the Far East was not warranted at the time.[16]

The announcement incensed the press. The *Ottawa Evening Citizen* claimed that "a major decision cannot long be postponed on Korea. Canadian co-operation with American troops ... offers the best prospect of effective Canadian help.[17] And the *Globe and Mail* stated: "It will be gratifying if the Cabinet at last acknowledges this country's duty to send ground forces ... The Cabinet should at once ... recognize Canada's obligation and give maximum support to the U.N."[18]

As the editors of Canada's newspapers waged a war of words over Korea, Mackenzie King, the former long-time Liberal prime minister, died. On the train home from King's funeral in Toronto, the Cabinet further debated sending Canadian ground forces to Korea. Although Lester Pearson firmly believed that Canada should send an expeditionary force immediately, other Cabinet ministers were decidedly less enthusiastic.[19] However, St Laurent apparently supported Pearson's position and reconsidered his earlier decision; on 7 August he announced that Canadian ground troops would go to Korea.

The decision to commit Canadian ground troops to the fighting in Korea quickly revealed the pathetic condition of the army and the inadequacy of Canadian mobilization plans. The need was for combat-ready troops right now, not twelve months from now.

Caught on the horns of an increasingly embarrassing dilemma, the government decided to recruit the all-volunteer CASF from the streets.

The core of the Special Force consisted of second battalions of the three Active Force infantry regiments – the Royal Canadian Regiment (RCR), the Princess Patricia's Canadian Light Infantry (PPCLI), and the Royal 22e Régiment (R22eR). Rounding out the order of battle was a squadron of tanks from Lord Strathcona's Horse (LDSH), a field regiment from the Royal Canadian Horse Artillery (RCHA), and a squadron of Royal Canadian Engineers (RCE). By mobilizing second battalions (and squadrons) of these renowned regiments, organization and training time would be minimized. It was also hoped that the Active Force units would quickly instill the requisite regimental ethos in their respective second additions, an important consideration, given the fact it can take years for a new unit to develop its own traditions and esprit de corps. Initial strength of the force was set at 4,960 all ranks, plus a reinforcement pool of 2,105.

Thus the CASF came into being. Command of the force was given to Brigadier J.M. Rockingham. When the formation of the CASF was announced, Rockingham – "Rocky" to the troops – was a civilian executive with the British Columbia Electric Company in Vancouver. He had commanded the 9th Canadian Infantry Brigade during the Second World War and was hand-picked by the minister of national defence, Brooke Claxton, to lead the Canadians in Korea. The decision to recall Rockingham from civilian life, rather than appoint a senior officer from the Active Force, was threefold: first, Rockingham had proved himself to be an extremely capable brigade commander in Northwest Europe; second, he was perceived to have the ability to work well within the American-dominated U.N. Command; and third, the minister of national defence wanted to maintain the character of the Special Force by appointing a commander who was also a veteran from civilian life.[20]

Similar guidelines were used in the selection of commanding officers for the Special Force infantry battalions. Command of the 2 PPCLI was given to Lieutenant-Colonel James R. Stone. One of the most capable fighting soldiers in Canadian military history, Stone had enlisted as a private in the Loyal Edmonton Regiment in 1939; by 1944, now a lieutenant-colonel, he was in command of the unit. Command of the R22eR was given to Lieutenant-Colonel J.A. Dextraze. He had commanded the Fusiliers Mont-Royal in

Northwest Europe and, like Stone, was commissioned from the ranks.[21] Unlike Stone and Dextraze, Lieutenant-Colonel R.A. Keane, the commanding officer (CO) of 2 RCR, was a regular soldier in the Active Force. He had commanded the Lake Superior Regiment in Northwest Europe and was with the Directorate of Military Plans and Operations before his Special Force appointment.[22]

The orderly appointment of Special Force senior officers was in sharp contrast to the recruitment of the enlisted men. Despite initial concerns that the high level of employment would lead to a shortage of recruits, there was no difficulty finding enough "soldier of fortune" types to fill the ranks of the Special Force. In the days following the Canadian government's call to arms, scores of eager volunteers descended upon their local personnel depots. Oral sources reveal that the overwhelming majority of volunteers enlisted with the sole intention of seeing combat in Korea. For example, a young soldier from Quebec informed a recruiting officer that while he had "no ambition for an army career," he "wanted the experience of action."[23] Similarly, when asked why he wanted to join the 2 RCR, Kenneth Blampied stated that he wanted "to fulfil his dream of serving for his country overseas."[24]

Recruiters, however, were not prepared for Kenneth Blampied and the thousands of eager volunteers like him. The confusion that soon prevailed in the nation's personnel depots has been capably described elsewhere and need not be retold here.[25] Rather, it is instructive to explore the experiences of No. 6 Personnel Depot (Toronto) in some detail. This depot provided more recruits for the Special Force than any other and was at the centre of the recruiting fiasco.[26] The recruiting problems there reflect those of the CASF as a whole.

On the morning of Tuesday, 8 August, the CO of the depot, Major R.G. Liddell, was shocked to find the lawns of Chorley Park swarming with hundreds of "male civilians of every description."[27] Apparently, he had not heard the prime minister announce the formation of the Special Force on the radio the night before, nor had he seen a morning paper. Moreover, as the previous day had been a civic holiday, he had not yet received recruiting instructions for the Special Force in the mail.

When the doors of No. 6 Personnel Depot opened at 0800, the bemused Major Liddell and his staff were overwhelmed. Normally, the enlistment process took several days per man, with recruits actually lodging in a barracks at the depot. They were required to fill out myriad forms, pass a series of aptitude tests and interviews, and have a medical examination. Only after satisfying these requirements was a recruit accepted for service and sworn in. Using this process, No. 6 Personnel Depot provided the Active Force with up to six new soldiers each day. Obviously, it was totally incapable of dealing with the hordes of Special Force volunteers, and total chaos quickly ensued.

As recruiting for the Special Force commenced, No. 6 Personnel Depot received instructions to provide hourly returns showing the number of enlistments. The first of these showed only the five recruits who had passed selection the day before. Meanwhile, seeing the throngs of men cavorting around the depot, a reporter from the *Toronto Daily Star* erroneously announced in the evening paper that the city had enlisted 600 men in the Special Force. Unable to reconcile the *Star's* enlistment figures with those of his own department, Minister of National Defence Brooke Claxton flew to Toronto to sort things out.

Arriving in the city on 10 August, the minister and his entourage quickly made their way to No. 6 Personnel Depot. "While medical officers 'thumped and listened' and naked men coughed and stretched," Claxton darted from room to room pumping hands and slapping backs."[28] At one point the minister asked a potential recruit if he had experienced any problems with the enlistment process. The young man responded that, as he was under twenty-one, he was ineligible for the army's marriage allowance. A jovial Claxton informed him that he would indeed receive the allowance, despite repeated attempts by the depot's paymaster to convince the minister otherwise. The paymaster even went so far as to cite the regulations, but to no avail. Commenting on this unexpected change in policy, an officer wrote: "I believe this later caused legal headaches as members of the Regular Army were not included for some months in this 'ruling.' I believe the [depot's paymaster] carried this ball on the [minister's] verbal authority and instructions 'out of the blue' to ensure marriage allowance was paid even if recruits were under 21."[29]

Claxton's impromptu change in the regulations governing the army's marriage allowance was a boon to public relations but did nothing to simplify the recruitment of the Special Force. With the press shadowing his every move, the minister jumped at an opportunity to pose in a photograph with the first soldier to enlist in the

Special Force. The photograph later appeared in the national press, although the soldier in question was subsequently released for not meeting the minimum-age requirement of nineteen.[30]

Claxton's visit to No. 6 Personnel Depot was not just for publicity's sake. Concerned that recruitment procedures were too elaborate and time consuming, the pencil-chewing minister continually challenged the overworked clerks to justify why so much documentation was required. Their responses confirmed Claxton's suspicions, and at the end of the visit he retired to the officers' mess, where he reportedly imbibed "three doubles" in quick succession.[31]

The next day, Claxton implemented a number of measures designed to expedite recruitment of the Special Force: all applications were to be processed within twenty-four hours, interviews of prospective recruits were cut from thirty to five minutes, and the two-and-a-half-hour Educational Survey Test was jettisoned.[32] Henceforth, all Special Force recruits were to be attested before they were processed – meaning that recruits were sworn in as soon as they entered a personnel depot and were issued with a chit instructing them to return at a later date for documentation and a medical examination. In actual practice, few recruits were able to return as instructed once they reported for training. Instead, they were documented and medically examined on an ad hoc basis at their respective regimental training establishments. However, according to one cynical recruiting officer, the "attest first, process second" method of recruiting allowed the minister "to publicly state the enlistment figures he wanted."[33]

Not surprisingly, Claxton's reforms rendered the army's method of screening and selecting recruits ineffective. Lieutenant-Colonel Stone complained, "They were recruiting anybody who could breathe or walk. Brooke Claxton pushed the enlistment along because he was a politician at heart and didn't really give a damn about what else was happening. He was recruiting an army."[34]

As the Special Force inductees commenced training, the consequences of Claxton's political expediency became painfully apparent. At the RCR training establishment in Petawawa, Lieutenant-Colonel Bingham, CO of 1 RCR, recalled meeting a recruit who was old enough to have served in the South African War, and another who had a wooden leg! He also remembered "a milkman who paraded himself with a request for compassionate leave. He had left his milk truck parked outside No. 6 Personnel Depot while he went in to inquire about the Special Force. He had been swept up in the stream of recruits, and had emerged at Camp Petawawa, leaving his milk truck in the hot August sun of Toronto."[35]

Other regiments reported similar occurrences. The sudden influx of recruits into the PPCLI training establishment at Calgary included a large number of what Lieutenant-Colonel Stone classified as "undesirables." This euphemism encompassed "dead-beats, escapists from domestic and other troubles, cripples, neurotics, alcoholics, and other useless types," all of whom had to be weeded out before the battalion was fit for deployment.[36] The scores of recruits arriving without documentation also made it difficult to determine who had actually been enlisted; at least one civilian is known to have joined the PPCLI on the spur of the moment without ever setting foot in a personnel depot.[37]

While chaos reigned at the training establishments, the Chief of the General Staff, Lieutenant-General Charles Foulkes, reported to Cabinet on 18 August that the Special Force was up to authorized strength. However, it was decided that recruitment of reinforcements would continue for several months to come.

Ironically, as the CASF hurriedly prepared for battle, it appeared as if it might not be needed in Korea after all. On 15 September, after two months of bitter fighting along the Pusan perimeter, U.N. forces under the command of General Douglas MacArthur captured the strategic port of Inchon and began an advance up the Korean peninsula. With the North Koreans on the brink of defeat, there was talk that the war would be over by Christmas. Consequently, the Canadian government reduced its planned contribution of the CASF and decided to send only one infantry battalion to "show the flag" and assist with any U.N. occupation duties. At the same time, the remaining units of the CASF moved to Fort Lewis, Washington, to complete training.

As the Canadians established themselves at Fort Lewis, there was much uncertainty over what would become of the CASF. Many believed that once training was completed it would be deployed to Europe as part of NATO. Once again, however, events in Korea intervened. On 24 November, MacArthur launched a general offensive across the U.N. front. As his troops moved northward, they encountered stiff resistance from Chinese forces, who had crossed into North Korea in mid-October. Since then, although they had been appearing on the battlefield in considerable numbers, the U.N. Command had been slow to recognize Chinese involvement.[38]

This time it was different. On 26 November, Communist Chinese Forces (CCF) descended from their mountain sanctuaries and launched a massive counteroffensive in the west, followed two days later by an equally large attack in the east. Division after division of United Nations and ROK forces were either destroyed or forced to make a hasty retreat in the face of the advancing Chinese juggernaut. Recent scholarship suggests that the Chinese made the decision to enter the conflict well before the Inchon landing, although military unpreparedness and North Korean intransigence delayed intervention.[39] In any event, China's entry sealed the fate of the CASF. With the war now destined to drag on for the foreseeable future, the Canadian government reversed its earlier decision and decided to send the rest of the CASF to Korea.

Meanwhile, the situation at the nation's personnel depots gradually returned to normal. This, however, was small consolation to the Special Force units left to deal with the results of Claxton's hasty recruiting program. The administrative and disciplinary headaches caused by these undesirables defies description, although a review of the Special Force's predeployment absent-without-leave (AWOL) and discharge figures provides some measure of the gravity of the problem. When recruiting for the Special Force was terminated at the end of March 1951, 10,208 men had been recruited, 2,230 had been discharged or were awaiting discharge, and 1,521 cases of desertion had been processed, including 501 who were still unaccounted for.[40] As the army's official historian observed, "The figure for discharges and unapprehended deserters, which is more than 25 percent of the total numbers enlisted, compares with 7 percent for the first seven months of the First World War and 12 percent for the same period in the Second World War."[41]

These decidedly sombre statistics should not allow us to lose sight of the several thousand keen young men who enlisted in the Special Force and proceeded overseas with their respective units. Although they were always in the majority, these men have been overshadowed in the literature by the undesirable minority. Consequently, we currently know very little about the social background of the Special Force soldiers who actually served in Korea. Viewing the entire CASF through the lens of the initial recruiting fiasco, popular historians have characterized these units as comprising poorly educated, unemployed swashbucklers.[42] While this is certainly true of some of the soldiers who made it to Korea, it is by no means an accurate depiction of the vast majority of Special Force soldiers. It is also assumed that most CASF soldiers had previous military experience, either in the Second World War or otherwise. These impressions have never been subjected to rigorous analysis and have resulted in an exaggerated social distinction between the allegedly footloose and fancy-free soldiers of the Special Force and the spit and polish regulars of the Active Force first battalions.[43] While there were differences between the two, some of the generalizations that have appeared in recent years are completely unfounded.

The exaggerated social distinction between Special Force volunteer and Active Force regular is largely the result of reliance on anecdotal evidence. Regimental histories and archives abound with apocryphal tales of swashbuckling Special Force soldiers who learned their trade not on Canadian parade squares but on the tough battlefields of Europe. Indeed, Special Force soldiers often referred to themselves as the "bums from the slums."[44] One such legendary figure was Tommy Prince, a Canadian Native person who served with the elite Devil's Brigade during the Second World War. With little formal education and a severe drinking problem, Prince found it difficult to adjust to civilian life after the war. Promoted to sergeant shortly after his re-enlistment in the 2 PPCLI, he was supposedly overheard addressing a group of enlisted men: "You're in the Princess Patricia's now. You are hard! You drink hard! You play hard! You love hard! You hate hard! You fight hard! You can decide what you drink, how you play, who you love. We'll decide who you hate and who you fight."[45]

Legendary figures like Tommy Prince and the myths that have grown up around him are all too often used to characterize the entire Special Force. In actuality, CASF soldiers were slightly older than their first battalion counterparts.[46] The average age of Special Force men when they sailed for Korea was 25.2 years, compared with 23.6 years in the Active Force. The average level of formal education attained in both formations was grade 8, and the number of soldiers who were unemployed at the time of their enlistment was identical at 7 percent.

There also was little difference in their geographical origins. A full 79 percent of CASF and 77 percent of Active Force soldiers were born in their regiment's traditional recruiting areas,[47] while 84 and 80 percent, respectively, resided in these areas at the time of their enlistment. Religious affiliation in the CASF and the Active Force was almost identical, with just over half (51 and 52 percent) adhering to the Roman Catholic faith – a reflection, no doubt, of the R22eR presence. The rest of the men in both formations belonged to a variety of predominantly Protestant denominations, of which the Anglican Church was the largest.

Family status also was similar. Contrary to popular belief, CASF soldiers were slightly *less* likely to be single than first battalion soldiers, although of the married men, those in the Active Force were more likely to have a family. However, the difference between the two (69 and 62 percent respectively) was minor.

In terms of previous military service, CASF soldiers had a wealth of experience: a full 75 percent of them had served in the military (cadets, militia, or Second World War) before their Special Force enlistment. Significantly, the first battalions also contained a surprisingly large number of men with previous military experience. Nearly half of them (44 percent) had served in the military before their initial Active Force engagement. Thus, in terms of age and military experience as well as social background, the exaggerated distinctions between Active Force regular and Special Force volunteer are tenuous at best.

The debacle of CASF recruitment was, alas, only the first in a series of blunders and oversights that ultimately shaped the Canadian infantry's Korean experience. Some were the result of the army's total unpreparedness for war in Korea, while others stemmed from a seemingly indifferent Canadian high command. Either way, the consequences for individual foot soldiers were nothing short of horrendous, making their Far Eastern tours far more difficult and dangerous than they need have been.

From the outset, Canadian soldiers were not suitably prepared for combat in Korea. Their training was more appropriate for European-style warfare. Equipment was also a problem. Although they had first-rate support weapons, the Canadians were forced to rely on outmoded personal weapons and equipment. In the close-quarter patrol clashes that were such a feature of the fighting in Korea, Canadian soldiers were at a distinct disadvantage. Their Chinese adversaries, armed with the latest Communist bloc automatic weapons, routinely brought superior firepower to bear and won the firefight. Inadequate weaponry and the Canadians' obvious training deficiencies combined to undermine battlefield performance and shape the image of the Chinese soldier as superman. Combat motivation and the willingness to engage the enemy in active combat, as evidenced by the Canadians' increased reliance on support weapons, suffered accordingly.

The infantry's problems extended into other areas. Insufficient indoctrination left soldiers poorly prepared for the non-combat aspects of service in the Far East, leading some to question the purpose of Canadian involvement in Korea. The lack of indoctrination also shaped Canadian impressions of, and relations with, the people of the country they were sent to defend. Soldiers were shocked by the primitive conditions they encountered, and some allowed their Western prejudices to develop into open contempt for the Korean people.

On the battlefield, relations with Koreans were influenced by more pragmatic concerns. The porters and labourers of the Korean Service Corps – who kept the forward positions supplied with food, water, and ammunition, and who dug trenches and evacuated the wounded – were held in high esteem by the Canadians. The Korean Augmentation Troops, Commonwealth, or KATCOMS, on the other hand, were generally despised. Poorly trained and seldom fluent in either English or French, the KATCOMS were integrated into front-line Canadian infantry units during the last few months of the war. This unprecedented move demonstrated a fundamental misunderstanding on the part of certain Canadian commanders of the importance of group cohesion to combat soldiers. The results were disastrous.

The Korean War also witnessed the battlefield debut of two medical/technical innovations: the armoured fragmentation vest and the medevac helicopter. Unfortunately, the limited availability of these American-designed and -manufactured items prevented their having a major impact on the Canadian casualty experience in Korea. Only during the last three months of the war were sufficient numbers of vests available to outfit most Canadian fighting men. Helicopters were also in short supply and, as a consequence, all Canadian requests for evacuation had to be approved by American medical authorities. Thus, only the grievously wounded could expect a helicopter medevac. Moreover, ground fire and inclement weather often resulted in men with life-threatening injuries making the uncomfortable journey to the casualty clearing post by jeep ambulance instead.

Although Canadian soldiers enjoyed a reasonable standard of medical care in Korea, they were susceptible to a variety of infectious diseases with which Canadian medical officers had little experience. Hepatitis, malaria, Japanese encephalitis, and the horror-movie-calibre haemorrhagic fever all posed serious threats to the health of Canadian soldiers in Korea. Far more prevalent, however, was venereal disease. Unpreparedness and the failure of defence planners to institute the appropriate preventive measures resulted in a VD rate that surpassed not only those of the other Western allies in Korea but also that of the Canadian Army in the world wars and also Canada's NATO brigade in Germany.

Contributing to the Canadians' staggering VD rate was the general lack of concern for the soldiers' welfare. In the combat zone, they lived like beggars without even the most basic comforts and amenities. The Canadian Army postal service compared unfavourably with its British and American counterparts, and it was only during the final year of the war that a frugal Department of National Defence agreed to send civilian concert parties to the Far East to entertain the troops. Reading and writing material was practically non-existent in the forward areas, nor were there enough blankets or stoves to go round.

One item that was abundant was beer. The austere conditions in Korea, coupled with the failure of the Canadian rotation and rest and recreation policies to sustain morale, encouraged heavy drinking amongst front-line troops. Issued on an almost daily basis and easily obtainable from regimental canteens just behind the front line, beer was *the* pillar buttressing Canadian morale in Korea. This wholesale dependence on alcohol often undermined operational performance and created disciplinary problems. But perhaps the greatest tragedy was the number of men whose alcohol dependency did not end with Korea.

Not that the Canadian public did anything to assist returned men. Korean veterans returned to a prosperous country that cared little for the war in Korea and even less for the men who had served there. Many felt marginalized by such veterans' groups as the Royal Canadian Legion, finding solace with their comrades in the Korean Veterans Association. Only recently have plaques bearing the inscription "Korea, 1950–53," been added to war memorials across the country, and it was not until 1992 that the government approved issue of the Canadian Volunteer Service Medal for Korea.

For too long, public and governmental apathy have obfuscated the experiences of the Canadian infantry during the Korean War. In Korea, the Canadians encountered a land, a climate, a people, and an enemy that were more unfamiliar and unforgiving than anything Canadian soldiers had ever faced before. Yet the impression remains that Korea was a "conflict" or "police action," or even a "peacekeeping" operation. For the men who spilled their blood on those anonymous Korean hills it was nothing of the sort. Their Far Eastern tours were twelve-month journeys through hell from which some never returned. Korea was most certainly a war, and it is high time the public acknowledged this fact. Canadian infantrymen fought and suffered in that far-off Asian land because we, through the medium of the Canadian government, asked them to. As the benefactors of their sacrifice, can we justifiably ignore the ordeal of Canadian combat soldiers in Korea any longer?

CHAPTER ONE

Slit-Trench Attitude

Military training prepares soldiers to fulfil their duties in an operational context as part of a fighting unit. As Richard Holmes observed, "A great part of a man's behaviour on the battlefield, and hence of the fighting effectiveness of the army to which he belongs, depends upon training."[1] In order to be truly effective, then, training should be tailored to the theatre of operations in question. Paradoxically, the theatre that exerted the most influence on the direction and substance of Canadian infantry training during the Korean War was Northwest Europe. With few exceptions, the training Canadian soldiers received was predicated on the assumption that they would be participating in combined-arms operations across the open expanses of Northwest Europe, not small-unit conflict in the mountains of Korea. As a result, the Canadians found themselves unprepared for the exigencies of the Korean battlefield in three important areas: individual weapons handling, patrolling, and, as the war progressed, the construction and maintenance of defensive positions. In Korea, these constituted the combat soldier's holy triad of battlefield skills – skills that were given short shrift during the Canadians' preparation for battle.

Because of the confusion that arose in Canada when so many soldiers of the Special Force poured into the regimental training establishments, it was not possible to begin training in earnest until the middle of August. The experiences of the PPCLI during this tumultuous period are particularly well documented and generally reflect those of the CASF as a whole. In the days following the Canadian government's call to arms, the 1 PPCLI commenced drafting and setting up a training program for its second addition.

However, there was not enough time to prepare fully for the flood of new recruits. Despite 1 PPCLI's best efforts to maintain some semblance of military order, the regiment's base at Currie Barracks, Calgary, was overwhelmed. In retrospect, it is a wonder that the base's administrative and logistical framework did not crumble under the sheer weight of numbers. The kitchen, for example, operated at nearly twice its normal capacity until 20 August, while the Regimental Quartermaster's Stores ran for nearly a month on a 23-hour-a-day schedule.[2]

As already noted, a training cadre from the 1st Battalion was responsible for training and administering the 2nd Battalion until it was ready to function on its own. To this end the sixteen officers and fifty-two other ranks of the 1 PPCLI training cadre divided themselves into schools of instruction, through which recruits progressed until they were basically trained and ready for advanced training.[3] This system maximized precious training time by making provisions for recruits with previous military service. Thus, when 2 PPCLI began to train in earnest on 14 August, twenty-six recruits who had previous military experience started advanced training at neighbouring Camp Sarcee. Upon completing advanced training, these veterans became the 2 PPCLI's first section leaders. As such, they formed the foundation on which the battalion command structure would be built.

As the enlisted men of the battalion trained at Currie Barracks, their officers, all of whom were either veterans of the Second World War or serving members in the militia or the Active Force, were undergoing a refresher course at Calgary. The CO of the battalion, Lieutenant-Colonel Stone, supervised the course and ensured that it kept up with recruit training.[4]

At the beginning of September, the Advanced Wing from Camp Sarcee, consisting of 7 officers and 208 other ranks, together with the 1 PPCLI training cadre, moved to Camp Wainwright, Alberta. Wainwright today, with its sprawling barrack blocks and computer-controlled firing range, bears scant resemblance to the camp the soldiers of Advanced Training Wing encountered five decades ago. To the chagrin of the troops, the camp was situated in a sparsely populated region some 125 miles east of Edmonton, and access was limited to a rail line and dirt road.[5] As a further complement to their austere surroundings, the troops were billeted in the same prefabricated, tar-papered H huts that had quartered German soldiers when

Wainwright was a prisoner-of-war camp. But the officers of Advanced Wing welcomed the isolation of Wainwright; here, training could proceed unfettered by the remaining vestiges of the enlisted men's civilian lives.[6] The 2 PPCLI was beginning to take shape.

So were the other infantry units of the Special Force. In Valcartier, the R22eR adopted a similar approach to training and by late August had begun to train its Special Force recruits in earnest. In Petawawa, meanwhile, the now up to strength 2 RCR organized its surplus manpower into an ad hoc reinforcement company.[7] By early November, all of the first battalion training programs had come to an end, and 2 PPCLI, 2 R22eR, and 2 RCR were officially recognized as independent units.[8]

It is instructive to outline the organization of a Canadian infantry battalion. At the time of the Korean War, a full-strength battalion comprised approximately 1,000 men all ranks. At the top of the battalion hierarchy was Battalion Headquarters, consisting of 5 officers (including the battalion commander) and 45 other ranks. The backbone of the battalion was the four rifle companies – Able, Baker, Charlie, and Dog companies – each with 5 officers and 122 other ranks. The rifle company was subdivided into three platoons, each consisting of one officer and 36 other ranks. Within the battalion, platoons were numbered one through twelve, beginning with those from Able Company. Thus, 1, 2, and 3 platoons would be from Able Company, 4, 5, and 6 platoons from Baker Company, 7, 8, and 9 platoons from Charlie Company, and 10, 11, and 12 platoons from Dog Company. The platoon in turn was further subdivided into three sections, each with two non-commissioned officers (NCOs), and eight enlisted men. Rounding out the battalion was a Headquarters (HQ) Company (4 officers and 91 other ranks), and a Support Company (7 officers and 185 other ranks). Support Company was subdivided into four platoons – Mortar, Carrier (machine-gun), Antitank, and Pioneer platoons – which provided the battalion with close battlefield support.

It will be recalled from the previous chapter that in the aftermath of General MacArthur's capture of Inchon in September 1950, the Canadian government reduced its planned contribution of the Special Force and decided to send only one battalion of infantry to Korea, the 2 PPCLI, to assist with any U.N. occupation duties. With the departure of the 2 PPCLI to Korea in late November, the remaining units of the Special Force (now known as the 25th Canadian

Infantry Brigade Group) concentrated at Fort Lewis, Washington, to complete training. Fort Lewis was selected for its mild climate and large training area; in peacetime it was the home station of the 2nd U.S. Infantry Division. At this time the 25th Canadian Infantry Brigade (25th CIB) was left with a large pool of first-line reinforcements who had been enlisted during the August recruiting drive. At the beginning of December, these reinforcements were organized into three understrength training battalions.[9] The new units were designated third battalions of the RCR, R22eR, and PPCLI.[10]

All Canadian soldiers who served in Korea, whether in the Special Force or the Active Force, began their military service with individual training. "Individual training," as defined by the 1950 Canadian Army training pamphlet *Training for War*, is "a comprehensive term which embraces instruction at a staff college or senior officers' school as well as the most elementary instruction in the use of arms, and implies that the student is being trained as an individual rather than as a member of a team."[11]

For enlisted personnel, individual training had two distinct phases. The first, commonly referred to as recruit training, was six weeks in duration and endeavoured to break recruits and then remold them in the military ethos. This was achieved by subjecting them to extreme mental and physical privations. These included excessive drill, sleep deprivation, relentless physical training, harassment, and draconian group punishment for individual transgressions.[12] Paradoxically, the first phase of individual training also cemented small-unit cohesion. Under such conditions of shared hardship, the individual recruit's civilian values and identity were expunged and replaced by those of the group.[13] As Richard Holmes has shown, the harshness of basic training has a direct impact on the cohesiveness of the unit that undergoes it.[14]

For most recruits, the first few weeks of recruit training were almost unbearable. The seemingly egalitarian atmosphere of the personnel depot was replaced by an entrenched hierarchical rank structure, in which the raw recruit clung precariously to the bottom rung. All vestiges of his civilian past, including his hair, were stripped away, and he was no longer permitted to wear civilian clothes. He seldom heard his first name and had minimal contact with the outside world. He quickly learned that his well-being was inextricably bound to that of his fellow recruits, and that even the slightest infraction would be rewarded with a series of expletive-laced insults from the training staff. A recruit whose turnout or performance was judged to be below standard was harassed and assigned extra duties. At the time of the Korean War, he could even be punched by an instructor. Private Stanley Carmichael recalled that his "instructors were real hardasses": "I thought they would have been a little easier since most of them were not much older than me, but boy was I wrong."[15] And according to Private Bill Nasby, "The instructors were really strict and didn't have time for any whiny bullshit. I remember on one occasion a guy in my unit made the mistake of showing how well he could twirl his rifle when he should have been cleaning it. It worked out well for the rest of us because the sergeant had him clean all our rifles for the remainder of the week. It was the last time he showed off in front of the guys."[16]

A recruit who persistently fell below the required standard also faced the wrath of his peers. A soldier in the 1 R22eR remembered "a way within the unit to keep the guys in line, because if one guy messed up, the whole section was in trouble."[17] In actuality, there were several ways, but the most common was the nocturnal blanket party. The offender was pinned in his bunk under a taut banket, and systematically beaten by his peers. One blanket party was usually sufficient incentive for the offender to clean up his act.

Recruits were also subjected to more official forms of military socialization. Lectures on regimental history were given frequently, and visits to the regimental museum were *de rigueur*.[18] They also learned the motto and traditions of their regiment, which they would be expected to uphold once they completed training. In the RCR, for example, recruits learned the meaning of the regimental motto, *Pro patria*, and discovered that on 27 February the regiment commemorated the Battle of Paardeberg.[19]

To civilians, instruction in the minutiae of regimental life might seem picayune; however, it did perform an important function. On the one hand, immersion in regimental lore reinforced the recruit's sense that he was now part of an organization whose ultimate purpose was to wage war.[20] On the other, it solidified his new identity as a member of the regimental family. Lance-Corporal John Murray reminisced, "I knew as part of the Patricias, I was expected to maintain a strong sense of pride and loyalty. That was something that was drilled into our heads constantly."[21]

Military socialization was the first objective of recruit training, but it was not the only one. The latter stages also included instruction in basic military skills, such as first aid, weapons handling, elementary fieldcraft, and an introduction to small-unit tactics.[22] Many veterans found this stage of recruit training to be a rehash of their earlier experiences. While Lance-Corporal William Powell rated the training by his NCOs as "fair," he felt that when they were training him, "they were still thinking about the Second World War."[23] Similarly, Private Kenneth Blampied, a veteran of the Second World War, found that many of the things he had learned five years earlier "were still the same."[24]

After receiving a grounding in the basic military skills, the soldier progressed to advanced infantry training. This six-week course prepared the soldier for the individual duties he would carry out as a member of an infantry battalion. For example, if posted to a rifle company, he received further instruction in small-unit tactics, weapons handling, fieldcraft, field fortifications, map using, and battle drill.[25]

There is a substantial body of evidence which suggests that the Canadian Army's Advanced Training Program failed to produce what Captain W.R. Chamberlain of the Royal Canadian Dragoons called a "functional rifleman."[26] By this, he meant a combat soldier who was aggressive and willing to engage and destroy the enemy at close range.[27] Heavily influenced by S.L.A. Marshall, and citing Canadian Army Operational Research Team reports from the Second World War, Chamberlain argued that 75–85 percent of the men in the rifle platoons did not fire their weapons at the enemy.[28] Chamberlain (like Marshall) held that this reluctance to fire was attribual to the soldiers' pre-enlistment civilian values and inadequate training. In a *Canadian Army Journal* article that appeared one month before the first Canadians were committed to battle in Korea, he wrote: "The civilian enters his military training with this reluctance to kill firmly implanted in his mind. Nor does he at any period during his training receive any purposeful indoctrination that will motivate him in such a way that he is prepared to shoot his enemy on sight without having first received a direct order to do so."[29]

Insofar as training was concerned, Chamberlain suggested that the Canadian infantryman's reluctance to fire – the "slit-trench attitude," as he called it – was the result of the army's emphasis on the mechanical and physical aspects of weapons handling.[30] He argued that most weapons training was dull and boring, and primarily concerned with teaching recruits the parts and characteristics of their weapons and how to strip and clean them.[31]

The Canadian infantry may not have received adequate instruction in even these basic skills. The 3 RCR's Lieutenant-Colonel Campbell complained that his men's "great fault (and it is the fault of the whole army) is that they have no proper regard for their equipment, weapons, [and] ammunition."[32] The 2 PPCLI's Major R.K. Swinton reported a similar problem in his battalion.[33]

The drill-hall approach to weapons training was replicated on the firing range. Troops marched out, by day, to a level field, where they were lined up and instructed to lie down in the prone position. On command, they commenced firing at a two-dimensional black-and-white target that was always posted at hundred-yard intervals to correspond with the graduations on their rifle sights.[34] Firing was by the book, and woe betide any soldier who displayed initiative in either his firing position or his choice of target. As Chamberlain correctly pointed out, this method of weapons training had little in common with actual battlefield conditions. In combat, the soldier was rarely presented with an unobstructed field of view and level firing surface.[35] Moreover, the target was rarely stationary, almost never at a fixed range, and he usually fired back.

To overcome the Canadian rifleman's slit-trench attitude, Chamberlain recommended that recruits be subjected to constant indoctrination to foment aggressiveness. "It is not a question of engendering hatred for the enemy in the recruit's mind," he wrote, "but of impressing upon him that his sole function is to kill the enemy, and if he does not perform that function when the opportunity presents itself, he is useless."[36] The available evidence suggests that the Canadian Army did not take Chamberlain's recommendation to heart: in a report published in June 1953, Major Harry Pope identified a strong reluctance to close with the enemy on the part of Canadian troops in Korea.[37]

Chamberlain advocated a more realistic weapons training program that would make use of three-dimensional targets, encourage initiative, and teach soldiers to fire the instant they encountered enemy action.[38] This was easier said than done, for the process of familiarizing recruits with the audio and visual characteristics of the battlefield was fraught with insurmountable bureaucratic hurdles during the Korean War. Known as "battle inoculation," this type of training called for the use of live fire and pyrotechnic devices in a manner not normally deemed safe in peacetime. Battle inoculation exercises during the Second World War, for example, had often used Vickers machine guns mounted on tripods to fire live rounds five degrees to the flank of soldiers negotiating assault courses.[39] In 1950, however, peacetime rules governing the use of live fire in training were still in effect. Thus, when it was decided that Canadian ground troops would take part in U.N. operations in Korea, there were severe restrictions on the use of live fire in training schemes. Astonishingly, the Department of National Defence refused to relax the peacetime restrictions, and no Canadian soldier to serve in Korea took part in live-fire battle inoculation exercises during individual training in Canada.[40]

The inadequacy of Canadian weapons training was brought to the attention of the Vice-Chief of the General Staff, Major-General H.A. Sparling, in November 1952 when he visited Canadian units in Korea. He was informed that the level of individual weapons handling under battlefield conditions was depressingly low.[41] On his return to Canada, Sparling instructed the Directorate General of Military Training (DGMT) to determine how individual weapons training could be improved.[42] The DGMT duly investigated the matter, but no instructions for an amended individual training program appear to have been issued before the soldiers of the third battalions, the last Canadian troops to see combat in Korea, embarked for the Far East. Indeed, in summarizing his battalion's experiences after the war, Lieutenant-Colonel Campbell reported that it was always necessary to run weapons-handling courses in Korea.[43]

A possible explanation for the general inadequacy of Canadian weapons training is that it simply reflected the doctrinal belief that individual rifle fire meant very little to the overall conduct of operations. Certainly, on the European battlefield, masses of armour and artillery were expected to decide the outcome of any conventional engagement. In such a scenario, rifle fire was relegated to a marginal role, reinforcing the popular dictum that armour and artillery conquer, and infantry occupies. In the mountains of Korea, however, where the roles were largely reversed and a high standard of individual weapons handling was absolutely essential, the results of inadequate weapons training quickly became evident.

Another oversight that reflected this European focus was the lack of instruction in the maintenance and construction of defensive works. As has been seen, the latter stages of advanced training included instruction in fieldcraft and field fortifications. It was at this time that recruits were introduced to the infantryman's second-best friend: the spade. Most soldiers despise digging, and the training Canadian recruits received during the Korean War certainly did nothing to correct this. Aside from the occasional hastily dug foxhole or shell-scrape (a trench with overhead protection), recruits did comparatively little digging of the kind that was called for in Korea.[44] With the shift to static warfare in late 1951, the inadequacy of Canadian training in the construction and maintenance of defensive positions gradually became apparent. According to a bulletin entitled *Training Hints for a Battalion Destined for Korea*, issued by the DGMT in late 1952, Canadian troops required more training in laying barbed wire, constructing and maintaining fighting trenches and bunkers, and filling and laying sandbags.[45]

The available evidence suggests that the soldiers of the 3 RCR and 3 R22eR were given extra instruction in these areas before they embarked for Korea in the spring of 1953. At Valcartier, for example, the soldiers of 3 R22eR built a Korean-style defensive position on a small hill in the centre of the camp just before their deployment.[46] While this was undoubtedly a step in the right direction, it was, in hindsight, too little, too late. *Training Hints* was issued too late to be of any use to the soldiers of 3 PPCLI who embarked for the Far East in October 1952, and as Lieutenant-Colonel Campbell explained, it was "not possible to do effective field training after the summer of 1952."[47] Thus, although he considered his men to be better trained than those in the second or first battalions when they embarked for Korea, Campbell still found himself confronting a serious shortcoming in the individual training of his men.[48]

On completion of advanced training, the individual infantryman was ready to take his place in the order of battle, but he still had to be trained to function as part of sub-unit within the infantry battalion. This was the object of collective training. According to the 1950 Canadian Army training manual *Training for War*, "Collective training means exercises and manoeuvres, the keynote of both being realism."[49] Collective training, like individual training, may be divided into two distinct categories. The first, sub-unit training, is progressive, starting with the smallest sub-unit, the infantry section, and continuing upwards to the company level. On completing sub-unit training, companies undergo formation training at the battalion, or unit, level. Unit training, therefore, is synonymous with battalion training and is the final stage of training before an infantry soldier is ready for battle.

With the exception of 2 PPCLI, all Canadian infantrymen underwent collective training at North American camps. When 2 PPCLI embarked for Korea, the soldiers of the battalion had not yet started collective training. Few were troubled by this, because it was believed that the Patricias would not be taking part in active operations. However, the changed tactical context that greeted the soldiers of 2 PPCLI on their arrival in Korea made it absolutely imperative that they complete collective training as soon as possible. To this end, the Patricias moved to a training camp at Miryang, fifty miles north of Pusan. As it turned out, the necessity of having to complete collective training in the rugged hills above Miryang was a blessing. From the outset, the Patricias learned how to survive and manoeuvre over the type of terrain they would be fighting over. Their close proximity to the front also ensured that their training program incorporated the tactical lessons that were being learned by U.N. forces already engaged in active operations.[50] Mastery of these tactical lessons was one of the contributing factors to the battalion's successful defence of Hill 677 during the battle of Kap'yong in April 1951. But while the Patricias' tailor-made training program proved beneficial in the short term, it shared an important deficiency with the collective programs of the other Canadian units to serve in Korea – a lack of emphasis on patrolling.

Patrolling is an inseparable part of field operations to the extent that an army that does not patrol vigorously and effectively quickly surrenders the tactical initiative to the enemy. This was particularly the case in Korea, where the mountainous terrain placed a premium on small-unit patrol skills. Moreover, with the occupation of static lines of defence in late 1951, it became essential to control the approaches leading from the valley floors, or "no man's land," to the hilltop defensive positions. Failure to dominate this vital ground gave an attacking enemy the element of surprise and the ability to harass or ambush one's own patrols.

The Canadian infantry used four different types of patrols in Korea.[51] The first and most common was the standing patrol, which varied in size from three or four men to a complete section. Standing patrols went out regardless of the weather, usually at last light, and occupied a stationary position to the Canadians' front. Their purpose was to observe and report enemy movement and to call down artillery fire on any troop concentrations in the area. The second type was the reconaissance, or "recce," patrol, which seldom numbered more than three men; its purpose was to provide field commanders with intelligence on enemy dispositions. Recces would often "lie up" in no man's land for several days, placing an enormous physical and emotional strain on the men in the patrol. Third were the nuisance, or roving, patrols, containing up to twenty men, whose job it was to harass the enemy in no man's land or on the approaches to their own positions. Finally, there were fighting patrols. These varied in strength, but could at times involve an entire company; their purpose was to seek out and destroy the enemy through one of two means: an ambush or a raid. Ambushes usually required fewer men than a raid and were set along routes or paths thought to be travelled by the enemy. Raids, on the other hand, were launched against enemy positions to destroy field fortifications and capture prisoners. With the renewal of peace talks at Panmunjom in the fall of 1951 and the U.N. Command's concomitant policy of "active defence," ambushes and raids became the primary means through which the enemy was brought to battle.[52]

Patrolling in Korea was therefore an art.[53] Success was dependent on sound collective training, particularly at the section and platoon levels. According to the Canadian Army training pamphlet, *The Infantry Battalion in Battle*, "The successful collective training of an infantry battalion depends above all on ... a high standard of rifle and specialist platoon training. Each platoon must be thoroughly trained as a team in the various phases of battle and every rifle platoon must be capable of carrying out the role of a fighting patrol."[54] However, patrol reports and training bulletins from the Korean War indicate that the Canadians did not meet the standard outlined in the official doctrine. The first indication that Canadian soldiers were not adequately trained in patrol techniques came shortly after the 2 PPCLI was committed to battle. A training bulletin prepared for Army Headquarters in Ottawa reported:

Conduct of foot patrols by day and night has not been up to required standards. Patrols have failed to penetrate to depths required to gain contact and locate forming-up areas; they have failed to observe the area they were to patrol prior to departing, to select alternate routes, to obtain the information required by their missions, and to return by previously designated routes. Often they have been incapable of reporting what they have seen. Our training must cover more thoroughly these basic subjects and place more emphasis on night patrolling.[55]

Most other Canadian infantry units to serve in Korea appear to have experienced the same problems as the Patricias.[56] So pronounced was the 25th Brigade's inability to patrol vigorously and effectively that in May 1953 Brigadier Jean-Victor Allard[57] instructed one of his most capable staff officers, Major Harry Pope, to look into the matter. Pope published his findings on 2 June 1953 in a paper entitled "Infantry Patrolling in Korea." He argued forcefully that the enemy had held the tactical initiative since the beginning of 1952.[58] Reiterating many of the shortcomings in Canadian patrol techniques cited above, Pope averred that with very few exceptions, the Canadians had not conducted a successful patrol in no man's land.[59] The 25th Brigade had simply been outclassed by a skilful and determined opponent, who used specially trained troops to raid and ambush Canadian patrols "at will." Pope was not solely concerned with the training implications of the 25th Brigade's inability to patrol effectively; his paper raised a number of related issues, which will be discussed in a subsequent chapter. Nevertheless, his findings did expose the extent to which Canadian infantry units had neglected patrolling in their predeployment collective training programs.

Predictably, not all Canadian battalion commanders were impressed with Pope's findings. Chief among them was Lieutenant-Colonel H.F. Wood, the Canadian official historian and commanding officer of 3 PPCLI in Korea. In *Strange Battleground*, Wood summarized some of Pope's more salient findings at length and then attempted to discount them in a decidedly condescending footnote that questioned Pope's battlefield credentials.[60] In actuality, Major Pope was a highly experienced field officer, having served with distinction in the Italian campaign and in Northwest Europe, as well as in two tours in Korea with the R22ER before his appointment to Brigadier Allard's staff.[61] Perhaps Pope's resignation from the army in 1959 over NATO nuclear policy and his subsequent affiliation with the Co-operative Commonwealth Federation[62] afforded Wood some leeway in attacking him in an official Department of National Defence publication. Moreover, contrary to what the official historian claimed, there is evidence supporting Pope's conclusions and his thesis that Canadian infantry units did not place enough emphasis on patrolling during their collective training programs – evidence that Wood either did not see or chose to ignore.

During his visit to Korea in late November 1952 (by which time Lieutenant-Colonel Wood's battalion had been in Korea for a month), Major-General Sparling had also been informed that Canadian collective training programs needed to place more emphasis on patrolling.[63] *Training Hints*, which appeared towards the end of 1952, made a similar appeal.[64] However, patrolling was supposed to be an integral part of any collective training program, regardless of the operational situation in Korea or elsewhere. Why, then, did the Canadians find themselves inadequately trained for patrol operations in Korea?

With the obvious exception of 2 PPCLI, whose collective training program was largely devoted to the tactics of hilltop defence,[65] the training of Canadian infantry battalions ws not geared to the Korean situation. As David Bercuson has observed, the Canadian Army of the early 1950s was "structured, equipped, trained, and located to fight a major all-arms battle alongside Canada's NATO allies against the Soviet army."[66] Even the units of the Special Force who completed collective training at Fort Lewis focused on combined-arms operations rather than small-unit patrols, though it must be admitted that at this time the war in Korea had not yet become static.[67] To make matters worse, it was subsequently discovered that the camp's climate and terrain was not entirely appropriate for troops training for battle in Korea.[68]

The infantry battalions who subsequently prepared for battle on the open expanses of Canadian training areas seem to have adopted a similar focus. Commenting on the collective training he received at Wainwright, Alberta, Private Stanley Carmichael of 1 PPCLI stated: "I was shipped out to Currie Barracks ... and then up to Wainwright where we really learned most of our training. Looking back on my Korean experience, I realize [we] were not prepared for the Korean terrain ... Most of the area we would occupy in Korea was pretty mountainous and deep terrain, yet at Wainwright we practised a lot of open exercises which at the time seemed to make sense to me."[69]

The focus on European-style mobile warfare was also in evidence at training camps in the East. Corporal James Wilson of 1 RCR averred that during training at Camp Petawawa, "the young snot-nosed officers" were constantly "trying to establish a battlefront like Germany as opposed to the realities of Korea."[70] And according to Lieutenant-Colonel L.F. Trudeau, CO of 1 R22eR, "When faced with training men for [Korea], [I] knew there would be difficulties, given that most training had prepared [me] and others for the European landscape, and not the Korean terrain."[71]

As has been seen, the third battalions made an attempt to orient their training to Korean conditions.[72] For example, during training at Camp Wainwright in the summer of 1952, provision was made for the third battalion rifle companies to attend the Canadian Army Mountain Warfare Course at Jasper, Alberta. Although this was a step in the right direction, these exercises were the exception to the rule: collective training continued to be devoted primarily to cross-country combined-arms exercises at the battalion and brigade levels.[73] Moreover, as was the case with individual training, the DGMT bulletins that appeared towards the end of 1952 calling for an increased emphasis on patrolling in Canadian collective training programs appeared too late to be of any significant use to the 3 RCR and 3 R22eR.

The end result of the 25th Brigade's insufficient patrol training was that Canadian infantry units deployed to Korea were ill prepared for the operations they would subsequently be called on to carry out. Several battalion commanders in Korea attempted to compensate for their men's lack of training by conducting patrol courses when their units were in reserve. However, it was not until May 1953 that the 25th Brigade finally opened a patrol school in Korea. As the official historian himself conceded, this was too little, too late.[74]

Canadian infantry training during the Korean War thus contained serious deficiencies at both the individual and collective levels. Weapons training was not entirely suited to combat conditions, and there was a general disregard for training in the construction and maintenance of fieldworks. At the collective level, there was a lack of emphasis on patrolling, since training was largely geared towards preparing soldiers for European-style combined-arms operations. Deficiencies in these areas meant that, with few exceptions, the Canadian infantry took to the field largely unprepared for the combat conditions encountered in Korea. Although efforts were made to improve the standard of individual and collective training in the 25th Brigade, these usually came too late to offer any practical benefit. A similar pattern emerges in regard to the infantry's small arms and personal equipment.

CHAPTER TWO

A Lot of Good Men Died

One of the key factors in soldiers' combat performance is the quality of their equipment. During the two world wars, this had been based on British designs to the extent that it was often difficult to differentiate Canadian infantry units from their Commonwealth counterparts. In Korea, however, 25th Brigade fighting men were outfitted with a mixture of Canadian, British, and American equipment.[1] Like their predecessors, they carried British-pattern small arms, but this was the first time Canadian troops had used Canadian kit or relied on American support weapons. Thus, the Korean War may be considered a watershed in the technological evolution of the Canadian infantry. Yet, with the exception of the support weapons, this evolution was not to Canadian soldiers' advantage. As the war in Korea progressed, they found themselves increasingly ill equipped to meet the operational exigencies of static warfare.

When the Korean War broke out, the Canadian Army was still largely equipped with Second World War, British-pattern equipment. As World War gave way to Cold War, plans to re-equip the Active Force with the latest in American military hardware were countenanced.[2] Due to many factors, including U.S. export laws and Canada's shortage of American dollars, little new equipment had reached Active Force units by June 1950.

The Chief of the General Staff, Lieutenant-General Charles Foulkes, discussed the state of Canadian infantry equipment with Prime Minister Louis St Laurent in July 1950, when they met to examine the feasibility of sending a Canadian expeditionary force to Korea.[3] Foulkes recommended that Canada raise an infantry brigade to operate within a yet to be formed Commonwealth division.

Fighting as part of a Commonwealth division would allow Canadian field forces to use British supply lines and hence would reduce costs. Moreover, Canadian field commanders were used to British methods of command, control, and communications, since all of their training and indoctrination had been done on British lines. Finally, it was alleged that the enlisted ranks of the Canadian expeditionary force would likely contain a large number of veterans, who were accustomed to British traditions, small arms, training, and tactical doctrine.

Following the government's decision to commit Canadian ground troops to Korea, Cabinet formally decided that the 25th CIB would be equipped with British-pattern small arms. However, as the 25th CIB began to take shape, it became obvious that operational capabilities demanded that some of the infantry's equipment be replaced immediately. A review of existing stocks of kit and equipment concluded that the Canadian Army's berets, greatcoats, boots, putties, socks, mitts, groundsheets, blankets, underwear, undervests, steel helmets, entrenching tools, and tents were unsuitable for issue to the 25th Brigade.[4] The standard-issue Canadian battledress uniform was also considered unsuited to Korea's extreme climatic conditions.[5] The quarter-master general (QMG), Major-General N.E. Rodger, was instructed to procure suitable replacements, including new winter combat suits, ponchos, and peaked caps.[6]

The Canadian infantry's British-designed 2 and 3 in. mortars and 2.36 in. "bazooka" rocket launcher were also deemed unsuited to operations in Korea, because of their limited range. Situation reports from the 27th British Commonwealth Infantry Brigade (27th BCIB), which by September 1950 had already been fighting in Korea for a month, described actions during which North Korean mortars outranged the 27th BCIB's 3 in. mortars by as much as 2,000 yards.[7] During such engagements, the need for fire support placed an even greater strain on field artillery regiments. Similarly, reports from the front during the first crucial weeks of the war described infantry-armour engagements in which the 2.36 in. rocket projectile bounced off the armour of North Korean tanks at ranges of only thirty yards.[8]

In view of these shortcomings, Foulkes asked his American counterpart for assistance. After a series of lengthy discussions, the Americans agreed to provide the Canadians with their latest infantry-support weapons.[9] Meanwhile, as expected, the British agreed to allow the Canadians to use their lines of supply in Korea, to maintain the 25th Brigade's British-type small arms, and to supply ammunition for British-type weapons. The Canadians themselves were responsible for providing non-common-user items, such as combat clothing and personal kit.[10] Thus, for the first time in Canadian military history, Canadian soldiers would go into battle outfitted with weapons and equipment from three different national sources. As will be seen, this ad hoc mixture was not entirely suited to combat conditions in Korea. Nowhere was this more apparent than in the 25th Brigade's kit and clothing.

In battle, the individual infantryman must be self-sufficient to a certain point. Extra ammunition, clothing, rations, water, rain gear, and emergency medical supplies must be carried if the soldier intends to survive on the battlefield for any amount of time. The web equipment used by the soldiers of the 25th Brigade during the Korean War was the Canadian version of the British 1937-pattern webbing. The British had themselves discarded the despised 37-pattern shortly after the Second World War, in favour of their superior 44-pattern.

In any event, the Canadians' 37-pattern webbing was completely unsuited to battle conditions in Korea.[11] Assembling and adjusting the webbing's numerous straps was inconvenient, the small pack lacked space, and miscellaneous items of equipment could not be clipped onto the belt.[12] The pouches were too short to carry Sten magazines, leaving soldiers to stuff them into their pockets, where they rattled around and were damaged.[13] More ominously, there was no provision for carrying hand grenades on the 37-pattern webbing. These too were jammed into pockets, where they bounced around with a metallic clang. Even worse, some soldiers hooked them through their belts, sometimes with tragic results. Lieutenant Brian Munro recalled, "Everybody was issued two grenades; we carried them on our belts. One time we were moving by vehicle; one of the soldiers was sitting at the back of the truck, near the tailgate. One grenade shook loose of his webbing and fell out the back of the truck. It landed on the road, the pin fell out and it exploded."[14]

Several salient items of Canadian combat clothing were equally unsuited to the operational conditions encountered in Korea. In 1950 the Canadian infantry's standard combat headdress was still the wide-brimmed 1914-pattern Mark II steel helmet. Originally designed to protect soldiers in the trenches of the First World War from shell fragments and air-dropped flechettes, the Mark II steel helmet became obsolete in the early 1940s with the advent of the American MI helmet and the British assault helmet.[15]

Defence planners had initially hoped to outfit the soldiers of the 25th Brigade with American helmets, but this was scrapped when it was discovered that the earphones of the Canadian no. 19 wireless set were incompatible with the new headgear.[16] As signalmen comprised only a fraction of an infantry battalion's strength, the decision not to equip Canadian soldiers with American helmets was totally ludicrous. There was no reason why Canadian signalmen, most of whom had no operational requirement for protective headgear, could not have continued to use the old Mark II helmet while their compatriots in the fighting echelon wore the superior American, or indeed the British, helmet. In any event, when the Canadians deployed to Korea, they did so with the same helmets that their fathers had worn in the trenches of the First World War.

Because the Chinese initially possessed little in the way of mortar and artillery support, steel helmets were rarely worn during the first year of the war. Veterans of 2 PPCLI fondly recall throwing their steel helmets overboard as their troopship approached Pusan harbour.[17] However, with the shift to static warfare and the concomitant increase in Chinese artillery capabilities, helmets became a battlefield necessity. In this changed tactical context, the obsolescent Mark II helmet proved to be less than satisfactory. According to Lieutenant-Colonel Campbell, "The steel helmet of the Canadian Army is the most poorly designed, uncomfortable, useless, stupid-looking and unpopular piece of equipment issued to Canadian soldiers."[18] As usual, Campbell's recommendations for a new design fell on deaf ears, and the Mark II remained in Canadian service until the late 1950s.

Helmets were seldom worn on patrol. Instead, soldiers wore the equally useless Canadian peaked cap.[19] Designed in late 1950 with the parade square in mind, the cap came in two patterns. The winter version was made of heavy serge and had no provision for ear coverage; the summer version was made of cotton and incorporated a folding tailpiece that could supposedly be extended to protect the back of the neck from sun glare. This was seldom used,[20] for its tight design prevented the free movement of the head and neck.[21]

Both patterns of peaked cap were incompatible with the hood of the poncho – another item of kit first used by the Canadians in

Korea – and undermined its effectiveness. During the battle of Chail-li, for example, the peak capped- and poncho-clad soldiers of 2 RCR were drenched by a vicious 30-minute wind and rainstorm that left them soaked and chilled.[22] Reporting on the incompatibility of the peaked cap and poncho, the battalion intelligence officer (IO), claimed, "There is a great variety of opinion on the poncho. It is useful for bed rolls and shelters and may be efficient as a rain cape if suitable headdress becomes available."[23] The report went on to recommend that a water-repellent, wide-brimmed headdress based on the British tropical bush hat be developed.[24] This was not done, leading several companies in the brigade to request a re-issue of the Second World War British-pattern gas cape.[25] The hoodless gas cape could be cinched tightly around the neck, thereby compensating for the Canadians' lack of a suitable headdress.

Winter combat suits were also a problem. The first troops to arrive in Korea wore the 1949-pattern Canadian arctic parka and windproof trousers. The outer shells of both parka and trousers were made of heavy $6\frac{1}{2}$ oz. khaki-coloured cotton poplin. Insulated by a heavy wool pile liner, the fabric was impermeable to wind, was quiet, and generally gave good service.[26] Oral sources unequivocally confirm this assertion; during the winter of 1950–51 a Canadian winter suit fetched upwards of US$100 on the Korean black market.[27] Indeed, even the enemy was known to strip dead Canadians of their 1949-pattern parkas and windproof trousers.[28]

During the winter of 1951–52 the 25th Brigade was issued with an "improved" winter combat suit, constructed of a loose-weave nylon. In hindsight, nylon was a poor choice for the suit's shell material. It was neither windproof nor water resistant, and it generated far too much static electricity.[29] As most of the 25th Brigade's heating devices were fuelled by gasoline, the Canadians wore their winter suits in close proximity to a bunker stove at their peril. Nylon was also extremely noisy. Lieutenant Bob Peacock recalled that "the noise the nylon made from rubbing together as you walked was audible for quite a distance on crisp, clear nights. A patrol wearing nylon parkas and windpants could be heard long before it could be seen."[30] As we shall see later, excessive noise was last thing Canadian soldiers needed in the silence of no man's land.

The poor quality of the winter combat suit also made Canadian soldiers susceptible to environmental injuries. In Korea's subarctic climate, improper clothing could kill a soldier nearly as fast as an enemy bullet. Commenting on the sorry state of Canadian winter clothing, Lieutenant-Colonel Campbell wrote: "It seems unbelievable that Canada is far behind the United States and U.K. in the design of winter clothing ... The U.K. pattern was preferable. The nylon ... used in Canadian winter clothing is completely unsatisfactory. Also its appearance is bad."[31] Outfitted with shoddy winter kit, many Canadian soldiers attempted to re-equip themselves with superior British or American clothing, or even with the old 1949-pattern parka and windproof trousers.[32]

The Canadians' wool battledress uniforms were marginally better. Originally designed in the late 1930s for use in Western Europe, battledress was considered obsolete by the 1950s.[33] During the Second World War, the Americans had set the trend in modern field uniforms with the development of a general-purpose cotton uniform. At war's end, the British began testing their own version of a general-purpose combat uniform. The Canadian Army adopted a wait-and-see policy with regard to new field uniforms, resolving to replace battledress with a general-purpose uniform once an acceptable design became available.[34] At the outbreak of the Korean War, testing was not complete, and Canadian troops were issued with modified versions of their respective Second World War – pattern battledress uniforms.

Battledress was not completely unsuited to the climatic conditions encountered during the winter months in Korea, but most Canadian soldiers found the heavy serge material of the uniform scratchy and uncomfortable.[35] Moreover, battledress was extremely difficult to keep clean in the lice-infested bunkers of the Jamestown line – the east-west axis of defensive positions that served as the U.N. front line for the last two years of the war. As a result, at least one battalion in the 25th Brigade allowed its soldiers to wear the marginally superior Canadian summer uniform,[36] supplemented with thermal underwear, throughout the winter months, reserving battledress for leave in Japan.[37]

Boots were equally troublesome. The Canadian-pattern ammunition boots wore out very quickly and were not considered suitable for the Korean theatre.[38] Moreover, in Korea's wet monsoon season the Canadian-issue puttees restricted circulation and caused lameness.[39] Ammunition boots were totally inadequate for patrolling. They were clumsy and noisy, and were a constant source of blisters.[40] Several battalions in the 25th Brigade compensated for the lack of appropriate footwear by issuing their men with superior British or American boots.[41] But what the Canadians really needed was a lightweight canvas patrol boot similar to the one worn by the Chinese. This they did not receive, and for the duration of the war they were forced to tramp around no man's land in their heavy ammunition boots.

Overall, then, the army's first operational experience with uniquely Canadian kit and combat clothing left much to be desired. While some Canadian kit and clothing did perform well in Korea, the most important items were unsuited to static warfare in general, and to patrolling in particular. A similar pattern emerges with regard to small arms.

Small arms are the weapons the soldier operates at the section level – the smallest sub-unit in the Canadian Army's order of battle. At the time of the Korean War they included the light machine gun, the rifle, the submachine gun, and the hand grenade.[42] These were considered basic infantry weapons, and all who served in the 25th Brigade were trained, to varying degrees of competence, in their operation.

The light machine gun (LMG), or section automatic weapon (SAW) in contemporary military parlance, was the most powerful weapon that a soldier could expect to operate at the section level. During the Korean War the Canadians, and indeed all the Commonwealth forces in Korea, used the .303 Bren LMG. Fed from a 30-round magazine, the weapon could deliver up to 120 rounds, or four magazines, per minute.[43] At this rate of fire, the barrel had to be changed every two and a half minutes.[44] Barrel changing was a simple procedure, taking an experienced Bren gunner only seconds to complete. A red-hot barrel could be cooled by air after removal or dipped in water without damaging the metal.

The 22 lb. gun was serviced by a two-man crew and was primarily designed to be fired from a bipod in the prone position. It could be fired from the hip in the "assault" position, but this required considerable training (not to mention upper-body strength) to be effective. In other words, the Bren was not especially suited to the type of small-unit, hit-and-run skirmishes over rough terrain that were such a feature of the fighting in Korea, especially during the last eighteen months of the war. The commanding officer of the 3 R22eR, Lieutenant-Colonel J.G. Poulin, maintained that the Bren "proved an awkward weapon whenever taken on patrol and would have been advantageously replaced by the machine carbine or a semi-automatic rifle."[45]

The Bren also lacked a suitable tripod. This was not a concern when the battlelines in Korea were fluid, but with the shift to static warfare there was a requirement for a tripod so that the Bren could be fired from bunkers along fixed lines. The 3 RCR's Lieutenant-Colonel Campbell explained: "The provision of inter-locking small arms fire was a problem. Because of the steepness of the slopes and many ridges and re-entrants it was often only possible to get fire in front of a [section position] by getting it from another platoon. The only solution was found to be in the use of fixed lines ... Unless the bren-gunner had a definite task he tended to wait for the enemy to appear directly in front of him. As a result the weapon was useless."[46]

Unfortunately for the Canadians, the Bren's tripod was clumsy and not suited to bunker use.[47] This had an adverse effect on the Bren's ability to fire on fixed lines and led to a greater reliance on rifle fire. As Canadian tactical doctrine dictated that rifle fire develop *around* Bren gun action, the result was a significant decrease in the amount of firepower available at the section level.

The Bren's reduced effectiveness would not have been so serious had Canadian soldiers been equipped with a better rifle. The standard Canadian rifle during the Korean War was the bolt-action no. 4 – the last in a long pedigree of Lee Enfield rifles to see service with Canadian troops.[48] Fed from a 10-round magazine, the no. 4 had to be reloaded after each shot by operating the bolt. In the hands of a trained soldier, the rifle could fire up to 15 rounds per minute.[49] This rate was generally found to be adequate during the first year of the Korean War, when rifle and Bren gun fire could be properly coordinated according to tactical doctrine.[50] Although it did not fire as fast as the semi-automatic M1 Garand (the standard American infantry rifle), the no. 4 rifle initially had one important advantage over its American counterpart: it was virtually jam-proof.

Adverse battlefield conditions were a fact of life during the first year of the Korean War. Snow, freezing rain, mu, and dust all conspired to wreak havoc on the mechanisms of semi-automatic and automatic weapons. American accounts from the winter of 1950–51 often describe action during which M1 Garands failed to fire, their mechanisms having been locked into place by heavy frost and freezing rain.[51] Moreover, one official American report stated: "Casualties have been incurred by our troops because of malfunctioning of automatic or semi-automatic weapons at critical times. Investigation revealed that the malfunctions were caused by excessive dirt or dust on moving parts."[52]

The no. 4 rifle, on the other hand, seldom failed under even the most difficult conditions. According to Bill Rawling, an obstruction or jammed casing was almost always cleared by the first turn of the bolt.[53] Commenting on the superiority of the no. 4 rifle over the M1 Garand, Lieutenant-General G.G. Simonds wrote: "I have recently had a report from 2 PPCLI in Korea which includes a statement to the effect that under the conditions of frost and mud in the theatre they have found that a hand-operated rifle is more reliable than the automatic."[54]

With the shift from mobile to static warfare, the primary advantage of the no. 4 rifle became its greatest liability. The construction of semi-permanent defensive positions reduced the exposure of weapons to the elements, and cleaning kits and graphite lubrication were readily available in the front line. Lulls in the fighting also provided ample time for routine cleaning and maintenance. Thus, the conditions that initially gave hand-operated mechanisms the edge over automatic mechanisms largely ceased to exist with the consolidation of the Jamestown defensive line. More importantly, in the close-quarter combat of patrol actions and in the defence of positions against massed attack, the no. 4 rifle's bolt action was dangerously slow.[55]

As the war progressed and the unsuitability of the no. 4 rifle became increasingly obvious, several Canadian officers, including Lieutenant-Colonel Campbell and Major Harry Pope, called for its immediate replacement.[56] It must be noted, however, that Campbell's handling of the rifle question was much more cautious than Pope's.[57] While Pope advocated the wholesale abandonment of the no. 4 rifle in favour of a new light automatic weapon for the Canadian Army, Campbell emphasized that his opinions applied only to static warfare in Korea. In an interview with the brigade's historical officer, he maintained: "In a completely static war such as this, almost everyman now armed with a rifle should have instead [an automatic]. In a mobile war the difficulties of ammunition supply make it unfeasible to have the men so armed but here in Korea, at this time, there is no particular problem in getting ammunition to the front and everyone can be armed with an automatic weapon."[58]

Campbell's obligatory references to the unique circumstances surrounding the fighting, and to the inherent superiority of a rifle over an automatic in mobile warfare, reflected the general impression in Ottawa that the war in Korea was an aberration. To the army brass, mobile warfare on the Central European front was the real war for which Canadian soldiers ought to be equipped and trained.[59] Anything that deviated from the European model was of secondary importance and could be brushed aside. Moreover, those at the top of the military hierarchy could always sidestep the rifle issue by pointing to the generally satisfactory performance of the no. 4 during the mobile operations of 1951. Not surprisingly, Pope's and Campbell's calls for a new weapon fell on deaf ears, and the no. 4 rifle remained the standard Canadian infantry weapon until the late 1950s.

Outgunned by their adversaries who were well equipped with Soviet-designed "burp guns,"[60] Canadian soldiers went to extraordinary lengths to acquire replacements for their no. 4 rifles. The weapon of choice was the American M2 carbine, a light, .30-calibre self-loading rifle issued to NCOs and specialist personnel. These could be obtained on the black market that flourished behind the front line, or through barter with American soldiers. The usual price was one bottle of Canadian whisky, though it could increase according to demand.[61]

Having obtained an M2 carbine was no guarantee that a soldier could use it. While some units, notably 2 PPCLI and 1 RCR, permitted their men to carry non-issue weapons, others did not. Moreover, NCOs and junior officers often requisitioned their men's M2 carbines for their own use. "I got my hands on an M2 carbine," a soldier recounted, "but it was taken away from me by the same lieutenant who couldn't read a map if his life depended on it. He took it away, and I knew for a fact that the other officers made damn sure they had a .30-calibre M2 handy. The guys at HQ didn't understand our situation."[62]

Indeed they did not, for the Canadian submachine gun (SMG), the only other weapon officially available to Canadian enlisted men, was also dangerously inadequate in the close-quarter combat of static warfare. The standard Canadian SMG of the Korean War was the 9mm Sten gun. With only forty-seven parts, the Sten was designed in England for cheap mass-production during the early stages of the Second World War. Still in Canadian service at the outbreak of the Korean War, it was initially issued only to NCOs, medics, radio operators, drivers, and the crew of support weapons. However, with the advent of static warfare in Korea there was a tactical requirement for more SMGs, and Stens were issued on an increased scale.[63]

The Sten suffered from a number of mechanical and design flaws that became increasingly pronounced as the war progressed. The weapon's safety catch was unreliable, making it a continual source of battle accidents; standing Orders in 1 RCR forbade soldiers from loading their Sten guns unless an enemy attack was imminent.[64] As well, the lips of the Sten magazine were easily bent and were the primary cause of morale-sapping battlefield malfunctions.[65] A driver in the 54th Transport Company recounted how he and his navigator were almost killed by a sniper after their Sten gun jammed in the middle of a firefight.[66] Another soldier was adamant that "a lot of good men died because they were stuck with shitty [Sten] guns."[67] A 1 RCR patrol report for 31 May/1 June 1952 noted that several Stens failed to operate during a firefight with a Chinese patrol.[68] Perhaps the most telling indictment of the Sten was expressed in the laconic words of an anonymous soldier from 3 PPCLI: "The Sten gun was a fuckin' piece of crap."[69]

In examining the battlefield performance of the Sten gun in Korea, one is reminded of the Ross rifle fiasco of the First World War. However, unlike their fathers in the trenches of Flanders Fields, the soldiers of the 25th Brigade never received a replacement for their Sten guns. Although battalion commanders routinely criticized the Sten in their after-action reports, no attempt was made to equip the Canadians with a more reliable submachine gun.[70] In an official report prepared for the commander of the 25th Brigade, Major Harry Pope explicitly called for the adoption of the superior British Patchett SMG or, even better, the Australian Owen gun;[71] but to no avail.[72] Faced with a Hobson's choice, soldiers routinely ditched their Sten guns in favour of the equally unsuitable but more reliable no. 4 rifle.[73] Not until *after* the Korean War did the Canadian Army finally replaced the notorious Sten with the British Patchett.[74] In the meantime, combat performance in Korea suffered accordingly.[75]

The Canadian infantry section's paucity of firepower led to an increased reliance on hand grenades. This was particularly the case in the defence, where the Canadians' British-designed Type 36 hand grenades were trundled down the steep slopes of hilltop positions into the masses of attacking Chinese infantry. Used in this manner, and in the more conventional bunker-busting role during the advance to the 38th parallel, the Type 36 hand grenade was extremely effective. But in the routine patrol actions of the static war, it was far from ideal.[76] The grenade's substantial weight limited its range, and the thrower often found himself in the bursting area of his own weapon. The Chinese, on the other hand, made extensive use of lightweight concussion grenades.[77] The stick-shaped Chinese grenade could be hurled much farther than the heavier egg-shaped Type 36 and had a smaller bursting area. In the featureless terrain of the valley bottoms, the Chinese could shower Canadian patrols with grenades with little danger to themselves.[78] Using this tactic, they were often able to gain the initiative, which they were quick to exploit with fire from their burp guns.[79] At this point, the rifle-equipped Canadians could do little to regain the tactical initiative.

In view of the Type 36's unsuitability in Korean patrol actions, several Canadian officers, Lieutenant-Colonel Campbell and Major Pope included, pushed for the development of a new "offensive" grenade. Once again, calls for a new weapon went unanswered, and the Canadians were forced to make do with the weapon at hand. Thus, the lack of an effective offensive grenade in the latter half of the Korean War was the final chapter in a sorry tale of High Command ignorance. From improper LMG tripods to dangerously unreliable submachine guns, the Canadian infantry section was improperly armed for static warfare in Korea. As we have seen, several battalion officers in Korea called for the development of more appropriate weaponry, but Defence headquarters in Ottawa ignored their requests. Consequently, soldiers were forced to carry out their duties with weapons that were unsuited to the tactical conditions they encountered. Fortunately for the Canadians, their American-pattern support weapons were better designed.

The most powerful weapons used by the Canadian infantry in Korea were mortars. According to the Canadian Army training manual *The Infantry Battalion in Battle* (1952), a mortar is "a close support weapon with a high trajectory. It can give overhead fire support from behind steep cover and can engage targets which are themselves defiladed from flat trajectory weapons. The mortar is capable of producing a high rate of fire which is limited only by the amount of ammunition available."[80] The Canadians generally used two types of mortars in Korea, the 81 mm and 60 mm.[81]

Procured directly from American sources, these replaced the British 3 and 2 in. mortars in 25th Brigade service just before the first Canadian ground troops were committed to battle in Korea.

The 81 mm mortar was a battalion-support weapon; its primary purpose was to kill enemy personnel.[82] It was capable of firing a 7½ lb. high-explosive shell to a maximum range of 4,000 yards – 1,200 yards farther than the 3 in. mortar.[83] The rapid rate of fire was twelve bombs per minute, though this could be considerably increased in an emergency. Their substantial weight (107 lb. each, not including ammunition) made them too heavy to be man-packed into action. Obviously, this was not a problem during the static war. During the earlier mobile phase, however, the "81s" were mounted for travelling on U.S.-pattern M3A1 halftracks, another new addition to the Canadian infantry's arsenal.

The 81 mm was generally regarded as a superb weapon. Lieutenant-Colonel Stone believed that it played an indispensable role in saving his battalion from annihilation during the battle of Kap'yong in April 1951, as did Lieutenant-Colonel Dextraze during the battle of Hill 227 seven months later.[84] Lieutenant-Colonel Campbell also considered the 81mm a good weapon and claimed that his battalion had complete faith in it.[85]

The 60 mm mortar was essentially a smaller version of the 81 mm. It could fire an M492A high-explosive bomb to a maximum range of 1,939 yards – nearly five times farther than the weapon it supplanted.[86] The 60 mm mortar's maximum range was often used with devastating effect, but it was not without its detractors. Canadian soldiers often grumbled about its complexity, and its illumination round was often unreliable and in very short supply. Moreover, according to the 3 RCR, the place of the 60 mm "in the battalion organization has not yet been found. It was used in the defence satisfactorily at company level ... but it was really duplicating the role of the 81 mm mortar."[87]

Another new American-pattern support weapon whose role was not clearly defined was the 3.5 in. rocket launcher. Antitank weapons had been critical during the first few months of the war, but by the time the first Canadians took to the field in early 1951, enemy armoured vehicles were seldom encountered.[88] In any event, the 25th Brigade's 3.5 in. rocket launchers were truly state-of-the-art. Constructed of aluminum, the tube could be broken into two sections for carrying, a useful feature when operating in Korea's mountainous terrain. More importantly, the weapon was capable of penetrating the frontal armour of a T-34 tank – a target the Canadians never had an opportunity to fire on – at 100 yards.[89] Still in the laboratory stage of development in June 1950, the 3.5 in. replaced the 2.36 in. in time to be taken into combat with the 2 PPCLI in February 1951, when it was used with some success in antipersonnel and bunker-busting roles.

With the shift to static warfare, the 3.5 in. rocket launcher became redundant. But the Canadians continued to use the heavier 75 mm recoilless antitank rifle, a tripod-mounted, direct-fire weapon with an effective range of 6,000 yards. Another first-rate American weapon,[90] the 75 mm gradually superseded the British-designed 17 pounder in 25th Brigade service, a weapon that Lieutenant-Colonel Campbell claimed was "as extinct as the Dodo."[91] With no tanks to shoot at, the Canadians used their 75 mm recoilless rifles to knock out enemy snipers and observation posts. They also used it in the indirect role of bolstering the firepower of the mortar platoon's 81 mm mortars.[92]

Rounding out the 25th Brigade's battalion-support weapons were machine guns. The Canadian Army's standard medium machine gun (MMG) during the Korean War was the British-designed Vickers .303 Mk 1.[93] This was a water-cooled, belt-fed gun, capable of impressive feats of battlefield endurance.[94] Operating on a simple gas-assisted short-recoil system, it could fire 10,000 rounds an hour – as long as it had an ample supply of water, ammunition, and spare barrels – making it especially suited to the static defensive role. Although the Vickers was heavy (90 lb. including water and tripod) and emitted a stream of water vapour when hot, most Canadian soldiers had nothing but praise for the gun. Indeed, the Vickers's extraordinarily long service life testified to its quality, a factor, no doubt, in the decision to retain this weapon for service in Korea. First used by the Canadians in the trenches of Flanders, it was not officially declared obsolete until 1968.[95]

Although the Canadians refused to trade their Vickers for the American M1917 Browning – a weapon that shared many of the same characteristics and fulfilled the same role as the Vickers – the 25th Brigade did use two other U.S.-pattern machine guns in Korea: the .30 and .50 in. Browning. These modern, air-cooled weapons had originally been fitted to the M3A1 halftracks to provide protection for the dismounted mortar crew, but with the advent of the static war they were incorporated into the front-line defences. Both were considered fine weapons, though at least one Canadian battalion commander felt that proper tripod mounts for the Bren would obviate the need for the .30 in. Browning.[96] This did not prevent both weapons from being officially adopted by the Canadian Army after the Korean War.

The official adoption of the Browning family of machine guns was yet another example of the technological evolution that occurred in the Canadian infantry at the time of the Korean War. As has been seen, the Canadian Army's break with the British technological model went simultaneously too far and not far enough. Korea was the first time that Canadian soldiers went into battle wearing uniquely Canadian kit. However, British kit was generally superior and would have been a better choice for Canadian fighting men. Although they performed well enough during the mobile phase of the Korean War, the Canadians' outmoded British-pattern small arms were completely unsuited to static warfare. Insofar as SMGs were concerned, anything – the newly developed British Patchett, the Australian Owen, or even the American "grease gun"[97] – would have been better than the Canadian Sten gun. The one area in which the technological evolution was indeed to the 25th Brigade's advantage was in infantry-support weapons. With the exception of the Vickers, for which no superior American replacement could be found, the Canadian Army went to war in Korea equipped with the very latest in American infantry-support weapons. This, together with improper training, had a pronounced impact on the Canadians' battlefield performance in Korea.

CHAPTER THREE

Domain of the Golden Dragon

If the soldiers of the 25th Brigade were improperly trained and equipped for battle, they were equally unprepared for the non-combat aspects of service in the Far East. Most possessed only a superficial knowledge of Korea before their deployment, and the 25th Brigade's shipboard indoctrination program certainly did nothing to improve this. Thus, when the Canadians disembarked from their troopships in wartorn Pusan harbour, they recoiled from the smell, dirt, poverty, and cultural mores that confronted them. By the time they reached the front line, many soldiers in the 25th Brigade had formed the impression that Korea was a God-forsaken place, populated by a primitive and even brutal people. Some went so far as to question the purpose of Canada's involvement in the war. But all this still lay in the future. Before they even reached Korea, the Canadians had to endure a monotonous and at times unbearable voyage across the Pacific into the "Domain of the Golden Dragon."[1]

The long voyage to Korea began when the soldiers of the 25th Brigade clambered aboard their transports for the move to the Seattle docks, the point of embarkation for most Korea-bound Canadian fighting men.[2] For the Special Force battalions this entailed only a short bus ride from nearby Fort Lewis;[3] for later battalions, especially those from the RCR or R22eR, it involved a considerable overland journey by rail. Fresh from embarkation leave, many of the men were in a festive spirit, and reports of drunkenness and harassment of civilian passengers were common.

On arrival at the Seattle docks, the departing Canadians formed up to hear their CO's embarkation orders. These normally outlined the men's duties and explained what was to be expected of them on their impending voyage: "On board ship, it being a U.S.A. vessel, there will be no liquor ... In its place there will be lots of training. Instead of drinking beer, we'll be studying tactics, learn the odd word of the Korean language, do PT and generally get so fit that we will be worthy representatives of our country."[4] On dismissal, the Canadians heaved their personal weapons and kit onto shoulders that still ached from the most recent round of pre-deployment vaccinations, and climbed up the narrow gangplank into the bowels of their American troopships. Having stowed their kit and secured their weapons, most scurried up to the top decks for a final glimpse of the North American continent. For some, it would be their last.

The reference to learning the Korean language in the embarkation orders is revealing, for it was during the month-long sea voyage that the Canadians were to receive their Korean indoctrination.[5] But from the outset, the shipboard indoctrination program was far from satisfactory. Lectures were ostensibly given for one hour each week by a senior NCO (who himself knew next to nothing about Korea) in an informal setting known as Soldier's Forum.[6] These rarely dealt with specifically Korean topics but instead focused on the reasons for Canadian involvement in Korea, the principles of the U.N. Charter, and the threat of international communism.[7]

Attendance at Soldier's Forum was highly irregular.[8] With so many last-minute administrative and technical details to attend to aboard ship, men routinely missed their weekly classes. Moreover, the seas seemed to conspire against the successful conduct of any training whatsoever, as many men were seasick from the time they left Seattle to the time they arrived in Pusan. For example, during their voyage to Korea in October 1951 on board the USS *Marine Alder*, the 1 PPCLI encountered a typhoon off the coast of Japan which lasted for three interminable days. The waves were so large and powerful at times that the propellors actually came out of the water, causing the entire ship to shake violently.[9] With most of the battalion incapacitated by seasickness, very little training was accomplished. Later contingents experienced similar problems. Private W. Hummer of the 3 RCR recalled being "as sick as a fucking dog" and spending much of the voyage above ship "hurling over the side," while Lance-Corporal William Powell of the 3 PPCLI remembered that both officers and enlisted men were too "sick over the railing to be any good."[10] Thus, shipboard training, when it took place at all, was usually on a small scale.

The indoctrination of Korea-bound troops was also bedeviled by a dearth of suitable instructional material. As late as mid-1951, the 25th Brigade gleaned most of its information on Korea from a series of reports published by the Advanced Headquarters, British Commonwealth Base Korea. These reports, collectively entitled "Notes on Korean Police Action," included general information on Korea, such as population, religion, language, education, and government. They also contained an extremely racist section on Commonwealth impressions of the Koreans. The anonymous author began by noting: "In the short time of four months over here, one can only get impressions of Koreans, or Gooks as they are commonly known."[11] Following this blunt disclaimer, the author delineated what were in his opinion some of the more salient characteristics of Korean civilians. These included a propensity for thievery, a "foul smelling" body odour, and "a very perverted sense of humour."[12] He went on to note that while "the male member of the species [sic] is a poor worker, the female is good."[13] The women, he wrote, "work from sun up to sun down washing clothes and tilling the fields."[14]

The obvious unsuitability of the 25th Brigade's shipboard indoctrination program became painfully apparent by the fall of 1951. The behaviour of at least some Canadian servicemen, particularly those assigned to support duties behind the front line, was endangering Canadian-Korean relations.[15] Backing for this viewpoint was furnished by the fact that six Canadian soldiers were court-martialled in August and September for perpetrating violent criminal acts against Korean civilians (see chapter 10). Moreover, the reports of Canadian war correspondents in newspapers and on the radio seemed to point to a general disrespect for Korean culture on the part of Canadian servicemen. Canadian Press war correspondent Bill Boss reported an incident in which Canadian soldiers chopped down a tree that was sacred to local villagers to create an unobstructed field of fire during a *training* exercise.[16] Similarly, as a correspondent for *Maclean's* magazine, Pierre Berton witnessed Koreans being removed from their mud huts at bayonet point so the Canadians could take a photograph.[17] Berton also recalled a Canadian soldier who wanted to unload the magazine of his Bren gun.[18] He did so into a Korean burial mound.

Another manifestation of Canadian soldiers' cultural insensitivity identified by the war correspondents was their tendency to treat all Korean women as prostitutes.[19] While prostitution was a tolerated survival strategy for many impoverished women in Korea's male-dominated society, only certain women were permitted to sell their services. Prostitutes were usually identifiable by their "pageboy" hairstyle and predominantly Western style of dress; married Korean women, who did not engage in prostitution, wore traditional Korean clothing "with their hair parted in the middle and tied tightly in a bun at the back."[20] Few Canadian soldiers recognized these subtle but important differences in appearance and social function. Obviously, an attempt to solicit the services of a married woman was an affront to Korean culture and did little to cement harmonious relations between Canadians and Koreans. However, Pierre Berton cautioned, "Let's not blame the soldiers. They've had no training in this business of being an ambassador. Nobody's given them any really thorough training in how to behave [in Korea] ... In my mind, this business of teaching men how to behave is getting to be as important as teaching them first and second stoppages on the Bren gun."[21]

As evidence of tactless Canadian behaviour in the Far East continued to mount, Lester Person wrote a letter to Brooke Claxton requesting him to look into the matter. Claxton duly instructed the Acting Chief of the General Staff, Major-General H.A. Sparling, to prepare a paper on Canadian attitudes towards Koreans and the suitability of 25th Brigade's predeployment indoctrination program. As might be expected, Sparling refuted all accusations of improper behaviour in the 25th Brigade. He claimed that Canadian soldiers were friendly towards Koreans and went out of their way to give them food, clothing, and medical attention.[22] But Sparling's paper did hint at the gross ineffectiveness of the Canadian indoctrination program. In the appendix he outlined several measures that had recently been implemented to better prepare Canadian soldiers for service on the Korean peninsula. The most important of these was the provision of handbooks and pamphlets on Korea to Canadian units destined for the Far East.

As it turned out, the handbooks were almost always in short supply and of rather dubious value. For example, *A Precis on Korea*, which covered topics such as agriculture, transportation and communications, trade and industry, and natural resources, was prepared by the Directorate of Military Training and issued to the

25th Brigade on a scale of one copy per battalion.[23] Eight hundred reprints of the U.S. Army's *A Pocket Guide to Korea*[24] were also issued to the 25th Brigade, but few veterans recall ever having one in their possession.[25] To make matters worse, the guide scarcely mentioned the dismal social situation in Korea. However, it did contain hard-to-find information such as "Swinging used to be exclusively a girl's sport but, because of its danger, has come to be shared by boys as well"; "Koreans may have wives and concubines [and] enjoy a good joke or a laugh like the rest of us," and they "produce a strong potato alcohol."[26] Tips of this sort obviously did little for the edification of Canadian soldiers. Having said this, the guide did make a half-hearted attempt to familiarize its readers with such things as Korean religious practices, diet, and appearance. But even here it lacked useful information, as reflected by the simplistic chapter titles: "Confucius Says," "Fire-Eaters?" and "They've Fashion Worries, Too."[27]

Overall, the 25th Brigade's Korean indoctrination program was a failure. While Canadian soldiers were relatively well informed about the political implications of containing communism on the Korean peninsula, they knew very little about the country and people they were sent to defend.[28] In hindsight, the 25th Brigade's ineffective indoctrination program can largely be attributed to the Canadian Army's limited experience in Asia. The Canadian Army did not deploy to Korea with the benefit of a well-developed institutional memory of service in Asia, as it had of Europe during the Second World War. Even though this collective memory did not include Italy, the Canadians and Italians clearly had far more in common than the Canadians and Koreans ever could have.[29] Furthermore, the practice of leaving indoctrination on Korea to the last possible moment, while travelling on the troopships, prevented the effective dissemination of information based on first-hand experience from returned veterans to those en route to the Far East. In any event, the absence of an effective indoctrination program left the door wide open for the Canadians to form their own impressions of Korea – impressions that were based on racist assumptions and fleeting glimpses of Korean society from the back of a truck or from behind the window of a passing troop train, rather than on sustained contact with the local civilian population.

In all likelihood, few Canadian soldiers worried about their inadequate indoctrination as their troopship steamed across the Pacific;

at this early stage of their tour there were other concerns of more immediate importance. Chief among them were the condition of their quarters and the quality of their rations. Troopships are notoriously crowded, and the ships of the U.S. Military Sea Transport that carried the Canadians to Korea were no exception. Normally, officers and senior NCOs were billeted in relatively comfortable cabins on the upper decks. Enlisted men were always quartered in the lower decks, and shipboard discipline dictated that these be kept as clean and orderly as possible. With hundreds of men and their kit crammed into the narrow corridors between the racks of bunks, it was hard enough to move, let alone maintain some semblance of military order.

Restrictions on access to shower and laundry facilities made the journey across the Pacific even more uncomfortable, especially when the ships approached the warm, tropical waters off Hawaii. For men sweltering in the overcrowded, claustrophobic troop compartments, the pungent odour of unwashed humanity and vomit from seasick comrades was more than an unpleasant inconvenience; it was a health threat. On the advice of battalion medical officers, the Canadians countered the threat by implementing open-air laundry parades. Under this arrangement, troops moved to the top deck by platoon, then stripped and tied their heavy woollen battledress uniforms to a long line that was weighted at one end. Once all the uniforms were securely fastened, the line was tossed overboard and dragged alongside the ship. After approximately thirty minutes the line was reeled in, uniforms reclaimed, and the process began anew.

Other measures implemented to combat the spread of bacteria in the lower decks included the formation of special fatigue parties to swab the heads and the enforcement of the highest standards of personal hygiene. At least one Canadian battalion, the 2 PPCLI, is known to have taken the latter measure to extremes. During its voyage to the Far East the battalion launched Operation Haircut.[30] A group of Patricias with shaved heads, aptly known as the "cue ball club," were given the responsibility of executing the operation. Armed with hair clippers, the cue ball club prowled the troop compartments of the USS *Private Joe P. Martinez* looking for unwary comrades with full heads of hair. Most submitted willingly to the "cue ball treatment." Those who did not were unceremoniously pinned to the deck and their heads shaved clean. In addition to improving comfort and hygiene, Operation Haircut undoubtedly contributed to the maintenance of morale on an otherwise arduous voyage.

Another feature of shipboard life which required some adaptation on the part of Canadian soldiers was the practice of responding to commands and instructions issued over the ship's intercom. "Each message [was] prefixed [by], 'Now hear this ...' then the message."[31] Thus, the announcement ordering the soldiers quartered in compartment E5 on the USS *Marine Alder* to the "galley"[32] would sound like this: "Now hear this. Compartment Easy-Five, chow now."[33]

Meals were, in fact, the highlight of most soldiers' day. Served cafeteria style, they usually knocked several hours off each day, since the men had to wait in a queue that wound around the ship and down into the lower decks. The food on the American troopships was generally good and plentiful,[34] although during 2 PPCLI's voyage to Korea many of the men complained that they were constantly hungry. On one occasion, when the meal consisted of that old military standby, spaghetti and meat sauce, all that remained by the time the men at the end of the line reached the meal counter were a few pots of plain pasta noodles.[35] But as with any highly coveted commodity, food could be procured from the ship's under-deck economy. An after-hours ham sandwich from the galley cost a hungry Canadian an outrageous five American dollars; for those with more modest tastes, a stale loaf of bread could be had for two American greenbacks.[36]

Little concern was shown for the soldiers' welfare during off-duty hours; when not incapacitated by seasickness, many veterans recall having the evenings to themselves. This is surprising given the fact that the Canadians were on their way to an unfamiliar operational theatre. Surely, some of their free time would have been better spent brushing up on weapons drills or first-aid techniques. In any event, the off-duty hours represented a temporary escape from the monotony of the shipboard routine. For some, the respite presented an opportunity to win back the money lost in the previous night's poker game; for others, it was a time to write letters or to contemplate the immediate future. For most, it was a time to smoke and socialize and, if they were lucky, to catch a movie on the ship's upper deck after dark. But even movies could become tiresome, especially when the same ones were played over and over again. On the USS *Private Joe P. Martinez*, for example, *The Boy with the Green Hair*, starring Barbara Hale and Pat O'Brien, was shown no fewer than five times.[37]

To help alleviate the boredom of shipboard life, most Canadian units published daily news bulletins. These included the "Gaffey

Gazette" on the USS *Hugh J. Gaffey*, the "Freeman News" on the USS *General Freeman*, and the joint American-Canadian "Eagle-Leaf" on the *Private Joe P. Martinez*. All provided news and sports results from home, as well as a lost and found service, movie, worship, and dining schedules, birthday announcements, weather reports, a classified ads service, and a humour column.[38] For example, the 11 December 1950 edition of the "Eagle-Leaf" advised its readers that, among other things, today was their sixteenth day at sea, that a Canadian bayonet had been found in the Chaplain's Office, and that Lance-Corporal Finn was repairing Ronson cigarette lighters in compartment B3 for 25 to 75 cents.[39] The edition also ran a cartoon depicting a Canadian soldier doubled over with bare buttocks in front of an angry-looking medical officer. The caption read: "I don't care what your Sergeant says, there's no lead in there!" It goes without saying that comic relief of this nature was especially appreciated by men who had spent the better part of two weeks living in close proximity to their senior NCOs.

As their troopships steamed across the international dateline, the Canadians were treated to another form of comic relief: the U.S. Navy's Neptune Ceremony. Following a humorous display of dancing, horseplay, and singing, participants were presented with a Domain of the Golden Dragon certificate, which read in part:

To all ... GREETINGS ... Know ye: Ye that are chit singers, squaw men, opium smokers, ice men, and all-round land lubbers that [name of soldier] having been found worthy to be a numbered dweller of the FAR EAST has been gathered in my fold and duly initiated into the Silent Mysteries of the Far East ... I do hereby command all money lenders, wine sellers, cabaret owners, Geisha managers, Sergeant Majors and Military Police, and all my other subjects to show honour and respect all his wishes whenever he may enter my realm.[40]

Raucous behaviour notwithstanding, for many soldiers the Neptune Ceremony served to underline their sense of having crossed the Rubicon. From this point on, there was no turning back. They were now in the Domain of the Golden Dragon, a mysterious region that contained people and images of which they had only the faintest knowledge.

The Canadians were treated to their first glimpse of the Domain of the Golden Dragon when their troopships steamed into the port of Yokohama in Japan. All Korea-bound troopships stopped here to take on supplies and, in some instances, American replacements. Battalion commanders typically used the layover to give their troops an opportunity to shake their sea legs and take in some of the local attractions. To the chagrin of their officers, the route marches around Yokohama revealed just how unfit the men had become after twenty-three days at sea.

Depending on their battalion, the Canadians either proceeded directly by sea to Pusan or boarded a troop train for the ports of Kure or Sasebo in western Honshu, whence they embarked for Korea.[41] The 1 PPCLI was one of the Canadian battalions to follow the latter itinerary. The unit's war diary records the Patricias' first glimpse of Asia:

3 October 1951,
Docked at Yokohama 0940 hrs ... Entraining was handled efficiently ... Faces were glued to the window until darkness. This was our first close-up view of the Orient and the troops were not going to miss a thing.

4 October 1951,
0500 hrs we passed through Osaka; it was a miserable night, the constant rocking of the train making sleep nearly impossible. However, the discomforts of the night were soon forgotten as we passed through such large cities as Kyoto, Kobe, Hiroshima, all of them offering strange and wonderful sights.

5 October 1951,
Embussed at 1600 hrs and were taken to the port Sasebo ... Troops were allotted compartments and boarded [a Japanese] ship ... Officers and Senior NCOS have state rooms; the other personnel are occupying compartments and sleeping on straw mats.[42]

Now only thirty-six hours from Pusan, the Canadians settled down for the final leg of their journey.

If the Canadians' initial impression of Japan was generally positive and coloured with an intense curiosity, their initial reaction to Korea hovered between apathy and contempt. According to a Department of National Defence press release, the first thing the newcomer to Korea noticed was the rugged topography.[43] With the exception of the Chorwon plain north of Seoul, Korea is a mountainous country, and at the time of the Korean War few of the mountains were covered with trees. Perpetually short of natural resources, the Japanese had effectively deforested much of the countryside during their thirty-five years of occupation. As the Canadians approached the waters off Pusan, the vast granite monoliths that ring the city came into view: "The realization that they would have to fight over [this type of terrain] spoiled the enjoyment, because it was not easy fighting country."[44]

Nor did the climate particularly appeal to the Canadians. One report characterized it as having a schizophrenic personality.[45] During the summer, monsoon winds off the South China Sea blow across the peninsula, bringing high temperatures and heavy rainfall. During the winter, the pattern is reversed: dry subArctic winds from Manchuria and Siberia blow down the peninsula, freezing rivers and bringing subzero temperatures. Some of the first Canadian soldiers to arrive in December 1950 were shocked to discover just how cold a Korean winter could be. A soldier in the 2 PPCLI recalled: "We thought we were going to a tropical country. Nobody had heard of Korea or thought of snow and ice. If I thought it to be snow and ice, I would never have gone."[46]

Whether the temperature was blisteringly hot or bitterly cold, the soldiers of the 25th Brigade had other things to worry about as their ship slipped into Pusan harbour. On arrival, they packed their fifty pounds of combat kit and stumbled down the gangplank on legs still reeling from three weeks at sea. Barely audible above the din of heavy combat boots on wood and the grumbling and cursing of men locked in strenuous physical exertion were the familiar refrains of "If I Knew You Were Coming, I'd a Baked a Cake." This song, performed by the resident U.S. Army band, greeted every Canadian unit that arrived in Pusan and remains an enduring feature of most veterans' initial impressions of Korea.

Two other features that shaped initial Canadian impressions were the smell and the abject poverty of Pusan's civilian population. Today, Pusan is a modern, relatively clean, cosmopolitan city; at the time of the Korean War, it was a shambles. The city's Japanese-built infrastructure (where it existed) was in a dilapidated state and totally incapable of dealing with the hundreds of thousands of civilian refugees who had flocked to Pusan in the aftermath of the bloody battles of 1950. Thousands of homeless and despondent civilians, without the bare necessities of life, congregated in the vermin-infested shanty towns that ringed the port.

The depth of their misery defies description, crammed as they were into crude shelters constructed of corrugated iron, discarded ration boxes, and loose bricks. Cooking was conducted outside over open fires, often only feet away from the communal privy. Where none existed, people simply relieved themselves amid the piles of rubble. Sewage and refuse mixed freely in the gutters which, combined with the powerful (and unfamiliar) smells emanating from several thousand cooking pots, created an odour that assailed the Canadians' nostrils. Veterans often recall that it was possible to smell Pusan several miles out to sea, long before the city came into view.

Commenting on Pusan's appalling odour, Brigadier Rockingham reminisced: "The lack of sanitation when a normal population is present is bad enough, but when a place like Pusan has its population increased from 600,000 to 2,000,000 by refugees, you can imagine the result. The stench was so bad that it seemed to slow the motors of the vehicles as we drove through a particularly heavy concentration."[47] Lance-Corporal William Powell also remembered Korea as "a really smelly country," while Private Louis McLean recalled, "When I arrived in [Pusan], the smell of human waste was a shock and almost made me puke. I had done enough puking on the [troopship] and was really tired of feeling like crap."[48]

As repulsive as Pusan's unmistakable odour was to the Occidental nostrils of Canadian soldiers, most found the pitiful conditions of the refugees the hardest to bear. According to Lance-Corporal John Murray, "When we arrived in Pusan I was terrified about the prospect of getting ashore and meeting the population ... I was not prepared for the dismal conditions of South Korea. I was really depressed after my arrival."[49] And in Corporal James Wilson's opinion, "If anything sticks out in my mind it was the total destruction and destitution which the [civilian] population, particularly the people of Pusan, had to survive in. We were not trained for those conditions, and man I still can't shake the shitty conditions out of my mind."[50] That both soldiers identified a lack of training as the cause of their emotional difficulties is not surprising, given their inadequate indoctrination in the social aspects of operational service in Korea.

The Canadians were equally unprepared for some of the sights and cultural mores they witnessed as they moved through Pusan and up the Korean peninsula to the front line. Shortly after the 25th Brigade's arrival in Pusan in May 1951, a Canadian convoy was treated to what Brigadier Rockingham later referred to as "our first experience of the Oriental disregard for human life."[51] As the convoy made its way from the port to the railway station, a truck struck and killed a young Korean child. To the Canadians' utter disbelief, the ROK soldier who was driving the truck jumped out of his cab and casually dragged the child by one foot to the side of the road, whereupon he returned to his vehicle. The by now dismounted Canadians intercepted the hapless driver before he could get back in his truck and proceeded to rough him up. Fearing his soldiers were going to kill the man, Rockingham was forced to intervene.[52] The next day he reported the incident to some seemingly indifferent ROK army officials, who "did not actually say 'so what,' but managed to convey that impression."[53]

Fresh from North America, Rockingham and his men were understandably shocked by the seemingly ghastly insouciance of both the offending driver and ROK officialdom. However, what they could not possibly understand was that the combined impact of war and thirty-five years of Japanese subjugation had made survival in this unhappy nation precarious, to say the least. Had the Canadians been properly indoctrinated before arriving in the Far East, they would have recognized that the behaviour of the truck driver and the ROK officials reflected the mass desensitization to capricious death that is such a feature of life in a war zone. In no way did this sordid episode reflect a uniquely "Oriental disregard for human life." To the average Canadian soldier in Brigadier Rockingham's convoy that day – and it is with perception that we are dealing – the callous disregard for a dead child was proof positive of the primitive and brutal nature of Korean culture. As the Canadians completed the final leg of their journey to the front line by train, this impression became even more pronounced.

The train ride from Pusan to the battleline north of Seoul took two days and was notoriously uncomfortable, eroding any enthusiasm the Canadians might have had for the passing Korean countryside. There was no heat in winter (and, save for the occasional broken window, no air-conditioning in summer). The wooden seats were extremely uncomfortable, and men and kit competed for every available space.[54] Tempers were dangerously short as the narrow-gauge train rocked from side to side over the rugged Korean terrain. To make matters worse, the ablution facilities were horrendous:

> The worst was the toilet. It was situated at the end of the coach, a small cubicle with a hole in the floor. No windows, no door, nor rails to hold onto as the train rocked back and forth, no toilet paper, just three narrow walls and a hole in the wooden floor. There was shit everywhere. Layers and layers of it, shit on the floor, shit on the walls and as proof of man's endeavour, shit on the ceiling. We were prisoners on that train ... each and every one of us had to use that shit hole at least once.[55]

The little food available on the train – normally some hardtack biscuits and jam from the men's ration packs and a canteen full of heavily chlorinated water – was scarcely any better. In the event, few Canadians had much of an appetite; the sight (and smell) of Korean farmers (condescendingly referred to as "smiling Sams")[56] carrying "honey" buckets of human excreta to fertilize the vast rice paddies that flanked the rail line, helped suppress the pangs of hunger.

The Korean housing and clothing also failed to impress. At the time of the Korean War, most rural Koreans still lived in the same type of mud and brick thatched-roof villages as their ancestors had done.[57] The Canadians viewed these humble abodes as quaint anachronisms, though few could understand why they were being sent over ten thousand miles from home to defend them. To a lesser degree, this feeling was directed against the Koreans themselves. Dressed in baggy clothing and often wearing what were considered to be "comic" pointed hats, the average Korean farmer appeared to Canadian eyes like something out of medieval times.[58] Even the Korean women were considered to be unattractive and dirty[59] – although, as we shall see, this did not keep the soldiers of the 25th Brigade out of the bawdy houses.

The Canadian impression of Korean civilians was not enhanced by the desperate acts of some of the poverty-stricken individuals they encountered at train stations along the way. These incidents could range from innocuous attempts by shoeshine boys to overcharge their Canadian customers to instances of outright thievery. The latter were never violent, and usually involved the theft of rations or personal effects such as blankets and greatcoats.[60] Nevertheless, they only confirmed the racist stereotypes proffered in the early indoctrination literature.

In an effort to come to terms with the dismal conditions that confronted them, Canadian officers and men with Second World War experience often commented how primitive and undeveloped Korea was compared with anything they had seen in Europe. It was widely accepted that Korea was even more backward than either Sicily or southern Italy.[61] Following a brief visit to Korea during the summer of 1951, Lieutenant-Colonel D.S.F. Bult-Francis of the Adjutant-General's Office wrote that "the terrain, the climate, the time and space factor, the filth and poverty ... in Korea ... forbid comparison with conditions met during the last war in Europe."[62] This assessment was corroborated by the soldiers themselves. A veteran of the Second World War claimed that he "had seen destruction in Europe late in '44 and '45 ... but nothing compared to [Korea] ... Rice paddies fertilized with human waste, no plumbing, the place stank and the food was scarce."[63]

The seemingly primitive and brutal nature of Korean society shocked most soldiers, leading some to question the purpose of Canadian involvement in Korea. Shortly after his arrival in Korea a young soldier informed a Canadian war correspondent, "I suppose this really must be a war for an ideal. There's obviously nothing else to fight for in this god-forsaken country."[64]

The Canadians' scepticism was further exacerbated by the questionable combat record of their Korean allies. It is not the purpose of this work to assess the battlefield performance of the Republic of Korea (ROK) army in the Korean War; nevertheless, it is important to note that long before the first Canadians reached the front, the ROK army had already gained the reputation as unreliable "bug-out artists."[65] Although this reputation had first been bestowed on ROK units by the Americans, the Canadians quickly picked up on it after the disintegration of the 6th ROK Division at the battle of Kap'yong in April 1951. During the battle, the 2 PPCLI had occupied defensive positions overlooking the Kap'yong River Valley in a successful attempt to hold open an escape route for the beleaguered Korean division. As the Canadians made their way up the Kap'yong River Valley, they passed scores of panic-stricken ROK soldiers fleeing in the opposite direction. The sight did not impress the advancing Patricias, and for the rest of the war the Canadians generally viewed their ROK counterparts as cowards who were more than happy to let others do the fighting for them.

Koreans were not the only thing on the Canadians' minds as they neared the front line. As their train chugged northward, the villages and farmers that had dotted the rail line gave way to ammunition dumps and military traffic. The Canadians were now in the rear areas of the battle front, and tension infused the air.[66] The sense of adventure that had characterized the initial stages of the journey to Korea was replaced by a feeling of foreboding as the soldiers came to the realization that they were now at the sharp end. This feeling was reinforced when they detrained and clambered aboard the Royal Canadian Army Service Corps trucks for the final run to the front. There they would remain for twelve long months, save for the occasional rotation into divisional reserve and a five-day "rest and recuperation" (R&R) in Japan. Otherwise, the only way out of the front line was on a stretcher or wrapped up in a blanket.[67]

The journey to the front had been long and difficult for the soldiers of the 25th Brigade. Life aboard the U.S. Navy's troop transports had been anything but a picnic; for almost a month the men had had to cope with cramped, foul-smelling troop compartments, boredom, seasickness, and, in one instance, insufficient food. Things had not improved when the Canadians disembarked from their "floating prisons" in Pusan harbour.[68] Inadequately indoctrinated on the non-combat aspects of service on the Korean peninsula, the vast majority recoiled from the smell, poverty, dirt, and cultural mores that confronted them. By the time they reached the front line, many had formed the impression that Korea was a God-forsaken place, populated by a primitive, and even brutal, people. But like all first impressions, this one would undergo a metamorphosis once the Canadians found themselves in sustained contact with Koreans. And in the crucible of combat, other variables would emerge that would shape Canadian impressions of, and relations with, the Korean "other" on the field of battle.

CHAPTER FOUR

Rice Burners and KATCOMs

During their Far Eastern tours the soldiers of the 25th Brigade were in almost continual contact with the men of the Korean Service Corps (KSC), an indigenous service organization that provided porters and labourers to each front-line unit.[1] Later in the war, the soldiers of the third battalions served in combat alongside Korean Augmentation Troops, Commonwealth (KATCOM). Canadian battlefield relations with these two distinct groups of Korean servicemen were characterized by an ambivalence that transcended the immediate concerns of race. While the Canadians generally respected the men of the KSC, the KATCOM were resented and poorly treated. The explanation for these contradictory battlefield relations with the Korean "other" is found in the Canadian soldier's sense of comradeship and group cohesion. So long as the Koreans contributed to the maintenance and support of the Canadian group, they were viewed in a positive light and generally treated as equals. When they were perceived as a threat to the group, they encountered intense hostility and even harsh treatment.

One of the most important insights to emerge out of Richard Holmes's exceptional book, *Firing Line*, was the importance of comradeship – and, by extension, small-group cohesion – to the combat soldier. While recognizing the role played by abstract ideals such as patriotism and religion in certain historical contexts, Holmes argued forcefully that neither could account for what he termed "the valour of simple men."[2] "To the [soldier] crouched behind a hummock of peat and heather while bullets snap over his head," he wrote, "neither ideology nor religion give much incentive ... to get up and sprint for the next cover ... For the key to what makes men fight – not enlist, not cope, but fight – we must look hard at military groups and the bonds that link men within them."[3]

As we saw in an earlier chapter, the entire process of cementing the men of the 25th Brigade together into small groups began in basic training. Harsh collective punishment for individual transgressions and relentless drilling were not simply anachronistic hangovers from an earlier age; from the outset, these practices were utilized to draw recruits closer together under conditions of intense but controlled hardship. Group cohesion assumed a new importance once the soldier was posted to an infantry section within his regiment. Although he was now a member of the regimental family, his strongest loyalties were to his section mates – the primary group of ten[4] men with whom he trained, bunked, whored, and drank on a daily basis. The army has long recognized that soldiers who socialize together fight together, and this precept was not lost in the messes and brothels frequented by the men of the 25th Brigade.

In Korea, the bonds of comradeship and the small-group cohesion that stems from it became even more pronounced. Commenting on the intensification of comradeship in a battlefield context, a Second World War British medical officer wrote: "The sense of separation from home, from its security and comforting permanence and its familiar reassurance of one's personal status, is a permanent stress. A camaraderie is the only human recompense for a threatening sense of importance in the face of death and the waywardness of elemental forces and the decisions of the mighty who use soldiers like pawns."[5] Isolated on their lonely hilltop positions, fighting a war that was not even officially recognized as such, and faced with the daily threat of death or mutilation, Canadian soldiers turned inward to their immediate comrades to the exclusion of almost everything else. Mail and parcels from home were shared amongst the group, and food was prepared communally whenever possible.[6] All that mattered to the individual soldier was the continued survival and well-being of his primary group.

S.L.A. Marshall has argued that soldiers in the line of fire do not even think of themselves as subordinate members of a formal military organization; they see themselves as more or less equals in a very small and exclusive group. In combat, the members of the group fight for their personal survival, which, as John Keegan noted, is inextricably bound to group survival.[7] At the same time, individual soldiers fight to avoid drawing the cowardly contempt of the group.[8] This is the essence of the combat soldier's existence, and it goes without saying that any threat to this group – be it real or imagined, friend or foe – will be met with extreme hostility.

This perilously brief overview of the importance of the primary group to the combat soldier in no way does justice to the complexity of the subject. Nevertheless, it is included here to give the reader some appreciation of the nature of small-group dynamics on the battlefield, because the Canadians' conflicting battlefield perceptions of and relations with the KSC and KATCOM were largely shaped by these two organizations' relationship with the Canadian primary group.

As the Canadians moved up through the echelons to the front line, they could not help but notice the large numbers of KSC workers unloading trucks, hauling equipment, and digging latrines. Formed as a paramilitary organization on 4 July 1950, the KSC provided workers to serve in combat-support roles.[9] Although technically part of the ROK army, the men of the KSC did not normally carry weapons, nor did they wear the standard ROK combat uniform.[10] In its place, they wore a padded blue jacket and baggy khaki trousers. Despite their unwarlike appearance, they were commanded by their own officers and NCOs and organized along military lines: each KSC regiment consisted of three battalions of four companies each. In October 1951 the Canadians were officially assigned one battalion of KSC personnel from the 120th Regiment. This battalion was employed by the 25th Brigade for the rest of the war, on a scale of one KSC company per Canadian infantry battalion;[11] the remaining company was divided between Brigade Headquarters and the Engineer Squadron.[12]

In fact, Canadian soldiers and Korean workers had served together long before the official allocation of a KSC battalion to the 25th Brigade in October 1951. Shortly after the 2 PPCLI took to the field in February of that year, the battalion was allocated several dozen Korean porters to assist in packing food, water, ammunition, and the other sundry supplies that an infantry unit requires in the field. As the Koreans were not yet officially part of the KSC – most would be integrated into the corps within the year – but were locally recruited labourers, they were organized into a company under the command of the battalion adjutant. Initially known as G Company (which, according to the 2 PPCLI's Japanese Canadian war diarist, stood for "Gook") the Korean porters quickly became known as the "rice burners," in reference to their dietary staple.[13]

There was, however, another reason for the shift in terminology. At this time, the war in Korea had not yet bogged down into a static, attritional affair. During the day, the Canadians advanced on a north-south axis along the valley floors and occupied hilltop defensive positions for the night. The absence of serviceable roads dictated that all supplies had to be man-packed up the steep and at times treacherous slopes that led to these positions. Imbued with incredible stamina and intense physical strength, each Korean porter carried a load of more than 55 lb. on a traditional Korean backpack known as an A-frame. An A-frame consisted of "three poles lashed together to form a crude triangle with shoulder straps of roughly-woven straw."[14] Cargo such as ammunition crates, water cans and hayboxes (insulated metal containers used to transport food prepared in the company kitchens) was simply lashed onto these frames, and the Korean porters did the rest. The battalion war diary recorded that Korean "supply trains continued to arrive in the battalion area until late at night ... due to a nearly ten mile cross-country endurance test in the course of which they crossed three 300 metre passes and climbed to 900 metre ridge lines through snow and ice."[15]

Watching the porters clamber up the narrow ice-covered mountain tracks under their back-breaking loads, the Canadians could not help but be impressed. Corporal Earl Richardson recalled that the KSC "were something to see with the big loads they carried. They climbed those hills at a steady clip and seldom rested. Some of them only had one eye or arm. They were a cheerful people and worked long hours."[16] Although today we might find the term "rice burner" offensive and laced with racism, Patricia soldiers used the term out of respect for the indefatigable travails of their Korean porters.[17] Hence the shift in terminology. The Canadians who served in Korea were products of Second World War society, and from their point of view "rice burner" was certainly an improvement over the term it supplanted. An official (and decidedly racist) Canadian report ruefully commented in mid-1951 that "the men of the [Korean] labour battalions [are now referred to] as 'the rice-burners,' the term 'gook' having gone out of fashion."[18]

With the occupation of static defensive positions along the Jamestown line in late 1951, the KSC assumed an increased importance; hence the official allocation of a KSC battalion to the 25th

Brigade in October. Where previously they had been used almost exclusively as porters, the KSC now found themselves performing myriad tasks for the Canadians. They constructed and repaired trenches; they filled the critical link in the medical evacuation chain by acting as stretcher bearers between the forward fighting positions and the jeep-heads on the reverse slopes of the Canadian positions; they unloaded supply trucks; and, of course, they kept the front-line troops supplied with the combat soldier's holy triad of ammunition, water, and food.

Given their close proximity to the firing line, it was inevitable that members of the KSC would periodically become casualties. As was the case with the Canadians, most KSC casualties were caused by routine enemy artillery harassment. The Chinese artillery often fired around mealtimes, and the Korean porters carrying the hayboxes to the hungry Canadian riflemen manning the forward defensive positions were frequently caught in the midst of this fire.[19] On other occasions, such as the Chinese attack on Hill 355 in October 1952, members of the KSC were killed bringing ammunition to the Canadian fighting trenches.[20] The unit's war diary recorded the wounding of a KSC man just before the attack: "Shelling and mortaring continued throughout the day and one casualty was sustained, a Korean labourer. It has made it rather uncomfortable."[21]

The almost daily interaction between Canadian soldiers and the men of the KSC gave rise to a form of rudimentary front-line pidgin.[22] The most common expressions included "Hava yes" and "Hava no" for "yes" and "no," "Idawa" for "Come here," "tok son" for "lots," "chop chop" for "food," and "number one" for "the best."[23] Thus, if a Canadian soldier wanted to ask a KSC porter if the evening's rations had been brought forward, he might say: "Idawa boy-san, hava yes number one chop chop?" Similarly, the KSC porters used front-line pidgin to communicate with the Canadians. Lieutenant Bob Peacock reminisced: "One of our corporals in B Company was a native western Indian from the Blackfoot tribe and was called Corporal 'Same Same' by the Koreans. They would point to him, and then to themselves, and say, 'You, me, Same Same!'"[24]

When not on duty, the men of the KSC were quartered in canvas cantonments just behind the front line but well within range of enemy indirect artillery fire. Here, they enjoyed a vibrant social life, frequently imbibing "Kickapoo Joy Juice," a potent moonshine produced in stills fashioned out of scrap trench stores.[25] Not surprisingly, the KSC received frequent visits from the Canadians. Cigarettes and food (usually C-ration tins of fruit cocktail, which were popular with the KSC)[26] were the standard medium of exchange, though the thirsty Canadians might also pay cash for a jug of the Korean shine.

Besides such illicit sources of income, the men of the KSC received wages. They were paid on a monthly basis, in Korean currency, out of the British Commonwealth Occupation Forces' account in Japan.[27] A private in the KSC earned only 3,000 Korean *won* per month (about 75 cents Canadian),[28] leading one officer to comment that KSC labour was "dirt cheap."[29] While this was undoubtedly true, the wages of the KSC were significantly higher than those the ROK government paid the KATCOMS. As we shall see, the pay differential between the two formations led to problems once the KATCOMS took to the field.

By performing essential battlefield-support tasks, albeit for a mere pittance, the men of the KSC made an important contribution to the Canadian infantry battalion in the defence.[30] The 3 RCR's Lieutenant-Colonel Campbell reported: "It would be a hell of a job to defend these hills without [the KSC]. Because of the work they do by digging and bringing up supplies, almost every fighting man in the battalion is left free to fight. If the KSC were not here the size of the battalion's frontage would have to be reduced by at least 20%."[31]

The enlisted men of the 25th Brigade also recognized the importance of the KSC. Korean veteran and author Robert Hepenstall called them the "unsung heroes of the Korean War."[32] Countless other veterans have echoed Hepenstall's words. Private Louis Vincent McLean recalled that the KSC personnel attached to "our units made us realize the spirit and enthusiasm of the people and what they were fighting for," while Corporal James Wilson admired the KSC "because they had the will to survive in adversity and smile."[33] According to Sergeant Ken Blair, the KSC "were good workers, and no matter what job you gave them, they would eventually get it done ... The Canadians treated them as equals more or less. The average Canadian soldier in Korea was well aware that he was a peasant, the same as the Korean workers. A strange bond developed between the two races."[34]

Of course, this was not true of all Canadian servicemen. Some continued to view Koreans through the lens of racism. Their initial impression of Korea and its people was lasting, and their blinkered views were applied with equal vigour to the men of the KSC.³⁵ For example, a Canadian veteran has recently commented on the alleged brutality of KSC discipline and the frequent use of summary execution for even minor offences.³⁶ Another veteran, perhaps recalling the 1st Commonwealth Division's order prohibiting KSC personnel in front-line fighting positions after dark, has questioned the loyalty of some KSC personnel.³⁷ But overall, the available documentary and oral evidence strongly suggests that most Canadian soldiers held a tremendous amount of respect for their allies in the KSC and treated them accordingly.

On the other side of the fence, the handful of KSC veterans who were interviewed during the preparation of this work have nothing but praise for their treatment by the Canadians. Choi In Wa, a KSC porter who served with the PPCLI, recalled that the men were always happy to see him when he arrived with food and ammunition. "The Canadians would give me presents," he said, "which I would give to my mother. My family was very poor and the presents [normally food and cigarettes] helped a great deal."³⁸

It would be convenient to end the foregoing analysis with the conclusion that, on the whole, the soldiers of the 25th Brigade viewed their Korean allies in a positive light and treated them with the dignity and respect of an esteemed battlefield ally. In all probability, this would have been the case had it not been for the KATCOMS. The British official historian has recently suggested that despite "some reservations the [KATCOMs] were wholly accepted" in the 25th Brigade.³⁹ This clearly was not the case. While the Canadians generally respected if not admired the KSC, they despised and resented the KATCOMS.

Unlike the KSC, which provided essential battlefield support for the 25th Brigade and so contributed to the maintenance and identity of the Canadian primary group, the KATCOMS were officially integrated *into* these groups as de facto Commonwealth soldiers to bolster combat strength.⁴⁰ Predictably, the Canadian riflemen forced to serve with the KATCOMS viewed them as interlopers at best, and dangerous battlefield liabilities at worst. Accordingly, the KATCOMS' treatment by the Canadians was characterized by an intense hostility, which could at times lead to battlefield practices of extreme heartlessness.

The origins of the KATCOM program can be traced back to August 1950. At that time the U.S. Army, desperately short of replacements, initiated a scheme whereby surplus ROK personnel were integrated into understrength American field units.[41] Known as the Korean Augmentation to the U.S. Army, or KATUSA, the program had provided the understrength Eighth Army with several thousand replacements by the time of the Inchon landings.

From the outset, the KATUSA program was bedevilled by problems. Very few of the KATUSA replacements could understand a word of English, and many had never fired a rifle before. To complicate matters further, the U.S. Army did not possess sufficient quantities of small-sized clothing to outfit the KATUSAS, and it was found that the standard-issue American infantry rifle was too long and bulky for the average Korean to use effectively. Finally, there were major differences in culture, sanitary habits, and diet between the KATUSAS and their American hosts. In spite of these obstacles, the program proceeded as planned, and by war's end more than 23,000 KATUSAS were serving in American combat units.[42]

Despite the Americans' early integration of Korean troops into their order of battle, it was not until July 1952 that the units of the Commonwealth Division considered accepting Koreans for service with the infantry.[43] The proposal to integrate Korean soldiers into Commonwealth fighting units was in line with the overall Canadian policy of making the South Koreans responsible for the defence of their country as much as possible.[44] Moreover, from the international relations perspective, the integration of Korean troops would enhance Canada's image by showing that it was prepared to operate with non-white troops on an equal basis.[45] In light of these considerations, the Canadian government quickly approved the integration scheme in principle, though several months passed before it was actually implemented, during which time the various Commonwealth governments conferred on the matter. Meanwhile, defence planners in Ottawa voiced concern about the practicality, and indeed desirability, of attaching Korean troops to Canadian fighting units. As the Canadian official historian noted, "Such a proposal, coming at a time when an Armistice seemed to be a distinct possibility," seemed to present defence planners with "more difficulties than solutions."[46] Chief among the difficulties were those associated with equipping, administering, immunizing, and disciplining foreign nationals assigned to Canadian units.[47]

Not to be discouraged, the commander of the 25th Brigade and the integration scheme's leading proponent, Brigadier M.P. Bogert,[48] rebuffed his critics by stating that the Korean soldiers would not be issued with a complete set of Canadian kit but would eat the same food as the Canadians and would be re-examined and inoculated as necessary to prevent the spread of communicable diseases.[49] Insofar as discipline was concerned, Bogert claimed that there was no problem. "From experience in American Divisions," he wrote, the "threat of being sent back ... to the ROK Army for disciplining ... has been found to be good cure."[50] Finally, he assured the sceptics at Defence Headquarters that Koreans were capable fighters.[51]

Bogert's optimism carried the day in Canadian military and diplomatic circles.[52] The Chief of the General Staff, Lieutenant-General Simonds, appears to have been particularly impressed with Bogert's handling of the issue, claiming – erroneously as it turned out – that "the process will be a gradual one and will develop from the integration of fully trained sections to the formation of Korean platoons and companies under their own officers and eventually, the substitution of a South Korean battalion for one of the Canadian battalions of the brigade."[53] When official approval for the integration of Korean soldiers into the Commonwealth Division was received in early 1953, Bogert's headquarters commenced drafting the terms of reference that would govern the integration of the KATCOMs into the 25th Brigade. One hundred KATCOMs were to be assigned to each Canadian infantry unit on a scale of three per section.[54] The Canadians were to be responsible for arming, partially equipping, and feeding the KATCOMs, although, as Korean nationals, the KATCOMs would be paid by the ROK government.[55]

The first KATCOMs arrived at their host units towards the end of March 1953. It must have been a horribly disheartening experience for these young Korean soldiers as they made their way up through the echelons to join their respective rifle companies. Inadequately trained, unable to understand English, and unversed in Canadian cultural mores, these poor souls were expected to become instant members of what is arguably the most exclusive club on earth: the front-line infantry rifle section.

History has shown that individual replacements have always had a difficult time being accepted by the men in their section, particularly when the group has served together for an extended period.[56] That the replacements or augmentation troops might speak a different language or be subject to a different code of discipline made their acceptance into the group even more unlikely; but it does not change the fact that the plight of the combat replacement is tenuous at best. In his remarkable study of the allied fighting man in the Second World War, John Ellis described the unenviable experience of the front-line infantry replacement. Fresh from a holding unit and often improperly trained, the replacement was thrown into combat in the company of men who could not even bother to learn his name.[57] As an outsider, the replacement's life was not worth as much as a veteran's. This, combined with his "often infuriating ignorance, sometimes tempted the veterans and their officers to use them almost as cannon fodder."[58]

And cannon fodder the KATCOMS quickly became. Although they were supposedly basically trained when they joined their host units, experience showed that this was rarely the case. A postwar Brigade Headquarters report concluded that the majority of KATCOMS were useless and more of a liability to the brigade than a help.[59] Lieutenant-Colonel J.G. Poulin of the 3 R22eR explained why: "During shell fire, the KATCOM cower in their trenches and are undependable. On patrol they are unreliable. None of the company commanders like the KATCOM. They take them because they are ordered to."[60]

Another report noted that the KATCOMS almost always fell asleep as soon as it became dark, violating the infantryman's adage of "stay alert and stay alive."[61] The 3 PPCLI's Lieutenant Chris Snider recalled: "I was on a night patrol and part way through the night was alarmed to hear loud snoring. It was a KATCOM who had fallen asleep. He was awakened and quietly warned to stay awake. The next day, back in the platoon area, I was told by my NCOs that this had not been the first time this particular individual had fallen asleep."[62]

As might be expected, very few Canadians relished the idea of going on patrol or occupying defensive positions with the KATCOMS. This was especially true of the KATCOMS' Canadian "buddies" – the three soldiers in each section who were ordered to keep an eye on the seemingly unreliable and unpredictable KATCOMS. At the same time, these soldiers were to rely on the KATCOMS to watch their backs in a firefight. How the KATCOMS and their Canadian buddies were expected to have faith in one another in a firefight when they could not even speak to one another remains a mystery.

In any event, the complete lack of faith in the KATCOMS' battlefield reliability left their Canadian buddies, and by extension the entire section, with two choices. On the one hand, they could attempt to train the KATCOMS. However, the communication barrier (front-line pidgin was hardly up to the task of explaining how to set the fuse on a hand grenade), not to mention the absence of suitable training areas in the front line, hampered the successful conduct of useful, realistic training.

At best, the KATCOMS might be given "a few rudimentary lessons on their personal weapons, and then they were assimilated into trench warfare, which meant going on patrol at night."[63] Obviously, such training was far from satisfactory and did little to increase the confidence of either party. On the other hand, the KATCOMS could simply be abandoned by their buddies and left to fend for themselves. On patrol, this meant that they were positioned in the most vulnerable places in the formation, either at the very front or very back.[64] While the man walking point found himself performing the role of a human mine and ambush detector, the man in rear was a prisoner of war (POW) in the making. While it is impossible to know with any certainty the extent to which this form of patrol stacking occurred, circumstantial evidence indicates that it happened regularly.[65] Moreover, the apparent certainty of a truce agreement being reached in Korea after May 1953 would have made this practice seem all the more desirable, at least from the Canadian perspective.

Unlike the combat replacement in other wartime contexts, the KATCOM soldier faced the additional hurdles of culture and nationality. An NCO recalled: "The KATCOM's first meal after arriving in our unit was breakfast; here they were in the line up, with all this good food, and not a clue as to what was what. Our troops really put it to them. They showed them how to put pepper in their oatmeal, peanut butter and salt in their coffee. There were lots of stomach complaints."[66]

In addition to suffering gastronomical discomfort at the hands of their Canadian tormentors, the KATCOMS had reason to feel ill over their pay – or, more precisely, the lack thereof. As noted earlier, the KSC were paid, albeit indirectly, by the Canadian government, and the KATCOMS were paid by the ROK government. Compared with their compatriots in the KSC, the KATCOMS were poorly paid indeed. While a private in the KSC earned 3,000 *won* per month, or approximately 75 cents, a KATCOM private earned only 30 *won* – less than one cent per month![67] A Canadian private serving alongside a KATCOM, meanwhile, earned a whopping $47 per month. Not surprisingly, the disparities in pay created problems.[68]

The KATCOMS resented the fact that they were paid less than their KSC compatriots; in their opinion, serving in a front-line combat unit certainly entitled them to equal, if not greater, pay than the KSC porters. Similarly, it was difficult for the KATCOMS not to feel cheated when the other soldiers in their section were earning over 4,700 percent more than they were for performing the same duties. There is also some evidence to suggest that the KATCOMS' lack of money may have undermined their acceptance into the group.[69] There is a tradition in the Canadian Army that the new guys buy the beer.[70] Beer was readily available in the front line, and there were no prohibitions on its consumption when the men were not on duty. Thus, to the hard-drinking soldiers of the 25th Brigade, the KATCOMS' inability to spring for a crate of beer may have been construed as a sign of antisocial behaviour.

Another bone of contention between the Canadians and the KATCOMS was discipline. As the ROK army was responsible for disciplining the KATCOMS, the latter were not subject to the Canadian code of service discipline.[71] This meant that KATCOM troops could not be disciplined in the same manner as Canadian troops. Although this was not a major problem when serious breaches of discipline were involved, in which case the KATCOM was handed over to ROK authorities for punishment, the same cannot be said for minor offences. The distances involved, not to mention the impracticality, of pulling a KATCOM out of the line each time he committed a minor offence gave rise to a disciplinary double standard in the sections in which they served. While a Canadian soldier might be fined or assigned extra duties for losing an item of kit or for having a dirty rifle, a KATCOM could not. Thus, there was little that could be done when a KATCOM committed a minor infraction.[72] Canadian soldiers were understandably annoyed when a KATCOM went unpunished while the same transgression committed by one of their own number could result in a fine or, more seriously, a forfeiture of R&R. In such instances – and they were by no means rare – justice was usually served after dark by a clenched fist or the heavy sole of a Canadian combat boot.[73]

Another problem was that some of the Canadians, particularly those who shared bunkers with KATCOMS, were troubled by the Koreans' mannerisms and sanitary habits. A young Bren gunner in the 3 PPCLI remembered the way the section split in two as soon as meals were served. "The KATCOMS," he remembered, "would find a quiet corner of trench and squat on their haunches and just grin at you. So much for comradeship."[74] Another common Canadian complaint centred on the KATCOMS' dietary staple, *kim-chi*. Although they were fed Canadian rations, most KATCOMS kept a small supply of their own food, a wise precaution given the behaviour of some of the Canadians in the mess lines. Made from fermented cabbage, hot peppers, and garlic, *kim-chi* exuded a heavy odour which, in the close confines of a front-line bunker, most Canadians found revolting. Indeed, the Americans often referred to the KATUSAS as "those damned *kim-chi* eaters."[75] A final complaint centred on the KATCOM habit of constantly spitting and of standing on latrine seats.[76] Such fundamental differences in behaviour did little to promote cohesion and comradeship between the Canadians and the KATCOMS.

Nevertheless, the friction generated by differences in pay, discipline, and culture were not the primary cause of the Canadians' hostility towards the KATCOMS. The problem was that these differences, together with the language and training difficulties, combined to ensure that the KATCOMS remained, in effect, replacements for the duration of their service. Treated with hostility from the outset by virtue of the threat they imposed to the survival of the Canadian primary group, they were never able to transcend their new-guy or outsider status as any other replacement might; that is, of course, if they survived their baptism of fire.

The KATCOM program did not end when the shooting stopped in Korea on 27 July 1953, but the ceasefire did pave the way for a certain amount of reflection about the program's advantages and disadvantages. Lieutenant-Colonel Campbell spoke for many in the Canadian brigade when he concluded that the KATCOMS "remain[ed] a separate element in what was once a homogenous body."[77] Similarly, 3 R22eR's Lieutenant-Colonel Poulin opined that KATCOMS "think and act quite differently to Canadians. You can't integrate them and expect them to be Canadians."[78] Campbell's and Poulin's dissatisfaction with the KATCOMS was reflected in a report prepared by Major D.S. MacLennan in May 1954.[79] Citing the questionable value of the program, he recommended that it be cancelled forthwith; six months later the KATCOM program came to an end.[80]

So ended "one of history's most unusual socio-military programs."[81] Although the Canadian official historian was reluctant to condemn the KATCOM program,[82] there can be little doubt that from the perspective of the parties involved, it failed miserably.[83]

Indeed, Robert Hepenstall concluded that "in support of the KATCOM plan, [Brigadier Bogert] showed a remarkable misunderstanding of the men of his brigade."[84] More accurately, perhaps, Bogert, and by extension the Departments of National Defence and External Affairs, demonstrated a fundamental misunderstanding of the importance of small-group cohesion and comradeship to frontline soldiers. By introducing a poorly trained, culturally disparate element into the Canadian infantry section, the powers that be were tampering with a time-proven, combat-tested organization. At least one Canadian battalion commander, Lieutenant-Colonel Poulin, recognized this and wanted to organize his KATCOMS into their own sections and platoons. However, as Poulin later reported in an interview with the brigade historian, he was prevented from doing this.[85]

To the Canadian soldiers in the firing line, the KATCOMS represented a dangerous liability in that they threatened the survival of themselves and their comrades. That the Canadians considered the KATCOMS untrainable and unassimilable only served to perpetuate this point of view. Thus, in their perceived threat to the Canadian primary group, the KATCOMS, through no fault of their own, found themselves subjected to intense hostility and callous treatment. We can only imagine the fear, loneliness, and frustration which the embattled KATCOMS were forced to endure at the hands of their unwilling allies.

Canadian perceptions of and relations with the Koreans they encountered on the battlefield were thus characterized by an ambivalence that transcended the immediate concerns of race. While this is not to say that racism was not the most important factor in some soldiers' dealings with Koreans, the vast majority appear to have shaped their views of the KSC and KATCOMS around these organizations' very different relationship with the Canadian primary group. While the KSC reinforced and perpetuated the Canadian group, the KATCOMS threatened its very existence. Unlike the KATCOMS, the men of the KSC were not integrated into Canadian infantry sections. Their sole battlefield purpose was to ensure that the Canadian infantry section was provisioned, supplied, and evacuated as the tactical situation dictated. The KATCOMS, on the other hand, were dumped into 25th Brigade infantry sections without due regard for the ramifications this would carry for both Canadian and Korean alike.

Although the KATCOM soldier shared many of the same difficulties that the combat replacement faced in other wartime contexts – most notably, improper training – he faced the additional hurdles of language, nationality, and culture. Unable to overcome these, the Korean soldier was condemned to languish on the margins of the Canadian primary group, where he often found himself employed as cannon fodder. But it was not only the KATCOMs who found the exigencies of the Korean battlefield harsh and unjust. Within the 25th Brigade itself the infantry bore the brunt of the fighting and dying to an unprecedented degree, in what the Canadian government euphemistically labled a "police action."

CHAPTER FIVE

Keeping the Gunners in Good Training

Combat is a harrowing experience at the best of times. As we have seen, Canadian soldiers in Korea faced the additional hurdles of shoddy equipment and improper training. They also encountered an enemy who was himself well prepared for the type of small-unit, hit-and-run action that was such a feature of the fighting in Korea. Together, these disadvantages undermined battlefield performance and shaped Canadian soldiers' view of the enemy. Contrary to what the popular historians have claimed, the Canadians did not perform particularly well in Korea.[1] While there were exceptions – notably, the 2 PPCLI's stand at Kap'yong and the 2 R22eR's successful defence of Hill 227 – the impression is that the 25th Brigade was generally outfought by a better-equipped and better-trained Chinese enemy, particulary during the last eighteen months of the war.

The Canadians' decidedly lacklustre performance was in many ways apparent from the outset. It will be recalled that much of the 2 PPCLI's pre-battle training was devoted to tactical defence. Ironically, by the time the battalion commenced active operations as part of the 27th BCIB in late February 1951, U.N. forces had recovered from their earlier strategic setbacks and resumed their advance to the 38th parallel. At this time, the Canadians launched a series of small-scale attacks against Chinese rearguard positions, with mixed results. The most significant of these occurred on 7 March when they attempted unsuccessfully to dislodge expertly camouflaged Chinese troops from their positions atop Hill 532. In the ensuing attack, which saw some of the Patricia assault platoons bunch up on exposed ridge lines and become lost, the 2 PPCLI lost seven killed and thirty-three wounded. Only after the Chinese rearguard broke contact the following day were they able to gain the height.

Difficulties were also encountered during the 2 RCR action at Chail-li. Shortly after landing at Pusan with the rest of the 25th Brigade on 4 May, the RCRs were ordered to join the advance to the 38th parallel. Three weeks later, the battalion was in the rugged P'och'on Valley in central Korea, pursuing an elusive enemy. Initially, the Chinese were unwilling to engage the advancing Canadians in a set-piece battle. Meanwhile, the Canadians took several prisoners who, according to an intelligence report, "were dirty, ill-kept specimens, poorly dressed, without boots and inadequately equipped, whose reaction to capture appeared to be a combination of indifference, resignation, and fear."[2]

The pathetic condition of the prisoners belied Chinese capabilities and inspired a sense of false confidence in the as yet untried Canadians. For this reason, perhaps, the 2 RCR was given the difficult task of capturing Hill 467, a formidable twin-peaked height that overlooked the village of Chail-li. The attack began in the early morning hours of 30 May, with a flanking manoeuvre reminiscent of the Normandy campaign. Almost immediately the Canadians came under heavy fire and were unable to make any appreciable progress up the steep granite precipices. Unbeknownst to the Canadians, the hill was the backbone of the Chinese defences in the vicinity of Chail-li and was well fortified with trenches and weapons pits. The Canadians, however, continued to press their attack, calling for supporting fire from the 2 RCHA's 25-pounder field guns. But artillery fire failed to dislodge the well-entrenched Chinese. Smoke from the shooting mixed with the heavy monsoon mist that hung over the crest of the hill, reducing visibility to several yards and denying critical supporting fire to the Canadians. In view of the hopelessness of the attack, Brigadier Rockingham ordered the battalion to fall back short of its objective.

As at Hill 532, the price for failure at Chail-li was high: six Canadians were killed and twenty-five wounded. Commenting on the battle, a Canadian officer wrote: "If one can reach any positive conclusion from such limited experience, that conclusion would be that some of the tactics we had been told were being employed in Korea, are not in fact necessarily the proper ones."[3] In the 25th Brigade's first significant engagement in Korea, the Canadians had employed the familiar tactics of mobile warfare in Northwest

Europe.[4] That, after all, was what they had been trained for. In the mountainous Korean terrain, fighting against a well-equipped and highly resolute enemy, a different, more flexible approach was required. Even the official historian considered the botched RCR attack a tactical mistake.[5]

As we shall see, the Canadians never succeeded in modifying their tactics to suit conditions in Korea – a failure that became increasingly apparent as the war progressed. During the late summer and early fall of 1951, the 25th Brigade, now part of the 1st Commonwealth Division, participated in a series of operations that saw U.N. forces advance to the Jamestown line. These were relatively uneventful affairs – the RCR regimental historian dismissed them as "sundry operations"[6] – as evidenced by the low number of Canadian casualties. More significantly, the consolidation of the Jamestown line coincided with renewed efforts to end the war in Korea.

Truce talks were first initiated in July but broke off after the two sides failed to reach an agreement on the location of a demarcation line. On 25 October they were resumed in the village of Panmunjom, only to stall over the question of prisoner repatriation. The truce talks were destined to drag on for another two years before the two sides were able to agree on the terms of an armistice. Meanwhile, on 12 November the U.N. Command ordered the Eighth U.S. Army, of which the 25th Brigade was a part, to desist from further offensive operations and maintain an active defence.[7]

The opening of truce talks and the U.N. Command's concomitant policy of active defence represented a watershed in the Korean War. Previously, the fighting had been relatively mobile and the battle lines fluid. During that period, the U.N. forces' ultimate objective had been to defeat the enemy in the field. Now, the fighting became static and attritional, with the belligerents occupying semi-permanent defensive positions on opposite sides of the Jamestown line. Henceforth there would be no victory in Korea. Operations were confined to raiding and patrolling while the two sides attempted to reach a political solution to the war.

In this changed strategic and tactical context, the Canadians' equipment and training deficiencies became readily apparent. In a 1953 paper on infantry patrolling in Korea, Major Harry Pope wrote: "For the past year and more the enemy has held the tactical initiative in no-man's land. He has raided our outposts and forward positions and ambushed our patrols at will. We, on the other hand with only one or two exceptions, have not carried out any successful operations forward of our lines."[8]

Korean veterans have themselves commented on the lack of success. Second-Lieutenant C.E. Goodman of the 2nd and 1st R22eR recalled: "The patrols I took out were singularly unsuccessful"; and 1 PPCLI's Sergeant John Richardson observed: "No-man's land was a huge wide area. We needed, but didn't get, new techniques to deal with the distance involved in crossing the valley ... Still, the brass would not change their policy."[9]

Despite these difficulties,[10] the Canadians continued to partake in patrol operations.[11] The operational directive issued by the U.N. Command in May 1952, ordering each forward battalion to conduct one strong fighting patrol per week against recognized enemy positions and to capture at least one prisoner every three days, obviously had a role to play in this.[12] This policy was extremely unpopular with both the 1st U.S. Marine and the Commonwealth divisions. They maintained that patrols should be dispatched by commanders in the field according to the tactical situation at hand, rather than adhering to a rigid timetable formulated by staff officers in the comfortable surroundings of their air-conditioned offices.[13] The patrol policy was eventually amended to accommodate Marine and Commonwealth objections, but this did not translate into improved performance in the 25th Brigade. The reality was that Canadian patrols were routinely outgunned and outfought by a highly capable Chinese enemy. A postwar report summed up the Canadian patrol experience in Korea this way:

> We despatched a large number of patrols, the greater part of them ambush patrols, to operate in no-man's land. Very few of them made contact; the contacts which were made occurred, on more occasions than would seem desirable, *when our ambushes were ambushed by the enemy.* In June 1952, for example, we set 25 ambushes in no-man's land; only one of these resulted in a contact. On this occasion, our patrol was surrounded and engaged by an enemy group.[14]

All this is not to say that every Canadian patrol ended in failure. The most obvious exception was the recce-cum-snatch patrol led by Lieutenant H.R. Gardner and Corporal K.E. Fowler in late September 1952. Following a forty-eight-hour lie-up in no man's land, where they observed activity in a Chinese field kitchen, the two men snatched a lone enemy soldier and returned to Canadian lines. Underlying the patrol's success was exceptional planning and preparation and an emphasis on "stealth and surprise – key elements in the success of Canadian trench raids in the First World War" that had been all but forgotten in Korea.[15] This decidedly minor episode would have passed unnoticed in an earlier war, yet Gardner was awarded the Military Cross and Fowler the Military Metal. The lavish decorations underscored the fact that even such modest success was far from routine. Even in the 25th Brigade, the Gardner-Fowler patrol was regarded as the exception that proved the rule of poor Canadian patrol performance.[16]

Another reflection of the Canadians' inability to conduct successful patrols was their increasing reliance on support weapons. Through the summer of 1952 there was a growing tendency to use artillery, in the form of 81 mm mortars and 25-pounder field guns,[17] to compensate for the infantry's inadequate small arms and training. Encounters with the enemy that could have just as easily been settled with quick-firing personal weapons and effective small-unit tactics now hinged on the timely and effective use of overwhelming firepower. An Operational Research report noted, "a tendency to let artillery and mortars do jobs which at one time might have been done by a good sniper. Artillery has frequently been used when a single individual movement has been observed, in hope that other enemy were in the vicinity. As far as the damage done is concerned, artillery has frequently been wasted, but the large amount of firing has had the beneficial effect of keeping the gunners in good training."[18]

There were several other problems associated with the overreliance on artillery fire. Patrols became utterly dependent on radio sets and their operators for survival in a firefight, an uncomfortable prospect at the best of times. Poor weather, a dead battery, or a panicked operator could spell the difference between living to see the sun rise and a one-way trip to the U.N. cemetery at Pusan. To make matters worse, Canadian radios were not notably reliable.[19]

Nor did the lavish use of artillery fire necessarily translate into heavy enemy casualties. Using language that has come to be associated with a subsequent Asian conflict, a postwar Canadian report lamented the absence of accurate body counts to confirm the effectiveness of the fire support allocated to Canadian patrols.[20] As a further reflection of indifferent Canadian tactical performance, body counts became an increasingly popular yardstick for measuring the success of patrol contacts as the war dragged on. After-action reports usually attributed the absence of enemy dead and wounded to their penchant for "policing the battlefield" after an engagement. However, the RCR regimental historian had this to say about the overreliance on support weapons and the absence of enemy casualties:

It was an excellent plan to have someone outside the range of the enemy to do the killing for the forward troops, but the cold fact was that unless such weapons had more or less stationary targets their fire was often wasted on empty arcs. There would seem to be little reason to believe that the Chinese carried away their dead and the few bodies found suggested that the enemy groups were much smaller than their fire volume indicated. The smaller the group, the lesser the target, the greater its mobility.[21]

What the RCR historian was referring to was the tactic of dispersion, the practice of scattering troops to present as small a target as possible to enemy gunners. Rapid dispersal was relatively easy to effect in the undulating terrain of no man's land, and it helped negate the destructive effects of Canadian artillery fire.

Alternatively, Chinese troops might hug a beleaguered Canadian patrol. By maintaining close contact – ten yards distance was not uncommon[22] – the Chinese avoided the destructive wrath of Canadian supporting fire. They were also in a fortuitous position to exploit the superior firepower of their individual weapons. Using this tactic, the Chinese often pursued the Canadians all the way back to their own lines, inflicting casualties along the way.[23]

The net result of the 25th Brigade's inability to patrol effectively was that the Chinese were able to dominate no man's land.[24] Korean veteran and writer Robert Hepenstall sarcastically suggested that a better name for no man's land "might have been 'Joe Chinks Front Yard,' as he owned and controlled the territory."[25] Official sources corroborate this assessment through a clutch of euphemistic phrases such as "The Chinese ... demonstrated an uncomfortably intimate knowledge of ... our side of no-man's land"[26] and "[Patrol contacts] have detected the presence of enemy in areas which constituted a threat to friendly positions."[27]

One of the most startling examples of the price paid for letting the enemy control no man's land occurred during the Chinese attack on Hill 355 in late October 1952. The hill was the dominating feature in the Canadian sector of the Jamestown line and at the time was occupied by the 1 RCR.[28] The raid on Hill 355 developed over the course of several weeks, during which the Chinese consolidated their control of no man's land.[29] Following the destruction of the Vancouver outpost on 2 October and the successful ambush of an RCR fighting patrol on the night of 12–13 October, the enemy began to send reconnaissance patrols right up to the forward defensive positions. They were able to get so close that they pelted the Canadians with stones in an attempt, sometimes successfully, to draw small-arms fire and disclose defensive arrangements. With the Chinese just outside their wire, the RCRs were unable to send out their own patrols. They were now in the unenviable position of fighting blind.

On 22 October nearly 2,500 shells fell on Hill 355.[30] Holed up in their flimsy bunkers, the RCRs could do little but wait for the imminent Chinese assault. This came on 23 October, when several hundred Chinese troops who had been laid up in specially constructed caves in no man's land rushed into the RCR trenches on the heels of a massive bombardment. The Chinese quickly overran the forward RCR company and engaged a neighbouring company in a fierce firefight. The Canadians called for artillery and mortar fire on the overrun position, which they eventually regained with a counterattack. By this time, however, the Chinese, having satisfied their objectives, had pulled back.

The raid on Hill 355 was a costly lesson in the failure to patrol vigorously and effectively. In the month leading up to the attack, more than 150 Royals had become casualties, and 14 prisoners were taken during the raid itself. Although the RCR retained the height, the battle can hardly be considered a Canadian victory, for the Chinese objective was not to seize ground but to capture prisoners, destroy defensive positions, and weaken Canadian resolve. In this regard, they succeeded marvellously. Such was the price for allowing the enemy to dominate no man's land.

As the static war raged on, the 25th Brigade's defensive positions along the Jamestown line also left much to be desired. Fighting trenches were insufficiently revetted, lacked overhead cover, and were not situated to provide effective mutual support. Bunkers were not deep enough and were too far from the forward trenches. Communications trenches were not covered with wire, and they were clearly outlined to the enemy by the piles of spoil, rubbish, and beer bottles[31] that accumulated on the lips. Wiring along the

Canadians' front was too thin and, in most cases, unable to withstand Chinese artillery bombardments because it was strung too taught. Finally, the protective minefields that skirted the Canadians' positions were easily breached by enemy sappers, thus inspiring a false sense of security in the defenders.[32]

Obviously, many of these shortcomings had their roots in improper training. This was especially true in regard to trench maintenance and the uniquely Canadian practice of disposing "of rubbish by the simple expedient of throwing it out in front of the wire"[33] or over the lip of a communications trench. According to the Australian historian Jeffrey Grey, these practices and others were routinely condemned by the Commonwealth units who relieved the Canadians in the line.[34]

It is deceptively easy to blame this type of behaviour on poor discipline. Yet as has been shown in an earlier chapter, the Canadians were not properly trained in the construction and maintenance of defensive positions. When faced with the apparently mundane question of what to do with an empty c-ration tin or beer bottle, and in the absence of proper training, even the most unimaginative soldier would resort to the seemingly logical yet tactically dangerous expedient of tossing it out of his trench. To dismiss such behaviour as evidence of poor discipline ignores the very real shortcomings in Canadian infantry training. Brigadier Bogert's successor, Brigadier Jean Victor Allard, hinted at this when he wrote that "deliberate defence is in many respects foreign to the average Canadian officer."[35]

Training aside, to fully understand the origins of the 25th Brigade's defensive difficulties it is necessary to go back to the consolidation of the Jamestown line.[36] According to Major Harry Pope:

Convinced that we knew all about the art of war, merely because of our own happy war-time experiences, we applied our ... defence techniques without variation to the Korean hills we occupied in October-November 1951. As the enemy shelling increased – and with its nasty-minded probes – we remembered the stories of our fathers and began digging and wiring in the positions we had first occupied in the 1940–45 pattern. By simply developing our hills on the ... defence techniques of 1940–45 and on the dug-in techniques of 1914–1918 we made the mistake of not extracting all the lessons of the Great War.[37]

From the outset, the Canadians and their Commonwealth allies should have developed their hilltop defensive positions as if they were castles, heavily fortified with several lines of First World War–style mutually supporting fighting trenches.[38] As it was – and this is true of all the Commonwealth formations, though not the Chinese – the Canadians relied on a single ring of fighting trenches just below the crest of the hills they occupied. To make matters worse, Commonwealth units occupied too many hilltops (almost every one in their sectors). As David Bercuson has noted, "This was the Italian model, good for troops planning to move up against an enemy not planning to move back, but tempting to a habitual attacker."[39] The failure to develop defensive positions properly was usually blamed on any non-Commonwealth units that might have previously occupied the position. Yet as will shortly be shown, the so-called capital investment theory[40] – that it was too time consuming and laborious to re-dig a defensive position – was hardly an adequate excuse for the very serious defensive deficiencies that characterized Commonwealth positions in general, and Canadian ones in particular. In the 25th Brigade, the failure to develop defensive positions properly was not fully appreciated until the final year of the conflict, in the aftermath of the bloodiest Canadian battle of the Korean War.

In April 1953 the 3 RCR replaced the 1 R22eR in the front line in the vicinity of Hill 187 as part of the third annual rotation. Over the course of the next month, the battalion tried unsuccessfully to wrest control of no man's land from the enemy through a series of patrol actions. At the same time, the Royals apparently tried to shore up their dilapidated defences. After the war, Lieutenant-Colonel Campbell blamed the previous occupants from the 2nd U.N. Division for the position's poor condition. What he failed to realize was that the Canadians themselves had occupied the position for several months before the 2nd U.N. Division.[41] In any event, the 3 RCR was unable to make any appreciable progress on account of what appeared to be constant artillery harassment. An examination of the shell fragments that littered the Canadians' positions, however, revealed that many different kinds of guns were being used in the bombardments. This suggested that the Chinese were preregistering their artillery in preparation for a major attack.

The attack came on the night of 2–3 May 1953. Following an intense artillery concentration, Chinese grenadiers and assault troops stormed the Canadian trenches and succeeded in overrunning the forward positions of Charlie Company. The Canadians responded by calling for supporting fire to be brought down on their positions. This was followed by a combined infantry-tank counter-attack that appeared to drive the remaining Chinese out of the position;[42] but in reality the enemy, having satisfied his objectives, was already pulling back under a thick cover of protective smoke.[43]

The attack cost the Royals dearly. Thirty Canadian and KATCOM soldiers were killed, forty-one wounded, and eleven taken prisoner or missing. Brigadier J.V. Allard clearly considered the attack a Canadian defeat. The Chinese had inflicted casualties, captured prisoners, destroyed defences, and cleared their dead and wounded from the battlefield.[44] In short, they had satisfied all their objectives. In retrospect, it is unlikely that the Canadians would have suffered such grievous losses had their defensive positions been better prepared. The extent to which the positions had been allowed to deteriorate, combined with their unsatisfactory layout and wiring, made defence of the forward RCR company position practically impossible.

As noted earlier, the Canadians' defensive positions were developed during the consolation of the Jamestown line. As the British official historian observed, many of these had been hastily situated in captured enemy trenches or bunkers.[45] At that time, however, the Chinese possessed little in the way of artillery support. The following year witnessed a steady increase in Chinese artillery capabilities to the extent that the Canadians' flimsily constructed fighting trenches no longer offered adequate protection against a sustained bombardment. One alternative was to seek shelter in bunkers situated *behind* the fighting positions and wait for the fire to lift before making the thirty-yard dash back to the fighting trenches (if they were still intact) to engage the attacking enemy with small arms and grenades. All too often, however, the Chinese assault troops were on top of the Canadians before they had a chance to reach their fighting trenches. As was the case on Hill 355, vicious close combat quickly ensued, in which the rifle-equipped Canadians were at a decided disadvantage. As Major Harry Pope remarked, "Rifles at five paces at night, with or without bayonets fixed, give no confidence against a burp gun."[46]

The other and indeed preferred option was to stay in the bunkers and call for supporting fire on the position itself. This tactic was effective during the battle of Kap'yong in April 1951, when an impressive volume of proximity-fused shrapnel shells were brought to bear on the 2 PPCLI positions. Caught out in the open, the attacking Chinese were decimated by the fire, while the defenders hunkered down in their foxholes. This approach was also successful during the 2 R22eR's successful defence of Hill 227 in November 1951. An after-action report recounted: "When the Chinese attacked it was merely a matter of increasing the rate of [supporting] fire ... The mortars, which were located on the reverse slope ... fired 9,400 rounds between 1600 hours on the 23rd and 0800 hours on the 26th. At one stage ... the barrels became so hot that they were transparent and the rounds could be seen going up the spout even before they left the barrels."[47]

Sitting tight in a bunker while friendly artillery and mortar fire was brought to bear became less effective as the fighting solidified into a static, attritional affair and as the Chinese abandoned the Kap'yong and Hill 227 style of using "human wave tactics under light supporting fire."[48] Since the maze of communications trenches connecting the fighting positions along the Jamestown line were conveniently outlined by the garbage and spoil that had accumulated along their lips, and since they lacked any sort of protective wire, they now provided the attacking Chinese with a source of cover.[49] Safe from the destructive wrath of Canadian supporting fire, the enemy assault troops could go about their business of destroying defences and capturing prisoners.[50] This is exactly what happened to the 3 RCR; it was only after the raid that Brigadier Allard finally ordered the tops of all trenches to be covered with barbed wire.[51]

All in all, there can be little doubt that Canadian tactical performance left much to be desired, particularly during the last year and a half of the war.[52] Insofar as defensive doctrine was concerned, this was a shortcoming shared with other Commonwealth forces. Yet there is compelling evidence that in the areas of patrolling and the construction and maintenance of defensive positions, the Canadians were far less adept than some of their Commonwealth cousins.[53] The gulf between the Canadians and their Chinese enemies was even greater.

By all accounts, the Chinese were excellent at patrolling; according to a Commonwealth Division Intelligence Summary, there were "many lessons to be learned from contacts with Chinese patrols."[54] They excelled at night fighting, their field craft was first rate, and their training was sound.[55] On making contact, the Chinese used fire and manœuvre to outflank and encircle an enemy patrol, giving the impression that they were attacking from all sides simultaneously.

Ruses were frequently used to lure enemy patrols into ambushes, leading one after-action report to warn that "cries of 'help' must always be investigated with suspicion."[56] Lying in ambush, the Chinese made maximum use of foliage – or, in winter, white sheets in the snow – to conceal themselves. It was not uncommon for an ambush party to remain hidden in the waist-high scrub of no man's land, their caps and belts stuffed with grass and leaves, for up to twenty-four hours, waiting for an unwary patrol to stumble into their killing zone.

Camouflage and concealment was aided by their field uniforms and equipment. During the winter months the Chinese wore a khaki padded-cotton suit[57] that made very little noise and blended well into the overgrown rice paddies and brownish scrub brush of no man's land.[58] In summer, the winter suit was exchanged for a light olive cotton uniform that was equally effective. Light canvas sneakers were used in preference to the heavy, noisy, cumbersome combat boots worn by most U.N. soldiers. As a further reflection of the emphasis placed on mobility, Chinese soldiers seldom wore elaborate load-bearing equipment, and they carried only the bare essentials. A cloth ammunition bandolier, water bottle, and bag containing a rice ball and some salt comprised the standard combat load.[59]

Individual weapons were also selected with mobility and efficiency in mind. Early in the war the Chinese had been armed with a hodgepodge of Japanese, Soviet, American, and Commonwealth weapons, including a large number of cumbersome bolt-action rifles. As was the case with artillery, the quality of the Chinese infantry's small arms improved dramatically during the second year of the war. The preferred weapons were the Soviet-designed PPS-43 and PPSH-41 burp guns.[60] The latter weapon was especially suited to the type of fighting encountered in Korea after the consolidation of the Jamestown line. Firing 900 rounds per minute from 71-round drums,[61] a PPSH-41-equipped squad could produce a tremendous amount of quickly adjusted fire at close range.

As noted in an earlier chapter, the Chinese made extensive use of grenades. After-action reports frequently alluded to the Chinese grenades' insufficient killing power, but such assessments missed the point. Chinese grenades were of the offensive variety in that they were primarily designed to induce shock in a defender through concussion and by inflicting minor wounds. As a Commonwealth Division Intelligence Summary despondently noted, this "increased the chances of capturing wounded prisoners without disclosing the enemy's position."[62]

As the U.S. Army discovered in Vietnam, first-rate weapons are no guarantee of battlefield success. Proper training is even more important. At the root of the Chinese success was their use of specially trained patrol troops, who were held in the rear areas until a patrol was ordered.[63] This contrasted markedly with the Canadian practice of rotating patrol tasks among all front-line units. From the perspective of Canadian soldiers, patrolling was an occasional task interspersed with a myriad other front-line chores, such as sentry duty and weapons cleaning.[64] The use of general-purpose troops who were inadequately trained in the fine art of patrolling led some to conclude that "'the basic sense of mission' was lacking"; as no special training was provided and there was rarely any rehearsal over the type of ground to be covered, there was scarcely time for patrol members to begin to move and act as a team.[65]

Although the Chinese do not appear to have manned their defensive positions along the Jamestown line with specialized fortress or mountain troops, the overall standard of defensive training among Chinese formations seems to have been high. As Pope noted, "1st Commonwealth Division made no attacks and only a few company sized raids on the enemy in the last 18 months before the ceasefire. No deep penetration was effected. It is therefore not possible to describe in detail enemy defences and defensive techniques apart from his patrolling."[66] Nevertheless, it is possible to make some general points about Chinese field defences. First, the Chinese appear to have developed their defensive positions according to the castle principle, using three lines of mutually supporting trench lines connected by deep tunnels.[67] Tunnels permitted the rapid withdrawal or reinforcement of a trench line without exposing the defenders to U.N. artillery fire. They also kept the attackers out in the open, making them vulnerable to fire from the trenches farther up the hill. Canadian soldiers were extremely reluctant to enter these tunnels, preferring to blow the entrances with hand grenades.[68]

Paradoxically, Chinese field defences owed much of their success to U.N. air superiority and, at least initially, to the U.N.'s preponderance of field artillery.[69] They were therefore constructed, from the outset, to withstand the very worst the U.N. had to offer. Finally, the Chinese were able to draw on apparently unlimited manpower resources to construct and maintain their elaborate fieldworks. Yet all this must not allow us to lose sight of the defensive acumen of the individual Chinese soldier. According to a Commonwealth Division report, "The Chinese soldier digs in quickly and deeply which effectively protects him from U.N. bombardments. He immediately takes up his fighting positions to defend his sector when the shelling subsides."[70] The Canadians obviously had much to learn from their opponents across no man's land.

This discussion of Canadian tactical shortcomings and the corresponding strengths of the Chinese has carried us some distance from the social focus of this work. This deviation has been necessary to understand another important aspect of Canadian soldiers' Korean experiences: their views of the Chinese enemy. The average Canadian combat soldier had a tremendous amount of respect for his Chinese counterpart. This was not the result of an innate appreciation of the Chinese culture or languages, but rather a recognition of the tactical proficiency of a very capable opponent. Indeed, the available evidence strongly suggests that this respect became more pronounced as the Canadians' tactical difficulties increased.

Having said this, it should also be pointed out that traditional racist stereotypes characterized some of the Canadians' early encounters with the Chinese. Just prior to the 2 RCR's ill-fated attack on Chail-li, the Laundry and Bath platoon of the 25th Brigade Ordnance Company managed to capture two Chinese deserters. The platoon captured three more in the days that followed, leading one platoon commander to comment that "it was rumoured at the time ... that the poor fellows had heard that there was a laundry in the vicinity and had merely come in looking for a job."[71]

Images of the yellow peril were also present in some of the Canadians' early situation reports. On at least one occasion 2 PPCLI's Lieutenant-Colonel Stone spoke of the necessity of properly prepared defensive positions to "kill at will the hordes that rush the positions."[72] As Craig Cameron noted, the comparatively large numbers of enemy troops seen out in the open during the early stages of the Korean War helped perpetuate "yellow horde" imagery.[73] Certainly, the human wave attacks encountered at the battle of Kap'yong reinforced the impression of a beleaguered force making an epic stand against the Asiatic hordes. Such was also the case during the 2 R22eR's successful defence of Hill 227 in November 1951. A platoon commander recalled: "Small groups of 10 to

15 each could be seen moving down the hill and concentrating in larger groups in the valleys. These in turn would concentrate in still larger groups closer to our lines. They were in plain view and beautiful artillery concentrations must have killed and wounded a great many. I [the commander of Major Liboiron's left platoon] would estimate that the largest group of Chinese numbered approximately 500."[74]

Such large concentrations of enemy, combined with their apparent disregard for casualties – it was claimed that Chinese assault troops attacked *through* their own supporting fire – shaped another racist perception, namely that the enemy was high on opium. Major Liboiron, the officer commanding 2 R22eR's Dog Company, claimed that most of his men believed "the Chinese were doped before they were committed to battle because they were completely oblivious to danger. They stood up fully exposed when the heaviest of our mortar and artillery concentrations were coming down and apparently had absolutely no regard for their own personal safety."[75] It was also rumoured that the doped-up Chinese assault troops were led by a woman. "She was described as being dressed in black or dark coloured clothing and was easily recognizable as a woman by her long black hair."[76] A 2 R22eR soldier later claimed to have killed the so-called Dragon Lady, but there is no proof of this.

Images of bedraggled laundrymen and doped-up Asiatic hordes led by sinister yet erotic dragon ladies became increasingly tenuous as the war progressed, and as the Chinese abandoned human wave tactics and the Canadians found themselves increasingly outfought by a highly skilled enemy. It would have been extraordinarily difficult for even the most parochial Canadian soldier to maintain a sense of condescending superiority in such circumstances. In the aftermath of the attack on Hill 355, Commonwealth Division Headquarters found it necessary to circulate a memorandum stating that "the Chinese soldier is not a superman."[77]

Contributing to this superman image was the nature of the fighting along the Jamestown line. Very, very few soldiers ever had more than a fleeting glimpse of their Chinese counterparts during patrol clashes or raids. That almost all of the fighting was conducted in the dark, or under the half-light of descending parachute flares, contributed to the sense of unreality and fear. The enemy became a deadly shadow of a man, who stalked the overgrown rice paddies of no man's land with the cunning and skill of a professional hunter.

The superman image of Chinese soldiers combined with their elusiveness to make them objects of intense curiosity. The day after the ceasefire came into effect, for example, Major-General West, the commander of the Commonwealth Division, found it necessary to issue orders banning fraternization with the enemy and to put a stop to "the hundreds of military 'tourists' [who] converged on the front lines, armed with cameras and an insatiable curiosity."[78] As one soldier put it, "Everyone wanted to have a look at the little bastards who kicked our asses up and down the Sam'ichon Valley."[79]

Even Chinese corpses became objects of curiosity. Sergeant John Richardson recalled: "The Chinese looked so young and small in their baggy uniforms, with their small hands and feet. There was a Chinese corpse hanging on our defensive barb wire; he looked no more than fifteen years old, with his little peaked cap and deathly pale face and hands."[80] Korean veteran and artist Ted Zuber captured this haunting image in his painting *Welcome Party*.[81] In it, two Canadian replacements are greeted by a forward platoon sergeant as they make their way along a communications trench. Both soldiers are transfixed by the Chinese corpses that hang in the wire, one of whose arms is outstretched as if to post a grenade, only yards away from where they are standing.

Being left to hang in the enemy's wire or eviscerated by a hand grenade was, of course, a fate to be avoided at all costs. Facing a well-prepared enemy without the benefit of proper training and equipment, Canadian soldiers confronted the prospect of imminent death every time the sun dipped below the horizon. In the inky blackness of the Korean night, survival became the end that justified the means.

CHAPTER SIX

Pucker Factor

The indifferent battlefield performance of the 25th Brigade had a pronounced effect on combat motivation or, as John Keegan called it, "the will to combat."[1] Expected to fight a deadly opponent on what can only be considered unequal terms, a minority of Canadian soldiers became psychological casualties or resorted to self-inflicted wounds as a way out of the combat zone. But what was most remarkable about the Canadian combat experience in Korea was not how many men succumbed to the strain of battle but how many soldiered on in spite of it.

In his scathing indictment of patrolling in Korea, Major Harry Pope noted the Canadian troops' defensive attitude and reluctance to close with the enemy.[2] Yet aggression does not appear to have been lacking during the operations[3] that took the 25th Brigade to the Jamestown line,[4] nor was there any shortage of it at the battles of Kap'yong and Hill 227. Indeed, the 2 R22eR's Major Liboiron considered that the willingness to fight was one of the main factors in the successful defence of Hill 227.[5] Similarly, Lieutenant-Colonel Stone recalled a strong fighting spirit in his men at Kap'yong.[6]

This was not to last. As Canadian tactical fortunes declined through 1952, fighting spirit at the sharp end was blunted. The British official historian suggested that this was a problem throughout the entire Commonwealth Division,[7] though oral sources contradict this blanket characterization,[8] as does Jeffrey Grey. He argued that the Australians were too aggressive and occasionally found themselves dangerously overextended on the Chinese side of the valley.[9] He also suggested that poor Canadian performance underlay Major-General West's decision in late November 1952 to assign the 25th

Brigade its own permanent sector of the Jamestown line, a move that was heartily endorsed by both the British and Australians.[10]

A number of explanations have been posited to account for this lack of aggressiveness in the 25th Brigade. One is that the perennial shortage of infantry replacements precluded aggressive patrolling, because field units were unable to absorb large numbers of casualties.[11] Although there is some truth in this, Major Pope did not think numbers were the primary cause of Canadian tactical difficulties in Korea. "Our routine recce patrols and so-called fighting or ambush patrols would be engaged and defeated on our side of the valley by enemy forces of up to company size," he wrote. "Our static, night-time outposts would be raided or destroyed. Our reaction to this would either be to send stronger forces into the valley – but for some unaccountable reason never strong enough to defeat the enemy company – or be to withdraw our patrols and outposts and sit tight. Either technique was disastrous."[12]

Another explanation is that commanders believed the peace talks at Panmunjom would eventually be successful, and they wished to avoid risking the lives of their men in what might be the last days of the war. As was shown in chapter 3, some officers and men definitely had second thoughts about the necessity of sacrificing their lives for freedom and democracy in Korea shortly after their arrival in the Far East. However, it is important to remember that Canadian soldiers were all volunteers; and from mid-1952 onward, they were regulars from the Canadian Army's Active Force. Recalling the casualty lists from the Second World War, these men could have entertained few illusions about the business end of their profession when they enlisted. Moreover, according to Richard Holmes,

Professional soldiers are encouraged to think of themselves as servants of the state, whose task is to defend their country against its internal and external enemies. They are unlikely to inquire too closely into the nature of those enemies: indeed, for them to do so might introduce a potentially dangerous element of uncertainty ... Regular soldiers also share an intense professional curiosity as to how well their weapons, tactics and training will work in a real war. War is – and I mean this in no derogatory sense – the opportunity for them to apply what they have studied.[13]

In Korea, the Canadians were given the opportunity to test their weapons, tactics, and training against a real enemy and found them lacking. Canadian soldiers knew they faced specially trained and equipped patrol troops in no man's land while they themselves performed what amounted to a routine task with routine equipment.[14] This, perhaps more than anything else, was behind any lack of aggression or the reluctance to close with the enemy. Certainly, the promise of a ceasefire from late 1951 on does not appear to have weakened Chinese resolve in the slightest.

This was not the first time that improper training, equipment, and tactics eroded the martial spirit of fighting men. Richard Fox clearly demonstrated that military unpreparedness and the resultant breakdown of morale contributed to the U.S. 7th Cavalry's defeat at the Little Bighorn.[15] But unlike Custer's ill-fated command, the Canadians could, with decidedly mixed success, always substitute supporting fire for their tactical and technical shortcomings. On more than one occasion, overwhelming supporting fire saved Canadian infantry units from their own last stands. Still, from the perspective of the individual soldier, who had to live and die with the consequences of improper training and weaponry, the desire to avoid contact with the enemy must have been great.

It is impossible to know how many Canadian patrols purposely avoided contact with the enemy. British sociologist Tony Ashworth documented this phenomenon on the First World War battlefield,[16] and it is a well-known fact that U.S. ground forces in Vietnam routinely avoided combat. In Korea, the Welsh Regiment was said to have a live-and-let-live arrangement with the Chinese[17] on account of the socialist leanings of a large number of its enlisted men. There exists no comparable data for the 25th Brigade. Two Canadian veterans interviewed during the preparation of this work claimed to have been part of patrols that purposely avoided contact with the enemy.[18] In both cases, the patrols went to ground a short distance from the Main Line of Resistance (MLR)[19] and radioed false situation reports.

Although the available evidence strongly suggests that front-line relations between enlisted men and their officers were good,[20] tensions must have run high in cases where there was a lack of unanimity on combat avoidance. Again, there are no recorded cases of "fragging" – the practice of killing overaggressive officers, which reached alarming proportions in Vietnam[21] – or of outright mutiny in the 25th Brigade. Nevertheless, there is evidence that suggests the reluctance of some junior officers to dispatch patrols.[22] Such reluctance could have easily had its origins in the desire of a handful of enlisted men to avoid combat.

The avoidance of combat was not necessarily confined to patrols. There were several cases of Canadian soldiers feigning death and hiding in bunkers during enemy raids. In the attack on Hill 355, for example, Lieutenant Gardner of patrolling fame feigned death when the Chinese swept through his position.[23] So did a lightly wounded Private George Griffiths, who found himself cut off and alone in a Canadian communications trench: "I knew the Chinese were just above me, so I threw a couple of grenades and stumbled along until I came to a dead end, a bunker with a blanket across."[24] Griffiths climbed into it and hid among the four dead Canadians who lay sprawled across the floor. Moments later two Chinese soldiers entered the bunker, and began bayonetting the corpses. "But when they came to me," Griffiths recalled, "I turned and they realized I was alive. They motioned for me to drop my rifle, get my hands up, and get out of the bunker."[25]

Self-preservation also appears to have been the primary objective of some senior Canadian officers in Korea. It has even been suggested that many officers with Second World War experience "were most concerned not to get themselves killed in a sideshow like Korea."[26] Along the Jamestown line, this meant minimizing one's exposure to hostile fire. The way to do so was to take refuge in a deep bunker well behind the MLR or, if you were a battalion commander, to go on leave, as the 1 RCR's Lieutenant-Colonel Bingham did during the build-up to the attack on Hill 355.[27] Such behaviour set a poor example for one's subordinates and accentuated the "sit tight and call for supporting fire" attitude among front-line fighters. In all fairness, the lowly soldier at the sharp end was only following the example of his superiors. His platoon commander fought from a bunker on the reverse slope, sufficiently removed from the fighting to preclude direct observation or control of a battle. One or two hills behind, his company commander fought a "map board and telephone war" from the safety of a subterranean command post.[28] Commenting on the officers in his battalion, Lieutenant-Colonel Campbell said:

It was poor policy to post to 3 RCR as company commanders officers who had been company commanders during the Second World War ... They had not progressed and in many cases lacked drive and enthusiasm. Even where they retained these important qualities, age and/or physical condition made them unsuitable ... Company commanders must be fighting fit. The young officers are "pretty damn good." But they could be better disciplined, particularly self disciplined and they are inclined to take the easy way out. They are not fully acquainted with the technical side of their profession. Patrolling skills have been neglected.[29]

All this is not to say that there were no aggressive officers and men in the 25th Brigade. In every battalion there was that hard core of soldiers and junior officers who thrived on the intense thrill of combat. A handful of men even volunteered for patrol duty "to prove [themselves] and make a 'name' in the battalion."[30] According to army photographer Paul Tomelin, some junior officers cultivated a macho image that required periodic affirmation through aggressive behaviour and reckless courage.[31] These men were, however, a minority. The vast majority of Canadian soldiers did what was required of them, nothing more and nothing less, not wanting to draw the contempt of their comrades.[32] What they were required to do included killing the enemy.

The foregoing discussion should not cause us to lose sight of the fact that Canadian soldiers could kill with extreme aggression, especially when the enemy posed an immediate threat to the survival of their primary group. Such a perceived threat underlay the seemingly cold-blooded killing of a group of Chinese soldiers in February 1951. The incident occurred when several enemy approached a 2 PPCLI platoon position in the middle of the night, apparently with the intention of surrendering. Well aware of Chinese infiltration techniques, and not completely sure of the approaching group's motives, a terrified Bren gunner emptied a full magazine into the Chinese soldiers, killing them instantly.[33]

Sometimes the tables were reversed. Only days after the Bren gun incident, a six-man Canadian patrol was caught in a Chinese ambush. Instead of patrolling through the bush, the point man led the patrol along a clearly marked path, right into the beaten zone of a Chinese machine gun.[34] There were no survivors.

Assuming that one survived the staccato of automatic weapons fire and explosions of hand grenades that initiated an ambush, there was only one thing for anyone caught in the killing zone to do: charge the enemy directly. Once the firing started, there was no time to ponder a course of action. The enemy had chosen the ground and had positioned their weapons to deliver the maximum amount of firepower into the killing zone. It therefore became essential to get out of it as quickly as possible, and the best way to do this was to get in among the ambushers. Here, of course, the Canadians were at a distinct disadvantage. Their unreliable Sten guns and single-shot Lee Enfields were hardly suited to close combat. Nor did their training emphasize the instant, aggressive, offensive action drills required in such circumstances.

A wiser course of action was to avoid being ambushed in the first place. To do this, soldiers had to become one with their surroundings – their ears strained to pick up any sounds that portended imminent danger, such as the rustling of bushes or the metallic clang of a weapon's safety catch being disengaged. They also listened to the wildlife. A soldier in the 3 PPCLI claimed that when the crickets stopped chirping or a pheasant broke cover, there was trouble ahead.[35]

The embargo on noise applied to the Canadians themselves. Patrols wore their noisy nylon winter suits and heavy combat boots at their peril. In the deafening silence of the Korean night, the squawk of a radio, the rattling of equipment, the unrestrained rupture of flatulence, or even a muffled sneeze could spell the difference between life and death. Lieutenant Bob Peacock reminisced that coughing was especially dangerous. "The only way it could be controlled on patrols," he wrote, "was to chew gum or candies or suck on a small stone to keep the throat moist."[36] However, not all Canadian soldiers were as concerned about noise as they should have been. Sergeant John Vallance recalled: "One night on patrol, while laying on the ground, I heard this clicking noise; I couldn't figure out what it was; I got a grenade ready. Then I saw this spurt of flame, and here he was, trying to light a cigarette with his lighter. I told him to put it out or I would jam it down his throat."[37]

Sharp eyesight was equally critical. Eyes darted back and forth in their sockets, lizardlike, scanning the patrol's axis of advance for the slightest movement or incongruous shape. Small trees and bushes always required a double-take: the Chinese were experts at camouflage and concealment. In such circumstances it was imperative to maintain one's night vision. This meant not looking at flares as they descended across the horizon and using only filtered light to examine maps.

Towards the end of the war, the 25th Brigade was issued with a very limited number of first-generation night-vision devices known as snooper scopes. These used infrared to illuminate the dark recesses of no man's land, but their effectiveness was undermined by mechanical failures. A postwar report noted their tendency to malfunction at the most inopportune times. Notwithstanding this, they were a highly desirable piece of equipment.[38]

A keen sense of smell was also useful. A 1 R22eR soldier claimed that it was possible to smell the enemy. "If you smelled onions or garlic you were guaranteed to have a contact," he recalled.[39] By the same token, the smell of Aqua Velva aftershave or soap could disclose the presence of a Canadian patrol.

In this environment of heightened sensory perception, patrol dogs were invaluable.[40] Dogs had been used by both sides during the First World War, but the Canadian Army never established its own canine corps. In Korea, patrol dogs were used exclusively by the third battalions, but only during the last month of the war. As Lieutenant-Colonel Campbell noted, patrol dogs allowed the patrol to move much more quickly, since the possibility of ambush was "almost eliminated."[41] "Almost" was the operative term, for a well-known patrol dog in the Commonwealth Division, a female German shepherd named Killer, was killed in an ambush while accompanying a Canadian patrol.[42]

Another way to avoid ambushes was by not following a set routine. In theory, Canadian patrols should have gone out at different times of the day and used different routes. The only place the Chinese would lay an ambush was along a recognizable track; there was no point in lying in wait in an overgrown area of no man's land. However, the self-imposed prohibition on daytime movement along the Jamestown line made avoiding a fixed routine extremely difficult.[43] The Canadian patrols went out at more or less the same time each day, and they used the same well-worn routes. The thick minefields that skirted the Canadians' positions channelled movement, because patrols could pass through them only at specially marked gaps.[44] It did not take long before the Chinese caught on to this and laid ambushes there.

Errant mines were also a problem. These might be planted by enemy sappers, who made a habit of digging up Canadian mines and relaying them. Mines might also work their way into the minefield gap following a heavy rain, or they might be inaccurately marked on the minefield map. Either way, the consequences were the same. Only six days before the ceasefire, a Canadian soldier was killed and three KATCOMs wounded after one of them accidentally stepped on an antipersonnel mine known as a Bouncing Betty.[45] A similar accident claimed the life of a young platoon commander in the 2 PPCLI. Lieutenant Brian Munro recalled: "He stepped into the minefield by mistake. He was stripped clean, from his pelvic area down, totally devoid of flesh and muscle, or anything else. We called for a helicopter; he was still alive when we loaded him aboard. He died before he reached the hospital."[46]

Booby traps were another constant worry. One type favoured by the Chinese was the so-called mud bomb. It was made by covering a Soviet-pattern F-1 fragmentation grenade in a thick layer of mud until only the pull ring was exposed. Once it had dried, the ring was pulled. So long as the mud remained unbroken, it held the detonating lever in place and prevented the grenade from exploding. When laid in paths where it could easily be mistaken for a rock and stepped on or kicked, the mud bomb was a highly effective antipersonnel device.[47]

Whether a booby trap was safely side-stepped or triggered often depended on the alertness of its intended victim. But alertness was often eroded by the mind-numbing fatigue that was such a feature of the Canadian soldier's combat experience in Korea. Whether they were attacking a Chinese-held hill, patrolling, or manning defensive positions, Canadian soldiers almost always went into combat tired. The 2 PPCLI soldiers from Dog Company who attacked up the treacherous slopes of Hill 532 were so exhausted and disorganized by the time they reached the first line of Chinese defences that Lieutenant-Colonel Stone ordered them to fall back before they had even reached their objective.[48]

Things were little better at Kap'yong. After a two-mile march from Tungmudae to the base of Hill 677, the rifle companies had to hike to their positions on the hill itself. The climb up Hill 677 is difficult enough when equipped only with a camera, as this author discovered during a research visit to Kap'yong; but each Canadian soldier was carrying a rifle, several hundred rounds of .303 SAA,[49] grenades, an entrenching tool, a full water bottle, and a twenty-four-hour field ration pack. To make matters worse, many in the battalion were nursing wicked hangovers, as the night before had been spent clustered around bonfires imbibing bottles of Labatt's lager.[50] On reaching their allotted positions, the soldiers of 2 PPCLI still had to dig defensive positions, lay signal wire and trip flares, and clear fields of fire through the dense underbrush.

Combat was an equally exhausting experience after the consolidation of the Jamestown line. Trench routine provided limited opportunities for soldiers to maintain their physical fitness, particularly cardiovascular fitness, yet they were still expected to be fighting fit for patrol duty. This could cause problems, as a 1 RCR fighting patrol discovered when it was unable to keep up with its timed tankfire barrage.[51]

The return trek could be equally harrowing, especially if trailed by the enemy or carrying a wounded man. Even if unmolested, the climb back up to friendly lines was a heartwrenching affair, as lungs gasped for breath and legs heavy with fatigue struggled for balance. The sheer physical effort required just to make it safely up the slopes leading to the Canadians' positions often meant that caution gave way to haste.[52] As seen above, this could have tragic consequences as the patrol approached the minefield gap.

Repelling a Chinese assault was even more exhausting. Few men were able to relax while shells slammed into their positions, and a prolonged bombardment often meant that they were exhausted even before the battle began. Yet this was only the beginning of their ordeal. Once the shelling stopped – and assuming they did not sit tight and call down supporting fire – the race to the forward fighting trenches was on. The entrances to the Canadians' bunkers were usually choked with debris, making an easy exit impossible. Next came the dash of thirty or so yards over more rubble to the forward fighting trenches, which were usually destroyed or caved in.[53] Then came the real work. Cycling the bolts of their single-shot rifles like men possessed, and hoping for the best, the Canadians attempted to pour fire into the attacking Chinese ranks. This was far easier said than done, and it was only a matter of time before friendly supporting fire was brought down on the position itself. Commenting on the Chinese raid on 3 RCR, Corporal W.D. Pero recalled: "The Chinese were hard to hit with small arms fire ... You had to lean way out of the trenches to bring a weapon to bear on them. I finally had no choice but to call VT artillery on top of our position. All we could do was find shelter in a bunker, or lie on the floor of a trench. The VT fire caused many casualties to the Chinese; it killed some of our boys also."[54]

The extensive use of supporting fire reduced but did not completely eliminate hand-to-hand encounters between Canadian and Chinese soldiers. During the attack on Hill 355, for example, a

Canadian soldier killed a Chinese grenadier with an entrenching tool as he came round the corner of a narrow communications trench.[55] There was also a hand-to-hand melee during the battle of Kap'yong. A Baker Company soldier recalled: "Lieutenant Ross gave us the order to move out. Just as I jumped up ... I fell over a Chinaman who was running up the side of the hill. He let fly and got me in the neck then ran into the end of my bayonet ... I met [Wayne] Mitchell later in hospital. He knew my rifle because I had a couple of notches carved in it. He had gone back the next day and found it. He told me, 'You got him. The rifle was still in him.'"[56]

One of the more frightening close-quarter confrontations occurred during the earlier attack on Hill 532. As he struggled up the hill, a Dog Company platoon commander came face to face with a Chinese soldier as he emerged from a concealed position. Armed with a captured American rifle, the Chinese soldier fired but missed.[57] He attempted to fire again, but his rifle jammed. The Canadian raised his pistol to fire, but his mud-caked weapon would not work either. With less than ten yards between them, both men struggled frantically to clear their weapons in a macabre race to the death. The young Canadian officer managed to bring his weapon back into action first. He recounted what happened next: "I was so frightened that I let go eight rounds before I realized he was falling forward. I reloaded my magazine. To go forward up the trench, I had to crawl over him. There was not much evidence of his wounds, just a row of white puffs on the back of his quilted winter uniform showed where the bullets had come out. I will never forget that experience of crawling over a still warm body."[58]

This encounter underlines another aspect of the combat experience in Korea: fear. Fear is the common bond between combat soldiers and takes a variety of forms.[59] Some men channelled it into action, as the young officer above did, while others became withdrawn and sheepish. Others still became agitated and pugnacious. Fear had other manifestations. One soldier ruefully remarked that the best way to gauge fear was according to the "pucker" factor: "The more your asshole puckered up, the more frightened you were. It gave a whole different meaning to being scared shitless."[60] More scientifically, a 1952 study of blood and urine samples taken from American soldiers shortly after being exposed to enemy fire showed definite physiological changes occurring as a result of combat.[61] These changes included interference with the body's diurnal cycle, or internal clock,[62] often making men hungrier and thirstier than they normally were. A Kap'yong survivor remembered the fear-induced appetite of one of his comrades: "He had a metabolism like you wouldn't believe. We were issued two rations, two C-rations per man. Bishop sat down on the edge of his trench and ate two C-rations. There were three meals in each one. Then he went around seeing if anyone had any old ham and lima beans they didn't need."[63]

Just as the symptoms of fear varied from individual to individual, so did its causes. Some men experienced a surge of fear at the sound of a bugle or shepherd's horn. The Chinese used them for battlefield communications and to demoralize the enemy. However, in the words of an intelligence report, "Chinese Communist battle noises ... are effective on morale only to the extent that UN troops are not conditioned to expect them."[64]

Far more ominous was enemy weaponry. According to a 1951 American study of ineffective soldier performance under fire in Korea, mortars and machine guns, including the PPSH-41, were the most frightening.[65] With the advent of static war, artillery surpassed both as the leading fear-inducer among U.N. infantrymen, especially when large numbers of shells fell over a prolonged period of time.

Reflecting on his experiences under enemy shellfire, a Canadian soldier commented that "he was very fucking lucky not to have his head and balls blown off."[66] As we shall see in the next chapter, there was more than a little truth to this. But it was not only the body that could be destroyed by shellfire; the mind was, arguably, even more vulnerable to the effects of an enemy bombardment. The blood-curdling whine of shells as they descended along their banana-shaped trajectory, the rumbling of earth as it was churned by high explosive, the ringing in the ears punctuated by the sound of more explosions and the screams of frightened men, all conspired to make shelling a terrible ordeal – an ordeal made even worse by the Canadian practice of counting shells[67] for the "shellrep," a daily tabulation of incoming fire maintained by each infantry battalion.[68]

Completing this vision of hell on earth were the dark, dank, dusty, claustrophobic bunkers in which the men sheltered. There can be few things more frightening and demoralizing than counting incoming rounds, each one with your name on it, crouched in the sinister shadows of a flickering candle, your lungs screaming for oxygen as the walls draw ever closer, while high-explosive shells rearrange the topography of your hilltop warren. Few men endured this agony without reaching the very limits of their emotional endurance. In the words of a senior RCR regimental officer, "It's knowing that you can't walk around or you'll get hit. It gets so that even when there is no shelling at all you still get nervous. And when they pour in 1,275 shells a day you've got a problem. The odd man breaks and then you risk getting a run for it."[69]

That all men did not break and make a run for it is the truly astonishing aspect of the Canadian combat experience in Korea. Endurance in such extreme conditions depended on a variety of factors, such as comradeship, an adventurous spirit, or deeply held religious beliefs.[70] Yet it was inevitable that some soldiers would give way under the strain of battle. These were the so-called exhaustion cases, the men who suffered acute neuropsychiatric breakdown after exposure to combat.[71] Then there were the SIWs, the men who resorted to the traditional battlefield expedient of a self-inflicted wound as a way out of their horrible predicament. The boundary between the two was anything but firm, and many of the SIWs would have eventually been diagnosed as exhaustion cases. The differences between the two are, in any event, more apparent than real; both saw the ugly face of battle and were unable to come to terms with its diabolical visage.

As was intimated above, intense and prolonged enemy artillery fire was responsible for most battle exhaustion cases in Korea.[72] During the softening-up phase of the battle of Hill 355, for example, eleven men were evacuated for neuropsychiatric breakdown.[73] Although Hill 355 was responsible for the largest proportion of Canadian exhaustion cases during the Korean War, they amounted to less than one percent of the total casualties suffered by the 1 RCR during the month-long action.[74]

During the 2 PPCLI's first month in action, a period that included the disastrous attack on Hill 532, there were only two cases.[75] A Baker Company soldier recalled: "One guy shot two [enemy] with startling accuracy. It was a classic down on one knee, bang, bang, and that was it. Then he went completely out of his mind and ran hysterically down the hill to [Major] Lilley. I never saw him again."[76]

Because most of the battles fought by the Canadians in Korea were counted in hours rather than days or weeks, battle exhaustion was comparatively rare.[77] There were exceptions to this, such as

Hill 355, but on the whole battle exhaustion was not a major problem. Yet there is evidence that the Canadians had a higher rate of neuropsychiatric breakdown than the British.[78] However, as the Canadian adjutant-general pointed out, "The British practically ignore what we term battle exhaustion. It may well be that our doctors are so anxious to avoid retaining a man in action if he is in fact suffering from battle exhaustion that they may withdraw a substantial number of men who are not in fact suffering from nervous disorders at all."[79]

There is also evidence that the Australians and New Zealanders had a higher proportion of battle exhaustion casualties than the Canadians.[80] The contradictory nature of the available evidence therefore makes it impossible to assess the relative rates of battle exhaustion in each Commonwealth formation. Even if firm statistics were available for each contingent, as they are for venereal disease, it would still be impossible to reach any reliable conclusions. A diagnosis of battle exhaustion was far more subjective than that of VD and was dependent on the attitude of the attending physician towards psychiatric illnesses in general. Sergeant Paul Tomelin recalled that although Canadian battle exhaustion "cases in Italy and the Netherlands were much more severe ... those suffering from battle exhaustion were treated more compassionately than those in Korea."[81]

Nevertheless, the treatment of battle exhaustion was the same as it had been during the Second World War.[82] Men showing its symptoms, anything from paralysis and uncontrollable shaking to total hysteria,[83] were evacuated to the Regimental Aid Post just behind the MLR. Mild cases were returned directly to duty, while the more severe cases were sent along the evacuation chain to the Field Dressing Station, where they were sedated and given short-term psychotherapy.[84] Most exhaustion casualties returned to their units after a few days, though acute cases might be reassigned to support units or even sent home.

This method of treatment revolved around the proven principles of immediacy, proximity, and expectancy.[85] By treating cases in a timely fashion as close to the fighting as possible – and always under the assumption that they would return to duty – the number of recoveries was maximized and malingering minimized.[86] This is not to say that some men did not feign a neuropsychiatric breakdown as a way out of the combat zone. However, there were very specific taboos attached to this behaviour. A psychiatric report penned just after the ceasefire recorded:

Now there is no longer any shame or social disapproval attached to evacuation from Korea – Thus the soldier who would otherwise be held to his post by fear of appearing a "coward" should he be removed psychiatrically can now cheerfully accept this consequence ... It is now acceptable amongst a certain class to strive to attain such a disposal to the more congenial surroundings of Japan – and posting to that country (or better still to home) would be regarded as a mark of achievement.[87]

Another, arguably more effective, way to remove oneself from the combat zone was with a self-inflicted wound (SIW). Most of the 25th Brigade's medical records remain classified, so it is impossible to know the incidence of SIWs in Korea. However, no Canadian soldiers were court-martialled for SIWs in Korea.[88] It was extremely difficult to prove an SIW because of the difficulty of finding witnesses.[89] This dovetails with the anecdotal evidence, which generally suggests that most SIWs occurred during lulls in the fighting when soldiers "mistakenly" shot themselves in the foot or hand while cleaning their rifles in a forward weapons pit or in a lonely corner of the communications trench. The one bona fide SIW in 1 RCR on Hill 355, for example, occurred during a lull in the shelling, when a young Bren gunner turned his LMG on his left foot.[90] Commenting on the experience in his battalion, 1 PPCLI's Sergeant John Richardson recalled: "There were five or six [SIWs] in the battalion. I only recall one in [Dog] Company, a replacement; he shot himself in the foot, with the boot off, while cleaning his rifle. No witnesses. We gave him a rough ride on the stretcher going back to the Regimental Aid Post. This incident happened at a very quiet time and there were no physical hardships involved."[91]

Before the arrival of a Canadian medical formation in Korea (see chapter 7), the 25th Brigade faced the additional problem of disciplining cases of SIWs.[92] An Adjutant-General's Report claimed that SIWs were on the increase in Korea but noted that it was difficult to take disciplinary action because cases were quickly evacuated to U.S. medical installations.[93] With the arrival of the No. 25 Canadian Field Ambulance in Korea and the formation of the Commonwealth Division, it became easier to identify SIW cases. However, this did not necessarily translate into increased disciplinary action. During a visit to the Commonwealth General Hospital in Japan, the British Director General of Army Medical Services was disheartened to discover that of the 83 soldiers undergoing treatment for wounds, 24 (14 British, 6 Canadian, 1 Australian, and 3 New Zealand) were "accidental" gunshot wounds to the hands or feet.[94] However, the New Zealanders had the highest rate of SIWS. A whopping 75 percent of their admissions were for SIWS, followed by the British (38 percent), the Canadians (18 percent), and the Australians (17 percent).[95] Commenting on these disheartening but highly irregular[96] figures, he wrote: "I saw no soldier under arrest for any of these [SIWs], and I consider it is bad for morale for those who are wounded due to enemy action to see their comrades in the same ward with self-inflicted wounds being treated on an equal footing. I feel that instructions should be given that all [SIWS] should be treated in a special ward in hospital until it has been proved beyond doubt that the self-infliction was not deliberate."[97]

Despite the recommendations of the British medical officer, SIWS continued to be treated alongside comrades who had been wounded by enemy fire. The impact this had on morale is questionable, as men with SIWS were most certainly viewed as cowards, or "lead-swingers," by their fellow soldiers.[98] As we have seen, however, cowardice, battle exhaustion, and SIWS were anything but synonymous in Korea. Although the available evidence strongly suggests a reduced will to combat in the 25th Brigade, the vast majority of Canadian fighting men soldiered on in spite of their very serious deficiencies in training and equipment, and the resultant lacklustre battlefield performance. That even more men did not succumb to battle exhaustion or resort to self-inflicted wounds is perhaps the most astonishing aspect of the Canadian combat experience in Korea – an experience made even more taxing when soldiers saw their comrades being killed and wounded.

CHAPTER SEVEN

Butcher's Bill

Compared with the carnage in the two world wars, Canadian casualties in Korea were extremely light. In only eight hours of fighting at Dieppe, for example, the Canadian Army suffered more than twice as many casualties as it did in the entire Korean War.[1] This was little consolation to the soldiers of the 25th Brigade, who faced death and mutilation on a daily basis. For although the numbers of wounded were far smaller in Korea, the dangers were universal. Men could be cut in half by machine-gun fire, eviscerated by shell fragments, or burned beyond recognition just as surly in Korea as in the world wars. The Korean War did, however, mark the battlefield debut of two medical technical innovations: the medevac helicopter and protective body armour. Unfortunately, the limited availability of these American-designed and -manufactured items prevented their having a major impact on the Canadian casualty experience in Korea.

Battle casualties are sustained through direct enemy action and are distinct from psychological and accidental casualties. Soldiers who were killed in action (KIA), officially presumed dead, died of wounds (DOW), wounded in action (WIA), injured in action, missing,[2] or captured as prisoners of war (POWs) were all considered battle casualties. The butcher's bill was highest in the infantry. Of the 1,543 Canadian battle casualties in Korea only 101, or less than 10 percent, were from non-infantry units.[3] A similar pattern emerges in regard to fatal casualties. Of the 309 KIAs, DOWs, or officially presumed dead, only 15 were from non-infantry units, the majority of these (9) being in the artillery.[4] Clearly, the infantry bore the brunt of the fighting and dying in Korea.

Table 1
Fatal Battle Casualties

Unit	Killed in action	Presumed dead	Died of wounds	Total
1 RCR	40	3	8	51
2 PPCLI	40	1	9	50
2 R22eR	31	–	4	35
3 RCR	26	4	5	35
1 PPCLI	27	2	5	34
1 R22eR	27	3	3	33
2 RCR	30	–	1	31
3 PPCLI	18	–	–	18
3 R22eR	4	2	–	6
Total	243	15	35	293

Source: NA, RG24, 18,502,133(D4), "Statistical Report on Battle Casualties (Far East), 4 February 1955"

The 1 RCR and the 2 PPCLI lost the most men, with 51 and 50 fatal battle casualties, respectively. In 1 RCR, approximately 38 of the 51 battle fatalities, or 70 percent, occurred in October 1952 while the battalion occupied positions atop Hill 355.[5] The 2 PPCLI, on the other hand, suffered 33 battle fatalities during the first three months of its operational service in Korea.[6] The fluid nature of the fighting at this time and the attendant difficulty of evacuating casualties over difficult terrain is reflected in the comparatively high number of deaths from wounds. Finally, it is worth noting that 16, or nearly half, of the 2 R22eR's fatal casualties were sustained during the battalions's two-day defence of Hill 227. Obviously, a set-piece engagement could have a drastic impact on a unit's casualty rate.

Since the truce was signed during their Far Eastern tour, the third battalions generally suffered a lower number of fatal battle casualties. There is, however, one important exception. It will be remembered that the 3 PPCLI arrived in Korea five months before the 3 RCR and six months before the 3 R22eR. However, it was not the 3 PPCLI but the 3 RCR that experienced the worst bloodletting. What the statistics do not tell us is that 26,[7] or 74 percent, of the battalion's battle fatalities were suffered by one single company during the attack against Hill 187 on 2–3 May 1953.[8]

The distribution of non-fatal battle casualties by battalion was similar to the fatal ones; with the exception of 3 RCR's and

Table 2
Non-Fatal Battle Casualties

Unit	Wounded in action	Injured	Prisoners of War	Total
1 RCR	204	13	14	231
1 PPCLI	178	25	–	203
2 PPCLI	141	22	–	163
2 R22eR	136	9	3	148
2 RCR	134	10	–	144
1 R22eR	84	6	1	91
3 RCR	71	1	7	79
3 PPCLI	61	7	1	69
3 R22eR	17	–	4	21
Total	1,026	93	30	1,149

Source: NA, RG24, 18,502,133(D4), "Statistical Report on Battle Casualties (Far East), 4 February 1955"

1 PPCLI's altered positions, the order of units was more or less the same. While the 3 RCR ranked fourth in fatalities, only the 3 PPCLI and 3 R22eR had the fewest non-fatal battle casualties. Conversely, the 1 PPCLI ranked fifth in fatalities but had the second-highest number of non-fatal battle casualties. It is not clear why this should be the case. A possible explanation would include the high number of non-fatal casualties suffered by the 1 PPCLI (and 1 RCR) in May–June 1952 when the battalion patrolled in accordance with the U.N. Command's raiding policy.[9] The relatively high proportion of fatal to non-fatal battle casualties in the 3 RCR, on the other hand, can largely be attributed to the unusually high proportion killed during the attack on 2–3 May 1953: 26 men were killed and 27 wounded.[10] Put another way, for every soldier who was wounded, another was killed.

As noted above, POWs were counted among the non-fatal battle casualties. The experiences of Canadian POWs in Korea are relatively well documented and need not detain us here.[11] Nevertheless, several observations are in order. The figures once again reflect the 1 RCR's and 3 RCR's unhappy experiences on Hills 355 and 187; all of the RCR POWs in the Korean War were captured during these two engagements.[12] Similarly, all three of the 2 R22eR POWs were taken on 24 November 1951;[13] and three of the four 3 R22eR POWs were captured on 20 May 1953, the fourth being taken during a patrol clash on 22 June 1953. The only other battalions to have men captured were the 3 PPCLI and 1 R22eR, which lost one man apiece. Lance-Corporal Paul Dugal, the 1 R22eR POW, was captured in June 1952 during a routine patrol in no man's land. Like the other Canadian soldiers captured during the Korean War, Dugal survived his stint in a Chinese prison camp. He was released in April 1953.[14]

From the information presented above, excluding the POWs, it is possible to calculate the ratio of fatal to non-fatal battle casualties in the 25th Brigade during the Korean War. The number killed or dying of wounds was 293 out of 1,412, or approximately 21 percent of all wounded. In other words, there was one death for each five wounded in the 25th Brigade. This corresponds exactly with the figure for the Second World War.[15] Clearly, the fighting in Korea was far more lethal than the euphemism "police action" suggests.

Although the ratio of killed to wounded remained constant throughout the Korean War,[16] the percentage of casualties by weapon appears to have changed. A 25th Brigade report released in December 1951 identified bullets as being responsible for 33 percent of all battle casualties in Korea, shell wounds for 52 percent, and "other" (mines, grenades, edged weapons, etc.) for 15 percent.[17] The percentage of gunshot wounds (GSW) is probably low, as it includes casualties from October and November 1951 when heavy fighting erupted along the newly consolidated Jamestown line. This period coincided with the Canadians' first real taste of the destructive potential of enemy heavy artillery. The casualty list from the 2 R22eR action of 23-5 November, for example, records only one GSW in the entire battalion. The circumstances surrounding this lone GSW are hazy, though the nature and location of the wound, a .303 rifle bullet through the right foot, suggest a self-inflicted wound.[18] All of the 2 R22eR's other 62 casualties, including the 16 fatalities, were caused by shell or mortar fire.

One of the most upsetting direct hits of the war occurred at this time. Three "Vandoo" privates were clustered around a small hexamine fire in front of their dugout, cooking lunch and enjoying a brief respite from the fighting. Sergeant Paul Tomelin, a Canadian Army photographer on assignment with the 2 R22eR, stopped to chat with them.[19] Pressed for time, he declined their offer of lunch and continued with his work. No sooner had he left the scene then a Chinese shell exploded right on top of the three men. When the smoke cleared, nothing remained of them, leading the battalion adjutant to list them as "Missing – Presumed Dead," until enough eyewitnesses could be assembled to confirm their fate.[20]

As the 2 R22eR casualty statistics suggest, the occupation of defensive positions and the attendant increase in enemy artillery fire was accompanied by a relative decrease in the number of GSWs in the 25th Brigade. An official breakdown of casualties by weapons is not available for the period December 1951 to July 1953; however, an examination of the 1 RCR casualties for October 1952 yields some valuable clues.

The 1 RCR suffered 38 killed and approximately 114[21] wounded during this period. Only two of the fatalities can be attributed to GSWs, both of which occurred during the Chinese infantry assault against Baker Company on the night of 23–4 October;[22] one soldier was cut in half by a series of burp-gun hits, which stitched across his upper torso from his left scapula to his right shoulder, while another took a burst in the face.[23] The remaining 36 RCR fatalities (95 percent) were caused by shell or mortar fire. Some of the bodies were mutilated beyond recognition. On 2 October, for example, a soldier was killed after sustaining multiple fragment wounds from a high-explosive shell. The man suffered abdominal evisceration, complete destruction of the frontal cranium, and a shattered right femur.[24] Most of his clothing was torn off by the blast. It was only after his identity tags were recovered that he was positively identified as KIA.

Artillery was also responsible for most of the RCR wounded. Of the approximately 114 non-fatal battle casualties, only 11 (10 percent) were officially listed as GSWs.[25] However, there is reason to believe that most of these were self-inflicted, since at least six and possibly a seventh were caused by bullets of Canadian calibre and were inflicted in non-threatening regions of the body, such as the hands and feet.[26] Moreover, none of them coincided with the Chinese infantry attack on 23–4 October. Four of the eleven were, however, directly attributable to Chinese small arms fire.[27] Thus, a more plausible percentage of non-fatal GSWs due to direct enemy action would be in the 4 percent range, with shell and mortar fire accounting for the overwhelming majority of 1 RCR casualties.

Field artillery and mortars, then, were the greatest killers of Canadian infantry. This was hardly unique to Korea. The fathers and older brothers of the men in the 25th Brigade had faced the same threat from shells in the two world wars. What was unique to Korea was the use of armoured vests to reduce casualties from shellfire. Developed by the Americans, the eight-pound vests were "filled with overlapping plates of moulded fibreglass and nylon."[28] When worn properly, they could prevent 60–70 percent of chest and upper abdominal wounds and reduce fatal casualties by 10–20 percent.[29] Tested by the Canadians on a limited basis in May 1952, it was not until the following spring that sufficient numbers became available to outfit most of the troops manning the forward fighting positions. In other words, armoured vests arrived too late to have a significant impact on the overall Canadian casualty rate during the Korean War.[30] In October 1952, for example, the 1 R22eR, the first Canadian unit equipped with armoured vests, had only enough to outfit thirty men. This number increased to sixty in February 1953, and when the unit last entered the line in April, it was equipped with three hundred armoured vests[31] – though this was still not enough for all the men in the 1 R22eR support and rifle companies.

Although American body armour research teams had specifically warned against issuing insufficient numbers of armoured vests to front-line troops, citing an adverse impact on morale, 25th Brigade Headquarters continued to dole them out as they became available.[32] Lieutenant Robert Peacock of the 3 PPCLI recalled that the issue of ten armoured vests to his platoon in mid-December 1952 "caused a bit of a dilemma."[33] With enough vests for only one-third of his command, the young subaltern restricted their issue to sentries and men manning the observation posts. Other platoons may not have been so egalitarian. A private who served in the same battalion as Peacock has stated that his platoon's ten vests were allocated according to rank, beginning with the platoon leader;[34] considerations of risk simply did not figure in the decision.

The Canadian soldiers fortunate enough to be issued an armoured vest certainly liked them.[35] But even armoured vests had their limits. Although they could stop shell fragments, they were not bulletproof. This did not prevent some soldiers from foolishly relying on their armoured vests to stop snipers' bullets.[36] A careless soldier in the 3 PPCLI, for example, was gut-shot by a Chinese sniper while returning from a patrol. The bullet passed clean through his vest, killing him instantly.[37] Nor did they offer much protection from a direct shell hit; a high-explosive blast could still vaporize a man wearing an armoured vest.

Assuming that a man was not vaporized by a shell and that he survived the initial impact of bullet or shell fragment, it was imperative to get him to an advanced medical treatment facility as quickly possible. This was, of course, far easier said than done. The evacuation of wounded men under fire has always been difficult, and Korea's rugged terrain and climatic extremes made the task no easier.[38]

First, the casualty had to be removed from the scene of the fighting. As in every other war, this crucial first step along the evacuation chain was made with the help of the soldier's immediate comrades. He would be carried, dragged, pushed, rolled, or helped along, depending on the nature of his wounds and the tactical situation. If under artillery fire in a defensive position, he would be pulled into the nearest bunker; on patrol, he would be carried back to the "firm base," or patrol rallying point.

Having removed the casualty from any further danger, the next step was to render any life-saving first aid. This could include anything from putting a shell dressing on a sucking chest wound to tying a tourniquet on a severed limb.[39] The timely and effective provision of emergency first aid at this stage could often mean the difference between life and death.[40] Private D. Bateman described the first crucial seconds after his three-man patrol was caught in a mortar barrage:

I heard the cries [of a wounded man] but before I reached him, I came upon [the signalman]. I bent down and felt his pulse and it wasn't beating so I knew he was dead. I then went over to [the other wounded man] and he told me he was hit in the legs, arms, and body. I was laying a blanket over him when a mortar bomb landed about 15 to 20 feet away. I caught a piece of shrapnel in the left cheek. It started to bleed so bad that I put a field dressing on it ... I then put a tourniquet around [the wounded man's] leg.[41]

With the casualty stabilized, the next step was to prepare him for evacuation – or, in the case of Private Bateman, to return to Canadian lines as quickly as possible and organize a stretcher party. Either a large M was painted on the casualty's forehead or the empty surette was hooked through his front breast pocket, indicating that the medic had given him morphine – though, of course, morphine was withheld if he was wounded in the head. The standard four-man wood and canvas stretcher was the most convenient way to transport a wounded man, but its awkward size and shape presented a problem in the narrow communications trenches leading back from the forward positions, and regimental or KSC bearers often had to carry the stretcher over their heads.[42] Patrols, on the other hand, seldom carried stretchers. Until the appearance of a specially designed light telescopic stretcher in early 1953, the preferred method was to fashion a crude litter out of a blanket and extra rifle slings.[43]

The journey to the Regimental Aid Post (RAP), the first medical facility along the evacuation chain, could be excruciatingly slow, especially for patrols forced to bring their wounded in under fire. Even in the absence of hostile fire, there was always ice, mud, ambushes, or minefields to contend with; it was not usual for a patrol with wounded to take two or three hours to reach Canadian lines.[44] For this reason, the 25th Brigade introduced the Forward, or Advanced, Regimental Aid Post in June 1952. This was essentially "a small medical establishment centred about the Regimental medical officer. It [could] be set up quickly at any given point in forward positions where moderately heavy or heavy casualties [were] anticipated."[45]

The introduction of the Advanced RAP spared the wounded the long and difficult journey to the rear without the benefit of medical attention, drastically reducing treatment time. At the Advanced RAP, the medical officer (MO) quickly assessed each case and commenced treating the most seriously wounded. He was often assisted in this by listening in on the commanding officer's radio net, a practice that allowed the MO to follow the patrol from the moment it left Canadian lines to the time it returned.[46] If any casualties were sustained, he was able to take appropriate measures, such as preparing blood plasma, for their reception.

After being examined by the MO and given any necessary life-saving treatment, casualties were released for transport (usually by stretcher) to the RAP. If enemy shelling had not cut the wires, the MO would telephone his counterpart at the RAP to pass on any relevant information concerning the type and number of casualties being evacuated. Minor wounds were dressed at the RAP, while cases requiring more advanced treatment were prepared for the move to the Casualty Clearing Post (CCP), located just behind the front line with the Canadian Field Ambulance. Most made the journey over the pot-holed dirt tracks leading back to the CCP by jeep ambulance. A driver recalled the emotional turmoil engendered by his sombre job: "Our main task was to transport the wounded as quickly as possible with the least amount of time available. There were times when the screaming from the wounded was a little too much. They made a point to rotate us as often as possible as ambulance drivers and guard duty so that we wouldn't go crazy looking at the wounded and all the blood all the time. I challenge anyone to spend six months caring for wounded and dead and not go crazy."[47]

A small minority of wounded men were spared the jeep ambulance ride to the rear by being evacuated directly from the RAP by helicopter. The request for a helicopter medevac was made by the MO and relayed through Battalion Headquarters to the appropriate American MASH authorities. The helicopter's limited availability and two-stretcher payload meant that only the most seriously wounded or injured could expect to be evacuated in this manner.[48] Head wounds, penetrating chest wounds, penetrating abdominal wounds, fractured femurs, and burns were all likely candidates. Helicopters were not used to evacuate the dead.

In ideal conditions, it took about half an hour for a medevac helicopter to reach the designated pickup site. A number of factors could conspire to lengthen this considerably. The helicopters of the day were extremely fragile by modern standards and prone to damage from even light hits, so all requests for evacuation had to be accompanied by a verbal confirmation that the pickup area was free from enemy fire.[49] The helicopters' fragility and lack of sophisticated navigational equipment prevented their use in winds over 35 mph and in heavy rain, sleet, or snow, and also at night. Finally, all pickup sites had to be clear of obstructions, measure a minimum of 50 sq. ft. (in hot, windless conditions an area 400 by 100 sq. ft. was needed), and be clearly marked with smoke grenades and aircraft identification panels.[50]

Because helicopter evacuations in forward areas were extremely delicate operations at the best of times, they were relatively rare; only thirty-one Canadian soldiers were evacuated by helicopter between 1 July 1951 and 29 February 1952.[51] Assessing the utility of helicopter evacuation from a strictly medical point of view, a 25th Brigade report concluded: "It would seem that the helicopter as used in Korea has a limited role in the evacuation of casualties.

The present day motor ambulance car still remains the reliable method of evacuation and must continue to be looked upon as such when the problems of casualty evacuation are considered."[52]

There can, however, be no doubting the positive impact of helicopters in Korea. No other mode of evacuation could match the helicopter's speed and comfort. When available, they could have a dramatic impact in reducing the number of fatal casualties. Lieutenant-Colonel Stone was adamant that the evacuation of the wounded by helicopter during the battle of Kap'yong helped keep the number of fatalities in his battalion to a minimum. He was also convinced that they boosted morale.[53]

In view of the helicopter's technical and tactical limitations in Korea, it is understandable that the vast majority of wounded men made the journey to the CCP by jeep ambulance. Here, the wounded were re-examined and triaged according to wound severity and required treatment. Men who required less than four days' treatment were admitted to the CCP's casualty ward; those requiring intensive care were evacuated by air transport to the British Commonwealth Hospital in Kure, Japan; and minor surgical cases were placed in a Royal Canadian Army Service Corps "box ambulance" and moved to either an American or Norwegian MASH unit or to the No. 25 Canadian Field Dressing Station (FDS) north of Seoul.[54] Finally, men who required casual hospitalization (usually less than two weeks) for illness, minor wounds, and postsurgical convalescence were admitted to the Canadian hospital in Seoul.[55]

Canadian soldiers had little cause for complaint in the American or Norwegian MASH units or the No. 25 FDS. The food was good and plentiful, the wards were comfortable, and the standard of care was generally high – especially when it was provided by a young Norwegian nurse! The same cannot be said of the Canadian hospital in Seoul. A soldier hospitalized for a burned hand wrote his parents:

They talk about how well the boys that are sick and wounded are getting treated ... You would figure that in a hospital forty or fifty miles from the line that treatment would be good. But this hospital that is Canadian is one living hell. To tell you the truth it is not fit for pigs to live in. They have about ten of us in one room, the windows are all knocked out and the stoves won't stay lit. There are holes in the floor big enough for a horse to fall through. We even have to go and get our own meals. Its hard to believe that I got better medical treatment and fed better up in the front lines ... When you get hurt or wounded you get treated worse than a pig pen full of pigs ready to go to the market. Its no wonder we are losing so many men ... They want to get killed because they say they would be better off dead than get the treatment we are getting.[56]

Conditions continued to deteriorate at the Canadian hospital through the spring and summer of 1952, prompting the vice-adjutant general, Brigadier J.W. Bishop, to make a special visit in October. Not only was the brigadier disappointed by the ramshackle nature of the facility, but he was surprised to discover that its two hundred patients did not have proper beds or sheets. Apparently, the Commonwealth Division officer responsible for the overall administration of the hospital (who also was a brigadier) "felt that it was in a vulnerable position and should not be hampered with equipment which might be difficult to move."[57] Brigadier Bishop retorted that "he did not consider the loss of a few hospital beds as particularly significant in the case of a severe military reverse," but to no avail.[58] The obstinate officer refused to recognize the absurdity of his position. Bishop was therefore forced to pull rank and broach the matter with the newly appointed commander of the Commonwealth Division, Major-General Alston-Roberts-West, who agreed to inspect the hospital forthwith.[59] Bishop's ploy worked; there was a marked improvement in conditions at the hospital in the months following the general's visit.

Seriously wounded men evacuated directly to the British Commonwealth Hospital in Kure did not have to worry about inadequate bedding or missing floorboards. With one important exception (see chapter 8), the equipment and standard of care was first-rate. Sergeant John Richardson of the 1 PPCLI was especially impressed by the surgeons: "The two Australian surgeons were built like football players. Both joined from private practice to receive additional experience with traumatic injuries. Never a day passed that we didn't have visits from other Commonwealth surgeons ... That my knee holds up to this day is directly attributable to their care."[60]

As comfortable as the British Commonwealth Hospital may have been, nothing could match the elation of being selected for air evacuation back to Canada. A young ambulance driver remembered the laughter and banter that reverberated off the cavernous interior of the Douglas Dakota transport planes as the wounded were hoisted aboard. "They were happy because they were going home, and it rubbed off on me. It made my tour that much easier."[61]

To qualify for repatriation, a wounded man had to be incapable of returning to duty within 120 days.[62] A soldier could also be eligible under the 25th Brigade's tri-wound policy. On the surface, this policy allowed for the early rotation of any soldier who had been wounded three times. However, the fine print dictated that all three wounds had to be serious enough to receive medical attention at the RAP level or higher, and also be the result of direct enemy action. Since 25th Brigade medical records remain classified, it is not known how many – or indeed if any – Canadian soldiers qualified for early rotation under the tri-wound policy. At least one soldier did come close, only to be turned down at the last moment by a medical review board. The soldier in question had received two wounds early in his tour: one from a mortar fragment and the other from a mine blast. His third, so-called million dollar wound, was a severe burn caused by an improperly constructed field stove. To his chagrin, a medical review board at the CCP ruled that an accidental stove burn "was not a 'wound' proper."[63] He was therefore deemed ineligible for early rotation and was unceremoniously admitted to the Canadian hospital in Seoul for treatment.

It was an unfortunate fact of life in Korea that men often became casualties through accidents. Patrols were ripped to shreds after stumbling into an uncharted minefield; the pins retaining the striker mechanism on the no. 36 grenade worked themselves free after being subjected to the wear and tear of life in the field; artillery fire fell short, landing among friendly troops; motor transports slid off ice-covered mountain roads into deep ravines; tired men could not be bothered to clear their weapons before cleaning them; friends were mistaken for enemies in the dark communication trenches along the Jamestown line; heavily burdened men plunged through the ice of a frozen river and drowned. All of this and more happened in the 25th Brigade during the Korean War, claiming the lives of forty-three men and wounding countless others.[64]

However, it was not drowning, friendly fire, or even minefields that were responsible for the majority of accidents in the 25th Brigade. As the experiences of the man denied repatriation under the tri-wound policy suggest, that distinction belonged to improvised field stoves. Burns caused by the careless use of gasoline stoves had been a problem in the Second World War, but not to the extent they were in Korea.[65] From the time the first Canadians arrived in the Far East, there was an acute shortage of proper stoves and fuel. In their absence, soldiers were forced to improvise, with tragic results.

Korean winters are notoriously cold. In the mountains along the 38th parallel, freezing temperatures combine with strong winds to make life out of doors difficult and dangerous. The long hours of darkness are particularly frigid, with temperatures plummeting well below zero degrees Celsius. Hypothermia is a constant threat, tired, wet, and undernourished bodies being particularly susceptible to the deleterious effects of this silent killer. Without recourse to a warm shelter and a hot drink, those afflicted will surely die.

Thus, as winter descended over the Korean peninsula towards the end of 1951, the 25th Brigade found itself in need of several thousand field stoves. As most of the infantry were quartered in bunkers and firewood was extremely scarce, what was required was a liquid-fuel field stove that could be safely installed and operated in the confines of the troops' cantonments. However, as with so many other items of military kit and equipment, there was an acute shortage of field stoves in Korea. To make matters worse, the two types issued to the Canadians, the M37 cooker and the U.S. M1951 tent stove, both operated on kerosene, another rare commodity in the Far East.[66] As is usually the case in war, shortages were most pronounced in the font line; REMFs ("rear echelon mother fuckers") on the other hand, always seemed to have an abundant supply of both stoves and kerosene.[67]

Stuck on a wind-lashed Korean hilltop in a freezing cold bunker, soldiers were forced to improvise. Even if they were fortunate enough to have "acquired" a proper field stove, chances were they did not have any kerosene. It was difficult enough to keep the men in the front line supplied with ammunition, water, and food, let alone with a steady flow of scarce kerosene. However, the few troops who did have proper field stoves soon discovered that gasoline could be used instead. It was easier to obtain at the front, and as long as it accomplished the immediate objective of fuelling his stove, the average soldier was unlikely to concern himself with the dangers associated with its use. Lieutenant Robert Peacock explained: "We had [an American] tent stove which we adapted to use gasoline for fuel instead of kerosene which was in short supply. Quite often the fuel control generators would malfunction and a pool of heated gasoline would collect in the base of the stove where it would eventually explode."[68]

Soldiers unable to steal, trade, or scrounge a proper field stove had to make their own. A number of different designs appeared during the war, but the "drip" and "can" types were the most popular. Both were constructed around a burner compartment, usually a metal 25-pounder ammunition box filled with several inches of sand and fitted with air intakes and a stovepipe.[69] A metal 4.2 in. mortar transport tube was normally used for this purpose. The drip stove was fed by a gravity system, normally a rubber surgical hose with a small brass valve affixed to one end that regulated the drip of gasoline into the burner compartment.[70] The operation of the can stove was far less technical; a can filled with gasoline was simply inserted into the burner compartment and ignited.[71] Both designs usually incorporated features to facilitate cooking, and neither "could be called environmentally friendly by today's standards."[72] Both were also potentially dangerous.

With the onset of cold weather in Korea, the Canadians' field-expedient stoves began to take their toll. In October 1951 six soldiers were admitted to No. 25 FDS with grievous burns; by January, the number had jumped to thirty-eight, and that was just the severe cases.[73] Not included in the statistics were the scores of soldiers who were treated for minor burns in the front line by platoon medics.

By early 1952 it was apparent that the Canadians were suffering a disproportionate number of casualties due to accidental burns. The experiences of the 1 PPCLI on 9 January reflect, in microcosm, the gravity of the problem. At 1100 hours a stove fire in the Mortar Platoon Command Post completely razed the bunker.[74] Over the course of the next few hours, errant stoves destroyed the Battalion Command Post, Tactical Headquarters, the CO's bunker, and a tent containing small-arms ammunition. Miraculously, only three men were wounded, all by exploding ammunition.

It was initially believed that the stoves issued to the 25th Brigade were unsafe and hence were responsible for the large number of Canadian burn casualties.[75] But as the majority of troops were not issued with proper fuel, let alone proper stoves, this was not simply a case of defective equipment. That such an assumption could even be countenanced was a measure of the distance between defence planners in Ottawa and the troops in the firing line.

As the number of burn casualties continued to mount, DND ordered the No.1 Canadian Army Operational Research Team (CAORT) into action. The team duly conducted a detailed study of burn casualties in Korea, releasing its findings in an official report in January 1953. The CAORT report is thorough and forthright and provides the historian with a window into this important but neglected aspect of the Canadian casualty experience in Korea. CAORT's most significant finding was that the majority of burn incidents occurred in the three infantry battalions.[76] This is not surprising, as the infantry accounted for the vast majority of the 25th Brigade's fighting strength. However, recalling that the shortage of stoves and kerosene were most pronounced in the front line, numbers alone are not sufficient to explain why the infantry suffered a preponderance of burn casualties in Korea.

The CAORT report provides further details. In April 1952, 1,500 stoves were in service with the 25th Brigade, of which half were improvised.[77] All of the latter were located in forward positions with the infantry. Significantly, the accident rate for these was found to be three times greater than that for issue stoves.[78] Close scrutiny of the type of accidents most commonly associated with improvised stoves explains this discrepancy and provides a glimpse of the danger the Canadian fighting man confronted each time he retired to the specious safety of his front-line abode.

Half of the accidents occurred during refuelling.[79] In the case of drip stoves, accidents occurred when the fuel reservoir was placed too close to the burner plate – normally the result of an inadequate length of rubber tubing. When the gasoline became hot enough it exploded, engulfing the bunker in a shower of flames. Accidents involving can stoves usually happened after a fresh can of gasoline was placed in the burner compartment while the stove was still hot. According to the CAORT report, "failure to take reasonable precautions against the hazards of gasoline vapour in an enclosed space" accounted for most of the other accidents involving improvised stoves.[80] What precautions should (or could) have been taken in a front-line bunker designed to withstand enemy shelling the CAORT report did not say.

All gasoline burns were extremely painful. Patients with third-degree burns, the most serious type, had their fluids restored and special National Research Council burn dressings applied.[81] Treatment was often complicated by the presence of foreign matter in the burns, making debridement necessary. The Canadian nylon combat parka was especially prone to fuse with the skin when exposed to the intense heat of a gasoline explosion, a lesson that seems to have been lost on the current generation with its nylon-shelled Gore-Tex military parkas. Less severe burns were usually treated by the exposure method, although this was not practical when casualties had to be evacuated by ambulance over Korea's dust-choked roads.[82] Finally, minor burns that did not require specialized treatment could be left open to heal on their own.

Treatment of burns could be excruciatingly slow. A burn casualty required an average of thirty days of treatment. Of the fifty-five severe cases examined in the CAORT report, approximately one-half required less than fourteen days, while the rest required anywhere from several weeks to several months; the average loss of time away from duty was fifty-seven days.[83] In terms of manpower loss, burns were quite significant.[84]

Burned soldiers were almost certain to carry the scars of their misfortune for life. These could range from small, aesthetically unpleasing blemishes to gross disfigurements in which the soldier's hands and face disappeared under layers of shiny scar tissue. Fortunately, two world wars' worth of experience and advances in skin grafting techniques kept these to a minimum. However, this was hardly a consolation for the handful of men who returned to civilian life without the use of their hands or without a face.

The available evidence strongly suggests that accidental burns from runaway stoves remained a serious threat through the winter of 1952-53. In October 1952 (three months before the appearance of the CAORT report) Brigadier Bogert issued routine orders dealing specifically with fire prevention and stove safety. Unfortunately, they dealt almost exclusively with fire safety in stove-equipped tents. As the vast majority of accidental burns involved improvised stoves in front-line bunkers, Bogert's safety recommendations were considerably off mark. Granted, the CAORT report was not yet available; however, a survey of No. 25 FDS admission records from January 1953 (the month the CAORT report appeared) onward shows that the Canadians never really succeeded in reducing the number of accidental burn casualties in Korea.[85] This can be attributed to the continued use of improvised stoves in the front line. Even in the aftermath of the CAORT report infantrymen were compelled to use the same improvised stoves they always had. The results were predictable.

Whatever the type of injury, the fact that so many men survived their wounds is testimony to the effectiveness and flexibility of the evacuation chain in Korea. But as this chapter has shown, exaggerated assessments of the medevac helicopter's role in the 25th Brigade, as well as the impact of body armour on the overall Canadian casualty rate, must be made with caution.

The treatment of wounded men was, alas, only one facet of the larger Canadian medical experience in Korea. Disease also posed a threat to the health of soldiers. In its treatment and prevention, Canadian medical authorities enjoyed far less success.

CHAPTER EIGHT

Permanent Souvenirs

Despite advances in preventive medicine and the widespread use of antibiotics, many men were incapacitated by disease during their Far Eastern tour. Most of these ailments were easily treated, but others led to painful and ghastly deaths. Nevertheless, the mortality rate from disease was the lowest in Canadian military history.[1] What is significant about the Canadian epidemiological experience in Korea is the number of diseases, ranging from hemorrhagic fever to chancroid, that had rarely been encountered in the past. As a result, the 25th Brigade suffered a disturbingly high number of non-battle casualties, which placed an enormous strain on its already overtaxed manpower resources.

Disease has always posed a serious threat to soldiers. Typhus ravaged the Bavarian army in 1812, and during the notoriously unhealthy Crimean War nearly 10 percent of the total British force was lost to disease.[2] Armies can be vast incubators for disease and must go to great lengths to prevent the disaster of an outbreak. Thus, over the course of the first weeks after their induction, the soldiers of the 25th Brigade received a series of basic vaccinations – against typhus, typhoid, smallpox, tetanus, polio, cholera, and plague.[3] The latter two were especially unpopular with the troops as they often became quite ill after receiving them.

Canadian medical officers were understandably shocked by Korea's unhygienic conditions, and their early situation reports portended a fierce struggle against disease in the Far East.[4] A report from the 2 PPCLI laconically stated: "Korea is a land of filth and poverty ... Diseases, except venereal ones will not be a problem during the winter, but as all fertilizing of fields is done with human excreta there is no doubt that there will be a health problem in spring and summer."[5]

Thanks to the immunization program, however, the epidemiological killers from the past were seldom a problem in Korea, though at least one Canadian soldier contracted smallpox. He was 2 PPCLI's Lieutenant-Colonel Stone, who in March 1951 was evacuated to Canada after developing the high fever, nausea, headache, and pinkish red spots characteristic of smallpox. Stone had contracted the disease in the village of Wol-li, where he had established a temporary headquarters in a thatched hut filled with the bodies of dead children.[6] Apparently, the two injections he had received prior to embarkation were reported as "no take," and the whole battalion was subsequently revaccinated in Korea with a special Japanese-type smallpox vaccine.[7] This incident, while isolated, served to remind the Canadians that preventive measures were not always effective and that serious illness or death were not confined to the battlefield.

Many of the diseases endemic in the Far East were new to the Canadians. Some of these were parasitic, most were highly infectious, and some could be fatal. Canadian medical authorities were not always prepared or equipped to cope with them, though treatment often improved with experience. A selective examination of the most problematical of these diseases provides yet another window into the 25th Brigade's continuing struggle with the unfamiliar conditions encountered in the Far East.

Korea's primitive sanitary conditions made gastrointestinal infections such as dysentery, acute diarrhea, and hepatitis inevitable. Dysentery appeared early in the war; several soldiers from the 2 PPCLI contracted it during the winter of 1951.[8] At that time the battlefront was still fluid, and the Patricias in question developed the disease after drinking untreated paddy water. Apparently, the exigencies of operations during this period precluded the proper use of the halazone water-purification tablets included in the Canadians' daily ration packs. However, with the occupation of semi-permanent defensive positions in the fall of 1951, chemically treated water from portable trailers was widely available and the incidence of dysentery dropped substantially.[9]

Far more common, though sharing many of the same symptoms as dysentery, was acute diarrhea. Not only could it make life in the field incredibly uncomfortable (with up to thirty explosive bowel movements a day in severe cases), but it could lead to severe dehydration. Diarrhea could be caused by anything from indigestible c-ration meals (ham and lima beans were especially bad) to food poisoning. The latter was the case in May 1952 when an entire section of the 1 RCR occupying a forward outpost became violently ill after consuming their evening meal. Clyde Bougie, a hygiene orderly from the No. 25 FDS, who investigated the outbreak, recalled:

I was told by the kitchen NCO that the food had been taken out to the outpost [by the KSC] ... in hayboxes. I inspected all the hayboxes and found one had a small cut at the bottom ... I inquired as to what was put in this one and the sergeant said hamburger patties and that the container was always used for meat. It was concluded that the juices that soaked into the insulation had contaminated all of the patties that came in contact with the juice and that the men at the very end of the trenches were the last to be served and had been poisoned.[10]

As in the Second World War, jaundice due to infectious hepatitis was relatively common.[11] Although it never reached epidemic proportions in Korea,[12] it was a continual source of non-battle casualties, accounting for 18 percent of all Canadian infective and parasitic diseases.[13] To make matters worse, hepatitis patients typically required fifty days' hospitalization.[14] Hepatitis A was transmitted in three ways: by the oral-fecal route (when a healthy individual consumed food or water containing the fecal matter of an infected person); through person-to-person contact; and through contaminated food and water. The oral-fecal mode of transmission was common during the first year of the war, when the Canadians found themselves operating in Korea's notorious rice paddies. It is no coincidence that the incidence of hepatitis A in the Commonwealth Division as a whole decreased by 43.6 percent with the occupation of the Jamestown line.[15]

Hepatitis B was usually transmitted by infected blood. In contrast to the Americans, who used disposable plastic intravenous equipment, or Bernard kits, the Canadians (and indeed all the Commonwealth forces) relied on the outmoded Baxter kits.[16] Made from glass, the Baxters were reused over and over again. Improperly sterilized, they became conduits for the spread of homologous serum jaundice, an advanced form of hepatitis B. Obviously, this was the last thing that a wounded soldier needed. The switch to Bernard kits came too late to save several men who might have recovered from their wounds had they not contracted the disease in this manner.[17]

Malaria, Japanese encephalitis, and hemorrhagic fever shared at least four important characteristics in the context of the Korean War: they were spread by insects; all were potentially fatal; they were endemic to the Far East; and they were more or less new to the doctors of the Royal Canadian Army Medical Corps (RCAMC). The Canadian Army already had experience with some tropical diseases. In August 1943 the 1st Canadian Division in Sicily had experienced a malaria epidemic that required quinine therapy for the whole division.[18] The cause of the outbreak was subsequently attributed to inadequate training and a general disregard for antimalarial precautions.[19] Only nine years after the Sicilian debacle, the Canadian Army found itself confronting yet another malaria outbreak – this time, in Canada.

Malaria is a serious and sometimes fatal disease caused by a parasite injected into the bloodstream through the bite of an infected female *Anopheles* mosquito. The early symptoms are flulike and are followed by fever, chills, and, at worst, multiple organ failure and death. Canadian medical authorities recognized the threat posed by malaria in Korea and instituted a preventive program based on the suppressive drug paludrine.[20] However, paludrine only suppresses the clinical symptoms of malaria and does not necessarily prevent infection by the malaria parasite. To complicate matters further, the four different types of parasite that cause malaria in different parts of the world require different kinds of suppressive drugs. Thus, if the malaria parasite endemic to a given area is paludrine-resistant, an individual using this drug stands a very good chance of developing the disease. This is precisely what happened in the 25th Brigade. Following the return of the second battalions to Canada in early 1952, more than a thousand cases of malaria were reported.[21] These so-called breakthrough cases were promptly treated with a combination of primaquine and either quinine or chloroquine. Fortunately, there were few recurrences.[22]

As this example shows, the Canadian Army had not fully digested the lessons learned in Sicily, though treatment in Korea did improve as medical officers gained experience.[23] Moreover, in contrast to the Sicilian campaign, Canadian medical authorities advised against the wearing of shorts during Korea's hot summer months in order to reduce the risk of exposure to mosquito bites. Not all soldiers were happy with this decision. Lance-Corporal Ted Smyth commented that "khaki pants were great, but when it reached ninety degrees, even khaki became uncomfortable ... It was at these times that shorts would have been appreciated."[24]

Whether they realized it or not, long pants were clearly the right choice for troops serving in the Far East. Paludrine alone, however, was not. This might have been obvious to the Canadians had they possessed up-to-date malaria maps – charts detailing the geographical locations of the different types of malaria parasite.[25] It is not entirely clear why these were unavailable, though the Northwest European focus of the post–Second World War Canadian Army may have been to blame. In their absence it was impossible to prescribe the correct chemoprophylatics, let alone identify the type of malaria parasite endemic to Korea. Clyde Bougie explained:

There were times when everyone in the lab gave up the search for parasites in particular blood samples as they could not find anything after looking through a microscope for more than twenty minutes. This one man had all the symptoms of malaria, but no parasite could be found ... I had a little time on my hands so I must have spent about two and a half hours looking over several stained blood samples, when bingo! Out of nowhere I found one lonesome little parasite in a cell, which I had each of the more experienced Lab Techs have a look, and sure enough ... it was a positive case of malaria.[26]

Although Canadian troops continued to take paludrine for the rest of the war, in the aftermath of the 1952 outbreak it was decided to supplement it with primaquine.[27] Taken together, these drugs proved extremely effective.

The shift to static warfare also permitted more effective use of other malaria control measures. All soldiers were issued head nets and twelve yards of mosquito netting.[28] These were far less likely to be used in the open field than in a bunker, where they could be set up properly and left hanging for as long as soldiers remained in the front line. Also, they were less likely to be damaged – and hence were more effective – when not subjected to the daily wear and tear of life on the march. The occupation of semi-permanent defensive positions also facilitated the saturation of nearby mosquito-breeding areas with residual insecticides containing DDT. When combined with the revised chemoprophylactic program, these measures resulted in a drastically reduced malaria rate; by early 1953, the incidence of malaria was only one-fifth of what it had been the year before.[29] Nevertheless, the Canadian rate continued to be slightly higher than that experienced by the British or Australian armies.[30]

It is unlikely that the 25th Brigade, or for that matter any other national contingent, could have succeeded in totally eradicating malaria from its ranks. As Korean veteran David Hackworth commented, there were always "some slackers who did not take their antimalarial pills and then went around inviting mosquitoes with their sleeves rolled up and shirts unbuttoned when the sun went down."[31] So long as at least some soldiers viewed contracting the disease as a way out of the front line, the Canadians were bound to continue to suffer malaria casualties, no matter what preventive measures were implemented.

Like malaria, Japanese encephalitis was endemic to the Far East. A viral infection spread by ticks and mosquitoes, its early symptoms included fever, headache, muscle pain, malaise, lethargy, and seizures. About one-fifth of Japanese encephalitis infections resulted in death.[32] After much indecision, the RCAMC decided in mid-1951 to vaccinate all Canadian troops who were at risk of contracting the diesease (namely, front-line troops in regular contact with mosquitoes and ticks). The highly effective vaccine, combined with the insect-control measures discussed above, limited the Canadian cases to a mere handful. Nevertheless, as the No. 25 FDS's "Interesting Case" log makes abundantly clear, Japanese encephalitis caused Canadian medical officers considerable anxiety. The war diarist wrote: "Patient admitted ... suffering from abdominal pain with a temperature of 102.4 and pulse of 110 was diagnosed variously as gastro-enteritis, appendicitis, and malaria. There was no diarrhoea or vomiting, no rigidity or guarding and smear for malaria parasite was negative. The pain however was acute. Final diagnosis was Japanese encephalitis and the patient was evacuated."[33]

Even more alarming than Japanese encephalitis was the horror-movie-calibre hemorrhagic fever. Brigadier Rockingham reminisced that "this deadly Oriental disease upset our medical people terribly because they never heard of it before."[34] The entries by RCAMC doctors in the No. 25 FDS war diary confirm this. The monthly progress report for November 1951 recorded that while there had been a slight decrease in infectious hepatitis, "a new (for us) disease has shown itself ... This is epidemic hemorrhagic fever."[35] Identified by the Japanese Army Medical Corps in Manchuria and Korea in 1943, the first cases of epidemic hemorrhagic fever appeared in U.N. field hospitals in June 1951. Known simply as "the fever" by the troops, the disease was spread by chigger mites carried on the bodies of rodents. Early symptoms included nausea, vomiting, headache, high fever, and chills. As the disease progressed the patient began to cough blood, pass bloody stool, and bleed from the skin. The mortality rate was between 8 and 20 percent, with coma or death usually occurring in the third or fourth week.[36] There was, and still is, no specific treatment for the fever.

It is difficult for the historian writing nearly five decades after the fact to express in print the fear induced in front-line troops by the ever-present threat of contracting hemorrhagic fever. Their bunkers and fighting trenches were crawling with large, aggressive rodents, and the war diarists certainly considered the fever worthy of mention. The 4 January 1952 entry in the 1 PPCLI war diary recorded that in addition to an ambulance being ambushed in the rear of the Patricia position, "the incidence of an undiagnosed fever is increasing in the battalion ... Another man was evacuated today."[37] Rumours about this mysterious disease circulated freely among the troops, embellished by graphic accounts of its victims' agony. Lance-Corporal Earl Richardson recalled: "Sergeant Crowen ... contracted the dreaded disease. The medical staff could do nothing for him, except watch him die, bleeding from every orifice of his body, including his navel and eyeballs; nothing would stop the hemorrhaging."[38]

Although the available statistics preclude a precise breakdown of hemorrhagic fever cases by national origin, there is reason to believe that most of the twenty-six Canadian soldiers who died of disease in Korea perished after contracting the fever.[39] Moreover, there is some evidence to suggest that in mid-1952 the Canadians had the highest rate of infections in the Commonwealth Division. According to a report released in September 1952, forty-three Canadian soldiers were evacuated with hemorrhagic fever between October 1951 and August 1952, compared to only nineteen in the joint British-ANZAC 28th Brigade, and twenty-six in the all-British 29th Brigade.[40]

One explanation for the higher incidence of hemorrhagic fever in the Canadian brigade is that medical officers may have wrongly diagnosed a number of less serious illnesses. As we have seen, the fever was virtually unknown before the Korean War; in the aftermath of the general panic invoked by its appearance, doctors were more likely to err on the side of caution. Sergeant George Elliot of the 1 PPCLI, for example, was evacuated for what was believed to be hemorrhagic fever; but after spending two leisurely weeks in an American hospital, he was diagnosed as having a mild form of trench fever and was returned to duty.[41]

As Sergeant Elliot's experience intimates, a man suspected of having the fever was quickly evacuated to a special American MASH unit. Even if he was later found to be suffering from another, less serious, illness, the statistics of the No. 25 FDS still listed him as a hemorrhagic fever case. Although his personnel file would eventually reflect the changed diagnosis, it is unlikely that it would have been communicated to the No. 25 FDS.[42] In other words, the statistics may not be entirely accurate.

Another possible explanation for the high Canadian rate is that the 25th Brigade's forward positions contained an inordinate number of rodents. This would certainly support Jeffrey Grey's contention that the Canadians did not employ proper rubbish-disposal methods.[43] This explanation becomes even more convincing when viewed in the context of the Commonwealth Division's hemorrhagic fever-control program, implemented in the fall of 1952. Perhaps the Canadians had finally realized that such unheroic and painful deaths were avoidable, for the program was executed with a zeal seldom surpassed in the annals of Canadian military history.

The program outlined rigorous standards for food storage and refuse disposal, and enforced them through periodic inspections by the Division Hygiene Inspection Team. Other measures included impregnating clothing with mite repellant (di-butyl-phthalate) at fortnightly intervals and a front-line rodent-destruction plan. The expressed purpose of the plan was to quickly kill as many rodents as possible.[44] To this end, breadmash, soaked rice, or oatmeal was mixed with rat poison (Red Squill or Warfarin) and left at strategically situated baiting points.[45] Each platoon maintained a record of these, along with the daily body count. Thousands of rodents were killed in this way, their bodies burned just behind the forward positions in large fifty-five-gallon drums.

Whatever the cause of the Canadians' seemingly high hemorrhagic fever rate, the No. 25 FDS statistics clearly point to a dramatic decrease in the number of cases from the fall of 1952 on; only three men were diagnosed with the fever between September 1952 and July 1953.[46] But while the Canadians were making dramatic inroads in the fight against hemorrhagic fever, they were enjoying less success in their battle against that age-old ailment, venereal disease.

As already noted, early situation reports from the 2 PPCLI portended a fierce struggle with communicable diseases in general and venereal diseases in particular. During the battalion's first two months in the Far East, sixty-four men (70 percent of all non-battle casualties) were treated for VD.[47] But despite the Patricias' warning, it was not until early 1952 – nine months after the arrival of the rest of the 25th Brigade in Korea – that defence planners woke up to the reality of VD in the Far East. By then, hundreds of Canadian troops had become infected, and the 25th Brigade found itself confronting a VD epidemic unparalleled in Canadian military history.

Venereal disease has a long tradition in the Canadian Army. The Canadian Corps had a higher rate of VD than any other belligerent army in the First World War, with one in nine soldiers becoming infected.[48] During the Second World War, the Canadian Army's VD rate remained relatively high, reaching a wartime peak of 68.4 per thousand in 1945.[49] During its first two years in Korea, however, the 25th Brigade's VD rate surpassed all of the above, peaking at an unbelievable 611 infections per thousand per annum![50] Thus, the VD rate among Canadian soldiers in Korea was ten times what the Canadian overseas rate had been in 1945.

In view of the 25th Brigade's VD problem, DND instructed the Defence Research Board (DRB) to conduct a statistical analysis of the cause and incidence of infection among Canadian troops. In initiating the DRB study, DND was less concerned with the moral fibre of Canadian troops in Korea than with the problem of personnel wastage from non-battle causes. The DRB analysis was, in fact, based on an earlier report prepared by the 1 CAORT, which had noted that one in three non-battle casualties were caused by VD.[51] The DRB analysis may therefore be viewed as an extension of the CAORT report.

The DRB's analysis of VD in the 25th Brigade was based on medical records obtained from the Directorate General, Medical Services (DGMS) between June 1951 and February 1952. The vast majority of the DGMS's records were in the form of nominal roles, which listed the name, number, rank, unit, diagnosis, date of diagnosis, and place of contact for each case of VD; information relating to the use of condoms was obtained from the accompanying case record forms.⁵² A veritable gold mine for the historian, the DRB report retained its original "Secret: For Canadian Eyes Only" security classification until 1976, when it was downgraded to "Restricted." For the next two decades it languished in the Directorate of History's vault, but in July 1995 the remaining restrictions on access were removed, and the DRB report became public property.

A logical place to begin an examination of the DRB's findings is with a comparison of Canadian, British, and American VD rates during the first two years of the Korean War. If cases of nonspecific urethritis (NSU) are excluded,⁵³ the rates per thousand per annum are 25th Canadian Infantry Brigade, 414; 28th British Commonwealth Infantry Brigade and 29th Independent British Infantry Brigade, 387; American forces, Eighth U.S. Army, 208.⁵⁴ A comparison with Canadian troops stationed in other theatres is especially instructive. In February 1952 the 25th Brigade's VD rate was fifteen times greater than that of the 27th Canadian Infantry Brigade in Germany.⁵⁵ Clearly, something was amiss in the Far East.⁵⁶

Within the 25th Brigade, the DRB identified significant differences in VD rates between units.⁵⁷ The difference in rates was not, as might be expected, between the allegedly footloose and fancy-free units of the Special Force and the spit-and-polish regular units of the Active Force; the DRB found no evidence that Special Force soldiers had a higher rate of VD than Active Force soldiers.⁵⁸ Rather, it was a case of teeth versus tail, with units situated in the rear having a much higher rate of VD than those at the sharp end. This was the result of support personnel having far more opportunities for contact with the local civilian population. The DRB report substantiates this assertion, identifying units of the Royal Canadian Ordnance Corps, the Royal Canadian Engineers, Headquarters, the 25th Canadian Infantry Brigade, and the Royal Canadian Electric and Mechanical Engineers (in that order), as having the highest VD rates in the brigade.⁵⁹ All these units were situated well behind the front line, and their personnel had easy access to prostitutes, or "sexy-sexys," in the nearby cities of Seoul, Tokchon, and Uijongbu.⁶⁰ As Private Jacket Coates explained, the support-unit guys were mobile: "They get around the country, see? Into the rear areas. The infantry are stuck up here on the hills and have what you might call limited opportunity for play."⁶¹

Although support units had the highest rate of VD in the 25th Brigade, the greatest number of Canadians who contracted venereal infections were from the infantry units. Of these, the 2 R22eR was purported to have the lowest rate; however, there is some evidence to suggest that "a certain number of infections within the unit [were] not reported through the regular channels."[62] In any event, by March 1952, 2 R22eR's VD rate had matched 1 PPCLI's and surpassed 2 RCR's.[63] Unlike their compatriots in support units, soldiers in the combat arms usually acquired VD while on leave in Japan. Each soldier was eligible for two five-day blocks of "special" R&R leave in Kure or Tokyo.[64] Often referred to half-jokingly as "rape and rampage," R&R was the highlight of the Canadian soldier's Far Eastern tour.

In contrast to the British and Australians, the Canadians did not open a leave centre in Japan until the last year of the war. Although they were more than welcome to use the British and Australian facilities, few Canadians wanted to spend their leave "eating mutton and listening to how great the British and Australians thought they were."[65] Not surprisingly, most elected to make their own travel arrangements.[66] For months they had lived like beggars, endured the extremes of the Korean climate, and faced the threat of sudden, violent death. Now, only twenty-four hours' distant from the combat zone, they were free to choose where they stayed, how they ate, what they drank, and who they slept with.

They almost invariably began their leave with a hot bath. The younger soldiers particularly appreciated the chance to clean themselves up, several months having passed since the last "zit patrol."[67] Next came the drinks and women. Neither was particularly hard to come by, for Kure and Tokyo both contained extensive red-light districts. Kure's notorious red-light district included 115 licensed prostitute brokers, 54 beer halls and cabarets employing approximately 300 waitresses; 119 hotels with 357 chambermaids; 640 tea shops licensed to serve alcohol; 6 dance halls; countless massage parlours; and 24 high-class (for officers only) geisha houses.[68]

The sights, sounds, and smells of an Asian red-light district were unlike anything the Canadians had ever experienced. Rickshaws jockeyed for position amid the flickering glow of neon lights, as the din of a foreign language reverberated down the narrow alleyways. The smell of putrid fish mingled with steam from boiling rice cauldrons, making the air heavy and oppressive. People filled the streets, exuding a carnival-like insouciance. Many Canadians were taken aback by the exoticism of their surroundings. One soldier characterized the prevailing attitude in Kure as being one of "Why fight? ... Drink and fuck instead."[69]

Most Canadians did just that. According to Private Jacket Coates, Canadian soldiers "just loved screwing and they didn't care what they screwed."[70] With US$200 burning a hole in their battledress pockets, few wasted any time on smalltalk or pleasantries.[71] A soldier recalled: "You had a choice of girls at the hotel; I had three in rotation. On the last day of my leave, I was in a communal bath house and this gorgeous Japanese girl gives me the eye. The next thing I know we are up in her room. It cost me money, of course; no free sex in Japan or Korea."[72]

Nor was sex necessarily worry free. Soldiers who did not take measures to protect themselves during their forays often spent their first couple of weeks back in Korea wondering whether they had left Japan "with a permanent souvenir."[73] There were several different kinds of souvenirs, though three were most common. Unlike the situation in the First and Second World Wars, syphilis, the most serious type of sexually transmitted disease before the appearance of HIV, was rarely encountered. According to the DRB's findings, syphilis accounted for only 1.4 percent of the 25th Brigade's venereal infections.[74] Gonorrhea, on the other hand, was a major problem, accounting for 33.1 percent of all Canadian VD cases.[75] Soldiers infected with the gonococcus bacillus, the causative organism of the disease, became acutely aware of their predicament three to seven days after sexual contact.[76] The first manifestation of the disease assumed the form of a greenish stain in the soldier's underwear. If this was not enough to convince him to seek medical treatment, the next symptom most certainly would. As the disease progressed, the soldier's meatus would swell, making urination difficult and extremely painful; some likened the process to "pissing fire."[77] By this stage, the infected soldier would be compelled to seek medical attention, thus becoming a non-battle casualty.

The second most prevalent form of venereal disease in the 25th Brigade was nonspecific urethritis (NSU), which accounted for 32.3 percent of all infections.[78] Those infected with NSU became painfully aware of their condition four weeks after contact and experienced some of the same symptoms as those with gonorrhea.[79] Soldiers diagnosed with NSU were instructed to avoid alcoholic beverages during treatment – no mean feat for a soldier in the 25th Brigade. Apparently, alcohol increased the rate of relapse in NSU cases.[80]

Chancroid, the third most common form of VD in the Korean theatre of operations, accounted for 30 percent of all Canadian cases.[81] Rare in Europe and North America, chancroid was endemic in the Far East. Not surprisingly, Canadian medical officers had little experience in treating it.[82] Chancroid patients required from five to fifteen days hospitalization, making it especially costly from the manpower perspective.[83]

From the figures presented above, it is apparent that syphilis, gonorrhea, NSU, and chancroid accounted for 96.8 percent of all Canadian VD cases. Commonwealth Division records indicate that the remaining 3.2 percent of cases encompassed a host of minor venereal ailments, such as balantitis (white blisters on the glans penis), penal warts, and inflammation of the foreskin.[84]

Sixty percent of gonorrhea cases were successfully treated with penicillin at the Regimental Aid Post by the "one/two shot" method.[85] Cases requiring further treatment joined those diagnosed with NSU at the No. 25 Canadian Field Dressing Station, where they were given a five-day course of sulfa drugs.[86] Patients undergoing sulfa treatment were ordered to drink six pints of fluid daily to prevent kidney complications. Chancroid, as we have seen, almost invariably involved prolonged hospitalization, because patients required routine blood surveillance. Even so, the treatment of VD in Korea posed no major challenges to the professional skills of Canadian medical officers.[87] This was partly attributable to the low number of syphilitic cases encountered in the Far East, but it was also due to the widespread use of antibiotics, which made the effective treatment of VD possible.

Antibiotics had made their battlefield debut during the Second World War, and by the time of the Korean War were in the medicine chest of every major U.N. army. Their use in the treatment of a host of previously fatal infections quickly earned antibiotics the dubious title of wonder drugs. However, not everyone at National Defence Headquarters in Ottawa thought they were so wonderful. Shortly after replacing Lieutenant-General Foulkes as Chief of the General Staff, Lieutenant-General G.G. Simonds complained that Canadian soldiers in Korea viewed penicillin as a panacea for the consequences of their sexual indiscretions.[88] In singling out the liberal use of antibiotics as the reason for the 25th Brigade's high

VD rate, Simonds was ignoring the failure of his own department. British and American soldiers presumably found Asian prostitutes just as inviting as Canadians did, nor were there any differences in the use of antibiotics in those armies.[89] Yet the British and Americans were able to maintain a VD rate that was consistently lower than that of the Canadians.

Under intense pressure from Ottawa to bring the 25th Brigade's VD problem under control, Brigadier Rockingham issued orders in early April 1952 that any soldier who contracted VD during the last ninety days of his tour would have to serve an additional three months in Korea. Rockingham later admitted that he did not have the legal authority to issue the order but justified his action by claiming that the VD rate had dropped immediately.[90] However, Commonwealth Division VD statistics tell a different story; they show that by June 1952 the 25th Brigade's VD rate was the same as it had been before the announcement of the VD rotation policy.[91] Moreover, as Korean veteran and author Robert Hepenstall observed, "All units ignored this order, except the infantry; it was another shameful means of keeping men in the line for another three months. The rule applied only to the lower ranks; no officer of any regiment or corps served an extra three months for contracting venereal disease."[92]

Once again, the soldiers in the firing line suffered the most from their superiors' ignorance. Fearing a three-month extension of their Korean tour, many infantrymen hid their condition until they were safely on board the troopship taking them back to Canada.[93] "I had an infection in my urinary tract," a soldier recalled. "On the boat going home, I heard there was an American doctor taking sick parade. What a shock; the sick parade line up extended half way around the boat, all Canadians."[94]

By the late fall of 1952, the 25th Brigade's VD rate at last started to decline.[95] This was not, however, the result of the illegal VD rotation policy; rather, after a year's service with the 1st Commonwealth Division, the 25th Brigade was starting to learn how to handle its VD problem, just as it had done to a lesser extent with hemorrhagic fever. With years of operational experience in Asia, the British army had developed a number of preventive measures to combat the spread of VD. As an integral part of the Commonwealth Division, the 25th Brigade was able to draw on British experience and reduce its VD rate. Thus, the 25th Brigade's struggle with VD during the first two years of the Korean War can be attributed to a lack of operational experience in a Far Eastern context and inadequate preventive measures.

Prior to the outbreak of hostilities on the Korean peninsula, the Canadian Army had little operational experience in Asia. Two infantry battalions had participated briefly in the doomed defence of Hong Kong in late 1941, but with this obvious exception few Canadians had served in the Far East during the Second World War. (And it is interesting to note that the most serious medical problem during the Hong Kong deployment was VD.)[96]

The Canadians' inexperience in the Far East was reflected in the 25th Brigade's training lectures on hygiene. Of the three hundred lecture periods the soldiers of the brigade attended during their basic training, only five were allocated to personal hygiene.[97] Of these, maybe one might be allocated to a discussion of VD; the remainder dealt with issues such as how to defecate in the field, brushing one's teeth in the combat zone, and foot care in a cold, wet climate. Indeed, an Adjutant-General's Report identified the lack of education as the primary cause of the 25th Brigade's high VD rate.[98] To make matters worse, when the Canadians deployed to Korea they did so without the support of a specially trained VD unit.[99] Apparently, defence planners in Ottawa did not believe VD would be a major cause of non-battle casualties in Korea.

As noted above, the British army had a wealth of operational experience in the Far East.[100] Based on this knowledge, the British, and by extension the 1st Commonwealth Division, instituted a number of preventive measures, which reached the peak of their effectiveness by the fall of 1952. The first of these was a comprehensive VD training program, carried out under the auspices of the No. 10 Field Hygiene Section.[101] The program consisted of a day-long series of lectures. Only officers and NCOs were permitted to attend, the idea being that they would take their newly acquired knowledge of VD back to their units. The senior chaplain usually made a brief appearance at these lectures to remind students of the moral issues surrounding the acquisition of VD. According to a Commonwealth Division report, the chaplain's "section particularly was well received by the students."[102]

The second preventive measure adopted by the Commonwealth Division was to restrict the movement of personnel in rear areas and to reduce the number of Korean prostitutes in nearby villages.[103]

To this end, the No. 1 Commonwealth Provost Company conducted routine vice raids on nearby towns and villages. While these raids did not reduce the incidence of VD among soldiers returning from R&R in Japan, they did help lower the VD rate in support units.

Rounding out the Commonwealth Division's approach to VD control was the creation of prevention stations around leave centres and base areas.[104] No questions were asked at the time of admission,[105] and soldiers were instructed to:

1. Scrub the hands thoroughly with soap and water.
2. Pass water in short, sharp gushes, holding the urine back by pinching the top of the penis and letting go with a rush.
3. Remove trousers and underpants, and tuck up your shirt.
4. Wash thoroughly with soap and water the genitals, especially under the foreskin, the thighs and lower abdomen. Continue to wash these parts for five minutes.
5. Dry the genitals, thighs and abdomen with the paper towel provided.
6. Take the ointment provided and rub well onto the genitals and surrounding areas, pull back the foreskin and rub onto the glans (knob), and under the foreskin, be sure that the ointment is applied to the whole of the genital area including the scrotum. Continue for five minutes.
7. Wrap the genitals in a paper towel, do not wash these parts again for at least six hours.

DO NOT PUT OINTMENT INTO THE PIPE[106]

These measures did not guarantee that a soldier would not develop a venereal infection, but they could reduce the chances if carried out immediately after exposure. However, Canadian infantrymen who developed VD in the last ninety days of their tour still faced an additional three months' service in the Far East.

Finally, the Canadians followed the British and Australian examples and opened a leave centre in Tokyo.[107] Known as the Maple Leaf Club, it provided the Canadian atmosphere that was clearly lacking in the British and Australian centres. It was popular with the troops because the amenities included a reading room, a snack bar, guided tours, shopping service, and wet canteens.[108] There can be no question that the Maple Leaf Club kept some soldiers out of the red-light districts and reduced their exposure to VD.[109] An Adjutant-General's Report even suggested that the VD problem and instances of disorderly conduct among Canadian troops in Japan could have been avoided had the Maple Leaf Club been available from the outset.[110]

Although the Canadians never quite succeeded in bringing their VD rate down to British or American levels, by the end of the war the disease was no longer the threat it had once been. By July 1953, the Canadian rate had plummeted to 416 infections (including NSU) per thousand per annum – a significant improvement over the 610 infections recorded only a year earlier.[111] Credit for reducing the 25th Brigade's VD rate must go to the British. Without their direction, it is highly unlikely that the 25th Brigade would have been able to bring its VD problem under control by war's end.

Summing up the Canadian epidemiological experience in Korea, a medical officer concluded that the "conflict may have been a localized war but it was a dirty, difficult one."[112] As this chapter has shown, the silent battle against disease was anything but easy. From the outset, the Canadians were clearly not prepared to deal with the epidemiological dimension of service in the Far East. Although treatment tended to improve with experience, the struggle with disease would likely have been even more difficult had the Canadians not been able to draw on British experience. In the end, it was the lowly soldier in the firing line who paid the price for the army's unpreparedness. From needless hemorrhagic fever deaths to a patently unfair VD rotation policy, the Canadian infantryman faced the consequences of improper planning and preparation – in addition to the threat of imminent death from enemy action – on an almost daily basis. Canadian unpreparedness was not, however, confined to disease prevention. Another area given insufficient forethought was the provision of basic comforts and amenities to help assuage the hardships of life in the field.

CHAPTER NINE

Forgotten People

Compared with their compatriots in the rear, the infantry led a life of extreme hardship and deprivation in Korea.[1] While most support personnel enjoyed three square meals a day, slept in proper beds, and could look forward to such things as regular mail service and the occasional live show, the soldiers in the firing line lived like tramps without even the most basic comforts.

One indication of a soldier's proximity to the sharp end was the type of food he ate and the manner in which it was consumed. Soldiers in the rear seldom ate prepackaged combat rations, whereas men in the firing line often subsisted on them for extended periods. The combat, or hard, rations used by the 25th Brigade in Korea were the infamous American C-rations. During the latter stages of the Second World War, Canadian fighting men had largely subsisted on British-type composite rations. These had been developed in the early-1940s to replace the traditional but immensely unhealthy battlefield diet of bully beef and hardtack biscuits. As John Ellis observed, a "'Compo' pack contained the ingredients for the daily meal of fourteen men, though where necessary it might have to provide one man with 14 day's food, two with seven or whatever combination seemed easiest."[2] Compo meals were all tinned and included traditional English fare such as bacon, bangers, Irish stew, steak and kidney pie, pudding, fruit, butter, cheese, and jam.[3] Rounding out the compo rations was an accessory pack containing cigarettes, matches, toilet paper, candies, and a small solid-fuel cooker.

As with so many other things, the Canadian Army was deficient in compo rations at the outbreak of the Korean War. This led to the decision to feed the soldiers of the 25th Brigade with American

C-rations. Thus, for the first time in Canadian military history, Canadian soldiers would officially eat American-style food in combat.

Not all of the soldiers in the 25th Brigade were impressed with the new American grub.[4] Like the earlier compo meals, C-rations were packaged in tins, but unlike the compo meals they were packaged for individual issue in small cardboard boxes. Each individual C-ration pack contained two cans: one contained a vegetable and meat combo, the other instant coffee, sugar, and some biscuits.[5] As a result, the social aspect of cooking and eating was partially eroded. This was particularly irksome to the veterans in the brigade, who were accustomed to the banter and comradeship that accompanied the breakdown and preparation of compo meals. Moreover, the self-contained C-rations complicated cooking in forward areas. Lieutenant-Colonel Campbell complained, "The C-ration is far from the ideal ration in static warfare. I feel that something in the nature of the last war compo pack where cooking could be done on a group basis, say section or half section, would be preferable."[6]

C-ration menus were not completely to Canadian tastes.[7] While wieners and beans and spaghetti and meatballs were popular with Canadian troops, turkey loaf and ham and lima beans – or "ham and motherfuckers" in military parlance[8] – definitely were not. During the battle of Kap'yong, for example, the famished soldiers of 2 PPCLI left their air-dropped stocks of ham and lima beans largely untouched.[9] Later in the war, rewards were posted in the third battalions for any recipe that would make ham and lima beans edible.[10] Predictably, Canadian soldiers attempted to pawn off their tins of turkey loaf and ham and lima beans to their Commonwealth allies. For some inexplicable reason, the New Zealanders often accepted these unpopular entrees in exchange for their coveted compo tins of cheese and butter.[11]

Like the earlier compo meals, C-rations were accompanied by an accessory pack. With the possible exception of the toilet paper, few of the items or brands were suited to Canadian tastes. American cigarettes were not especially popular with Canadian troops, though there were few smokers in the brigade who would decline a Lucky Strike or a Marlboro in a pinch. American pipe tobacco was also included in each accessory pack, even though the total number of Canadian pipe smokers was estimated to be less than two hundred.[12] Another superfluous accessory was old-fashioned Gem razor blades. As straight-razors were not issued to the soldiers of the 25th Brigade, the Gems were totally useless.[13] A final complaint about the American accessory pack was the manner in which the contents were arranged. Lieutenant Bob Peacock recalled that the Hershey Bars "were packed in the box next to the soap whose taste permeated the chocolate. This simple placement has, unfairly, influenced my selection of chocolate bars ever since."[14]

Another problem with c-rations was their susceptibility to temperature extremes. In hot weather, the unappetizing layer of fat that surrounded such culinary favourites as turkey loaf melted, saturating the entree and leaving soldiers with a greasy film on the roof of the mouth. In extremely cold weather, the fat could be scraped off, but the entree itself often froze solid. There were few things more demoralizing to a cold and hungry man than the prosect of eating a frozen c-ration meal with the shape and consistency of a hockey puck.[15] With hunger being the only alternative, soldiers went to extraordinary lengths to defrost their c-rations. The easiest way to heat the tin was to hold it over a burning solid-fuel tablet. However, these could not be used in bunkers or other confined spaces because of the danger of carbon monoxide poisoning. In the fighting positions, c-ration tins were warmed in the pockets of parkas or windproof trousers or, if a soldier was desperate, under an armpit or in the crotch.

Worse still, c-rations could cause acute diarrhea and severe gastrointestinal discomfort when consumed for extended periods. As well, soldiers subsisting exclusively on these rations faced a daily deficiency of between 400 and 1,800 calories.[16] During the battle of Chail-li, for example, several soldiers in the 2 RCR fell ill after subsisting strictly on c-rations for several days. The battalion after-action report recommended that c-rations be supplemented with A- or B-rations (fresh food) whenever possible.[17]

Fortunately for the Canadians, fresh food was frequently available in forward areas. The staples included lamb from New Zealand, hamburger patties, bacon, and pork chops from the United States, bread from the Commonwealth Division's bakery, and vegetables grown on special hydroponic farms in Japan.[18] The palatability of these rations was largely dependent on the acumen and technical expertise of the cook who prepared them. Cooked in company kitchens, they were transported to the front line in hayboxes on the backs of KSC porters, and soldiers waited in trepidation to taste the cook's latest creation. Some companies, notably those in the

3 PPCLI, were renowned for their excellent food. Others suffered in silent anguish as they choked down flaccid pork chops and shrivelled potatoes, whose flavour and texture had literally been boiled out of them.

Even well-prepared rations could become unappetizing by the time they reached the front line. Hayboxes seldom kept food warm during the winter, and the standard-issue mess tin was useless.[19] The rectangular, $2\frac{1}{2}$ in. deep, aluminum mess tin was supposed to double as both a frying pan and a plate. Without a partition, the various components of a meal spilled together into one unappetizing mess. Equally ineffective were the standard-issue knife, fork, and spoon – or "gobbling irons"[20] – which were poorly designed, with no provision for clipping them together, so that Canadian soldiers frequently lost their knives and forks, and, more importantly, their spoons.[21] The loss of something so mundane as a spoon passed unnoticed in the rear. At the front, where it was used for digging, prying, tightening screws, and chipping ice and snow, in addition to its more conventional role as an eating utensil, the spoon was counted as one of the combat soldier's most important tools.[22]

Rear-echelon personnel did not need to worry about inadequate eating equipment; their meals were normally dished up on proper settings. They were also spared the rigours of masticating frozen C-rations, as well as the suspense that accompanied the opening of a haybox. For them, fresh food prepared by some of the best cooks in the brigade was the norm. And with their quarters situated behind the front line, they had plenty of opportunity to supplement their official rations with wild game.[23] The Korean countryside possessed an abundance of wildlife, and a successful hunt might translate into roast venison or baked pheasant.

The closest the lowly soldier in the firing line came to savouring such delicacies was during Christmas, when a turkey dinner was served to all ranks. The tactical situation permitting, soldiers were brought down from their hilltop positions in rotation to enjoy their festive meal. The hundreds of turkeys required to feed the brigade were obtained from the Americans, who were, it was rumoured, using Korea as a dumping ground for frozen birds left over from the last war. Despite the dubious origins of the Canadians' turkey dinners, most soldiers wolfed them down like men possessed.

A further discomfort of life in the field was caused by the primitive bivouac arrangements. When the fighting was mobile, soldiers simply slept under a poncho, which was fashioned into a crude shelter using local materials such as sticks and rocks. Such spartan accommodation was uncomfortable, to say the least. The open-floored layout did not deter snakes or rodents,[24] and during the monsoon season water streamed through as if passing under a bridge.

The lack of an official-issue camp mattress added to the discomfort.[25] A proper sleeping pad is essential to curtail radiant heat loss to the ground, and its absence meant that men woke up colder, not to mention stiffer, than would otherwise have been the case. In especially cold weather, such as that experienced by the 2 PPCLI in late January 1951, soldiers improvised by lining their poncho shelters with pine boughs or rice straw.[26]

Further contributing to the misery of life in the field was the prohibition on sleeping bags in the front line. Men forward of A echelon were expressly forbidden to have a sleeping bag in their possession.[27] This was because of a design flaw which made it impossible for a man to extricate himself rapidly from the Canadian-issue sleeping bag in an emergency.[28] The U.S. Army sleeping bag suffered from a similar flaw, but this did not stop some American troops from using it. The results were catastrophic. In February 1951 the 2 PPCLI came across the bodies of sixty-five American soldiers of the 2nd Reconnaissance Company.[29] The Americans had zipped themselves into their sleeping bags and gone to sleep without digging defensive positions or posting sentries. During the night they had been surprised by the Chinese. All of the Americans were promptly bayonetted where they lay, their sleeping bags becoming body bags. The skewering of these Americans convinced the remaining sceptics that perhaps it was best to leave their sleeping bags behind. For the duration of the war, Canadian fighting men did just that, providing the "rear-echelon commandos" with a convenient medium of exchange on the black market. Meanwhile, soldiers in the firing line shivered under flimsy woollen blankets. Although issued on a scale of three per man, the blankets were hardly adequate protection against the Korean cold.[30]

Living in the field under a poncho, soldiers became dirtier than beggars. Mosquito repellant, camouflage cream, sweat, and dirt combined to form a greasy film that covered the skin and assailed the nostrils. Underclothes became crusty with the accumulated filth of living rough. Diarrhea, which "everyone in Korea got ... sooner or later," was a constant annoyance, leading some men to forgo underwear altogether.[31]

Aside from the occasional visit to the mobile bath unit, there were few opportunities to wash oneself in the field. Rivers were used for bathing whenever possible, but this could be dangerous during the monsoon season, when flash floods created powerful currents: eight Canadian soldiers are officially listed as having drowned.[32] Creeks provided another source of water for bathing. However, as George Cook discovered, a wash in a Korean creek did not necessarily make one feel cleaner. After washing his face and brushing his teeth in what appeared to be a pristine mountain creek, he was shocked to discover the decomposed bodies of two Chinese soldiers just upstream from where he had been bathing![33]

Opportunities for bathing improved somewhat with the occupation of the Jamestown line. Crude showers were built just behind the front line, and bath parades were held at regular intervals. Proper latrines were also constructed in the forward areas, although the increased comfort was largely negated by the smell and the clouds of flies that hung over them. Where soldiers had previously practised "cat sanitation" – defecating into shallow holes scratched into the earth – they now visited "the library."[34] Located at the end of a narrow communications trench, the library, contained both toilets and urinals. The former were usually constructed of discarded 45-gallon oil drums. The drum was cut open at each end, and the bottom dug into a hole in the ground. A doughnut-shaped piece of plywood placed on top of the drum served as the seat.[35] Urinals, also know as "piss tubes," were fashioned out of empty mortar casings. Normally four feet in length, the long metal tubes were between eight and ten inches in circumference – "the right size to accommodate us all," as a soldier in the PPCLI commented.[36] One end of the tube was dug into the ground; the other was angled upwards, the exact height being determined by the regimental sanitaryman.

The sanitaryman was also responsible for the maintenance and cleanliness of the latrines. Each morning he inspected the battalion's forward latrines, spreading lime and creosote where necessary. To control the musty odour emanating from the urinals, a small amount of gasoline was occasionally poured down the tubes and lit. Assuming that all of the gas in the tube ignited, this practice was reasonably safe; but when it did not, the tube became a time bomb. On one occasion, a sergeant from the 3 PPCLI with bushy eyebrows and moustache dropped a still smouldering cigarette end down a tube containing unburnt gasoline. A fireball belched out of the tube, singing all of his facial hair. Miraculously, no other part of his anatomy was affected by the blast.[37]

The shift to static warfare brought about changes in the bivouac arrangements. Soldiers were henceforth accommodated in sleeping bunkers just behind the forward fighting positions. A soldier described their construction under ideal conditions: "The bunker began as a large hole, with smaller holes at its edges to hold the log frame. The logs were brought up from the rear and fastened together with spikes and communications-wire lashings. More logs made up the roof, and both the roof and sides were covered with sandbags."[38]

Designed to hold two to four men, a bunker constructed in this manner was impervious to light mortar fire.[39] Unfortunately for the Canadians, few of their bunkers lived up to the ideal. Robert Hepenstall, an engineer in Korea, described the average Canadian bunker as a "hovel" that "offered very little protection from artillery fire" and was prone to collapse in heavy rains.[40] Sergeant John Richardson of 1 PPCLI concurred, identifying a lack of building materials as the primary reason for their shoddy construction. During a severe storm in April 1952, a platoon in his battalion had all but three of their fourteen bunkers collapse in a single day.[41] "Most of the material went to the rear areas," he recalled, "both for the construction of rear defences and the comfort of rear area troops. The forward areas were always short of ... construction material."[42]

Other shortages included proper field stoves which, as mentioned earlier, were practically non-existent in the front line. Also in short supply were cots and chairs – items that proliferated in the rear but were seldom seen in the austere surroundings of the Jamestown line. On the other hand, the forward areas possessed an abundance of discarded signal wire. Used to connect the hand-cranked field telephones in the fighting positions to a central switchboard in the rear, signal wire criss-crossed through the trenches for miles like a giant spider's web. Extremely vulnerable to shellfire, the exposed cables were damaged with annoying regularity. Rather than dispatch a linesman to locate and repair the offending cable, the Canadians adopted the simple expedient of laying a new line. Experience had shown this to be the preferred method while under fire.[43]

It did not take long for the more imaginative soldiers in the 25th Brigade to find a use for the nests of abandoned signal wire that accumulated in their positions. Using angle-iron pickets driven into the floor of the bunker as a frame, the signal wire was interlaced until a crude box-spring bed was formed. At twenty-five cents a foot, the troops liked to joke that they slept on the most expensive beds in the world.[44] A similar method was used to make chairs. Rounding out the well-furnished front-line bunker was a ration-crate table, a signal-wire clothesline, an improvised stove, and a door fashioned out of a scrounged poncho or blanket. Interior illumination was provided by a candle jammed into a c-ration tin.

Ration crates were also used to construct crude floors, although soldiers who were afraid of rats or snakes might question their desirability. The space between the floor boards and the barren earth provided the ideal habit for a variety of Korean fauna, but rats and snakes were the most common. The role of rats in the spread of epidemic hemorrhagic fever has already been noted. Disease aside, rats made life inside the claustrophobic confines of a forward bunker uncomfortable to say the least. A soldier returning to his bunker after a hard day's work would find rat feces in his kit, on his bed, and on the furniture. Rat urine was equally disgusting, leaving the Canadians' bunkers smelling musty and pungent. But there was worse. Corporal Earl Richardson explained: "[The rats] came out at night. They ran around squeaking and squealing above your head. They knocked dirt on you, and would occasionally drop on you. It was necessary to keep a blanket over your head when sleeping to keep them away from your face. There wasn't too much air in the bunkers, so it was an added discomfort. One fellow jumped up from a sound sleep and hollered; we lit a candle and found a rat had taken a bite out of the nape of his neck."[45]

With the rats came snakes. Of the twelve varieties indigenous to Korea, two are poisonous. Like the North American rattlesnake, they belong to the pit viper family. Their bites are potentially fatal, but with prompt and effective treatment, deaths are rare. At least two 25th Brigade soldiers were bitten, but no Canadians died from snake bites during the Korean War.[46] To avoid a bite, soldiers were advised to shake all clothing before putting it on and to kill any snakes they encountered.[47]

All the above activities, of course, accounted for only a small portion of the Canadian infantryman's daily routine. When not engaged in active combat, a seemingly endless array of menial fatigue duties demanded the soldiers' attention. Together, these duties conspired to create a monotonous existence that at times seemed unbearable. A typical day in Korea began with reveille just before first light. Shaken or prodded to life by one of their platoon mates, soldiers clumsily dressed themselves and made their way to their assigned positions for the morning stand-to. Still dopey with that mind-numbing buzz brought on by lack of sleep, they stared out into the morning gloom, more asleep than awake, waiting for the order to "stand down." After daybreak, the watch was reduced to 30 percent unless an attack was imminent. Men not assigned to sentry duty were fed a quick breakfast and given the opportunity to visit the latrines. Assuming that sufficient water was available, a quick wash and shave followed. The next couple of hours were spent cleaning weapons.

Korea's climate posed a formidable challenge to weapons maintenance above and beyond the regular cleaning regimen. In winter, the standard-issue lubricating oil had to be wiped clean from the weapon lest it freeze and render the weapon inoperable. In its place, the Canadians used a specially formulated graphite lubrication that was immune to freezing; but like so many other items, graphite was always in short supply. In summer, rain coupled with high humidity conspired to rust weapons and corrode ammunition. During one engagement, a Canadian platoon fired eleven mortar illumination rounds, all of which failed to ignite because of rotten fuses.[48] Preventive maintenance such as frequent oiling delayed deterioration, but as Robert Peacock recalled, "Humidity won over man's technology."[49]

A strict procedure was laid down for weapons cleaning. First, the soldier carried out an individual safety check to ensure that his weapon was unloaded. He then removed its bayonet (if fixed), sling, magazine, and bolt, in that order. These were laid out on a poncho in preparation for a systematic cleaning. However, in reality, weapons cleaning was seldom this orderly. Such crucial steps as performing an individual safety check might be skipped by a tired, overconfident, or careless soldier. Such was the case in November 1951, when a 1 PPCLI private cleaning a Sten gun failed to clear the weapon and accidently shot two of his comrades. Both men survived their injuries, but the hapless private was himself fatally wounded several days later when he wandered off a path and stepped on a booby trap.[50]

Weapons cleaning was almost invariably followed by intense physical labour. When the fighting was fluid, this could include the additional burden of marching long distances over extremely difficult terrain to reach a distant objective. Apart from this, the afternoon and evening routine of the combat soldier was much the same in both the mobile and static phases of the war. Stores had to be brought forward, defensive positions (or foxholes) constructed and maintained, sandbags filled, barbed wire laid, and signal wire strung between positions. If a soldier was going on patrol, weapons needed to be test-fired and equipment made ready.

Sundown was followed by a quick meal, after which the men prepared for the long night ahead. Some continued with their day's work, while others settled down to a few hours' sleep before patrol or sentry duty. At last light, the men were ordered to "stand to" for one hour. This was taken far more seriously than the morning stand-to, because it was well known that the Chinese preferred to attack under the cover of darkness when U.N. air power was least effective.

The order to "stand down" was followed by a final inspection of defensive positions by the platoon NCOs and, tactical conditions permitting, by a hot meal. At the same time, the first shift of sentries assumed their positions in the firing line. While their comrades slept, wrote letters, or socialized, the sentries gazed out into the darkness. Although they were normally replaced at two-hour intervals, many found it impossible to stay awake. After a hard day's work, with little rest, eyes quickly became heavy with sleep. Men might doze for several minutes before an involuntary reflex action jolted them back to consciousness. Others might actually fall asleep at their post, endangering not only their own lives but those of their comrades. Not surprisingly, sleepers were dealt with harshly. Private Dan Johnson recalled: "Sergeant Tommy Prince, while making his rounds one night, found a soldier, leaning over the lip of his trench, asleep at his post. He came up behind him, grabbed him around the neck and began choking him. Some off duty soldiers, awakened by the noise, grabbed Prince and with some difficulty managed to pry him off the soldier's back."[51]

At the opposite extreme was the jumpy novice sentry, whose overactive imagination turned bushes into enemy soldiers and gusts of wind into enemy voices. Sergeant John Richardson recounted:

I came upon a sentry in a long lonely trench, and he was terrified. I asked him, "What is the matter?" He replied, almost sobbing in despair, "Listen to that noise! They must be all around us!" I listened, and heard the weirdest noise; it sounded like a huge bird flapping its wings. We traced the sound and discovered it was loose signal wire flapping on the barbed wire, every time the wind would gust. It was a good thing I came across that sentry when I did; if I hadn't, we would have had a nut case on our hands in the morning.[52]

Although jumpy sentries were preferable to sleeping ones, they too could cause problems. Repeated false alarms, much like the boy who cried wolf too many times, met with increased scepticism and reduced vigilance. A jumpy sentry was also more likely to pop flares and take potshots at mysterious shadows, alerting any bona fide enemy in the vicinity of his exact position.

The elements made their own contribution to the sentry's ordeal. In winter, frigid temperatures and bitter winds tore through their flimsy clothing. Toes and fingers became numb with cold and inactivity as the sentries stood motionless, gazing out across the frozen landscape. A standing order in the 25th Brigade forbidding the wearing of parka hoods in forward areas – they restricted hearing and peripheral vision – left ears and faces dangerously susceptible to frostbite. Sentries were instructed to rub their ears and contort their faces at regular intervals to prevent the onset of this insidious injury.

The summer months could be equally uncomfortable. Clouds of mosquitoes in search of their evening meal swarmed around the uncovered sentries with an aggravating buzz. The only respite came with the monsoon rains, those ferocity proved too much for even the most pertinacious mosquito. Clad in olive-drab ponchos, sentries watched passively as their positions turned into mud holes. Wet feet swelled in their boots, inviting ringworm and a host of fungal infections. More ominously, the driving rain reduced visibility and masked the sound of an approaching enemy.

Sentry duty in the combat zone was a nerve-racking experience at the best of times. Men literally counted the minutes until their shift was due to end and they could return to the comparative safety and comfort of their front-line abode. For soldiers working the predawn shift, relief and the realization that they had survived to see another day came with the morning stand-to.

According to one soldier, life at the front was 90 percent boredom and 10 percent pure terror.[53] To make matters worse, very few recreational amenities were officially supplied for the men. During the world wars, these had been provided by private civilian organizations such as the YMCA, Knights of Columbus, Salvation Army, and Royal Canadian Legion. In 1949, however, the Defence Council decided that henceforth the armed forces themselves would be responsible for welfare in their ranks.[54]

In Korea, the Canadian Army quickly proved incapable of tending to the needs of its men. According to an Adjutant-General's Report, comforts and amenities of Canadian origin were "conspicuous by [their] absence."[55] Movies were sometimes shown just behind the line, but there were never enough film projectors to go round. Even when projectors were available, there was no guarantee they would work, since most were in a poor state of repair.[56] Magazines and newspapers were appallingly out of date by the time they reached the front, and there was a severe shortage of paperback novels. This was especially the case in the R22eR battalions, where French-language reading material was practically non-existent.[57]

A number of civilian auxiliary organizations attempted to compensate for the Department of National Defence's inability to meet the demand for pocket books and other comfort items. By the end of the war the Canadian Legion and the Red Cross were providing most of the reading and writing material in the Far East.[58] But the improvements may have been more apparent than real. Two months after the cessation of hostilities, 3 RCR's Lieutenant-Colonel Campbell was still imploring Ottawa to send more.[59]

Entertainment of Canadian origin was also in short supply. For the first two years of the war, the Department of National Defence steadfastly refused to allow Canadian civilian entertainers to visit the troops in Korea. The reason for this is not entirely clear, though the fact that there were no restrictions on British or American entertainers visiting Canadian troops suggests cost as the governing factor.[60] In practice, the reliance on non-Canadian entertainers translated into very few shows for the soldiers of the 25th Brigade. A veteran of the 1 PPCLI remarked, "We were the forgotten people; nobody ever came to see us on our hilltop positions."[61] British and

American performers were understandably reluctant to visit the Canadians when there were thousands of their own troops in Korea who also needed entertaining. Accordingly, visits to the 25th Brigade were given a low priority.

The lack of entertainment did not go unnoticed on the other side of the Pacific. In 1951 alone, nine civilian concert groups requested permission to visit the 25th Brigade in Korea. All were denied on the grounds that it was not army policy to send concert parties overseas to entertain the troops.[62] Not to be discouraged, several group members commenced a letter-writing campaign to convince the Department of National Defence to reconsider its decision. Their efforts paid off, and in the spring of 1952 the first Canadian concert party, the Cammie Howard Show, was given permission to tour the Far East.

The party left Vancouver on 10 June 1952 for a sixteen-day, twenty-five-show tour of the Commonwealth Division. Rear-echelon troops were the primary beneficiaries of the tour, as only a handful of infantrymen could be pulled out of the line at any one time to watch a show. This was not necessarily a bad thing. Critics claimed that Cammie Howard's "music was too slow for troops in the field"[63] and that the show "appeared to be lacking rehearsal and continuity."[64] They did, however, concede that Cammie Howard compared favourably with some of the earlier British acts.[65]

Only four more Canadian concert parties toured the Far East before war's end. They performed to a predominantly rear-echelon crowd, and none was in danger of taking Broadway by storm. This was especially true of the Western Five. This act toured the Far East in the fall of 1952 and was not very popular.[66] Not surprisingly, the troops made no attempt to hide their disapproval. A post-tour report recorded that "the general attitude of the Western Five was that they made very considerable personal sacrifices to entertain the boys. This naturally did not meet with a great deal of favour from troops in the face of the enemy."[67]

Another organization that met with little sympathy from front-line troops was the army's postal service. Postcards, writing paper, and envelopes were scarce, and there was a perennial shortage of qualified postal clerks.[68] Few men arrived in Korea knowing their military postal address, a fact that delayed the arrival of their first letters from home. Mail was supposed to be delivered twice a week, but most front-line men counted themselves lucky to receive something even once a week. On average, it took ten days for a letter to reach Korea and a fortnight for one mailed from the front line to arrive in Vancouver.[69] This fell far below the standard set by the British army's postal service, which provided four deliveries a week and needed only six or seven days to deliver a letter to Korea.[70]

Mail was immensely important to men at the sharp end. A letter transcended distance and reminded soldiers of their alter egos as friends, fathers, or family members. When they read a letter, they were temporarily released from the deprivation and hardship of their tenuous front-line existence. Mail, or its absence, could literally make or break a man's day, as the letters of a young soldier in the 1 PPCLI to his parents clearly demonstrate:

18 October 1951
I sure hated to leave Calgary but there wasn't much I could do to stay there. It sure is monotonous riding on the train ... This is the fourth letter I have wrote today.

23 November 1951
[The Chinese] started to attack just after six o'clock and went on going till about two thirty in the morning ... It sure helps a fellow out [to receive mail] in a time like this.

20 February 1952
Was sure glad to hear that you received your parcel with the souvenir from Japan as I was starting to worry myself if they had got lost in the mail. But they tell me that all parcels sent from over here go by boat instead of airplane. Haven't been getting mail through to us.

29 July 1952
Something sure has gone wrong with the mail service over here. We were getting our mail at least twice a week now we are even lucky if it comes once every two weeks.[71]

Hardship and deprivation have always been the lot of infantrymen; Korea was no exception. From the time they entered the firing line, Canadian soldiers endured a lifestyle that can only be described as primitive. Yet as this chapter has shown, it need not have been as hard as it was. Little things like good food, proper bivouac equipment, and sufficient writing paper, which often get overlooked in the comfort of a headquarters building, can make all the difference to lowly combat soldiers. But in Korea it was neither food nor concert parties that ultimately sustained the morale of Canadian fighting men. It was something stronger.

CHAPTER TEN

Rum and Coke

The austere conditions in Korea, coupled with the Department of National Defence's inability to provide even the most basic comforts to troops in the field, led to the introduction of two policies designed to sustain the morale of Canadian fighting men: annual rotation and rest and recreation (R&R) leave. Neither enjoyed complete success, and as the war dragged on and the ineffectiveness of the official policies became apparent, the officers and men of the 25th Brigade found themselves increasingly reliant on the traditional tonic for military lugubriousness: alcohol.

Morale, the mental attitude and bearing of a group of soldiers, is an extremely nebulous concept that resists objective analysis. The limited official documentation generally suggests a reasonable level of morale among Canadian soldiers in Korea, but the reasons for it are seldom explored in any detail.[1] Part of problem is that a seemingly endless array of variables come into play when dealing with something as complex as human emotions during wartime. Morale is, then, an incredibly subjective concept, approachable from a variety of angles.

One way to approach it is from the perspective of the defence planners themselves. In Korea, difficult and unfamiliar operational conditions were regarded as the greatest threats to morale.[2] As has been seen, the Department of National Defence did little to ameliorate the discomfort of life in the field through the official provision of comfort items and basic amenities. Instead, it decided to follow the British and American examples and limit the duration of soldiers' operational tours.[3] If life in the field could not be made more tolerable, at least it would be limited.

When the first Canadian troops arrived in the Far East, the Department of National Defence had not yet settled on a firm rotation policy. Since the original Special Force's term of service was set to expire in February 1952, it was obvious that a clear rotation policy must be articulated in order to avoid any morale problems. This was done in July 1951, when Chief of the General Staff announced that the 2 PPCLI, the first Canadian infantry unit to arrive in Korea, would be replaced by the 1 PPCLI in the fall. The relief measure provided the blueprint for the Canadian rotation policy in Korea, which was summed up in an official dispatch in October 1951:

Rotation will be on a unit and sub unit basis except for certain units for which no counterpart exists in Canada, which will be on a man for man basis. Service in the Far East will be reckoned from the date of despatch from North America. Only personnel who have served 12 months in the Far East will be eligible for return to Canada except that [the commander of the 25th Brigade] may use his discretion on individual cases and in such cases may exercise a leeway of one month plus or minus from the 12 month policy.

Personnel whose period of engagement terminates before they have completed the period of service required for eligibility for rotation will be retained in the theatre.[4]

The rotation policy seems to have been a double-edged sword insofar as morale was concerned. The prospect of having to serve only twelve months in Korea gave men an objective to work towards – assuming that they survived their tour of duty and that they returned home at the prescribed time. The rotation policy therefore eliminated the uncertainty of the First and Second World Wars, in which soldiers were committed for the duration. It also helped keep down the number of battle exhaustion cases.

The rotation policy may have been a boon to morale over the long term, but it did little in the short term. A year can seem like a very long time to soldiers, including volunteers, when forced to exist without even the most basic comforts or amenities and faced with a seemingly endless routine of eating, sleeping, fatigue, and sentry duty. Moreover, the rotation policy may have undermined the will of Canadian soldiers to combat. Paradoxically, the primary strength of the policy – that men arrived at the front line not as complete strangers but as integral members of a primary group, whose bonds had been established during training in Canada – may have become its greatest weakness as the repatriation date approached. Lieutenant-Colonel Poulin and Major Harry Pope both hinted at the overall lack of aggressiveness in the 25th Brigade.[5] The approach of the rotation date would have served to make aggressive action even more unlikely.

If the impact of the rotation policy on the day-to-day morale of Canadian soldiers was marginal at best, so was the other scheme designed to sustain morale in the 25th Brigade – R&R leave. All Canadian soldiers qualified for two seven-day periods of R&R in Japan. Although R&R was an intensely enjoyable experience for most soldiers, it is unlikely that the promise of leave in Japan made a palpable contribution to the maintenance of morale in Korea.

Very few men received their second allotment before they were due for rotation, and most counted themselves lucky to get even one. Ostensibly, this was the result of insufficient air transport.[6] The 2 PPCLI, for example, still had soldiers waiting for their first R&R leave in July 1951, only three months before they were due for rotation.[7] Things were little better in other Canadian units. With "a Brigade quota of only 80 men at one time," the Adjutant-General's Report noted, "it will be a long time before all men can have this leave."[8]

The reluctance of field commanders to release men for the second R&R must also not be discounted.[9] Canadian infantry units were often understrength, and the loss of even a couple of men going on leave could translate into gaps in the firing line. The commanding officer of 3 RCR claimed that most of his soldiers were happy to have only one R&R,[10] but no veterans have corroborated this. Sergeant Don Urquhart summarized the feelings of many enlisted men when he said, "It would have been better to give us one [R&R] every six months instead of once a year. This would really have [helped] to keep morale up."[11]

Also undermining the effectiveness of the R&R scheme was the way soldiers were chosen for it. They seldom knew when their turn would come, and there was speculation that those with connections at Battalion Headquarters were the first to be selected. According to one Korean veteran, these men "became outcasts within the platoon. They were shunned, and their upbeat behaviour viewed as poor taste."[12] In short, the questionable selection process may have actually undermined morale.

The imperfect R&R scheme convinced the Canadians (and their Commonwealth allies) to rely increasingly on local leave. The idea was that if soldiers could not count on a second visit to Japan, they could at least look forward to a seventy-two-hour respite at the Commonwealth Division rest centre in Seoul. Most of the men who visited the so-called rest centre were far from impressed. A decidedly racist report noted: "It takes three hours driving over ghastly 'roads' to get there. Once there the soldier finds himself in a half-gutted city with only other brassed-off soldiers as companions and no entertainment if one excepts the simian types, alleged to be human and female, that invest the off-limits area. Result – the man returns to his unit dirtier and more brassed-off than when he left."[13] Local leave facilities improved somewhat later in the war, with the opening of another rest centre at Inchon. Although better equipped than its predecessor, it still "wasn't much of a leave centre,"[14] and it could accommodate only forty Canadians at any one time.[15]

In sum, it is unlikely that either the rotation policy or R&R leave had much influence on the day-to-day morale of Canadian fighting men. While soldiers certainly welcomed rotation and R&R, these remained abstract concepts, divorced from the reality of the front line by time and space. Most field officers recognized this and looked beyond the official policies for a manna to steel their men's morale. They found it in alcohol.

Alcohol use by soldiers is as old as military history.[16] Only recently have some Western armies begun to question their relationship with alcohol. To understand the role of alcohol in the 25th Brigade it is necessary to outline its use in the broader context of the Canadian Army in the years following the Second World War.

The enlisted men of the 25th Brigade first experienced the army's insatiable thirst for alcohol shortly after their enlistment. At this early stage of their military service, they were "Cee Bee'd" (confined to base). Thus, their first drinks as soldiers were taken not at the local civilian watering hole but in the Enlisted Men's Wet Canteen, usually the only recreational outlet for off-duty soldiers. "Back then it was no big thing to get drunk, I mean really drunk when you were off duty," Private Ratchford reminisced. "That is part of what being a soldier was all about."[17] Invariably the canteen was the oldest, most decrepit building on base and had few amenities. The fictitious Private Jacket Coates recalled that "beer drinking was usually done sitting on a rickety bench ... to the tune of breaking bottles and violent talk. The floor was usually awash with stuff and you could cut the fug with a bayonet."[18]

The officers had their own drinking establishment – the Regimental Mess. Festooned with regimental curios and war trophies, and furnished with fine leather sofas and crystal glassware, the mess was a far cry from the Enlisted Men's Wet Canteen. Unlike the men in the ranks, officers were privy to the entire gamut of alcoholic beverages, with scotch and port ranking among the favourites. Its opulent decor and fine single malts notwithstanding, the Regimental Mess performed the same function as the Enlisted Men's Wet Canteen, namely to provide a modicum of entertainment and cement cohesion. As the drinks flowed, however, things could get out of hand. Lieutenant Bob Peacock recalled: "As ordered ... I took a pinch of snuff and inhaled. The result was a tremendous sneeze which delighted the commanding officer until he realized I had blown the lining in my nose and there was blood over everything within sneezing distance."[19]

The exigencies of life in the field prevented the construction and maintenance of elaborate drinking places in Korea. The Enlisted Men's Wet Canteen might be a poncho shelter or bunker, the Regimental Mess a marquee or Quonset hut. Atmosphere and material trappings were irrelevant. What was important was that the hard-drinking culture nurtured in the canteens and messes of Canadian bases was transplanted to Korea.

Another Canadian Army practice to appear in Korea was the official rum ration. Rum, or SRD (service rum demerara) in military vernacular, had traditionally been used as a stimulant in the combat zone. After the Second World War, a handful of general officers and defence bureaucrats began to question the desirability of issuing rum to soldiers.[20] Citing its negative effects on a cold and overtaxed body and pointing out that rum was not a stimulant but a depressant, they contended that SRD served no practical physiological purpose. Their assault on it met with intense hostility from many former field officers, including Brigadier W.L. Coke, director general of medical services, who wrote a three-page report in 1950 defending the official rum ration.

Although Coke agreed that SRD served no practical physiological purpose, he emphasized its morale-enhancing properties.[21] He divided these into two broad categories: the gift component, and the alcoholic beverage component. Because SRD was not considered a necessity of life and was issued after an arduous task by order of a higher authority, it was a gift.[22] At the same time, its high alcohol content imbued it with important symbolic qualities. Coke explained:

It is probable that the morale effect of "a shot of rum" is greater than would result from a gift of a chocolate bar, hot soup, or cigarette. This is because of the symbolic value of "a drink" in our society.
(i) It symbolizes being "off duty," of being relieved of responsibility temporarily, it marks the end of a job, e.g. the cocktail or beer at the end of the day's work.
(ii) Rum, particularly, is a masculine drink and he who can take it straight is "a he-man."
(iii) It symbolizes comradeship and cements group bonds, e.g. toasts, stags, wassail.
(iv) It awakens associations of past memories of happier times – parties, holidays, festivals.[23]

Coke did not specify the exact quantity of SRD required to achieve the desired psychological results, but recommended a shot of between one and four ounces. Coke won a temporary reprieve for the rum ration; two more decades passed before the Canadian Forces officially retired SRD from active service.

In Korea, the rum ration was delivered to front-line troops in one-gallon wicker-bound stone jars that had changed little since the eighteenth century. As SRD moved with the ammunition supply, it was the company sergeant-major's responsibility to ensure that the precious liquid reached the appropriate troops. Inevitably, cynics at the sharp end maintained that SRD actually stood for "Sergeants receive double." Others claimed it stood for "Seldom reaches destination."

Assuming that the precious crocks of SRD reached their destination, the men lined up in anticipation to receive the one fluid ounce of thick, black, navy rum (though Lieutenant Bob Peacock claimed that in the 3 PPCLI the issue was one and a half ounces per man).[24] The rum had to be consumed in the presence of an officer to prevent hoarding, but as one soldier recalled, "There was always some to be had if you knew the right connections."[25] Most soldiers downed their dram in one gulp, savouring its fiery bite as it slid down their gullets into empty stomachs. The 2 PPCLI war diarist laconically recorded: "Despite the miserable state and the prospect of a very cold, wet and hungry night the morale of the men was very high. First rum issue authorized by the Brigadier tonight."[26]

As this entry suggests, the decision to issue SRD originated at the very top of the chain of command. Indeed, according to army regulations, no commander below the rank of brigadier could order a rum ration.[27] In other words, the only Canadian officer with the authority to issue rum in Korea was none other than the 25th Brigade commander himself! This meant that field officers, the very men with their fingers on the pulse of Canadian fighting units, were powerless to use officially supplied alcohol as they saw fit. There were exceptions, though, notably in 1 RCR's Easy Company during the Chinese attack on Hill 355 in October 1952. Easy only in name, the ad hoc company had been cobbled together a month earlier in less than ideal circumstances.[28] Consisting of rear-echelon personnel and men siphoned off from other RCR rifle companies, it had been formed to fill the gap in the line that had resulted from the decision to disband 1 R22eR's Able Company to provide reinforcements for the other understrength Vandoo companies.

Morale in Easy Company was low, to say the least.[29] The company's fighting positions were terribly run down, it had a dearth of warm clothing and blankets, and it was severely understrength in NCOs, even lacking a platoon sergeant to act as nursemaid to a green second lieutenant.[30] As the Chinese stepped up their bombardment, the commander of the 25th Brigade arrived on the scene, and the rum began to flow: between 10 and 31 October, SRD was issued to Easy Company eight times. Rum does not appear to have been issued to any of the other RCR companies during this period, not even to Baker Company, which endured the full weight of the Chinese onslaught on 23–4 October.[31] Easy Company was the exception that proved the rule. The pedantic regulations governing the rum issue, combined with the fact that all requisitions for SRD had to pass through an increasingly unsympathetic defence headquarters in Ottawa, ensured that it was doled out in only the gravest of circumstances, and then only on the authority of the brigade commander. Private Louis McLean was "never issued SRD during [his] nine months at the front,"[32] and Lance-Corporal William Powell felt that the "rum rations were not frequent enough" for his liking.[33]

What was needed was a supplement to the official rum ration – something that had the gift and alcoholic aspects of SRD but was free from the red tape. The answer was beer. An integral part of garrison life in Canada, beer did not possess the stigma, at least to official eyes, of SRD. It was readily available in the Far East, cheap, and, thanks to the Canadian Transport Company and the KSC, relatively portable. More importantly, field commanders could dole it out at their discretion (every day if they liked) without having to ask Brigade Headquarters for permission.

Beer quickly became the pillar buttressing Canadian morale in Korea. The 3 R22eR's Lieutenant-Colonel Poulin considered it essential to high morale,[34] while Lieutenant Bob Peacock viewed the daily beer ration as "one of the joys of life."[35] Private Bill Martin, a driver in the 54th Canadian Transport Company, whose truckloads of beer were "given top priority" at all traffic points leading up to the front,[36] reminisced: "If there was one highlight of [my] duties, it was the looks on the faces of front-line troops when I arrived with the beer run ... That was one duty I feel helped make a difference."[37] The scale of the issue varied from battalion to battalion, though two bottles per man per day seems to have been the norm.

It is important to note that the beer issued was free, in that it was provided to the men out of battalion stocks or by one of the major Canadian breweries that periodically donated several thousand cases to the 25th Brigade. For many soldiers, however, two beers a day simply were not enough, especially during the hot summer months or after a difficult task. Fortunately for them, there was the battalion canteen.[38] As Lance-Corporal William Powell recalled, "Beer was always available and was cheap to buy once you drank your daily ration ... Hell, coming off a rough patrol ... it was almost expected that you would have more than your share of booze."[39]

Situated just behind the front line, the canteen did a brisk business quenching the thirst of parched soldiers. In the 3 RCR, for example, gross sales averaged $14,000 per month, leading Lieutenant-Colonel Campbell to comment that "the volume of sales puts the canteen in the category of a business."[40] Most canteens stocked a variety of British and American beer, although at only seventeen cents for a quart bottle, Japanese brands such as Asahi and Kirin were the most popular.[41] Sergeant Harry Repay remembered Japanese beer as "really sweet," and claimed that "it took some getting used to, but once you did, you realized how good it was for so cheap."[42]

Whether soldiers chose Western or Japanese beer, they were encouraged to choose a brand and stick with it; switching between the two could wreak havoc on the digestive system when a significant volume was consumed. Corporal James Wilson recalled getting "the shits after [drinking] a little too much rice beer,"[43] while Lieutenant Bob Peacock said that "there weren't enough people able to leave the latrines for patrols" following an issue of Canadian beer: "As I remember, no one turned down the beer – we just shortened our patrols and the time spent on various duties until the body adapted to the change in beer. Of course, when the Canadian beer ran out, we were back to [Japanese beer] and the problem, appeared again."[44]

Some of the officers were also drinking heavily. Lance-Corporal Clyde Bougie of the 1 RCR recalled that the battalion's surgeon and his sergeant assistant "were always in a jovial mood." He explained why: "The medical officer and sergeant appeared to me to be half smashed most of the time, and on several occasions I noticed the sergeant pull half a gallon of liquid from under his cot and pour some into two cups, mixing it with fruit juice. When they were both out one afternoon I slipped into the RAP and had a good look at this bottle to find it was 65 proof alcohol."[45] The 1 PPCLI War Diary recorded: "The supply of liquor in Korea is a delight to alcoholics. It is plentiful and cheap ... An ounce of Canadian Club or Haig sells for ten cents in the [mess] and that gives the mess a respectable profit ... There was a tendency toward excessive drinking by both officers and sergeants ... probably a result of boredom and the new found plenty."[46]

Boredom and an excess of alcohol contributed to at least two officers' unauthorized forays, or "whisky patrols,"[47] into no man's land. One of the most notorious of these occurred on Christmas Day 1952. Shortly after noon, a sentry from the PPCLI reported that a lone Canadian soldier was observed stumbling across no man's land towards the Chinese lines. With a pistol in one hand and a bottle of whisky in the other (witnesses claim it was Crown Royal), the drunken soldier, an officer from the R22eR, exhorted the enemy to come out and fight.[48] As he neared the Chinese line, Canadian machine-gun teams were ordered to stand by with covering fire. A sniper was also instructed to fire on the officer if captured. Only steps away from certain death, the inebriated officer was intercepted by a patrol from his own battalion and dragged back to Canadian lines to face disciplinary action.[49]

A similar incident occurred in the 3 PPCLI. Second Lieutenant Pare Vik recalled:

> My company commander, who was known to have a drink or two, came into my bunker one night and said ... 'I'm going on patrol; get me your best rocket launcher man!"
> "Well," I said, "it would be best if you went back to your bunker." He was determined to go on patrol, so I told him I was the best rocket launcher man. We carried the launcher and one rocket and he stumbled down the hill ... There was a bit of an argument as to which hills were the enemy; he ... fired the rocket ... [and it] landed with a satisfactory bang on the Chinese hill.[50]

Such behaviour might be construed as evidence of rock-bottom morale and a complete breakdown of discipline, but there is reason to doubt this. In his remarkable study of the hard-drinking French Foreign Legion, Douglas Porch suggested that drunkenness and disorderly conduct can reflect high morale, a way of maintaining aggression in the absence of combat.[51] Certainly, neither of the officers involved in these episodes lacked aggression, as evidenced by their willingness to close with the enemy. Rather, excessive drinking appears to have loosened their inhibitions and stimulated their Dutch courage.

All this is not to say that alcohol could not cause problems, especially in rear or reserve positions. As mentioned earlier, infantry battalions were periodically rotated out of the front line into reserve positions to reorganize, re-equip, and absorb replacements. Time in reserve was also supposed to give the men a break from the monotony and morale-sapping routine of life in the front line, though this was seldom the case. They usually spent most of their time training, laying wire, digging bunkers, and filling sandbags along the secondary defensive lines south of the Jamestown line. The reserve positions contained little in the way of comforts or amenities. With the exception of warmed tents, proper shower facilities, marginally better food, and the absence of enemy fire (although armed guerrilla bands were a constant threat), there was little difference between conditions at the front and in reserve.

Not surprisingly, consumption of alcohol was *the* feature of life behind the front line. Combat-weary soldiers often bragged about how drunk they were going to get when their battalion went into reserve.[52] There, they could attain a level of intoxication even greater than what was possible in the front line. Not only was there more alcohol available, but the troops did not have to worry about going on patrol or repelling an enemy attack. Moreover, officers were likely to turn a blind eye to drunken excess behind the lines as the men blew off steam.[53] Thus, soldiers could throw all caution to the wind and temporarily lose themselves in a blur of drunken bliss.

It has been shown that such excess might have been a factor in the maltreatment and murder of several Korean civilians by a handful of deranged Canadian and British infantrymen during the first year of the war.[54] What is less well known is that a poisonous moonshine known as Lucky Seven purchased from Korean vendors was responsible for the death of several Canadian soldiers.[55] Robert Peacock recalled having to claim the corpse of an RCR soldier who perished after drinking some of the deadly liquid disguised as Canadian Club.[56] In a similar incident that claimed the life of another young Canadian soldier, medical authorities conducted a laboratory analysis of the poisonous mixture. It was found to contain methylated spirits, formaldehyde, and human urine.[57]

As these examples suggest, the most likely victims of the misuse of alcohol were Canadian soldiers themselves. As usual, the officers set the example for their men to follow. During their evenings in reserve, most officers could be found in the marquee designated as the temporary Regimental Mess, their feet up and a glass close to hand. A popular drink was Black Velvet, a combination of stout and champagne, lauded for its smooth texture and hefty kick. Mass drinking binges and all-night parties were common, once again testifying to the successful transplantation of Canadian mess culture in Korea. On New Year's 1952, for example, a joint party of British and Canadian officers assembled in the neighbouring Black Watch Officer's Mess to ring in the new year. According to Lieutenant Bob Peacock, "What happened after that is a matter of conjecture. I awoke the next morning in the shreds of a partially burned tent, very cold and frost-bitten suffering the morning after to beat all mornings after."[58]

The enlisted men mixed their own drinks, often with fatal consequences. On 17 March 1951, for example, the soldiers of the 2 PPCLI celebrated the birthday of their honourary colonel-in-chief. In recognition of the important day in regimental history, all ranks were given half a day off. In the evening a large bonfire was lit, and a concert was given by a Commonwealth pipe band. At this time the men received a substantial beer ration: three bottles from the battalion scale and two from the colonel-in-chief.[59] For some, the beer ration was not enough to quench their insatiable thirst for alcohol, especially hard alcohol. One soldier recalled: "[Some men from Able Company] were making alcohol from canned heat and mixing it with fruit juice someone stole from the mess. I didn't try any but a friend of mine did ... It made him sick and didn't remain in his stomach for even a minute. It is the only reason he is alive today."[60]

Some soldiers were not so lucky. The next day two men died from alcohol poisoning. Four others were rushed to a nearby MASH unit to have their stomachs pumped after consuming the lethal concoction, but two were permanently blinded.[61] The morning after the poisonings, Lieutenant-Colonel Stone paraded the entire battalion in front of the bodies of the dead men.[62] He admonished the wide-eyed Patricias for their foolish behaviour and announced that the battalion would no longer be using canned heat. Nevertheless, beer continued to be supplied to the battalion in liberal quantities.[63]

The misuse of alcohol manifested itself in other ways. The case of a 2 RCR mortar fire controller (MFC) is revealing, and although, admittedly, extreme, it clearly points out the potentially dangerous consequences of excessive drinking. The soldier in question was an old salt from the Second World War, who joined the Special Force to provide financial security for his wife and two children.[64] After enlistment, he was posted to the 2 RCR mortar platoon. During routine training while his battalion was reserve, he was tested on his ability to lay down mortar fire on a set of prearranged grid coordinates. However, he was unable to accomplish the requisite mathematical calculations. It quickly became apparent to his examiners that he was stone-cold drunk. Immediately relieved of his duties as MFC, he was ordered to appear before a committee of officers the following day, which he did – drunk! Struggling to overcome the alcohol-induced vertigo that threatened to topple him over, he admitted to the frequent misuse of alcohol. The committee concluded that he was a chronic alcoholic and ordered his immediate repatriation to Canada on medical grounds.

Less severe cases of alcohol abuse seldom resulted in anything more than a fine. William Powell recalled that "if there was a major problem in the ranks with too much beer while on duty, a fine would be issued and that would be that."[65] Alternatively, the offender might be dealt with on the spot. Corporal Don Hibbs recounted:

I ... was in a really shitty mood and took it out on my buddy ... The Sarge stepped in, and I just walloped him ... Right there and then he could have brought me up on charges ... Instead he got up and just laid me out good ... I was out cold. Next day, I saw the sergeant and he told me that if it ever happened again, he'd let the Chinese have me and be done with it. Well, it never happened again, that's for sure! Would a young lieutenant or captain let me get away with that? No fuckin' way ... but Sarge was an old timer and looked out for us.[66]

So long as alcohol achieved the broader objective of maintaining morale, field commanders appear to have accepted a certain amount of misuse. Far from being viewed as an antisocial or potentially disruptive activity, communal drinking was seen to cement cohesion and was thus actively encouraged. However, individuals who habitually misused alcohol or who were drunk while they committed a more serious offence could expect little leniency from their commanding officers.

With the exception of a crime survey prepared by the Canadian Army Operational Research Team (CAORT) in late 1951, the disciplinary records of the 25th Brigade largely remain classified. Nevertheless, this report provides a window into the nature of crime in the 25th Brigade in general, and into alcohol-related offences in particular.

Between May and November 1951, only seven Canadian infantrymen (two from the PPCLI, and five from the RCR) served sentences in the field punishment camp for drunkenness,[67] whereas seventeen soldiers from support units did. Since the PPCLI, RCR, and R22eR comprised over half of the 25th Brigade's total strength, the infantry was significantly underrepresented in the official statistics. This suggests one of two things. As we have seen, the casual attitude towards drunkenness may have translated into few soldiers being formally charged with drunkenness. Alternatively, support personnel may indeed have been more likely to abuse alcohol than the infantry. This seems plausible in view of the tendency towards excessive drinking in reserve positions. Either way, the small number of infantrymen who were formally charged with drunkenness clearly suggests that the minor misuse of alcohol was not – at least, from the perspective of field commanders – in itself synonymous with indiscipline.

This interpretation is even more convincing when other offences are considered. Between May and November 1951, for example, 117 infantrymen served sentences in the field punishment camp for offences other than drunkenness (45 from the PPCLI, 46 from the RCR, and 26 from the R22eR).[68] These included such traditional service offences as absence without leave, forcing or striking a sentinel, acts to the prejudice of good order and military discipline, and disobeying a lawful command (which Canadian infantry commanders seem to have taken very seriously).[69] It is worth noting that drunkenness was not accepted as a defence in any of these cases. In fact, the average length of sentence in which drunkenness was a secondary charge (approximately 13 percent of all cases) was forty-three days, which suggests that it was viewed more as an aggravation of the offence than as a mitigating circumstance.[70] The only other crime that warranted such a long sentence was "making away with equipment."[71]

By comparison, the supporting arms sent a total of 103 men to the field punishment camp.[72] Thus, of the 220 soldiers detained between May and November 1951 for offences other than drunkenness, 53 percent were from the infantry and 47 percent from the supporting arms. Drunkenness notwithstanding, there appears to have been very little difference between the teeth and the tail insofar as general military discipline was concerned.

An analysis of the overall crime rate for each Canadian unit in Korea at this time further suggests that the infantry's disciplinary record was by no means the worst in the brigade. The monthly crime rate per thousand men was six in the infantry, compared with eight for the rest of the 25th Brigade. Indeed, figures recorded in the PPCLI (seven), the RCR (eight), and R22eR (four) compared very favourably with those in the 54th Transport Company (twelve), the RCOC (fourteen), and the No. 25 Canadian Field Dressing Station (sixteen).[73]

Whether they were from the infantry or the supporting arms, few relished a stay in the field punishment camp: a lengthy sentence was very hard time indeed. This was especially true of the temporary camp operated by the 2 PPCLI during training at Miryang. This brutal institution, usually referred to as "Stone's Stockade" or "the piss can," consisted of a small tent enclosed by a thick belt of barbed wire.[74] Inmates had their heads shaved and a large yellow circle painted on the backs of their uniforms.

The day in the life of detainees began at 0430 with reveille. They had ten minutes to run down to the Miryang River to collect water in a one-gallon can, run back to the prisoners' tent, wash, shave, and put on their battle order, including packs filled with 60 pounds of river sand. At 0440, they formed up and were ordered to run, with rifles at the slope, round a fifty-foot stone perimeter known as the bull ring. This regimen went on for the rest of the day, with only short breaks for meals. In the evening, the exhausted prisoners returned to their tent to clean their weapons and prepare their kit for another day in the ring.

Unsatisfactory performance could land an inmate in the hole, a tomblike cavern carved out of the side of a cliff for solitary confinement.[75] The front of it was blocked by sandbags and a wooden door, which had a small opening to allow a mess tin to be passed through. The hole was lined with odd-shaped rocks to make sleeping difficult, and large spiders inhabited its dark recesses. A blanket and a one-gallon can to defecate in were the only comfort items allowed.[76]

Conditions were little better in the No. 25 Canadian Field Punishment Camp (later renamed the No. 25 Field Detention Barracks). Opened in May 1951 north of Seoul, the camp's motto was "Discipline by Example." Sergeant-Major Jim Holland of the Canadian Provost Corps recalled: "The routine in 25 FDB was tough, not only on the inmates but on the staff as well. The excess shouting and the constant doubling had its effect on everyone. The daily routine was as follows: All inmates had to be up at dawn and all vigorous routine completed before the heat of the day. The physical training was done in the hills near 25 FDB, as all inmates had to be in top physical condition when they returned to their units."[77]

The exacting physical regimen and regular beatings[78] that inmates were forced to endure led Lieutenant Bob Peacock to conjecture "that some of our very best NCOs got religion serving a term [at the field punishment camp] before they became corporals."[79] Some U.N. allies thought conditions at the camp were too harsh.[80] An Indian Army doctor was especially troubled by the practice of placing incorrigible inmates in solitary confinement on bread and water.[81] A.R. Menzies of the Department of External Affairs defended these draconian methods, stating, "There evidently have been no cases of hospitalization on account of physical exhaustion from the Camp and there have been few repeaters."[82]

Time in the field punishment camp was the most serious punishment an infantry battalion commander could dole out. More serious offences were brought before Canadian courts martial. As to be expected, of the sixty-four courts martial during the Korean war, most (forty-six) were for the so-called traditional service offences. Less than half of these involved Canadian infantrymen (five in the PPCLI, seven in the R22eR, and nine in the RCR, including three for drunkenness), which suggests once again that the infantry was by no means the worst-behaved element in the 25th Brigade.[83]

The rest of the Canadian courts martial in Korea were for violent crimes, such as murder, rape, manslaughter, robbery with violence, and attempted murder. These have been covered elsewhere and need not be re-examined here.[84] Suffice it to say that very few men who were actually found guilty of these crimes served their full sentences after being returned to Canada; in fact, most were released within a year or two.[85] This travesty of justice was yet another example of the institutional racism that seems to have permeated the upper echelons of the Department of National Defence. Yet the failure of Canadian military justice at the highest levels can hardly be blamed on Canadian field commanders. The evidence clearly indicates that they immediately took the appropriate disciplinary action in cases involving serious criminal offences, whether perpetrated against civilians or fellow soldiers.[86]

It is necessary to point out that serious criminal activity was by no means widespread in Korea, nor was it confined to any one army. All the national contingents to serve in Korea contained that small percentage of sick men responsible for the vast majority of serious crimes; the 25th Brigade was no exception. However, the sensational nature[87] of these admittedly "isolated occurrences"[88] has created the false impression that the ranks of the Canadian infantry, and especially the 2 PPCLI, were overflowing with murderers and rapists. This clearly was not the case. The available evidence strongly suggests that the number of crimes of a serious criminal nature were not disproportionate to the number of Canadian troops who served in Korea.[89]

Of the eighteen courts martial for violent criminal offences in the 25th Brigade, nine were in the infantry (six in the PPCLI,[90] one in the R22eR, and two in the RCR).[91] Recalling once again that these units accounted for over half of the 25th Brigade's strength, the infantry cannot be said to have had a monopoly on violent crime in Korea. It is, however, worth noting that most of the violent crimes involving civilians occurred when the Special Force was in Korea.[92] Shoddy recruitment may have been partially to blame, but as already seen, this period coincided with the mobile phase of the war, when Canadian soldiers had far more opportunities for contact with Korean civilians than was the case following the consolidation of the Jamestown line. Any attempt to account for the disproportionate number of cases involving Special Force personnel would therefore have to consider such factors as inadequate indoctrination and training, the absence of clearly demarcated "no civilian" lines, and the complete lack of comforts and amenities, as well as changes in Canadian military law.[93]

During the last year of the war the tables appear to have been turned somewhat. The Canadians' comparatively well-stocked reserve positions south of the Jamestown line presented enticing targets for the scores of poverty-stricken Koreans who lived just beyond the perimeter wire. Looting and pilfering were everyday occurrences.[94] Several civilian infiltrators were shot by Canadian sentries after being challenged, foreshadowing events in Somalia forty years later. But unlike in Somalia, it was sometimes the infiltrators who initiated the firefight: "The RCR had [an] incident when a sentry challenged a group of intruders in their bivouac area. The response was automatic fire from the intruders as they made a sweep of the tent lines, stealing whatever they could get their hands on. This group had done a proper wire cutting operation and had operated as a platoon in the assault. We were not dealing with amateurs."[95]

It has been suggested that like the 25th Brigade's VD statistics, its crime rate was the highest in the Commonwealth Division.[96] The current restrictions on access to the disciplinary records of Canadian soldiers make it impossible to substantiate this assertion. If this was in fact the case, there is every reason to believe that, as with VD, it was more the result of unpreparedness and inadequate indoctrination than any natural predilection for crime amongst 25th Brigade soldiers. An Adjutant-General's Report warned:

One must not lose sight of the fact that foreign service is comparatively new for the Canadian Army when the country is not engaged in a world war, whereas in the British and United States forces foreign service has always been accepted as a normal matter in a soldier's career and it may be that absence from home in a foreign country, coupled with the totally different conditions and way of life in the Orient, have resulted in a loosening of many bonds which would not be the case were Canadian troops employed in Occidental countries where conditions are not so dissimilar from those in Canada.[97]

Reflecting on the discipline of Canadian soldiers, a Canadian officer ruminated, "Sure there were some bad weeds in Korea. Where are there not any bad types? The army didn't go to churches looking for choir boys to sign up did they?"[98] If the Canadians were not choir boys, they were not criminals either. Although the ranks of the infantry undoubtedly contained both, it is misleading to view the question of discipline from such extreme perspectives. It is a truism that the vast majority fell somewhere in between. Certainly, the disciplinary record of the Canadian infantry was comparable to that of the rest of the 25th Brigade. There is even some evidence that it may have been marginally better.

More disturbing, perhaps, was the Canadians' relationship with alcohol. As has been shown, at times the misuse of alcohol caused problems. This was the price to be paid for alcohol dependency, albeit self-induced, on a massive scale. But it must be remembered that alcohol, and especially beer, was one of the few comforts available to Canadian fighting men. In the absence of officially supplied comforts and amenities, and the failure of the rotation and the R&R policies to ameliorate the discomfort of life in the field, alcohol filled the void. In hindsight, this should not be surprising. Alcohol had been used to steel soldiers' morale long before the first Canadians arrived in Korea. The increased volume of alcohol available in the Far East was simply incorporated into an ethos that was already hard drinking and accustomed to the effects of heavy alcohol use. For many soldiers, however, the dependency on alcohol did not end with the Korean War.

CONCLUSION

Kap'yong Couldn't Have Been Much of a Battle

In the evening of 27 July 1953 the guns along the Jamestown line fell silent. It had been a hot, muggy day, with some last-minute desultory shelling in the afternoon. As the sun dipped below the horizon and the hour of the ceasefire approached, the day's tension gave way to excited anticipation. At 2200 hours sharp, a salvo of flares erupted along the front, officially announcing the end of open hostilities. While the flares hissed and fizzled, the first Asahi beer bottles were prised open to mark the occasion. Many, many more were consumed before the night was through. Gazing, between sips of warm beer, at the brilliant pyrotechnic display, the soldiers of the 25th Brigade came to the realization that they had survived their Far Eastern tour.

Except for the pyrotechnics, this scene had been played out every time a Canadian infantry battalion rotated home: nervous days as the tour came to an end, excited anticipation on the rotation date itself, and, finally, intense elation. Said one soldier, "When I got close to my time being up in Korea, it really felt weird ... I thought all the time that something bad was going to happen, because I had been lucky up to that point ... The good thing is nothing bad did happen."[1]

For many soldiers, the feeling of euphoria was brief. In the 2 PPCLI, for example, elation gave way to indignation when soldiers discovered they were assigned to the same troopship, the notorious *Private Joe P. Martinez*, for the voyage home. Private Dan Johnson recalled, "When we saw the ship, we stared in disbelief. A few soldiers refused to board the ship. They were not charged and were flown home by [Trans-Continental Airlines]. The Army didn't want it known that they allowed their troops to be so badly abused, and had done nothing about it."[2]

On an individual level, soldiers left Korea with their mental baggage tightly packed. Some, like Private Bill Nasby, "could not forget the guys we left behind,"[3] while others just wanted "to forget Korea, forget the army, and get the hell on with life."[4] Others struggled with the guilt of knowing that they had killed people, or of having survived when close friends had not. Few soldiers returned home without at least some regrets or painful memories, and most were "not at all sorry to say goodbye to Korea."[5] Fewer still "would have done it all again without hesitation."[6]

The difficulty many men experienced in coming to terms with their Korean experience was not made easier by the Canadian public's apparent indifference towards the war. As Private J. Robert Molesworth put it: "When I hear people today say that Korea was not a war but a 'conflict' or 'peacekeeping,' it really pisses me off. You tell people it was a war and people died. It's that simple."[7]

Although several communities organized official receptions for returned soldiers, these were a far cry from the VE and VJ celebrations of 1945. As Sergeant George Thwaites noted, "With the exception of my family, I don't think the Canadian public gave one thought to what we were doing over there ... It wasn't like 1945 when I came home I can tell you that!"[8] Similarly, Private Kenneth Blampied recalled: "If there was any disappointment, it was the lack of recognition when I got back to Canada. I mean, I wasn't expecting a big parade or anything like they had in 1945 but, shit, something would have been nice."[9] And Private James Morrice said: "I was just a simple kid who should have stayed in Canada. But I had to shoot and kill over there, and I knew I killed people, and I sometimes have trouble with that. That's the hard part about remembering ... knowing that I did that and my country really didn't give a shit."[10]

Public indifference was one thing, but many Korean veterans found the condescending attitude of some of their fellow soldiers even harder to bear. In the smoke-filled beer parlours of the Royal Canadian Legion, Second World War veterans sometimes remarked, "Kap'yong couldn't have been much of a battle if you only had ten killed; why we had over 900 killed at Dieppe."[11] Understandably, many Korean veterans shied away from the Legion, finding solace with their comrades in the Korean Veterans Association. But perhaps the greatest blow to veterans was the Canadian government's lack of concern. Only recently have plaques bearing the inscription "Korea, 1950–53," been added to municipal cenotaphs across the country, and not until 1992 did the Department of Veterans Affairs finally authorize the Korea volunteer service medal for "all those Canadian personnel who participated in the Korean War."[12]

The belated recognition of Canada's Korea veterans was the final chapter in a story of governmental neglect and high command imprudence that began more than four decades earlier, on that hot August morning following Prime Minister Louis St Laurent's call to arms. As this book has shown, the wartime experiences of Canadian infantrymen in Korea were far more difficult and unpleasant than they need have been. That these men were expected to soldier on in spite of such difficulties was a measure of the distance between defence planners in Ottawa and the troops in the firing line.

From the outset, Canadian soldiers were not properly trained for the combat conditions they encountered. Trained with European-style combined-arms operations in mind, they were unprepared for the small-unit, hit-and-run patrol actions that were such a feature of the fighting in Korea, particularly during the last eighteen months of the war. Training in the construction and maintenance of defensive positions also left much to be desired, as evidenced by the condition of Canadian defences along the Jamestown line.

Equipment was also a problem. With the exception of their American-pattern support weapons, the Canadian infantry was not well equipped, especially in small arms. This was not a major problem when the fighting was fluid, but the shift to static warfare revealed just how poorly equipped they were for modern, close-quarter infantry engagements. Their Chinese enemies, on the other hand, were well armed with Soviet-designed submachine guns which, as the RCR historian noted, "in a short clash gave them six times the fire power of riflemen. This meant that they offered one-sixth of the target of adversaries armed with rifles."[13] Together, improper training and shoddy equipment undermined battlefield performance and had a pronounced effect on Canadian soldiers' will to combat.

The infantry also experienced problems off the battlefield. Soldiers arrived in the Far East with only a cursory knowledge of the country and people they were sent to defend. Unprepared for the smell, abject poverty, and seemingly primitive and brutal nature of the alien society that confronted them, some soldiers immediately questioned the purpose of Canadian involvement in Korea. In the third battalions, inadequate indoctrination was also a factor in the failure of the KATCOM scheme.

For the soldiers themselves, the lack of foresight and planning translated into unnecessary casualties. The infantry lacked a suitable field stretcher for most of the war, making casualty evacuation from forward areas extremely difficult and time consuming. There was also a dearth of body armour, field stoves, and fuel. Shortages of the latter two items were especially serious, as soldiers were forced to rely on improvised contraptions, with disastrous results.

Infectious diseases presented another danger. The Canadian Army's unfamiliarity with the epidemiology of the Far East resulted in unacceptably high rates of infectious diseases in the 25th Brigade. Venereal disease, the most common ailment, was not particularly difficult to treat, but far fewer soldiers would have been infected had medical authorities and defence planners followed British practices sooner. The infantry ultimately paid the price for this failure through the patently unfair – not to mention, illegal – VD rotation policy.

As if all this were not enough, Canadian combat soldiers also had to endure miserable living conditions without even the most basic creature comforts. Attempts were made to assuage the discomforts of life in the field by limiting soldiers' tours to one year and instituting an R&R program, but neither did much to enhance the day-to-day morale of Canadian soldiers, who compensated by an increasing reliance on alcohol.

In an interview with the 25th Brigade's historical officer shortly before the ceasefire, a Canadian commander claimed that "from the viewpoint of the professional soldier with Second World War experience the lessons of the Korean War are ones which can have but limited application."[14] In view of the many problems and difficulties encountered by Canadian combat soldiers in a variety of wartime contexts, the absurdity of this statement is obvious.

Having examined the unhappy experiences of the Canadian infantry in Korea, it is clear that something was drastically wrong at Defence Headquarters in Ottawa. How senior commanders and defence planners could allow Canadian soldiers to endure such needless danger and hardship remains a mystery, for we currently know nothing about the structure and internal workings of the Canadian high command during this period. Having said this, there were two factors that clearly contributed to the infantry's ordeal in Korea.

The first was that the army was seriously overextended during the Korean War era. As David Bercuson has shown, from the the decision to recruit the CASF onward, the army played catch-up to the St Laurent government's burgeoning military commitments to the United Nations, North American air defence, and NATO.[15] Indeed, this period witnessed the largest peacetime expansion of the Canadian military in history. In June 1950, for example, the Active Force's total strength stood at just over 20,000 men; one year later, the number had mushroomed to nearly 43,000 all ranks.[16] The navy and air force also expanded apace. With the military's limited resources stretched to breaking point, there simply was not enough material or equipment to meet every need or contingency.

In this era of scarcity and mushrooming military commitments, it was inevitable that the 25th Brigade in Korea would suffer most from the army's growing pains. Defence Minister Claxton made no bones about his desire to keep the Canadian military commitment in the Far East to the bare minimum, and Defence Headquarters clearly shared the outlook of the Department of External Affairs that the Korean War was a sideshow. Almost three decades ago, Dennis Stairs argued persuasively that the thrust of Canadian external and defence policies during the Korean War was to avoid becoming bogged down in Korea at a time when there was a more important theatre to safeguard in Europe.[17] Certainly, the European focus of the Canadian infantry's training, equipment, indoctrination, and medical preparation would seem to suggest that the Canadian high command was more concerned with fighting a major land war in Europe than a so-called police action in some distant Asian land. As the Canadian official historian himself conceded, Korea was only one of several Canadian "defence preoccupations" during the early 1950s.[18]

Although overextension and the European focus of Canadian policy makers helps explain the combat soldier's ordeal in Korea, there is still need for an in-depth analysis of the Canadian high command during the war. This work has also laid the foundation for subsequent studies of Canadian soldiers on post-Korea U.N. deployments, and it has provided the analytical perspective the military needs to understand its own recent history. As recent events have shown, the Canadian Army really did not learn from its Korean experience. The extent to which this fact influenced the behaviour and performance of Canadian soldiers on peacekeeping missions in the Middle East, Indochina, the Congo, and Cyprus has not yet been addressed. Only when defence planners finally take the lessons of the Korean War to heart will future generations of soldiers be spared the unnecessary hardships that were such a feature of the Canadian infantry's Far Eastern tour.

Notes

INTRODUCTION

1 Bercuson, *Blood on the Hills*, 17.
2 Ibid., 14.
3 Security Council Resolution, 25 June 1950, cited in Canada, Department of External Affairs (hereafter DEA), *Canada and the Korean Crisis*, 17.
4 Pearson, *Mike: The Memoirs of the Right Honourable Lester B. Pearson*, vol. 2: 1948–1957, 145.
5 Security Council Resolution, 27 June 1950, DEA, *Canada and the Korean Crisis*, 21.
6 Both the Liberal and Conservative press reflected this consensus over the Korean question.
7 "Canada on the Sidelines," *Globe and Mail*, 1 July 1950, 6.
8 "Canada and Korea," *Winnipeg Free Press*, 1 July 1950, 19.
9 "July 1, 1950," Halifax *Chronicle Herald*, 1 July 1950, 4.
10 House of Commons, *Debates*, 30 June 1950, 4: 4959.
11 "Drew Blames Russia for Korea Attack," *Montreal Daily Star*, 26 June 1950, 4; *Debates*, 26 June 1950, 4: 4119–20.
12 Granatstein and Bercuson, *War and Peacekeeping*, 101.
13 "Victory in Korea," *Vancouver Sun*, 9 July 1951, 4.
14 "War in Korea," *Globe and Mail*, 27 June 1950, 6.
15 "Korea, an Historic Aim of Russian Policy," *Montreal Daily Star*, 21 Aug. 1950, 10.
16 Statement by Louis St Laurent, 19 July 1950, DEA, *Canada and the Korean Crisis*, 28–30.
17 *Ottawa Evening Citizen*, 28 July 1950, cited in Wood, *Strange Battleground*, 22.

18 "Ottawa's New Brainstorm," *Globe and Mail*, 31 July 1950, 6.
19 They included Minister of National Defence Brooke Claxton.
20 Wood, *Strange Battleground*, 33.
21 Interview with J.R. Stone, Victoria, Nov. 1994.
22 Stevens, *Royal Canadian Regiment*, vol 2: *1933–1966*, 373. The CO of 2 RCHA was also a member of the Active Force.
23 Interview with anonymous soldier, Calgary, Aug. 1996.
24 Interview with Kenneth J. Blampied, Calgary, Aug. 1996.
25 See Wood, *Strange Battleground*, 27–34, and Rennie, "Mobilization for War," 47–50.
26 National Archives of Canada (hereafter NA), Department of National Defence Record Group (RG) 24, War Diary (WD), Adjutant General Branch, vol. 18,221, "Canadian Army Recruiting State," 28 Aug. 1950.
27 Directorate of History and Heritage, National Defence Headquarters (henceforth DHH), file 112.3H1(D9), "Narrative of Special Force Recruiting," 2.
28 Ibid., 3.
29 Ibid., 3.
30 The maximum age limit for CASF volunteers was thirty-five.
31 DHH, 112.3H1(D9), "Narrative of Special Force Recruiting," 5.
32 Wood, *Strange Battleground*, 28; Rennie, "Mobilization for War," 48.
33 DHH, 112.3H1(D9), "Narrative of Special Force Recruiting," 5.
34 J.R. Stone, quoted in Granatstein and Bercuson, *War and Peacekeeping*, 104.
35 DHH, 145.2R13(D12), "Interview with Lt-Col P.R. Bingham, 10 May 1962," 1.
36 Princess Patricia's Canadian Light Infantry Archives (hereafter PPCLI Archives), box 130-1, file 130(6)-1, "Kap'yong – A Speech by Colonel J.R. Stone, 18 December 1973," 1.
37 Wood, *Strange Battleground*, 29–30.
38 Cummings, *The Origins of the Korean War*, 2:70–1.
39 This contradicts the earlier interpretation that MacArthur's advance to the Yalu River precipitated the Chinese intervention. See ibid., 734, and McGibbon, *New Zealand and the Korean War*, 2:30–2.
40 Wood, *Strange Battleground*, 32.
41 Ibid.
42 See, for example, Melady, *Korea: Canada's Forgotten War*, 38–42.

43 The alleged differences between the CASF and the Active Force do not apply to the third battalions that were subsequently formed, since they drew their manpower from both formations.
44 PPCLI Archives, uncatalogued file, "Bums from the Slums."
45 Tommy Prince, quoted in Granatstein and Bercuson, *War and Peacekeeping*, 105.
46 This study consulted the randomly selected dossiers of 300 soldiers from the Special Force second battalions and the Active Force first battalions, or 50 enlisted men from each of the six battalions for a 5 percent sample. This provided the basis for a comparison of Special and Active Force enlisted men. Unfortunately, officers' files were not as readily available. In any event, all of the Special Force officers had either held commissions during the Second World War or were serving members of the Active Force on loan to the CASF.
47 These were as follows: PPCLI, west of Ontario; RCR, English-speaking regions of central and eastern Canada; R22eR, French-speaking regions of central and eastern Canada. Based on the personnel files examined, French- speaking recruits from Manitoba tended to gravitate to the PPCLI.

CHAPTER ONE

1 Holmes, *Firing Line*, 36.
2 NA, RG24, WD, 2 PPCLI, 20 Aug. 1950.
3 NA, RG24, WD, 2 PPCLI, 9 Aug. 1950; Wood, *Strange Battleground*, 40.
4 Wood, *Strange Battleground*, 40.
5 Wood, *The Private War of Jacket Coates*, 68.
6 Interview with J.R. Stone, Nov. 1994.
7 Wood, *Strange Battleground*, 40.
8 Stevens, *Royal Canadian Regiment*, 2:219.
9 Wood, *Strange Battleground*, 82.
10 The 3 PPCLI was subsequently attached to the 25th CIB at Fort Lewis to facilitate brigade-level training.
11 PPCLI Archives, *Training for War*, 26.
12 It is significant to note that drill accounted for 40 of the 300 instructional periods in CASF recruit training. See PPCLI Archives, uncatalogued file, "2 PPCLI Basic Rifle Wing Block Syllabus, 12 August 1950."

13 Holmes, *Firing Line*, 36.
14 Ibid., 46.
15 Interview with Stanley Carmichael, Calgary, Aug. 1996.
16 Interview with Bill Nasby, Calgary, Aug. 1996.
17 Interview with anonymous soldier, Ottawa, July 1997.
18 PPCLI Archives, "2 PPCLI Basic Rifle Wing Block Syllabus."
19 Stevens, *Royal Canadian Regiment*, 2:241–2, 53.
20 Holmes, *Firing Line*, 31–2.
21 Interview with John Murray Thomas, Calgary, Aug. 1996.
22 PPCLI Archives, UD163.I5, *The Infantry Battalion in Battle*, 4.
23 Interview with William Powell, Calgary, Aug. 1996.
24 Interview with Kenneth Blampied, Aug. 1996.
25 PPCLI Archives, uncatalogued file, "1 PPCLI Advanced Infantry Training Syllabus."
26 Chamberlain, "Training the Functional Rifleman," 25.
27 Ibid., 30.
28 Ibid., 26.
29 Ibid.
30 Ibid., 28.
31 Ibid., 27.
32 DHH, 410B25.013(D57), "Interview with Lt-Col Campbell, OC, 3 RCR, 7 September 1953," 2.
33 DHH, 145.2P7031(D1), "Interview with Major R.K. Swinton, OC, D Coy 2 PPCLI," 1.
34 Chamberlain, "Training the Functional Rifleman," 27.
35 Ibid., 28.
36 Ibid., 29.
37 DHH, 410B25.0033(D5), "Paper on Infantry Patrolling in Korea by Major W.H. Pope, 23 June 1953," 1.
38 Chamberlain, "Training the Functional Rifleman," 28.
39 DHH, 327.039(D5), "Training Syllabus for 2 PPCLI."
40 NA, RG24, 18,229, WD, Headquarters Western Command, 11 Sept. 1950.
41 DHH, 111.41(D22), "Training – 25th CIB, 12 December 1952."
42 Ibid.
43 DHH, 145.2R13019(D1), "Summary of Experiences – 3 RCR, 25 March 1954," 13.
44 PPCLI Archives, "2 PPCLI Basic Rifle Wing Block Syllabus" and "1 PPCLI Advanced Infantry Block Syllabus."

45 DHH, 111.41(D22), "Training Hints for a Battalion Destined for Korea," no date, 2–3.
46 DHH, 410B25.013(D53), "Interview with Lt-Col J.G. Poulin, 3 R22eR, 4 July 1953," 1.
47 DHH, 410B25.013(D57), "Interview with Lt-Col Campbell," 1.
48 Ibid.
49 PPCLI Archives, *Training for War*, 34.
50 DHH, 419FE.009(D4), "Sitreps by 25th CIB," 4.
51 The engineers also sent out patrols to repair wire and lay minefields.
52 Truce talks had first been initiated on 10 July 1951 at the village of Kaesong but had broken off after the two sides failed to reach an agreement on the location of a demarcation line. Shortly after the resumption of talks at Panmunjom, the U.N. Command ordered the Eighth Army to desist from offensive operations and maintain an active defence.
53 Granatstein and Bercuson, *War and Peacekeeping*, 158.
54 DHH, UD163.151952, *The Infantry Battalion in Battle*, 9. This passage also appeared in *Training for War*.
55 DHH, 111.41(D22), "Extracts from OCAFF Training Memorandum No. 3, 13 March 1951," 1.
56 See, for example, DHH, 145.2R13019(D1), "Summary of Experiences – 3 RCR," 7.
57 Brigadier Allard assumed command of the 25th CIB on 21 April 1953.
58 DHH, 410B25.0033(D5), Pope, "Infantry Patrolling in Korea," 1.
59 Ibid.
60 Wood, *Strange Battleground*, 241.
61 Gardham, *Korea Volunteer*, 126–7.
62 Ibid., 133.
63 DHH, 111.41(D22), "Training – 25th CIB, 12 December 1952."
64 DHH, 111.41(D22), "Training Hints for a Battalion Destined for Korea," 2–5.
65 Watson, "From Calgary to Kap'yong."
66 Bercuson, *Significant Incident*, 93.
67 NA, MG31, G12, Brig-Gen J.M. Rockingham, "Recollections of Korea," 10.
68 Wood, *Strange Battleground*, 83.
69 Interview with Stanley Carmichael, Aug. 1996.
70 Interview with James Wilson, Calgary, Aug. 1996.

71 Interview with L.F. Trudeau, Calgary, Aug. 1996.
72 DHH, 410B25.013(D53), "Interview with Lt-Col Poulin," 1.
73 Stevens, *Royal Canadian Regiment*, 2:263.
74 Wood, *Strange Battleground*, 241.

CHAPTER TWO

1 During the Second World War, the 6th Canadian Division, the joint American-Canadian Special Service Force, and the Canadian troops who participated in the Kiska invasion were issued some American equipment.
2 Wood, *Strange Battleground*, 85.
3 NA, RG24, 18,220, WD, Vice Chief of the General Staff, "Extract of Minutes, 17 July 1950."
4 DHH, 112.3M2(D410), Equipment, General, vol. 2, Oct. 1949 – Sept. 1951, 1.
5 Wood, *Strange Battleground*, 35.
6 Ibid.
7 DHH, 111.41(D22), "British Information from Korea," 1.
8 NA, RG24, WD, Chief of the General Staff, "Notes on Korean Situation," July 1950.
9 The Americans were also asked to provide field rations.
10 DHH, 111.41(D19), vol. 8, Equipment, General, 25th CIB. Although based on British designs, Canadian small arms also fell under the rubric of non-common-user items.
11 Most Canadian battalion commanders considered the British 44-pattern webbing, with its eyelet belt, snap-on pouches, and roomy pack ideally suited to conditions in Korea. See DHH, 410B25.003(D2), "Notes on Equipment in Korea," 2.
12 Results from historical questionnaire circulated among former members of 2 PPCLI, Nov. 1994 (hereafter Questionnaire); DHH, 410B25.003(D2), "Notes on Equipment in Korea," 2. Lt-Col Campbell was especially critical of the 37-pattern webbing's inability to carry the Canadian-issue poncho and cup, two things that soldiers were almost never without.
13 NA, RG24, 18,339, WD, 1 RCR, Nov. 1952, app. 28, "Report on 1 RCR Night Action 23/24 October 1952," 6.
14 Brian Munro, quoted in Hepenstall, *Find the Dragon*, 318.
15 The American steel pot helmet had a removable fibreglass liner, which supported the helmet's suspension system. In the field, the

liner could be removed and the steel shell used for cooking and washing. The design of the M1 helmet and the British assault helmet were decided improvements over that of the Canadian Mark II helmet, in that they afforded far greater protection of the neck, temples, and forehead.

16 NA, RG24, 18,225, WD, Branch of the QMG, 2 Oct. 1950.
17 Interview with George Cook, Kelowna, June 1994.
18 DHH, 410B25.013(D57), "Interview with Lt-Col Campbell," 9.
19 Balaclavas could also be worn on patrol during the winter months.
20 Photographs from the Korean War clearly show that the tail flap was seldom used.
21 This assertion is based on an examination of a Canadian summer peaked hat in the author's possession.
22 DHH, 145.2R13013(D2), "The Battle of Chail-li, 20 May 1951," 3.
23 Ibid., 8.
24 Ibid.
25 Ibid., 1.
26 NA, RG24, WD, 2 PPCLI, 4 Jan. 1951.
27 Results from Questionnaire; interview with George Cook, June 1994.
28 NA, RG24, WD, 2 PPCLI, 28 Feb. 1951; Wood, *Strange Battleground*, 64.
29 Peacock, *Kim-Chi, Asahi, and Rum*, 77.
30 Ibid.
31 DHH, 145.2R13019(D1), "Summary of Experiences – 3 RCR," 3.
32 Peacock, *Kim-Chi, Asahi, and Rum*, 77.
33 Wood, *Strange Battleground*, 35.
34 DHH, 112.3M2(D410), Equipment, General, October 1949 – September 1951.
35 DHH, 145.2R13019(D1), "Summary of Experiences – 3 RCR," 3.
36 During the monsoon season, a cotton poplin "bush" uniform was issued in lieu of battledress. The jacket of this uniform was found to be unsuitable for service in Korea, but it was an improvement over battledress. See DHH, 145.2R13019(D1), "Summary of Experiences – 3 RCR," 3.
37 Ibid.
38 WD, 2 PPCLI, 4 January 1951; DHH, 145.2R13013(D2), "The Battle of Chail-li," 7.
39 DHH, 410B25.003(D2), "Notes on Equipment in Korea," 1.
40 DHH, 145.2R13019(D1), "Summary of Experiences – 3 RCR," 4.

41 NA, RG24, WD, 2 PPCLI, Jan. 1951; Wood, *Strange Battleground*, 58; interview with J.R. Stone, Nov. 1994; DHH, 410B25.003(D2), "Notes on Equipment in Korea," 1.
42 DHH, UD325.15, *Infantry Training*, vol. 4: *Tactics*, 14.
43 Archer, ed., *Jane's Infantry Weapons 1976*, 340.
44 Ibid.
45 DHH, 410B25.013(D53), "Summary of Experiences – 3 R22eR, 4 February 1954," 2.
46 DHH, 145.2R13019(D1), "Summary of Experiences – 3 RCR," 2.
47 Ibid.
48 Canadian troops first used an early version of the Lee Enfield during the South African War.
49 Interview with George Cook, June 1994.
50 Results from Questionnaire.
51 See, for example, Marshall, *The River and the Gauntlet*, 49.
52 DHH, HQS 3201-151/25 (trg 5), 28 May 1951, Training, General, 25th CIB, 1: 2.
53 Rawling, *Surviving Trench Warfare*, 12.
54 DHH, 314.009(D464), "Sitreps and Notes on Fighting in Korea," Simonds to Wrinch, 2 Apr. 1951, 2.
55 DHH, 145.2R13019(D1), "Summary of Experiences – 3 RCR," 1.
56 DHH, 410B25.0033(D5), Pope, "Infantry Patrolling in Korea," 13.
57 DHH, 145.2R13019(D1), "Summary of Experiences – 3 RCR," 1.
58 DHH, 410B25.013(D57), "Interview with Lt-Col Campbell," 8–9.
59 Stairs, *The Diplomacy of Constraint*.
60 Contemporary military vernacular for a submachine gun.
61 Interview with Lorne Warner, Calgary, Aug. 1996.
62 Interview with Bill Lee, Calgary, Aug. 1996.
63 DHH, 410B25.0033(D5), Pope, "Infantry Patrolling in Korea," 11. According to official Canadian doctrine, there was one Sten gun per rifle section.
64 DHH, 410B25.013(D57), "Interview with Lt-Col Campbell," 9.
65 Archer, *Jane's Infantry Weapons*, 285.
66 Interview with Bill Martin, Calgary, Aug. 1996.
67 Interview with Bill Lee, Aug. 1996.
68 NA, RG24, 18,314, WD, 1 RCR, June 1952, app. 4, 2.
69 Interview with anonymous soldier, Calgary, Aug. 1996.
70 DHH, 410B25.003(D2), "Notes on Equipment in Korea," 3. The Sten remained in service until the late 1950s.

71 The Australian Owen gun had a reputation for reliability under the most adverse battlefield conditions.
72 DHH, 681.009(D11), "Paper on Infantry Defences in Korea by Major Harry Pope," 7.
73 DHH, 145.2R13019(D1), "Summary of Experiences – 3 RCR," 2.
74 The Patchett, subsequently renamed the Sterling, was adopted by the Canadian Army under the designation SMG C1A1.
75 Results of interviews, Calgary, Aug. 1996; DHH, 410B25.013(D57), "Interview with Lt-Col Campbell," 9.
76 DHH, 145.2R13019(D1), "Summary of Experiences – 3 RCR," 2.
77 DHH, 410B25.0033(D5), Pope, "Infantry Patrolling in Korea," 13.
78 Canadian soldiers often referred to stick grenades as "Chinese firecrackers."
79 DHH, 410B25.0033(D5), Pope, "Infantry Patrolling in Korea," 13.
80 PPCLI Archives, UD163.15, *The Infantry Battalion in Battle*, 28.
81 The Canadians also used the heavier American 4.2 in. mortar towards the end of the war, but only in very limited quantities. Some battalions also retained the British 2 in. mortar.
82 Marshall, *The River and the Gauntlet*, 370.
83 Archer, *Jane's Infantry Weapons*, 509–10, 528.
84 See Stone and Castonguay, *Korea 1951: Two Canadian Battles*.
85 DHH, 145.2R13019(D1), "Summary of Experiences – 3 RCR," 2.
86 Archer, *Jane's Infantry Weapons*, 527. The 60 mm mortar, like the 81 mm mortar, could fire training, illumination and smoke rounds, in addition to high explosive.
87 DHH, 145.2R13019(D1), "Summary of Experiences – 3 RCR," 2.
88 Unlike the North Koreans, the Chinese did not possess a significant armoured capability.
89 DHH, Training, General, 25th CIB, vol. 1, "Notes on Fighting in Korea, 28 May 1951," 2.
90 The Commander of the 1 R22eR, Lt-Col Trudeau, was very impressed with the 75 mm recoilless rifle. See DHH, 410B25.013(D41), "Account of Interview with Lt-Col Trudeau, 21 April 1953," 1.
91 DHH, 145.2R13019(D1), "Summary of Experiences – 3 RCR," 2.
92 DHH, 410B25.013(D57), "Interview with Lt-Col Campbell," 7. The 3 RCR actually employed its antitank platoon as a mortar platoon.
93 During the Korean War era, a Canadian machine-gun platoon was equipped with six Vickers guns.

94 Archer, *Jane's Infantry Weapons*, 335.
95 Ibid.
96 DHH, 145.2R13019(D1), "Summary of Experiences – 3 RCR," 3.
97 Military vernacular for the American M3 SMG.

CHAPTER THREE

1 Contemporary naval term for the Far East.
2 Some Canadian soldiers sent to Korea as reinforcements were flown by USAF or RCAF transport.
3 With the departure of the second battalions to Korea, the third battalions concentrated at Wainwright for training.
4 NA, RG24, WD, 2 PPCLI, Nov. 1950, app. 17.
5 Ironically, the officer who issued these orders later stated in an official report that his men made absolutely no attempt to learn Korean. See DHH, 145.2P7013(D6), "Reports by Lt-Col Stone," 9.
6 DHH, 112.1(D157), "Training, 25th CIB on Current Affairs," no date, 1.
7 NA, RG24, 18,237, WD, HQ 25th CIB, Aug. 1950, app. 4, 3.
8 Soldier's Forum was subsequently renamed Platoon Commander's Hour.
9 PPCLI Archives, uncatalogued file, "The Papers of B.A.J. Franklin" (hereafter Franklin Papers).
10 Interview with W. Hummer, Calgary, Aug. 1996; Interview with William Powell, Aug. 1996.
11 DHH, 81/229, "Notes on Korean Police Action, 1 March 1951," 2.
12 Ibid., 2–3.
13 Ibid., 3.
14 Ibid.
15 DHH, 112.2(D157), "Correspondence ref. Behaviour of Canadian Troops in Korea," 1.
16 Bill Boss, "PPCLI Engage in Hard Training," *Calgary Herald*, 22 Jan. 1951, 2.
17 NA, RG24, acc. 83-84/167, box 5079, file 3415-2, part 1, "If Koreans Don't Love Us This Is Why: Excerpts of Talk by Pierre Berton," 1.
18 Ibid.
19 Ibid.
20 Dave Cyr, cited in Hepenstall, *Find the Dragon*, 42.

21 NA, RG24, 83-84/167, 5079, 3415-2, "If Koreans Don't Love Us," 2.
22 DHH, 112.2(D157), "Correspondence ref. Behaviour of Canadian Troops," 2.
23 DHH, 112.1(D157), "Training, 25th CIB on Current Affairs," 1, and "Correspondence ref. Behaviour of Canadian Troops," 2.
24 The guide was reprinted, complete with Canadian illustrations, by DND in December 1951 under the nondescript title "Korea."
25 DHH, 112.1(D157), "Training, 25th CIB on Current Affairs,"; this observation is based on interviews with over fifty Korean veterans.
26 NA, RG24, 20,290, 934.009(D373), "Booklet on Korea," 29.
27 Ibid., 1.
28 PPCLI Archives, uncatalogued file, "Kap'yong Remembered: Anecdotes from Korea," 4.
29 This was certainly the opinion of Korean veterans interviewed during the 1996 KVA Conference in Calgary.
30 Miscellaneous file, provided to the author by E.A. Higham (hereafter Higham Papers).
31 Jack Hayward, quoted in Hepenstall, *Find the Dragon*, 43.
32 A kitchen is usually referred to as the mess in army parlance, but in the navy it is known as the galley.
33 PPCLI Archives, Franklin Papers.
34 Jack Hayward, quoted in Hepenstall, *Find the Dragon*, 43.
35 Interview with George Cook, June 1994.
36 PPCLI Archives, boxes 130-1 to 134-3, file 130(6)-1, "2 PPCLI in Korea."
37 Higham Papers.
38 PPCLI Archives, uncatalogued file, Walter O. Holt Papers.
39 Higham Papers.
40 PPCLI Archives, uncatalogued file, "Domain of the Golden Dragon."
41 Two companies of the 1 RCR landed at Inchon instead of Pusan.
42 NA, RG24, 18,312, WD, 1 PPCLI, 4-6 Oct. 1951.
43 DHH, 81/229, "Canada's War in Korea, Article No. 1," no date.
44 Wood, *Private War of Jacket Coates*, 92.
45 DHH, 81/229, "Canada's War in Korea, Article No. 1," 2.
46 PPCLI Archives, "Kap'yong Remembered," 4.
47 NA, MG31, G12, Rockingham, "Recollections of Korea," 19.
48 Interview with William Powell, Aug. 1996; interview with Louis McLean, Calgary, Aug. 1996.
49 Interview with John Murray, Calgary, Aug. 1996.

50 Interview with James Wilson, Calgary, Aug. 1996.
51 NA, MG31, G12, Rockingham, "Recollections of Korea," 19.
52 Ibid., 20.
53 Ibid.
54 Wood, *The Private War of Jacket Coates*, 91.
55 Jack Hayward, quoted in Hepenstall, *Find the Dragon*, 47.
56 DHH, 81/229, "Notes on Korean Police Action," 3.
57 DHH, 112.1(D157), "Korea," no date, 4–5.
58 Wood, *The Private War of Jacket Coates*, 92.
59 DHH, 145.2P7013(D6), "Notes on Talk Given by Lt-Col Stone, 5 June 1951," 6.
60 DHH, 81/229, "Notes on Korean Police Action," 2.
61 DHH, 81/229, "Canada's War in Korea, Article No.1."
62 DHH, 112.009(D87), "Report by Lt-Col Bult-Francis on Visit to Japan and Korea, 2 July to 4 August 1951," 1.
63 Interview with George Thwaites, Calgary, Aug. 1996.
64 DHH, 81/229, "Canada's War in Korea, Article No. 1."
65 Hepenstall, *Find the Dragon*, 180.
66 Wood, *The Private War of Jacket Coates*, 92.
67 Body bags were not used by the Canadians in Korea. Instead, fatal casualties were wrapped in a waterproof poncho and covered by a standard-issue wool blanket.
68 PPCLI Archives, Franklin Papers.

CHAPTER FOUR

1 DHH, 81/229, "Canada's War in Korea, Article No. 1."
2 Holmes, *Firing Line*, 291.
3 Ibid.
4 Ibid., 293.
5 Lt-Col T.F. Main, quoted in Ellis, *The Sharp End of War*, 340.
6 Peacock, *Kim-Chi, Asahi, and Rum*, 89–90.
7 Keegan, *The Face of Battle*, 51.
8 Ibid.
9 Eighth U.S. Army Historical Office, Yongsan Garrison, Seoul, Republic of Korea (hereafter Eighth U.S. Army Historical Office), 700.016, "The Value of the Korean Service Corps, 24 March 1971," 1.
10 DHH, 410B25.009(D2), 1 Commonwealth Division Operational Instruction No. 21, 1.

11 There were approximately 300 men in a KSC company.
12 DHH, 410B25.009(D2), HQ Instruction No. 18, 19 Oct. 1951: Civil Labour, 1. Twenty-five KSC personnel were normally allocated to each Canadian infantry company. The remaining 240 were formed into a labour pool under the command of the regimental sergeant-major.
13 NA, RG24, WD, 2 PPCLI, 23 Feb. 1951. "Gook" was a derivative of the Korean word *han-guk*, which meant Korean "person."
14 Peate, "No Pay – No Uniforms – No Glory," 2. The title of this article is misleading, as the KSC were paid – albeit a paltry sum – for the work they performed for the Canadians.
15 NA, RG24, WD, 2 PPCLI, 28–9 Mar. 1951.
16 Earl Richardson, quoted in Hepenstall, *Find the Dragon*, 154–5.
17 Peacock, *Kim-chi, Asahi, and Rum*, 76.
18 DHH, 81/229, "Canada's War in Korea, Article No. 1."
19 NA, RG24, 18,338, WD, E Company, 1 RCR, 31 Oct. 1952.
20 DHH, 145.2R13(D12), "Interview with Lt-Col Bingham, 1 RCR, 10 May 1962," 1.
21 NA, RG24, 18,388, WD, E Company, 1 RCR, 19 Oct. 1952.
22 Peacock, *Kim-chi, Asahi, and Rum*, 76.
23 Ibid.; "Korea War-Born Vocabulary Vigorous," *Winnipeg Free Press*, 11 Dec. 1951, 28.
24 Peacock, *Kim-chi, Asahi, and Rum*, 76.
25 Peate, "No Pay – No Uniforms – No Glory," 29.
26 Peacock, *Kim-chi, Asahi, and Rum*, 90.
27 The BCOF, in turn, billed the Canadians government for the cost of KSC services rendered to the 25th CIB.
28 Values are in 1951 Canadian dollars. A KSC sergeant received double this amount.
29 DHH, 410B25.009(D2), "Miscellaneous File Strippings of the 25th CIB, 1951–1952."
30 DHH, 410B25.013(D53), "Summary of Experiences – 3 R22eR," 10.
31 DHH, 410B25.013(D57), "Interview with Lt-Col Campbell," 9. 1 RCR's Lt-Col Bingham was equally impressed with the KSC. See DHH, 145.2R13(D12), "Interview with Lt-Col Bingham," 2.
32 Hepenstall, *Find the Dragon*, 132.
33 Interview with Louis Vincent McLean, Aug. 1996; Interview with James Wilson, Aug. 1996.
34 Ken Blair, quoted in Hepenstall, *Find the Dragon*, 181- 2.

35 The available evidence suggests that this was especially the case with some R22eR officers. See DHH, 410B25.013(D53), "Interview with Lt-Col Poulin," 6.
36 Interview with anonymous soldier, Calgary, Aug. 1996.
37 See Peate, "No Pay – No Uniforms – No Glory," 29.
38 Interview with Choi In Wa, Naech'on, Republic of Korea, Oct. 1997.
39 Farrar-Hockley, *The British Part in the Korean War*, 2: 375.
40 DHH, 410B25.019(D267), "Orders, Instructions and Reports on Organization and Administration of KATCOM in the 25th CIB, February 1953 to August 1954."
41 Skaggs, "The KATUSA Experiments," 53.
42 Ibid.
43 Brigadier Bogert to the Canadian General Staff, cited in Wood, *Strange Battleground*, 220.
44 DHH, 111.41(D14), Memorandum for Cabinet Defence Committee, 10 Nov. 1952, 1.
45 Ibid., 1–2.
46 Wood, *Strange Battleground*, 220.
47 DHH, 111.41(D14), HQS 2715-151/25(178), app. A, 13 Aug. 1952.
48 Bogert replaced Rockingham in April 1952.
49 DHH, 111.41(D14), HQS 2715-151/25(178), app. A.
50 Ibid.
51 Ibid.
52 DHH, 111.41(D14), "Proposed Integration of South Korean Personnel in the Commonwealth Division, 17 November 1952," 1.
53 DHH, 111.41(D14), Minutes of CGS Conference No. 145, 26 Nov. 1952, 1.
54 Wood, *Strange Battleground*, 221.
55 DHH, 410B25.019(D245), "Administration of KATCOM Troops, 12 May 1953," 1.
56 It is interesting to note that all of the Active Force first battalions experienced problems with cohesion in sections that contained battle-hardened, former second-battalion men. See DHH, 410B25.013(D41), "Interview with Lt-Col Trudeau," 2, and DHH, 145.2R13(D12), "Interview with Lt-Col Bingham," 1.
57 Ellis, *The Sharp End of War*, 336.
58 Ibid.
59 DHH, 410B25.013(D53), "Summary of Experiences – 3 R22eR," 10.
60 DHH, 410B25.013(D53), "Interview with Lt-Col Poulin," 5.

61 DHH, 145.2R13019(D1), "Summary of Experiences – 3 RCR," 11; Hackworth, *About Face*, 635.
62 Chris Snider, quoted in Gardham, *Korean Volunteer*, 180.
63 Hepenstall, *Find the Dragon*, 180.
64 Ibid.
65 Several veterans have disclosed, in strict confidence, that patrol stacking was common.
66 Earl Richardson, quoted in Hepenstall, *Find the Dragon*, 181.
67 DHH, 410B25.019(D245), "Administrative Order No. 9, 12 May 1953," 2.
68 DHH, 410B25.013(D57), "Interview with Lt-Col Campbell," 9.
69 See Skaggs, "The KATUSA Experiment," 57.
70 Davis, *The Sharp End*, 207.
71 DHH, 410B25.019(D267), "KATCOMS: A Brief on the Situation for Commander, 25th CIB, 14 May 1954," 3.
72 Ibid.
73 Interview with anonymous soldier, Calgary, Aug. 1996.
74 Ibid.
75 Skaggs, "The KATUSA Experiment," 56.
76 Ibid.
77 DHH, 410B25.013(D57), "Interview with Lt-Col Campbell," 9.
78 DHH, 410B25.013(D53), "Interview with Lt-Col Poulin," 6.
79 MacLennan was the 25th CIB brigade major from 8 May 1954 to 5 November 1954.
80 DHH, 410B25.019(D267), "KATCOMS: A Brief," 4. The KATUSA program continued in the U.S. Army.
81 Skaggs, "The KATUSA Experiment," 53.
82 Wood, *Strange Battleground*, 221. It is worth noting that Wood was in command of the 3 PPCLI when the KATCOM program was introduced.
83 This was probably the case in the U.S. Army as well, although it is likely that the Americans' individual (as opposed to the 25th CIB's unit) replacement system made KATUSA integration easier. See Hackworth, *About Face*, 117, 246–7, and 633–4.
84 Hepenstall, *Find the Dragon*, 180.
85 DHH, 410B25.013(D53), "Interview with Lt-Col Poulin," 5. The transcript of the interview was later submitted to Brigadier Allard, Bogert's successor, for vetting. Allard penciled in the margin that Poulin had indeed been granted permission to organize his KATCOMS into their own sub-units, but there is no evidence to support this.

CHAPTER FIVE

1 See, for example, Barris, *Deadlock in Korea*.
2 DHH, 145.2R13013(D2), "The Battle of Chail-li," 2. The POWs may have been deserters.
3 DHH, 145.2R13013(D2), "The Battle of Chail-li – C Company Report," 1.
4 Wood, *Strange Battleground*, 105.
5 Ibid.
6 Stevens, *Royal Canadian Regiment*, 230-1.
7 Wood, *Strange Battleground*, 160.
8 DHH, 410B25.0033(D5), Pope, "Infantry Patrolling in Korea," 1.
9 C.E. Goodman and John Richardson, quoted in Hepenstall, *Find the Dragon*, 201.
10 The failure of Canadian fighting patrols was due in part to inadequate reconnaissance and the practice of establishing firm bases, followed by small group advances. Harry Pope considered the Chinese method of patrolling in-depth to be far more effective.
11 See, for example, WD, 1 PPCLI, July 1952, app. A.
12 Wood, *Strange Battleground*, 186.
13 NA, RG24, WD, 1 PPCLI, June 1952, app. 1.
14 DHH, 681.011(D2), "Address by Maj-Gen H. Murray, 16 December 1954," 4. Emphasis is the author's.
15 Doary, "Miniature Set-Piece Battles," 29.
16 DHH, 681.011(D2), "Address by Maj-Gen H. Murray," 3; DHH, 410B25.0033(D5), Pope, "Infantry Patrolling in Korea," 12.
17 These were located just behind the MLR with the RCHA.
18 DHH, 112.3W1013(D13), "CAORT Notes on Operational Research in Korea, 18 Apr. 1952," 4.
19 DHH, 410B25.013(D53), "Summary of Experiences – 3 R22eR," 4.
20 DHH, 681.011(D2), "Address by Maj-Gen H. Murray," 4.
21 Stevens, *Royal Canadian Regiment*, 275.
22 DHH, 410B25.0033(D5), Pope, "Infantry Patrolling in Korea," 13.
23 This tactic was used with devastating effect on 3 May 1953 when a 3 RCR fighting patrol was pursued from the valley floor all the way up to the forward Canadian positions.
24 DHH, 410B25.0033(D5), Pope, "Infantry Patrolling in Korea," 1.
25 Hepenstall, *Find the Dragon*, 136.
26 DHH, 681.011(D2), "Address by Maj-Gen H. Murray," 3.

27 NA, RG24, WD, 1 RCR, Nov. 1952, app. 28, "Chinese Tactics and Lessons Learned," 4.
28 Coverage of all the raids launched against the 25th Brigade are clearly beyond the scope of this work. The raids that have been selected for analysis were chosen for their instructive abilities and because of the relative abundance of primary source material generated in their aftermath. They are also among the most significant and best-known Canadian actions of the Korean War.
29 NA, RG24, WD, 1 RCR, Nov. 1952, app. 28, "Report on 1 RCR Night Action," 1.
30 Ibid.
31 DHH, 410B25.0033(D5), Pope, "Infantry Patrolling in Korea," 7.
32 DHH, 145.2R13019(D1), "Summary of Experiences – 3 RCR," 8–9.
33 Grey, *The Commonwealth Armies and the Korean War*, 150.
34 Ibid., 151.
35 NA, RG24, WD, 25th CIB, May 1953, "Notes on Defence."
36 Farrar-Hockley, *The British Part in the Korean War*, 2: 354.
37 DHH, 681.009(D11), "Paper on Infantry Defences in Korea by Major Harry Pope," 2.
38 For a more detailed account of the inadequacy of Commonwealth defensive doctrine, see David Bercuson, "Fighting the Defensive Battle on the Jamestown Line," 13–16.
39 Ibid., 14.
40 DHH, 681.011(D1), "Personal Recollection of the Field Works of Wyoming, Jamestown and Kansas lines in Korea, prepared by Capt Maden, September 1954," 1.
41 DHH, 681.011(D1), "Personal Recollection," 2.
42 DHH, 681.009(D11), Pope, "Infantry Defences in Korea," 4.
43 DHH, 410B25.013(D57), "Interview with Lt-Col Campbell," 6.
44 WD, 25th Canadian Field Historical Detachment, December 1953, cited in Wood, *Strange Battleground*, 236.
45 Farrar-Hockley, *The British Part in the Korean War*," 2: 354.
46 DHH, 681.009(D11), Pope, "Infantry Defences in Korea," 3.
47 DHH, 410B25.013(D12), "Interview with Maj R. Liboiron, and Lts W. Nash and T.R. Webb, 2 R22eR, concerning Battle of Hill 227, 23–25 November 1951," 11.
48 Farrar-Hockley, *The British Part in the Korean War*, 2: 370.
49 DHH, 681.011(D1), "Personal Recollection," 11.
50 DHH, 681.009(D11), Pope, "Infantry Defences in Korea," 3.

51 Wood, *Strange Battleground*, 228.
52 DHH, 681.009(D11), Pope, "Infantry Defences in Korea," 5.
53 Grey, *The Commonwealth Armies and the Korean War*, 150-3.
54 NA, RG24, WD, 1 RCR, Nov. 1952, app. 28, "Chinese Tactics and Lessons Learned," 1.
55 Farrar-Hockley, *The British Part in the Korean War*, 2: 370-1.
56 NA, RG24, WD, 1 RCR, Nov. 1952, app. 28, "Chinese Tactics and Lessons Learned," 2.
57 NA, RG24, WD, 1 PPCLI, 6 Nov. 1951.
58 Chinese winter uniforms are on display at the Canadian War Museum in Ottawa.
59 PPCLI Archives, 132(2)-1, "Uniforms of the Korean War," 4.
60 Hogg and Adam, *Jane's Guns Recognition Guide*, 263-4.
61 Ibid.
62 NA, RG24, WD, 1 RCR, Nov. 1952, app. 28, "Chinese Tactics and Lessons Learned," 2.
63 DHH, 410B25.0033(D5), Pope, "Infantry Patrolling in Korea," 6.
64 Ibid., 9-10.
65 Ibid., 10.
66 DHH, 681.009(D11), Pope, "Infantry Defences in Korea," 5.
67 NA, RG24, WD, 1 RCR, Nov. 1952, app. 28, "Chinese Tactics and Lessons Learned," 4.
68 DHH, 681.009(D11), Pope, "Infantry Defences in Korea," 5.
69 NA, RG24, WD, 1 RCR, Nov. 1952, app. 28, "Chinese Tactics and Lessons Learned," 4.
70 Ibid.
71 Maj. R. Ringma, quoted in Wood, *Strange Battleground*, 101.
72 DHH, 419FE.009(D4), "Sitreps by 25th CIB," 2.
73 Cameron, *American Samurai*, 232.
74 "Interview, 1 December 1951," reprinted in Wood, *Strange Battleground*, 156-7.
75 DHH, 410B25.013(D12), "Interview with Maj R. Liboiron," 10.
76 Ibid., 8.
77 NA, RG24, WD, 1 RCR, Nov. 1952, app. 28, "Chinese Tactics and Lessons Learned," 4.
78 Wood, *Strange Battleground*, 243.
79 Interview with anonymous soldier, Calgary, Aug. 1996.
80 John Richardson, quoted in Hepenstall, *Find the Dragon*, 178-9.
81 In the Canadian War Museum, 90026.

CHAPTER SIX

1 Keegan, *The Face of Battle*, 114.
2 DHH, 410B25.0033(D5), Pope, "Infantry Patrolling in Korea," 1.
3 Stevens, *Royal Canadian Regiment*, 230–1.
4 See, for example, NA, RG24, 18,342, WD, 2 RCR, Aug. 1951, after-action report for Operation Rodger, 13–15 Aug. 1951.
5 DHH, 410B25.013(D12), "Interview with Maj R. Liboiron," 10.
6 Interview with J.R. Stone, Nov. 1994.
7 Farrar-Hockley, *The British Part in the Korean War*, 2: 366.
8 According to Robert Hepenstall, the Canadians were the battlefield equals of the Dutch and Belgians, better than some of the American and British units, and completely outclassed by the Australians, the French, and the U.S. Marines. See Hepenstall, *Find the Dragon*, 125.
9 Grey, *The Commonwealth Armies and the Korean War*, 153.
10 Ibid.
11 Farrar-Hockley, *The British Part in the Korean War*, 2: 366.
12 DHH, 681.009(D11), Pope, "Infantry Defences in Korea," 2.
13 Holmes, *Firing Line*, 286–7.
14 DHH, 410B25.0033(D5), Pope, "Infantry Patrolling in Korea," 9–10.
15 Fox, *Archaeology, History, and Custer's Last Battle*, 260–74.
16 See Ashworth, *Trench Warfare, 1914–1918*.
17 NA, RG24, WD, 1 PPCLI, 11 Mar. 1952.
18 These men have, understandably, wished to remain anonymous.
19 The main line of resistance, or MLR, was the ring of weapons pits on the forward slope of a defensive position.
20 This is clearly the impression that has emerged out of interviews with Korean veterans.
21 Holmes, *Firing Line*, 329.
22 NA, RG24, WD, 1 RCR, Nov. 1952, app. 28, "Chinese Tactics and Lessons Learned," 4.
23 Wood, *Strange Battleground*, 209.
24 George Griffiths, quoted in Melady, *Korea*, 133.
25 Ibid.
26 Pope, quoted in Gardham, *Korea Volunteer*, 130.
27 NA, RG24, WD, 1 RCR, 11 Oct. 1952.
28 DHH, 681.009(D11), Pope, "Infantry Defences in Korea," 3.
29 DHH, 410B25.013(D57), "Interview with Lt-Col Campbell," 1–2.

30 Hepenstall, *Find the Dragon*, 199.
31 Interview with Paul Tomelin, Kelowna, Aug. 1997.
32 John Richardson, quoted in Hepenstall, *Find the Dragon*, 173.
33 Interview with anonymous soldier, Calgary, Aug. 1996.
34 Hepenstall, *Find the Dragon*, 76.
35 Interview with anonymous solider, Calgary, Aug. 1996.
36 Peacock, *Kim-chi, Asahi, and Rum*, 12.
37 John Vallance, quoted in Hepenstall, *Find the Dragon*, 201.
38 DHH, 145.2R13019(D1), "Summary of Experiences – 3 RCR," 12.
39 Interview with anonymous soldier, Hull, July 1997.
40 DHH, 410B25.013(D53), "Summary of Experiences – 3 R22eR," 7.
41 DHH, 145.2R13019(D1), "Summary of Experiences – 3 RCR," 12.
42 Hepenstall, *Find the Dragon*, 213.
43 DHH, 410B25.0033(D5), Pope, "Infantry Patrolling in Korea," 3.
44 DHH, 681.009(D11), Pope, "Infantry Defences in Korea," 7.
45 NA, RG24, WD, 3 RCR, 21 July 1953.
46 Brian Munro, quoted in Hepenstall, *Find the Dragon*, 307.
47 NA, RG24, WD, 1 RCR, Aug. 1952, app. J.
48 NA, RG24, WD, 2 PPCLI, 7 Mar. 1951.
49 Small-arms ammunition.
50 Interview with George Cook, June 1994.
51 NA, RG24, WD, 1 RCR, May 1952, app. 4, "Preliminary Report on 1 RCR Fighting Patrol, 31 May – 1 June 1952," 2.
52 Hepenstall, *Find the Dragon*, 201.
53 NA, RG24, WD, 1 RCR, Nov. 1952, app. 28, "Report on 1 RCR Action," 5.
54 W.D. Pero, quoted in Hepenstall, *Find the Dragon*, 237.
55 Interview with anonymous soldier, Calgary, Aug. 1996.
56 PPCLI Archives, uncatalogued file, "Kap'yong Remembered," 24.
57 Interview with Rod Middleton, Calgary, Oct. 1994.
58 Middleton, quoted in Hepenstall, *Find the Dragon*, 77.
59 Holmes, *Firing Line*, 204.
60 Interview with Bill Martin, Calgary, Aug. 1996.
61 Eighth U.S. Army Historical Office, 870-5a-220.515, "Lessons Learned: Operations Research Office," 3.
62 Ibid.
63 PPCLI Archives, uncatalogued file, "Kap'yong Remembered," 28.
64 PPCLI Archives, uncatalogued file, "Noise as a Chinese Communist Weapon," 1.

65 Eighth U.S. Army Historical Office, 870-5a-220.515, "A Study of Ineffective Soldier Performance under Fire in Korea, 1951," 3.
66 Interview with R.W. Granville, Calgary, Aug. 1996.
67 Stevens, *Royal Canadian Regiment*, 276.
68 The after-action report for the battle of Hill 355, for example, records a total of 1,466 incoming rounds for the period 17–20 October.
69 Senior regimental officer, RCR, quoted in Stevens, *Royal Canadian Regiment*, 276.
70 Farrar-Hockley, *The British Part in the Korean War*, 2: 365.
71 NA, RG24, 18,396, WD, No. 25 Canadian Field Dressing Station (FDS), July 1952, "British Commonwealth Classification of Wounds."
72 NA, RG24, WD, No. 25 FDS, "Monthly Psychiatric Report – September 1952," 1.
73 NA, RG24, WD, 1 RCR, Oct. 1952, app. 7, "Monthly Report, Battle Adjutant, 1 RCR." This figure does not include the five men evacuated to A Echelon with anxiety state, a mild, temporary reaction to stress.
74 Ibid., 1–31 Oct. 1952.
75 NA, RG24, acc. 83-84/048, box 977, file 3105-151/25, "Statistics – Korea," 1.
76 PPCLI, uncatalogued file, "Kap'yong Remembered," 11.
77 DHH, 147.013(D4), Brigadier K.A. Hunter and Colonel J.E. Andrew, "The RCAMC and the Korean War," 9.
78 NA, RG24 acc. 83-84/048, box 5210, file 3701-151/25, part 2, "Medical Arrangements – CASF – 1951–1953," Brigadier J.W. Bishop, Acting Adjutant-General, to Brigadier W.L. Coke, Director General of Medical Services, 11 Oct. 1951.
79 Ibid. The seemingly high number of Canadian battle-exhaustion casualties may have also been a reflection of the practice of repatriating cases directly to Canada
80 NA, RG24, WD, No. 25 FDS, "Monthly Psychiatric Report – September 1952," 1.
81 Interview with Paul Tomelin, Calgary, Aug. 1996.
82 See Copp and McAndrew, *Battle Exhaustion*.
83 Holmes, *Firing Line*, 265–9.
84 DHH, 147.013(D4), Hunter and Andrew, "The RCAMC and the Korean War," 9.

85 Holmes, *Firing Line*, 258.
86 DHH, 147.013(D4), Hunter and Andrew, "The RCAMC and the Korean War," 9.
87 NA, RG24, WD, No. 25 FDS, "Monthly Psychiatric Report – August 1953," 1–2.
88 Judge Advocate General, Court Martial Charge Cards and Court Martial Ledger, "Korea," kindly supplied to the author by Dr Chris Madsen, Canadian Forces College, Toronto.
89 Public Record Office (hereafter PRO), War Office (WO) 216/515, "Adjutant-General Report, 1 Commonwealth Division," no date, 3.
90 NA, RG24, WD, 1 RCR, "Monthly Report, Battle Adjutant, 1 RCR, 1–31 October 1952," 6. Officially, there was only one SIW in the battalion during this period, but there were probably at least three others. All involved gunshot wounds to the hands or legs.
91 John Richardson, quoted in Hepenstall, *Find the Dragon*, 322.
92 DHH, 112.009(D87), "Report by Lt-Col Bult-Francis," 11.
93 Ibid.
94 PRO, WO216/515, "Adjutant-General Report, 1 Commonwealth Division," 1.
95 Ibid., 2–3.
96 The available Canadian casualty lists clearly do not support the conclusion that 18 percent of all wounds were self-inflicted.
97 PRO, WO216/515, "Adjutant-General Report, 1 Commonwealth Division," 2–3.
98 25th Brigade vernacular for a shirker or coward.

CHAPTER SEVEN

1 NA, RG24, "Casualty Statement, 5 December 1952."
2 No Canadian soldiers are officially listed as missing in Korea.
3 NA, RG24, 18,502, 133(D4), "Statistical Report on Battle Casualties (Far East), 4 February 1955."
4 DHH, 79/704, "Canadian Army, Fatal Casualties – Korean War."
5 NA, RG24, WD, 1 RCR, "Monthly Report, Battle Adjutant 1 RCR, 1–31 October 1952."
6 DHH, 79/704, "Canadian Army, Fatal Casualties."
7 This figure does not include the four KATCOM soldiers attached to the 3 RCR who were also killed.
8 NA, RG24, 18,502, 133(D4), "Statistical Report on Battle Casualties."

9 Wood, *Strange Battleground*, 185.
10 Ibid., 236. The seven RCR POWs are not included.
11 See Vance, *Objects of Concern*, 229–37.
12 DHH, 410B25.065(D9), "Prisoners of War – Korea," 1.
13 Ibid.
14 Ibid.
15 DHH, 410B25.065(D1), "Preliminary Report on Battle Casualties of the 25th CIB, 5 December 1951," 2.
16 The ratio of killed to wounded was found to be one to five during the first ten months of the Korean War as well.
17 DHH, 410B25.065(D1), "Preliminary Report on Battle Casualties," 2.
18 NA, RG24, 18,357, WD, 2 R22eR, Nov. 1951, "Casualty List for the Period 23 to 27 November."
19 Interview with Paul Tomelin, Aug. 1997.
20 NA, RG24, 18,357, WD, 2 R22ER, Nov. 1951, "Casualty List for the Period 23 to 27 November."
21 This figure does not include psychiatric or KSC casualties.
22 NA, RG24, WD, 1 RCR, Oct. 1952, "Monthly Report, 1 RAP RCR."
23 The film *Korea: Canada's Forgotten War*.
24 NA, RG24, WD, 1 RCR, Oct. 1952, "Monthly Report, 1 RAP RCR."
25 Ibid.
26 Ibid. As mentioned earlier, however, only one of these was officially classified as an SIW.
27 NA, RG24, WD, 1 RCR, Oct. 1952, "Monthly Report, 1 RAP RCR."
28 Peacock, *Kim-chi, Asahi, and Rum*, 78.
29 NA, RG24, WD, HQ 25th CIB, Feb. 1952, app. 20, "Notes on Body Armour in Korea," 1.
30 The 1 RCR war diary for October 1952 does not mention armoured vests, but it records the issue of steel helmets.
31 DHH, 410B25.013(D41), "Interview with Lt-Col Trudeau," 2.
32 NA, RG24, WD, HQ 25th CIB, Feb. 1952, app. 20, "Notes on Body Armour," 3.
33 Peacock, *Kim-chi, Asahi, and Rum*, 78.
34 Interview with anonymous soldier, Calgary, Aug. 1996.
35 DHH, 410B25.013(D57), "Interview with Lt-Col Campbell," 9.
36 Peacock, *Kim-chi, Asahi, and Rum*, 78–9.
37 Hepenstall, *Find the Dragon*, 325.
38 Caswell, "Medical Unit Completes Years's Service in Korea," 126.
39 Each soldier carried a sterile shell dressing in his pocket or looped through his rifle sling.

40 United States, Headquarters, Department of the Army, FM 21-11, *First Aid for Soldiers*, June 1976, 4.
41 Interview with D. Bateman, Calgary, Aug. 1996.
42 NA, RG24, 18,350, WD, 3 RCR, Mar. 1953, app. 12, "The Advance Regimental Aid Post in Static Warfare," 2.
43 Peacock, *Kim-chi, Asahi, and Rum*, 31.
44 NA, RG24, 18,350, WD, 3 RCR, Mar. 1953, app. 12, "The Advanced Regimental Aid Post," 2.
45 Ibid., 1.
46 Ibid., 8.
47 Interview with B.J. LeFrancois, Calgary, Aug. 1996.
48 NA, RG24, WD, No. 25 FDS, July 1952, app. 9, "Helicopter Evacuation of Casualties in Korea," 1.
49 PRO, WO281/27, WD, 1st Commonwealth Division, Aug. 1951, app. G, "Evacuation of Cases by Helicopter," 1.
50 Ibid., 2.
51 NA, RG24, WD, No. 25 FDS, July 1952, app. 9, "Helicopter Evacuation of Casualties," 4.
52 Ibid.
53 J.R. Stone, cited in Gardham, *Korea Volunteer*, 41.
54 Keith Besley, quoted in ibid., 43; DHH, 681.001(D1), "Report by Mr A.R. Menzies of the Department of External Affairs on His Impressions of His Visit to the 25th CIB in Korea, 12–17 October 1951," 11.
55 NA, RG24, 18,224, WD, Adjutant General Branch, Oct. 1952, app. A, "VAG Liaison Visit, Far East – Medical Aspects."
56 PPCLI Archives, 111(4)-1, Ray Dooley letter to parents, 23 Nov. 1952.
57 NA, RG24, 18,224, WD, Adjutant General Granch, Oct. 1952, app. A, "VAG Liaison Visit, Far East – Medical Aspects."
58 Ibid.
59 Ibid.
60 John Richardson, quoted in Hepenstall, *Find the Dragon*, 326.
61 Interview with anonymous soldier, Calgary, Aug. 1996.
62 NA, RG24 acc. 83-84/048, box 2153, file 5835-1, part 1, "Evacuation Policy – Korean Theatre of Operations, 23 May 1951," 1.
63 NA, RG24, Personnel Records Survey, file no. 73.
64 DHH, 79/704, "Canadian Army Fatal Casualties."
65 MacNalty and Mellor, *Medical Services in War*, 442.

66 Peacock, *Kim-chi, Asahi, and Rum*, 78.
67 NA, RG24, 18,247, WD, HQ 25th CIB, Jan. 1953, app. 37B, CAORT, "Burns and Fires in the 25th CIB," 514.
68 Peacock, *Kim-chi, Asahi, and Rum*, 78.
69 NA, RG24, 18,247, WD, HQ 25th CIB, Jan. 1953, app. 37B, CAORT, "Burns and Fires in the 25th CIB," 513.
70 Peacock, *Kim-chi, Asahi, and Rum*, 78.
71 NA, RG24, 18,247, WD, HQ 25th CIB, Jan. 1953, app. 37B, CAORT, "Burns and Fires in the 25th CIB," 513.
72 Peacock, *Kim-chi, Asahi, and Rum*, 78.
73 NA, RG24, 18,396, WD, No. 25 FDS, Monthly Progress Reports, Oct. 1951 to Jan. 1952.
74 NA, RG24, WD, 1 PPCLI, 9 Jan. 1952.
75 NA, RG24, 18,247, WD, HQ 25th CIB, Jan. 1953, app. 37B, CAORT, "Burns and Fires in the 25th CIB," 510.
76 Ibid., 514.
77 Ibid.
78 This does not include official-issue stoves improperly fuelled by gasoline.
79 NA, RG24, 18,247, WD, HQ 25th CIB, Jan. 1953, app. 37B, CAORT, "Burns and Fires in the 25th CIB," 514.
80 Ibid.
81 DHH, 147-013(D4), Hunter and Andrew, "The RCAMC and the Korean War," 12.
82 Ibid.
83 NA, RG24, 18,247, WD, HQ 25th CIB, Jan. 1953, app. 37B, CAORT, "Burns and Fires in the 25th CIB," 515.
84 Ibid.
85 NA, RG24, WD, No. 25 FDS, Monthly Progress Reports, Jan. to Mar. 1953.

CHAPTER EIGHT

1 DHH, 147.013(D4), Hunter and Andrew, "The RCAMC and the Korean War," 7.
2 DHH, WO, *Handbook of Army Health*, 1.
3 NA, RG24, acc. 83-84/167, box 5210, file 3701-151/24, "Medical Arrangements – CASF, part 1."
4 DHH, 419FE.009(D4), "Sitreps by 25th CIB," 3.
5 DHH, 145.2P7013(D6), "Reports by Lt-Col Stone," 3.

6 Wood, *Strange Battleground*, 63. Stone survived his bout with smallpox and returned to duty after a short convalescence.
7 NA, RG24, acc. 83-84/167, box 5210, file 3701-151/24, "Medical Arrangements – CASF, Part 1," 1.
8 NA, RG24, acc. 83-84/048, box 977, file 3105-151/25, "Statistics – Korea, 20 March 1951."
9 NA, RG24, WD, No. 25 FDS, June 1950 to Dec. 1953.
10 Interview with Clyde Bougie, Calgary, Aug. 1996.
11 MacNalty and Mellor, *Medical Services in War*, 523.
12 DHH, 147.013(D4), Hunter and Andrew, "The RCAMC and the Korean War," 9. It is not possible to compare the hepatitis rates in the various Commonwealth contingents because the divisional statistics normally placed cases in the "Other" infectious disease category.
13 NA, RG24, WD, No. 25 FDS, Monthly Progress Reports, "Breakdown of Morbidity," Sept. 1951 to Dec. 1953.
14 MacNalty and Mellor, *Medical Services in War*, 523.
15 PRO, WO281/888, 1st Commonwealth Division, Monthly Liaison Letter, June 1953, app. A, 1.
16 Grauwin, *Doctor at Dienbienphu*, 174.
17 The existing documentary evidence does not contain statistics on how many Canadians actually died after contracting hepatitis B during the Korean War. One estimate puts the number at five.
18 MacNalty and Mellor, *Medical Services in War*, 486.
19 Ibid.
20 DHH, 147.013(D4), Hunter and Andrew, "The RCAMC and the Korean War," 8.
21 Ibid. The British also reported a small number of breakthrough cases.
22 DHH, 147.013(D4), Hunter and Andrew, "The RCAMC and the Korean War," 8.
23 PRO, WO218/887, ADMS 1st Commonwealth Division, Monthly Reports, Sept. 1951 to July 1953; DHH, 147.013(D4), Hunter and Andrew, "The RCAMC and the Korean War," 8.
24 Interview with Ted Smyth, Calgary, Aug. 1996.
25 The difficulties experienced by Canadian medical planners in securing reliable malaria maps is partially to blame for the epidemic in the 1st Canadian Division in Sicily.
26 Interview with Clyde Bougie, Aug. 1996.
27 DHH, 147.013(D4), Hunter and Andrew, "The RCAMC and the Korean War," 8; Peacock, *Kim-chi, Asahi, and Rum*, 43.

28 NA, RG24, 18,225, WD, Branch of the Adjutant General, Sept. 1950, app. A.
29 DHH, 147.013(D4), Hunter and Andrew, "The RCAMC and the Korean War," 8.
30 See PRO, WO218/887, ADMS 1st Commonwealth Division, Monthly Reports, Apr. 1952 to Aug. 1953.
31 Hackworth, *About Face*, 484.
32 NA, RG24, acc. 83-84/167, box 5210, file 3701-151/24, "Medical Arrangements – CASF – Part 1."
33 NA, RG24, WD, No. 25 FDS, Monthly Progress Report, Oct. 1953, 4.
34 NA, MG31, G12, Rockingham, "Recollections of Korea," 57.
35 NA, RG24, WD, No. 25 FDS, Monthly Progress Report, Nov. 1951, 1.
36 NA, RG24, acc. 83-84/167, box 5216, file 3760-EHF, "Epidemic Haemorrhagic Fever," 1.
37 NA, RG24, WD, 1 PPCLI, 4 Jan. 1952.
38 Earl Richardson, quoted in Hepenstall, *Find the Dragon*, 320.
39 DHH, 79/704, "Canadian Army, Fatal Casualties."
40 PRO, WO281/888, ADMS 1st Commonwealth Division Monthly Liaison Letter, for the four-week period 28 June to 31 Aug. 1952, 6.
41 George Elliot, quoted in Hepenstall, *Find the Dragon*, 320.
42 NA, RG24, acc. 83-84/167, box 5210, file 3701-151/25, "Medical Problems – Korea, December 1950," 1.
43 Grey, *The Commonwealth Armies and the Korean War*, 150-3.
44 NA, RG24, 18,325, WD, 3 PPCLI, May 1953, app. 3, "Rodent Control," 2-3.
45 Ibid., 2.
46 NA, RG24, WD, No. 25 FDS, Monthly Progress Reports, Sept. to July 1953.
47 NA, RG24, acc. 83-84/048, box 977, file 3105-151/25, "Statistics – Korea."
48 Morton, *When Your Number's Up*, 200.
49 DHH, 112.009(D95), "CASF Statistics as of 31 March 1952," app. D.
50 DHH, 76/14, J. Eastcott and K.W. Smillie, Defence Research Board Operational Research Memorandum No. 26, "A Statistical Investigation of Venereal Disease Incidence within the 25th CIB, October 1952."
51 DHH, 112.3W1013(D13), CAORT, "Notes on Operational Research in Korea, 18 April 1952," 13.
52 DHH, 76/14, Eastcott and Smillie, "A Statistical Investigation," app. A.

53 As NSU is a form of urethritis for which the presence of a specific virus or bacillus has not been detected, it is often excluded from VD rates. See Elliot and Ryz, *Venereal Diseases*, 58–9.
54 DHH, 76/14, Eastcott and Smillie, "A Statistical Investigation," 2. If cases of NSU are included in the calculation of VD rates, the margin between Canadian and British figures increases considerably.
55 DHH, 76/14, Eastcott and Smillie, "A Statistical Investigation," 2.
56 According to CAORT reports, the incidence of VD amongst the civilian population of the Far East was much higher than that of Europeans.
57 NA, RG24, acc. 83-84/048, box 977, file 3105-151/25, "Statistics – Korea," 1.
58 DHH, 76/14, Eastcott and Smillie, "A Statistical Investigation," 2.
59 NA, RG24, acc. 83-84/048, box 977, file 3105-151/25, "Statistics – Korea," 1.
60 Burns Sexton, quoted in Hepenstall, *Find the Dragon*, 48.
61 Wood, *The Private War of Jacket Coates*, 105. David Bercuson claimed that Wood's novel had "all the colour and atmosphere that *Strange Battleground* is lacking, and tells the story that Wood dared not write in the official history." See Granatstein and Bercuson, *War and Peacekeeping*, 105.
62 DHH, 76/14, Eastcott and Smillie, "A Statistical Investigation," 4.
63 Ibid., 2.
64 R&R leave was not chargeable against annual leave.
65 Interview with anonymous soldier, Hull, July 1997.
66 Ibid.
67 PPCLI Archives, uncatalogued file, "R&R Leave."
68 "Wide Open City of Sin," *Winnipeg Free Press*, 18 Dec. 1952, 23.
69 Interview with David Cathcart, Calgary, Aug. 1996.
70 Wood, *The Private War of Jacket Coates*, 104.
71 Hepenstall, *Find the Dragon*, 291–2.
72 Chester Nalewajik, quoted in ibid., 294.
73 DHH, 112.009(D87), "Report by Lt-Col Bult-Francis," 6. The DRB report found that VD rates among the Japanese were ten times those of North Americans.
74 DHH, 76/14, Eastcott and Smillie, "A Statistical Investigation," annex. B.
75 Ibid.
76 Elliot and Ryz, *Venereal Diseases*, 44–5.
77 Ibid., 46.

78 DHH, 76/14, Eastcott and Smillie, "A Statistical Investigation," annex. B.
79 Elliot and Ryz, *Venereal Diseases*, 59.
80 Ibid., 60.
81 DHH, 76/14, Eastcott and Smillie, "A Statistical Investigation," 2.
82 NA, RG24, acc. 83-84/048, box 977, file 3105-151/25, "Statistics – Korea," 1.
83 Ibid.
84 DHH, 410.B25.059(D1), "VD Treatment Policy, 13 July 1951," 1; Hazel and Ryz, *Venereal Diseases*, 72.
85 DHH, 410.B25.059(D1), "VD Treatment Policy," 1.
86 Ibid.
87 DHH, 147.013(D4), Hunter and Andrew, "The RCAMC and the Korean War," 8.
88 DHH, Lt-Gen G.G. Simonds to Minister of National Defence Brooke Claxton, 2 Sept. 1952
89 NA, RG24, acc. 83-84/048, box 977, file 3105-151/25, "Statistics – Korea," 2.
90 NA, MG31, G12, Rockingham, "Recollections of Korea," 78. Commenting on the obvious illegality of the order, Rockingham stated, "Who was to argue with me?"
91 PRO, WO281/887, 1st Commonwealth Division Monthly Liaison Letter, Sept. 1952, app. F, "VD Rates Monthly," 1.
92 Hepenstall, *Find the Dragon*, 261-2.
93 NA, RG24, 18,224, WD, Adjutant General Branch, Oct. 1952, app. A, "VAG Liaison Visit, Far East – Medical Aspects," 2.
94 Anonymous soldier, quoted in Hepenstall, *Find the Dragon*, 262.
95 PRO, WO281/888, 1st Commonwealth Division Monthly Liaison Letter, Dec. 1952, app. D, 3.
96 MacNalty and Mellor, *Medical Services in War*, 501.
97 PPCLI Archives, "2 PPCLI Basic Rifle Wing Block Syllabus."
98 NA, RG24, 18,224, WD, Adjutant General Branch, Nov. 1952, "VD – Far East," 1.
99 DHH, 112.3W1013(D13), CAORT, "Notes on Operational Research in Korea," 3.
100 See, for example, the discussion of VD treatment in DHH, WO, *Handbook of Army Health*.
101 PRO, WO281/887, 1st Commonwealth Division, "VD Treatment, 16 October 1952," 1.
102 PRO, WO281/887, Col G.L. Morgan Smith, ADMS 1st Commonwealth Division, to Commander, 25th CIB, 16 Oct. 1952, 2.

103 PRO, WO281/887, 1st Commonwealth Division, "VD Treatment," 1.
104 DHH, WO, *Handbook of Army Health*, 84.
105 NA, RG24, WD, 1 PPCLI, Oct. 1952, app. 56, Routine Daily Order part 1, 27 Oct., 4.
106 NA, RG24, 18,441, WD, Canadian Military Mission Far East, Feb. 1954, app. 1, "PAC Instructions."
107 It is not clear why the Canadians took so long to learn from the British and Australian examples. It may be, as Jeffrey Grey suggested, that the Canadians tended to keep to themselves and avoided direct liaison with other Commonwealth officers at divisional headquarters. See Grey, *The Commonwealth Armies and the Korean War*, 151.
108 NA, RG24, acc. 83-84/167, box 4903, file 3125-33/29, "Welfare Facilities in the Far East, 5 December 1952," 2.
109 The vice-adjutant general, Brig-Gen J.W. Bishop, believed that the high Canadian VD rate could largely be attributed "to men who had no intention whatsoever of getting themselves into trouble but did not realize the effect of the surroundings to which they were exposed." See NA, RG24, 18,224, WD, Adjutant General Branch, Nov. 1952, "VD – Far East," 2.
110 DHH, 112.009(D87), "Report by Lt-Col Bult-Francis," 5.
111 PRO, WO281/888, 1st Commonwealth Division Monthly Liaison Letter, July 1953, app. C, 3.
112 DHH, 147.013(D4), Hunter and Andrew, "The RCAMC and the Korean War," 13.

CHAPTER NINE

1 The disparity in living conditions between the soldiers of the 25th Brigade and those of the 27th Brigade in Germany was even greater. An Adjutant-General's Report noted: "The brigade in Germany can make use of civilian facilities in adjacent towns. Further, living conditions, such as tents, services and climate compare very unfavourably with those in Germany where modern barrack accommodation, services and heat are provided. Further, the serviceman in Korea is separated from his dependants whereas elsewhere dependants can, or will in the very near future, accompany the servicemen. Further, there is a constant tension created by the continuous standing-to in battle position to fend off a possible attack. The hazards to health are far greater in this primitive Asiatic country than in Western

Europe. Further, there is no contact with people and customs of the Western civilization." See NA, RG24, 4904, 3125-33/29, part 6, "Welfare Facilities in the Far East, 13 January 1954," 2.
2 Ellis, *The Sharp End of War*, 275.
3 Ibid.
4 Peacock, *Kim-chi, Asahi, and Rum*, 89.
5 Levenstein, *Paradox of Plenty*, 94.
6 DHH, 145.2R13019(D1), "Summary of Experiences – 3 RCR." Also see DHH, 681.001(D1), "Report by Mr A.R. Menzies," 16.
7 Peacock, *Kim-chi, Asahi, and Rum*, 89.
8 Interview with anonymous soldier, Calgary, Aug. 1996.
9 PPCLI Archives, uncatalogued file, "Kap'yong Remembered," 28.
10 Peacock, *Kim-chi, Asahi, and Rum*, 89.
11 John Richardson, quoted in Hepenstall, *Find the Dragon*, 151.
12 NA, RG24 acc. 83-84/167, box 4912, file 3127-33/29, part 1, "Purchase of Pipes and Tobacco, January 1951."
13 Peacock, *Kim-chi, Asahi, and Rum*, 90.
14 Ibid.
15 Earl Richardson, quoted in Hepenstall, *Find the Dragon*, 152.
16 Ellis, *The Sharp End of War*, 281-2.
17 DHH, 145.2R13013(D2), Memorandum, Historical Section, Army Headquarters, Ottawa, 18 Jan. 1952, 7.
18 NA, MG31, G12, Rockingham, "Recollections of Korea," 19. Local vegetables were considered unsafe.
19 Peacock, *Kim-chi, Asahi, and Rum*, 89.
20 Eighth U.S. Army Historical Office, Franklin Papers.
21 DHH, 145.2R13019(D1), "Summary of Experiences – 3 RCR," 5.
22 Hackworth, *About Face*, 172-3.
23 NA, MG31, G12, Rockingham, "Recollections of Korea," 53.
24 NA, RG24, WD, 1 PPCLI, May 1952, app. A, "What You May See in Korea," 1.
25 DHH, 112.3M2(D410), "Equipment, General, 25th CIB, Volume 1."
26 Bill Boss, "PPCLI Engage in Hard Training," *Calgary Herald*, 22 Jan. 1951, 2.
27 NA, RG24, WD, 1 PPCLI, May 1952, "Q Notes."
28 Ibid.
29 NA, RG24, WD, 2 PPCLI, 19 Feb. 1951.
30 NA, RG24, WD, 1 PPCLI, May 1952, "Q Notes."
31 NA, MG31, G12, Rockingham, "Recollections of Korea," 14.
32 DHH, 79/704, "Canadian Army, Fatal Casualties."

33 Interview with George Cook, June 1994.
34 Higham Papers, in possession of author.
35 Eighth U.S. Army Historical Office, Franklin Papers, "Korea Outdoor Plumbing."
36 Ibid.
37 Ibid.
38 Weir, "Sandbag Redoubt Defended," 70. Weir was a public information NCO with the U.S. Army in Korea.
39 Ibid., 71.
40 Hepenstall, *Find the Dragon*, 134, 170.
41 Peacock, *Kim-chi, Asahi, and Rum*, 21.
42 John Richardson, quoted in Hepenstall, *Find the Dragon*, 135.
43 Peacock, *Kim-chi, Asahi, and Rum*, 88.
44 Weir, "Sandbag Redoubt Defended" 71.
45 Earl Richardson, quoted in Hepenstall, *Find the Dragon*, 321.
46 NA, RG24, WD, No. 25 FDS, Monthly Reports, Oct. 1952 to July 1953.
47 NA, RG24, WD, I PPCLI, May 1952, app. A, "What You May See in Korea," 1.
48 Peacock, *Kim-chi, Asahi, and Rum*, 56.
49 Ibid.
50 NA, RG24, WD, I PPCLI, 22 Nov. 1951.
51 Dan Johnson, quoted in Hepenstall, *Find the Dragon*, 68.
52 John Richardson, quoted in ibid., 162.
53 Interview with David Cathcart, Calgary, Aug. 1996.
54 Wood, *Strange Battleground*, 139.
55 DHH, 112.009(D87), "Report by Lt-Col Bult-Francis," 5.
56 NA, RG24, acc. 83-84/167, box 4903, file 3125-33/29, "Welfare – Far East, 25 September 1952," 1.
57 NA, RG24, acc. 83-84/167, box 4903, file 3125-33/29, "Report by Dr Stanby of the Canadian Red Cross on His Visit to the Far East, 26 April to 9 May 1952," 3.
58 NA, RG24, acc. 83-84/167, box 4903-4904, file 3125-33/29, part 4, "Welfare Amenities, Equipment and Supplies Sent to the Far East during the Past Three Years, 29 July 1953," 2.
59 DHH, 410B25.013(D57), "Interview with Lt-Col Campbell," 10.
60 NA, RG24, acc. 83-84/167, box 4914, file 3128-33/29, part 1, "Concert Parties for Troops Overseas, 13 May 1952," 1.
61 John Berwent, quoted in Hepenstall, *Find the Dragon*, 152.

62 NA, RG24, acc. 83-84/167, box 4914, file 3128-33/29, part 1, "Concert Parties for Troops Overseas," 1.
63 NA, RG24, acc. 83-84/167, box 4914, file HQ3128-33/29, part 1, "Canadian Concert Party – Cammie Howard, 1 July 1952," 1.
64 Ibid.
65 Ibid.
66 NA, RG24, acc. 83-84/167, box 4903-4904, file 3125-33/29, part 4, "Welfare Canadian Forces – Far East, 1 November 1952," 3.
67 Ibid.
68 NA, RG24, 19,074, 1675-151/25, "Postal Inspection Trip – Far East, 2 October 1952," 19.
69 DHH, 112.009(D87), "Report by Lt-Col Bult-Francis," 23.
70 Ibid.
71 Eighth U.S. Army Historical Office, Ray Dooley, letters to parents, 18 Oct. and 23 Nov. 1951; 20 Feb. and 29 July 1952.

CHAPTER TEN

1 See, for example, DHH, 410B25.013(D57), "Interview with Lt-Col Campbell," 10; and, NA, RG24, acc. 83-84/167, box 4903, file 3125-33/24, "Welfare Canadian Troops in Korea, 27 October 1951," 2.
2 DHH, 145.2P7013(D6), "Notes on Talk Given by Lt-Col Stone on Activities of 2 PPCLI in Korea, 5 June 1951," 6.
3 NA, RG24, acc. 83-83/167, box 4903, file 3125-33/29, "Welfare in the Canadian Army, 13 November 1952," 1.
4 DHH, 410B25.069(D1), "Rotation Policy File of 25th CIB, 1951," 2.
5 DHH, 410B25.013(D53), "Interview with Lt-Col Poulin," 4; DHH, 410B25.0033(D5), Pope, "Infantry Patrolling in Korea," 1–2.
6 PPCLI Archives, uncatalogued file, "Brief Respecting 25th CIB in Korea," 2.
7 DHH, 112.009(D87), "Report by Lt-Col Bult-Francis," 5.
8 Ibid.
9 NA, RG24, acc. 83-84/167, box 4903, file 3125-33/29, "Talk with Capt Fenny on Welfare in Far East, 21 May 1952," 2.
10 DHH, 145.2R13019(D1), "Summary of Experiences – 3 RCR," 13.
11 Interview with Don Urquhart, Calgary, Aug. 1996.
12 PPCLI Archives, uncatalogued file, "R&R Leave."
13 DHH, 112.009(D87), "Report by Lt-Col Bult-Francis," 6.

14 W.R. Newton, quoted in Hepenstall, *Find the Dragon*, 294.
15 Wood, *Strange Battleground*, 141.
16 See Hanson, *The Western Way of War*.
17 Interview with Gerrard Ratchford, Calgary, Aug. 1996.
18 Wood, *The Private War of Jacket Coates*, 52.
19 Peacock, *Kim-chi, Asahi, and Rum*, 5.
20 See NA, RG24, acc. 83-84/167, box 5767, file 5503-Rum, letter from Maj Gen S.F. Clark to Dr O.M. Solandt, 6 Dec. 1950.
21 NA, RG24, acc. 83-84/167, box 5767, file 5503-Rum, "Physiological and Psychological Effects of Single Doses of Ethyl Alcohol (Rum), 21 December 1950."
22 Ibid., 2.
23 Ibid.
24 Peacock, *Kim-chi, Asahi, and Rum*, 57.
25 Interview with David Cathcart, Aug. 1996.
26 NA, RG24, WD, 2 PPCLI, 21 February 1951.
27 NA, RG24, acc. 83-84/167, box 5767, file 5503-Rum, "Issue of Rum, 6 November 1951."
28 Wood, *Strange Battleground*, 203.
29 Interview with Paul Tomelin, Kelowna, Aug. 1997.
30 NA, RG24, WD, E Company 1 RCR, 10–31 Oct. 1952.
31 NA, RG24, WD, 1 RCR, 10–15 Oct. 1952.
32 Interview with Louis McLean, Aug. 1996.
33 Interview with William Powell, Aug. 1996.
34 DHH, 410B25.013(D53), "Summary of Experiences – 3 R22eR," 11.
35 Peacock, *Kim-chi, Asahi, and Rum*, 56.
36 Hepenstall, *Find the Dragon*, 254.
37 Interview with Bill Martin, Aug. 1996.
38 Interview with William Powell, Aug. 1996.
39 Ibid.
40 DHH, 410B25.013(D57), "Interview with Lt-Col Campbell," 10.
41 NA, RG24, acc. 83-84/167, box 4903, file 3125-33/29, "Talk with Capt Fenny," 2.
42 Interview with Henry Repay, Calgary, Aug. 1996.
43 Interview with James Wilson, Aug. 1996.
44 Peacock, *Kim-chi, Asahi, and Rum*, 56–7.
45 Interview with Clyde Bougie, Aug. 1996.
46 NA, RG24, WD, 1 PPCLI, May 1952, app. 46, "Operation of Officers' Mess in Korea," 2.
47 Hepenstall, *Find the Dragon*, 209.

48 Peacock, *Kim-chi, Asahi, and Rum*, 82.
49 Ibid.
50 Pare Vik, quoted in Hepenstall, *Find the Dragon*, 209.
51 Porch, *The French Foreign Legion*, 135.
52 PPCLI Archives, uncatalogued file, "Temporary Receipt of Artifacts – Korea."
53 Interview with J.R. Stone, Nov. 1994.
54 Madsen, "The Canadian Army and the Maltreatment of Civilians: The Korean Example." The author thanks Dr Madsen for sharing his courts martial records from the Korean War.
55 It was also known as "tiger's piss."
56 Peacock, *Kim-chi, Asahi, and Rum*, 57.
57 NA, RG24, 18,342, WD, 2 RCR, 4 July 1951, Part One Orders.
58 Peacock, *Kim-chi, Asahi, and Rum*, 87.
59 NA, RG24, WD, 2 PPCLI, 18 Mar. 1951.
60 PPCLI Archives, uncatalogued file, "Kap'yong Remembered," 14. Canned heat, or methyl alcohol, was used to heat rations.
61 NA, RG24, WD, 2 PPCLI, 18 Mar. 1951.
62 Ibid.
63 See, for example, DHH, 145.2P7013(D6), "Reports by Lt-Col Stone."
64 NA, dossier survey conducted by the author, Personnel file no. 264.
65 Interview with William Powell, Aug. 1996.
66 Interview with Don Hibbs, Calgary, Aug. 1996.
67 DHH, 410B25.059(D1), CAORT, "Preliminary Report on Crime Casualties in the 25th CIB, 14 February 1952," 5.
68 Ibid.
69 Madsen, "The Canadian Army."
70 DHH, 410B25.059(D1), CAORT, "Crime Casualties," 4.
71 Ibid.
72 Ibid., 5.
73 Ibid., 4.
74 PPCLI Archives, uncatalogued file, "A Day in the Life of a Detainee," 2.
75 Ibid.
76 Ibid.
77 Jim Holland, quoted in Gardham, *Korea Volunteer*, 141.
78 Gordon Duholke, quoted in Hepenstall, *Find the Dragon*, 255.
79 Peacock, *Kim-chi, Asahi, and Rum*, 119.
80 DHH, 681,001(D1), "Report by Mr A.R. Menzies," 4.

81 Ibid.
82 Ibid.
83 Madsen, "The Canadian Army," table 2.
84 See Ibid.
85 Ibid.
86 Ibid.
87 Dick Pucci, quoted in Hepenstall, *Find the Dragon*, 262- 3.
88 Madsen, "The Canadian Army."
89 DHH, 122.009(D95), "Memorandum from the Adjutant General to the CGS, 22 August 1952," 2.
90 Three of these occurred on 17 March 1951.
91 Madsen, "The Canadian Army," table 2.
92 Ibid.
93 The National Defence Act replaced the King's Regulations in July 1951.
94 Peacock, *Kim-chi, Asahi, and Rum*, 120.
95 Ibid.
96 Bercuson, *Significant Incident*, 51.
97 DHH, 122.009(D95), "Memorandum from the Adjutant General," 2.
98 Interview with George Thwaites, Calgary, Aug. 1996.

CONCLUSION

1 Interview with Robert Molesworth, Calgary, Aug. 1996.
2 Dan Johnson, quoted in Hepenstall, *Find the Dragon*, 340.
3 Interview with Bill Nasby, Aug. 1996.
4 Interview with anonymous soldier, Calgary, Aug. 1996.
5 Interview with Harry Repay, Aug. 1996.
6 Interview with Louis Vincent MacLean, Aug. 1996.
7 Interview with Robert Molesworth, Aug. 1996.
8 Interview with George Thwaites, Aug. 1996.
9 Interview with Kenneth Blampied, Aug. 1996.
10 Interview with James Morice, Aug. 1996.
11 Ken Blair, quoted in Hepenstall, *Find the Dragon*, 344.
12 Department of Veterans Affairs, DVA press release, "Korea Volunteer Medal."
13 Stevens, *Royal Canadian Regiment*, 275.
14 DHH, 410B25.013(D52), "Interview with Lt-Col H.W. Stern, 81 Field Regiment, RCHA," 4.

15 Bercuson, *Blood on the Hills*, 225.
16 NA, RG24, acc. 83-84/048, box 977, file 3105-151/25, "Statistics – Korea."
17 Stairs, *The Diplomacy of Constraint*, xi.
18 Wood, *Strange Battleground*, ix.

Bibliography

PRIMARY SOURCES

Archives

DIRECTORATE OF HISTORY AND HERITAGE, NATIONAL DEFENCE HEADQUARTERS, OTTAWA

Canadian Army Manual of Training. *Infantry Training, Part 1: The Infantry Battalion.* 1944
- *Infantry Training, Part 4: The Mortar Platoon.* 1944
- *Infantry Training, Part 8: Field Craft, Battle Drill, Section and Platoon Tactics.* 1944
- Military Training Pamphlet no. 23. *Operations, Part 2: Defence.* 1939 (91/251)
- Military Training Pamphlet no. 37. *The Training of an Infantry Battalion.* 1940
- Notes from Theatres of War no. 20. *Italy, 1943/1944.* 1944
War Diary, 27th British Commonwealth Infantry Brigade
War Office. *Handbook of Army Health.* 1950

The Directorate of History and Heritage currently holds a large number of documents relating to Canadian involvement in the Korean War that are awaiting transfer to the National Archives of Canada. They are not organized on a record group basis.

EIGHTH U.S. ARMY HISTORICAL OFFICE, YONGSAN GARRISON, SEOUL, REPUBLIC OF KOREA

Files relating to Eighth U.S. Army's participation in the Korean War, 1950–53

NATIONAL ARCHIVES OF CANADA, OTTAWA

RG24 Army Central Registry Files
RG24 Army War Diaries, 1950–53
MG31 Manuscript Collection
G12 Recollections of Korea by Brigadier-General J.M. Rockingham

OFFICE OF THE JUDGE ADVOCATE GENERAL, OTTAWA

Court martial charge cards
Court martial ledger, "Korea"
The author wishes to thank Dr Chris Madsen for sharing these files.

PRINCESS PATRICIA'S CANADIAN LIGHT INFANTRY ARCHIVES, CURRIE BARRACKS, CALGARY

Box 130-1 to 134-3, the Princess Patricia's Canadian Light Infantry in Korea
Canadian Army Manual of Training. *Training for War.* 1950
– *Infantry Training – Tactics.* Vol. 2: *The Infantry Battalion in Battle.* 1952 (UD163.15)
– *Infantry Training – Tactics.* Vol. 4: *Infantry Section Leading and Platoon Tactics.* 1950 (UD325.15)
Papers and Letters of Private Ray Dooley
Papers of B.A.J. Franklin
Papers of Walter O. Holt
PPCLI scrapbook. 1950. Vol. 1.
PPCLI scrapbook – Korea. 1951. Vols. 1 and 2
USS *Private Joe P. Martinez*, Daily Bulletin: "The Eagle-Leaf," November–December 1950

PRIVATE COLLECTION OF AUTHOR

Papers and photographs of E.A. Higham

PUBLIC RECORD OFFICE, LONDON, ENGLAND

All War Office files used in this work were kindly supplied to the author by Professor David J. Bercuson.

Published Documents

Canada. Department of External Affairs. *Annual Reports*. Ottawa: King's Printer, 1950
- *Canada and the Korean Crisis*. Ottawa: King's Printer, 1950
- *External Affairs* (monthly). Ottawa: King's Printer, 1950
- *Statements and Speeches*. Ottawa: King's Printer, 1950

Canada. House of Commons. *Debates*. 1950. Vol. 4

United States. Headquarters, Department of the Army. *FM21-11, First Aid for Soldiers*. Washington, D.C.: Department of Defense, 1976

Newspapers

Calgary Herald
Globe and Mail
Halifax Chronicle-Herald
Montreal Daily Star
Ottawa Evening Citizen
Vancouver Sun
Winnipeg Free Press

CORRESPONDENCE AND INTERVIEWS

I am grateful to the following veterans for their information and assistance. A number of veterans who assisted in the preparation of this work have requested anonymity.

Correspondence

Don Hibbs, letter, November 1995
A.T. Lynch, letter, December 1994
H. Rollinson, letter, January 1995

Interviews

Unless otherwise indicated, all interviews were conducted by the author or Mr Bruce McIntyre in August 1996 during the KVA annual reunion in Calgary, Alberta.

J.D. Atkinson
D. Bateman

Frank Bayne
Kenneth John Blampied
Clyde Bougie
Stanley Carmichael
David Cathcart
Choi In Wa, Naech'on, Republic of Korea, 10 October 1997
George Cook, Kelowna, British Columbia, 24 June 1994
J. Ralph DeCoste
W.H. Ellis
Paul Gauci
R.W. Granville
Hubert Gray
Don Hibbs
W. Hummer
William Martin Keil
William Lee
B.J. Le Francois
Joseph Leichester
Louis Vincent McLean
Bill Martin
Rod Middleton, Calgary, Alberta, 13 October 1994
J. Robert Molesworth
James W. Morrice
John Thomas Murray
Bill Nasby
John Pember
William Powell
Gerard L. Ratchford
Harry Repay
Henri St Laurent
Ted Smyth
F.J. Spicoluk
James R. Stone, Victoria, British Columbia, 8 November 1994
George Thwaites
Paul Tomelin, Kelowna, British Columbia, 12 August 1997
L.F. Trudeau
Don Urquhart
Lorne E. Warner
Ross Wilkes
R. James Wilson
Micheal Yandel, Kelowna, British Columbia, 17 November 1997

SECONDARY SOURCES

Allard, Jean V., with Serge Bernier. *The Memoirs of Jean V. Allard.* Vancouver: University of British Columbia Press, 1988
Appy, Christian. *Working-Class War: American Combat Soldiers and Vietnam.* Chapel Hill: University of North Carolina Press, 1993
Archer, Denis H.R., ed. *Jane's Infantry Weapons.* London: Paulton House, 1976
Ashworth, Tony. *Trench Warfare, 1914–1918: The Live and Let Live System.* London: Macmillan, 1980
Barclay, C.N. *The First Commonwealth Division: The Story of the British Commonwealth Land Forces in Korea, 1950– 1953.* London: Gale & Polden, 1954
Barris, Ted. *Deadlock in Korea: Canadians at War, 1950–1953.* Toronto: Macmillan, 1999
Beevor, Antony. *Inside the British Army.* London: Corgi Books, 1993
– *Stalingrad.* New York: Viking Penguin, 1998
Bercuson, David J. *Blood on the Hills: The Canadian Army in the Korean War.* Toronto: University of Toronto Press, 1999
– "Fighting the Defensive Battle on the Jamestown Line: The Canadians in Korea, November 1951." *Canadian Military History* 7, no. 3 (1998): 7–22
– *Significant Incident.* Toronto: McClelland & Stewart, 1996
– *True Patriot: The Life of Brooke Claxton, 1898–1960.* Toronto: University of Toronto Press, 1993
Bidwell, Shelford. *Modern Warfare.* London: Allen Lane, 1973
Blumenson, Captain Martin. "KATUSA." *Military Review,* August 1957, 51–6
Brereton, J.M. *The British Soldier.* London: Bodley Head, 1986
Brosseau, Lieutenant-Colonel B.L.P. "Notes from Korea: Medical Services." *Canadian Army Journal* 7, no. 1 (1953), 107–20
Cameron, Craig. *American Samurai: Myth, Imagination, and the Conduct of Battle in the First Marine Division, 1941– 51.* Cambridge: Cambridge University Press, 1994
Carew, Tim. *Korea: The Commonwealth at War.* London: Cox & Wyman, 1967
Caswell, Lieutenant-Colonel C.B. "Medical Unit Completes Year's Service in Korea." *Canadian Army Journal* 7, no. 1 (1953): 122–30
Chamberlain, Captain W.R. "Training the Functional Rifleman." *Canadian Army Journal* 4, no. 9 (1951): 25–30
Clark, Alan. *The Donkey's.* London: Hutchinson, 1961

Cohen, Eliot, and John Gooch. "Aggregate Failure: The Defeat of the American Eighth Army in Korea, November–December 1950." In *Military Misfortunes: The Anatomy of Failure in War*, 165–282. New York: Free Press, 1990

Copp, Terry. *The Anatomy of Poverty*. Toronto: McClelland & Stewart, 1974

Copp, Terry, and Bill McAndrew. *Battle Exhaustion: Soldiers and Psychiatrists in the Canadian Army, 1939–1945*. Montreal and Kingston: McGill-Queen's University Press, 1990

Costello, John. *Love, Sex, and War: Changing Values, 1939–1945*. London: Collins, 1985

Cummings, Bruce. *The Origins of the Korean War*. Vol. 1: *Liberation and the Emergence of Separate Regimes, 1945–1947*. Princeton: Princeton University Press, 1981

– *The Origins of the Korean War*. Vol. 2: *The Roaring Cataract, 1947–1950*. Princeton: Princeton University Press, 1990

Davis, James. *The Sharp End: A Canadian Soldier's Story*. Vancouver: Douglas & McIntyre, 1997

Directorate of Public Relations (Army). "The Patricias In Korea." *Canadian Army Journal* 5 (Jan. 1952): 14–25

Doary, Christopher. "Miniature Set-Piece Battles: Infantry Patrolling Operations in Korea, May–June 1952." *Canadian Military History* 6, no. 1 (1997): 20–33

Dower, John. *War without Mercy*. New York: Pantheon, 1986

Du Picq, Ardent. *Battle Studies: Ancient and Modern*. Translated by Colonel John Greely and Major Robert C. Cotton. New York: Macmillan, 1921

Dynes, Robert J. *The Lee: British Service Rifle from 1888 to 1950*. Bloomfield, Ont.: Museum Restoration Service, 1979

Edgerton, Robert. *Like Lions They Fought: The Zulu War and the Last Black Empire in South Africa*. New York: Free Press, 1988

Elliot, Hazel, and Kurt Ryz. *Venereal Diseases: Treatment and Nursing*. London: Bailliere and Tindall, 1972

Ellis, John. *On Infantry*. New York: Praeger, 1984

– *The Sharp End of War*. London: David and Charles, 1980

Farrar-Hockley, Anthony. *The British Part in the Korean War*. Vol. 1: *A Distant Obligation*. London: HMSO, 1990

– *The British Part in the Korean War*. Vol. 2: *An Honourable Discharge*. London: HMSO, 1995

Fox, Richard Allan. *Archaeology, History, and Custer's Last Battle: The Little Big Horn Reexamined*. Norman and London: University of Oklahoma Press, 1993

Gagnon, Jean-Pierre. *Le 22e Battalion (Canadien-Français), 1914–1918.* Quebec City: Les Presses de l'Université Laval, 1986

Gardam, John. *Korea Volunteer: An Oral History from Those Who Were There.* Burnstown, Ont.: General Store Publishing, 1994

Giesler, Patricia. *Valour Remembered: Canadians in Korea.* Ottawa: Veterans Affairs, 1982

Granatstein, J.L. "The American Influence on the Canadian Military, 1939–1963." Reprinted in *Canada's Defence,* ed. B.D. Hunt and R.G. Haycock. Toronto: Copp Clark Pitman, 1993

Granatstein, J.L., and David Bercuson. *War and Peacekeeping: From South Africa to the Gulf – Canada's Limited Wars.* Toronto: Key Porter, 1991

Grauwin, Paul. *Doctor at Dienbienphu.* New York: John Day, 1955

Graves, Donald. "Naked Truths for the Asking: Twentieth-Century Military Historians and the Battlefield Narrative." In *Military History and the Military Profession,* ed. David Charters et al. London: Praeger, 1992

Grey, Jeffrey. *The Commonwealth Armies and the Korean War.* Manchester: Manchester University Press, 1988

Griffith, Paddy. *Forward into Battle.* Sussex: Antony Bird, 1981

Hackworth, David. *About Face.* New York: Simon and Schuster, 1989

Hanson, Victor Davis. *The Western Way of War: Infantry Battle in Classical Greece.* Oxford: Oxford University Press, 1989

Hastings, Max. *The Korean War.* London: Michael Joseph, 1987

Hepenstall, Robert. *Find the Dragon: The Canadian Army in Korea, 1950–1953.* Edmonton: Four Winds Publishing, 1995

Hermes, Walter G. *Truce Tent and Fighting Front: The United States Army in the Korean War.* Washington, D.C.: Office of the Chief of Military History, United States Army, 1966

Historical Section, General Staff, Army Headquarters. *Canada's Army in Korea: The United Nations Operations, 1950–52, and Their Aftermath.* Ottawa: Queen's Printer, 1956

Hogg, Ian, and Rob Adam. *Jane's Guns Recognition Guide.* Glasgow: HarperCollins, 1996

Holmes, Richard. *Firing Line.* Harmondsworth, Middlesex: Penguin, 1985

Holmes, Richard, and John Keegan. *Soldiers: A History of Men in Battle.* New York: Viking Penguin, 1986

Johnston, William, and Stephen Harris. "The Post-war Army and the War in Korea." In *We Stand on Guard,* ed. John Marteinson. Montreal: Ovale, 1992

Keegan, John. *The Face of Battle.* London: Penguin, 1976

Lanning, Michael Lee, and Dan Cragg. *Inside the VC and NVA.* New York: Ballantine, 1992

Levenstein, Harvey. *Paradox of Plenty*. New York: Oxford University Press, 1994

Linderman, Gerald. *Embattled Courage: The Experience of Combat in the American Civil War*. New York: Free Press, 1987

Lotz, Jim. *Canadians at War*. London: Bison, 1990

Lowe, Peter. "The Origins of the Korean War: Civil War." In *Major Problems in American Foreign Policy. Vol. 2: Since 1914*, ed. Thomas Paterson. Lexington, Mass.: D.C. Heath, 1989

McAndrew, Bill. "The Soldier and the Battle." In *Military History and the Military Profession*, ed. David Charters et al. London: Praeger, 1992

McGibbon, Ian. *New Zealand and the Korean War. Vol. 2: Combat Operations*. Auckland: Oxford University Press, 1996

MacNalty, Arthur Salusbury, and W. Franklin Mellor. *Medical Services in War: Principal Lessons of the Second World War*. London: HMSO, 1968

Madsen, Chris. "The Canadian Army and the Maltreatment of Civilians: The Korean Example." Unpublished paper presented to the Qualicum History Conference, Qualicum, B.C., 5 Feb. 1994

Marshall, S.L.A. *Men against Fire*. New York: Morrow, 1947

– *The River and the Gauntlet: Defeat of the Eighth Army by the Chinese Communist Forces, November, 1950, in the Battle of the Chongchon River, Korea*. Westport, Conn.: Greenwood Press, 1953

Matray, James I. *Historical Dictionary of the Korean War*. New York: Greenwood Press, 1991

Melady, John. *Korea: Canada's Forgotten War*. Toronto: Macmillan, 1983

Miller, Carman. *Painting the Map Red: Canada and the South African War, 1899–1902*. Montreal and Kingston: McGill-Queen's University Press, 1993

Moran, Lord. *The Anatomy of Courage*. Boston: Houghton Mifflin, 1967 (American edition)

Morton, Desmond. *When Your Number's Up: The Canadian Soldier in the First World War*. Toronto: Random House, 1993

Morton, Desmond, and Glenn Wright. *Winning the Second Battle: Canadian Veterans and the Return to Civilian Life, 1915–1930*. Toronto: University of Torornto Press, 1987

Nicholson, G.W.L. *Canadian Expeditionary Force, 1914–1919: The Official History of the Canadian Army in the First World War*. Ottawa: Queen's Printer, 1964

O'Neill, Robert. *Australia in the Korean War, 1950–53. Vol. 1: Strategy and Diplomacy*. Canberra: Australian Government Publishing Service, 1981

– *Australia in the Korean War, 1950–53.* Vol. 2: *Combat Operations.* Canberra: Australian Government Publishing Service, 1985

Peacock, Robert S. *Kim-chi, Asahi, and Rum: A Platoon Commander Remembers Korea, 1952–1953.* Toronto: Lugus, 1994

Pearson, Lester B. *Mike: The Memoirs of the Right Honourable Lester B. Pearson.* Vol. 2: *1948–1957*, ed. John Munro and Alex Inglis. Toronto: University of Toronto Press, 1973

Peate, Less. "No Pay – No Uniforms – No Glory: A Salute to the 'Rice-Burners.'" *Esprit de Corps* 4, no. 5 (1997): 28–9

Pierson, Ruth Roach. *"They're Still Women After All": Canadian Womanhood in the Second World War.* Toronto: McClelland & Stewart, 1986

Porch, Douglas. *The French Foreign Legion.* New York: Harper, 1991

Pottle, Frederick. "The Teaching of Battle." *Yale Review*, March 1977, 423–5

Rawling, Bill. *Surviving Trench Warfare: Technology and the Canadian Corps, 1914–1918.* Toronto: University of Toronto Press, 1992

Reader's Digest. *The Tools of War, 1939–1945.* Toronto: Reader's Digest Association, 1969

Rennie, C.G. "Mobilization for War: Canadian Army Recruiting and the Korean Conflict." *Canadian Defence Quarterly*, Summer 1995, 43–62

Richardson, Frank. *Fighting Spirit.* London: Ovale, 1978

Ridgway, Mathew. *The Korean War.* New York: Doubleday, 1967

Ronksley, Major P., ed. PPCLI: *The First Seventy-Five Years.* Calgary: Regimental Headquarters, PPCLI, 1989

Schnabel, James. *Policy and Direction: The First Year. The Official History of the United States Army in the Korean War.* Vol. 3. Washington, D.C.: United States Government Printing Office for the Office of the Chief of Military History, United States Army, 1972

Sheppard, George. *Plunder, Profit, and Paroles: A Social History of the War of 1812 in Upper Canada.* Montreal and Kingston: McGill-Queen's University Press, 1994

Skaggs, David Kurtis. "The KATUSA Experiment: The Integration of Korean Nationals into the U.S. Army, 1950–1965." *Military Affairs*, April 1974, 53–8

Stacey, Charles P. *Six Years of War: The Official History of the Canadian Army in the Second World War.* Vol. 1: *The Army in Canada, Britain, and the Pacific.* Ottawa: Queen's Printer, 1955

Stairs, Dennis. *The Diplomacy of Constraint: Canada, the Korean War, and the United States.* Toronto: University of Toronto Press, 1974

Stanley, George F. *Canada's Soldiers: The Military History of an Unmilitary People*. Toronto: Macmillan, 1960

Stevens, G.R. *Princess Patricia's Canadian Light Infantry*. Vol. 3: 1919–1957. Montreal: Southam Printing, 1958

Royal Canadian Regiment. Vol. 2: 1933–1966. London, Ont.: London Printing, 1967

Stone, Colonel James R., and Jacques Castonguay. *Korea 1951: Two Canadian Battles*. Ottawa: Balmuir, 1988

Stouffer, Samual A. *The American Soldier*. Vol. 1: *Adjustment during Army Life*. Vol. 2: *Combat and Its Aftermath*. Princeton: Princeton University Press, 1949

Travers, Tim. *The Killing Grounds*. London: Unwin Hyman, 1987

Vance, Jonathan. *Objects of Concern: Canadian Prisoners of War Throughout the Twentieth Century*. Vancouver: University of British Columbia Press, 1994

War History Compilation Committee, The. *The History of the United Nations Forces in the Korean War*. Vol. 2. Seoul: Ministry of National Defence, Republic of Korea, 1973

Watson, Brent. "From Calgary to Kap'yong: The 2 PPCLI's Preparation for Battle in Korea, 1950–51." MA thesis, University of Victoria, 1995

– "Recipe for Victory: The Fight for Hill 677 during the Battle of the Kap'yong River, 24–25 April 1951." *Canadian Military History* 9, no. 2 (2000): 7–25

– "Tonight's the Night: The 25th Canadian Infantry Brigade Group and the Riot at Wainwright, 18 June 1951." *Prairie Forum* 25, no. 2 (2000): 233–43

Watson, Peter, *War on the Mind: The Military Uses and Abuses of Psychology*. London: Hutchinson, 1978

Weir, William. "Sandbag Redoubt Defended." *Military History*, October 1992

Winter, Denis. *Death's Men*. London: Penguin, 1978

Wood, Herbert Fairlie.*The Private War of Jacket Coates*. Don Mills, Ont.: Longmans, 1966

– *Strange Battleground: The Operations in Korea and Their Effects on the Defence Policy of Canada*. Ottawa: Queen's Printer, 1966

FILM

Korea: Canada's Forgotten War. The War Amps, 1991

Index

Advanced Regimental Aid Post (RAP), 115
air superiority, 89
alcohol, 48, 73, 159; abundance of, 165; black velvet, 167; drunkenness and excessive drinking, 166–70, 178; ill effects of, 100, 174; impact on morale, 160–9; impact on VD relapse rate, 136–7; "kickapoo joy juice," 66; poisoning, 167, 168; rum, 161–3, 164; "whisky patrols," 165
Allard, Brig. J.V., 29, 84, 86, 87
antibiotics, 125, 137, 138
armoured vests. See equipment
artillery, x; U.N., 89
Ashworth, Tony, 95
Australian army, 93, 94; incidence of battle exhaustion, 105; leave centre, 135, 140; malaria rate, 130; self-inflicted wounds, 107. See also units and regiments in Korea: 1st Commonwealth Division; 27th BCIB; 28th BCIB

Baskin and Robbins, xii
Bateman, D., 114
battle exhaustion, 93, 104–7, 158, 201n79; in Australian army, 105; in New Zealand army, 105
battle inoculation, 24, 25
bedding, 146
beer, 16, 73, 83, 160, 168, 174, 175; daily ration, 164; donations of, 164; ill effects of, 165; impact on morale 163–5
Bercuson, David, 30, 85, 179, 197n38, 208n61
Berton, Pierre, 49, 50
Bingham, Lt-Col. P.R., 10, 96
Bishop, Brig. J.W., 118
black market, 36, 53, 146
Blair, Ken, 67
Blampied, Kenneth, 8, 176
body counts, 81
Bogert, Brig. M.P., 84, 123; support for KATCOM program, 69–70, 75
booby traps, 100, 151
boredom, 153, 165
Boss, Bill, 49
Bougie, Clyde, 127, 129, 165
bouncing betty. See mines
British army, 94; credit for reducing Canadian VD rate,

141; equipment,
32, 33, 34, 36, 37,
44, 46; leave centre, 135, 140;
malaria, 130; previous experience in
the Far East, 138–9, 141, 173–4; self-inflicted wounds,
107. *See also* units
and regiments in
Korea: 1st Commonwealth Division; 27th BCIB;
28th BCIB
British Commonwealth Hospital,
Kure, 117, 118
Bult-Francis, Lt-Col.
D.S.F., 60
bunkers, 74, 83, 86,
96, 101, 103, 121,
122, 148–9, 153;
improvised furnishings for, 149
Burger King, xii

Calgary, 11, 155
Cameron, Craig, 90
Cammie Howard
Show, 154
Campbell, Lt-Col.
K.L., 24, 25, 85,
153, 159, 164; on
C-rations, 143; on
equipment, 35, 37,
40, 41, 43, 44, 45;
on KATCOMS, 74;
on KSC, 67; on
patrol dogs, 99;
on patrolling, 97;
on personnel
policies, 96–7

Camp Casey, xii
Camp Sarcee, 18
Canada, Government
of, 4–6, 69, 72, 76;
decision to commit
ground troops, 6;
indifference to
Korean War veterans, 176, 177
Canadian Army, post–
Second World War,
3, 6, 24, 46, 99,
175; European focus
of, 7, 29, 41, 60,
129, 179; organization of an infantry
battalion, 20; overextension of, 179;
unfamiliarity with
Asia, 51, 139
Canadian Army
Active Force, 7, 8,
9, 13, 94; alcohol
use in, 73; equipment, 32; expansion of, 179; failure
to learn from
Korean experiences,
178–80; social profile, 13–14, 183n46;
VD rates in, 134–5
Canadian Army Journal, 23
Canadian Army
Mountain Warfare
Course, 31
Canadian Army Operational Research
Team (CAORT), 23,
121–3, 133, 169
Canadian Army Special Force (CASF),
3, 158; formation

of, 7–8; recruitment, 8–11, 173,
179, 183n47; social
profile, 13–14; 18,
20, 183n46; statistics for, 12; VD
rates, 134. *See also*
units and regiments in Korea
Canadian hospital,
Seoul, 119; conditions in, 117–18
canned heat, 168
Canadian Volunteer
Service Medal for
Korea, 16, 177
Carmichael, Stanley,
22, 30
casualties, 15, 79,
83, 86, 101, 178,
192n67; accidental, 99, 100, 119,
123, 147, 151; battle, 108; burns, 119,
121–3; by weapon,
111–12; compared
to the world wars,
108, 111, 112, 119;
evacuation of, 109,
114–17, 123–4;
fatal, 109; impact
of armoured vests
on, 113, 203n30,
124; non-battle,
127, 133; non-fatal,
109–10; ratio of
fatal to non-fatal,
111, 203n16; use
of medevac helicopters, 116–17, 124
Casualty Clearing
Post (CCP), 115,
117, 119

Index

ceasefire, 74; possibility of, 69, 79, 94, 95, 185n52
cenotaphs, 177
Chail-li, battle of, 36, 78, 90, 144
Chamberlain, Capt. W.R., 23–5
chigger mites, 131
China, 4. *See also* Communist Chinese Forces
chloroquine, 128
Choi In Wa, 68
Chorwon Plain, 55
Christmas, 145
Chronicle Herald, 5
civilians, Korean, 56–7, 59; and attacks on Canadians, 173; Canadian impressions of, 49, 55–61, 68, 75, 125–6; Canadian relations with, 49, 50, 75, 167, 172, 173
Claxton, Brooke, 7, 50, 179; and CASF recruiting, 9–12
Coates, Pte. Jacket, 134, 136, 160
cohesion, 62–4, 75, 194n56; effect of alcohol on, 161, 162, 169; of primary group, 63–4, 74, 97, 158
Coke, Brig. W.L., 161
Cold War, 3, 32
communism, 4, 48, 51
Communist Chinese Forces (CCF), 11; alleged use of opium, 91; artillery, 35, 66, 83, 85, 86, 148; attack on Hill 187, 85–6; attack on Hill 355, 83, 201n68; camouflage and deception, 88, 98; corpses, 92; defensive positions, 89–90; entry into Korean War, 11–12, 182n39; fighting spirit, 95; human-wave attacks, 87, 90; specialized patrol troops, use of, 89, 94; superman image of Chinese soldier, 92; tactical abilities, 87–9; tactics, 91, 151; training, 77; weapons and equipment, 14, 41, 43, 77, 88, 177, 189nn78, 88
compo meals, 142–3
condoms, 134. *See also* venereal disease
Congo, the, 180
Cook, George, 147
Co-operative Commonwealth Federation, 29
courts martial, 172
cowardice, 107
c-rations, 67, 102, 126, 127, 142–4, 145
crime, rates, 173; role of alcohol in, 169–70; statistics by unit, 169–70, 172–3; violent, 167, 172–3
Crimean War, 125
Currie Barracks, 19, 30
Custer, Brig.-Gen. G.A., 95
Cyprus, 180

daily routine: in the front line, 149–53; in reserve, 166–7
defence budget, Canadian, 3, 32
defence policy, Canadian, 3, 69, 179
Defence Research Board (DRB), 133, 134
Department of External Affairs, 75
Department of National Defence (DND), 6, 16, 29, 55, 70, 75, 137, 153, 154, 155, 158, 172, 178, 179, 180
Department of Veterans Affairs, 177
Dextraze, Lt-Col. J.A., 7, 44
Dieppe, 107, 176
Directorate General, Medical Services, 133
Directorate General, Military Training (DGMT), 25, 26, 50
discipline, 70, 84, 166, 174; collective

punishment, 63; noise, 98. *See also* alcohol; beer; crime
disease, 16, 70, 124, 125, 141; compared with Second World War, 128; diarrhea, 126, 144, 146; dysentery, 126; hemorrhagic fever, 16, 125, 128, 130–3, 138, 141, 149; hepatitis, 16, 126, 127, 206n17, 131; Japanese encephalitis, 16, 128, 130; jaundice, 127; malaria, 16, 128, 129, 130; malaria rates of Canadians compared with British and Australians, 130; mortality rate from, 125; ringworm, 152; smallpox, 126; trench fever, 132; typhus, 125; unpreparedness for, 125, 141, 178; vaccinations against, 48, 125, 126, 130. *See also* venereal disease
Douglas Dakota, 118
Dragon Lady, 91
Drew, George, 5
drugs, elicit: opium, 91
Du Picq, Ardent, xiii

"Eagle-Leaf," 54
Eddy, Col. Keith, xi
Edmonton, 18
Eighth U.S. Army Historical Office, xi
Elliot, George, 132
Ellis, John, 71, 142
Enlisted Men's Wet Canteen, 160–1
equipment, 14, 100; armoured vests, 15, 108, 113, 178; battledress, 37, 52, 187n36; boots, 37–8, 88, 98; Bren gun, 38–9, 46; Browning .30 and .50 machine guns, 45–6; clothing, 34; deficiencies, 33, 79, 92, 94, 95, 107, 177; Garand M1, 39, 40; grenades, 42–3, 119; helmets, 35; M2 carbine, 41; M3 "grease gun," 46; mortars, 33, 43–4; night vision, 98–9; no. 4 rifle, 39–41, 86, 98, 101, 188n48; Owen gun, 42, 46, 189n71; Patchett submachine gun, 42, 46, 189n74; peaked caps, 35; ponchos, 35–6, 146, 150, 152; quality of, 32, 34–46, 77; radios, 35, 81; rocket launcher, 33, 44–5, 166; small arms, 38; sources of, 32, 186n1; Sten gun, x, 41–2, 46, 98,

188n70; Vickers gun, 45, 46, 189n93; webbing, 34, 186n11; winter combat suits, 36–7, 98, 122–3, 152
Esquimalt, 4
external (foreign) policy, Canadian, 69, 179

fatigue, 100–1, 151
fear, 102–4; effect on diurnal cycle, 102–3; reactions to enemy fire, 102–3
First World War, 42; defensive positions in, 85; dogs used in, 99; rotation policy in, compared with Korea, 158; trench raids, 81
food, 53, 59, 67, 127, 142, 144, 150, 151, 156; fresh, 144; poisoning, 127; sources of in Korea, 142–3, 145
Fort Lewis, 11, 21, 30, 47
Foulkes, Lt-Gen. C.G., 11, 32, 33, 137
Fowler, Cpl. K.E., 80–1
Fox, Richard, 95
fragging, 95
Freeman News, 54
French Foreign Legion, 166
friendly fire, 119
front line, 61, 66, 73, 74, 89, 95, 123,

129, 145, 146, 148, 154, 155, 164, 178
frostbite, 152

Gaffey Gazette, 53
garbage: in Canadian defensive positions, 132
Gardner, Lt. H.R., 80–1, 96
General Freeman, 54
Globe and Mail, 4, 5
gobbling irons, 145
Goodman, Lt. C.E., 80
Gore-tex, 123
Grey, Jeffrey, 84, 93, 132, 210n107
Griffiths, George, 96

Hackworth, David, 130
halazone tablets, 126
halftracks, 44, 45
handbooks on Korea, 50–1
hand-to-hand combat, 86, 101–2
hayboxes, 144, 145
Headquarters, Canadian Army, 28, 43
helicopters, 15, 100, 108; limitations on use in forward areas, 116–17, 124
Hepenstall, Robert, 67, 75, 82, 138, 148, 199n8
Hibbs, Don, 169
Hill 187, 85, 109
Hill 227, 44, 77, 87, 90, 93

Hill 355, 82, 83, 91, 96, 101, 104, 105, 106, 109, 163
Hill 467, 78
Hill 532, 77, 100, 102, 104
Hill 677, x, 27. *See also* Kap'yong, battle of
Hiroshima, 55
HIV, 136
Holland, Sgt-Maj. Jim, 171
Holmes, Richard, 18, 21, 62, 94
Hong Kong, 139
Honshu, 55
Hugh J. Gaffey, 54
Hummer, W., 48

Imjin River, xii
Inchon, 11, 20, 69
insecticides, 130
intravenous kits, 127

Jamestown line, 40, 65, 67, 79, 82, 83, 84, 86, 87, 88, 91, 96, 99, 101, 111, 127, 147, 148, 166, 173, 175, 177
Japan, 48, 55, 106, 155; Canadian impressions of, 55, 135–6; hydroponic farms in, 144; occupation of Korea, 56, 58, 131; R&R in, 61
Jasper, 31
jeep ambulances, 117
Johnson, Dan, 151, 175

Kap'yong, battle of, xi, 27, 44, 60, 77, 86, 87, 90, 93, 100, 102, 117, 143, 176
Keane, Lt-Col. R.A., 8
Keegan, John, 63
Killer, 99
kim-chi, 74
King, W.L. Mackenzie, 3; death of, 6
Knights of Columbus, 153
Korea: climate, 36, 56, 58, 152; effect of climate on weapons, 39–40, 150; sanitary conditions, 125–6, 177; terrain, 56, 59, 157. *See also* civilians, Korean; Republic of Korea
Korean Army Service Corps (KSC), 15, 62, 115, 144, 193n12; Canadian perceptions of, 64–6, 75; Canadian relations with, 66–8; casualties in, 66; discipline in, 68; pay in, 67, 73, 193nn27, 28
Korean Augmentation Troops, Commonwealth (KATCOM), 15, 62; Canadian perceptions of, 64, 68, 75; Canadian policy towards, 69–70, 74–5;

Canadian relations with, 70-6; casualties among, 72, 86, 99; discipline, 73; failure of KATCOM program, 74-6, 178; lack of training, 71-2; language difficulties, 71; pay, 67, 72-3
Korean Augmentation Troops, United States Army (KATUSA), 68
Korean Veterans Association, 16, 176
Kure, 55, 135
Kyoto, 55

latrines, 147-8
Liboiron, Maj. R., 91, 93
Liddell, Maj. R.D., 8
Lilley, 4
Little Bighorn, battle of, 95
live-and-let-live, 95
Lucky Seven, 167. *See also* alcohol: poisoning

MacArthur, Gen. Douglas, 11, 20, 182n12
McLean, Louis, 57, 67, 163
Maclean's, 49
MacLennan, Maj. D.S., 74
Madsen, Chris, 215n54
mail, 142; postal service in Korea, 154-5; writing paper and envelopes, 154, 156
Main Line of Resistance (MLR), 95, 96, 105, 199n19
malaria. *See* disease
malaria maps, 129, 206n25
Maple Leaf Club, 140-1
Marine Alder, 48
Marshall, S.L.A., 23, 63
Martin, Bill, 164
Menzies, A.R., 171
militia, 3
mines, 84, 99, 100, 119
Miryang, 27, 170
Mitchell, Wayne, 102
Mobile Army Surgical Hospital (MASH), 106, 116, 132, 168. *See also* casualties: evacuation of
mobilization, 3
Molesworth, J.R., 176
Montreal Star, 6
morale, 16, 178; and alcohol, 160-9; effect of armoured vests on, 113; and R&R, 159, 174; effect of shelling on, 103-4. *See also* discipline
morphine, 114
Morrice, James, 176
mosquitoes, 128, 129, 130, 152; netting, 129
Murray, John, 22, 57

Naech'on, xi
Nasby, Bill, 22, 176
National Archives of Canada, x
National Research Council, 122
Neptune Ceremony, 54
New Zealand army, 143; and battle exhaustion, 105; self-inflicted wounds, 107. *See also* units and regiments in Korea: 1st Commonwealth Division; 27th BCIB; 28th BCIB
no man's land, 27, 36, 80, 82, 83, 85, 88, 90, 95, 99, 165
non-commissioned officers, 55
North Atlantic Treaty Organization (NATO), 3, 5, 11, 29, 179
North Korea: invasion of South Korea, 4, 5; tanks, 33, 45

officers, 55, 161, 165
Operation Haircut, 52
Ottawa, 28, 41, 43, 69, 121, 137, 138, 139, 153, 163, 177

P'och'on Valley, 78
Paardeberg, battle of, 22
paludrine, 129

Panmunjom, ix, 28, 94
patrol dogs, 99
patrolling, 27, 79, 80; lack of emphasis in training, 29, 31; preparation for, 151; school in Korea, 31; types of, 27–8
pay, 72
Peacock, Lt. Robert, 36, 66, 98, 113, 120, 150, 161, 162, 164, 165, 167, 171
Pearson, Lester B., 6; reaction to alleged mistreatment of Korean civilians, 50; response to North Korean invasion, 4
Pero, W.D., 101
Petawawa, 10, 20, 30
Pope, Maj. W.H, 24, 159; on battlefield performance, 94; on defensive difficulties, 84–5; on equipment, 40, 42, 43, 86; on patrolling, 29–30, 79; on reluctance to close with the enemy, 93
Porch, Douglas, 166
Poulin, Lt-Col. J.G., 159; views on beer, 164; opinion of Bren gun, 38; on KATCOMS, 71, 74, 75
Powell, William, 48, 57, 163, 168

primaquine, 128
Prince, Sgt. Tommy, 13, 151
prisoners of war (POWs), 72, 79, 89, 110; losses by unit, 110–11
Private Joe P. Martinez, 52, 54, 175
prostitutes, 50, 59, 134, 139
Pusan, 27, 55, 56, 57, 58, 61, 78

quinine, 128

racism, 49, 51, 60, 67, 75, 90, 91, 160, 172
Ratchford, G.L., 160
Rawlings, Bill, 40
rear-echelon personnel, 145, 146, 154
Red Cross, 153
refugees, 56–7
Regimental Aid Post (RAP), 105, 106, 115, 119, 137, 165
regimental mess: in Canada, 161; in Korea, 167
REMFs ("rear-echelon mother fuckers"), 120
Repay, Harry, 164
replacements, 21, 70–1, 72, 76; shortage of, 94, 159, 163
Republic of Korea (ROK), 4, 58; army, 60, 61, 64, 67, 69, 70; government, 70, 72

rest and recuperation (R&R), 61, 73, 135–6, 159–60; Inchon rest centre, 160; local leave, 159–60; impact on morale, 159, 174; Seoul rest centre, 160
rice paddies, 59, 127
Richardson, Earl, 65, 92, 131, 149
Richardson, John, 106, 118, 148, 152
Rockingham, Brig. J.M., 7, 57, 58, 78, 130; and VD rotation policy, 138, 209n90
rodents, 131; in bunkers, 149; destruction of, 132
Rodger, Maj-Gen. N.E., 33
Ross, Lt., 102
Ross rifle, 42
Royal Canadian Air Force, 3, 6, 179
Royal Canadian Legion, 16, 152, 176
Royal Canadian Navy, 4, 179

St-Laurent, Louis, 177, 179; and feasibility of sending ground troops to Korea, 6, 32; response to North Korean invasion, 4–5
Salvation Army, 153

Sam'ichon Valley, 92
Sasebo, 55
Seattle, 47
Second World War, 3, 5, 23, 65; battle exhaustion in, 105; Italian campaign, 29, 51, 60; Normandy campaign, 78; rotation policy in compared to Korea, 158
self-inflicted wounds, 93, 104, 106, 107, 111, 112, 202nn90, 96; consequences of, 106–7
sentries, 151–3
Seoul, 55, 58
service rum demerara (SRD), 164; authorization to issue, 163; impact on morale, 161–3; use during battle of Hill 355, 163
sex, 136
shellreps, 103
shorts, 129
signal wire, 148–9
Simonds, Lt-Gen. G.G., 40, 70, 137–8
snakes, 149
Snider, Lt. Chris, 71
Soldier's Forum, 48, 190n8
Somalia, 173
South Korea. *See* Republic of Korea
Soviet Union, 5; boycott of Security Council, 4

Sparling, Maj-Gen. H.A., 25, 30
Stairs, Dennis, 179
Stone, Lt-Col. J.R., 7, 10, 11, 19, 44, 90, 93, 100, 117, 126, 168, 206n6
stoves: field, 119–21; improvised, 121–3; shortages of, 120, 148, 178
Strange Battleground, 29
support weapons, 15, 32, 33, 189nn81, 86; at Kap'yong, 86–7; overreliance on, 81–2, 87, 96, 101; quality of, 43–6. *See also* equipment
Swinton, Maj. R.K., 24

tanks, x, 101
thirty-eighth parallel, 4, 77
Thwaites, George, 176
ticks, 130
tobacco: cigarettes, 67, 142, 143; pipe, 143
Tokchon, 134
Tokyo, 135, 140
Tomelin, Paul, 97, 105, 111
training, 14, 18, 183n12; advance, 23–6; collective, 26–30, 31; in the construction and maintenance of defensive positions,

25–6, 84; deficiencies in, 31, 79, 92, 94, 95, 107, 177; European focus of, 30, 31, 78–9; hygiene, 139; importance of, 89; individual, 21–6, 31, 63; recruit, 21–3; and reluctance to fire, 23–5; weapons handling, 23–5
tri-wound policy, 119
Trudeau, Lt-Col. L.F., 31
Truman, Harry, 4
Tungmudae, 100

Uijongbu, 134
United Nations, 179; Charter, 48; Emergency Force (UNEF), 180; Security Council, 4, 6
United Nations Command, Korea, 12, 80; patrol policy, 110; air power, 151
United States, 4, 6
United States Army, 102; experience in Far East, 141, 173–4; indoctrination, 51; KATUSA program, 68–9, 195n83; rotation policy, 157; VD in, 138; 2nd Reconnaissance Company, 146; 7th Cavalry, 95; Eighth Army, 79
United States Marine Corps, 80

United States Navy, 48, 61
units and regiments in Korea:
- 1st Commonwealth Division, 32, 33, 68, 70, 79, 85, 91; bakery, 144; crime rate in, 173; defensive doctrine, 87; disease in, 127, 131, 206n12; fighting spirit in, 93; formation of, 106; Hygiene Inspection Team, 132; rest centre, 160; VD preventive measures in, 139–41; VD rate in, 138, 173
- 25th Canadian Infantry Brigade Group (25th CIB), ix, xii, 20, 21, 76, 164, 179; assigned permanent sector of Jamestown line, 93–4; battlefield performance, 77, 93; comforts and amenities in, 210n1; condition and quality of defensive positions, 83–6, 151; conduct of troops in Japan, 140–1; defensive doctrine, 87; failure to develop defensive positions properly, 83–5; failure to dominate no man's land, 82–3, 85; headquarters, 134; inability to patrol effectively, 29, 31, 82, 83, 196nn10, 23; inadequate indoctrination of, 47–51, 57, 58, 60, 61, 157; lack of aggression in, 93–6, 107, 159, 177; life aboard troopships, 48, 51–5, 61; mess culture in, 167; mobile bath unit, 147; morale, 157–69; prohibition on fraternization with enemy, 92; relations between officers and enlisted men, 95; rotation policy, 61, 157–60, 174, 178; tactical shortcomings, 78–9, 94; unpreparedness for service in the Far East, 139, 141, 173–4, 177, 179–80; VD in, 138–9, 178; views on the Chinese, 90–2. *See also* casualties; discipline; equipment; patrolling; training; welfare
- Princess Patricia's Canadian Light Infantry (PPCLI), ix, 7, 172; first battalion, 11, 18, 19, 48, 121, 135, 158; second battalion, 19, 20, 27, 28, 30, 40, 45, 47, 52, 60, 64, 77, 86, 104, 128, 146, 158, 159, 167, 169, 170, 172, 175; third battalion, 21, 26, 29, 31, 143, 145, 162, 178, 183n43, 190n3
- Royal Canadian Regiment (RCR), ix, 7, 172, 173; first battalion, 10, 41, 83, 104, 106, 112, 127, 163; second battalion, 20, 36, 47, 78, 79, 90, 128, 135, 144, 169, 170; third battalion, 21, 26, 31, 85, 87, 96, 101, 143, 164, 178, 183n43, 190n3
- Royal 22e Régiment (R22eR), ix, 7, 172; lack of French-language reading material in, 153; first battalion, 20, 85, 113, 163, 165; second battalion, 20, 47, 77, 87, 90, 128, 135, 169, 170; third battalion, 21, 26, 31, 143, 178, 183n43, 190n3
- Other: 27th British Commonwealth Infantry Brigade (27th BICB), 33, 77; 27th Canadian Infantry Brigade Group (27th CIB), 134, 210n1; 28th British Commonwealth Infantry Brigade (28th BCIB),

131; 54th Transport Company, 42, 164, 170; Lord Strathcona's Horse (LDSH), 7; No. 1 Commonwealth Provost Company, 140; No. 6 Personnel Depot, 8–11; No. 10 Field Hygiene Section, 139; No. 25 Canadian Field Dressing Station (FDS), 105, 121, 132, 170; –, admissions for accidental burns, 123; –, "interesting cases," 130, 137; No. 25 Field Detention Barracks, 169, 170; –, experience of a detainee in, 170–2; Royal Canadian Army Medical Corps (RCAMC), 130; Royal Canadian Army Service Corps (RCASC), 61, 117; Royal Canadian Electrical and Mechanical Engineers, 134; Royal Canadian Engineers, x, 7, 64, 134, 185n51; Royal Canadian Horse Artillery (RCHA), 7, 78; Royal Canadian Ordnance Corps (RCOC), 134, 170

Urquhart, Don, 159

Valcartier, 26
Vallance, John, 98
Vancouver, 154, 155
Vancouver outpost, 83
Vancouver Sun, 5
VE day, 176
venereal disease (VD), 16, 105, 133–41, 178, 208n73; balantitis, 137; Canadian VD rates in Korea compared with British and American rates, 134, 208n54, 138, 141; Canadian rates in Korea compared with those in the two world wars, 133, 139, 210n109; chancroid, 125, 137; comparison of 25th and 27th CIB rates, 134; gonorrhea, 136, 137; inflammation of the foreskin, 137; non-specific urethritis, 136–7, 208n53; penal warts, 137; prevention stations, 140; preventive measures (and lack of), 138–41; rates among 25th CIB units, 134; syphilis, 136, 137; training program, 139; treatment of, 137; VD rotation policy, 138, 140, 141

Vik, 2nd Lt. Pare, 166
VJ day, 176

Wainwright, 19, 20, 30
war correspondents, 49, 40
water, 59, 126
weapons: Canadian, 14; Chinese, 14–15; maintenance in the field, 39–40, 150–1. *See also* equipment
Welcome Party, 92
welfare: lack of attention towards, 53–4, 141, 153–6, 157; live shows and concert parties, 142, 153–4, 156; magazines, 153; movies, 53, 153; newspapers, 153; in Second World War, 153. *See also* mail; rest and recuperation
West, Maj-Gen. Michael, 92, 93
Western Five, 154
Wilson, James, 30, 51, 67
Winnipeg Free Press, 4
Wol-li, 126
Wood, Col. H.F., 29, 195n82

"yellow peril," 90
YMCA, 153
Yokohama, 55

Zuber, Ted, 92

When Conchi Blows

Omar Sheriffe Vernon el Halawani

Copyright © 2013 Robert Vernon
Trustee Estate Omar Sheriffe Vernon el Halawani
Vernon el Halawani Book Trust
All rights reserved. No part of this publication may be reproduced, stored in a retrieval system or transmitted in any form or by any means electronic, photocopying, recording, or otherwise, without the prior written permission of the Publisher, except for brief quotations used in conjunction with a review written specifically for inclusion in a magazine or newspaper.
Inquiries regarding rights and permissions should be addressed to:
Vernon el Halawani Book Trust
43 Millsborough Cres. Toronto, Ontario, M9C 5E7, Canada.
Library and Archives Canada Cataloguing in Publication

Vernon el Halawani, Omar Sheriffe, 1935-2005, author
When conchi blows / Omar Sheriffe Vernon el Halawani.
ISBN 978-1-4637-1223-5 (pbk.)
I. Title.
PS8643.E753W54 2013   C813'.6   C2013-903301-7
United States Copyright Office Registration Number/Date: TXu001226131/2005-02-04
Library of Congress Control Number: 2013909098.
A catalogue record of the book is available from the National Library of Jamaica.
A catalogue record of this book is available from the British Library.
ISBN-10: 1463712235
EAN-13: 9781463712235
Afterword: Rachele Evelyn Vernon. Ph.D
Glossary: Robert Vernon.
Cover design: Robert Vernon.
Cover art: Painting IMP by famous Jamaican artist Judy Ann MacMillan, who kindly granted permission for its use. She was a close friend of the author. It was chosen as the painting mirrors the image of Neddy, the central character in the novel.
Printed in the United States of America
CreateSpace Independent Publishing Platform
North Charleston, South Carolina

*This novel is dedicated to
my mother, Dr. Kathleen Alberta Vernon, FRCP,
her sisters, my aunts, Lillian Evelyn Vernon, RN,
and Cynthia Valentine Vernon, RN, MBE,
all of whom inspired me
with family lore from I was very young.*

*One such tale is the basis of this novel but ironically
is only incorporated in the seventeenth chapter of
the book—the
story of Eliza Stevenson's adventures traveling with
her slave nurse from
Lapland Estate to Montego Bay. I regret to say that,
in truth, Neddy was not with them, but how could
I leave him out? There would be no novel without him.*

*Also, I wish to extend my heartfelt gratitude to
Mr. Roy Clark, Mrs. Shirley Arnold Kay, Mrs.
Norma Reiss, Mr Robert Vernon and Rachele
Evelyn Vernon, PhD.
Without their help and encouragement, this book
would never have been completed.*

Chapter 1

Jabbering Crow

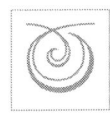

Galloway mounted his mule, nearly vomiting with the effort. It was sometime between midnight and dawn, October 21, 1831. His right foot straddled the animal's back, and he fought to steady himself in the saddle. At that moment in the unending blackness, he didn't give a damn about the date or the time. He could not see to hook his foot through the rope loop that took the place of a metal stirrup, which annoyed him in his inebriated state. Only his natural aptitude for riding and years of experience with horses in Ireland kept him from going arse over tit to the ground. He was still very drunk but in the first stages of sobering up—the worst part of an orgy—but through the haze that clung about his senses, his brain whispered that boredom and the few prospects of any kind on this accursed island drove him and his class to drink, eat, and wench too much. That, along with yellow fever, black water fever, dengue fever, lockjaw, yaws, and driving Negroes to produce sugar and rum for others, destroyed a man's body utterly. There was no soul to destroy, he reckoned, for only soulless men took the work of overseers.

His stomach churned. The mule's gait recalled the sensation of an ancient coracle spinning in slow motion down a river, bouncing off rocks and over rapids. Indistinguishable shapes in the nightscape rose and fell, and in his gut the rum, water, pepper pot, salt pork, beans, plantain, and yam from the excesses of the night before agitated like firebrands and ricocheted off his stomach walls. Pepper pot, full of okra, yam, callaloo, crab…foods unknown in Ireland, England, or anywhere else in Europe were the main cause of his agony. The spices—so different from the bland potato soup he'd eaten growing up in Ireland. He could not get enough of pepper pot. But he regretted those extra helpings, now. The acid came up into his throat, burned, and left a sour taste as he forced it back. He tried to keep it down, but it swilled up again. Again he swallowed back. "Willpower, willpower, willpower, I need willpower to come through these desperate times," he said, choking the contents of his stomach back.

He slouched over the saddlebow as the animal moved forward. All might yet be well, as long as the pace remained unhurried and steady along the shortcut to the road. He was glad to have a sure-footed mule under him instead of a horse. The hybrid was less likely to shy or stumble. Once on the road, he would make it back to Newman Hall all right.

Five miles in the cool of the morning would wake him up to face another day of sameness, driving blacks to produce and produce and, if they didn't, whipping them into producing. Behind him, on Retirement estate, where he had caroused with fellow overseers, a similar day was beginning, and all for the enrichment of Sir Simon Clarke, baronet, lord and master of Retirement and many other plantations. At least that gentleman had been born in the island and lived here. Not like his employers. They had never set foot on this hell rock. "No, not him; the good life in London sustained by molasses, sugar, and rum is all William Peat-Litt, Esquire, knows," Galloway mumbled to himself. Although he had never met his employer, he knew the English for what they were, according to the historical Irish experience.

He could hear the fop now, through the haze of stale rum that exuded from his pores, "Jamaica! Yes, mi dear, turns a pretty penny for mi, don't you know. Not as much as in mi father's day, but able to keep up appearances—don't you know. Couldn't do much without it. Been there! No, mi dear. That is for attorneys and overseers. Employ them, you see. Irish and Scots mostly. What else would we do with that sort? Gads! Couldn't have them in England, don't you know—could we now, mi dear?"

At last Galloway's stomach had started to settle down, but now came the struggle to stay awake and keep from falling down onto the gravel road. He turned right and let the reins go slack. Instinctively, the mule stopped, and Galloway stared down a slight incline along the narrow road before it turned uphill again. The glisten of the dew on the white marl surface reminded him of a dusting of snow in winter on Irish roads. He could just make out the way as the moss-laden branches of great cotton trees overlapped each other across the road, like a vaulted roof, hindering the morning light that tried to force itself through the overhang. Leaving the reins slack, he kicked the mule, and off it ambled, heading toward Worcester, then up to John's Hall past Spring Mount, and then eventually to Newman Hall.

Perched in the branches overhead, doves on their way from the hills to their feeding grounds on the flats cooed to each other, their calls replacing the whistling of the tree frogs of the tropical night. Galloway wished them silent, for their sound added weight to his throbbing head. There seemed to be more birds than usual, and he remembered, through the ache that grew with each step of his mule, that the second half of the year had already begun. That meant more birds. Breeding was over—the young ones were on the wing.

In his effort to stay awake, he tried to distinguish the dove calls. That one was a baldpate, and that one a pea-dove, over there a whitewing, or maybe it was a white-belly. Struggling against sleep he listened to the *coo-co*, or *co-coo, co-cocaroo*. He strained to catch a ringtail call, but they must still have been high in their mountaintops, up around Lapland and Catadupa. You did not get many of them in this part of Jamaica.

St. James did not really have the high mountains that the birds liked. One had to go up around the Blue Mountains in St. Thomas to find them in abundance, or on the other side of the range in Portland. He recalled the experience being exhilarating, the one time he had been on a shooting expedition there. Cool mountain air washed over him and reminded him of damp morning shoots at home. He wished for some of it now. Even October was hot here. In Ireland it would be cooler. His thoughts turned to the shooting parties that began there on August 12. The gentlemen would be out on the heather from then on. He wished he were there now, instead of here.

A smile crossed his lips when he thought how they carried on the same tradition here in this faraway island. No heather softened by rising mist in the morning to traverse with your gillie and beater, but a bush tangle to cut through and slaves doing your bidding. Lord! How pretentious they were in Jamaica. You owned a few slaves and a piece of land, and you were God almighty in the island, with almost the power of life and death over those under you.

One day he would be so privileged, when his uncle died and Unity Hall became his. Yet he did not take much comfort in this prospect. There was, to Galloway, something unholy about this island. He would much rather have gotten some place in Ireland where, despite the English, it was still green and fresh, as if touched by the hand of saints. Until Unity Hall passed his way, he, Matthew Conner Galloway, was just another lowly employee on a Jamaican estate.

Resentment filled his very being at the idea. The voices of the owners rumbled in his aching head, referring to overseers and bookkeepers nonchalantly as *my white people*. The arrogance of it all! Negroes were valuable property, while subservient whites were not. They were less than chattel, there to be used and discarded when done with. That was the reality of Jamaica, and his stomach churned again in rebellion.

Wa-Ca-ca-fa-ca-sta-ca-crab. The sound drilled into his head. *Do-ca-Baka-ca-ca-ca-cra-wrk*, it sounded again. *Bakkkkkaaaaraa-win-win-caca*. How could a bird make so awful a noise when the daylight was in its infancy?! His head throbbed. "It sounds like mad Welshmen quarreling in hell!"

"Here's a knocking indeed at hell's gate! Who's there, in the name of Beelzebub?" He laughed to hear himself, trying to remember his Shakespeare, learned all that age ago, the Jesuit strap never far from his backside. He should have been an Irish poet; he was worthy of that honor, Galloway contended to himself. Like the Irish, Shakespeare was a man who understood men.

Again, *ca-ca-ca-bakraa*. The sound seemed to bounce off the rocks along the side of the road, singing straight into the very darkest recesses of his skull. Galloway looked up into the canopy of the trees overhead for a sight of the creature making the infernal racket. Through a break in the branches, he saw a John Crow circling high above the ground, probably looking for a rotting corpse on which to feed. Then, out of the treetop above him flapped slowly, without grace or resilience, a large black crow he had never seen before. Heavily it moved to the higher branches of the great cotton tree and was lost to sight. The noisemaker revealed at last. What else could it be? As the mule moved on, Galloway craned his neck backward, looking for the bird. "*What a strange creature*," he thought. Its wings seemed to strain lifting it between the branches. "Is it native to this island?" he wondered. So many strange things do happen here, and stranger yet were the many things foreign, brought in on ships from Spain, England, France, America, Africa, even the damned Dutchman had his say in the Antilles.

Tis unnatural,
Even like the deed that's done. On Tuesday last,
A falcon, towering in her pride of place,
Was by a mousing owl hawk'd at and killed.

Galloway shouted the verses at the birds high above him, as if to warn the jabberer and its cousin the buzzard that far up there was no safer than down here on the ground. With its rocking motion the mule plodded on. Sleep began to make his head nod forward again. Almost off, he forced himself back in the saddle and heard his neck crack with the effort. "Shit! Stay awake, stay awake," he told himself. The only way to do this was to recite poetry. He should be on the Abbey Theatre stage in Dublin. Macbeth it was. Oh! But instead of an Irish stage, the blackness of the tragedy would be played out here on this lonely Jamaican road. And it would be a tragedy if Galloway was not careful and fell to the ground breaking his neck.

Overseers had been known to topple drunk from their horses and be killed, or, worse, crippled and useless for life. Lying in bed or confined to a chair, a man dependent on handouts and free drinks from those friends who stuck by him; family and homeland gone forever. If he was lucky there would be a black slave to fetch and carry for him, but there would be the worry that the food contained more poison than goodness. Some even begged their attendants to end it for them and were granted their wish.

Others suffered long days of relentless heat torturing the body with sweat that made clothes stick to their skin in the armpits, down the back bone, around the crotch. Their nights were filled with incessant buzzing insects, stings injecting venom into them. Only daylight chased those pests away, and the cycle continued. The heat again, and with it the trickling sweat, until night returned with the annoyance of insects. Relief came only with death.

In such a situation, they urged the pale horseman along with rum and yet more rum, the ambrosia of forgetfulness that even numbed the insects' attacks and turned the sweaty clothes into a cooling shroud around the body. Then restless sleep, until the permanent sleep that eventually comes to all of us drew them in to the next stage of existence.

"Faith, sir," Galloway began again and followed with a dramatic pause. "We were carousing till the second cock; and drink, sir, is a great provoker of three things." More pause—this time not stage direction but failing memory—until the unseen prompter in his brain whispered, and loudly he recited to the treetops and the birds:

"Marry sir, nose painting, sleep, and urine.
Lechery, sir, it provokes and unprovokes:
it provokes the desire but it takes away the performance."

Another dramatic pause as the mule plodded on.

"Makes him stand to and not stand to. Equivocates him
in a sleep, and giving him the lie, leaves him."

He could remember no more. To hell with Macbeth and his porter anyway. Galloway looked above him again for the turkey buzzard, but the John Crow was gone. In its place a chicken hawk soared overhead. Sunlight flashed off its red feathers, giving it the richness of blood color. Suddenly its harsh war scream, *pin-yay!* and again *pin-yay!* warned that the hunter was abroad, danger was aloft. Magically the cooing in the treetops stopped, as if suddenly emptied of life. In the uneasy silence, Galloway pulled his mule to a stop and listened, as if making sure of the stillness surrounding him. "Red-headed, unappreciative black bastards! Buzzards all!" shouted Galloway, laughing. His answer came with *Cacacabakara*. Obviously one black bastard up there was not afraid of the hawk and would sing the devil song, come hell or high water. Galloway pressed his hand hard against his forehead in a futile effort to stop the ache.

That was the problem in the island—it was not civilized. One had to leave it to appreciate the finer things life had to offer and to be appreciated by one's fellows. No wonder those who could leave did so, never to return. Lord, he could do with a drink! Perhaps he would stop along the way and have one. As a rule he didn't believe in the hair of the dog, but he did acknowledge that sometimes a hangover was eased by an early morning drink.

It was early yet, but the sun had begun its daily task in earnest. The shirt had begun to stick to him. Sweat ran down his neck and back. Rum always caused water to run from his body and dry him out. Unless he could replace it with a drink from somewhere soon, discomfiture would harass him all the way home. But the so-called hair of the dog that bit him would be welcome when he got back to Newman Hall. Perhaps he should stop at Worcester? A rum and water would be offered as the natural course of hospitality. They had taken to adding it to coconut water, and that was sweet and refreshing. He would not stop. Rum, he decided, was killing him before his time. "Discipline, my good man!" he said aloud to himself.

Without his being aware of it, his head began to nod forward with sleep again. Just in time, he caught himself as he slumped forward on the mule's back. As if dreaming, he caught the sound of bagpipes. That is, at first he thought it pipes. He strained to listen. The sound was a flute somewhere in front of him. Drifting down in the valley, the notes seemed to be heading in his direction. What a strange morning. Doves that turn into crows, vultures that turn into hawks, sounds that echo from nowhere, and pipes that are flutes. "I must be delirious. It's not the drink but a fever upon me!" His hand patted the mule's neck, as if to reassure the animal that what he said was the truth of the matter.

Then, off in the hills, on his right, a powerful baritone voice took up the tune, *Amazing grace! How sweet the sound.* No sooner had he begun than a female joined in. Then another followed her. Galloway reined in the mule to listen to these unseen singers, harmonizing with each other across the hills, with the flute player leading them somewhere along the road in between.

He shivered at the sounds. Then again he shivered with the clawing dampness of his shirt. And he shivered again as a young boy appeared in front of him through the remnants of the morning mist, playing his flute.

Coming face to face with a white man so early on a Sunday morning caused the youth to stop in his tracks. The long bamboo flute made a pathetic note and fell silent at his lips. Slowly the boy lowered his arms to his side. He did not move but looked straight in front of him at the bedraggled man on the mule, noting the sad shape of the saddle he sat in. Still, the man was a Backra Massa, and being careful was wise. His mother had taught him to be wise. "Look, listen, learn, and move slowly in the presence of backra," she had told him many times, but she said the same thing when he was in the presence of respectable black men too. He had learned the advice applied to anyone in authority.

Galloway stared at the boy in front of him. His eyes roved up and down before focusing on the face. "Lord God! What a beautiful face. A black cherub appears among us," he muttered.

"Wat dat, sah?"

"Never mind, boy." Galloway continued to study him. No doubt about it, a sparkling sable youth. They did not come like this every day. The head was round with perfectly shaped ears at each side to keep the balance. Close-cropped hair showed the shape of the skull with slight undulations at the side above his ears. The boys eyes were jet black, like ackee seeds, set wide in his head, his stare unwavering. Above them, delicate eyebrows flickered up and down in a puzzled fashion, questioning what was before him. His nose, with slightly flared nostrils, ended an inch above the upper lip and came straight down from the forehead to divide his face evenly. His soft lips were closed, each line clean-cut and perfect in shape. The upper lip was slightly more prominent than its lower counterpart, which turned down sensually at the point where the flute would have sat. Moisture left from the flute playing added to the appeal. Truly, it was the face of a prince. Yet, a blemish on the right side of his chin reminded all who gazed upon him of his humanity and youth. Lower too, an eruption on his collarbone peeped out of his clean white Sunday shirt. Below his neck, his form, similar in perfection to his face, showed through tight white homemade pants to his bare feet.

Galloway moved his mule across the road and dismounted with effort. He sat on a large rock by the side of the road. The boy watched him settle down, not knowing what to expect next. Galloway pointed with his whip to the sandals tied together by a string, hanging down around the boy's neck. "You are meant to wear those to protect your feet." Slaves were always coming down with jiggers, cuts that festered and turned into cocoa-bay, as they called yaws; and if they caught that, it would mean the end of them prematurely. As a good overseer, he was always conscious of his charges' well-being, for the good of the estate. Others of his class never gave a damn; after all, they didn't own them.

"I wear dem in church, sah."

"Well, you should wear them *to* church as well. What's your name?"

"Neddy, sah."

"Neddy what?"

"Lawrence, sah."

"Where are you from, Neddy Lawrence? Who do you belong to?"

The boy straightened up, his left eyebrow arched upward. "No one but mi modder, sah." There was much pride in his answer.

"You are free, no one's slave?" queried Galloway again.

"After mi barn, mi fader buy mi modder's and fi mi freedom paper, so mi free, sah." Again there was the ring of pride in the boy's answer to the overseer.

"But you were born a slave?"

"Yes, sah, right up on Kensington, when Miss Fowler own it," he explained.

"Who is your father, Neddy? He must be a rich man to be able to buy your mother and yourself?" The boy was definitely not mulatto; he did not show any mixture at all. Galloway could not imagine anyone but a white man being able to buy the freedom of a young slave woman and her child in this age, when estates were quitting production because there were fewer and fewer slaves in the island.

"Mi fader di carpenter pon Kensington still, sah."

"Oh!" Galloway paused. "I know him. He comes up to us at Newman Hall sometimes to fix things and make furniture for me. Yes, I do know him—a good man. He is still a slave though?"

"Yes, sah. Im say a man of his importance doesn't need freedom paper. Who going look after im when im got it, im say?"

"Why did he buy you and your mother and not himself?"

"Mi modder, sah. She want it." Then with a serious expression, eyebrows coming together for emphasis, Neddy added, "Di people round say she tell mi fader no pum-pum till she and her baby get freedom."

Galloway let out a boisterous laugh at his answer. This time there was joy in the sound. "That's the best yet. Do you know the power of pum-pum, boy? No, I suppose you don't, not yet anyway. Wars, in ancient times, have been stopped when pum-pum was withheld. It still works its power today."

Hearing the word pum-pum used so freely by the white man in front of him, the boy half-smiled with embarrassment, unsure how to react. He wondered if he had gone too far. His mother always admonished him for chatting too much and being friendly. "Yu jus like a fool-fool gal," she would say.

"How old are you, Neddy?"

"Mi born in 1816, sah."

"Fifteen or sixteen, then? You gone a bush yet, Neddy?" inquired Galloway, half catching himself with the question. He shouldn't have said it. Why drag himself down by asking such a thing? But it was too late. He felt like a common island white, whose jaded eyes despoiled all the good and beautiful they came into contact with. Watching the boy's discomfort, Galloway knew he had been in the island too long. His head seemed to throb harder as punishment.

The boy shifted his gaze from the overseer to the ground and began moving his weight from leg to leg nervously at the question. Tension built where none had existed before. Neddy could feel tears of fright begin to well up in his eyes, and they blurred the vision of the white man sitting on the rock, now gently slapping his leg with the riding jack he carried. His figure seemed to enlarge through the lenses of the eye water. The mule he had tethered to a bush beside the rock swished its tail to and fro, as if keeping time with the riding whip. Neddy fought back the tears. The struggle became harder, and he could feel the trickle begin down his cheeks.

Galloway, fully aware of the boy's unease, said gently, "Neddy, boys don't cry. No one here is going to hurt you. Bush time will come soon enough, but not with me. Come now, boy, play me a tune. All I want is to listen to that flute of yours. Who taught you?"

As the consolatory words sank in, Neddy sniffled and wiped the tears away from his cheeks on the back of his clean white Sunday shirt sleeve. He held up the flute, his eyes still glistening. "Reverend Waldrich, sah. Im bring di music from America, when him go and come back." Neddy choked nervously. Wiping his cheek again, this time with the wrist of the hand holding the flute he added, "Is me make di flute out of bamboo."

"Did you, now?" Galloway paused, as if thinking along a different track before changing direction to say. "Obviously, Neddy, you know what the tune you were playing means?"

A little smile appeared around Neddy's lips, signaling relief that the innocence of his boyhood would continue a little longer. He looked down at the road, a bit fretful to be on his way again, but Galloway quickly added, "Play what you were playing when we met, Neddy. I would like to hear your rendition."

"'Amazing Grace,' sah?"

"Yes, boyo. I heard tell of the man and his redemption," Galloway smirked. "Redemption is the password into heaven for you Baptists."

"Is di Moravian church we a go, sah. Not di Baptist!"

"Never mind, it is touching music and almost worthy of being a Gaelic lament. Play it, boy."

Neddy put the bamboo flute to his lips, his fingers nervously searched for the right holes of the six to block, and then, with a hesitant breath, a note of sorts came out.

Galloway shuddered, slapped his leg with his whip impatiently, and barked, "Play it with feeling, boy. All music, no matter what, must be played with feeling, or it has no meaning, no feel to it. Music is life, and it has to have meaning, or why bother to go on? Now play for life, youth."

Neddy began again. This time his flute filled with pathos. His fingers blocked the six holes, then four, then two, then four again, back to two, three, four, five and a half, and six. His eyes closed, and his music seemed to take wing, gliding above and beyond the treetops. This time there were no singers to accompany him, just the one white man sitting stock still with his eyes closed, for audience. Neddy had never played like this before. "Was lost but now am found," came through the simple instrument so distinctly that there was no need for a human voice to sing the words. The meaning was clear. On he went, with the notes lifting higher and higher. Galloway sat on the rock in front of him, also with his eyes closed. So intent were they on the music and the moment that neither heard the horseman rounding the corner from the Williamsfield road.

"What's this, a roadside concert? Too early in the morning for such things. Is that you, Galloway?"

At the interruption, a discordant note from the flute ended the recital. Galloway did not have to open his eyes; he knew who it was.

"It is never too early for music. But Mr. Breary, is it not too early for Mr. Breary?" Galloway opened his eyes and looked at the horseman before him. Apart from his broad-brimmed raffia hat, he was dressed for riding in English fashion. He wore a carefully pressed black coat with white tights that bulged with the lumpiness of the late thirties. Each leg was encased in carefully handcrafted knee boots, which some slave had spent hours rubbing to the highest gloss. All the horse's accouterments sparkled and formed a sharp contrast to Galloway's mule, with its disreputable saddle, rope stirrups, and bridle. Obviously, Breary was dressed for going calling and not for church.

"Like going for an early morning ride on Sunday, Galloway—like it much indeed. Usually ride with Forbes-Dunbar, but he is taken down with fever this day."

"More like drunk and hung over, if I know the major. Are you currying up to him now? You know they kicked him out of the East India Company? That's why he is here rather than there. Not worth knowing, that one." There was a pause before Galloway went on. "His people sent him out to look after the last place they own in Jamaica." Galloway looked up at Breary, his lips twisting at the left corner in a half-smile as Breary struggled with his horse. "And he is botching it, you know. By the time he is dead, the creditors will have it all."

"Good soldier, though," said Breary, defending the reputation of his friend.

Galloway smirked. "So he tells us."

"We need men like him in the militia," Breary insisted. "The slaves are restive these days."

"They are always restive. What do you expect from chained animals?"

"Yes, well—that's maybe," said Breary, not really knowing what more to say.

Neddy stood listening quietly, not fully understanding what the white men were talking about. He wanted to leave them but was not sure how. The sun was getting higher, and if he did not get down the road quickly, he would be late for church. The Erwin estate and village, where the Moravian church stood on a small hill, was still a good three miles' walk. Reverend Waldrich would be none too pleased if his prize flute player were not there at the beginning of the service.

"I gots to go now, sah, if yu please," said Neddy to Galloway.

"Oh yes, boy, thank you for the playing." Galloway put his hand in his pocket and brought out a penny for him. With further kindliness he added, "Avoid Friendship, or you will go a bush with Backra

Roy. Then you will have the seed of the devil in you while you listen to the word of God."

"Yes, sah." Neddy's eyes turned down again to the road by his feet. At the warning, they did not seem too motivated to walk. Friendship estate lands bordered Erwin. He would have to pass by them on his way to the church.

"Yea, though I walk through the valley of the shadow I will fear no evil, for thou art with me," intoned Galloway followed by a laugh. "You passed by there all the time, and the Lord looked after you—and you did not know it, Neddy ! You don't have to be afeared, he will look after you yet again." Galloway chuckled. He was not being vicious, but the horseman and the boy did not understand the humor.

"Roy does have a penchant for that vice; but, I must say, he is a comely boy," broke in Breary. The last part came hesitantly, as if afraid to admit the obvious, which could be misconstrued.

"Well, you English introduced the Negroes to it, and like ducks to water, you know? Not that they did not indulge before. You planters have rued the day for they now prefer to breed each other than their womenfolk." Galloway waved his hand expansively toward the hills and flats. "Look around you and see; the plantations are running out of slaves since you can't import them, and here they are buggering each other."

"Unnatural practice."

"No more so than bulls mounting bulls and rams tupping rams. That is a daily occurrence."

"Yes, but they are dumb animals."

"And we are?" Galloway's left eyebrow lifted with his rhetorical question to Breary.

"What is so wonderful about the whole thing," he went on, "is watching the guilt you Protestants have after you have gone a bush with one of these boys."

"And I suppose you Catholics don't suffer guilt?"

"Oh yes, but we have the confessional box, and you have only your little, little selves to look to for absolution. We Catholics have the Almighty himself."

"Damn your papist sophistry, Galloway."

"Better be a papist than a Baptist, Mr. Breary. We stand by, while they bring the whole house of cards down on your heads. I hear one of your future relatives horsewhipped one of their rabble-rousing preachers over in Falmouth a week or so ago."

"One of my future relatives? Where did you get that from?"

"Come on, mi boyo, as a Welshman would say; everyone knows you are after Miss Mary Vernon, gentlewoman and heiress. That is where you are heading now I bet. Was it not a Vernon who beat the poor parson man in Falmouth?"

Breary's horse began to prance and sidestep as it felt its rider stiffen in the saddle at the mention of the Vernons. Galloway smirked as Breary tried to settle the horse. He did not have a very good seat, and the big gray gelding sensed this and danced sideways across the road, tossing its head up and back. Luckily for Breary, it was held in check by a martingale.

"My, my, you do ride showy cattle for just a morning outing," Galloway said, as the animal settled down under the restraining hand of its rider.

"Im a ride harse, im don't ride cow, sah!"

Both white men were caught off guard by the remark. They had forgotten the boy standing there, taking their conversation in. They looked at each other trying to figure what he meant, and it was Galloway who twigged first. He began to laugh and the effort made his head throb, reminding him yet again of the night before. "Lord, boy! Gentleman in England sometimes refer to their fine horses as cattle. Like many things they do, it is wrong way round."

"Why bother explain, Galloway? He won't understand."

"We all need explanations, Breary."

Richard Breary stiffened at being addressed in the familiar by the overseer. "Remember your place, Galloway," he admonished haughtily.

"How could I forget it, Breary? I am in my place because I own nothing; you are in your place because you own two slaves and are courting Miss Mary Vernon, heiress to the Mount Vernon, Keith Hall, and Stonehenge estates. If she be foolish enough to take you on herself, then, and only then, will you be truly esquire."

The two men stared at each other, one sitting on the rock, and the other uncomfortably on his nervous horse. Both knew the truth had been spoken. Breary was the first to break the tension by forcing a laugh before adding, "I suppose you could be right. She is not the only one inheriting, you know? She ain't in Stonehenge; that is her cousin James, the doctor's son, and a share goes to her father's quadroon bastard, William."

"You mean her brother?"

Quickly, Breary turned that observation aside, by conveniently remembering that Galloway was also well connected. As a matter of fact, better connected than he himself. "But ain't you in line for some property yourself, Galloway?"

Galloway grunted, shrugged. "Maybe."

Time anyway to get moving. He made the effort to stand. Once more he mounted his mule and turned its head toward Newman Hall, giving it a nudge with his heel. "Coming my way, Breary?" Then he stopped the mule with a light tug on the reins. Turning in the saddle he looked at the boy still standing there, obviously reluctant to continue on his original path. "Get along to your church, Neddy. You will be late." He added, "Walk with care." For an instant his eyes scanned the youth yet again, then he turned and kicked the mule into motion. Breary followed.

"When is your wedding going to be?"

"Galloway!" Breary exclaimed. "How the deuce did you know Miss Vernon had accepted my proposal?"

"Every Negro and white person from St. Elizabeth to Trelawny knows that you have been after her. The Negroes knew the moment you asked her, and then everyone knows in the Parish."

"Yes, we tend to forget they listen to all our conversations. They are never out of earshot."

"Let's face it, Breary, the Negro is invisible to our eyes. He is colorless." The pun was lost on his companion.

"What do you mean, Galloway?" asked Breary, a puzzled look clouding his normally bland features.

"Furniture, man. It's there. You use it and forget it. If it could talk, we all would be in great trouble with each other. Well, that's the damned Negro. Only he can talk, and does." Galloway turned in his saddle and looked straight at Breary, who was still trying to control his jittery gray. The horse showed signs of stress. Lather on his neck and saliva where he wrangled the bit showed his rider's poor horsemanship. "Has she accepted you, then?"

"Yes, we are going to be wed in Falmouth. She will be over at Stonehenge then. Yes, the wedding will be on the twenty-sixth, November. All the family will be there."

"Then damned good luck to both of you, Mr. Richard Breary, Esquire, sir," said Galloway with a half-smile.

At John's Hall village square, a mile above Worcester, Breary and Galloway dismounted. Sunday was no time to hurry. Literally, it was the day of rest and prayer on the plantations. Slaves went to their provision grounds to work them and collect fruits and vegetables for their weekly supplement. Surplus produce they sold to the Jews who traded in the towns. And so Jacob da Lazarus was in the square when the two rode up.

Four of his donkeys were straining under loaded wicker hampers, while the peddler sat on a stool by the door of the thatch-roofed wattle-and-daub rum shop. It was owned and run by Tinka Jackson, a free mulatto. As the two riders made toward the door of the establishment, they were greeted by the stool sitter.

"Marning, gentlemen. What you doing bout ya before di sun ready to set up on di hills? Hope yu nah go set up in competition with a poor peddler like me and buy up all di produce de naygar man got to sell?" said da Lazarus, in exaggerated Creole manner. He was a thin man, with parrot-like features and a sallow complexion that suggested a heavier tarring of Moor than da Lazarus would freely admit to having.

Like so many of his ilk, they had been here long before the British arrived. When the Spanish were kicked out, the Portuguese Jews stayed and made the most of it. Protestants suited them; they were far easier to get along with than the Catholics. It did not matter that Jews were looked down on as second class and to be kept at arm's length. They were free to come and go, do business, and attend their own synagogue.

"You are quite safe there, Jacob," answered Breary, who was familiar with his coming and going in the district. He was the most successful of his kind and had been at the game a long time. Every area had these peddlers; most were Jews. Montego Bay, Falmouth, and all other big towns depended on them for supplies, not only in produce but dry goods as well. They made a lot of money trading and being informal bankers, and they were the main conduit by which many a slave built up what would be envied as a small fortune. Thanks to them, the slave population had over three million pounds sterling in gold hidden under beds or buried in their provision grounds.

"What in the world would give the idea that a Christian gentleman would want to take over from a Jew? We have to leave certain things for you sons of Abraham to do, you know."

"Just funning, Mr. Breary. When you going get married, sah?"

"What do you know about such things?" Breary came back at the peddler haughtily, obviously irritated that such a type should know of his impending nuptials. "It's really none of your business, da Lazarus."

Galloway laughed at the question and his companion's indignation. "I told you that every man and his puss knows of your plans for the rich heiress, Mistress Vernon."

"Well, it's just damned well none of Jew business, Galloway. That's all there is to it." There was an arrogant sulkiness in the statement.

"All business is a Jew's business, Mr. Breary," said da Lazarus softly, with more than that tinge of studied obsequiousness Jews showed gentiles. "Dat's how we survive so long. All I want to do is wish you an di lady happiness and long life."

"Nothing else?" Breary asked with a suspicious look at the peddler.

"Well, now dat you asks, I was going to suggest dat you bring di lady to mi shop on St. James Street and let her look at di new damasks, calicoes, and silks just come down from New York. She may well find some ting dat would please her." His English was oddly overlaid with patois and back-of-the-throat Hebrew harshness that added a slur to many of his words.

"Produce and cloth. I hope you don't mix them up in the same basket or shelf?" smirked Breary.

"I sells every ting, sah. That is the way to do it. One year there is little produce 'cause of the hurricanes or drought, so you have to have more dan one string to your bow," the Jew explained.

"Yes, we all know about weather calamities in the island."

"Can I buy you gentlemen a drink?"

Galloway watched Breary begin to puff himself up again and knew a put-down was coming.

"No, thank you, Jacob. I just want water or coconut water, if it is available," Galloway said.

"Tinka, Tinka, come out ya, man. You got customers. Di gentleman want some water, an if unu got it, some coconut water. An while you de, bring me another of your ginger beers," da Lazarus ordered.

A minute or two later, the sound of cans banged against each other assured those waiting outside that they were being looked after. Tinka arrived on the scene with worn, bruised pewter mugs of coconut water and ginger beer. The Jew remained on the stool, the gentlemen on a bench just under the eaves of the thatched roof. Tinka walked over and served them first before turning to da Lazarus.

"You want any ting more?"

Da Lazarus signaled no with his hand and looked over at Galloway, sipping his coconut water. "Captain Galloway, you going to be called into Montego Bay for the Christmas to keep order among the naygars?" The militia would be in the towns around holiday time to control the drunken slaves overcelebrating their three days of freedom.

"I expect so, but we are only in November. That will be yet awhile."

"Captain?" Breary said, lifting his eyebrows in astonishment.

Galloway turned and looked at the dumpy little man. "What's the matter, Breary? Surprised to hear that an overseer has the rank of captain in the militia? What, not a gentleman and so highly placed? Sorry to disappoint you, Breary, but I was a captain in the regulars long before I came to this accursed island to do this ignoble job."

"Never meant anything by it, Galloway. Never knew that, not being in the militia and all. Closest I get to the military is Forbes-Dunbar, you know."

"It doesn't matter, Breary. You would hardly know my history, as we only met, what was it, six months ago?" Not waiting for his companion's corroboration, Galloway turned to the peddler. "Yes, Jacob, I will be in Montego Bay come the birth of our Savior. They always call us down at that time, I understand. This will be my first year on guard, so to speak."

Ignoring the Jew and determined not to be left out of the conversation, Breary interjected, "What regiment did you serve in, Galloway?"

"Sixteenth Bedfordshire Foot."

"That one used to be out here, if memory serves me correctly," Richard Breary added.

"As a matter of fact it has been out here on two tours of duty. I missed both tours. But you know, Breary, a sublieutenant with me, who is a major now, was Brabazon Vernon." He paused and crooked an eyebrow at his companion. "A relative of your Miss Vernon, perhaps?"

"Don't know, Galloway. Never heard them speak of him."

"They would have to be from Ireland to be related. Brabazon is Irish, like me."

"Hardly, Galloway! The Vernons are from the Midlands. Warwickshire, Derbyshire, Worcester, round those counties. They are the same family as the admiral. Don't think they have Irish relatives, Galloway."

"Not good enough for them eh, Breary? The Irish are never good enough for the English. Isn't that right? Good enough to do your fighting and your dirty work but not marry your daughters. Would you let one of those rascals marry your sister, Richard mi boy?"

"Hardly know that, Galloway. Have many friends who are Irish."

"Which admiral would that be, the one they call Old Grog, Mr. Breary?" Jacob said, reminding them there was a third party to their banter.

"Old Grog? Oh! You mean Admiral Vernon. Yes, that's the one."

"Me seems to remember," cut in Galloway, "there are two bastards out of Vernon by Nugent. One even governed this island."

Only the uncomfortable creak of their bench cut the silence after Galloway's quip. Jacob watched a cockroach creep from a crack in the bench the men were sitting on and make its way to Galloway's boot. Then, slowly, its feelers searched along the side of its sole to the boot's arch and under it to appear in the sunlight on the other side. Slowly it made its way to the toe.

Had the roach been cognizant of the realities of the world, it would have lived long. There would have been the realization that cockroaches were night creatures only, and the dark hours were best for survival. Trapped in broad daylight, a greenish brown lizard, close to a foot long from jaws to tail, streaked in from off the porch and made it breakfast. Clamped firmly in the lizard's griping jaws, the roach's legs worked furiously back and forth in a futile attempt to escape. Then it disappeared into the bushes as the reptile's meal.

"Hum! That's how we all go. One minute you tink you is safe, and the next you gone. What it doing in daylight, I ask you gentlemen? That's how it is going to be for all of us. And it coming sooner dan you tink."

"What are you talking about, da Lazarus?"

"The changing times we live in, Mr. Breary. Slavery will soon end, one way or t'other. You watch! Back in England the Parliament soon abolish it, just as they did the slave trade."

"If they do that, then we will join America. There is talk of doing that anyway, so we can trade in slaves again. Plantations are going to ruinate because there is no labor. If that happens, then it will change for the better, da Lazarus."

"That is so true from a planter's point of view. But Richard," Galloway continued, "England will never allow Jamaica to become Yankee."

"Never mind Yankee, never mind what Parliament does in England. What you rich planters have to watch out for are the naygars and them psalm-singing, hand-clapping, baptizing, Reverend Knibb people. Baptist blessed and Baptist led, they will be the cause of a Baptist hell here in the island!" the Jew exploded in plain English, with passion uncharacteristic of his kind. Galloway and Breary were taken aback.

"What have you heard, da Lazarus?" Breary inquired nervously. His interest was sufficiently aroused by the Jew's passion that, for a moment, he forgot he was a Jew. But before the Jew could make his answer, a garbled chatter from above turned all who heard it in its direction.

Kakakawasheebakrabakrabakradonebakradonebakkragone. Slowly a black crow flew overhead followed by a companion. Back and forth they gibbered at each other, as their wings labored with the effort of flight, taking them from treetop to treetop. Those below listened in puzzlement and tried to decipher what they said. Human chatter everyone knew it was, but what was the language? What were they saying?

"Christ!" exclaimed Galloway, "there they go again. They were at it this morning, further down the road. What the hell are they?"

"Lord God! Dem is jabbering crows, Mr. Galloway. Jabbering crows, sah. You never heard them before? Bud, dem are my specialty," Jacob da Lazarus said with some pride. He had slipped back into his creole talk. "Studied them from I was a likkle boye. That, a true Jamaican bud. Dey live way up in the cockpit mountains." He stopped, his brow furrowed as if in deep thought, and then went on, "Strange, dem crows never come down this far. It too low for them. Something must be wrong." He turned and shouted through the door, "Tinka, Tinka come ya-so. You understand crow talk, what dem say?

The rum-shopkeeper came out at the call. "What dem always sey, sah," he said.

"And what is that?" inquired Breary.

"Well, Massa, dem sey, 'don't do backra work, backra done, backra soon gone.' Dat's what dem say."

"Now you know, Mr. Breary, and I must be gone to Montego Bay miself. Business is business and must be done. Where mi man gone, Tinka? Cumberland, Cumberland!" shouted da Lazarus, "Where di rass you deh? Bring mi horse and di donkeys round front."

Galloway and Breary sat where they were and let the Jew depart. They watched him mount his ancient horse.

"Dammed Jew will work an animal to death," commented Breary softly as the procession got underway. "That animal should have been turned out to pasture long ago."

In no better condition than the horse, four donkeys laden with produce headed down the road toward the coast and Montego Bay, led by Cumberland.

"Can't stand his type. We shouldn't have let them stay after we kicked the Dons out of here. They always seem to have their hands in another man's pockets. Well, Galloway, can't sit chatting to you all day. Must get going mi-self." Both men got up at that, and Breary handed Tinka a three-penny piece to cover the cost of their drinks.

Galloway swung himself easily onto his mule, while Tinka gave Breary a leg up onto his gray. They turned up the road and were soon clear of John's Hall village and back in cane-growing hillsides. Only a few trees grew by the roadside. All the way up the valley, healthy green sugarcane sprouted on different estates. They'd had just enough rain and sunshine to make an excellent crop come January and February.

Tedious work was at hand now for slave, bookkeeper, and overseer alike. Keeping the weeds down and the fields clean so the ratoons, or fresh plantings, could get hold was the main concern from September right through until December. After that month, there would be little respite for any until the crop was in and the cane juice turned into the stuff of gold. But before that, Christmastime would come. Jonkunnu would be out and about, and the drinking and celebrating would be underway for three days of freedom.

"Big estate, this. Love to own it. Would go well with Mount Vernon lands."

"One day, Breary, all that could come to pass. That is, if you turn out to be a successful planter. Many great estates are going to come up for sale, the way things are going, I bet."

"You may be right, Galloway."

They had just reached Spring Mount Estate when Breary reined in his horse. "This is where we part company, Galloway. I am going to cut through here on to Mount Vernon lands."

"Go easily there. That track is steep, rough, and not well traveled. Your horse seems ready to shy at every step. We don't want Miss Vernon dressed in black before she has worn her bridal gown—do we?"

Richard Breary doffed his hat to Galloway and kicked the horse into a canter as he left the main road. There was nothing like showing his mettle to those who cautioned him. He rode through the cane piece. Before long, he was through Spring Mount bottom over the boundary wall and onto on one of the better sections of Mount Vernon lands.

He knew that this acreage had been left to old man Vernon's freeborn quadroon son, who, although he had not got the property had already changed its name to Cool Water. James Vernon was to get his piece, too. Richard Breary hated the estate being broken up. Mary would have a goodly share after her cousin James, but by the time the distribution was done, Mary's share of Mount Vernon would be down to about six hundred acres. Perhaps after the marriage, he could swap her share of Stonehenge in Trelawny with her cousin for his share of Mount Vernon. Then maybe he could get that arrogant quadroon William to sell. All these thoughts were going through his head as he came up to the gates and the carriageway to the Great House.

Through one of the open lattice cooler shutters in the piazza, Mary Vernon could see him riding up. She smiled to herself. She knew she was no great catch, heiress or not. He was white, and he was a man. There would be no question about their children, and that was what mattered.

Years had passed since Mary's mother and father had died. She had been brought up in Scotland with her aunt before disobeying her father's wishes and returning to the island. Coming out never really happened for her after her parents' deaths. Her guardian was not much of a social man. Besides, he thought it best to keep it all in the family. With this in mind, he planned to marry her off to his son.

Cousins married cousins regularly in Jamaica. The shortage of white women was one reason, and keeping land in the family the other. Thanks to her mustee status, she just met the requirements, so the necessary arrangements were made.

Prospects for her future looked bright, but Thomas died just three years after her parents. She never forgot that September. Her eyes seemed to have changed permanently to red from crying. She felt so alone and deserted. Nanny came into her bed at nights to rock her to sleep, as she had done when Mary was a baby and scared of duppies. Her only relief in those years was being sent to her aunt in Scotland and then to England to stay with relatives in Warwickshire.

Then tragedy came again: her guardian died. For a time the family was in disarray. It was her youngest brother, William, who stepped in to steady the situation. It was funny to think of her little brother taking charge and becoming her closest and dearest ally in the family. The last of eight children, until Hannah was born, no one paid William much attention growing up. Then, as her father's will dictated, he, like the rest of the children, was sent away to school. Like so many others with similar backgrounds, William was packed off to England. He would be as an equal there and not just a quadroon, as he was here. After all, he was still William Vernon's son and must be brought up a gentleman.

On William's return from England, he took up the duties of the overseer on Mount Vernon. That allowed their cousin James to concentrate on his Stonehenge estate in Trelawny, even though he had inherited most of Mount Vernon from his uncle because he was white.

Mary looked down from the window as Richard Breary dismounted by the welcoming arms of the steps to the entrance of Mount Vernon Great House. He was her last chance for a husband, and this time she would make sure not to miss out on the opportunity of being a wife. Besides, running an estate was a man's job. Eventually, William would want to be with his own young family on Mount Apfel, and James was far away on Stonehenge. So it was now dear Richard, and he was most welcome.

Galloway rode into the yard of the overseer's house on Newman Hall. Lucy stood at the entrance, waiting to welcome him. He had won her at cards from Doctor Waite when he first arrived in Montego Bay. She was so beautiful, and pregnant at fifteen. Three months later she had given birth to a healthy boy, obviously Waite's child. Octoroon by definition, he looked more of a mustee; and as he grew up, he would undoubtedly be taken for white if his mother was not in view.

Galloway insisted that the child be given his name and be registered as a mustee, and as such white by law in Jamaica. For that, he won Lucy's everlasting gratitude. She had been willing to become more than a housekeeper for him, but he had not taken advantage of her, as many other white men would have. It was the *droit de seigneur* to have a quadroon, octoroon, or mustee housekeeper who bedded with them regularly. Society and nature alike demanded it. Galloway shunned the idea of bastard children with the added stigma of caste thrust upon them. They were in the island, seemingly lost between the dawn and dusk of humanity, neither knowing nor able to choose their place.

"Welcome, Massa," she said, as he came up the steps to the door.

"Don't call me that! I have told you that!" He was not angry, just irritated by her subservience. Everyone was always "Yes Massa, no, Massa, can I get you dis or dat Massa? Massa, Massa, Massa." He needed a rest from being Massa.

Her eyes filled with tears at his irritation. People were ever ready to cry here in the island. He was never sure whether it was genuine or not. Lucy was the exception. If ever a man was certain of sincerity, Galloway was certain of Lucy. Tired and thirsty, he nevertheless reached out for her and pulled her close. He was very seldom so intimate. Hung over and road weary, he felt the need to touch soft, warm flesh just then.

"Never mind, Lucy, I did not mean to be brutal," he comforted her. His hand moved up to her face, and she turned her right side away, trying to hide the terrible scars where her ear had been torn to shreds. She always wore a bandana pulled down to hide the disfigurement. Galloway just stroked her cheek and hugged her closely. "Now, go and get me a glass of water and tell that lazy Hercules to get in here and take off my boots. After that, I do not want to be disturbed until the morning." He walked across the hall to the bedroom.

Five miles away, Jacob da Lazarus's horse labored with him as Jacob struggled to keep the donkey caravan in line and underway. They had not yet reached Erwin, but Neddy had. This time he had not taken the shortcut through Friendship estate. Galloway's warnings rang loud and clear inside his head, and he had run the long way by the road. The Moravian church bell rang out its appeal, "God's word is here." Neddy reached the door, slipped on his sandals, and crept in along the side of the pews up to where the little organist sat. Reverend Waldrich was pleased to see that his flutist had made it. Neddy had never missed, but the reverend had wondered this day at his lateness.

Chapter 2

False Prophets

The Reverend Waldrich placed his foot on the first of the seven steps that would put him in the pulpit. His mind was in a whirl. How could he dash their hopes? He knew that all who sat in front of him were waiting to hear that the freedom paper had come, and they would be free.

Those damned Baptists, always jumping the gun, he thought, as his right foot stepped on the second step. *They are always stirring up trouble by promising in the name of the Lord what only the Parliament in England can bring about.*

He had prepared a sermon on goodness and kindness to one's neighbors but realized it would be of no use. His flock was not interested in that today. There was a stir in the air, a buzz around. Rumor had it that Brother Sharpe had said this and that were going to happen, but Waldrich knew that to be wrong. Sam would never raise false hopes. He knew the man. Slave he was, but as educated and intelligent and well thought of as any white parson.

Waldrich was now on the third step, and a whirlwind churned in his mind. If he did not put a damper on the expectations, then there would be trouble. Planters and those who owned and expected the labor from the black bodies they had bought and cared for would come down hard. They could be harsh when their economic interests were threatened. Backs would be peeled by the cart whip. Trees would bear strange fruit. And the country would stink of rotting corpses as the wind carried the putrefaction forward to all corners.

Had not Richard Barrett gone to London and pleaded the planters' case eloquently? He climbed the fourth step. Only three to go before he faced them down there in the pews. All eyes stared at him, all ears listened to each word and phrase and nuance. They were not dumb animals, these blacks. They were different to look at on the surface from the whites, but they were the same when skinned. What to say? Could he be as convincing today as Barrett had been in front of the Parliamentary committee drawn up to investigate slavery in the colonies?

Man was so strange when he was threatened. Waldrich moved to the fifth step. Cruelty was intensified when a household turned in on itself, and that would happen not only in this island but in all the British colonies in the Antilles. Slave and master were one, black and white in a symbiotic relationship in this social order. How had this slave colony begun? Had the Lord intended it to bring white and black together?

Oh Lord! Help thy servant in this time of need, he silently prayed, as his foot raised him to the sixth step. At first a shadow and then the pitch black of nothingness engulfed his mind. So completely lost was he that even fainting to escape this moment was beyond his consciousness.

He was there, the seventh step. Now, he faced all faces, and eyes stared at him, wide and unblinking. They drew him in, every eye a black and bottomless pit. A lifetime of familiar greens, blues, and browns under blond hair were nowhere seen in the congregation. Irwin was not Munchen-Gladbach. Perspiration ran from Waldrich's face, along his neck, to the tight collar stiff with starch that his good wife insisted he wear, for appearances' sake. She insisted it let the entire world know he did the Lord's work, which was righteous.

"The Apostle John describes the seventieth week and warns all of you that the end is coming." The echo of his words came back to him from the walls of the church. Did he really say that? The pause had been dramatic and brought the congregation to the edge of their

False Prophets

seats. He could see them all lean forward in expectation of his next statement.

"The first seal is a white horse and a rider." His voice came from deep within, resonating and commanding those who were before him to listen. Never before had he sounded like this. Only back in Germany had he heard those taken with the spirit utter thus. One such voice had drawn him into the church and impelled him to go forth and teach the way of the Lord, to become a savior of those lost souls in slavery, in a world full of evil.

"He represents false prophets of the Antichrist, who conquers by deception. Revelation six, verses one and two. But where it is found in the Holy Scriptures does not matter; it is there and is the truth. Pay you heed." Both hands gripped the pulpit rail, and his head and upper body leaned forward and over, as if impelling each and every ear to listen on pain of eternal damnation.

He had got their attention. Now he was in the hands of God. Nothing prepared, all words that came from him now were those of the Lord. He was but the mouthpiece.

"The second seal," his voice had deepened and resonated as if coming from within a cave, "is a red horse and rider. The sword of war raised by his right hand, he conquers through war. Right and left does he swing the scimitar. Heads roll, and the blood of innocent and evildoer alike change the earth's green to red. Oh Lord, have mercy upon your children."

"Amen," came up from below him. Bodies moved and heads turned to look over their shoulders.

"A black horse and rider is the third seal. In his hands is the scale to measure food and goodness provided by the land. Famine is his weapon. He will bring it down upon us all. In place of humans, skin and bones walk the earth. Children crying for want in the land. Bloated bellies filled with the wind of hunger will be everywhere. No help cometh to you." His hand shot out over the congregation with his forefinger pointing like an arrow to the back of the church, his eyes staring as if seeing shadows materializing. There was an audible intake of breath and heads turned quickly to where he pointed. With a scream, a young girl flopped forward. A helping arm coddled and supported her. "Death is upon the land, and the black horseman rides into the night and with him all of us!" His words rose to hysteria.

"Mercy, Lord! Mercy, Lord! Have mercy!" The cry came in unison from the tormented below.

"But," he began, and paused. Below him was the silence when breathing stops. "The one most afeared is the fourth seal, the pale horse and rider. He cometh and is death and pestilence. Heads, arms, and legs lie in the dust as he rides by. A great two-handed sword he swings, to the right and the left, like a scythe among wheat. The beasts of the jungle gorge themselves on the corpses left scattered by his passage. Vermin of the earth invade those left standing and bring pestilence upon the living. That is the carnage the pale rider leaves behind." The reverend's voice dropped to a hoarse whisper.

Overcome by the oratory and heat, the leader of the choir fainted. She lay where she had dropped. Not one member of his congregation moved. They were transfixed. Their minister was glassy-eyed and standing in a trance, it seemed to them. He had caught the spirit. Many who watched had seen it all before, when the obeah man had been taken. Now they discovered obeah took black as well as white, and they were amazed. The strongest would win. Jesus was on the white man's side, and the black man had only his juju. They were impressed. Waldrich's funny German accent was dismissed. Their man was a true man of the spirit. They accepted this, and it pleased them. Lord! They had been given a speaker of spirit words.

"Revelation! Revelation! Revelation!" they cried in unison. A silence followed and seemed to last forever. A moan from somewhere brought them all out of the mantra state. A fellow chorister helped their leader back to her sitting position.

"If we are to avoid ze inevitable, it is the first rider ve must stop." The reverend took a deep breath. He was tired, and his German accent became more pronounced. "He represents false prophets. Follow him, and all the other riders follow." They could all hear him sucking in the breath. "They are the terrible four horsemen who have haunted mankind from the beginning of the world. We can stop them here in Jamaica, if we stop the first one." Again, the reverend paused. He raised his arms in a gesture to heaven and looked to God through the church ceiling. Suddenly his arms dropped to his sides, in weariness and in expectant rejection. No more words came from him.

"Speak, preacher! Let us hear di word of Gad! Yes, Lard, let us see di light. Di light!"

Rejuvenated by their shouts, he raised his arms again. "Rumor has it that the freedom paper is in the land, and the planters won't honor it. Freedom is withheld from us. He who says that is so is a false prophet. Believe them not; they lead those awful horses and riders out of the stable and let them loose upon the world, once the barn door is let fly." Reverend Waldrich knew that he had them all hanging on his oratory again. It gave him a sense of power he had never known before, and he was exhilarated. Even his wife down below, in the first pew, sat transfixed.

Never before had she heard her husband in full exhortation; she was mesmerized. Her mouth was slightly open, saliva running from the right corner to her chin. Looking down, her husband was slightly revolted but strangely impressed. She had always been the pushy one, a regular martinet in the household. Her wishes and orders had to be carried out without deviation. In the parish, though, she was a godsend. A pillar of fortitude, carrying the word of God to these unfortunate heathens was her life, apart from the welfare of her husband. What would he do without her? She was better at this missionary work than he was. However, this moment was his.

"Yes, ze owners and ze planters vill resist and fight as long as zey can." The tension broken, he went on, "But zey cannot vin ven Parliament enacts its legislation. No force in England or in Jamaica can vithstand ze order of Parliament. Ze mother of all parliaments, ze one zat teaches ze vorld vat is justice." Once again, it was time to pause and let what he had said sink into the dark minds below. Many he knew were bright, but many others were slow on the uptake. They were tied to the way it was, to the order laid out by known authority.

"Yes, the barn door is ajar. Close it quickly. Banish the false prophets and stop the other three horsemen from getting loose. If they do, we, the righteous children of this earth, will suffer most horribly." He had made his point. To go on would be like flogging a dead horse. Waldrich almost giggled at the thought. He so loved making puns. To think them up in English was an accomplishment. His knowledge of the language was improving. Zat vas goodt.

"Redemption! Redemption!" he shouted. "Let us sing a hymn, nay, the song from our zouls for redemption. If John Newton can find it, we too can find it. Let us hear and sing Amazing Grace." From the pulpit, he looked down at Neddy.

Given the cue for his big moment, Neddy felt a million humming birds had been let loose in his stomach. Their wings tickled his innards, the feeling spreading to his arms and legs. Luckily, being seated, his legs were not required to support him at that moment. He closed his eyes and lifted his flute. An image of the white man who had made him play that morning appeared in his head, and he heard him command, "Play it for life, Neddy."

His fingers began to move along the holes of the instrument. At first he heard his flute. Then he felt his flute, and then his flute became an extension of himself and his toes moved in unison with his fingers across the holes. It was he making music, not the bamboo stick at his lips. Powerful, sweet sounds sang out as his long fingers blocked and unblocked the holes. Voices around him took up the tune, and their great expanse resounded off the walls of the small, cut-stone church.

Reverend Waldrich was most pleased with his Sunday's work as he stood at the door of his church, shaking hands and giving out his little homilies. His best service ever had just ended. An inspired sermon, he knew. It had come to him—a revelation. God's word and God's warning. For the first time, God's work was his work. The Lord had made him shepherd of this flock, and they were his responsibility. It was up to him to see that they were not led astray with false hopes. Predators lurked, waiting to settle the slavery question once and for all, in their own favor.

Many planters encouraged the more brutish to burn Baptist chapels and talked about becoming Americans. Waldrich wondered when they would turn their attention to the Moravian establishments. They had been lucky thus far. Then again, they were not as outspoken or militant as the Baptists. All things in God's good time, Moravians knew. Pushing the timeframe could bring disaster on the

False Prophets

most worthy and divine cause of the century. Standing on the steps of the church, watching his satisfied and now joyous congregation meander off home, the reverend felt he understood the grand design. Neddy came by, and he caught the boy by the shoulder.

"Young man, zat vas ze most beautiful I have heard Amazing Grace played. You must have been practicing a lot. Zat is how you make a success of live. Vork and order, vork and order. Zank you. Again, zank you." He gave the boy a friendly pat on the back that sent him on his way.

Neddy felt as if he were floating on air as he walked home. Someone called to him, "You play nice do. It sweet wi. Di Lord love how you sound, boyee." He felt even better.

Up the road, far in front of the stragglers coming out of the church, the popular chant of the day began. It rolled back along the road, and all voices picked it up, as in a choir. You could tell they felt the words held their future.

One, two, tree
All de same,
Black, white, brown
All de same.
Yes, sah, Lord!
White, brown, black,
One, two, tree,
Brown, black, white,
All de same!

Waldrich heard them and had second thoughts. Had his moment extolling God's word been truly heeded? Or was it just the moment of passion that took them and now passed, as their own aspirations and anxieties took over once again? The questions puzzled him for a minute, and then he shrugged his shoulders as he heard his wife calling him to follow her back to their house.

Neddy felt nice. It made him forget to take off the sandals and hang them around his neck. He stopped in his tracks with the realization, looked down at them, and wriggled his toes; he thought about

35

taking them off but decided to leave the sandals right where they were, on his feet. They were supposed to be there. On Sundays, from now on, he would wear them all day. He nodded his head in agreement with the thought and went on his way. A few steps further along the path, he stopped again and frowned. In his excitement, he had forgotten the warning he had received that morning and was well on the shortcut across Friendship. Quickly he glanced back over his shoulder. Then his head cautiously turned right and then left to see if there was anyone about.

Go back or not go back? What to do? Another pressing need added to his quandary. Nature's demands, he knew, had to be taken care of, no matter what happened. So he pissed by the side of the path before he wet himself. As his internal pressure subsided, so his indecision vanished, and he boldly ventured onward.

As he made his way through the cane-piece, a big fat-belly rat scurried across his path. Neddy quickly looked around for a stone to throw. Already the rats were getting big and fat on the young shoots. Roasted cane-piece rat made nice eating. The memory made his eyes dart here and there for a stick or a stone, but the rat was gone out of sight before he could find either.

As Neddy turned a corner of the field, still looking for the right-sized stone for the next opportunity at cane-piece rabbit, as the whites called the rat, he accidentally bumped right into a donkey and rider. The surprise made him jump backward in fright. He lost his balance on the damp grass and fell flat on his back, spread-eagled.

Stars circled in front of his eyes from the jolt. Through them, he could see a donkey's head stretching forward toward him on the ground. Its lips curled back as if it was going to bite, with nasty big teeth stained brown and green from grass and dirt. Instead, it began to bray as if giving a victorious laughter. The *hee-haw* sound rasped across the field. Then its rider joined in, adding his own shriller laugh. At the sound, Neddy's elbows dug into the soft earth lifting his body off the ground at the same time his legs pushed him backward in rapid succession and, like a crab, he scrambled out of the way to safety. That brought even more laughter from the donkey's rider.

FALSE PROPHETS

Wiping away the tears running down his cheeks, he gurgled, "By God! That's the best I have seen since coming to Jamaica." Something tickled the rider's fancy even more, and he continued to laugh almost senselessly. He rocked backward and forward in his saddle and was in jeopardy of falling off the donkey himself, until the donkey began to walk in circles as he tugged, unthinking, on its left halter. To stop the animal, he dropped the long bamboo pole he was holding in his right hand and grabbed both reins, tugging them up to his chest.

"Whoa there, whoa there, Neddy. Whoa," he commanded. Finally, the donkey stopped circling with another of the rider's "Whoa, Neddy, I say whoa!"

From the ground, Neddy's view was now the tail of the donkey. It swished from right to left a couple of times in annoyance. Fearing a kick, Neddy scrambled further backward. With a tug on the reins to the right, the rider brought all three of them face-to-face once again.

Neddy did not move. If anything happened, he could scurry into the cane field and hide, or make a run through it for the road and the safety of the church. He wasn't sure what to expect. At last, the donkey stopped and stood still, giving him a good view of the rider.

He had on a big, floppy straw hat, like some white women wore in the garden when they pretended to plant flowers. The hats lent fashion to the rustic setting and shaded the ladies from the burning sun, as they gave orders to the garden boys to plant this or that flower there, or perhaps over there. Under the tattered brim, strands of sweaty blond hair stuck to the forehead; under that, blue-blue-blue eyes seemed to shine out from the shaded white face that was pleasantly round, with pinkish cheeks. A long neck came up from shoulders that held the promise of a big, muscular man in the future, but in his riding position he didn't look all that tall, and he looked very young. Still on his back, Neddy took it all in.

"Boy," said the donkey rider imperiously, "pick up my lance over there. Come, come, my good man, don't dawdle." A long forefinger pointed to the bamboo pole on the ground. At the same time he gave the order he must have nudged the donkey with his heels in the wrong place, for the next moment it had gone into a tantrum and began bucking and spinning and bucking. With its back arched, its hind legs kicked up and out, twisting at the same time. Once, twice, a couple of turns, another jolt, and the animal earned its reward. The straw hat flew through the air followed by the rider himself. His arms outstretched, as if going into a swan dive, he seemed to hang in midair. Then came a nasty thud as he belly flopped onto the grass. Its burden gone, the donkey *hee-hawed* again and leisurely wandered to the side of the field to munch on the sweet young cane shoots, its rider a forgotten burden of no consequence.

Not an insect moved, and not a bird flew across the sky. Paralysis had taken over the cane-piece. Still on his back, Neddy had heard the thud and felt the vibration but had not seen the actual meeting of the celestial bodies.

Fearing the worst, he did not move. "Lord! What if im dead?" flashed through his mind. Panic began to fill his stomach at the thought. All manner of frightening thoughts filled his mind. Cart whips, duppy tree, and his body hanging from it. Tongue swollen, turned black, stuck out of his mouth as the rope squeezed his neck. Legs danced in the air trying to find solid ground; finally black oblivion and duppy kingdom. Ghosts wandered to the front of his imagination. Complete panic was about to set in when he heard a groan.

Neddy lifted his head from the ground and looked between his knees at a very white scalp with a twirl of blond hair growing from its crown. With another groan, a face emerged from the grass. Blood trickled from the right nostril, and mud and grass stuffed the mouth. There was much spitting, splattering, and gasping for air. Neddy burst out laughing at the sight.

Much of his mirth came from the relief that a corpse did not lie on the ground in front of him, while the rest came from witnessing another's misfortune that did little harm to anyone. He rolled onto his side and drew his legs up into the fetal position in an attempt to restrain his glee. His sides ached; he gasped for breath and choked, struggling not to laugh.

By the time he got control, the other was sitting up and trying to wipe grass and mud from his clothes. Recent wet weather had softened the ground and made his tumble less severe, but the mud and grass stained more easily, and his attempts at cleaning only made the mess worse.

"Oh, God! Look at me!" He rubbed furiously at his coat with a large bandana produced from an inner pocket. "My aunt gave me this last week," he moaned. "Don't just sit there, boy. Help me up!"

"Who yu callin boye? Yu tink yu is a big bakra massa or some ting?" Neddy came back angrily.

"You're a slave, aren't you? Help me up, I say."

"Elp yuself up. I am no slave, and I ain't fi unu boye or slave." This was the second time that day he had been mistaken for a slave. The man was one thing, but this little backra boye was another. Neddy was not going to put up with it, coming from someone obviously his own age and at most a bookkeeper. He was not taking any lip from that class. The cheek of the boye taking him for a common slave made him furious.

"An anoder ting," he said, "ouw yu know mi name?"

The donkey rider was taken aback by the castigation and the arrogance of this black boy. This was not the subservient behavior he had been led to expect blacks gave to white masters.

The white boy scowled. His mind whirled with possibilities. What was he to do? Should he take the high road, or should he walk with caution along the low road? The black in front of him did not seem so fearsome. He would be cautious. He would take the low road. You never know with these Negroes: They could attack, and he was unarmed. The lance of Don Quixote was not at hand. He glanced over at the bamboo pole, lying on the ground a few yards away.

Move slowly and act cautiously was the best tactic, he decided. He would speak gently to the black boy. That would put him off guard and calm him down. Yes, that was the approach, to throw him off guard. If necessary, when it was more advantageous, he could attack. A wounded animal was the most dangerous. His uncle, who had been in India, had told him that. He must show no sign of weakness, or he would lose the upper hand, and it would attack him.

"What do you mean, *your name*? I do not know who you are. Who are you, my good man?" He would try blandishment.

"Yu call mi name."

"When did I do that?"

"Yu say, 'Whoa, Neddy.'"

For a short time silence stood between them. There was a puzzled look on the white boy's face. Then, cautiously he said, "Well, yes, that is my donkey. I was telling him to stop and stand still."

"Fi yu donkey named, Neddy?" asked Neddy, his eyebrows shooting upward in surprise.

"No, stupid, all donkeys are called Neddys." He knew that was a mistake as soon as it came out of his mouth.

"Who yu calling 'stupid'?"

Oh dear, thought the other. *Now, he may attack. What have I said?* Pacify him. Calm him down. Be perplexed? "I don't understand?"

"Yu call mi name. How yu know mi name? When wi meet before? Is obeah yu use to know mi name?"

"No, no, you don't understand. In England, all donkeys are called 'Neddy.'"

"They are! Why?"

"Well, I don't know, but I can assure you that it's so," he said firmly.

"Well, mi not a donkey." Neddy scowled. "Fi mi real name Edward. Mi fader's name Edward. So, dey call me Neddy. Dat is fi mi pet name. Yu understan? Mi no donkey! Yu understan? An mi no slave. Yu understan dat one? So don't come the bucky massa wid me, yu hear, boye?"

Silence descended upon the two again. They sat on the grass, staring at each other. One was not sure he should be there, and the other was amazed at himself for talking to one of the overlords in such a manner, even if just a young one like himself. Both wanted to say something, but there was the uncertainty who should go first. England was the first to speak.

"My name is Watt Tyler-Cope. What is yours again?"

"Edward Quashi Lawrence," came back Jamaica. "Mi name Edward for mi fader," Neddy repeated, "and Quashi for mi modder. Her name Quashiba, and mi barn on a Sunday," he further explained, half-expecting the other would understand the significance.

"What's that got to do with it? Sunday, I mean."

He sighed audibly, as one speaking to an exasperating child, and explained, "Anyone born in Africa on the seventh day of di week is Quashiba, or Quashi, if im a boye."

"But, you were born here?"

"What yu tink?" Neddy smirked.

"Don't know, really." A slightly vacant expression registered on Watt's face.

Neddy went on to try clarifying the situation and clear the dazed look from the other's face. "Mi barn right ya so. Jamaica is mi lan." A short silence interrupted the lesson, and then "What yu tink, because mi gran-modder come from there, mi going back to Africa when di freedom paper come?" He audibly sucked air through his teeth before adding, "No, man! Dat is for fool-fool people. Dey can go back de an get nyamed by all dem lion an wild dog." He let out another of those characteristic peals of laughter. Watt had heard the sound before in the island and had come to understand its defensive nature as well as its gaiety.

Silence again fell upon them on the grass. It lasted until the discomfort forced Neddy to speak. "What yu say your name is?" He looked sideways at the other, the merest suggestion of a smile playing on his lips.

"Watt Tyler-Cope," replied the other with a straight eye-to-eye look. Again there was a pause for a second as both boys stared at each other. This time Neddy had the puzzled look upon his face offset by a smile just parting his lips, exposing the glistening white of his teeth. Shaking his head from side to side as if completely baffled he finally broke out, "*What* can't be a name. *What* is *What?*" he insisted. The other's head went back and eyebrows shot up crinkling his forehead. Before he could throw in a defense, Neddy let fly, "What dat? What yu come for? What yu say? What yu want? Nobody can name so. Some ting wrong wid dat, man," he emphasized finally.

"No, stupid."

"Who yu calling stupid?"

Watt knew he had made another mistake but cleverly ignored it and went on with his explanation. "Not *what* but Watt. You don't spell it like *what*, the question, but like *Watt*, the name."

"What di difference?" shot back Neddy. "What is a Watt? Tink pon it. Dem going call una Massa What. What Massa say? What una say Massa what? No man," declared Neddy, "yu got to change dat der name in a dis ere lan. Di slave dem will kill yu wid di What-Watt, Watt-What."

Silence came again. "Well, I suppose you may be right." The concession did not come easily, but it moved the boys toward a more harmonious relationship. Neddy began to laugh, and like a fever it caught on with Watt. Soon both of them were rolling around the grass in fits of laughter like hysterical girls.

"I could tell them to call me Master Tyler. *Massa Tyler* will be all right?"

"It will do. Never heard dat name eider, but it not *what*!"

"Oh! If you were an Englishman, you would understand the name Watt. You see, my family name is Tyler-Cope, and my father thought it would be good to name me Watt when I was christened."

"Why im do such a stupid ting?"

"Not stupid, really; you see, there was a chap named Watt Tyler who led a peasant revolt, way back, against the king."

"What happened to dat Watt?" asked Neddy with a giggle.

"They killed him. But my father though he shouldn't have been killed. He had right on his side. It was murder, really. My father was on their side. You see, being a parson, he took the Christian way. He said the peasants were being oppressed and were right in revolting." Again there was a pause for thought, and then he ended with, "The king's side won. I guess justice is hard to come by."

A mosquito buzzed and interrupted the silence between the boys. Neither knew what to say. The question Neddy asked surprised even him: "What you are saying den, slaves have di right to cause ruckus for dere freedom?"

Watt twisted his mouth to the left and scrunched up his right eye before answering, "I suppose so." Then without hesitation, "I say, have you any food?"

At that unexpected question, Neddy sat bolt upright in amazement. "Like what?" he asked.

"Anything to eat. A crust of bread; some cheese will do."

There was a peal of laughter before Neddy replied, "Yes, sah! Mi just have a crust of bread and cheese in mi draws for every white boy who asks." He rolled on the grass in stitches.

"No, seriously, any food will do. I am starving!" exclaimed Watt Tyler-Cope, with a very set look on his face.

When he managed to get control of himself, Neddy studied his newfound companion with a playful look. "How long you been here?" he asked.

"You mean Jamaica or Friendship?"

"Jamaica, man."

"About two months."

"Yu just come to Jamaica, den?"

"Yes, you see my father died, and no one wanted me in England, and my Aunt Hannah in Montego Bay said she would take me. She does not have any children and was my father's youngest sister. She owns slaves, you see."

"What has owning slaves got to do wid it?"

"Well someone has to inherit her property, and I guess I am her heir."

"What heir means?"

"When she dies, I will get her property, and then I will be a slave owner."

"Dat make yu feel good?"

"Well, that is the way it is, isn't it? Someone has to own slaves."

"Dat not what the reverend say. He says it is against God's will. No man should own anoder man. Dat is what I believe, and dat is what di Reverend Waldrich say."

There was the crispness of certainty to Neddy's speech that brought a further silence between the boys. A cooling breeze made the young cane shoots flutter and sway. From where he had been feeding, another big rat emerged into the open. Nimbly, Neddy jumped into action; on his feet in an instant. Seeming not to aim, he let the stone fly with a swift arm motion, like a whip cracking. But his expertise let him down this time, and all he managed to do was neatly clip the rat's tail off, sending the creature scurrying back into the cane piece.

"You aren't very good, are you?" Watt said, with a tinge of superiority in his voice.

"Yu could do better?" snapped Neddy, disappointed with his near miss.

"Perhaps. If you had hit it, what would you do with a rat anyway?"

"Eat it, what do you expect? Yu said you were hungry. Dem is nice eating."

"A rat! Are you mad? I would not eat a rat. They are dirty and nasty!"

"In Jamaica yu could well eat much worse tings. Yu say yu hungry, and all around yu is food, and yu don't know it. Di rat is one food. Look pon di trees. Dere is mango, and over dere is a naseberrry tree full of fruit, and yu don't even know it, little white bucky massa," Neddy teased. "House rat nasty but cane field rat, unu white people call cane piece rabbit. An I tell yu, dem is cousin to di coney. Now, *dat* his nice eating," he said. "But yu don't see too many dose dese days. Di nayga-man kill dem off."

"What is a coney?" asked Watt.

"Boye! Yu don't know notting, do yu? Dem will be singing di song for yu in di boiler house soon if yu don learn bout dis ya country. Yu heard it yet?" Neddy asked, with a mischievous grin.

Watt Tyler shook his head and looked puzzled. "What song?"

"Well, if yu asked, den yu not heard it yet. What yu do?"

"Mr. Roy has me looking after the bullocks for the mill."

"So im got yu getting de cow dem. boye! Yu got the worse job, getting up when it still nighttime to get di cow dem. When it dark like dat, how yu tell if di cow dem is real cow or a rolling calf yu got in di pen?" Neddy went into another shrieking laugh, slapping his thigh at the same time.

"Rolling calf?" Watt made up his face as if he were dealing with an idiot. "Rolling calf! What the devil do you mean?"

"Is just dat, a devil. Yes, a rolling calf. Yu know what dat is?" Neddy shook his head in disbelief. Everyone in the world must know what a rolling calf was. How could anyone have reached his age and not know that wicked people turned into rolling calves when they died and that they haunted the countryside at night?

"No," Watt said.

"Rass, Massa! Yu know notting! Now me understand why your fader name yu 'Watt.' Yu always got to ask di question. If yu see a rolling calf, yu will know what a rolling calf is. It is a duppy."

"A duppy, what's that?"

"Dere yu go again wid di *what*." This time Neddy just smiled. His joke had made its point, and rubbing it in would only bring them back to their original face-off. "A duppy and a rolling calf is a dead person who walk bout at night. Dat is why yu don't go out at night. Yu run into a duppy, or worse, a rolling calf, yu is in trouble. Yu one of dem soon."

"Ghosts! Don't be a donkey. Only foolish superstitious people believe in ghosts. They are invented to frighten stupid people and children," declared Watt, trying to recover some of the dignity he felt should be his when dealing with a Negro, even if he was a free one.

"Yu tink so. Well, yu go down to Rose Hall, spend di night, and see if yu are not a madman come morning. When Miss Annie Palmer grab yu, is ta-ta time for you. Yu hair turn white, and yu do-do your pants. Dat is if yu lucky. If yu unlucky, she suck out your soul right through your nose-hole and take it right to hell with her. She sleep wid de devil an sex wid him."

Watt looked incredulously at his companion and giggled. "All she would get from me is a pile of snot," he said with a straight face then doubled over in laughter. At first, Neddy did not get the joke. When he did he giggled nervously, as if not to offend Mrs. Palmer, wherever she was.

"Oh! Come off it! You can't frighten me," Watt said. "Who is this Mrs. Palmer, anyway?" He sat up in the grass.

"Is true! She own Rose Hall down dere along the coast between Montego Bay and Falmouth. She kill four husbands and whip her slaves to death. Den she take out dere heart an eat dem. Blood a drip all over. She a big obeah woman. She learn it all from di French Africans in Haiti, where she barn. Now dem is bad people." Neddy's eyes opened wide at the prospect. "If yu don't believe me, just go down to Rose Hall and look pon di floor. The bloodstains still dere. She kill her slaves and stick dem head pon di gate post to Rose Hall. You watch!"

Neddy noticed the pink cheeks had become paler as his tale unfolded, a sure sign his words were having their desired effect. Now he was enjoying himself and would savor every word he spoke. "One night, dey find one of her husband after di devil she call get him. His head a rip off and him guts all bout di place. Di slave dem so frighten, dey would not touch a ting in di house. All di fine gentlemen from di other plantations nearby, like Cinnamon Hill, come over and pick up di pieces and bury dem." His eyes narrowed as he studied Watt's face to see if his words were sinking in.

Before the other could interrupt, Neddy had plunged in again. "Even up here, around Worcester, John's Hall," he said, his hand flicking backward in their direction. "We know bout her and di power she carry down on Rose Hall and all along di coast. All di way pass Trelawny and St. Ann. Everyone wid sense afraid of her. Nursemaids frighten children wid her name. Old people tremble, wet up demselves. Yes, sa!" Watt sat there saying nothing, and Neddy took that to mean he wanted to hear more.

"Obeah practiced by an African is one thing, but in di hands of a white woman is some ting else. Yu know where she learns it?" There was another intense pause. "She learns her arts from the hands of a Voodoo queen in Haiti." Neddy made a gesture two or three times with the palms of his hands toward the sky for emphasis. "It mek her strong-strong. No one in Jamaica can face her. None of di planters dem trust her—an boye!" His hand sliced the air. "Mek me tell yu, dem stay long ways from here—dem so frighten for dem soul." He finished with a flourish of his hand, like an actor completing a perfect scene.

Instead of the expected applause, however, his audience learned forward, jaw set, and exploded: "Oh, yes? Who are you joshing? I know..." Watt hesitated. "Well, I don't know them personally, but Edward Moulton-Barrett owns Cinnamon Hill and is one of the richest and most respected gentlemen, both here and in England." He continued, "Mr. Barrett would not be picking up the pieces of whatever his name was. The Barretts are among richest and biggest landowners in Jamaica. They are the crème de la crème." Silence followed, then he repeated, "They are very rich," as if wealth were a talisman against witchcraft.

"Oh! Yu tink so. Well, let mi tell yu, de crème de la crème get down and pick er up just di same," Neddy said. "An den im duppy and all dem dat she kill take over di Great House. Ask di Baptists." Neddy drew his knees up to his chin and hugged them with his arms, signaling the finality of his contentions.

"What have they got to do with it?" snapped Watt.

"Dey try to hold Bible meetings at Rose Hall. Dey don't stay long. Di duppy drive dem away. Nobody come to de meetings, and when dem come, di duppy grab dem." His hand shot out and the palm snapped shut, as if around a fly.

This Watt boy was getting an initiation he would not forget. An opportunity to stick it to a white boy did not come every day. They were around, but since he was not a slave, he did not meet them on a daily basis. When he went with his father to various estates, helping him and learning the trade of carpentry, he encountered the overseers and bookkeepers. Even then, his father was the intermediary who stood between his son and the whites.

Suddenly, Neddy said, "What dat mean?"

"What?"

"What yu say, *crème de la crème*."

"Oh! Top notch. The best of all."

Neddy nodded his understanding and regarded the boy on the grass in front of him. They were a pathetic lot, these boy bookkeepers. They were all about his age, but many looked much older. They aged before their time. Skin turned yellow and dry from bouts of malaria. Too much rum gave them bloodshot eyes that ran water all the time, and poor food left them looking meager and stunted. Syphilis or clap, and sometimes both, picked up in their desperate loneliness, gnawed away at their innards. They came to the island, acquired all its depravity, then died. Owners replaced them as quickly as overseers drank water and sweated it out, driving slaves in the cane fields and boiler houses, producing sugar and rum.

When Conchie Blows

Reverend Waldrich once spoke about them as being slaves, too. "For the most part," he said, "they are orphans, unwanted children without influence. Their only qualification is rudimentary literacy and a white skin to fulfill the Jamaican law, which requires a certain ratio of whites to blacks on the plantations. So, too, are they enslaved by the system. Have pity on them, may the Lord!" His hands extended heavenwards. "Have mercy on their lonely little souls," he sighed.

Neddy was woolgathering during most of the sermon that Sunday, but some of it got through to him, imposing on his dreams of heroic deeds and lovemaking. He recalled the words. They must have been important, if only because of all the passion with which the reverend delivered them. The drama had burned itself into Neddy's memory.

"Here, in ze Antilles, they served the greater good of ze growing empire, and zey pass from ze scene without recognition, or a thank you." Reverend Waldrich's face was red as he spoke. From his breast pocket, he pulled a blue cloth to wipe the sweat from his brow. The reverend was a master of the dramatic pause.

"England gets rid of a population that, if left to fester at home, has the potential to explode in social unrest and upset the rich, powerful, and beautiful." The words meant nothing to the people in front, but they sounded good. "Colonies like Jamaica are perfect devices for this jetsam. Together with all the Negroes from Africa, they produce wealth for those who stay at home." That struck a chord, and the church walls answered loudly. "Amen!" rose from the gathering. "Vor the poor and destitute, vhite or black, zere is nozing but enslavement. We must right zese wrongs. God demands zis, for ve are all his children." Again he wiped his brow. "Amen! Yes, Lord! Amen!" The cries filled the church. Then silence. The Reverend Waldrich stared at his flock. Slowly he turned and descended from the pulpit.

Watt Tyler-Cope did not seem to fit Reverend Waldrich's picture. He looked healthy and well-fed. Obviously he had influence, for his aunt in Montego Bay was quite well off; she owned slaves. Neddy stared at him, not sure about this one. He took in the fine blond hair, the round face with its pinkish cheeks that made Neddy wonder if he had pinched them, like he heard white girls did to bring color to the whiteness and make themselves pretty. But the large, silvery blue eyes held him. Angels' eyes, he imagined. They seemed to cut right thorough, to expose all hidden secrets. Yet, their unblinking steadiness made one trust that their owner would not take advantage of the nakedness they laid bare. For, amid the icy blueness was a kindly glint, like sunrays bouncing of the sea; these flashed and bespoke a friend.

"How come yu aunt owns slaves, since yu fader was a reverend, and reverends don't hold with slavery?" asked Neddy, changing the subject.

"Don't really know. She has a will of her own. Funny, I asked her that after I arrived. She just said, 'When in Rome, do as the Romans do.'"

"What dat mean?"

"Well, if they have slaves where you live, you have slaves. If they don't have slaves, like in England, then don't have slaves. She needs them to help around her school."

"She has a school?"

"Yes, for young ladies. That is why she came to Jamaica. My father said she was always strong-willed, and there was no chance for her at home, so she came to the colonies and she chose here."

"Where di school?" Neddy asked.

"Up the hill on Union Street. Beaconsfield School for Young Ladies is the name."

"What she teach?"

"Reading and writing and how to behave correctly in society. You know, the things girls should know to become ladies."

"Reading and writing, I learn at di church school," said Neddy proudly. "Mi modder says education is di only way I can learn to be better than a field-nigger."

"You can read and write?" asked Watt, surprised that a black boy in the countryside knew these arts.

"Yes." Neddy added carefully, "Some."

"That's good. Now, can we get back to food? How can I get some of that fruit?" Watt pointed to the naseberry tree. "Can you climb, or should I show you how?"

Like whippets, both boys rushed for the tree. Neddy got there first, tossed off his sandals, grabbed the trunk, and was up in the branches while the other struggled, unable to get a good grip on the trunk with his leather shoes. Each inch up cost him two, sliding backward. Neddy laughed, watching the struggle below.

"Go back down, and I will trow di naseberry down to yu," he advised.

"You think I can't make it up there? I will get there." Watt looked up and took a deep breath then shouted, "Never give up when faced with adversity. I am Don Quixote. This is but another windmill."

Even with this brave statement, he remained stuck to the trunk like a limpet, unable to move up or down. Not daunted, he tried up again—an unfortunate move. Losing his grip on the trunk, he slid back, tearing his trousers, and leaving skin pasted to the bark. There was a screech of agony as he hit the ground. A minute must have passed, perhaps two, as he gingerly inspected the damage to his right arm. Thereupon a large handkerchief appeared from a pocket, and he wrapped the wound.

Firmly on the ground, Watt performed admirably catching the naseberries that came down to him. Before long there was quite a pile at his feet. One or two had gotten squashed, but that was to be expected with their ripeness.

"Dat's enough," said Neddy, as he joined his partner in praedial larceny on the ground. "Yu ever eat dis before?" he queried.

"No, never seen this fruit before," answered Watt, but that did not stop him from taking a bite out of a big one he held in his hand. The naseberry was soft and deliciously sweet and slightly satiny. Down it went, quickly. "Boy! That is great!" Watt said as he grabbed another and, when that was gone, another and another, till brown juice ran down his chin. In his haste to eat, he outpaced Neddy two naseberries to one.

"If yu don't stop nyam dem dat fast, dey will make your belly run," came the warning that Watt paid not the slightest attention to.

"Lord! I am so hungry," said Watt, grabbing the last naseberry. "Can we get some more? Or some other fruit? I don't care what they do to my stomach. It has not had a lick of food for days," he exaggerated. No sooner had the last of the naseberries slipped down his throat than he pointed to a well-laden mango tree and suggested that they go after those next.

"Dem is green and will give yu colic," Neddy said. "Dem will bine up your belly." He ate a naseberry and laughed. "Nutting going stop dat wid all de fruit yu eat today. Have more, and yu will do-do for de next month. Di overseer not going like dat. Slave can get sick, but bookkeepers—dem can't afford sickness."

"But you don't understand," Watt said. "The food they give me is rotten. It is awful. It stinks and has worms crawling out of it."

Neddy shook his head dubiously. "Worms come out of it? Mi can't believe dat one. When yu cook it, di worms get cooked too. Dere is no worms dere," Neddy said.

"Bet you!" Watt stuck out his hand.

Neddy's eyes narrowed, trying to figure his move. He was not going to be taken in some bet by this one. He waved the hand away.

"All right, den, I believe yu. But mi not going get blamed for yu eating too much and getting sick. Besides," he went on, "I hardly know who yu is." After all, he had just met this little bucky massa.

"Well, perhaps you are right. You, after all, were born here and know all about the flora and fauna, so I bow to your expertise." Watt grinned.

Clamping his lips tightly, Neddy narrowed his eyes again. He wanted to rush the other and tussle some manners into him but restrained himself. There was that gulf of color that kept them apart and saved the English boy from a good Creole roughhousing.

"Let me get Rosinante over there, and I will walk with you to the road," said Watt. Until then they had forgotten the donkey, which had passed the time by chomping on some of the young sugarcane.

"What yu call de donkey?" Neddy asked, another puzzled look on his face at the donkey's new name.

"Rosinante, that's his name. He is named after the charger of Don Quixote, the great knight-errant. Behold, I am he!" shouted Watt, holding his arms aloft as if the countryside were an adoring audience.

When Conchie Blows

"Yu get touched by the sun or some ting? Yu call de donkey Neddy, and now yu call im Rosinante?"

"Ah, my young Sancho—that's it!" he yelled. "You can be my Sancho. I will teach you about Don Quixote and his mighty deeds, just as my father told me the tale. You will know about great literature, Neddy, my newfound friend. For now, learn that in England all donkeys are Neddys, but in Jamaica all Neddys are not donkeys. Boy!" he exclaimed, "I am such a wit."

Neddy rocked with laughter. "Yu fool-fool, eh," he said.

The boys walked toward the road. Watt led his donkey and wondered about each fruit tree they passed. He wanted to stop and sample some. Birds also came in for scrutiny, and he swung his bamboo pole like a fowling piece, left and right, as they flew by. Occasionally, a loud, ominous grumble came from his stomach.

Watt was all curiosity but did not ask any questions. He suspected there would be time for clarification later. Silence was the order now between them. Occasionally the donkey stopped for the odd, succulent cane that was within easy reach at the edge of the field. Inevitably a trial of strength followed between the animal and his owner, as the latter tried to curtail the donkey's browsing and speed up the procession. Much tugging and pulling ensued from one end of the halter and heehawing from the other. It was a one-sided affair most of the time. Usually, the *Equus asinus* won the battle.

Neddy remained tight-lipped throughout their slow progress and slipped into deep thought. There was no hurry, so he went along with the boy-beast battle and proffered no advice. For him, the day had been strange. He had enjoyed his musical triumphs, before both the man who had stopped him in the morning and Reverend Waldrich, but he felt apprehensive. The hair on the back of his neck tingled, as if at the touch of a deathly cold hand. He needed time to digest it all.

Then, without a by-your-leave, this fool-fool boy tugging at his donkey beside him now, had appeared out of nowhere. What was he going to do with him? He did not relish the thought, for it brought a feeling of responsibility, an added burden.

They stopped again at the command of the donkey, who insisted that a delightful young cane shoot in its pathway should join the others in its belly. Watt tugged at the reins to deny the animal the tidbit, launching another struggle between boy and beast.

This boy needed his guidance, Neddy realized. If he was not shown the ways of the island and made to understand the havoc they wrought upon the lowly bookkeepers, he would soon lose all that golden hair. Those shining blue eyes would become bloodshot and dull. The joy and sparkle for life that were in them now would be lost forever.

Watt did not even know how to feed himself with all the food about the land. A suckling babe ripped from its mother's breasts would better know how to suck a mango for survival. Watt instead would be asking *what, what, what?* A smile turned the corners of Neddy's mouth. How could yu get to be a man, almost, and not know a naseberry or a mango? Surly they had them in England? They were all over the world. What a sad place it would be without God's gifts. "Dees was the fruit in de garden of Eden," he mumbled to himself.

While he might not know the difference between a mango and a naseberry or star apple, Watt could sure chat up a storm of nonsense: *Whoa, Neddy! Hand me my lance, my good man. Don Quixote, Sancho, Pancho, and Rosinante.* Dangerous foreign words. They would not be popular in Jamaica. They could get him into trouble. "Di fool could not even make up his mind what the donkey name was. Den him say him is a wit and laugh," Neddy said to himself.

"Did you say something?" Watt said.

Neddy hadn't realized he was talking out loud. "No. Why yu aks?"

"Nothing, thought you said something." Watt went back to his struggle with the donkey.

When all was said and done, Neddy concluded this one was one mad rass in the making; he must be saved from himself. First thing, he must learn about the fruits upon the trees and the language of the island.

But why help him? Neddy continued his internal debate. What stirred within to make him reach out to this stranger, who came from a people he was told by the missionaries used and abused his people? He was pleasant to look on. Was this the answer?

By the time they hit the road, both knew that the testing time had come to an end. They could feel that an unspoken bargain, which comes between boys, had gathered them together as one.

Time had passed unnoticed. A slight breeze coming off the hills had begun to cool the land, getting it ready for the coming night. The earth had rotated, and the sun was just above the crest of the hills. Soon it would sink beneath the sea at Negril Point, and black night would take over the land.

Suddenly, with the fanning of the breeze reminding him of the time, Neddy realized he was in trouble with his mother for being late. Undoubtedly his father would have gone off to their provision grounds and would have expected his son to be with him. A boy had to learn a man's work early, to be ready for the day when he provided for his own family, his mother insisted time and again. It was the African way, coming down from his grandmother. Even though his mother had been born in Jamaica, she would tolerate none of this new Creole dishonest laziness. He could almost feel her switch on his batty already. Or, perhaps not that. For of lately, she had not switched him. He had heard her say to his father, "De boye is getting too big now for the switch, and yu going ave to take over and keep im in order." But that did not stop her giving him a tongue-lashing, and it was difficult to say which was worse, her switch or her tongue.

They walked a little way along the road, until the gates of Friendship came into sight on the left. They reminded Neddy of the morning's warning, and the feeling of unease came again.

"Yu like Friendship?" he asked nervously.

"It's all right."

"How bout Busha Roy?" Neddy said, glancing at Watt from the corner of his eye.

"That fat slug? He has not said much to me so far."

"Well," Neddy warned, "Yu be careful of im. Mi hear tings bout im."

"That's all right; I am able to take care of myself," boasted Watt. Then a worried look crossed his face for an instant. There was a tense moment as he worked up the courage to ask, "Will I see you again?" It was the question Neddy had waited for.

False Prophets

"Yu going to be in the same field next Sunday?"

"Yes, we could meet there. It will become our secret meeting place," Watt said, a grin on his face.

"Well, I don know bout dat, but I will ask mi mum to mek some food for you, since yu say dem is starving yu pon Friendship. But now mi know you can find fruit to eat until mi come next week after church."

"You will do that for me? Wonderful!"

Neddy stood at the entrance of Friendship, watching Don Quixote ride his war charger toward the Great House. From where he stood, it was out of sight, around a corner and two miles further in from the road. He waited until his newfound friend passed out of sight. Then Neddy smiled and, nodding his head up and down, acknowledged that something of great import had happened. He turned in the road and set out for Kensington and home at a slow jog.

Chapter 3

Friendship

Watt looked over his shoulder and waved back at his new friend, still watching him from the gate. Then Neddy was lost to sight, as the donkey plodded around the corner on the way to Friendship Great House. There was still a good way to go, as the road meandered through three miles of cane fields and pastures, ending in the yard of the building complex that was the heart of the estate. Four-foot-high stone walls lined either side of the road that separated the cane fields sprouting their young shoots from the opposite tracts of unused land. Had he not been a new arrival in Jamaica, Watt might have mumbled, on seeing the new growth to his right, "This will be a good year, for a change."

Rain had come at the right time, and the sun and wind had been gentle. The ground had absorbed it all and was giving back an abundance of new cane not seen for at least three years. Even the older ratoons looked to be coming in fresh. For the first time in a while, planters could meet their obligations and shake off the feeling of being beholden to the moneylenders, who hovered over their estates like vultures waiting for an animal to die.

Defaults on debts had made many a Shylock rich beyond his station in the island's society. Despised as hurry-come-ups, the moneylenders were kept at arm's length and never invited to the planters' clubs or homes. When they called in their debts, however, the moneylenders had their revenge, usually making their money back along with a hefty profit after selling off the slaves. The land was an added bonus, but, without slaves to work, it was forgotten and left to become ruinate.

Wherever he went and saw these unproductive fields, dreams of wealth formed in young Watt's mind. He became an early settler, bringing order to nature's chaos with nicely partitioned cane fields. His thoughts ran back to England and Bying Hall, with fat cows feeding on the manor's soft green fields of clover. There was no reason why this should not be the same here in Jamaica for him. Then he, too, could return home in clover. He smiled. His lack of capital for this venture did not bother him, nor were his dreams clouded by the question of why all this wealth-creating possibility was left unused.

He rode on, knowing that given half a chance, he would make it work and be rich beyond belief. Golden guineas in his imaginary purse jingled in unison with the silver bells on the traces, holding the four-in-hand of the gently swaying landau. Along the avenues of the great cities of Europe he traveled, footmen and outriders at his beckoning. He sighed as the image faded when he looked down at the grey neck of the ass beneath him.

Pulling up for a minute, he looked over to his left and sighed again, concluding that his overseer was a fool to have all this unused area on Friendship. Well, he had known the man was strange from the moment they met. If he was the owner of this estate, that dullard would be off and gone long since.

At the first opportunity, he, Watt, would speak to Mr. Fray about putting his ideas into practice. The attorney would appreciate his interest. As a keen young man with a future, he would be in favor and win the attorney's support; his job would be convincing his aunt's friend that he was much more than just her nephew to help out with a job. Besides, he knew, Mr. Fray despised the slug, Roy. With a resolute kick to the animal's sides, Watt started off again.

Little did Watt realize that there was a bigger issue weighing on the land than lack of labor, poor management, and bad weather. Jamaica was losing its monopoly on sugar. The price had been in

Friendship

decline for years. Competition from new colonies in the East, with the latest technology and manned by free or indentured labor, was undermining the sugar production of older slave colonies in the Caribbean. Mauritius and Ceylon were the Antilles' main challengers. Yet there was always the argument for slavery, on the grounds that the Negroes depended on the plantation and the white man, that God intended white men to rule the Negro. Who else would look after these simple people?

Watt thought about this contention. He took neither one side nor the other in the debate but reasoned to himself, "It is stupid not to use the latest methods for the production of wealth." Looking to his right, he declared aloud to the cane shoots he rode past, "No damned lazy slaves to look after."

From what he'd heard, the planters would never go back to the old system of indentured labor. He recalled one planter, vehemently opposed to the system, arguing the changing times over tea with his aunt. His aunt had smiled, not wishing to upset the father of one of her pupils, and he had taken it to mean she agreed and wished to hear him expound on the faults of the system and why it should never be brought back. He argued that white indentured labor always proved to be too frail to work in the tropics. "White men were made to rule, not to labor physically." Aunt Hannah smiled again and offered him more tea. Since being on Friendship, Watt had come to appreciate what the man had said. Working in sweltering heat with flies and bugs buzzing all the time and hunger in his belly was not to his liking at all.

The same matter had come up among the bookkeepers, as they barked at each other while yelling for refills of rum and limewater. The indentured labor idea was scotched by a slurring voice, pointing out that the planters would have to give land or money to those who had worked for them after their time ended, and the planters would never do that. Another pointed out that allegiance was no part of the indentured way. They were strangers who came and went, not like slaves who lived and died on the estate. Another grumbled, "Besides, who would need us, if that came back?" That brought silence for a few seconds as the prospect sunk in with those around the table.

One bookkeeper from another estate surfaced from his mug and said softly, "Perhaps, then, we would live to be old men. Maybe some of us would get to thirty?"

The unease was broken when someone suggested Indians from India could be replacements for white laborers. Watt recalled the yells of protest that rose about the room: "No, no, the coolie babu is too foreign for Jamaica!" Another shouted, "Better the nigger you know than the nigger you do not know!" Cups clattered on the tabletops as a roar of approval rose about the room.

The dilapidated saddle rubbed Watt's inner thigh, and he stood up in his stirrups to ease the soreness. "Oh, for a horse and equipment that suits my station," he said, patting the Jack's neck.

Truth be told, it was the whites who depended on the Negroes to keep them in a style of luxury and command unimagined by their relatives at home in England. He adjusted himself on the donkey. These whites liked owning their people. It made them feel safe and omnipotent—like the *pater familias* of old Rome. Watt remembered the conversation that drifted out to him on the veranda of the Planters Club in Montego Bay, as he waited for Mr. Fray.

Sir Charles Gordon was boasting that all his slaves were now the new Gordon clan. After all, had they not taken on his name when the church men came with their baptismal waters?

Not to be outdone by a fellow Scot, a Graham, owner of Carlton estate, said, "There are plenty Grahams here about in St. James." Little did they who talked or he who listened realize that they were on the cusp of change that would shake the society of the island for good.

As the cane fields came to an end, so did the walls on either side of the road. A gate opened into a large pasture. Watt was about to dismount and open the gate when a black man seemed to materialize from thin air. He must have been crouching behind the wall. Startled, Watt caught himself and straightened in the saddle. Remembering where he was, and remembering that as a bookkeeper on the estate he was supposed to give orders to these Negroes, he declared with authority, "Open the gate, my good man."

"Yes, sah, yes young Massa, sah," was the familiar response from the man. Watt nodded toward the black, not sure if that was the right thing to do, but figured it couldn't hurt to play the graceful squire in old England, acknowledging one of his serfs. He made a lordly gesture and nudged the donkey through the opened gate. The slave's obeisance was his answer.

Some way off, across the pasture, Watt could see Friendship Great House on its prominent knoll. Below the great pile, to the right, were the lesser buildings for housing the white staff. Of the two, the overseer's was the better built. Its foundation and walls were cut stone, like the Great House, although it was a much smaller structure. On his arrival on Friendship, Watt discovered that it was the head bookkeeper instead of the overseer who occupied the house.

The overseer's place was still comfortable. The second floor living quarters included two bedrooms and the inevitable wide piazza that ran the breadth of the building, for entertaining visitors at meals or just sitting, drinking, and conversing. Below were the ground-floor storerooms, where Watt and the other bookkeepers came to hand out implements and harnesses for the workers.

Further off to the right stood the bookkeepers' residence. Unlike the other two buildings, it looked old and dilapidated. Years had passed since its wooden sidings had been brushed with a new coat of whitewash; its boards had absorbed the damp and showed rot and mildew. Lacking a foundation, it leaned to the left, threatening to pitch over with the next earth tremor. So far, it had held its ground. The inner space was partitioned into three rooms—two bedrooms and a general room for lounging and eating. It was toward that dilapidation that Watt now headed. Looking at it now from a distance, he remembered his shudder when he first learned it would be his living quarters. At the time it seemed a storehouse. Now he knew it as the home he and two other junior bookkeepers shared.

Close by the bookkeepers' residence was the mill for grinding cane, the boiling house, and the trash house, with all the attending smells. The buildings were bunched together before the slave huts, standing neatly side-by-side in two rows, heading out to where the hospital stood. As Watt discovered, this substantial edifice was a most important building on the estate. It not only housed the truly sick but also was a refuge to those who feigned every malady they could to get out of work.

He eased himself up in the saddle again as the donkey moved relentlessly forward, closing in on the Great House. The red glow of the setting sun on its stone walls reminded him of the red-hot coals in the barbeque pits, where the slaves sometimes roasted yams and meat. But as the sun lowered, the long shadows of the hills darkened the Great House, making it even gloomier. It still surprised him how quickly night came in the tropics. No sun-lengthened days, like summers at home.

Friendship was no architectural masterpiece as Jamaican houses go, just a very large two-story, cut-stone box. The narrow windows on the upper story had no window coolers to allow air in and keep the heat out, only thick wooden boards to shutter the openings in times of hurricane or armed attack.

Climbing the front of the house, a narrow whitewashed stairway stood out like the bleached backbone of a prehistoric beast. From a small portico on the second floor, thirty-two steps ran like vertebrae to the ground, branching in two directions at the bottom like an upside-down *T*.

There was no doubt in Watt's mind that the stairway was designed for defense. An enemy could begin the climb from the right or the left sides of the *T* then continue up the main stairs. But the width of the stairs admitted only a single file ascent; two men abreast was impossible. A defender could pick them off one at a time. The first shot would leave a corpse blocking the stairs, giving the defender time to reload. From any of the upper-story windows, a defender could pick off the attackers. Only a brave fool would attempt to climb those stairs under gunfire.

At the top of the steps, a small portico jutted out. Two wooden columns cracked by sun and age supported its roof. Their white paint had peeled off, leaving only a faint reminder on the naked wood. Off the portico, a thick slab of a door blocked the entrance to a long, wide, dismal corridor running the length of the house. On either side of this main hall, which served as the house's main room for eating

Friendship

and entertaining, doors opened onto three large bedrooms. Any attacker penetrating this deeply into the house would face a gauntlet of fire from these rooms before claiming control of the building.

On the ground floor, the walls stood two feet thick and windowless. Light and air reached this region of the Great House only by loopholes. A studded double door, thicker than the one upstairs, was held closed by double crossbars reinforced with chains and formidable-looking iron locks. This fortified entry protected the main storerooms of the estate. It was a gloomy precinct that included a special corner reserved for miscreant slaves. There, among sacks of pimento, goatskins, and hogsheads of rum and sugar waiting to be shipped to England, they were shackled to the wall, whipped, and had their lashes doused with brine. In this darkness of rats and cockroaches, field slave and house slave alike were left to ponder their sins against their owner.

As Watt and his charger plodded past the gate, they sent scattering turkeys and curly-horned sheep feeding peacefully in the pasture by the path to the houses. Two milk cows lowed indignantly at the interruption. The bucolic scene for some reason made Watt think of the day he first arrived, when his new employer, the attorney friend of his Aunt Hannah, drove him to Friendship from Montego Bay.

Black clouds with their thunder and lightning had rolled in from the sea that day, turning bright day into grey half-light. Rain pelted the land with huge drops of water, like spent lead shot from a million muskets fired into the air. Buckets fell that day. Not the gentle stuff he had known all his life but a tropical downpour that undermined trees and left them clinging by their roots to the eroded roadsides. Bridges toppled into streams that turned into rampaging rivers, forcing them to make a long, treacherous detour. From under the tarskin provided for him, Watt saw the raindrops hit the ground and chip it away before joining the torrents of water racing along either side of the road.

Mr. Fray, muffled up in a sailor's tar-skin like the one he had given Watt, paid the deluge no mind. At this time of year, nature's wrathful blessings were expected and welcomed, as they rejuvenated the land for the young cane just planted, as well as those emerging from last year's ratoons. As they bounced through the rain, with the buggy rocking from side to side like a skiff blown about, Watt wondered if they would ever make safe harbor through this storm. His trepidation heightened when, to his amazement, the edges of the road peeled away with the falling torrent. Would any road be left by the time they reached their destination? In several spots, the horse dragged the buggy through water that reached its axle. None of this seemed to worry the attorney. On he drove, as if this were an everyday occurrence. Little did Watt realize that it was exactly that, during the rainy season.

Mr. Fray was really in charge of Friendship on behalf of the owner in England. There was no one out here to naysay him. Being Aunt Hannah's friend, he had offered to place Watt on the plantation and have him learn planting. She jumped at the opportunity for Watt. He could learn plantation business and work his way up from bookkeeper to overseer and, perhaps, attorney. One day he may even be able to own land and be part of the planter class. Well, that was the dream she put to him, and his mind readily absorbed the image. "What else can a high-spirited boy like you do here in the island?" his aunt said. "A school for young ladies is no place for you." Watt nodded agreement.

His imagination seized on the plantation romance: land, slaves, livestock, rum, sugar, coffee, and then a manor house at home in England. Who knows, maybe a seat in Parliament, even a title awaited at the end: Sir Watt Tyler-Cope Bart. He could hear the address clearly through the grinding wheels of the buggy and the deluge. His mind's eye watched the crowd lifting their hats and greeting him as he swept by, taking the air from his carriage. His mismatched four-in-hand, two blacks and two greys, were the envy of all horse aficionados who watched him pass in the park. "Good morning, Sir Watt." "Enchanting ball you gave last evening, Sir Watt." "Wonderful speech in Parliament, Sir Watt. That will have an impact throughout the empire." Voices called to him in unison with the beat of the rain and the clopping of the horse struggling toward Friendship.

With the rain still pelting down, they climbed the stairway up to the house. Mr. Fray led the way, and Watt, holding tight to the

Friendship

rails, followed. At the top, unseen hands pulled the heavy door open for them, and they entered that dark, gloomy hall. They were helped off with their heavy tar-skins, and unshod feet padded away, taking them to be dried and readied for the return journey to Montego Bay.

Within the walls of the Great House, the air was thick with a strong odor coming through the crevices between the floorboards. To Fray, it was the familiar mixture of rum, sugar, and pimento, mixed in with moldy half-cured skins of slaughtered animals and stale humanity. Watt, on the other hand, was taken aback by the olfactory assault. It was pungent, to say the least, his introduction to the heavy tropical essence that clung to storerooms. He didn't know whether to be accepting or revolted, but youthful curiosity, and the fact that he had no other place to go, made him stand his ground and take in the unfamiliar scene and smells in that strange room.

About halfway into the long room sat a toadlike man. Squat and very fat, he slumped in a huge chair that must have been made specially to accommodate his widely spread and immense belly. It was twice the width of a normal chair and had three legs on each side instead of the normal two. A thick, wide piece of leather formed the seat. Time and constant use had stretched the leather, so it sagged with the weight of his buttocks. Adding strength to the chair was a high, thronelike back, which extended from the floor to above his head, supporting him upright.

Crowning his head was stubble of kinky red hair clipped close to the scalp. Beneath this was a round face with thick lips and a fleshy Semitic nose separating pale, tawny eyes, like a cur's, staring through half-closed eyelids. Two or three days' growth of beard stuck to his fat chin and cheeks. This strange creature turned out to be the ruler of Friendship, the overseer, Bardolf Richard Roy.

He was covered, for one could not call it dressed, by immense pantaloons and cotton shirt that hung from his shoulders like a fat woman's skirt. Unlaced down the front, the shirt left open to view scraggly chest hair, like tufts of cactus in a sun-bleached desert. His unshod feet, elevated on a stool, were fleshy, with flat soles. Huge bunions protruded at the base of each big toe, twisting them to the right and left like gnarled branches of a withered tree.

At first sight, Watt thought he looked like the China Buddha that his uncle had brought back from the East for his father and that sat brooding on the mantle of the fireplace in the rectory study. His shape was right, but his color was all wrong. Even in this half-light, Watt could see blotchy, brownish-red skin instead of the ceramic's white face. The man's hands were the exception; they were bloodless appendages that rested on the leather handles of the huge chair. The long fingers reminded Watt of a spider's legs, and their translucent quality made it difficult to distinguish where the nails grew from the cuticles. The hands looked quite out of place on a fat man and were more suited to the arms of a thin, even bony, frame.

Hands made the man, said his father's housekeeper, the main female influence in his early life after his mother's death. "You can tell the character of the man, whether he is a gentleman or a scoundrel, by his hands," Martha claimed. Watt took all her pronouncements to heart, and hands became his point of reference in judging the souls of the new people he met. In his short life, he had found what Martha said to be true. In that unaccustomed room of his new home, Watt decided that he was in the presence of a creature beyond a scoundrel. He had never seen such hands before, and they made him very uneasy.

Bardolf had not been expecting guests, certainly not the estate attorney. On seeing Fray, he struggled to heave his fat body out of the chair to greet his superior. In his jumble, he toppled a small round table beside his chair. With it went a heavy rum glass onto the small rug that sat like a patch on the wide expanse of the cedar floor. Unbroken, the glass rolled off the carpet, across the floor, to gently stop beside the leg of a huge sideboard against the wall. Once its journey ended, an uncomfortable stillness settled in the room.

Like a truant caught out of school, the fat man broke the silence by excusing himself for not being out and about the estate: "Just resting, sah—getting over a bout wid di malaria fever, Mr. Fray." He released that false wooden laugh of inferiors in the presence of their superiors, then went on, simpering, "Di rain, you know, sah. Dat not good for di ague, but me glad to see you, sah—so I can tell you ow we a manage wid dis year's crop. So far, it goes good, sah. We going

Friendship

to ave good-good cane in January." His dropping *H* and flat Creole accent fit in with Watt's assessment of his hands. He had disliked this man instinctively at the sight of his hands, and his fawning now confirmed he was anything but gentility.

Fray indicated a straight-backed chair against the wall to Watt, while he walked over to a mahogany and leather plantation lounge chair and sat down. He did not make use of the arms that could be extended to rest the legs on; instead he sat fully square, facing Bardolf, with both feet firmly on the floor, like a judge on the bench about to don the black cap of final sentence.

"Sit you back down, Bardolf," ordered Fray, with the cut of irritation. "I know how difficult it was for you to get up, especially after a malaria attack." There was a distinct hardness in the attorney's tone of solicitude.

"Thank you, sah, thank you." Bardolf flopped back into the chair, which sagged with the returning weight.

"Mr. Fray, Mr. Fray, sah!" he repeated, "I did not expect you, sah. What you doing here, sah?" Without waiting for an answer, he continued. "Always glad to see you, even on a day when di cloud dem buss." The sound of Bardolf's ingratiating cackle bounced off the walls in the long, cavelike room. Watt cringed with embarrassment at the false display of subservience.

"Bibi!" shouted Bardolf.

From some gloomy crevice in the rear of the room, a male figure emerged. It was as thin as its master was fat and so black to be almost green in the half-light. His complexion and movements reminded Watt of the croaking lizard that would emerge from the vines hanging on his aunt's veranda to scurry along the rails.

"Yes, sah, Massa," answered the one summoned.

"Bibi, run down and get di cook to make up a hot…" he paused and looked at Watt for the first time. "No, two hot rum toddies for Mr. Fray and dis little gentleman here." His eyes returned and fixed on Watt. Expertly they went up and down, assessing every nook and cranny of the boy's form. It had been a long time since Bardolf had seen such a pretty and well-made-up white boy. If Bardolf could glow with expectant pleasure, he did then.

67

So intense was his interest that he almost forgot Mr. Fray standing there. None of this was lost on Fray. Knowing Bardolf's intent, he wondered if the boy should not return with him to the Bay and another position be found for him. But, no, Watt was old enough to look after himself. He should be exposed to all types and life in general. In all likelihood he would be living in Jamaica for a long, long time to come. He would have to get used to the unsavory and savory alike in the island.

The Negro brought the steaming toddies on a wooden tray and offered them to the visitors. Fray looked across to Watt as he took the pewter mug from the tray. "You are not to make a habit of this, young man. It is the ruination of our kind in this island. Occasionally, like today, to get the damp out of your bones, it is allowable."

"Yes, sir," acknowledged Watt dutifully.

"You mean he is not to have his own rummer glass, like the rest of us, Mr. Fray!" exclaimed Bardolf, following with his staccato laugh again.

Fray's eyebrow flickered with annoyance, the rest of his face registering disdain. *I really should get rid of the man*, he thought. But that would have to wait until after this crop season. He needed someone who knew the estate, and Bardolf had been holding sway over it from before Fray had taken over as its attorney. The attorney noted mentally the recommendation he would make to William Heath, Esquire, when he did his yearly report.

"Bibi," Bardolf said, "you can bring me one of dem too."

When the green Negro had disappeared, Fray said, "Unusual for you to be nice to a Negro, Bardolf. You must think a lot of that one to speak so sweetly to him." His sarcasm drew an immediate explanation from the overseer.

"Biblow is not one of Friendship's slaves, Mr. Fray. He is my personal man. He has been with me long, long time, ever since mi fader's death." Bardolf ran on as if he were in the room talking to himself. "Now, that was a tragedy. He was a good man dat, who always followed God's word and did his bidding." His voice trailed off, its soft reverence leaving a silence in respect to the unseen grave.

"Unlike you," broke in Fray, relishing the jibe.

Friendship

Bardolf ignored his superior and went on about his servant. "Bibi held me up all tru my loss. When the parson man was baptizing him, I claimed he was like a son to me, and Parson Hilbert baptize him Biblow Roy. Di parson man say di name would mark him as mi son. That was good enough for me."

"Not *Biblow*, Bardolf." Fray laughed. "*Bi-blow*, man." The parson must have had a tremendous sense of humor. Fray was laughing so much, he had to wipe away the tears with a wet handkerchief he pulled from his upper coat pocket. "It means *bastard*, Bardolf, *bastard*! I never would have thought of that had it been me pouring the water over him. I would have ennobled him with my blessing. I would have named the black bastard *Bibi*, which means the same thing." Mr. Fray almost forgot who he was, and let his mirth take over until finally he brought himself under control and blew his nose in the handkerchief.

The overseer looked back at the attorney, uncertain of his ground. He did not want to appear to be an ignoramus, but the fact was, he had no idea what Fray meant. Thinking it was time to put him down a notch, he added, "Di Parson man name dat, too." He waited.

Fray could not help himself and went into rollicking laughter. "This will be a good story to tell over many a drink at the Planters Club. Bardolf, you have been had, man. The names mean Bastard, Bastard of Roy." Fray did not miss the opportunity to needle the fat man and his pretensions.

The comment sent Bardolf into his defensive posture. He hoped his next pronouncement would place him level with the attorney, perhaps even elevate him above his superior.

"I bring Bibi here with me from down May Pen way, when I was learning the planting business at Halse Hall."

"Is that where you began, Bardolf?" Fray inquired.

Bardolf seized the opportunity to drop names and put Fray in his place and, at the same time, add to his self-importance. Stretching the truth to make him appear better than he was came as second nature to him. *Apocryphal* should have fit somewhere among his names.

"Yes, Mr. Fray, Sir Henry de la Beche was a close friend of my fader's, and he took me on at Halse Hall as a special favor to him. That was before him died, of course."

"Of course," was all Fray said, as he took another sip of the now lukewarm rum toddy. Then, "You were one of Sir Henry's bookkeepers, were you?"

There was no coming back with a rejoinder to Fray's scornful observation. Bardolf fell silent almost at the moment the rain stopped pelting the shingled roof of the Great House. In the pause that followed, all that hung between the three men and the unseen slaves was the smell that rose from the floorboards. Somewhere in the long room, water dripped from a leak in the roof.

Fray was the first to speak. "At last the rain is done. You will have to get that leak over there fixed, Bardolf. The water is dripping down on the floor and will soak through to the sugar and rum below. Get your people to put buckets there and mop it up."

"Go get Mark Anthony and some of di other house servants to clean it up," Bardolf ordered Bibi, hurriedly.

"Yes, sah, Massa!" the Negro replied.

At the order, Bibi displayed both rows of teeth, flashing that wide foolish grin that some blacks displayed in the presence of whites. Apparently the errand pleased Bibi—he was not the one designated to do the mopping up of the room—and his grin subsided into the sly smile of a slave.

Bibi's legs moved almost reluctantly for such a tall man. In England, Watt reckoned, a servant would never have taken so long to cross the room from behind his master's chair. Slow, reluctant movement by workers seemed natural in Jamaica. Negroes, he noticed, took three times as long to do a job as an Englishman—or even a Scotsman, and that was saying something. According to his Aunt Hannah, you needed three slaves to do the work of one white man, and then they eat you out of house and home. Not only did they expect to be fed but clothed as well. "Not worth it! Not worth it! Not worth a farthing, any of them!" she complained, often and loudly. After scolding one of her slaves for some infraction or for leaving work undone, her tirade on their worth would follow, and her face would turn red with the blood of anger and frustration. Then she would declare that they did it on purpose—whatever it was—to annoy her. She would not accept the premise espoused by many other owners that laziness was an inborn African trait, like a dog's love for his master. To Aunt Hannah, they were as capable as any white but, instead, were possessed by the devil and commanded to send their masters to early graves.

Watt's train of thought was interrupted when Bibi returned with half a dozen people, carrying buckets and rags to mop the floor and catch the last of the dripping water. Three began to work while three stood by to watch, directing sly glances toward the visitors. A young girl on her knees with the rags and bucket kept looking up at Watt. When he returned her curiosity, she giggled, which got her a kick in the buttock from Bibi.

"Marky," called Bardolf to the crowd, "behaving yourself now, or you needs a little tech again wid di whip?"

From their midst, a well put-together young man who seemed to be in charge of the crew answered with a knowing grin, "No, Busha, me is all right now. You don't ave to whip me." Obviously the whip had not been laid on with alacrity in the past, for there was no tremble to the words.

"Mr. Fray, dat is what I mean," said Bardolf. "You see dat boy dey? Most of the time he is good, but then sometimes he gets miserable, like a rancid dog, and just lie down and refuse to work, or im go off to another property to hide out."

"No, Busha, no sah, mi love yu. Would never leave ya side, Massa, never," protested Mark Anthony. A wide grin split his mouth, and very white teeth glistened through the dim room.

"Tellyou, Mr. Fray, if you give me permission," Bardolf's hand gave a lazy wave toward his superior, "I would sell im tomorrow, but di replacement, now, dat is anoder matter. Can you understan dis? I got twenty-nine people in di Great House to do what five could do. Niggers..." he spat sneeringly, shaking his head from side to side. "Boye!" he exclaimed, with arms opened in appeal and with eyes turned to the ceiling as if looking through it to heaven and the all-knowing God, "dem will be di deth of dis island." He looked at Fray and pointed to Mark Anthony, "Maybe I could sell im to the Dutch Jew. Den im could sell im to Cuba. Marky!" he called to the slave again, "you seems to like di Dutch man dat owns a piece of land up di road. If im don't buy you, den it is Cuba for you."

"No, Massa! No, Massa. Beg yu, Massa. Oh no, Massa! I loves yu, Massa," pleaded Mark Anthony. "Who else going look after yu when Bibi don't?" He threw out that last niggling comment with a sly grin, glancing at Bibi to see its effect. Obviously, in some way, they were archrivals.

Before Bibi could retaliate, Fray spoke. "Bardolf, I must say you seem to be as well-served as many a proprietor in the island. Perhaps too well-served." Fray indicated the six slaves attempting to clean the floor.

Bardolf's tack changed immediately. "Lord no, Mr. Fray! It just seem so." Before the attorney had time to speak, Bardolf tried to distract him from the chaotic scene of too many hands doing little or no work on the floor. "Another toddy, Mr. Fray?"

"No, Bardolf, one is more than enough. However, Bardolf, to my business with you." He looked over to Watt. "This young man is Master Watt Tyler-Cope, Bardolf." Fray paused to let it sink in, as if he was introducing someone of importance.

"How do you do, sir," Watt said, astutely picking up on the introduction, and walked over to offer his hand to the overseer.

Bardolf's long fingers grasped the outstretched hand willingly, and pressed it. The clasping fingers felt like the touch of a snake's underbelly, soft, cold, and clammy. Watt resisted the inclination to pull back in revulsion and knew to suppress the shudder that went with the contact. As quickly as good manners permitted, he pulled his hand away from Bardolf's; and, while the others were distracted by the entry of a woman, inquiring if they would be having guests for dinner, Watt dug in his pocket for his handkerchief to rid himself of the residue left by the overseer's fouling touch.

"Watt is under my charge, Bardolf. He is sent to this island by Mr. Heath to learn the planting business." A fiction that would protect the boy, Fray hoped. "To begin his education, Bardolf, I am leaving him with you on Friendship; only for the time being, mind you."

Friendship

From explaining the presence of Watt to Bardolf, Fray turned to the boy, "Next year, Watt," he said, "after the crop season…" Fray paused and took a deep breath, which gave him time to think. "I will be putting you on Springmount or Pitfour. To my mind, they are nicer than Friendship. In the meantime, I will leave you here with Bardolf. Friendship is near enough to the Bay for you to come in and report to me and your aunt, so we can keep your benefactor in England informed as to your progress." He said it with the intent that all in the room heard and understood.

Bardolf, like the bottom-feeding carp he favored, was unable to resist the tidbit thrown by Fray. Once again his hollow, obsequious staccato laugh reverberated off the walls, and he exclaimed, as if insulted, "Mr. Fray! How can you say dem other estates are better than mine?"

Fray looked at him over the half-rimmed spectacles that seemed to be a natural part of a notary public, attorney, or judge, and inquired with a gentle smile, "Did Mr. Heath give you Friendship, Bardolf?"

Bardolf knew he had been bested again, and he was back in his place as just another overseer.

"Don't let my allowing you to live in the Great House give you the idea that you have come into possession of the property," Fray said. "Mr. Heath would not like that. Perhaps you should return to the overseer's quarters?"

Again, Bardolf emitted that laugh he reserved for his superiors. When it ceased, he went into his most submissive mode. "Mr. Fray, I only meant that Friendship is run better than dem odder estates and turns a fair return on investment for Mr. William Heath, Esquire, sah."

"I don't recall that from the figures," Fray said. "I will have to look at Chalmers' books again. He does those for you, Bardolf, doesn't he? If his figures are right, then perhaps he should run Friendship, don't you think, Bardolf?"

That was Fray's second threat, and it did not escape the overseer. He shifted uneasily, and his chair creaked, its joints loosening from constant use and growing pressure as Bardolf aged.

"Morris Chalmers is a very good bookkeeper. Yes, sah, a very good bookkeeper," emphasized the overseer. "I don't know what I would do without him to look after de little things, which I cannot get around to because my day is so full keeping dese damned lazy niggers doing the work they have to do." He did not stop pleading his case there. "Lord! If only we could get some fresh skin from Africa, we could do more, Mr. Fray." It was a desperate attempt to divert Fray from the thought that the chief bookkeeper was in fact doing the overseer's job as well as his own.

Bardolf's ploy was not lost on the attorney, whose only response was a thoughtful, "Ah hum!"

"Like I said, Mr. Fray, dese niggers keep one going fulltime. I wish I could sell the lot of them and start all over again. Get us some fresh ones from Guinea coast, like we used to. Den I could teach dem to work."

"You remind me, Bardolf: I do hope that you and your Jewish friend, Lindies, or whatever his name is, are not dealing in slaves smuggled in from Cuba on this estate. I will not tolerate the law being broken here," Fray said.

The fat man wiped his forehead with the back of his hand and protested, "Oh, no, never, Mr. Fray! The law is the law, and I would never risk breaking it for the likes of niggers and Jews."

"Let it be so, Bardolf. Rumor, you know, rumor." There could be no doubt that all in the room got the message Fray conveyed.

Even Watt realized that an invisible wall of protection had been thrown around him, and he was not sure why.

"Send for Chalmers, Bardolf. I will put him in charge of the boy. That way you will be relieved of direct responsibility for him. Oh, I hope your people have taken his box off the back of the buggy, so it does not get soaked through and through."

Once again, feet scurried to orders yelled out by Bardolf, who attempted to rise from the chair and exert his authority. Bibi came over from his supervisory job and gave him a helping hand to get up. Mark Anthony, not to be outdone, raised himself from cleaning the floor and rushed to his master's other side. Together, they got him upright. Mark Anthony was shooed away by Bardolf, leaving him and Bibi standing together. An astute observer would have remarked how they complemented each other in their contrast.

Friendship

Eventually, Morris Chalmers arrived. Wet clothes showed that he had been about the plantation in the rain. "You will catch your death of cold, Chalmers," said Fray, on seeing the state of the man. "We can't afford to lose you to the fevers. Can we now, Bardolf? What would you do if his toes turned up, eh?" Fray said. "Better get changed, Chalmers."

"Yes, sir. That I will do, as soon as your business with me is finished." His stilted reply indicated a man who chose his words carefully, like a lawyer. There was no currying-up in the way he addressed Fray, and his accent was not of the island. He was an emaciated man with paper-white skin. Not a blemish or blush showed. Years under the tropical sun had made no difference. Not even a sallow cast marked him as a survivor of the dreaded fever that took eighty percent of those infected. He was as white as the blackest African was black. Neither showed signs of blood coursing through their veins beneath their respective skins. It was Chalmers, though, to whom all Friendship looked for survival. Without Chalmers no cane would be crushed, no juice boiled, no sugar made, no rum distilled. Only those who slaved on the property knew this for certain, but Fray suspected as much.

"Chalmers, this young man is my personal charge." He pointed to Watt. "Here to learn the business of planting. He is a white man, so I am putting him under your personal care and supervision. He is to be treated like any other apprentice bookkeeper. But…you will personally supervise his activities. I do not expect him to turn into a hard-drinking, wenching, washed-out fag like the others."

The significance of *white man* was lost on Watt, but not on the others. Black and white in the room knew what was meant, and a titter rose from the slave ranks. Bardolf especially seemed to be uncomfortable with the comment and took pains to say, "All us white men ere, sah, will look after di boye. He will make a good addition to the company." Again he laughed, like a hammer hitting wood in rapid succession.

"Well, I have to be going back to the Bay. Watt, buy yourself a donkey, boy. I am sure Mr. Chalmers can get you one." He turned back to Chalmers and added, "You will help him?"

"Yes, sir, if that's what you want."

Fray, nodded. "The donkey is a safe beast. Not spectacular, but it will take you anywhere you want to go, my boy. You can ride into Montego Bay on it at any time. Now, I will leave you with Mr. Chalmers."

"Before you go, Mr. Fray, sah, a word in your ear, hif I may, sah?" Bardolf said. He shuffled his flat, bunioned feet to where the attorney stood at the front door. Bardolf leaned forward in a conspiratorial manner, and in a low voice so that the slaves would not hear he asked, "What you hear bout di freedom paper for di slaves, sah?" he asked.

Backing away from the intrusion into his personal space, Fray said, "Nothing, nothing at all."

"Dere is talk about that it will come by Christmas. If it does, it will be the ruin of us. If it don't, watch my words, sah, dere will be trouble, Mr. Fray! Di Baptists are stirring up di niggers. Dat man call Sharpe is di ring leader of dem."

"Well, that may be," Fray said. "But I can assure you there will be no freedom paper in this or any other island by Christmas." His voice increased in volume so all in the room could hear. "And if there is trouble, it will be put down by the army, as it has always been. Jamaica is too valuable a colony to let go to ruin because of a few hotheads. Good day, Bardolf."

Mark Anthony ran to open the door. Before descending, Fray turned and made one last swipe at the overseer. "Take care of that malaria, or it may turn into blackwater fever. It favors your type, I am assured, Bardolf."

The rain had stopped. Placing his hat carefully on his head, Fray descended those thirty-two steps, holding onto the hand rail to make sure he did not slip. A slave at the bottom helped him back into his buggy as Fray's own man climbed up behind the buggy. The whip touched the horse, and off they trotted into the descending gloom of the failing day.

Standing beside Chalmers, Watt watched the buggy jolt off down the road. He was alone with strange men in a strange house.

Friendship

"Come, boy, let me show you where you will live." Chalmers turned to Bardolf, who had shuffled back to his chair, rum glass in hand. "Mr. Roy, I will be going now with our new bookkeeper. Watt, is it?"

"Yes, sir," Watt said.

"Chalmers to you. Reserve the *sir* for Mr. Roy."

"Take care of im. Let the other two saffen im up for me, Chalmers." Bardolf shouted back, as the door closed behind them. Then to Bibi he said, "Lard! Bibi. I hate them. Oh, how I hate di whites; di boyes only good for one ting, if dey got any ting." Bardolf let out an ear-splitting scream of laughter unlike anything Watt had ever heard. Although he was halfway down the front steps, he knew who it had come from, and he was shocked. Certainly it sounded nothing like the Bardolf laugh in Fray's presence. Again it was forced, but this time the sound was somewhere between terror and the manic scream of a girl being violated. So loud was it that the slaves below heard it and looked knowingly at each other, grinning.

"A new one come now, Marky. Where yu goin be dis time, eh?" said the girl, who had been on her knees mopping up the rainwater.

"Dem come and go like flies pon cow dung."

"Eh-heh! But dis one pretty-pretty an im not brown like you. It looks like is mi you gowin ave to come to when you want tings." The girl leered at Mark Anthony.

"Bibi going tek yu. An yu can ave im," Mark Anthony said.

"Lard Gad! Mi don't want dat maaga nigger ting in mi! Im not a nice cool brown color like yu. Im black." She smiled coyly at Mark Antony. "Is yu mi tink bout all di time."

"Well, tink!"

Chalmers led the way over to the bookkeepers' residence. Watt wanted to ask what the overseer had meant by his remarks but concluded it was better left for the time being and dealt with when it came up, whatever it was. He was a man now, and he had to act like one.

A cramping pain in his gut and an urgent need to empty his bowels brought Watt back to the present. *Oh, God! Neddy was right!*

When Conchie Blows

The fruit is going to make me run. His stomach began to growl. Would he even reach the latrine before his exploding intestines forced their contents into his pants? How embarrassing in front of slaves. Not good for a gentleman and a scholar. Not good for a knight of the round table. Not good for Don Quixote! Not good at all.

He kicked the donkey in its ribs. It stopped and brayed. "No!" Watt screamed. "Not now, Rosinante!" The noble steed must have heard Don Quixote and taken pity, because it moved again and quickened its pace. To counter the jerky motion and his growling belly, Watt gritted his teeth. He forced himself to think about that first day on Friendship.

They had entered the main room of what was to become Watt's lodgings. The room had been furnished with only the barest essentials in the way of tables and chairs. Most were crudely made, as if by an apprentice carpenter. Sturdy pieces built to withstand rough use. Wasting money and effort to make bookkeepers comfortable was not the estate's way. Many a slave dwelling was far better furnished, as Watt was to find out. Slaves were valuable property, after all.

In a corner stood one of the leather chairs reserved for owners and overseers. It had seen better days. Only one of the swing-out footrests remained still intact, but its right rear leg was broken off, its stub resting on a brick to keep it from tipping over. Sitting in the chair was a man who, at first glance, appeared to be in his middle to late twenties, but at a closer distance he appeared younger. His face, ravaged by the tropics, made him look older. His skin had the telltale yellow hue, and black circles ringed his watery, bloodshot rum eyes, the kind of sacks hanging beneath them that came from with constant dissipation. Between a stubby thumb and deformed forefinger, he held a crudely rolled cigar, which, as he puffed, smelled most strong. He dragged in and blew out a cloud of smoke to greet the head bookkeeper and the stranger.

"Chalmers, who is this charming young one? A sapling come to join our merry band?" he inquired arrogantly, spitting bits of the cigar on the floor before putting it back in his mouth.

"Don't be so damned nasty, Duar," Chalmers said. "If you don't know how to smoke that damned cigar like a gentleman, don't smoke at all."

"But he ain't a gentleman," piped up another boy, sitting at the table eating from a plate of stewed peas and plantain.

"Shut up, Shirley!" the cigar smoker said.

"This," said Chalmers, "is William Duar, one of our *merry band*." He mimicked the cigar smoker.

"Guillaume Du War. I wish you would get it right, Chalmers." He turned to Watt, "My people came from Haiti originally. We are not of this island," he added with contempt.

"Ah! Parlez vous francais?" asked Watt in his best school French. It was about the only phrase he could rattle off with ease. For a moment he was met with a blank stare, then a cloud of smoke.

"Oh, no," said Du War. "We have forgotten all that frog stuff. We speak only English now."

"Don't listen to im, you ear," the one called Shirley said. "His name is Duar. Not one of his family ever see this side of Haiti. Im barn right ere in Jamaica, like mi."

"Yes, but not a walk-foot backra like you," said Du War, or Duar, whatever his name was. The insult brought an instant response.

"Who you calling *walk-foot backra*—you rass! I suppose your family is class! Dem a *blood clart*, not class. If not, what you doing ya so?" He almost screamed his last sentence, and the tin plate with the stew peas flew across the room at Duar. Shirley's aim was poor, and the plate missed Duar's head, splattering its contents against the wall to his left before clattering to the floor. The food oozed down the wall, leaving a nasty brownish stain of red peas.

"Wasted food, Shirley. You may regret that. It's a long time to the next meal." A smile played about Chalmers's lips. "Watt, our plate thrower over there is Patrick Shirley, the other bookkeeper. His bark is worse than his bite. You might not think so, after his appalling exhibition of bad manners, but I assure you, it is."

The boy he referred to was small in stature but of not unpleasing countenance. His was a thin face, with soft brown eyes to match his hair and the odd blemish of his age on his cheeks. One look at him made it clear that life had not been an easy road to walk. Almost from the day he could add to his family's income, his life had been work. Surprisingly, in between his labors, he had managed to accumulate enough education to move to the position of bookkeeper on an estate. He nodded at Watt on the introduction.

"We are luckier than most, on Friendship, to have two bookkeepers born in Jamaica," Chalmers said. "Usually bookkeepers, like you, come from home. Duar, Shirley, this is Tyler-Cope. What is your full name again?"

"Watt Tyler-Cope."

"Proud of it, I can see. There you have it. Watt Tyler-Cope is his name. Here under the special care of Mr. Fray." Chalmers stopped and looked at both his underlings in turn. "So tread carefully, you two, or you may find you are out of work."

"Oh! So it's hands off for the Zulu, too," Duar said, laughing. "He will be disappointed."

"Don't call him that," Chalmers said. "*Mr. Roy* to you, Duar."

"Why? All the niggers call him Zulu. It suits him better than Bardolf or Mr. Roy."

"How can it? A Zulu is an African, William," Watt said.

The other laughed. "Boye! You can tell im just arrived." Duar gestured at Watt with what was left of his cigar. His accent had suddenly taken on the Creole distinction. "Im is a damned nigger like the rest—can't you tell? Im is a damn red naygar. That is what Bardolf Richard Roy is." Rum seemed to being playing its part in the bold, belligerent outburst. An empty mug stood on the ground beside the chair.

"Don't speak of the overseer like that, boy, or you will lose the work," Chalmers said. "Can the Duar family sustain you? I think not."

"Come on, Chalmers!" Duar said. "Don't be smarmy. You are only staying around to take over his job. That is, when Fray gets rid of the incompetent slug. Don't stand up for that shitting, fat mustee passing as white, Chalmers. It ain't honest." Duar looked over the table and pointed a deformed forefinger at Shirley. "Roy only keeps that one for his pleasure and because he can point to him as his white cousin. He is your cousin isn't he, Shirley?"

"Sort of."

"What the hell do you mean, *sort of?*"

"All right, damn you, Duar. He is my cousin."

"You are white, an he ain't. That's why he keeps you around. Right, Shirley?"

Shirley rose to leave.

"Shirley, don't go," Chalmers said. "Watt is going to share your room. So take him, and get somebody to make up his bed and get his things from over at the Great House." With that, he turned and left the three of them to get better acquainted.

The donkey came to a full stop at the paddock gate. Watt dropped the reins, threw himself off, and ran for the latrine as if the hounds of hell were snapping at his heels. He got there in time. As relief came, he decided it best to listen to Neddy's advice in the future. Maybe, too, he could explain a few things about Friendship.

Chapter 4

Daddy Sharpe

Emerging from deep sleep and the sorcery of dreams, Neddy sat straight up into a black void. Sweat ran down his neck and chest. Panic replaced strange excitement in his disorientation. There was an emptiness in which he seemed to float. Steadying himself, his hands tightly gripped the covering around him, and he began to shiver uncontrollably in the darkness. His breath came fast, and he wanted to yell for help, but his panting forbade it. All that came out was a strangled gurgle.

A peenywally flickered and broke the blackness. For one moment, and then another, and then another, and then again, it lit the walls of his little room. Gradually, with each flicker of the tiny light bug, the room reassembled itself into a known quantity out of nothingness; Neddy remembered where he was. The unholy agitation abated, replaced by the knowledge that he was wet, as wet as if someone had doused him with a bucket of cold water.

Unsteadily, he got out of his cot, dreading making a sound that would wake his parents in the next room. All were asleep except him and an animal he could hear cropping grass outside his window. His left hand felt along the wall until it discovered, hanging on its peg, the cloth he used to dry himself after a bath. Taking the cloth, he gently wiped from his naked body the sweat brought on by his dream.

Then he lifted the latch of the door to the outside and, standing in the doorway, urinated into the yard. Venturing to the outhouse was not worth the risk. Who knew if there was some unpleasant thing lurking out there.

Getting back into his cot and under the covers made him shiver again. The damp sheet had lost his body heat. Maybe drying off hadn't been worth it. He crunched himself up in the fetal position in an effort to minimize his nakedness against the clamminess and regenerate some warmth into his covers. Gradually he relaxed and again stretched himself out to his full length.

As he lay there, bits and pieces of the dream began to filter back. The noise: donkeys laughing, a blond boy braying at him. A bamboo pole tipped like a lance with a flag on its end that they passed between them, the blond boy and himself. Thunder and lightning flashed. Heavy rain fell. Water splattered him, and he shivered. The scene faded. The blond boy, spattered with blood, stared at him and smiled. Blue eyes changed to black as the light went out of them. Neddy reached out his hand to him, but the boy faded, leaving Neddy standing in burning fields of cane, where he felt the heat, but no fire touched him. A high wind blew the flames out and left blackened stalks of standing cane. As the cane bent and swayed, he saw rats gnawing on ghastly bodies, twisted and stiff, lying between the rows of cane. There was the acrid stench of corpses and gunpowder. He shivered in horror. "Lard Gad! Mi not going eating another of dem cane piece rat again," he whispered to himself. The images haunted him until sleep finally overtook him again.

His father's call, the clang of his mother's tin pots preparing breakfast for them, the cooing of doves in the trees, the crowing of the peel neck rooster perched on the log where so many of his kind had lost their heads—the sounds of morning woke Neddy. He yawned and stretched, the dawn lighting his room. His dreams and nightmares were gone, and he did not want to rise, but he had to. Soon his father would enter with a stern look, demanding that his apprentice hurry, as they were going to Newman Hall.

Neddy pulled his pants on and went outside to where the bucket stood for washing. Timidly, he splashed the water on his face so as not to let the early morning cold bite. His father, standing nearby, watched the precautions and laughed. "Afraid of a little cold water, boye? You better hurry up, or your modder will pour the bucket of water all over you." Knowing this to be true, Neddy splashed in the bucket quickly and even more quickly dried himself and donned his shirt. When it came to cleanliness, his mam tolerated no slackness, and he was just in time as Quashiba made her appearance, carrying a pot inside to the table where they breakfasted.

Although Neddy had plenty of his father in him, there was no doubt where he got his looks—he was his mother's son. She was a pure African, of astonishing beauty. Her finely chiseled features suggested she was perhaps a Masai. Whatever she was, whatever her ancestry, it certainly was not rooted in the common Bantu people. There was no portion of her being that was out of place, none too large or too small. Even in her middle thirties, a mother of one child, her form had not yet begun to give way under the rigors of wifehood and manual work. She stood straight, strong, and lithe. Her facial features looked finely carved from black onyx, unique in the island, and probably unique in the country from which she originated. Quashiba was made to be admired, as she was by all men who came into her realm. But only one man ever knew her.

"What you going do when mi an Neddy is at Newman Hall? You say you going somewhere?" Edward said.

His wife looked at him, knowing full well that her husband was trying to tease her. She had told him last night what she had planned.

"As I told you last night, me and Miss Dodd is going down to Montego Bay in her cart."

"Oh, yes!" exclaimed Edward, as if it had slipped his mind. "Mi forget, di two free lady dem going show off down in *Montego Bay*," he said, implying they were going to sport in the town rather than do serious business.

Quashiba's irises, deep black in her glistening white eyeballs, flashed in the morning light. *God! What a beautiful woman*, her husband thought, enjoying her reaction to his goading. He smiled, awaiting the response he'd angled for, knowing it was coming with just that tinge of acid to reassert her ground. So it had been from the day he had first noticed her. She, a tall, thin girl just beginning to show womanly promise, while he, an established man, was already the father of children. That nubile body with flashing ackee eyes drew him in.

"You would understand why we are going to Parson Sharpe's meeting, if you were an African." The corner of her mouth curled slightly with disdain.

"Well, I am not an African, and needer are you."

"I would have been if dem had not tief my mother away with mi inside her belly." As her anger grew, her language lost the refinement taught her by Mrs. Fowler when she was a young girl. Quashiba straightened up and looked at her husband, knowing that he had forced her into speaking broad Jamaican like all the slaves around. Her lower jaw clamped against its upper half and tightened hard. Her lips crimped together. It was the sign Edward had waited to see, and with the half-smile of someone who knew he was one up on another, he unmercifully tweaked her again.

"Well, you are a Jamaican now. You were barn right ya." He drove it in with his finger pointing at the ground by her feet. Then he braced himself for a verbal retaliation.

"I was barn on di slave ship. Mi not barn ya like all you slaves. In di middle of the sea mi barn, and so no country or man can claim mi." Her eyes were half-closed in defiance. Her logic was designed to throw men. Her husband knew he could not win an argument against her, but he loved to try. What really pleased him was knowing his wife was far better than most of the men and women around.

Neddy busied himself getting his father's tools together, while listening to his parents go back and forth, as they had done all his life. When he was younger, it had worried him sometimes when their arguments had become really heated. However, as he grew older, it became clear that it was their way of expressing a great love for each other. He looked to see his father shrug his shoulders at his mother's statement and heard him add, as if resigned to her victory, "Ah hum!" That was how it ended most of the time. Occasionally Edward had the last word, but Neddy was never sure if he'd won it squarely, or his wife had let him.

Breakfast time restored peace between them. The three of them entered the family room, where they gathered at mealtimes and other important family occasions. Quashiba had learned about family rooms from her late mistress, Mrs. Fowler, late owner of Kensington Pen.

She was acquired along with her mother as slaves for the estate, while still at her mother's breast. Probably on this account, and also because she had survived the middle passage, Quashiba took on special significance for the old white proprietress.

Mrs. Rachel Cornelia Fowler, as a planter and owner of slaves, was a strange woman, strong as a horse and God-fearing. She believed in God's word as written in the New Testament. The old one was just Jewish mythology, and she did not believe a word of it. In that, she was in advance of her time. Christianity began with Christ. Before that, no matter. Yet, when it suited her, she was quick to quote some reference that held the promise of fire and brimstone for those listening.

How she resolved the Apostles with slavery was another matter. For most of her life, Kensington was her kingdom, and her slaves were her subject people. God had put them together in this awful island to suffer before achieving a better life in the hereafter, and that was how she appeased her conscience. No whip, no ignorance, no devil worship, as she called obeah, and plenty of God; that was her constitution that all had to obey. No one ever did otherwise.

Every day, before work began in and around the house, the sugar mill, and the fields, Mrs. Fowler recited the Lord's Prayer to her people. If they didn't want to do double work—for that was her way of punishment—they listened, or pretended to listen. She knew them, knew every twitch of their being, and could tell insincerity at a glance. She prided herself on that fact. Yet, she realized that quite a few of her people had managed in their African way to sham sincerity and fool even her. She passed this over in the knowledge that they could not sham in the hereafter, and that thought gave her great comfort. Thus reassured, she would pat her stomach and smile contentedly. God would deal with them.

Quashiba and her mother had been taken into the Kensington household, an unusual privilege for a slave straight from Africa. As she grew, Mrs. Fowler began to teach Quashiba the rudimentary things whites knew. Reading and writing and how to speak and behave properly when company came. "I will make a lady out of you yet, my dear," she would declare with certainty.

Quashiba's mother resented the attention she got from the white woman at first, but she soon realized her daughter had the best chance for a reasonable life with her owner as guardian. She would never be condemned to the fields. So, she let the old lady indulge her fantasies with her daughter. The truth was, Mrs. Fowler missed her only daughter. She missed the bringing up and training of a child. The Vernon children over at Mount Apfel, although only a few miles away, were too far for daily supervision.

Quashiba's mother benefited from her daughter's position in the Kensington Great House. She was assigned to do light housework and sometimes sent over to help out in the estate hospital. Arduous estate tasks were left to other slaves. Further, she soon realized that in the island, the way to get along was to mix with the whites as much as possible. Going back to Africa would never happen. So, as a practical matter, she resigned herself to the new society but never forgot her origins.

In time, although unthinkable in Africa, she came to hope that a white man would look on her daughter with favor and set her up as his mistress. Most likely, her children by him would be set free. Her grandchildren would not have to slave for anyone. That was what mattered.

As it turned out, a white man never got into the picture. Edward Lawrence came along, and after a long tussle backward and forward and sometimes sideways, she made the compromise and surrendered for her daughter's sake. Quashiba wanted him as much as he wanted her. The old woman demanded and got her one wish for her child and grandchildren: freedom. Mother and daughter were at one with this wish.

Neddy played with his cornmeal porridge in the enamel bowl. His spoon searched for the lumps he knew to be hiding there. He hated them. That was the one thing his mam did not know how to cook. He grated the sugar cane furiously and then mixed the coarse brown sugar into the porridge, with the belief that the extreme sweetness it created would get rid of the lumps. He stirred furiously and, in the effort, mashed a few into smooth cornmeal.

His father watched him and smiled. His sympathies were with his son. He, too, suffered the cornmeal porridge and thought of it as the trial before the reward. Most of the time it was not bad, and it did help to fill them up to begin a long day's work. This morning though, his wife had not taken the time to stir continuously while pouring the dry cornmeal into boiling water. His spoon contained at least two lumps passing into his mouth, causing a shudder as they passed down his gullet. His son continued to churn his porridge, with the desperation of the young, afraid of the maternal consequences should he not eat most of her morning effort to appease their hunger. He wished it were corn pone rather than porridge. Neddy often wondered how she could be so good at cooking pone and so bad using the same corn when it came to porridge. One day he would ask her. But he would wait until he was grown before broaching the question. It would be safer that way.

His wife looked at both of them and said nothing. She should have been more careful when stirring the cornmeal into the water, she knew. This morning, her mind was not on cooking, it was on her upcoming visit to Montego Bay and the Baptist meeting, where Preacher Sam Sharpe would talk to them about the end of slavery. No longer a slave herself, she had been taught that men and women should not be in bondage. Funny, Mrs. Fowler, her one-time owner, said as much to her as she grew up under her tutelage. Her own mother was adamant, nay indignant, at belonging to another, no matter how benign an owner. Slavery was widespread in Africa but Quashiba was no man's slave, in Africa or anywhere else.

"What you going down to the Baptists for?" asked her husband, chewing on a lump of half-cooked cornmeal, trying to act as though that was the natural way to eat porridge.

"Miss Dodd want me to go wid her." She said no more, glancing over at Neddy to see how he was managing.

"You ain't a Baptist, so what business is it of yours? You go to di German man church."

"Lord! It bout slavery and the end to it. You can understan that? No, you wouldn't. You like belonging to someone else. You afraid to be free! You is one of dem good niggers. You is a *Yes, sah, massa* nigger, a *What you want, massa?* nigger, and a *Can I get it for you, massa-massa?* nigger." Quashiba said. Her face drooped with the frustrating situation. Free or not, they would remain condemned, because some in society were willing and able to accept the status quo of white on top and black below; master-slave, master-servant. She knew the slaves were divided into two groups, the good and those counted incorrigible—high-risk naygars. Most slaves were the latter kind, and although Quashiba would not have given them the time of the day, even they deserved freedom.

The good ones, like her husband, were the true obstacle to gaining the God-given right of freedom and equality. They loved the situation they lived in. All their needs were taken care of. Life went from day to day without a hitch. Freedom was a threat to them. It would force them to shoulder all the responsibilities their masters now took care of, as property owners. Their situations had only become more privileged with the death of the slave trade. The flow from Africa had stopped, and Negroes were hard to come by. Gone were the good old days when slaves were replaced seasonally, as trees changed their leaves. Now, the few leaves left on the tree had become more valuable, a resource to be nurtured and preserved.

Edward knew there was truth in what she said. He was afraid to be free. All the privileges he presently enjoyed would be lost. How could he get work? Who would employ him? Certainly not those damned niggers who worked in the fields. They could never afford his skills. Those thieving, conniving, murdering niggers would have no use for him anyway. Good cabinet making, furniture, and fine carpentry were matters beyond their comprehension. They were niggers, after all. Even oxen that drew the carts about the estate had more sense than them. Edward's work was for white people only. He should have been born white, not black.

Edward had been spoiled on Kensington estate. As a child he'd been just another little boy around the place, allowed to play with the other children, which included Mrs. Fowler's daughter. She was the only living creature that could have asked and received from her mother a denial of God's existence, so much was she adored. A pretty girl, with soft sunburned hair, big brown eyes shaded by long lashes, and a light golden complexion that suggested her father was more like the skin of the apple that his name signified in German than the fruit's white interior. Only the very oldest people in Kensington had known Mr. Apfel before the fever had taken him. They could tell you nothing about him, except that when he lived on Kensington, he had been Mrs. Fowler's man, taking the place of her late husband for a brief time.

Unlike on other plantations, the children on Kensington were never used to weed the cane fields. Perhaps it was because there were never many fields of cane to weed on Kensington, but pickney gangs did not exist. Kensington was more of a cattle and sheep pen than a sugar plantation.

Instead of hard manual labor under the scorching sun, the children performed simple tasks, such as feeding the turkeys, ducks, and chickens. From the fowls they graduated to bigger animals, like the goats and sheep, all the way up to cattle and oxen. Generally, they were taught the skills of farming and animal husbandry. With time, they fell into two distinct groups. Those with strong backs and little sense were destined for the fields, and those with more intelligence were put to learn a trade. Mrs. Fowler decided who went where, and thus lives were set and determined. The wheels of the plantation turned smoothly.

It was so with Edward. When old enough, he was apprenticed to the estate carpenter, learned his trade, and took over the chief carpenter's duties when the older man got sickly and too old to work.

Neddy gave up on scraping the sugar into his plate and slowly stirred, looking for more lumps in the cornmeal. He didn't want to eat it, but his mother would scold him. Better to try to finish what was before him, so he could enjoy the fried plantain, salt fish, and ackee that smelled so delicious on the cooking fire outside. Again, almost desperately this time, he mixed and churned the mess in his bowl, closed his eyes, and spooned the thick mush into his mouth, working his Adam's apple to choke it down. At last, the lumps seemed to diminish. And despite the odd one that had escaped his assault, it tasted good with the sprinkling of cinnamon and nutmeg she always added.

"What you tink im going tell you, dis Sam Sharpe?"

"I donuo, but im is a good man and wise. What im say will make sense. White and black is the same under di Lord, an we ave to realize dis and get together. In di Lord's view, one man cannot own another man."

"Dats may be. Who gots di power owns di man, is all I have to say."

Silence took over the small room as the three, mother, father, and son, finished their porridge. Neddy's bowl was not quite empty. There was still porridge left, but his mother knew there were lumps hidden there and did not press him to finish the food. There were boundaries that should not be crossed, if she wanted to keep the household peace. The yard dog got the scrapings in its bowl, which it lapped it up happily, not at all fussy about the lumps.

Quashiba went outside to get the next dish for them from her stove: the ackee and salt fish they had smelled while they struggled with the porridge. She scooped it out onto three plates. Edward loved the dish, despite the rumors that it could be poisonous.

"How come you can cook dis?" Edward said, pointing to the ackee with his fork.

"Because I am African," she said, with just the right hint of superiority.

"But when dem other cook dis, they get poison."

Quashiba laughed. "Ackee only poisonous when it not ripe and when dem pick it before it open up. These people, barn ya so, don't know. Mi mother taught me bout it. In Africa dem don't eat it unless there is nothing else."

"It is dangerous food, though—like you," he said, a grin spreading across his mouth.

Quashiba did not disregard his innuendo altogether; she followed up with a gentle lecture on the topic of food and love. "All tings dangerous, Edward. Food, if you eat too much, can do bad things to you. But just as dangerous, is what we calls love. You never know where that one going to tek you. Now, that can cramp you up an kill you, jus like the ackee."

As they finished breakfast, Quashiba quickly cleared away the plates. Neddy and his father went outside to see if they had missed anything and, if so, to add it to what the mule must carry for them to Newman Hall. All that was necessary to do the job had been loaded into the hampers, made specially to transport tools. After Edward inspected and found nothing wanting, he put his hand out and rubbed the back of his son's head affectionately.

"You getting good," he said.

"You sure you want him to come with you?" Quashiba cut in, pointing to her son.

"Yes, im got to learn to be a master carpenter like me," he said, proud of both himself and what he knew his son would be.

"There is learning and learning," she said.

"What you mean?"

"Well, him can learn carpentry business, and him can learn about him future in dis country."

"Lard! Dere you go again. Slavery is di only ting dat keeps us together as one. What you want to see? You want to see it end? For what? You tink we going to be better off? What di rass!—You is free! Why it bodder you? Mi buy your freedom. Mi buy your son freedom. What more you want, woman?"

"Mi want mi husband a free man. Dat is what mi want." Her answer came with exact rectitude, which only riled him more.

"You want dat. Well, mi is happy as an owned man. Nothing in this life mi want. Backra Massa supply it. Im look after mi till dead come." There was finality in his statement. It should have ended the spat there.

"How you tink mi feel, married in di church to a slave? You tink mi sleep well at night?" Quashiba's language slipped again, as her eyes flashed defiance.

Edward had been over this ground before, and he knew it was leading nowhere. He and Quashiba could not agree on this point. Her ideas and his were in constant conflict. So let it be.

"All right! You want Neddy to go with you to Montego Bay?"

"Yes."

"Den he can go. But when you get back, he must come over to Newman Hall and help mi. Dat suit you?"

"Yes." Quashiba suppressed a smile.

Neddy suppressed his involuntary jig of excitement. Montego Bay! He had been there a couple of times, but each trip to the big town was like a trip made in his dreams It was like going to foreign. The sights, sounds, and smells were so different from those in his district, where the most exciting place to visit was John's Hall Square. At that moment, when his mother got her way, Neddy loved her to distraction. He was getting out of work with his father and going off with her on an adventure. Montego Bay, yes!

The trio left home and headed down past the trash house and mill. They walked through the slave village and on toward the gates and the road, returning the usual salutations from women whose men had already gone to the fields for the day's work. Halfway to the road, they were hailed from the field by the overseer.

McCallums was new to the job on Kensington and still learning its traditions. Had he known them, he would not have bothered to stop Edward and his family. The attorney in charge of the estate had hired McCallums while the courts sorted out Mrs. Fowler's heirs. She had died three years before, and still nothing much had been done about the division of the property. As with many other properties, the attorneys and overseers skimmed what they could for themselves, leaving just enough for the heirs so they would not begin to ask for an accounting.

Edward halted his family and waited for the overseer to ride up to them.

"Morning, Edward." At least McCallums was polite—not like other overseers, whose whip was their tongue.

"Marning, sah," replied Edward, lifting his straw hat in respect.

"Where you going with your wife and son?" McCallums said.

Vernon el Halawani constructed various points of view about slavery and freedom that takes the reader beyond the binaries of slave and master, black and white, merchant and planter, crown and colony. Characters such as the Jewish peddlers, the prostitutes, the tradesmen, and the higgler women, making an independent living amid overseer gluttony, sports, debauchery, were very interesting. So were the characters that played their roles in spreading the Christian gospel through the Baptist and Moravian mission churches.

This complex story of slavery and emancipation struggles in Jamaica and the role of Christian ideas of freedom and equality, which Daddy Sharp was able to re-interpret from the Baptist and Moravians in contrast to the Anglican interpretation constitute another telling of the plotting of the Sam Sharp Rebellion. The aspirations of the enslaved Africans as articulated by Daddy Sharpe and his African co-leaders were carefully drawn, showing different attitudes to freedom as exemplified by the characters Edward Lawrence and is wife, as well as the overseers and investors.

I found the very powerful Galloway character most intriguing in the number of roles he occupied, and the ways in which he used his power. He resisted the sexual exploitation of the women as exemplified in his rescue and honouring of his brutalized "housekeeper" and her son. His advice to Neddy about homosexual exploitation of young boys was original. This topic is seldom dealt with so explicitly in the literature.

Vernon el Halawani's treatment of the oppressed Irish and Scots brought some historical complexity to the narrative. The "white" dispossessed, and displaced of the British Empire are often erased from historical accounts. The history of the Highland Clearances in Scotland by the Scottish and English capitalists and the wars of English colonization of Ireland are usually overshadowed by accounts of the potato famines as push factors, in their forced immigration to the Caribbean colonies and the US colonies, during the 17th and 18th centuries.

Even though class and race distinctions are clearly drawn, Vernon el Halawani skillfully leads the reader to see the entrapment and resultant persistent social and psychological pathologies that the set of circumstances bred.

The lifelong work of Jamaican psychiatrist, Fred Hickling has shown how these legacies of brutality and social division play out in the Island today. George Beckford's plantation thesis of underdevelopment has given us a historical material understanding of how and why structural poverty is endemic to the island even three hundred years later.

July 2014

When Conchi Blows
Omar Sheriffe Vernon el Halawani,
North Charleston, South Carolina:
CreateSpace Independent Publishing Platform, 2013. 558 pp.

Excerpts from Review by Yvonne Shorter Brown, author of *Dead Woman Pickney: A Memoir of Childhood in Jamaica.*

The general reader as well as humanities and social science academics of Caribbean literature should welcome this long needed epic novel of nineteenth-century sugar plantation regime in Jamaica. *When Conchi Blows*, written by the late Omar Sheriffe Vernon el Halawani fills a gap and complements the excellent historiographies that Jamaican historians have constructed, especially since independence

Vernon el Halawani recreates every imaginable detail of plantation life - its sights, landscape, sounds and smells. The brutal work regimes of the labour-intensive preindustrial capitalist enterprise of sugarcane plantation, sugar manufacturing, rum distillation, and molasses that required both man and horsepower are described by descriptive language that transports the reader to the various plantations of St James of the time.

This novel is chock full of details, no doubt gleaned over a lifetime of research, family history and participant observation of contemporary Jamaican society. I appreciated the details about the network of plantations and their social connections; descriptions of social and racial composition and hierarchy within each group; the labour regime around sugar and rum production; the related trades, and modes of transportation.

"Dem a going to Montego Bay, an I told you, sah, me have to do some work for Massa Galloway down at Newman Hall."

"You did tell me that, but when I saw you all like this I began to worry that you were moving away." McCallums grinned. "You know, Kensington would collapse if you ever left, Edward." There was more truth to that little jest than any of them would have liked to admit.

"Leave, sah? Where mi going to, Hingland?" The both laughed at that. "Dat never going happen. Besides, if in I ever try to leave, Miss Fowler get out of er grave and grab mi. You ever had duppy grab you, Massa Callums?"

The two men laughed. Quashiba did not find it funny, hearing her late mistress talked of lightly. She thought of her lying not far away, beside her husband in the family plot near the Great House garden, and imagined she could hear the old lady rumble her disapproval. But Quashiba said nothing until the overseer waved them on with the whip he held curled up in his right hand, the symbol that delineated the old ways from the new ways on Kensington.

As they moved out of the overseer's hearing, she said to her husband, "You see, if you was a free man, no man stop you an ask you about your business."

"And maybe when I is free, I don't ave any business. You hear what di man sey? Kensington mash-up wid out mi." He spread his arms wide as if to indicate an ownership and a belonging. "Where mi going go, woman?"

The trio moved on in silence. For the time being, there was nothing more to say. Edward had had enough badgering about his status. His wife realized he wanted to hear no more.

They reached the road just as the sun topped the great guango trees in the pastures next to the gate. The trees' huge canopies spread like giant green umbrellas to shade all beneath, and that was why they had been planted all those years ago. They were nature's barns in the tropics, which needed no maintenance. Under them, the animals of the estates were sheltered from sun and rain. White Brahmin cattle, newly imported from India, with huge horns and fleshy humps on their backs, moved slowly under the Kensington trees. They searched for the seed pods the great trees rained down on the ground like biblical manna. These they chewed, swallowed, and later regurgitated as cud to chew again, squeezing all the goodness out of them.

Like a sentinel at the entrance to Kensington, a young guango spread its branches halfway across the road. Edward, wife, and son stood beneath it, waiting for Quashiba's traveling companion.

They heard her before the cart rounded the corner. Miss Dodd's voice carried far, as she called to slave and free alike, asking who had produce to sell. She had her regular suppliers, but this was a special trip to Montego Bay, and why not make some money if she could? No opportunity to increase wealth was ever lost to Miss Clarissa Dodd. A freewoman and, by trade, a first-class higgler, she was chief rival in these parts to the Jew, da Lazarus.

"Marnin, all," she said with a broad, warm smile. It was difficult to describe Miss Dodd, except to say that she had a cocoa complexion with a lot of milk in it and just the suggestion of cocoa butter floating on top. Her countenance was round and smiling, and the rest of her was goodly proportioned. No one meeting her could mistake she was a woman who enjoyed life. The quality made her friends and kept them close.

"Boye! You looking good enough to nyam, as usual, Miss Dodd," Edward said.

"Lard, Mass Edward!" she exclaimed. "I just love you. You always say di nicest tings to mi. Quashiba better look out, or mi tek you away from her." The three grown-ups had a chuckle at that. Neddy found nothing funny in the banter. His eyebrows flickered, and he almost rolled his eyes to heaven to plead for deliverance from grown-up humor but restrained himself. Today was not the day to bring parental wrath down on his head.

Quashiba set herself on the cart seat beside Miss Dodd. When both were comfortable, the enlarged cavalcade moved down the road on the way to Newman Hall. Edward walked beside the cart, and Neddy led their mule behind.

They made good progress to Newman Hall, and time passed quickly as Miss Dodd brought them up to date with the latest this and that in the area. She missed nothing, it seemed. Not surprising, for she visited all the estates, trying to beat da Lazarus to the produce.

In her search for the choicest fruits and vegetables for her Montego Bay customers, she naturally gathered up the latest scandals along with the sweet potatoes, yams, and plantains. There was little else for entertainment.

At Newman Hall, Edward left the party. "Don't forget now, watch yoself down in Montego Bay. It is a jinnal town, full of jinnal man."

"What you worried about, Edward? Miss Dodd goes every week to Montego Bay. How many time ave you heard she get robbed? Don't fret yourself."

"It wasn't rob mi worry bout. Is dem jinnal Baptist you going listen to. When dem dunk you under di water, dem tief you soul and tief you pocket." He laughed raucously.

"Go wey, Edward!" Miss Dodd exclaimed. "Go on wid yu nonsense."

Edward went on laughing, took the mule's halter from Neddy's hands, and led the animal toward Newman Hall. As he got onto the property, he stopped and turned to shout at them: "Take care now, and when you get back, don't forget to sen di boye to mi, up ya at Massa Galloway's house."

The women watched him for a little while, allowing Neddy to jump up on the back cart and settle down to ride for the rest of the way. Then Miss Dodd slapped the reins on the beast's backside. The mule responded with a jerk, and the cart moved away at a faster pace than when they arrived. The clatter of the wheels precluded any conversation for a time. Then Miss Dodd blurted out between jolts, "Im is a good man."

Quashiba did not answer right away. She let the mule trundle them on a little way before agreeing. "Yes, mi know." The wheels of the cart ground the marl road a few more turns before she continued. "But mi must never let im know that mi know." The wheels completed several more revolutions before she finished. "If he knew mi know that im is a good man—he will stop being a good man."

Miss Dodd's head nodded acknowledgement. It was true of all men and especially, she believed, in Jamaica. Women knew these secret things about men. All too well, they knew that men about here were just boys, never growing up. Miss Dodd reckoned they reached about ten years old, and there they got stuck, even as the years rolled by. Women had to care for and cater to them and make them believe they were indispensable. And so they were. That was women's problem. In only one particular way were men indispensable, and Miss Dodd smiled at the thought. Quashiba looked at her friend and understood, as only women can understand each other.

Neddy paid them no mind. After all, it was only woman talk and of little interest to a man. He spent the time on the back of the cart, watching the road pass under his feet as they dangled over the edge of the backboard. His thoughts were in Montego Bay. He contemplated the possibility of sneaking off from his mother to explore the town, and he trembled with excitement at the prospect. He only wished he had some money to buy things. Some of those foreign sweeties in their bright wrappers, as he'd once seen in a shop there, would be nice. Or, better yet, a patty. He had had one before from a bakery. All that spicy, juicy meat oozing out when he bit into the light yellow, flaky crust! His mouth watered, and his hand rubbed his belly in appreciation. Hunger growled as if in answer. He was ready for a second breakfast, and the sundial in the garden of Kensington, five miles back up the road, was not even at ten o'clock yet.

They rolled into John's Hall Square. Miss Dodd pulled up in front of Tinka's establishment, assuring her passengers she would not be long. There were some jelly coconuts she wanted to pick up from Tinka. A good customer of hers had heard that there were medicinal properties in coconut water, and she now required a daily glass. For a constant supply of coconuts, she paid well. "There is no use going all the way to Montego Bay and lose the opportunity for making money," Miss Dodd declared and went inside to find the shopkeeper.

A young white girl, about fifteen years old, leaned against the shop wall, just to the left of the door. Under thick, wavy, tawny hair that caught the light and cascaded all about her forehead, was a pretty face. Freckles from long exposure to the sun dotted a small, upturned nose, adding a certain youthful charm and a suggestion of innocence.

A flimsy cotton blouse, provocatively unlaced at the neck, showed the outline of her full breasts, and a colorful broad woven belt around her small waist helped to raise them invitingly. A faded blue skirt, most likely a hand-me-down, stopped just above her ankles, exposing small, dirty bare feet. Neddy looked at these, and she wiggled her toes in response.

The girl shifted her stance to the left, giving a side view to anyone looking from the square. She hooked her left arm under her breasts and locked her hand in place with the elbow of the right arm. The effect was to enhance the size of her bosom. Then, as if unaware of any watcher, she pulled a ringlet from her hair and began expertly to twist it around her fingers. Now and then, she would let the curl go, and it would spring back into place, like a yo-yo on the up. Occasionally, she would put this lock of hair between her lips and nibble at it suggestively, then blow it back into place. Then she would glance across at the cart to see if anyone there was taking notice.

Her game continued until a flat-chested, tight-lipped white woman, with strands of prematurely graying hair hanging from under a droopy calico bonnet, came through the door, followed by Miss Dodd. The woman looked at the girl leaning against the wall of the shop and then across at Neddy sitting on the back of the cart, and she did not hesitate. Walking over to where the girl stood, she drew back her right hand and slapped the girl, hard and righteously, across the face. The girl cringed and let out a yelp like a kicked puppy. Ignoring the pain she had caused, the older woman grabbed the girl by the arm and dragged her off up the road, a four-year-old boy hanging onto her dress and stumbling to keep up.

Miss Dodd chuckled as she came alongside her cart. Her belly fat moved up and down with her laugh. "Poor Miss Dougal. She going ave grand pickney soon, wid di way dat Millicent go on wid de boye dem." Quashiba gave her a questioning look. "She mus of ave everyone of dem here about up in a di bush by now. You watch, soon she going ketch a pickney, and dem boye going ketch some ting else an spread it bout, you watch."

"You mean the white boys?"

"She don't mind which one she tek," Miss Dodd said, chuckling like someone who knew the pleasure of satisfying the desires of youth. "White or black, it don't matter, so long as dem big and can fill her up, I hear."

Listening to Miss Dodd, who knew all the scandal in the district, Quashiba turned around and looked at her son, sitting on the back of the cart. He met her eyes straight on. She felt reassured he was not one of the boys referred to by Miss Dodd. Quashiba hoped he never would be. If there was one thing she did not want, it was a diseased son. For that matter, she didn't want a half-black grandchild, either. She wanted them clean and black. After all, she had her pride. It did not matter that in her own husband's ancestral woodpile lurked an Englishman named Lawrence. Edward was the exception. The early prejudices of her mother died hard.

"I feel sorry for some of these walk-foot backra, you know," Miss Dodd said with conviction, looking over at her friend. "Dem got white skin and notting else but an empty belly. Dem is poorer than most slaves, but dey is mostly good people."

"Yes," Quashiba said. Then she added, in the English taught her those many years ago by Mrs. Fowler, "But you forget they got the most precious God-given treasure—freedom. They can come and go and do whatever they please without anyone's say-so. That is worth an empty belly."

Miss Dodd laughed. "Not if you is di one wid di empty belly."

"You beginning to sound like Edward."

Both women laughed at that.

Tinka appeared from the shop, carrying half a dozen coconuts. Following him with the same quantity was a young lad. Neddy jumped down from the back of the cart, and they stowed the nuts safely before he got back up.

"See dem don't roll aroun di place back dere, Neddy," instructed Miss Dodd as she climbed aboard. She handed Tinka money for the nuts, and they were off again, heading north to Montego Bay.

The cart passed estate after estate. On the roads they passed four- and six-wheel carts pulled by oxen, moving various implements and empty wooden barrels to hold the juice of cane or rum. Eventually, they rolled by the entrance to Friendship. Neddy looked at the gates and wondered how Watt was getting along. He had not yet told his mother about their meeting. He knew that before Sunday he would have to try talking her into cooking up some food for him, as he promised. But there were six days before Sunday came again. By then, he would work out a plan to convince his mother food for Watt was necessary. He had to keep his promise. After all, his pride was at stake.

White boys did not make friends of black boys, even if they were free. As for slaves, no intimacy lasted for long. Friendship between whites and slaves was not unheard of, but it was very rare. Slaves served and complied with their master's wishes, no matter what those wishes were, and the relationship solidified around the master-servant equation.

Without a let-up on the way, his mother and Miss Dodd debated the merits of freedom over slavery. Miss Dodd wondered how freedom would affect her business, and his mother knew that everything would be better in the land. The injustice of one human owning another would stop. Miss Dodd, even though she was a good Baptist, was skeptical. She generally agreed with Quashiba's views, but she wondered about the practical implications.

"You mean, when di freedom paper come and slavery end, they going pay good money for work to those they owned before?" The thought amused Miss Dodd. She slapped her side and gave a belly laugh.

"Yes, that's what is going to happen."

"Quashiba, mek mi tell you some ting. You live wid old Miss Fowler too long up on Kensington. Now, she dead, and dem bring in a new overseer to run di place. You notice how work get done now? You notice im ave to whip people?" She looked to her companion before continuing. "What you now got since she dead, is di slave split into bad niggers and good niggers. Just like on all the other estate. Well, let mi tell you some ting, dere is more bad nigger dan good nigger." Miss Dodd's voice contained no trace of doubt. "For every one of di good nigger, like Edward, dere is ten bad niggers, and dem not going to work for demselves or anybody! Not for money, not for freedom. Dem just going tief fi you work." Miss Dodd was most emphatic about it all. "But di Lord wills freedom." She shook her head from side to side with the resignation of one who believes a greater purpose to it all lies beyond her understanding. She chuckled. She would hold the faith.

They rode on, listening to the crunch of the iron-bound cartwheels cutting into the marl. Occasionally a wheel would slip into a larger rut and bounce, rocking the cart. When this happened, Neddy had to grab coconuts and stop them rolling in the back. Miss Dodd would look back to see if all was in order and her profit intact; she always had a good word for Neddy's efforts on her behalf.

They bounced in and out of a more potholes. "Lard, Quashiba!" Miss Dodd said, a tinge of envy in her voice. "You lucky, you know. You got a good man and a good boye back dere." She jerked her thumb at Neddy. "You free," she said. "Why mess wid tings? Better mi tink you let tings stay so."

Quashiba did not answer. All she had to say had been said, and her only reaction was to sit up straighter on the cart seat.

"You can tiffen up you back," Miss Dodd said. "But you know mi right."

At last they reached the outskirts of Montego Bay. Neddy could smell the place. Banished from his nose was the constant smell of crushed, discarded cane fermenting in the heat. Sea breezes swept the town clean of such odors and added a sting of salt. He could even pick up the smell of cooking from outdoor fires and kitchens set apart from the main houses they served.

They drove on to the center of town. The bustle became more intense. Carriages of the wealthy jostled with country carts, and coachmen cussed peasants for daring to get in their way. Sailors on shore leave were lolling about. Some stuffed their mouths with fresh fruit, and others, even at this time of the morning, were obviously two sheets to the wind with rum. Others were trying their best to get a local gal interested in what they had to offer. But even in this remiss society, propriety dictated that there would be no takers so long before midday. Those who would be interested were still abed from their work the night before; womenfolk out and about at this hour had reputations to protect.

"We have to deliver these coconuts to Miss Laird before we go to the meeting," said Miss Dodd, guiding the cart off St. James Street and up Church Street. They passed the Anglican Church, drove two more blocks to the Madison house—an imposing brick building standing in a large garden—then passed East Street, where the Presbyterian Church held sway. Soon they stopped at a small, neat cottage on the left side of the road, fenced by a brick wall topped with latticework for added privacy.

Miss Dodd got down from the cart and went through the gate. A middle-aged black man answered her knock. They spoke, and he went back inside. Then a young maid of about fifteen came out of the house with a basket. Neddy helped her with the coconuts. It took the girl two trips to complete the job. The middle-aged man reappeared and paid Miss Dodd; she said something more to him, and they both laughed.

"We are off again," Miss Dodd said, climbing back onto the cart. She turned them around in the middle of Church Street, where they were lucky not to block any carriage carrying someone of importance, and they returned the way they had come. Miss Dodd chuckled at her bold maneuver, and the mule went into a rough jog. They bounced down to East Street and wheeled right until Miss Dodd pulled hard on the reins. "Whoa!" she said, halting the cart at the steps of the Baptist Chapel.

"Well, now we have some time to wait. What time you tink it is, Quashiba?"

"Bout ten o'clock."

"Rev Sharpe said ee would come bout eleven o'clock. Let's go inside, out of di sun."

"Mama?"

They had almost forgotten Neddy. Quashiba turned to him.

"Can me go an walk about till im ready to speak?"

Quashiba looked at Miss Dodd questioningly.

"Let di boye go." Miss Dodd turned to Neddy. "But mine you mek sure you back here, and don't get loss."

His mother nodded, and he was free to explore the town.

"Neddy!" Miss Dodd said, as he was about to scurry off.

"Yes, Miss Dodd." He stopped midstride.

"Tek dis an buy youself some ting nice to eat and a drink." She handed him a silver threepenny piece.

"What you doing?" questioned his mother. "Why you spoil im so?"

Miss Dodd gave another merry little chuckle. "Mi not spoiling im, Quashiba. Mi paying di man for di work im do for mi."

"What work him do?"

"Im keep di coconut from rolling all over di place in di back of di cart. An im elp pick dem up. Dat no easy work for a boye, you know." His mother faced her friend with quizzical expression, and it was her turn to shake her head from side to side in resignation to things beyond her control.

"Im an me is in business today," Miss Dodd said. "I give Tinka sixpence for di nuts, and I charge Miss Laird one shilling. She now give me one shilling, and an extra treepence fi mi trouble. Now, Neddy ere, give me help. Im no mus get im pay? Im is a free man, not a slave, and dat is what wi fighting for. Na right?" Miss Dodd could not control herself and let out a crowing laugh at her logic.

Neddy awaited the outcome with a little trepidation His mother made no comeback—a good sign.

Resigned to losing this one to Miss Dodd, Quashiba waved her son on to his adventure. Secretly she was pleased that Neddy was getting spoiled; he deserved to be spoiled sometimes. Besides, she had no money to waste on him today, and it would be a pity to come all the way to Montego Bay and not enjoy something other than grown-up business.

"Jus remember, Daddy Sharpe is never late like di lazy nigger dem. When im say eleven o'clock at di chapel, im mean eleven. Im na mean one o'clock or two o'clock. So, young Massa Neddy, get yourself back ere by dat time. You understan?" Miss Dodd was adamant and wagged her fat forefinger to emphasize her point.

"Yes, Miss Dodd, mam." He was off before another word could be said, out and away from the clutches of the two women who ruled his day.

He rounded the corner to Church Street and was on his way down to Charles Square. Before long he was standing on the edge of the square, taking it all in. Street peddlers hawked their wares. Finely dressed ladies escorted by gentlemen passed by, out on a morning constitutional. Servants, male and female, looked for things to buy for their households from higglers who bravely dealt with them on the sidewalk, risking fines for trading outside the market behind the courthouse.

Carts and carriages vied with each other for passage on the narrow street. Skilled coachmen kept a tight hold on their animals to allow the drays to move out of the way. Most of these were heading for the waterfront with rum and sugar for ships awaiting cargo.

By the courthouse corner of the square, the back wheel of a dray slipped into a deep rut, tipping the conveyance to one side and throwing its weight on the right. There was a crunching, cracking sound, and the rear axle buckled. All went over. Oxen caught in the twisted shafts and tangled ropes bellowed. Women close by screamed. Men shouted orders and curses. A cask rolled off and crashed into the wall of the courthouse. Rum began to trickle between the staves. A few watchers grabbed any container they could and ran over to fill them, before the golden liquid was sucked in by the dusty ground. One man threw out some flowers from a handy pot on a windowsill, wiped it out with the tail of his shirt as he ran and used that to take his share of the liquid before it disappeared.

Rum filled the air in the square with its pungency. The reek made Neddy think he could taste the raw liquid itself and would get drunk. His mother would give him a bitch lick if she thought he had been drinking with his threepence. Best to move on down St. James Street to a bakery and buy his patties. His belly rumbled in anticipation.

Three cost him a penny-ha'penny. They were worth it. Freshly made, hot and spicy with scotch bonnet peppers, there was nothing like them. He remembered the first time he had tasted a patty; his father had bought one for him over a year ago, when they first began his training as an apprentice carpenter, and they had a job in Montego Bay. These smelled the same, and the first bite brought back that unforgettable first taste.

The first patty went down quickly, despite the heat of both the stove and pepper. That made him thirsty. He wandered toward the sea, looking for a vendor of fruit drinks. They were plentiful in the parade square, but down along the waterfront were only workers.

Male and female slaves carried sacks on their heads into and out of whitewashed warehouses with the names of their owners painted on the sides. Some belonged to town merchants and others to sugar estates. There were Fletcher and Company, Mills Brothers, and then Richmond Hill and Catherine Hall. Out of the last two rolled the great hogsheads, guided by men along the pier to where rope cranes lowered them into waiting lighters.

Naked boys plunged into the sea between transport vessels. As long as they did not get in the way of the lightermen loading the rum and sugar, no one around seem to care if the boys drowned or were crushed between the bobbing ships' hulls, which occasionally crashed against each other or against the jetty. Three-and-two masters lined up just offshore to Bogue Island, three miles out, waiting for their cargos. Merchants at home in England must not be kept waiting for their profits. The commerce of the Empire depended on it.

At last, Neddy spotted a drink seller. He was about to order a ginger beer when, cautiously, he asked the price. "Ow much for di ginger beer?"

The man looked Neddy up and down. "A country boye, it coss you a quattie."

The man was taking advantage of him, he knew. That was not going to happen, if he could help it. Boldly, Neddy bargained as he had seen Miss Dodd and others do on occasion, "Give you a penny," he said flatly.

The man sucked his teeth in contempt at the offer. "Go wey!" He waved Neddy away. The man turned his back and immediately began to quarrel, as much with himself as with his hopeful customer. "Facety boye, wan some ting for notting. What all dese damn naygar people come wid dese days, sah?" Again he sucked his teeth loudly.

"As you wish. I will take my business elsewhere," Neddy said in his best Sunday School English, attempting to put the man in his place.

Hearing white talk coming from a black brought the peddler round quicker than he had turned away. His jaw dropped, his mouth opened, he stared for a good five seconds, and then he exclaimed, "Where a boogu-yaga boye like you learn to talk so, eh?" Shrieking a crowing laugh, his hands gesticulated to the heavens and then came

Daddy Sharpe

down to slap both thighs at the same time—like a rooster flapping its wings. Finally, he exhausted his merriment. "Raatid!" He paused to catch his breath. Neddy could see he was choked up. His Sunday School English had devastated the man. "Rass, man!" came another cuss. "If a nigger boy can talk like unu, den Daddy Sharpe right. We is equal. Come ya. Mek mi give you a drink for free. Dat was worth di quattie I going lose."

"Penny," countered Neddy and then thought, enough said. He didn't press any further; obviously luck was with him today. As he sipped the ginger beer, sweet and strong, the thought crossed his mind that that was the second time today that he had heard Sam Sharpe referred to as Daddy Sharpe. He must be a very old man to garner such respect from the likes of Miss Dodd and this man, who was well past forty by any standard.

Neddy finished the drink and patties, which left him full and slightly dizzy from the alcohol in the ginger beer. His mouth tingled with ginger taste as he continued to explore the core of Montego Bay. It was the third bong of the clock on the Anglican Parish Church striking eleven that broke the spell, reminding him of his promise. There was an urgency in each clang and, by the fifth, he had broken into a trot to get back to Reverend Barchell's Baptist Chapel. By the eleventh bong, he was in a dead run up the street. He made it by two minutes past the hour.

Outside the chapel stood three carts, besides Miss Dodd's, and four mules and two donkeys were tied to the railings. The meeting was in progress. He would have to sneak in and pray his mother did not notice as he slipped through the half-open door. Staying close to the wall, he slowly made his way to a back pew. Too intent on what was before her, Quashiba did not turn around, so he slipped safely into the end seat.

"It cannot be right for one man to profit from the misery of another," said a voice from the front. "It cannot be right for one man to be captured by another and so lose his freedom. It cannot be right that there are marketplaces where one man sells another for profit. It cannot be right that there is master and slave upon this earth, which was given to us equally by the Lord God."

"Amen, oh Lord!" rose from the gathering in front of the speaker.

From his position, Neddy could see his mother and Miss Dodd right up front on the far side of the church. There must have been forty people listening to the well-built but medium-sized man standing in front of them. To his surprise, Sam Sharpe, Daddy Sharpe, was not the grey-headed old man Neddy expected. Instead he was about middle age. He could only be about his Sunday school teacher's age, who he knew to be thirty-two because his class gave him a gift of a cake with "32" in pink icing on it for the celebration.

The preacher wasn't preaching. Sam Sharpe just talked, and his audience hardly breathed, in fear the sound would blur his words. His voice was musical and the English spoken was that of a highly schooled man of the island. As he listened to the reverend Sharpe, Neddy began to understand why his mother insisted he be educated as much as possible and learn to speak properly. He had already profited from that ability, and here in front of him was a man, a slave, who had become a leader to his people and highly respected by the white Baptist community because of his education and presentable nature.

"It is near the end of October. Christmas will soon be upon us—the one time in the year our masters allow us to celebrate. Very unlikely that our freedom papers will be here by then. But I have a plan to hasten the day they come to this island and everywhere men and women are held in bondage, like the Hebrews in Egypt and Babylon."

"We goin rebel den, Parson? We going strike dem like the Lard did Babalon?" asked a man loudly, sitting two rows from the front. "Bun dem like Sodom an Gomorrah!" another said. "We mek it salt for dem!"

"No, brothers, not a rebellion like the old days. No killing, no burning. This plan is simple. We are going to stop work. We going sit down and refuse to work."

"How you mean? Stop work—jus so?"

"Yes. If we organize it properly, we stop work. What is the Massa going to do about it? We outnumber them by ten, twenty to one. What can they do? Nothing. There are not enough soldiers to force us back to work. We just sit down and refuse to work. That is it."

"Dat not going work. Dem will just shoot us down, like dem shoot bud for sport."

"It will work if we coordinate it properly," insisted Sharpe. "Granted, some of us could well get hurt and killed. But they can't kill us like birds. They won't do that. We are worth plenty money to them. You ever heard of any but a madman destroying what was valuable to him?"

"Lard, parson," said a little old man sitting way over to Sharpe's left. "Dere is many mad man in dis ya place. Mi know, mi live fifty years wid dem. Dem mad to rass!" Neddy stifled a giggle hearing the old man use a bad word in church. And his first sighting of Watt flashed through his mind. *Mad, yes!* he agreed.

None of them said a word more. Many sitting there probably thought only blood could settle the issue. One massive uprising to strike down their oppressors, once and for all! None spoke his mind on the subject. That was out of great respect for the man in front of them. Besides, should word of such a proposal get back to the whites, trees would bear strange fruit along the roadside, and none wanted to be that fruit.

Neddy studied Sam Sharpe from his corner. The light from the stained-glass window at the back of the chapel filtered through, outlining him clearly. He had a fine, open face, made more so by a receding hair line. His eyes were set wide apart, and his jawline was firm. Taken together, it all bespoke an integrity beyond the suggestion of the conviction of right over wrong.

"It is simple, brothers and sisters. We have to get this plan out to our people. We have got to explain it carefully and make them understand there will be no violence on our part. They have got to understand that when the time comes, we sit down and refuse to work. We do not take up machetes and guns to kill our owners. It is up to you to spread the word. You know how to do this from district to district, property to property. I am depending on each of you to speak for us all."

That got them. There was a general murmur of assent among the congregation. One big woman dressed in black spoke up.

"We will do our best for you and Jesus, Mister Sharpe."

"Nay, do it for yourselves and the Lord. And then, all of us will benefit. Unfortunately, I will not be in Montego Bay," he said. "For a little while, anyway, I will not be around. My master is sending me out to Cambridge to look after his jobber gang." Then he paused and looked over them, his voice dropping, "When all is said and done, we are all slaves still, and the law says we must remember that." Once again he paused and wiped his hands with a handkerchief taken from his inner jacket pocket. He passed it over his forehead. When he spoke next, his voice took on a new vibrancy. "But the law must change, and, come after Christmas celebrations, we must hasten that change. The New Year will bring about the New Man." Sharpe's voice rose to echo off the walls of the little chapel.

"Amen! Amen!" the crowd said.

"So be it."

Sam Sharpe ended the meeting.

As they rose to leave, a wizened man, the years of unrelenting taskmasters drawn upon his face, asked, "How we going know when to sit down and stop work, parson? Yes, sah," he said. "How we going know?"

"Ah, brother Gabriel, that is a good question. I had not thought that far as yet. We will have to have a signal that tells us all the time has come."

"You mean like when shell blow to signal food time and di end of di day, Parson?"

"Yes, brother Gabriel, yes!" A big smile spread across Sam Sharpe's face. "God moves in mysterious ways and speaks through his archangel here," he said, pointing to Gabriel. "Friends," he called, and they all stopped moving toward the door and turned back to where he was standing. "Brother Gabriel has given us the signal. I will pick the day on which conchi will blow for our freedom, yes sah! The conchi will blow our freedom, and the chains of slavery will tumble off, the way the walls of Jericho crashed down when Joshua blew the Lord's horn."

"Dat nice, Parson, di promis lan," Gabriel nodded, "but if mi remember di Bible story, it sey dere was plenty strife and blood before di Jew tek it over."

"True, brother Gabe, true. We are not going to have it go so. We have to be peaceful," Sharpe said.

Miss Dodd let the crowd go first, and then the three travelers got into the cart. A twitch of the harnesses set them off homeward. Miss Dodd and Quashiba argued the merits of the plan all the way. They explored every possibility they could think of. Neddy listened for a time and then curled up in the back of the cart, using some sacks for pillows and throwing one over him for shade, and snoozed. By the time they reached the entrance of Newman Hall, three hours later, the two women had come to a consensus that the plan was a good Christian one and should work for that reason alone.

When they came to a stop, his mother tapped Neddy's shoulder to awaken him. From the jolting and the awkward position he'd dozed in, he was stiff and sore. As he stretched to get the kinks out, his mother said, "Go on in an help your father." Then she smiled and added, "Tell him bout your day, and the day coming. Tell him he will be born again, a new man." Miss Dodd chuckled and ordered her animal into motion. Neddy watched them for a moment, then turned off the road and headed onto Newman Hall lands.

Chapter 5

Bookkeepers

Quashiba stacked the round enamel pots one on top of the other, using the bottom of one to cover the other below. They were the latest design for workmen to carry food with them and even had a handle that locked them together for easy handling. There was enough food in the four pots to feed two boys twice over: callalu with salt fish filled the top one; rice and peas the second; fried chicken the third; and at the bottom, sweet potato and cornmeal pudding, wrapped in the banana leaf in which it had been cooked, to keep it soft and moist. Thoughtfully, she tied to the stack a small bottle of thick, sweet cream made from coconut milk to pour over this stodgy dokunu, her son's favorite sweet pudding. It was a special treat for him today, and she knew the boy who would share the food was bound to love it. Quashiba prided herself on being a cook whose food was never pushed aside. There was the odd dish she made that was not well received by her family, but those did not count as special. They were everyday hurry-up food.

"Don't you come back and want to eat more, you hear me?" she said, knowing full well that he would come back and beg her for something to eat. Now, Edward could eat! She expected this from a hard-working grown man, but compared to his son, Edward was a beginner. She often wondered where Neddy put it all. Her friends told her boys of that age were all alike, and she was lucky that feeding one was all she had to worry about. But that could well change with this newfound friend, if Neddy begged for him.

As he took the pots from her hand, Neddy's face registered a smile of glistening white teeth. "Dis is for me one den, mama," he said. "Watt not getting a ting if no food for me when mi get back after di long walk to church and back."

She slapped him gently on the backside as he turned away. "Don't be greedy. You say he is your friend; dat's why he is getting the food." He was halfway down the path on his way when she added another warning: "Bring back those pots, and don't you chip them. Your father doesn't like eating his food out of chipped pots."

Neddy didn't even turn around at her cautionary word; he stuck his left hand up in the air, holding his flute and moving it from side to side in a wave. Had he turned around, he would have seen a look of resignation on his mother's face as she acknowledged to herself that he was fast becoming his own man and quickly moving away from her. She was not happy about it but accepted its inevitability. She had wished that along with him there had been a girl child. But her belly had dried up, and no other baby had come. They had tried, but it seemed God willed that they should be satisfied with one child. Her husband said nothing about it. Neddy was the sun that rose and set for him. He stood above all the others he had sired, and she knew that and was pleased.

As Neddy disappeared down the hill path and under the trees' overhang, she filled with pride. He was growing into a responsible boy. His mission to feed the white boy demonstrated this. Although not sure of the situation after hearing the story, it could do no harm to supply his request for food. Besides, those white boys were treated very poorly on many estates; in many instances, she reckoned, worse than slaves. They came here from foreign and died like flies stuck to treacle paper. Quashiba was satisfied with her son, and she thanked her maker for giving her a boy who showed he cared for the well-being of others.

Neddy hurried along the road, passing a few people going in the same direction to church. Some were parishioners of Reverend

Waldrich heading to the early service so they could get into their grounds and do a little farming for themselves. Neddy wished them a good day and moved on quickly. When they protested at his haste, he claimed the organist, Miss Foster, wanted him to practice the hymns.

Facety, fast, and forward—worst of all, gravalicious, he knew them all to be. If he took up and walked alongside, they would be asking what he was carrying in the pots. When they were assured that it was food, which to all but a fool was obvious, then the angling for a taste would begin. "Lard, it mus bi nice, you know. Mi love sal-fish and callalu. Any ackee in de? Lard! Hit always specially good when yu modder cook it!" Any listener would think they ate his mother's food often, and it was right that they should continue to do just that, especially so on a Sunday morning when people join in community with God.

It would go so, till they had the pots uncovered and the food gone. All would be gone lickety-split. Hospitality was a byword in the island, no matter where you were. It was not uncommon to have another nyam food right off your plate as you were eating and think that it was right you share. "Gimi a little taste, nuh?" Then it would be, "Gimi next taste, nuh?" After that it would be a quick gobble that left you feeling half-empty and cheated. But to refuse was impossible. Those refused would feel insulted. They had begged and were refused as common beggars.

His mother said that his grandma always told her, when you cook, always cook for the unseen guest, for surely they will come. His mother always did, and, oddly, there always seemed an extra body who sat down with them. If only the three of them ate, then what was left took on another form in the next day's meal. Or the ever-ready dog became the extra mouth.

Neddy was taking no chances. There would be no extra mouth this Sunday, or there would be nothing left for him and Watt. He moved on with his pots as quickly as possible without risking an upset. It was unlikely the churchgoers would quicken their pace to keep up with him. The only thing slower than a Jamaican walking or working was a pregnant sea turtle coming ashore to deposit her eggs. But even these ancient animals moved with compelling purpose.

He would tell them, if they asked, that the pots contained food for the reverend. That lie would keep their hands off. It was common for members of the congregation to give their parson a Sunday treat occasionally. But why bother say anything that could come back on him? And he certainly was not going to tell them about Watt. That would bring strange looks, comments, and nasty sniggers.

He did not even know if Watt would turn up, but a promise was a promise, and he had been taught never to go back on his word. After all, a man's word was all he had when the final trumpet sounded, and he stood naked in front of his Lord. Thinking about these things, he often wondered where his Sunday School teacher got his wisdom from. He dared not say so, but he strongly suspected Mr. Wilkinson made everything up as he went along. Still, they were good thoughts.

As it was, he lied anyway when he got into church. Miss Foster asked him what the pots were for, as he stowed them safely away behind the organ.

"They are for an old sick friend of mi mama's," he told her. She seemed satisfied with that and pried no more, just sniffed as she always did and wiped her nose with a little lace handkerchief that smelled strongly of camphor even at his distance from her.

During the sermon, Reverend Waldrich's voice intoned heavily. There was no sparkle, no tale to tell, no drama this week. The undulating voice and the heat caused Neddy's eyes to close, and his head drooped forward. Seconds passed in this posture, and he slipped into an uncomfortable semiconscious state. Sweat trickled down the crevice of his backbone and made him sit up and wriggle, only to nod off again. More sweat. His shirt stuck to his skin. He sat up and tried to unstick it but could not. He suffered it. Again his head dipped forward in that uncomfortable snooze.

None of those in the pews noticed. They were too intent on the parson's words. Besides, he was partially hidden behind the admirable Miss Foster, righteously upright on her organ stool. She noticed him from the corner of her eye. It was only as she expected: Negroes could not help their laziness. Undisciplined children, all of them. It had been so in America and was dependably so in Jamaica.

Bookkeepers

She was never comfortable accompanying Neddy when he played the flute. She blocked him from view and overplayed him at every opportunity. Last week, when he had the stage to himself with Amazing Grace, she deemed the performance not a triumph of musical accomplishment but a mortification of her own being and talent. She would have done it far better on the organ. The song would have thundered to the heavens, as its composer intended. The Lord would have heard it and would not have had to strain his ears to catch the simple notes of a bamboo flute.

In Miss Foster's view, the flute was inappropriate for the Lord's music. It was an instrument to tantalize the young and lead them astray into dark and forbidden places. It was almost a sinful instrument, like the pipes played by the half-man, half-goat in that book on Greek mythology in her late father's collection. She always promised herself she would burn it, but somehow she had never got around to actually doing so: "Just one last time," she would tell herself, as again and again she would flip through the pages, bent on casting the book into the flames once and for all but, each time, stymied by the pictures of naked Adonis and Apollo. And, so, a further reprieve from eternal damnation would be granted the tome, which she would replace carefully in the bottom desk drawer, depositing the key to its lock into the darkest reaches of her purse, attached to her wrist by a finely woven silk cord. After all, Miss Foster would tell herself, she was preserving her father's precious classical library—a sacred trust. If it was good enough for him, then the book must be all right, despite that animal-man thing. It must represent the devil in men, she assured herself, and she felt better for the reassurance.

Miss Foster did not want to say it outright to the reverend, but sharing the same stage with a little black boy, in front of a black audience, was not quite acceptable. Allowing them to rush forward would never do. It was setting a bad example. It did not matter when freedom came; whites must lead the way and blacks follow. If not, they would all end up as jungle creatures.

Her views were in step with those held by many who saw slavery as an evil to be controlled but still maintained. Negroes were simple, willful children, unsteady in the world, and not fitted by God to be much more than servants of the whites. "Nature made them subordinates," Mr. Foster, her father, always said—God rest his soul. He was an Empire Loyalist from the Carolinas and a good Tory. As a result, Miss Foster carried on his traditions. Change of any sort, if it had to be, must come at a slug's pace. Many years would have to pass before Negroes learned enough to be treated as equals. Slavery should be ended gradually over a long period of years. That would give everyone time to adjust to the new reality of a free society.

Miss Foster listened to the reverend's Sunday sermon on the innate goodness of man as provided by God, and she sighed. He was such a dreamer. Man had fallen; why did Reverend Waldrich not know this? It was in the Good Book. That was the trouble—these firebrand continental missionaries never understood this simple fact. They always wanted to rush forward, over the precipice, down, down into the black bottomless pit of eternity. She shuddered at the thought.

Perhaps they would understand the risk they ran if they had an empire to run like the British. Even they had stumbled in North America and, as a result, her whole family had to suffer. It must never be allowed to happen again. Yes, she would take it upon herself to help the reverend and Mrs. Waldrich understand this.

Strange, how they had been in Jamaica for at least two years and had not understood what was essential for the well-being of all its inhabitants. She would have to teach them it was not too late. Inviting husband and wife to tea on a regular basis would be the kindest approach, she decided. Surly, they could be made to see their way along the right path, even if they were Germans and Moravians. If only they had been of the established church, they would have understood, and she would not have to exceed what polite society required of her.

Attending the Moravian church had been a compromise for her father. With the constant cramps in his chest, the Parish Church in Montego Bay was too far for them to travel. Here were the Moravians, and with them they could worship the Lord. Besides, she got to play the organ for them.

But why had she not thought of this plan earlier? It must be their foreignness, Miss Foster decided. That explained it all.

Her left cheek twitched as the ache in her back began to press on her. She would not give in to it. Stretching or wriggling in front of the Negroes would be unseemly. That would never do. With hands folded in her lap, she endured the discomfiture, maintaining her rigid posture on the uncushioned organ stool. At last, relief came with the call for the final hymn. She could move and alleviate the hurt, and only the Lord would know. Her hands lifted dramatically, fingers extended above the keyboard like hawks' talons. They swooped down, striking and clawing at the keys as if they were defenseless quarries. Hunched over, she pressed hard, her fingers vibrating as if afflicted with palsy. The pipes shuddered and gave out a resonating moan. She sighed with relief; the pressure was off.

The sharp vibrations woke Neddy. His eyelids snapped open, and a second passed before his pupils focused and his mind comprehended where he was and what he had to do. He reached for the flute lying on the floor beside his chair and joined in. "Onward Christian Soldiers" resounded around the rafters of the little church. In his haste, he began out of cadence. Miss Foster heard the flute's misstep and turned to give him a scathing look that would have sent a younger child scurrying to hide under the nearest bed.

At last, the music ended. Neddy did not move from his chair or turn and look at Miss Foster, for he knew what was coming. "Next time, stay awake and follow the service, young man, or I will request another accompanist from the Reverend Waldrich."

"Yes, Miss Foster; sorry, Miss Foster, mam," he said, without looking at her. He knew she would complain, but she would not ask for anyone else. No, not her. She would try and get rid of him so she could be all alone at the organ, but she would not be about replacing him with another.

He never did quite understand her. Occasionally, when she thought he was unaware, he would catch her staring at him in a dreamy sort of way. Then, like a chameleon camouflaging itself with the color of its surroundings, her whole complexion would change. Always, it left him wondering if she liked or hated him. He knew she did not like his flute playing alongside her organ, but there seemed to be other things she wanted from him. He wanted to ask but knew no one trustworthy enough, so he kept his suspicions to himself.

After she stared, and he caught her at it, she would try to drown him out with the organ, and then, after the service, she would complain about his accompaniment to the parson. His friend the reverend would say, "Miss Foster, you have to be a patient teacher. The young depend on us." And that would put an end to it. She would agree and lift her nose slightly to the right, excuse herself, and be off to wherever she went.

At last the service was over. Miss Foster gathered her trim self together, sniffed at her lace handkerchief and, with small steps, moved rapidly down the center of the church, trying not to touch or be touched by any of those shuffling out of the pews. They, too, knew better than to approach her.

She disappeared through the door without a glance left or right, never mind who might be following behind. As the last of the congregation shuffled after her, it was time for Neddy to leave the church. As always happened, small knots of people would gather outside to talk about the latest events, rumors, and scandals. That was his opportunity to sneak out through the vestry and around the back to the path that would lead him into Friendship grounds. The tattlers would be there in front for a good hour, and stragglers would hang around even longer.

Retrieving the precious pots from behind the organ, Neddy started for the vestry. He hoped the reverend or Mrs. Waldrich would not be in there. Luck was with him. The little room was empty. Two big registers were open on the table with an inkwell and pen beside them. The door to the outside stood open; someone had been at work, obviously, and was not finished. They would be back shortly. He peered through the door to see if anyone was standing outside. Again, luck was with him. Voices came from around the side of the church, but the talkers were out of sight. Quickly he was through the door, across the church yard, over a couple of tombs, and onto the little path at the back that would lead him down the hill to the road, then to where the shortcut through Friendship began.

He reached the road and found it empty. Not a soul in sight. Luck had it that he was in between those who had headed home already and those still gossiping up at the church. He scrambled over the wall and walked rapidly the three hundred yards to where the shortcut began. He was on it and into the cane fields. A little further in, and he was out of sight. Only then did he feel safe.

The feeling of safety changed suddenly to panic swelling in his stomach. Stopping, he took a deep breath, hoping it would go away, but the sensation only expanded. Would he be spurned, he wondered? Would the food his mother made up be rejected? Would Watt be there as he promised? You never knew how white people were going to act. He'd had very little experience with whites and was never sure what to expect from them. No bookkeeper or overseer touched him on a daily basis. The whites he did know were always kind and helpful, but they were church people and had to be nice to all.

He reached the spot where they had agreed to meet and was relieved to see Watt hurling stones and sticks up the naseberry tree, trying to bring the fruit down. His untethered donkey was a few yards away, chewing on the canes along the edge of the field. Neddy crouched down and watched, hidden by the young cane stalks.

Unaware of Neddy's arrival, Watt turned around to pick up another stick and continue his assault on the fruit tree and spotted him.

"You came!" he yelled, throwing the stick to one side, and rushed forward at Neddy. Before the other realized what had happened, he was clasped in a bear hug that threatened to meld his body with Watt's. His arms were pinned to his side and he could hardly breathe. So close were they that he could see individual strands of reddish-blond hair and into the canal of the left ear. Neddy noted some wax in it, and an image of his mam reaming out with the twisted corner of a rag popped into his mind. Jesus! Watt was very strong.

"Rahted, man! You trying to kill mi?"

"Never, my loyal Sancho, never! Oh, I am so pleased to see you, Neddy. I was scared you would not come."

"What mek you tink I wouldn't come, Watt?" A mischievous grin spread over Neddy's face. "When me tell yu mi coming, mi coming. I always keep my word."

"You are true a gentleman, Neddy. Did you bring it?" Watt gave Neddy an intense look. His blue, blue eyes did not blink. "Did you bring food? Tell me you did before I die of hunger, and the buzzards pluck forth my sightless eyeballs from their sunken sockets."

Neddy stared back. *Dis one really nuts*, he thought again. "What if I said, Watt, I forget it?" He got no further.

"You didn't!" screeched Watt, the pitch of his voice increasing with anxiety. "Did you?" he asked. A distraught look soured his face. The sight of wide eyes, mouth hanging open expectantly, almost had Neddy feeling sorry for his inhuman teasing, as Watt would say. Before he could calm him down, Watt flung his hands over his head, "Oh, mercy! Watt is dead!" he said. "Come crows, feed upon this starved and frail body. Pick my bones clean. I am sorry there is not enough of me to feed you all." Neddy could not contain himself any longer. He curled up, falling to the ground with laughter.

"No, I am serious. You have no idea how grave my situation is," Watt said.

"Come on, then, let's go over to di naseberry tree and see what mi modder give us."

"She cooked for us?"

"What you tink, I cook it? Course she cook it."

"Wonderful! Thank God! If you had not brought food, I was going into Montego Bay. I could not stand it anymore." Watt gave Neddy a mischievous sidelong glance and pointed to the donkey. "If you had not turned up, I would have had to ride you all the way to Aunt Hannah's for a meal." For a moment, just for a moment, Neddy looked puzzled, then he smiled at Watt's attempt at humor.

They sat on the grass as Neddy carefully undid the string holding the stack of pots together and placed them side by side on the ground. Next, he took the top cover and put half the calalu and salt fish on it and handed it over to Watt. "Wait a minute!" exclaimed Neddy, as Watt grabbed the cover and was about to start eating with his hands. "I ave a spoon, you know?" Taking it from his pocket, he passed it over.

"Boy! You think of everything."

"Well, somebody got to roun ere."

Together they began to eat. Watt finished before Neddy and waited expectantly for more. Ignoring the silent appeal for a refill, Neddy continued slowly to spoon the food into his mouth and chew methodically.

"Elp yourself, but don't nyam it all off. Mi mam said she not going feed me when I get home." Neddy knew there was always food left. No one would ever go hungry in his mother's house. She was just fooling him, but it was a good test to see what would happen with the food.

"You mean she will starve you? You'll look like me? We will look awful, two bags of skin and bones walking about. That will give them a scare." Again Watt went into his merry laugh at his own *jeu d'esprit*.

"Huh! *You* starving?" Neddy said.

"Yes, I am. Look at me!"

"You don't look maaga."

"Maaga?" Watt said with a decidedly puzzled expression. "Oh, you mean meager?" He helped himself to the next pot. "The flesh you see upon me is left over from before coming to Friendship, but I assure you, my true and trusted Pancho, it is fast melting away in this hellhole." He waved expansively with the spoon at the surrounding countryside.

"Hmmm, strength ain't fading dough. When yu hug me up to you—yu nearly bruk me back!"

"Did I hurt you? Sorry. I am so glad to see you. You are the best and truest and only friend I have!" There was much truth to Watt's statement. His eyes were wide in astonishment at Neddy's not knowing that. Even back in England, Watt had no friends his own age. His father, the housekeeper, and his uncle, in that order, were the closest to him. Circumstances seemed to preclude happy relationships with boys his own age. At last, it seemed to him after their first meeting, which in Watt's imagination happened in a previous life, here was a true friend to fight dragons with—to the death.

"You only like me for the food mi get you," Neddy said, laughing.

"No, not so! How can you say that? How can I prove it?"

Neddy laughed outright at Watt's dismayed protest. But it was good to reaffirm ties with someone with whom he felt an affinity.

"Oh, I have been had again. Keep it up and one day I will ride you." But before Neddy could think of a comeback, Watt continued, "Boy! Your mother is such a good cook. She has saved my life."

"Most of di time she a good cook," Neddy said. "But you ave not eaten her carnmeal porridge, wid all the lumps in it." Closing his eyes, he shuddered at the thought.

"I wouldn't mind lumps. It would be hearty food to build up your strength, not like that rotten stuff they give you up there." Watt's finger pointed in the direction of the Great House.

"Do you know," Watt began, "what goes on there?" He stared straight into Neddy's eyes and for a moment appeared lost in the black pupils. A second passed, and then another, as his mind turned over events since his arrival at Friendship. Another world, yet it had become his. Strangeness he did not understand—excitement, attraction, and revulsion. Where to begin? He so needed to tell a friend. He was bursting with it. Innately, he knew the other would understand and perhaps explain many things that escaped his ken.

"After leaving you last Sunday, I rode back to the bookkeeper's dwelling, got there just in time, too," began Watt. "Your warning came through. I was nearly caught short, but I made it to the little house in time. The fruit did what you said it would."

"Told you." They both laughed.

"Mi just got to teach you, dat is all dere is to it," Neddy said with a decided, superior tone.

"Well, I hope so. What are friends for?" Watt said. He continued with what he wanted to say. Like an actor treading the boards, he mimicked the different players in the story. He was good. Neddy could almost see the scene developing in front of him.

"It was suppertime when I got there. Shirley was stuffing his face with the mess they had served up. He never seems to mind what he eats. Down his throat it goes. He always seems so grateful that there is anything at all. My guess is that he must have come from a very poor home where food was scarce. Is it true there has been famine here? I can't imagine people starving in an island where fruit grows on every tree, as you showed me." But he didn't give Neddy time to answer.

"Back to what I was saying. Shirley is not a bad type, really; at least, I prefer him to Duar. To tell the truth, they will never be my friends here, or in England. Both of them are awful. Come to think of it, they are just damned nasty brutes. Patrick Shirley is a strange bird. Sometimes you have to feel sorry for him and you don't know why. That is the problem with this place: very confusing. People are very kind or very hurtful; you never know what is right, what is wrong, which ones to trust, and which not to trust.

"We share a bedroom, but for the most part Shirley does not do much talking. We are about the same age. He may be a year older. From the way he was gobbling down the food last Sunday, I thought perhaps this time they had made a mistake and cooked it for us, rather than the dogs.

"'Had a good day?' he asked me.

"'Not bad, Patrick.' I answered. He usually never makes conversation at mealtimes. Coming out like this was a surprise. Perhaps he opened up because Duar was not around. 'What mess have they given us tonight?' I asked.

"'Not bad fare. Salt fish wid some ackee and yellow yam. And di same old tough crackers.' He pointed to them in the center of the table. I picked one up and knocked against the table, as I had seen sailors do on the voyage coming over. Just as I knew would happen, two fat maggots dropped out and began squirming around."

"Weevils," interrupted Neddy.

"No, maggots I tell you, maggots!"

Neddy shook his head side to side. "Maggots only live in meat kind, when it is rotten," he said. "Weevils come in bread and biscuits when dem stale."

"At Friendship, maggots come in everything! Even the overseer is a maggot. Wait till I tell you about that fat, greasy maggot."

There was no use arguing with him. He quieted down for a bit, until a resigned sigh from Neddy indicated Watt could continue.

"Fresh butter is another thing. Unheard of in this country! Unless you are rich, or have cows, or something." Watt screwed up his face in disgust, "They give us cold, rancid pork fat to use with those rotten biscuits. Just looking at it is enough to make your stomach churn as if you were at sea. You can see it moving on the plate."

Watt noticed Neddy's eyebrows flicker as if some objection was coming. Quickly, he forestalled it. "Let me continue, so you will believe how badly I am used there."

Neddy lay back on the grass, entwining his fingers together so that his hands formed a pillow behind his head. He would not interrupt again.

"I sat down, and Grace, the little maid who looks after us, brought in what was prepared. It looked awful. There was the rotten salt fish and what looked like lumps of yellow fat floating in oil."

"Yu mean ackee?" Neddy said, before he realized he had broken in again. He had not meant to. "Sorry bout dat, go on wid what you were saying."

"A huge piece of half-cooked yellow yam sat on the side of the plate. It looked awful, and my stomach did a somersault at least twice at the thought of eating it. Thank God for the fruit you had fed me earlier. Not only had it filled me up, but the aftereffect deterred me from eating any more that night. Two for one, eh!"

Not surprisingly, Watt found that amusing. As he laughed, Neddy wondered if he had a funny bone in his head rather than in his elbow like normal people.

"'You don't want yours?' Shirley asked me, pointing with his knife at the plate Grace had placed in front of me.

"'Not on your life, Shirley,' I answered.

"'Can I have it?'

"'By all means,' said I, pushing the plate toward him. You know, he isn't very big, certainly not as big as me, but, boy, he can out-eat me! Must have worms or something, the way he puts anything away in his gut. He grabbed my plate and emptied the contents into his.

"'It ain't good,' he said. 'But it is all we got. Bardolf ain't wasting money on us. He buys the cheapest food he can get from his Jew friends—all the rotten fish they can't get rid of down in Montego Bay. What he saves cheating us, into his pockets it goes. I heard Charmers tell it so to another head bookkeeper from Springmount.' Shirley chewed on for a bit, then he looked up at me. 'Said it amounted to three hundred or four hundred pounds currency a year.'

"'What does that mean?' I asked.

"'Oh, about two hundred sterling. More than we get in four years pay.' Shirley is very fast at figuring but can't read much. Sometimes I hear him attempting a book and struggling over each word aloud. Seems to be teaching himself. I could help him, but I don't think he would take kindly to the suggestion. Sometimes he is friendly and other times sour. Most of the time he is like that—just sits around or lies on his bed sulking, not saying a word. If you disturb him, he will shout at you angrily. A slave—he will hit him, and I have even seen him lay violence on a girl. She was only about twelve, fourteen at the most, skinny little girl not formed up yet. She told him Mark Antony was asking for him. All she said was, 'Marky want to know hif you like it?' Then she giggled. That's one of Bardolf's personal slaves. Shirley screamed some obscenity at her and struck her across the face. I could not believe it!

"'Shirley!' I protested, 'don't do that!'

"'Mind your own goddamn fucking business, Cope!' he screamed back at me. That was unexpected—took me right aback. Didn't expect that from him, not when we share a room and all.

"He dragged the poor sobbing girl into the bedroom and did her, before I could say or do anything. I could hear tearing cloth and her screaming. He had hooked the door with a chair, barred it, somehow, so I could not get in. Banging on it and shouting to let me in did no good; he was too far gone, in the throes of brutal rage. All-consuming, you know? There were muffled groans coming from inside and then silence. I tell you, I felt like a helpless fool, and a queasy emptiness inside. Where had all my gallantry disappeared to when a damsel was in distress? From behind me, Candy laughed.

"'Backra Massa Shirley tek im little ting. She a sweet virgin. She lucky if him breed her. Er modder will like dat.'

"'What are you saying, Candy?' I asked him.

"He looked at me with a broad, knowing smile. His very full lips parted, revealing a gap where a front tooth had been. 'Massa Watt, is better hif you don't pay mind. Hif Massa Shirley want to tek di little gal—den im tek er! She a ready. Her titty stan up. Is what happen all di time. It don't matter which one dem tek.' A good slap across his face would have cleaned the impertinent smirk off it because that is what his smile had become. Slapping him would have felt good, but hitting without great cause, such as defending the less fortunate or in defense of oneself, is wrong you know? He got away with it that time. The next time, I may give him a good one.

"Shirley came out of the room a few minutes later dragging the poor girl by the arm. You could see his clothes had been hurriedly reassembled on his body. The belt was still undone around his waist. Her flimsy had been torn off her, and she was holding it up against her naked breast. She was sobbing, and there was blood running down the inside of her legs, and her lips were swollen from being hit in the mouth. Without regard to her state, Shirley pushed her through the door.

"'Don't you dare talk to me like that again, you black bitch, or you will get it again!' he shouted, as the sobbing girl stumbled into the night.

"'What the hell do you think you are doing, Shirley? How dare you maltreat that little girl?' I said."

"'Mind your own fucking business, Watt!' he spat back, sharply turning and going back into our bedroom. The whole structure shuddered as he slammed the door behind him. I felt such a helpless fool. You should have been there, Neddy, you would have known what to do."

"Mi! You must be mad! You got to understan, Watt, white man business is white man business in dis ya country, and black man is white man business. For im own good, black man stays out of white man business—or he get worse dan what you tell bout."

Neddy had surprised himself with how wise he sounded. He wasn't sure of what he had said, but he knew it sounded good—like something his father would have said. Then he felt a flash of guilt when he thought of how his mother would have lambasted him for saying that. But Watt would probably be impressed.

Bookkeepers

Neddy's comment brought a quiet over the boys as both of them tried to assemble what had been said into everyday sense. Neddy scratched his right thigh to relieve an itch there. Grass lice crossed his mind. Hopefully, there was no nest hidden beneath him. He inspected what his thumb and forefinger captured and was relieved to discover the remnants of an ant.

Just over his toes, Neddy could see Watt sitting cross-legged in front of him. The shadow of the big floppy hat obscured his features, helping to hide whatever thoughts were going on inside his head. A pitchery chirped and was answered by another from in the trees behind. A baldpate, its white crown shining in the sunlight, flew low overhead, casting a shadow briefly across them below. Only Neddy saw it pass over as he stared at the sky through eyes half-closed against the glare, waiting to hear more.

"You know, after meeting you and all the fun last Sunday, I was dogged," Watt began again. "Just wanted my bed. That boy, Candy, wakes me up at four o'clock to get the bullocks from the paddock. It was time for me to turn in. Just as I was about to say good night, Duar came in. As usual, he looked his nasty self. All smarmy, stuck up, and full to the brim with gall. He is quite repellant with that deformed forefinger. Never trust a man with a deformed finger, Neddy. They do not hesitate to poke it into the porridge of life where it is unwanted."

The idea of lumps and stubby fingers in cornmeal porridge jumped to Neddy's mind, and he acknowledged it by waggling his foot left and right, letting Watt know he would remember the sage advice and to get on with his story.

The signal worked. Demonstrating Duar's finger action with outstretched hand and a crooked finger, Watt said, "He pointed his misshapenness in Patrick's direction and sneered, 'The Zulu wants you tonight, mi boyo. He wants his fun with his pretty little white cousin.'

"'Oh, God!' Shirley said, hoarsely. His head drooped down over his plate, and with the fork he began moving the food around on it, as a soothsayer would stir tealeaves in a cup that she had lost interest in and yet hoped to find answers there. You have seen them do that haven't you?"

Neddy's foot again acknowledged the point. He did not know what in hell a soothsayer was, but this was not the time for confessions. Satisfied with the shaking foot, Watt went on.

"Then Patrick asked, 'Who is up dere?'

"'The usual,' Duar said. 'His English friends and that damned Dutch Jew Lindorp. A jolly bunch of revelers whose gaiety will resound all through the night, and you will join in, sweet little white cousin Shirley.'" Watt again demonstrated the stubby finger pointing. "'Apart from fun tonight, the Zulu must be doing some sort of business with the Jew. Sell a slave or buy one, who knows? Whatever it is, it will be illegal. One day he will involve you in that too, little cousin, so look out!'

"'Jesus! Have pity.' I heard from Shirley, who by this time had put down his knife and pushed the food away. I swear, Shirley sobbed when he called upon the Lord. None of this, between Duar and Shirley, did I understand. Their conversation seemed coded to me. Like a secret language—the sort we make up as children. You know what I mean?" Neddy didn't, but stretched out on the ground, he corroborated the truth of it by waggling his right foot. Again Watt was satisfied, and resumed:

"To make matters worse and boil more bad blood between them, Duar began to chant:
'Batty-Shirley-Batty-Shirley-Batty-Shirley
Batty-Shirley is a boy
Batty-Shirley is a girl
Batty-Shirley is Bardolf's toy
Batty-Shirley tosses off his pearl.'

"'Shut up, Duar!' screamed Shirley. 'He uses you, too! You are his damned Sally!'

"'Not anymore. No, sah, not anymore. You and the black boys are his only meat.' Duar let out a shrieking cackle. 'Tonight he wants to dine on white batty meat, so off you go to your cousin, *dear little catamite*, as he calls you.'

"I listened to this bitter exchange, not really following what was happening. That slug, Bardolf, had sent for Shirley to come up to the Great House. Nothing strange in that. 'Why all the fuss?' I asked aloud.

"Both Duar and Shirley looked at me. It was Duar who answered, 'You'll find out soon enough. He must be saving you for something special.'

"'Something special! What do you two mean?'

"'All in good time, my pretty little English pigeon, all in good time.' Duar's mock had a sardonic ring to it. He is such a nasty fellow. I loathed him from the day we met. Like Bardolf, he could not keep his eyes off me. Always, he looks at me like a hungry boy with a sweet tooth outside a pastry shop window. But this time he did not pay much attention to me; he was after Patrick.

"'You better hurry up, Shirley. You know the Zulu does not like being kept waiting.'"

"'Which naygars are up there?'

"'Didn't notice,' Duar answered. 'You can bet, whichever nigger he brings in from the stable will be as big as a donkey. That's the sort he and Englishman like. You know that already, so why am I telling you? Just get a move on…and take this with you.' Duar pushed the plate of pork fat meant to spread on the crackers across the table toward Shirley. That was the second time I have seen Shirley propel his plate at Duar's head. Duar expected it this time and ducked quickly. It splattered all over the wall again. There are matching stains on it now. None of them have bothered cleaning off the first mess.

"For a moment, Shirley looked as if he would throw himself after the plate straight at Duar's head. My money would have been on Shirley; he is small but very strong. You should see him naked! Hard as rock, and muscles like sailors' ropes twisted together make up his arms, thighs, and calves. He ain't soft, like me."

Soft you ain't, thought Neddy, remembering the hug-up Watt had given him earlier. He had been surprised at how strong his body felt against his. Watt was not what he had been led to believe about whites, soft and easy to kill.

"They both left. Duar went out first, followed by Shirley. I went to bed. It did not take me long to fall asleep. Damn it! It seemed I had just dropped off when Candy came in to wake me up with a cup of lukewarm coffee. He does that out of a special kindness; the other two do not get that sort of special treatment. It's nice of him but a mouth full of coffee residue is awful at that unholy hour.

"As I dressed and sipped the noxious stuff, I noticed that Patrick was not back yet. His bed was empty and the covers were still rumpled, showing where he lay earlier, before I came back. Must have spent the night up at the Great House. Whatever went on must have been some show. But that is the habit in this island, or so I have been led to believe since coming to Friendship. I often wonder what it is like on other estates. Do bookkeepers get as poorly paid and looked after as it is with Bardolf the slug? Lord! I do hope Mr. Fray finds me another position on one of the other places in his charge. I am going to beg my aunt to ask him.

"I went outside with the lantern, chewing the hard crust of bread Candy had given me. I had to be careful that my teeth did not break on it, so stale was the morsel—supposed to keep me until they bring the second breakfast to me in the field. A hateful practice, which I will not put up with much longer. Two stinking half-cooked herrings in cold, congealed coconut oil with the same old plantain and stale bread to be washed down with cold coffee. That shit, Duar, put rum in his coffee. I have even seen Shirley do the same. Liquor can't be good for you at that time of the morning, can it?

"That's what they send out to us every morning. I am so sick and tired of plantain and rotten fish. How is a man supposed to survive on that, I ask you? Whatever happened to fat rashers of bacon and eggs? Roast leg of lamb with potatoes for dinner? Bet that slug gets that for his breakfast and dinner in the evening."

Watt did not wait for an answer.

"When I got outside, the mist was so thick that the feeble light from my lantern reflected back from it and showed only about a foot of the pathway in front. To make matters worse, that lout, Candy, had not trimmed the lantern's wick, and black smoke blackened the glass of the lantern, dulling it even more."

Neddy did not move. His eyes were closed; he felt comfortable after all that food and on the verge of niggeritis. But valiantly he struggled to stay awake, out of respect for Watt's story. He shifted slightly to assure the other he had an attentive audience.

"At that early hour, you have no idea how the fog swirled around and cloaked me, as if I were a corpse wearing my funeral wrapping. Only…" He paused and stared at the hills before continuing. "Instead of being in a coffin, I stumbled along the path like the ancient dead going to Hades—wispy strands of mist swirled up from the dew-laden ground and clawed at me on that path. They reached inside my shirt, wrapping around my innards like the cold fingers of the departed. I could feel the damp of the burial pit clawing at life's blood and threatening to whisk my God-given soul away to hell! Or, so it seemed that particular morning."

Neddy's right eye flicked open. He sighted Watt along his right leg, which crossed over his left as he lay on the ground. From his thigh to his foot and big toe his eye traveled. Had his leg been a musket barrel, the big toe sight was point-blank at Watt's body. Only his shoulders and head were visible.

Propped up by his hands flat on the ground, Watt had thrown his head back to face the sky like a sun worshipper. Luckily, the floppy hat covered his face completely and acted as a straw screen against the ravages of the rays as its owner continued to wax dramatic. The hat muffled his voice, giving it an unnatural sound. Watt was enjoying himself and entirely oblivious of the effect he was having on Neddy's imagination.

Even in the hot sun, Neddy shivered at the images conjured up. Watt's description fitted the Land of Look Behind, in the mountains behind Kensington. Old women told that only the dead and the desperate ventured into that land. Duppies of the murdered, rolling calves, and jujus lurked behind every tree and bush and walked alongside the Maroons who lived there. Only these fierce people were immune to those accursed specters. They warned, *mi no sen, you no come*. How did Watt know these things, he wondered? Neddy's eyes did not close again as the tale continued.

"Finally, I stumbled into the field where the dray animals are kept but it was impossible to see any of them. I felt my way slowly to Mount Joy—he is the biggest of them all. Lucky for me, really, because he is all white and the mist cloaked him perfectly."

"Yu lucky you don't buck-up a rolling calf," Neddy said.

"A what? What's that?"

Sitting up and giving his companion a searching look, Neddy asked earnestly, "You no member bout rolling calf, Watt?"

"What?"

" Watt, you no member what me tell you bout rolling calf!" Neddy's eyes bulged in astonishment and his mouth hung open, aghast that this white boy could still be alive and not bucked-up the dreadful beast of nighttime graveyards.

"Oh. That quaint native superstition," Watt said with a superior tone.

"Yu really needs looking hafter. Yu is a dead boye hif someone doesn't look out for yu," Neddy said, fixing the hat in front of him with a stern look. There was silence for half a minute or so. "Go on wid di story, Watt." But Neddy's tone had changed; there was gentleness in his request.

Cued, Watt began again: "I got the rope around Mount Joy's neck and mounted him bareback. He is so broad you don't need a saddle, and Mount Joy likes me riding him. I was damn sure not going to stumble around in that pea soup any longer."

"Where dat come from?"

"Where what come from?"

"Di pea soup?"

"Oh, that means fog."

"Fog is pea soup?"

"Yes. Sailors call it a pea souper, if it is really thick."

"Dat nice."

"Tell you what, Neddy, I will teach you the language, and you can teach me all about duppies, jujus, and rolling calves. Bargain?" Pushing his hat back on his head, Watt rubbed his hands together and then spat in the palm of his right hand. He stuck it out toward Neddy as he had seen farmers do in the markets back home to seal contracts.

Neddy ignored the proffered hand, "What dat, some kind of Hinglish superstition you just do?"

Watt let out his bubbling laugh. Neddy saw nothing funny in the situation. He watched as Watt rolled around the grass trying to control himself. Finally, his laughter subsided and he produced a huge bandana from an inner jacket pocket to mop his eyes and blow his nose.

"Neddy, I love you dearly, you are the best and funniest friend a fellow ever had." There was nothing flippant in the claim; he was sincere. Each boy looked at other for that long time waiting to see who would react first.

"Gowon wid di story, Watt." Neddy grinned and stuck out his hand for the other to shake. The reassurance pleased Watt. This was a true friend whom he could feel safe with and tell things to that he couldn't and wouldn't tell others.

On the other hand, Neddy didn't mind if Watt was maddy-maddy and knew nothing of the island's ways. *We can't all be perfect*, his Sunday school teacher took pains to tell them when a girl had a falling-down fit in the middle of church service. She rolled around on the ground between the benches and frightened the other children. They all thought the devil had taken her, as froth and bad breath came from her mouth, but she had an illness, not a possession. Watt was the same.

"Mount Joy let me get aboard. Boy! He would have made a magnificent bull if they had not doctored him. He let out a great bellow, ordering all the others to come to heel, so to speak. They all obey him. He is their leader: Where he goes, they follow along like sheep. If he were a bit faster, Mount Joy would have made a great battle charger. He knows Friendship better than me, so off we went through the murk toward the mill, with the other animals coming behind.

"The mist still swirled around but it had begun to get thinner. You could feel the warmth of the day beginning even though the sun was not yet up. Sweat had begun to form on my back and armpits.

"We got to the slave quarters, and some fool screamed as we emerged from the fog. A shadowy female ran across our path and went into one of the huts. Mount Joy stopped and snorted. Never understand why they love to scream. If they ain't cackling with laughter, they are screaming. She was sort of hugging herself and bent over."

"Hu! Told yu!"

"Told me what, Neddy?"

"Di gal see you on top of di cow tink you is a rolling calf."

"Hmm, never thought of that. I must have cut a dashingly awesome figure on old Mount Joy." The thought brought a smile to Watt's face, and for a moment it looked as if the pot of laughter was going to boil over again. Instead, he went on.

"The one good sound they make is singing. Listening to them is wonderful. Sometimes one thinks of the heavenly choirs my father said sing every day in heaven. When they are working in the fields, they have someone leading them, and they all join in. Great sound that. Sometimes, though, words can be nasty and hurtful. That is how I know they are not angels. Well, you know what I mean Neddy. You must have heard them?"

Neddy used his foot again to signal he had heard them. Once again, he had stretched out on the grass as Watt continued relating his week on Friendship.

"Chalmers was there when we came into the crushing house. At that time of the morning, he looks like a ghost. Never seen anyone as white or skinny as him. A walking corpse, if you ask me. Not enough on his bones for the vultures to pick off. Still, he ain't a bad sort."

"'Cope,' said he, 'Shirley is feeling sick today and won't be out and about. You take his place in the boiling house. You can manage that? It is not crop season yet, so there is only cleaning up to do and a small amount of boiling for distillation of rum. This will be your seasoning for the real thing to come.'

"It's not what I usually do, but this was something new and would be a nice change, or so I thought. The driver was there, so I got off Mount Joy and handed the animal over to his care. Nasty black brute of a man, with that great whip of his that he threatens everyone with. Haven't seen him use it on anyone, but I am told he loves to lay it on till the back is mincemeat. If let, he would go till they were dead. Lucky for the slaves, thirty-nine lashes are all he is allowed to give. Beastly awful! You know, that is the only privilege we have?"

"What's dat, Watt?"

"He cannot beat us white fellows. But let me tell you, sometimes he will snake out the lash in front of us, and I know he would just love to crack one of us bookkeepers with it."

He shifted his bottom around on the grass to get more comfortable, then dramatically threw his hands up as if appealing to the hills.

"I tell you, Neddy, entering the boiling house must be like entering the vestibule of Satan's dwelling. God! Ever been inside one of them? The temperature must be well more than a hundred degrees. How anyone survives that cauldron of hell is beyond me. Standing there, never mind working, pounds of good solid flesh must have melted from my bones. That's half the reason I appear so scrawny this week."

Neddy knew better than to contest the idea of Watt's thinning since they last met. He did look a bit scruffier than he had the previous Sunday. His clothes needed washing, and perhaps his body needed the same. Obviously, Watt needed someone like his mam to slap his batty. Then he would never wear soiled clothes, and he would have to bathe every day.

"Well, there I was, a stranger in the furnace room. All the workers stopped when I came in. I knew not one of them. Thought all on Friendship were in my ken by now. Not so. These stokers of hellfire were strangers to me. They must keep these firemen of sugar buckets locked away in a dungeon and let them out only for their job. Never seen them before.

"One fireman laughed at the sight of me, standing among them nonplussed. Another began to clap hands. Then all began to clap their hands in rhythm. At first I thought they were about to sing as they worked. Then the chant began. At first that seemed all right, for it sounded good, but then the words seeped into my brain.

> 'New-come backra,
> All white and fair
> Fever a tek him
> Soon dead im dead, dead ho
> Yellow shrivels him up, dead ho
> Blackwater drains im, dead ho
> Red rum lashes im, dead ho
> Pussy a clap im, dead ho
> To bed him go
> Yo ho, him die, im dead ho.'

"They began to laugh after they finished the ditty. Not nice of them at all, wishing me dead." Watt's voice dropped to just above a whisper. "After all, we really did not even know each other. What could I do? Just sat there and watched them work. Suspect many shirked off. Lazy buggers, all of them. Never seen the like. Just take your eyes off them for a second, and all work stops. Yell at them, they shrug and give you a toothy grin of innocence.

"Candy came in with that awful food I was telling you about. 'Massa Charmers say you is to eat dis ere, massa,' he said.

"'Not a damn!' I came back. 'It is bad enough having to eat that slop, but to eat it in this hot house, not one damn! Tell him that and take that muck with you back to our lodging. I will come and eat it there. You understand, Candy? Out of here!' I said, pointing to the door.

"'Yes, sa, but who going stay in di boiling ouse?' he said.

"'Tell Chalmers to come and stay here while I eat, or that fool William.'

"'Can't do dat, massa, dem will beat me.' He looked truly frightened at the prospect.

"'Can't help that. I am not eating in here. I don't care if they get rid of me. There will always be something for an intelligent chap to do. Now, tell Chalmers to get in here, Candy!'

"Chalmers turned up ten or so minutes later.

"'What do you think you are doing, Cope?' he said.

"'For one, Chalmers, not eating my breakfast in this dungeon of hell!'

"'You will do what we say you are to do,' he yelled.

"'Really. Well, not this time.'

"'We will see about that. You will have to leave Friendship when I report this insubordination to Mr. Roy.'

"'Oh!' I said. 'Then you want Mr. Fray to know all about what goes on here, do you?' That flummoxed him.

"Frankly, I had no idea what went on there, but I swear, if it was possible, he turned even more pallid at my threat. Boy! I played that card well. I watched him sway as he struggled for some statement to mollify me, to seek some way out of the dilemma.

"As we faced off, the Negroes stopped work and stared at us. I suppose they liked watching white men quarrel. Don't know whose side they were on. Probably they hoped we would kill each other. Can't say I blame them.

"'What do you mean?' Chalmers snapped at me. He had chosen to attack. But it was no time for me to go on the defensive, so I struck back.

"'You damned well know what I mean—all the thieving and filthy doings!' This time, I thought he was going to faint away like a simpering, flirty girl. I seized the opportunity and stormed out of that reeking oven and headed back to the bookkeeper's digs."

Chapter 6

Carousal

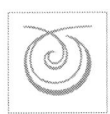

"Candy was standing by the table when I came through the door," Watt said. "He had laid the table with knife and fork and put the plate of rotten mackerel and plantain down where I was to sit. The coffee was still as cold as a witch's tit when I picked up the mug. Stale, cold coffee was not going down my throat. Not after what had transpired that morning, I can tell you. So what for Watt! If the slug, as Chalmers warned, asked Mr. Fray to remove me, so be it. Nothing in the world could be worse than this place. There would be other jobs, even teaching young ladies at Aunt Hannah's school would be better than debasement at Friendship."

Neddy lay there on the grass, listening to the passionate build-up in his friend. He wondered at the idea of Watt teaching young ladies. Nothing he had said so far about his work at Friendship seemed unusual. That was how it was for lowly bookkeepers on estates. Everybody knew they counted above slaves only because whites couldn't get lashed like the black man, but no one gave a fig for them. They came, died, were buried, and forgotten.

Seasoning, that's what Watt needed, like when they used to bring new niggers from Africa and season dem to Jamaica. Make them accustomed to working on an estate, make them know that if they gave trouble the driver would beat them. Watt was being seasoned, that was all.

But as Neddy looked at him, he could see Watt was all worked up. The set of his jaw showed he was determined to denounce the whole system that was making life miserable for him. The seasoning was not working too well. There was a long way to go if he was to adapt.

"He had not even reheated the coffee, Neddy!" declared Watt with feeling. "If I would not eat or drink that muck cold in the sugar boiling house, why would I do so now in our quarters? Losing one's temper is not gentlemanly, but after getting up at four in the morning, one is not inclined to be a gentleman. You can't blame me, now, can you?" Watt spread his arms in appeal to Neddy. "Anyone else would have struck him, and I nearly did, but my hand was restrained by our Maker. It was a struggle. I tell you, Neddy, you would have hit him—I am sure. Any sensible person should have lathered the little poop.

"'Take this,' I yelled at the shit. 'And ask whoever is out there to put it back on the fire and heat it up. Throw this away, and bring me a fresh hot cup coffee.' Candy's face changed at my orders, and he immediately became the subservient slave he is. It was the first time he had been treated harshly by me. He is quite accustomed to the like from the other two and knows how to bow and scrape to them like a Chinese coolie.

"'Yes, Massa, yes, sah, Massa, right away, Massa.' Bowing and scraping like a sick sheep, he backed out through the door with the plate and mug. He almost lost control, as some of the cold coffee slopped onto the floor when he shuffled into the door frame. I would have laughed, but I kept a stern face so he knew who was master.

"When he was gone, I flopped into a drinking chair, put my feet up on the rests that swing out from the arms, and let my head back. A little nap would do me right; refresh the body and mind, you might say.

"Just began to nod off when Candy came back. His shuffling feet let me know of his presence. I supposed he was worried at what I might do to him after the yelling. Obviously, he was about to put me in with the other two. He just stood there with his head bowed. Finally he mumbled, 'Massa Patrick, sick.'

Carousal

"'Speak up, Candy! I can't hear a word you are saying if you don't speak up.' I didn't yell this time but was firm. I would tolerate no more slackness from him." Watt jerked his thumb at his chest to emphasize his point.

"'Mi sey, Massa Patrick come back dis marning sick, sick bad, Massa Watt,' said Candy, shuffling his feet like a chicken scratching in the yard.

"'Oh?'

"'Im a lie down inside dey. Place tink up. Im jus a lie in it and don't move. Mi na wan go in dey.' He pointed at the bedroom door.

"'Why not?' I said.

"'You can go in dey, sah. No sah, mi nah go in dey! Di room tink up just like di latrine tink up. Hit smell like dead dawg han dead rat togedder.'

"'Nonsense!'

"'You can go on,' he said with some spirit, when he realized I was not going to chastise him—more than a yell or two.

"I got out of the chair to investigate his claim. The smell that came out of the room hit me like a donkey's kick. It was overpowering. Hung from floor to rafters, reversing all that was sweet to the senses. Awful! Beyond belief! The very thought of it churns the stomach. Candy was right, 'dead dawg and rat,' rotting for two days in the sun and more.

"He was lying naked on the bed! You have never seen such a mess. His clothes were strewn about, as if he had just torn them from his body. He had made filth from top and bottom. Most of it on the bed, but some had gone on the floor. Making matters worse in that confined space, the windows were closed, so the early buildup of the day's heat exacerbated the foulness of the scene." Watt's arms stretched out dramatically, then came a pause while awaiting a response from his audience. After all, it was a great performance worthy of the best mummer, and now he expected applause.

"What dat word mean?" was Neddy's only query.

"What word?" Watt scowled, disappointed he had not got a greater reaction.

"Dat excsipate?"

"A ha!" Watt's face relaxed. "It means, to make worse. I found it in a book the other day. Great word, isn't it? Now, I have got to use it." Watt grinned.

"'Oh!" Neddy exclaimed softly. Then he added with a tinge of envy in his voice, "You read books?"

"All the time. My father used to read all sorts of books to me and taught me to read when I was very young. He used to say, 'A man cannot know God unless he knows all he can about his creations. You read all you can. Then, and only then, you will understand man's thoughts about himself, about others and things beyond this universe. You read to understand life. In other words, my boy, you read for life.' That's what he drilled into me."

"Dat's funny," said Neddy.

"What's funny about that?" said Watt with some indignation. "My father was very intelligent. He wasn't funny."

"I don't mean funny like when una wan a laugh, but it sound like what Backra Galloway would a sey. Im tell mi once ow to play mi music. 'Play it for life, boye!' Im say it as hif music was beyond dis world. So im tell mi, just like how your fader tell you bout reading."

"Who is Mr. Galloway?"

"Im is de busha up at Newman Hall. Mi fader tell me he is a captain in di army."

"He sounds a sensible-nice man. An officer and a gentleman, no less." For a moment, Watt seemed lost in his own mind before he mused aloud, "Perhaps he could give me a position on his property?"

As the other pondered the possibility of working on Newman Hall estate, Neddy moved out of the sun, which had marked time by crossing the sky with Earth's rotation and shifted the shadow of the tree that had sheltered him. Watt did the same, and the boys sat side by side, supported by the trunk of the naseberry tree, their shoulders touching.

"That's another thing," Watt said, as he settled into his new position.

"Anoder ting?" Neddy glanced across at Watt.

"A job with Captain Galloway, of course! Neddy, let me tell you more of what happened, and you will understand why I need such a position with Captain Galloway, far from here."

"I came out of the room furious with them. How could they let Shirley just lie in all that muck without trying to help him? Not even a dumb animal would be treated so ill.

"'Candy!' I shouted again at the boy. 'Go for a bucket and a mop and get in there. Clean the place up. Call Grace to come and help you.' With my orders, I handed him a broom and, to my amazement, Candy refused to take it from me.

"'Mi nah go in de. It too tink up, massa,' he said defiantly.

"Anger rushed through every fiber of my body and soul. I trembled with its onset. Beside myself with rage, I swore, 'Go in there; you damned well will!'

"Before I knew it, I had hit him with the broom handle across his backside. Not hard, mind you, but severe enough to let him know his duty. The little rat screamed as if I had slaughtered him. What an actor! It was a bad performance, so I hit him again. This time, I heard the sound of the broom handle whack him right on the soft part of his buttock. Tell the truth, Neddy, you could feel the broom handle sink into his flesh as if you had done the same to a feather pillow. But—I can't explain it—the feeling was different." Watt gestured as if whipping something.

"You wanted to hit again and again. Funny that. Candy stopped screaming and began to moan and groan, more out of hurt pride than out of hurt bottom. Then came his mumbling under his breath.

"'White man all di same, treat im like a black dawg,' but he took the broom from me and went inside the room.

"Then it dawned on me: He would be more than useless on his own. I went into that foul room where he was fiddling around with the broom, avoiding Shirley's stuff on the floor. There he was sweeping the corners of the room. It must have been the first time those corners had seen a broom. I ask you! He needed a good kicking, but instead I ordered, 'Go and get Grace to help, you little fool!'

"He did not wait to be told twice that time. He was out of the room and through the door, calling on Grace to come and help him because bucky-massa would beat her too, as he had been lashed till he bled. Why do they lie so?

"Anyway, Grace arrived. She is always helpful and looks after us as well as she can with what little we are given by the slug and what we add to the pot. She went into the room and came out nearly as quickly as she went in, shaking her head in disgust and disbelief. Just after Grace left to go and get the necessary things to clean up, Chalmers came into our quarters."

"'Why are you here, Cope? Get out to work this instant, sir, or I will report you for insubordination. Fray will have to go along with your dismissal,' he threatened. 'We can't have this kind of behavior on the estates, or we will never get any work out of the niggers.'

"'Have you seen the state Shirley is in, Chalmers?' I asked, fully expecting a sensible response, as he seemed a reasonable chap.

"Instantly he came back at me, 'Mr. Chalmers to you, brat.'

"'Bollocks!' I retaliated. 'Who the hell do you think you are calling *brat*, Chalmers? You stupid fool!' The *cheek* of the man, as my uncle would have said. 'I will not be trifled with by nature's underling.'

"'I will damn well call you what I want—you impertinent young pup!' Chalmers raged. Candy and Grace were all agog listening to us go at it. Seldom do they get a chance to hear a junior bookkeeper and the senior fight, and they expected at any moment we would come to blows; that would have pleased them to no end.

"As bull fighters do, I grasped the bull by the horns. There was nothing more to lose. 'A written report will be going to Mr. Fray and another to Mr. Heath in England from me. I certainly will be reporting to Mr. Heath on my return home.' Chalmers stiffened and cringed when he heard that.

"Truth is, Neddy, I don't know the gentleman who owns the estate, but Chalmers does not know that, and when I first came to Friendship, Mr. Fray made out I was his protégé."

"What dat word mean?"

"Protégé? Means someone who is under the special care of another, Neddy. Something like that. It's French, I believe. Sounds frog, anyway, you know?" Watt kept on, "As I said before, you teach me about how to live here, and I will teach you words and reading books and things. Fair exchange, no robbery, eh?" Again out shot Watt's hand to seal the bargain as he had earlier, but this time he did not spit in the palm. Neddy gave the proffered hand a long look and, with a mischievous grin, took it to seal the pact.

"I can read and write, you know," Neddy said. "But I will learn what you can teach. Mi not fussy, and me mam will like dat. She is always pushing for me to learn more."

"Done then! You will be my protégé," Watt said.

At that, Neddy's eyebrows shot up. He followed with, "Mi did tink you were mine?"

"We are each other's protégés," Watt said. "Now let me get on with my tale of misery. Chalmers stared at me in disbelief. You could see in his face what he was thinking, you know? It was as if Friendship had nurtured a viper in its bosom that could and would bite with fatal results. A feeling of exhilaration raced through my veins—like a fresh wind through my hair. I had won, and I rubbed it in. I felt strange, though. The same as when I struck Candy with the broom handle.

"'Chalmers,' said I, cocking my eyebrow at him. 'Consider this a peasant revolt. Our wrongs will be redressed.' Believe me, Neddy, the whole building shook as he slammed the door behind him going out.

"Nothing has been said to me since that incident, so I doubt he made a report. I understand he wants Bardolf's job. My bet, he will keep very silent and hope that I tell all."

"When he had gone, I sat back in the chair. Grace went into the room and began the cleaning. She left the door open, so as to allow a cross-draught from the open windows to clear out that awful smell. You could hear Candy mumbling and complaining under his breath as she drove him to clean the floor.

"'Keep yourself quiet, boye, and get on wid di work,' Grace told him more than once, but that did not stop him grumbling."

Neddy smiled at Watt's continued attempt to speak Jamaican. It wasn't too bad. *He will learn*, Neddy thought, but said nothing, letting Watt go on with the story. Judging from his agitation, there was lots to tell.

"He is such a grumbler. Candy is just a bit older than us, but to hear him, you would think he was a crippled old man with nothing better to do than groan and moan to himself.

"Grace could not stand him any longer, doing more complaining than work. She ordered him to get more water to do the floors again and at the same time put some on the stove to heat up, so she could bathe poor old Shirley. It was as though she was sorry for him, although he treated her so badly. Well, she had to do it, but she was nicer about it that you would have thought. Women are strange.

"When he returned with the bucket, Grace told him to go into Duar's room and bring out the other mattress that was there, unused. The one Shirley was on would have to be cleaned and sunned for days. Even then, it may have been beyond use by any but a half-dead rat. The stink would probably kill it anyway." Watt laughed at his joke. "One way of getting rid of the rats, eh?

"While all the cleaning was going on, Duar, that rat of rats, came in. Chalmers must have told him what had transpired between us and that Shirley was in a bad way, for he began with, 'Ah Cope, hear sweet little Shirley took sick last night and you are looking after him.' He then let out a nasty laugh, stabbing the air in my direction with that deformed finger of his. Quite ugly." Watt shuddered to emphasize his distaste.

"'What are you doing here, Duar?' I asked, putting on my sternest face. 'Have you finished collecting the eggs and counting the rat-tails? Did you enter the count of them into the books? You know how Chalmers is a stickler for accuracy and will check up on you. You had better go and check them again,' I said, hoping against hope he would do just that—but no such luck. So, for good measure, I slapped him with, 'You know you can't read, and counting is not your strong point.' If he could be nasty, I could be just as nasty. He would get as good as he gives from now on.'

"'Oh, shut up, Cope! You will get yours soon enough,' he said. 'Let me see how sick little Shirley is.' He pushed past me and went into the room, and then I heard him laugh again."

"'Jesus! It stinks in here! Grace, that mattress is not from my quarters, is it? If it is, take it right back. He is not going to use it.' He pointed that awful stubby finger of his at Patrick, while staring at the clean mattress they had rested on my bed.

"'Yes, he is,' said I. While he was being swinish, I had moved to stand in the doorway to see what he was up to.

"'Don't listen to im,' Duar said, jerking his thumb in my direction. 'Take di mattress right out of here, before Shirley shits it up. Let him lie in his own mess. Rub his nose in it like you do a puppy, when it shits and pisses on the floor.'

"'Do no such thing, Grace,' I said. 'Mr. Shirley will be using the mattress.'

"'Who the hell do you think you are giving orders to, Cope? I am senior to you, and the goddamned wench will do as I say!' he yelled.

"'No, she won't, Duar.' I spoke calmly. No doubt about it, I was fully prepared to take him on in a fight, should it come to that. After all, I am a master in the art of pugilism." Watt cocked his head in a defiant manner.

"What dat?" Neddy said, looking for another word lesson from Watt, who responded by jumping to his feet and striking a barefisted boxer pose.

"You can fight?" Neddy looked skeptically at Watt's pose.

"Yes. Any gentleman can defend himself using his fists."

"Who taught unu fist fighting?" The unbelieving look was still there on Neddy's face when Watt confessed.

"Umm…well, no one, but I have seen boxing matches." A left fist shot out and withdrew rapidly like a piston a couple of times and was followed with a right, again and again, punching holes in thin air, as Watt demonstrated his pugilistic prowess.

"Where you see dis boxing match?"

"At country fairs; they have them regularly. My father did not approve, but my uncle loved to watch and took me along with him. He even bet on them. Don't think he won very much. Always seemed to pick the loser."

Neddy rolled his eyes to the heavens, as if searching for God hidden in that vast expanse of blue, and grunted, "Ahhaa."

The day's shadows, he noticed, had grown longer. Watt, standing in front of him, cast a shadow twice his size. Soon night would come and absorb the shadows into itself. He didn't want to walk home in the dark, and if he returned late, his mam would not be pleased. He thought about calling it a day, but watching his friend dance around the place boxing against an invisible opponent convinced him it was his duty to hear him out. That was what true friends were about.

Finally, Watt flopped down beside him again, panting from his shadow boxing.

"Duar, the cowardly dog, was not going to risk a bloody nose. Candy and Grace had stopped work to watch me take on my senior for the second time that morning. They were not sure what to make of it. You could see the worry on Grace's face. If she followed my instructions, would the others punish her for disobeying them?

"'They will obey me, or there will be hell to pay, Cope.' Duar had gone red in the face as if about to keel over in a fit. My own blood was on the rise again, but one must keep very cool when on the verge of a fight for life and honor. The time had come to outfox him. Tactics and strategy: put the enemy on the defensive. First rules of battle, you know? Attack, attack, from all sides. Attack, keep them off balance!"

It sounded sensible. Nodding his head, Neddy acknowledged his second lesson with, "Ahu."

"'Chalmers didn't tell you, Duar?' My question pulled the pig up short. That's what I wanted.

"'Tell me what?' he barked back.

"'I will be putting in a written report to Mr. Heath and Mr. Fray on what has been going on at Friendship.'

"I forced myself to be calmly superior. Stopped the swine in his tracks, so it did. Duar's mouth dropped open. His eyes widened as if about to pop out of their sockets. He shook his head in disbelief to what he had just heard.

"Watching this display, I knew my first cannonade had struck home. The attack had been righteous. The gape shot had torn his balls right out of their sac. His undercarriage was gone, shot to smithereens. Power, Neddy, was mine!" Watt raised a clenched fist and brought it down in the palm of his other hand with a smack. "For the first time that day, I knew what power was and is. No wonder people love slavery here. It is the power over another human being. It's the thrill of thrills. The shiver down the spine of all time. Wait until you taste it, my friend. It's better than a big swig of laudanum." Savoring the thought, Watt took a deep breath.

"Like Chalmers before him, William Duar made his exit in great confusion. For a second time that day the door slammed, and the house shook as if an earth tremor were passing by. Both Grace and Candy looked at me with awe and respect. They knew whose side they were on from now on. The bread had been buttered on my side at last! Talking of food, is there any left, Neddy?"

"Look in dat pot. There is a piece of corn pone, mi think. Yu can have it."

"We will share the last morsel, my friend—as I hope we share all things in the future." Watt placed his hand over his heart and looked up into the naseberry tree as if that would sanctify his gesture.

Once more, Neddy's eyes rolled heavenward and then back to Watt. He watched as the other quickly shuffled on his bottom to the pots.

Watt reached for the one pointed out by Neddy. With the spoon he carefully cut the corn pone in half, with one piece slightly bigger than the other. Graciously he offered the bigger piece to Neddy.

"No, hif you is starving, yu can ave dat piece."

"Truly?" Watt said. "But you should have it. I am the guest and you the host."

"Lard Gad, man! Ave di food and stop yu nonsense."

Watt did not wait; the god of politeness had been prayed to and satisfied; it was now time to feed the belly.

"Mmmm, it is so good!" he mumbled, and a small piece of corn pone flew out of his mouth. A second huge bite followed the first.

Neddy was far more circumspect, eating his piece of pone. He watched Watt's crammed mouth work like a cow chewing its cud before swallowing for the second time.

"Watch yu don't choke, yu know," Neddy said.

At last, the final piece had been swallowed, and Neddy settled down to listen to the rest of the story, resigned to night catching him on the way home and his mam's scolding. Watt took up his place beside him again and, as if in need of reassurance, sat closer. He hunched forward, and Neddy could feel the heat of his body and the intensity of his temper as he spoke.

"With Duar gone, I sat down again. Grace fussed in and out of the room. She came by and gave me a bowl of thick soup with yams and dumplings and took another bowl into the invalid. I wondered what had made him so sick. What had they done to him up at the Great House? Got to say, though, the soup was the best thing that they had fed me since my arrival at Friendship. Grace must have used her own produce. There was even some green stuff in it. We never seem to get that in our meals. It's a wonder scurvy isn't rampant in our barrack. If I didn't suck the occasional lime, my teeth would be dropping out by now."

Neddy choked back a giggle so as not to interrupt this time. A Watt lecture on scurvy would have to wait for another time. It was getting late. He assumed scurvy was some illness you got from not eating green stuff. He hated green stuff, apart from calalu. He had heard that sailor men sucked limes, and Jamaica sold the navy ships lime juice for the sailors to have at sea. Now he knew what the lime was for.

"After finishing the bowl of soup, I wanted more but didn't ask. Not fair to Grace. Just then she came out, mumbling to herself.

"'What's that, Grace?' I said.

"'Not di fus time mi help di poor boye, you know, Massa Watt. Di Zulu treat im bad, sah. Dem use im like man use young gal. Dem hurt im bad. Mek im bleeds. Bad place, dis, for man and gals,' she said.

"She left me, still shaking her head. Now for the first time I realized what all those snide remarks and hints from the others meant. I was caught in a nest of sodomites!"

"Mi know," confirmed Neddy. "Captain Galloway warn mi to stay away from Friendship because of di batty man. Mi forget him warning an tek di short cut an buck up yu."

"I am glad you did, Neddy." Watt sounded solemn.

"Me too."

Watt smiled at the response and continued with his tale. "I went into the room. The smell was still there, but Grace had sprinkled some grass stuff over the floor to mask it. Cuss-cuss grass?"

"Yes." Neddy nodded.

"She used witch hazel on him as well. But all that did, the cuss-cuss and witch hazel, was mix right into the stink and change the odor, adding a sickly sweetness. Only fresh air would dispel that stench. The windows and door would have to remain open, but I worried about sleeping at night. If it came to it, I would sleep in one of the chairs in the other room. Certainly wouldn't sleep in Duar's room. Shirley was sitting up in his bed and looked very pale and drawn.

"'How are you, Patrick?' I said.

"He did not answer at first, just looked at me like a sheep who wants to bleat but doesn't know how. His voice was low, and he looked down away from me. 'You despise an hate mi?' He mumbled the question, as if it was a foregone conclusion.

"'No, why should I hate you?' Didn't really like him but have to live with him, you understand, Neddy.

"'What happened, Patrick? I don't really know.' I lied to keep Shirley talking."

"'You know,' he said.

"'I do not.'

"I scowled to stress the honesty of my statement, to emphasize the truth of it, you follow, Neddy?" Watt leaned in and cocked his left eyebrow.

"Shirley then said, 'You didn't like what I did to di little gal?' He looked straight at me when he stated that, as if daring me to deny it.

"'The truth, Shirley,' I said. 'That was damn nasty of you, not what a gentleman would do."

"'Boye! Let me tell you something. There is no gentleman around here. I goin tell you what go on in dis here place.' He wore a look on his face, as if there would be vengeance in the telling.

"But before he could begin, my curiosity got the better of me. 'Before you do that, would you tell me how Bardolf is related to you, and what he has got on you?'

"Shirley looked away from me as one ashamed. In a subdued voice he came out with it: 'Him father was mi mother's cousin and was a white man. Him mother was a free quadroon so, between him parents, him free, and dem together make him a mustee, so him is counted white. But him really a red naygar,' Shirley said.

"'Interesting, but how has he got you doing what he wants, Patrick?'

"Neddy, for about two minutes Shirley said nothing. He sat in the bed and must have been wondering how much he should tell. Waiting was my game. What he had to tell would come out in his creole English when he was ready, I presumed. That takes getting used to, from a white, you know? The slaves are hard enough to follow, but people like Shirley and Duar, even if they are born here, you expect them to speak properly. After all, they have some education."

"It's all right," Neddy said. "Yu go on telling it as yu have been doing; me hear how it suppose to sound in mi head." He laughed and added, "But yu doing all right. Yu learning to talk patois."

"Oh, all right. You'll understand eh? But it's good fun to try and speak like a native then. But you'll translate if I get confused?"

Neddy nodded. "Yes."

"Oh, Great Boney! Well, now," Watt said. "While waiting for him to say something, the need for fresh air in that room became pressing. I walked over and opened the window as far as it would go. Leaning on the sill, I stuck my head through and sucked deeply at the fresh air. It revived me. Funny how you can remember smells… Awful! Finally, Shirley came out of his pondering.

"'We don't have much. Mi father died when I was young. I have another brother, Franklyn, who is older, but him gone with another cousin to bring up. Mi mother was left with me and mi sister. She tried, but it's hard in this country if you poor. It don't matter if you white or black, you got to have something, like a piece of land, or somebody to look out for you. Before mi barn, mi fader sell di little piece we have. After dat, we got notting. On mi thirteen birthday, mi mother took me to Bardolf. That time he was over in Clarendon, an he was doing good. Im agree to tek mi and school mi, and mi mother left mi wid him. It start from den.'

"Once again he paused. Then he pulled his legs up and wrapped his arms around them and rested his chin on his knees. He began to talk again, but, from the position he had taken up on the bed, his speech was subdued and muffled, and to make things worse he lapsed into broad creole. I had to lean forward and listen carefully to catch all he said. I came away from the window and moved closer to the bed and sat down on a box that we use for a chair or table.

"'First ting him do, when she leave, was take me into his bedroom and mek mi tek mi clothes off and he put mi on the bed and play aroun. Then him calls all the niggers in and let them look at mi naked. An den one come over an feel mi up. Bardolf began jumping up and down laughing an clapping im hands—urging di nigger on. Telling im what to do to mi! It mek mi feel shame, you see, Watt.' Shirley looked at me, begging for sympathy.

"'Is one ting to sex wid a white man, all right, but wid nigger man? Dats some ting else!' He spat that out, shaking his head in bewilderment. Then he mumbled. 'Truth is, mi modder sell mi to im as if I am a nigger slave.' He finished there.

"A longer silence followed. I moved back to the window to wait. Phew! The smell was getting to me. Just stood there by the open window looking through it, leaning on the cooler, and gasping in the air. A light breeze had come up and fanned my head, which gave me further relief. He wanted to get his trouble off his chest, come hell or high water, and it would come from him.

"'Last night di Zulu sent for me. You remember Duar came and called me?' I nodded and kept silent to give him the space to say what choked his craw.

"'As soon as im sey, I knew what was up. It was all the time, and lately it had gotten worse. Bardolf, him is possessed. Like if a juju magic take over im mind and body. Him have books with all sorts of sex pictures an stories. The one named De Sade im loves best. Someone bring it out from England an give him. It always on him bedside table, like hif it is bible. Reads it all the time and tries what the book say with all the little nigger boys him tek up to his room.

"'Him got other things too, carvings of man and woman, man mostly. Those him keep locked away in a cupboard and takes them out for him special guests from foreign. And I knew that was why he had called me the other night. Some of im foreign friends would be dere.

'"When mi get outside and start to walk over to di Great House, there were some of di people there about. Must ave been di second gang, just come in from weeding in di fields. One of dem look at mi an I hear him say, "Im going gets di wok tonight. Di Zulu a really hop an skip bout up a di Great House."

'"If dey knew what was going on, den…boye!' Shirley stopped and raised himself further on the bed so his back rested on the wall, where the head board should have been.

'"Loose chat-chat gets around here like fire going through a cane piece," he said. "You can't fart an dem don't know. Some of dem must have seen di Zulu's guests coming up the road and guessed what dey come for. It a regulars ting wid Bardolf. Many of the young ones must have wondered if Bardolf would send for dem.

""'Tell im mi ready tonight, Massa," one shouted from di darkness.

""'Mi will do any ting Massa want."

""'Tell di backra mi ready fi im. Mi go a bush wid im," yelled another voice.

'"When they get a chance to go up to the Great House, dem tief. Tief you blind, and that's what most of dem wan do. They don't mind what Bardolf and all of him fren do to dem. Most of dem love it. Down here, a big man tek many of di little boye on for themselves, an go a bush wid dem. Dats all right, it done in private. You like di man and di man like you—you unstan? But Bardolf, now, im want grind your face into di dirt. Dats when im get him trill!'

"Shirley continued, 'You get to those long steps leading up to the Great House front door; you look up them, you just want cry an run wey. Where me going go, sah? America? England? Mi don't know nobody there. Jamaica is all I got. In a way, mi better off than all the little bookkeeper boye dat come from foreign. They can't go back and them die ya-so. When mi die, mi die where mi barn.'

"It was a passionate speech," Watt said. "Shirley gave me a look when he said that about English boys dying out here in a foreign land. Well, Jamaica isn't really foreign. It's part of England, isn't it? Not my intention to die for a long, long time, anyway. And I don't mind where I die, so long as it has been a good life or for a worthy cause.

"Shirley wasn't done yet. 'Halfway up dem long step, I turned back. Just couldn't bring myself to go in by the front door, Watt. Mi could hear laughing and shouting and Bardolf singing some ting, so you could imagine what was going on. Di party hard started and was well going on,' he said.

"'Back down the steps and round the back of di Great House mi went. Then I noticed di storeroom's doors were open and mi wondered why. One small lantern was over in the corner, so mi walk an pick it up. Couldn't see noting out of order at first. Rats running around di sugar and rum, same way they always do, dat's all. Then mi hear a whispering and some ting moving. A tiefing flash through my mind. So, mi walk round to where Bardolf chain up di niggers him wan beat to see what was going on. It wasn't no tief. Two niggers were shackled to the wall. Both of dem naked. Mi never seen dem before.' Shirley looked directly at me then and asked, 'How long you been here Watt?' He did not wait for my answer.

"'Ever seen a slave beaten here? You never, have you? Don't you tink that is funny? Di niggers on Friendship are di worse kind of nigger! They are all bad naygar. Run wey all the time, an them tief bad, dem lazy. Lard! Them worse than lazy! Bardolf let them get away wid it most times, because he want them for some ting else than work. But when im want, di whip come out. But not down here. Bardolf have them whipped up under the house. An you know why? Some of im friend like to whip. Di Zulu save the slave for im friend to whip, come fete time.

"'Funny thing, Bardolf can't stand to see blood. Him watch till it come. One day him faint when him fren cut right to di bone wid the cow whip. Flesh just peel wey, like you peel banana skin. Not much blood at first, and di bone stand out white, like the banana inside. Waste a good slave when im drop dead. Di doctor could not save im. Im friend pay, so Mr. Fray never find out noting bout it when im look through the slave register. Bardolf tell im he was a troublemaker, so he sold im an he got a replacement from the Jew man. Mr. Fray couldn't say anything.

"'What was down in the basement, none of my business. I left the storeroom an went up the back stairs. Bardolf was doing business on di side wid di Dutchman, was my guess. Both would mek money, whatever they were up to. They do it all di time. If the magistrate catch dem, den there could be big trouble wid the law.

"'You know, Watt, when slave trade finish, dey got to get slaves from somewhere, so they get dem from Cuba and anywhere dey can. The Custos of di Parish and all the Justice of di Peace turn a blind eye. Them own big estates an need new slaves all di time fi dem place. Bardolf an the Jew mek plenty money smuggling and trading slaves from Cuba and America.

"'Through the back door, I snuck in and took a look. They were eating. Lard! When I see di food pon dat table! Watt, I wish mi never tek the food you give me. Christmas, is what? Six, five weeks off? Well boye! Mi tink Christmas hurry up an come when I sees what pon dat table!

"'Turkey, roast of lamb, ham—two huge hams, one in front of Bardolf and di other in front of Lindorp, an him a Jew an all. Pork when it come in ham don't bodder dem at all! No sah, not at all! They nyam it just like a good Christian.'

"I gathered, Neddy, from what Shirley was saying this Jew Lindorp was in the forbidden trade of humans for profit and was eating of the forbidden flesh of the pig. How absolutely astonishing!" Watt chuckled. "He must be a fallen Jew." He broke up with that and almost rolled on the grass.

"Pork is nice, an ham nicer, man! What's di matter wid yu?" Neddy said.

"Don't you know, Neddy? Jews are forbidden to eat any part of the pig or even go near one. Not like us Christians. We can eat pork, ham, bacon, whatever we want." Another piece of information Neddy salted away.

Tropical day changes to tropical night almost violently in Jamaica, and both boys were slipping from each other into the dim of twilight.

Aware of this, Watt knew time was scarce. He must hurry on with the story if he was to get it out of his system.

"Anyway, back to the story. 'Lard a mussy!' Shirley said. 'When I looked at dem, it would have mek you buss out laughing, Watt. Bardolf dressed in a flowing frock-like ting, which covered im like a tent, from his neck down to the floor and out around him. Where him gets some ting like dat—mi na know Massa! You could almost see through it.

"'Lindorp and two others were there. One come from Nova Scotia an is captain of a trading sloop. Hanker im name, and im is a regular at Friendship. Smuggling is his business. Sloops are fast and carry guns. They don't carry much cargo, if you get my meaning. So you know im picking up slaves and selling them from island to island. Wouldn't surprise me if there wasn't a little piracy in there too.

"'The other one, a Hinglishman named Sir Horatio Blair. This one was new. Mi hear him come from a town called Bath, like ours over in St. Thomas.'

"'Hardly, Shirley,' said I. 'Bath, in England, is where ladies and gentlemen take the waters. A most fashionable place, or it used to be. Why would a gentleman like that be coming here? That is a puzzle. Does he have an estate in Jamaica?' I asked.

"'Di one from Bath? No, you could see him come to Friendship for some ting else. Di way he look pon the boyes through him spectacles tell you so. The glasses not on his nose like ordinary glasses. Him hold dem out in front of him face, fastened to a silver handle, and up and down him inspect, like you look on a new horse or cow or some ting you wan buy.

"'When you get close and look pon him now, is like looking at a duppy. Blond-blond and whitey-white. Like Bardolf's shimmy ting im have on, you could almost see through his flesh. Scabby little tings on him face an hand. Mi don't want him touch mi when mi get up close an see dem. Tell you, Watt, I would not want to buck im up on a dark night. Let im walk through the front door of the Great House on a moon night and down dem long steps, and no one tief notting from Friendship. No sir, not never again.'

"Neddy, when I heard that, it just broke me up. You Jamaicans are so afraid of ghosts and goblins and things that go bump in the night, I wonder you aren't all white with fear all the time. If that were the case, then there would be no slavery. Perhaps the people should see more duppies." After that quip, the black shadow which had taken over the landscape as the sun set was assailed by his rollicking laughter. Neddy's eyes roll heavenward, this time making their appeal to the God of the night sky.

Neddy said nothing. The half-moon had appeared on the edge of the hills, and its weak light illuminated ghostly things in the field where they sat. The munching of the forgotten donkey intruded on his thoughts, sounding ominously loud as the animal teeth tore at the grass and young cane shoots. Then, for no reason known to man, it brayed. It was a short, harsh bray, like the bark of annoyance emitted by someone who wanted to be gone from that place. Perhaps Watt's mount was a signaling to its master that it was time to go. Both boys ignored the shattering sound and remained where they were under the naseberry tree. The telling had to continue.

"Patrick's description of the scene was quite startling, to say the least. 'There were black boys all around. All naked except for little skirts round dem waist, nothing underneath. You could see what dey got hang below the edge of di skirts. Dey were set up like dat to tantalize di guests. That is Bardolf's way. Boye! Im can think up some tings, you see!

"'Most of the nigger boys I had seen before. They come from all bout, not just from Friendship. You know the driver named Prince? Him tief like all di rest, an Bardolf send him back to the fields for punishment. Well, him go to other estates and look for what the Zulu like. The bigger them ting is, the better. He check out their hoods, and hif they meet the measurement, then he bring dem to Bardolf. The Zulu love it. That is how Prince get him job back as driver.

"'Mark Antony, he from Friendship. I don't like im but Bardolf love im. That Bibi was there; he was di only one not naked like the rest of the niggers. Him special, you see. There was another one from Halse Delight Pen. Him is new. To look at im nothing special, but

Bardolf seemed really partial to im. All night he molests im in front of us.

"'One small skinny one named Tuck-Tuck, whose big toe stiff up where someone broke it, so im drag im foot slightly when im walk. That mek im swished round an look like a little gal a walk. The others, mi na know where dem come from. All were there to serve the food and what the guest dem want.

"'Well, sah, you should have seen them dancing and prancing round the table. As they came up with the dishes and stand beside the Hinglishman, Sir Horatio Blair, he would put his hands up their skirts and play with what he could find there. Hanker, now, was always asking im, after he had done that, hif *the portfolio was to his liking*? Dey thought that very funny. Bardolf shrieks with laughter, and dey pour more wine and toast each other.

"'Mi watch all this going on before Mark Antony spot me standing there, fraid to go in. He go over and whisper to Bardolf.

"'"Patrick boye, come ya, come in and let me introduce you to these gentlemen and join our little gathering." Mi didn't want to go in, but mi must. Mark Antony watching all the time. I know what him want. Ever since Bardolf mek us do tings together, him wan mi.

"'"Gentlemen," calls Bardolf. "Dis is my little cousin, Master Patrick Shirley. Im is my ward. Don't let looks fool you. Small as he is, and he is not, he can match any man here, or any gal."

"'They laugh an laugh and clap, stamping their feet, bang their fists on the table, making di plate and the glass jump up and down and vibrate. One special crystal glass drop off and shatter all over the floor. You could see Bardolf wasn't pleased, but he made out like that happened all the time an he could get another. He ordered Bibi to get a replacement and set a place for me at the table between di man Blair and himself.

"'I sat down at the table, and they brought a plate for me. It was passed around and piled high with food that could have kept all us bookkeepers eating very good for a week at Christmas time. Mi don't care if mi just eat, Watt.' Shirley smiled for the first time since he had come back to the land of the living. 'I was going to nyam everything on that plate and more, if I could get it. An when the chance come,

I was going tief some to bring back here. We never see food like that in this life.'

"Listening to him talk about all those good things to eat made me feel famished—even with the smell in that room!"

Famished must be another word for hungry, Neddy thought, but he wasn't going to ask.

"There was no use interrupting Shirley, Neddy. I let him just get on with it.

"'I tell you, Cope,' he said. 'Even full, di food tasted good, you see! Every time I finish my wine, Mark Anthony fill di glass back up. When he did that, he would come up close and ask me if ever ting all right. Soon even him didn't seem so bad. They were all making a lot of noise, and no one paid me much mind. They were too busy with the dancing and prancing naygar boyes.

"'Two now, at the table, were in full swing of the revelry. They had eyed their special fancies and at every opportunity reached for them. The Zulu urged them on and squeaked with joy when their hands played with di boye's privates.

"'Sitting over by di Zulu, Lindorp di Jew. Im just a nibble at his food, touching his lips with the drink like hif im is some delicate wench. A watch an wait him dey do. Di long Jew nose a twitch as it smell profit across the table from where im sit. He was there just for money sake, like all dem Jew boye. Him eye dem never left the man from Bath. Him was the one with money, you see, Cope.

"'In the middle of all this, Bardolf stood up, clapped his hands for attention, "Gentlemens," he call out. "For our entertainments, fitting to dis moment, we have the dance of the seven veils performed by..." he clapped his hands again, and he pointed to a bedroom door. "Her, our Salome!"

"'Di door fling open, and in prance skinny Tuck-Tuck, who had gone away and come back wrapped in bandanas roun im body. All di plates and glasses shook when dey banged dere fists on di table; you should ave heard di racket when dey cheered im coming in, looking like a market gal dress up for a set.

"'Bibi follow im in with a big some ting wrapped in a sheet. He put it on di floor in di middle of di room. Next ting, Bardolf gets up, goes over, grabs di sheet and pulls it. "Behold, gentlemens! A work of art!" him screech out. Massa! Mi tell you! It a mahoe carving of a man's hood. It di hood of woods, di wood of hoods.' Shirley let out a bitter laugh at his quip. He took a deep breath before saying, 'You know how grain of di wood changing from black to white, that make it look real good? Nothing missing! Big, you see! No man ever carry dat between im legs.

"'With im brok toe, Tuck-Tuck start a shuffle dance aroun di table, where im strip one bandana off and den another. The room shake with clap hand every time one fall pon di floor. It sound like di drum beat naygars shake to when Jonkunnu come at Christmas time or dem in a Baptist church meeting. The last bandana drop an all him got on is di gold chain with di cross round him neck like di Pope. Where he tief dat from, mi na know. Tuck-Tuck is standing right over di hood ting in di middle of di room. Slowly, wiggling and wiggle right down and sit on it. You should have heard dem yell. Di Zulu got out of his chair an was clapping and screeching. Di place go mad. Dem clap! Dem cheer! Hanker got up and stamped im foot pon de ground, and him and Blair throw money at Tuck-Tuck. All di boye dem scrambled and start to fight for de coins as dey hit di ground. They knock Tuck-Tuck off im perch and push im one side, grabbing de money before im could move. It was funny to watch.

"'When di fighting over, the coins stop. The Zulu orders more drink for everyone. That's when de rum start to flow.

"'Bibi go round and fill up all di boye dem mugs with rum. One of dem come over to serve to us more wine at de table. Him swaying and giggling like a little gal as dey feel im up. Wine spilling on di guests, di table, an di floor. Not one seemed to mind. Di boye was so drunk, he could hardly stan up straight. This party was going to go on all night, mi know.'

"'Zulu turns and looks at me sitting beside him an begins, "Mi lards, ladies, and gentlemens, for your added joyful entertainments, my young cousin will show you how a white gal does it. Any ting a black gal can do, a white one can do better. Na right, Patrick?' When me hear what im calling me and preposing, mi chest fall into mi stomach, and mi feel weak an sick. It going come up all over the table, mi tink.

""'Bibi," im say. "Bring di bandana over here and give dem to Massa Shirley," Bardolf points down at me, sitting next to im.

"'No more,' says I to myself. 'No sah, no more!' Bibi brings di bandana and holds them out for me to tek. With everyone watching, what me going do? Where de bravery come from? I don't know. But the Lard guided mi mouth an give mi de words to say. "Tek de bandana, you damn nigger!" Dey come out of me in a scream. "And push dem up the Zulu fat batty!" They must have tink I gone mad an was going pop. Bibi jump back away from me as I stan up to walk out of that place; in my hand is di eating knife, pointing right at his belly."

"'Standing there, shaking with rage, I couldn't seem to move. All of dem went silent. Bardolf looked faint. Im don't know what to do. The whites looking and di blacks waiting to see what im going do and what mi going do. Some of dem must have hoped I would stick the knife into his fat belly. All went silent, like you is in a church.

""'Vell done," says Lindorp, in the funny way he speaks. "Vell done, young man. We whites should never compete with de inferior blacks. Zey are at a disadvantage with us. Sit down, sit down boy, and allow zee gentlemens to enjoy zem selves." Bardolf laughs, and so does the captain and Sir Horatio. Bibi backs right off, gone like the coward he is.

""'Perhaps I may fill de breach an offer up zome entertainment for you gentlemens," Lindorp says. Im look round the table. "There will have to be a price for the entertainment. When it is over, my goods will be damaged, and I am a poor man and cannot afford de loss." His voice whined as he said the last few words.

""'A ha!" says Sir Horatio when Lindorp made his offer. "Moses here shall lead us out of the wilderness of boredom and then return to the tents of Abraham enriched, no doubt, with our geld." They all had a good laugh at that. Even Lindorp made a half-hearted effort to be merry at his own expense. He picked up a glass and sipped some rum to show he was one of us.

"Well, gentlemens, below us Bardolf has two of my prize offerings to those who know good Octoroon and African flesh. The octoroon can substitute for white, if you so wish, without compromising a true white man." He meant nothing special by what him sey, but mi see out of mi eye corner, Bardolf flinch when he said that.

""""They are young, handsome, and, as you will see, both are endowed by our maker to be stallions among men," Lindorp said.

""""What is your proposal, man?" Hanker said, impatient.

""""I have a very good offer for both of them, but I must deliver them free of blemishes tomorrow. I can get out of the transaction by pleading they turned out to be diseased. They can be yours, and you may do with them what you will. They are not of this island, you see. Magistrates would never know if anything serious happened to them.

""""What are you saying, we can kill them?"

""""If you so wish, Captain Hanker."

"'On hearing that, Sir Horatio turned to the Captain, whiter than white. "That would be a waste of good sable flesh, if they are young and well put up as Moses here brags. Don't you agree, Hanker?" he said.

""""Agreed," says the captain. "Especially if they have enormous portfolios, and Lindorp has assured us they are well above average. That is so, isn't it, Lindorp?" Hanker leaned forward, agog to hear the answer, and seemed pleased when he was reassured.

""""You want us to buy them?"

""""Or rent them, Sir Horatio, but that will be high. Buying suits you. They are yours, and you can get some of your money back by selling them, or you can keep them. If it selling you want, I may act as your agent."

""""For a price, of course."

""""Either way, you are the winner, Sir Horatio. Good entertainment tonight and the prizes to take with you afterward."

""""What is the entertainment, then?"

""""Come, gentlemens, I will tell you on the way down," said Lindorp. I did not hear what im said, but dey were to fight, and Sir Horatio and Captain Hanker would spin a coin three times to see who would buy the winner, and who got lef with di loser. That was how it worked out when they spun a coin: Sir Horatio would buy the one who win, and di captain would buy di loser. Lindorp set di price, and he did not give dem away. Even with the shortage of slaves, dese cost plenty, but the captain and de other one didn't seem to mind.

"'On the way down to the storerooms, Bardolf slides up beside me and grabs mi arm. "You going pay, Patrick, for insulting me in front of mi guests. After all I have done for you and your modder, you insult me. You going pay, boye." He stopped and called out, "Mark Antony, you stay with Massa Shirley and see him is looked after proper. Bring him some rum, and when the time comes, see him get back to his quarters safely. You in charge of him. Treat him like you would a young white lady," Bardolf said. "You is now a black gentleman, Marky." He left us together to follow his guests down to the storeroom.

"'What to do? I know what the nigger Mark after, an Bardolf set him up. Him right there beside mi. I don't want problems, so I tek the rum him offer me. Best thing, stick with the crowd. When them all busy with the entertainment, I would slip away and come back here, I thought. But every step I take, that rass Mark is with me. No way I can shake him.

"'Down in di storeroom, all of the naygars set up against the wall to hold the lamps. Them unchain the Jew's naygars from the wall and strip them down so we could all see them. Di two of dem were about the same size and healthy looking. Well built, and you could see they would make better fancy boys than field hands. The younger-looking one was the octoroon and the other a purebred African, not much older. Him look tougher, as if im bred for a fighting man. Lindorp was right when he said dey was stallions, more like donkeys if you ask me.

""'White versus Black, entertainment par excellence!" exclaimed Sir Horatio when he saw them in the light. "How old are they, Lindorp?"

""'About eighteen, Sir Horatio," he said.

""'Good-looking pair. Yes, yes, good-looking brace. Would do well in harness as footmen. Look good when I take the waters in Bath. May take them back to England with me, if Hanker will sell me his when we done here. Hanker!" he calls out. "Bet you mine against yours. Winner takes all. What say you?"

"'Captain Hanker start to feel dem up and down, so much so dat Sir Horatio says, "All right, Hanker, that's enough feeling. Let's get on with it, man. Take my bet, will you?"

""'All right, Sir Horatio, if I can bet on the white."

""'Taking the white, are you? Good! I wanted the black one. All squared away then, as you seamen say. Bardolf, you heard. Now, hold the stakes. Metaphorically, that is."

"'Bardolf swayed from drink, giggled like a stupid fat girl, and slurred, "I would love to hold dem stakes."

"'They all found it very funny. When the laughing calm down, Lindorp spoke Spanish to them. They looked afraid when he finished what he was saying. Then he took a chain from a bag he had with him. It about six foot long with cuffs on each end. These he locked on dem left wrists. If dey stand square to each other, the chain come across dem in the middle. Both were rubbed all over with oil, making them slippery, hard to hold, you unstan?

"'We stood back and let dem at it. Dey pull each other by di chain and try to grab each odder to wrestle, but dem can't hold onto each odder. De black one get fed up and clap di white one in de mouth with im fist. That rile dem up good. Fist and foot a fly. Don't know how im do it, but de black one jump suddenly, wrap de chain around the other and kick im foot from under im. Down dem go on the ground, on his knees. Quick as lightening de black one grab him at de back of de neck and hold im face on de ground and grind it in. All de time im tighten di chain aroun di odder's body wid him left han. No way im could move, and he start to grunt in pain.

"'All of us wonder what going happen next. Not a whisper come out of we. All a lean forward a look and hold our breath. The black one get into position behind the brown boye, rub against him batty, an when im ting stan up—him mount im like a dog mount a bitch. Di one under him scream wid pain. The sound of his anguish sent Bardolf into choking ecstasy.'"

"Im say dat?" asked an astonished Neddy, who, until then, had listened in complete silence.

"Well, not really, but that's what Shirley meant."

"What im truly sey?"

"'Di Zulu choke up wid joy when im hear di pain come out of di boye.'"

"Dat better," said Neddy.

"Did I say that well, Neddy?"

"Oh, yes, my young friend," Neddy said, imitating Reverend Waldrich. "You are coming along very well indeed—yes, very well indeed."

Watt got control of himself first when their laughter moderated.

"Where did you learn to speak like that?" he asked.

"Mi Sunday school teacher. Im always sound as if a mango seed stuck in im mout."

They sat there in the dark, neither saying what they were thinking. Both knew it was time to part. Both seemed reluctant to move. As Neddy got to his feet, Watt begged him, "Stay a little longer, and let me finish what Shirley told me. It will be a whole week before I see you again. Are we going to meet next week?" Anxiety came clearly with the question. Neddy said nothing, as he resumed his previous position beside Watt, reassuring him that all was well between them.

"There isn't much more. Patrick said that he does not remember all that went on after the fight. He was very drunk by the time they went back upstairs. He did say a girl and Bibi were in Bardolf's bedroom naked. He did remember Sir Horatio commenting, 'What! We missed a pum-pum competition? Is it never ending in your establishment and in your bedroom, Bardolf? How do you keep up with it all?' Or something like that," Watt said. "Bardolf just sniggered.

"Shirley remembered waking up in all his mess, feeling great pain and bleeding, with Grace trying to clean him up and help him. He did not want to tell me, but I knew that Mark Antony had taken him back to his quarters. I am sure Patrick got the same medicine he gave that girl.

"What an awful place Friendship is, Neddy. It is frightening! You are the only one I can admit that to." They stood up, facing each other, just able to make out the others outline in the darkness. It was time to part.

"Am I going to die, Neddy?"

Watt's question shocked Neddy. He did not know what to say. His mind raced for an answer. "What kind of question is dat?" Nothing seemed to come, but Neddy heard himself saying, "Di only ting dat going kill you is old age. Don't talk foolishness. Next week we going fishing together, and I will bring food."

"You will! And we will go fishing!"

"Yes, up a Worcester River for mountain mullet an crawfish. Great River too far, but dat better. We ketch di fish and cook dem same time."

"We will do that?"

"Of course. Yu meet me early, early at John's Hall. You know where dat is?"

"Just up the road from here."

"All right, den, next Sunday morning at John's Hall. Early, you understan?"

"That will be wonderful! Oh, Great Boney! You have fishing lines?"

"Of course I got dem."

There was nothing more to say. It seemed though, they did not want to part. Both boys stood their ground, waiting for the other to move.

"Neddy." Watt's voice was subdued. "If I go to Montego Bay to live, will you visit me regularly? Will we still be friends?"

Neddy was glad darkness hid his face, for daylight would have given away his feelings. When he thought about it, Watt was his first and only friend. Worse still, he was a white boy who treated him as an equal. It wasn't supposed to be so.

"You talk foolishness, you know, Watt. Of course we going to be friends forever. Montego Bay just seven mile away, don't take long to go there." That said, they still did not move. Finally, Watt gave in.

"Better let you get home, or your mother will bring out the switch and forbid us to meet again. Can't risk that. She is a great cook. Please thank her for me and tell her I owe her my life."

"Boye! Yu sure got a sweet mout, but mi will tell her."

Watt walked over to his donkey, just visible in the gloom. After a short tussle between animal and master, Watt won and mounted his steed. Neddy watched as the indistinguishable shapes of rider and beast melded together and moved away, disappearing behind a stand of sugarcane at the corner of the field.

Neddy was frightened. The panic mounted in his belly. His eyes watering made it even harder to see in the darkness. Standing straight, he took a deep breath, shook himself to be rid of the panic feeling, and wiped his eyes with his shirttail. He had much to think about; Watt, friendship, and Daddy Sharpe occupied his thoughts.

Carefully picking up the pots, which he had wisely tied together earlier, Neddy headed along the path. Instinctively he knew its winding and followed it without worry. Had his mind not be so preoccupied, he would have known rolling calves and duppies would be no problem this night. The half-moon had risen, and millions of scattered stars flickered like peenywally fireflies seeking mates, lighting his way. Yet he noticed none of this, heading for Kensington and home.

Chapter 7

Newman Hall

Lucy hurried by without noticing Badalia on her knees, waxing and buffing the floor with the dried coconut husk. Two steps past the cleaner, her foot skated on the polished surface, making her totter, nearly pitching to the floor.

"Careful ow you urry, Miss Lucy!" came from behind her.

The warning, along with the skid, slowed her steps across the floor's sheen until she reached the window. A tumble would be painful and dangerous. If she broke a bone, there was no telling what would happen—death, maybe, or crippled for life. Doctors were better able to look after horses than humans, but they were expected to treat both equally, and they did. Estate rolls had cattle and horses accounted in the first column and slaves in the next. These were valuable property, after all.

Her breasts heaved with the tightness in her stomach. Would she miss the daily ritual at the bottom of the steps of the house? The tightness passed as she made it to the window, looked down, and saw they were still standing together on the steps, waiting for their mounts to be brought up by John and his assistant. They had not yet left on the daily rounds of the estate. Every morning she watched half hidden behind the jalousie, not quite believing what went on below. It was her morning devotion. All she cared for in the world would mount up below the front steps and set out to see that the estate worked properly and nothing was amiss in the making of sugar and rum.

"Yes, sah!" Lucy's head half turned to signal she had heard before turning back to her watch.

"Massa going teach im to be a big Bucky Massa. You never tink dat could happen, eh, Miss Lucy?"

She did not answer. There was no need to include another slave in her private thoughts. Today was a special day. No longer would her son be carried on the saddlebow in front of the master. He would have his own mount. Her child was being trained to be a Backra Massa, as Badalia had said.

This, and what Massa had done for Lucy herself, had won her adoration. Yet, he took no advantage of this. Lucy wished he would notice that now she was much more than the child he acquired five years before. But he seemed unaware of her devotion.

With each passing night of her twentieth year, she felt great and growing needs. All alone in that huge four-poster bed, in the room across the corridor from his, she waited for the night he would enter to have his way and fall asleep beside her. Imagining what it would be like with him was her dread and desire. She felt pulled in two directions. Only one man had ever touched her, and the thought, even after five years, still caused trembling and a mouth full of bile.

Nothing ever happened between her and the master. Galloway made no demands on her, as was his right of ownership. It was puzzling. It was especially bewildering in Jamaica, where it seemed everyone took advantage of those who belonged to them or were beneath them in society. She often wondered if that was how it was over there, in the world outside the island. It must be so. After all, the Lord had willed men first and women after. That was in the Good Book. Adam first, Eve second, and this Lucy believed to be the order ordained by her maker.

Massa's mule was being led by John, who looked after the riding animals, and right behind him followed young Mungo, the stable boy, struggling with the prettiest little jenny you ever did see. Reluctantly, the animal came forward with its new saddle and harness, which made a mockery of the shabby gear on the mule being led in front.

Mungo pulled at the reins and slowly won the tug-o-war with the donkey as they approached the steps of the overseer's house. Its tail swished angrily, and it tried to dig in its heels more than once. When it did, its opponent was clearly heard to threaten in that uneven, piping voice of puberty: "Unu wan I licks you! Go on, hif you wan one bitch lick! Stop dat now!" A switch in Mungo's hand cut into the donkey's neck. Warned by the stinging blow, the animal instinctively gave in and walked forward after its handler. Occasionally, a toss of the head or a pull at its leader signaled that the war between them was not over yet.

Galloway, like a commanding officer reviewing his troops, watched the march toward where he stood on the steps of the house. He smiled, bent to the child beside him holding his hand, and pointed to the donkey with his whip. Lucy could not hear what he said, but she could guess.

Effortlessly, he picked the boy up so he could get a better view of the procession. Lucy heard a squeal of delight and watched the boy clap his small hands together excitedly in the realization that the donkey was to be his.

The warm feeling of motherhood came over her as she watched the scene unfold on the steps below. Tears rushed to her eyes as pride and love came together. It wasn't always so. She wiped the tears away with the back of her hand and recalled the swelling thing inside of her; foreign and terrible it was. She remembered how it had been planted there, and she hated the recollection. Everything she tried to rid herself of the burden had been no use. It just got bigger. Her young body stretched to accommodate its bulk. The weight pulled her forward, and she would struggle to stand up straight. Time came when each morning she vomited until weakness overtook her, and she cursed the child.

Not knowing how Lucy got into her pudding state, but suspecting it was her own fault, the servants laughed at her. Their hearts held no pity for the wantonness they suspected resulted from her white skin. Backra Massa like to have very young girls like her.

When Lucy arrived at Newman Hall, the slaves knew nothing of her past or how the Massa got her. All they knew was that Massa was treating her special. If she dropped the child and lived, then surely the day would come when she would be the mistress over them. They didn't mind white, but muddy white they did not care for. They tittered and whispered behind her back. What she said and did they ignored as much as possible. Only when Massa commanded did they pay heed and dissemble.

Four months passed; Lucy could barely walk. Some of the household females began to watch her efforts with womanly sympathy. They had come to realize that she was very young and not Massa's woman. They knew her baby was overdue, and that could only result in death if it did not come out soon. Many women died in childbirth in Jamaica, especially after birthing time passed. Then, at last, came the night it wanted to be rid of her belly and to come out into the world.

As Lucy stood by the window, looking down, she heard again the screams that seemed to come from the pit of despair deep inside her. They echoed inside her skull, where only anguish existed. Again, for a moment, she felt the bottomless pain from her middle down the inside of her legs, as it seemed they would tear away from her at the hips.

She smelled again the stench of smoking whale-oil lanterns in the airless room and saw in her mind's eye flickering candles in the glass hurricane shades on the dresser. Melting tallow swelled the candle's shafts. Black smoke from their uneven wicks coated the shades' rims with soot. Fanciful shadows constantly did a pavane across the plastered walls of the room. Voices that belonged to the shadow-makers gabbled in confusion against each other, belying the stately phantom dance on the walls. None of it made sense to her. She screamed, and they cackled on, paying no mind to her misery.

"Lard, it brok! Di water spew out."

"It turn di wrong way."

"It too big to come out a she. Di hole too small for a big some ting dat."

"It can open up wider, man! Young gal can stretch."

"She will split open! Blood will come out a she!"

"Di baby na come!"

"Lard! She dead now!"

"What wi do?"

"Only obeah can save er now."
"Dat not fi she. Massa will kill we."
"Call di white doctor den."
"What im know?"

Lucy closed her eyes and shook her head, trying to rid her memory of the voices and of the fear and hatred she had felt that night. Badalia, there on the floor, had come into the room as if sent by God and taken charge. "Call Gran-Gran," she had ordered.

The grandfather clock outside in the corridor began to toll an hour that seemed never to end. Nine, ten, eleven, twelve, thirteen, fourteen, fifteen it went on, vibrating through her, punctuating each heave for air. Sweat trickled down her face and along her neck, soaking the flimsy and making it cling to her small breasts and full nipples. She shuddered. She lost control. Her body was divorced from her.

An old woman with hands gnarled like Guango tree roots reached inside of her. She screamed one last time, and the utter blackness of death seemed to come and give relief. When she regained the land of the living, it was all over. Emptiness filled her, and a mewling something lay next to her on the bed. It was pink all over and wrinkled up like an old man. *Lord!* she thought, *what an ugly ting!* And she tried to push it away.

"No, no, missy, give it di love you have," said the old woman with the black twisted hands who stood beside the bed. She picked the thing up and put it to her breast. Its small mouth leeched to the nipple.

Why would he only hug her and never take her to his bed? She so wanted to mother his children. She would joyfully suffer that pain all over again. Yet, the result of that long-ago horror, the boy down there beside him on the steps, was all he seemed to care about. Puzzle—it was a puzzle, such a great puzzle, and looking down at them standing together, she stamped her foot in frustration.

Leading the mule, John reached the step first. He brought the animal forward for the master to mount and was immediately waved off to the side. Pointing to the stable boy, the overseer ordered, "Bring the donkey up here, and hold her head, Mungo. If she bucks—" He got no further with the instructions as the donkey snapped at her young handler, nearly taking a hunk out of his arm, and a greased lightning reaction resulted—Mungo let go the reins, yelped, and jumped backward, out of harm's way.

"Rass, man! Unu see dat!" he said. "She try bite mi like dawg." His eyes rolled. "Mi nah go near er no more, she will grab mi up."

His utterance and fright brought laughter from those watching. Mungo versus the donkey. Even Lucy could not help but giggle. It seemed not to worry her that her own child was about to get aboard that snapping turtle of a donkey. The Massa was there, and her child would be safe.

John pulled the mule with him as he went over and got hold of the donkey's head and brought it back to the step, from where it had wandered after attacking the stable boy.

"Up you go, Timmy." Lucy watched as the small left foot was carefully placed in the stirrup, and a strong hand supported him from behind as he attempted to straddle the donkey. The four-year-old struggled to get his right leg over the saddle, which was built to accommodate older children. With a little more help from Galloway, he made it. Galloway strapped him into the saddle, so he could not fall off if the donkey tried any antics. With the confidence only children have, he settled into his saddle and slapped both legs against the side of the animal. Jingling the bridle, as he had seen others do, the child urged his mount forward.

The donkey paid no notice to the command. Freed from restraint, her head turned to see what the extra weight was she carried. Her neck stretched around, upper lip quivering, and her neatly trimmed tail whisked in annoyance. Instantly, Galloway grasped the halter and pulled the jenny's head back and, staring straight in its right eye, barked words in Gaelic. His incantation was not lost on those standing by. They understood nothing of the tongue, but to them it was obviously the universal language of wizards and obeah men. Fear and astonishment possessed them. Eyes popped till more white than black showed in their sockets as the donkey stopped swishing its tail, relaxed its lips, and bowed her head in submission.

Looking up, Galloway was amused to see John and Mungo stuck to the ground like statues. He realized that the old horse-handling tricks from Ireland had been taken in as supernatural. He could almost hear them thinking, *Lard Gad! Di Massa ave di powers!* He was not about to disabuse them of these newfound beliefs; the news would be spread far and wide, and that would do no harm. Let them think what they wanted, if it made life easier for him and his. Maybe they would compare him to Mrs. Palmer down in Rose Hall. But that was not a pleasant thought, and his skin ruckled, as if the cold hand of death had touched him.

From the Galloway stricture, the jenny seemed to understand whom she could bite and whom she could not bite or buck against. Not even flicking away the odd fly with her tail would be allowed when the little boy was on her back and riding alongside the mule that bore the master.

"Sit straight, Tim. Learn to sit your mount. A donkey is an animal you learn on; a horse an animal you depend on and live with. It will be far more frisky and have you off its back in two shakes if you do not sit like its master. A good seat is the sign of a gentleman. You will soon see the difference, when we are far from here and you ride your own pony, and I ride a good horse once again." He sighed wistfully.

At first, the words did not register on Lucy's consciousness, for she was more intent on watching her son ride by himself. It was after Galloway got on his mule that the meaning became clear. Instantly, her earlier anxiety returned tenfold. "O God! O God!" she cried out. "Him going leave here!"

The cleaner heard the cry of desperation from where she knelt upon the floor. Badalia could see her young mistress's hands gripping the windowsill. From ten feet away, she saw the knuckles turn white in the sunlight as the blood was forced from under the skin.

"You don't tink di Massa going leave wid out unu, Miss Lucy? Him would neber do dat! Im loves you an di pickney too much."

She knew he loved the boy—but love her? That was the first time Lucy had heard such a suggestion or even thought it possible. How could a house slave be given that impression? Especially middle-aged Badalia, who was wise and the person on whom the household depended. This time she had to speak. "What give you dat idea, Badalia?"

"Lard, missy!" Badalia said, for a moment stopping her buffing. "Even a blind man can see how im feel fi you. Um-hmm!" Her shoulders shrugged with the reassuring grunt. "All of we know im na bodder you at night time like most white man. But look pon ow im treat you, like if you is a white lady!" She paused and added almost inaudibly, "Not one of us." She had to get that little reminder in to Lucy. She may have been the mistress of the household, but only because the massa made it so. When all was said and done, he could sell her as he could sell all of them on the estate. Or, if he so chose, have them whipped for the slightest infringement of his rules.

"Di little boye, is fi him son, you know? What im do? Im have di parson man baptize him wid him name. Yes, sah, Timothy Matthew Galloway; an from den on we have to call him Massa Timothy."

Lucy remembered that day. Right here in this room of the house, where she stood watching this latest rite of passage at the foot of the steps.

Reverend D'Arcy Newcombe had come all the way from the Montego Bay Parish Church to perform the christening, just as if her son were some white planter's child.

Newcombe was a friend of Galloway's, and it was education and background that told the tale between them, rather than religious affiliation. For some reason better known to himself, Galloway thought the boy should be brought up Protestant, rather than Catholic like him. Thus the Reverend D'Arcy Newcombe, an Ulster man originally, had come to Newman Hall and performed the induction. In Jamaica it would be better for the child's future to belong to the established church. He had one strike against him already, why give him another? A greater acceptance would be extended to him as he grew up a Church of England man.

Lucy knew none of this at the time but came to understand as she grew up alongside her son in that household. At the time of the baptism, she had refused to attend the ceremony. Her master had not insisted. Leaving the door slightly ajar, she hid in her room but could watch and listen to what was going on, hidden from them in the drawing room.

Before handing him over for the blessing and the naming, Galloway held the baby high above his head and loudly declared,

"Timothy for mi father, Matthew for me, and Galloway for all of us."

"And how do I register him?" asked Reverend D'Arcy Newcombe.

"With those names, of course, D'Arcy."

"No, that's not what I mean."

"What do you mean then?" Galloway said.

Newcombe took a deep breath and looked at the ceiling of the room as if asking someone beyond it for help. "White, colored, free, or slave?"

Galloway shook his head side to side in disbelief. He did not bother to look at the ceiling for guidance. "I would have thought that is obvious, Parson. Can you imagine a son of mine being anything else but white and free?"

"But he is not your son!"

"Come on, D'Arcy! If the Caesars can adopt Jews, Arabs, and Negroes as their sons and heirs, why can I not do the same?"

"Because you are not Caesar."

"What makes a Caesar? Power. Did Caesar have more power than I have on this estate?"

"No, I suppose not." He paused and, stone-faced, looked straight at Galloway, "And the mother's registration?"

"Enter it in the records as Lucy Galloway."

"But that is not her baptismal name, is it?" Newcombe's question was emphatic.

"Perhaps not, but God won't mind. It is for a good cause, D'Arcy," Galloway answered with a whimsical smile.

Reverend Newcombe did not argue. He knew when to call a halt to his polemics. His friend was being charitable—and, under the circumstances, right. No one but himself, Galloway, and the Almighty would ever know that the truth had been stretched slightly to make a human's life more palatable on this earth.

Lucy understood little of the back-and-forth between the men. What she did understand was that her baby was being given a name and, above all, being registered as a free white. She couldn't believe her ears. If the baby was being made white, what was she then? Since that day nearly five years ago, that question had yet to be resolved.

After the ceremony, Galloway said nothing to her. He continued to treat her like a girl, which she was, even though the mother to the child he had taken for his. And the boy grew to understand: She nursed him, and Galloway played with him and spoiled him, and all the servants called him Massa Tim and obeyed his every wish. They even saved the mother crabs, with eggs, for him in the pepper pot soup. "Only the best for Massa Timmy," they would as one declare.

The slaves seemed delighted at the idea that a boy with their blood had become little Massa. They did not understand how, but if Mass Timoty wanted to kick dem like dawg, den im could kick dem like you kick dawg.

However, he was never allowed to do this. If he treated one of them badly, and Busha saw or heard, Timothy would get a good slap upon his rump. If he was very bad, a lecture as well as the slap was laid on. Banishment to his room to a supper of bread and water and bed had been a sentence once, to the astonishment of the household. Harsh treatment, they thought, for his spitting on passing slaves walking beneath his nursery window. And what the master didn't know was that two of them snuck some sweeties to him. "Im couldn't treat dem little boye like dat—no, sah!"

As she thought about these matters, Lucy realized her turn to be the center of his attention must come. She hoped it would be soon and caught herself just in time from uttering her thoughts aloud again.

Badalia raised herself on her knees and reached with both hands to the small of her back, arching backward for relief. She looked at the woman standing by the window, still gripping the sill, and she took pity on her fellow slave. "Miss Lucy, im don't own Newman Hall, but di Captain is a true Backra Massa. Yes sir, a Backra Massa. Don't worry; im love unu. Hif him go away, you gone wid him."

Lucy did not turn or say anything to the cleaner.

In its morning ascent, the sun's light scored the pattern of the open jalousie like iron bars across her breasts, as she stood watching the scene unfold below. The only sound in the room was the coconut brush's hard scrub against the floorboards, as Lucy's thoughts turned back to the night Galloway got her.

She had been sent for and brought to the tavern where her master was, not knowing the purpose for which she had been dragged from her bed at that hour of night. A big man, slightly the worse for drink, came out and asked, "Are you Lucy, who belongs to Doctor Waite?" She nodded.

"I did not hear your answer, girl." Annoyance came through in his voice.

All she could manage was a hoarse, "Yes, sah," and a sob.

"How old are you?"

"Fifteen, sah," she managed between sobs.

He looked down to her bare feet and up again, as if inspecting a horse or a cow. But he did not run his hands along her legs and body as other would have. Instead, unblinking, ice-blue eyes seemed to tear every stitch of clothing away and leave her naked. Hot as the night was, she shivered, whether from fright or the frigid look, she did not know. Her life was about to change. Familiar people, places, and cruelty would be no more; and she would have to get used to new people, places, and cruelty. At that moment, more than ever, she wished for that dim memory of her mother to take shape and wrap comfortable, safe arms around her.

His hand reached out for hers, and they walked over to where his mule stood waiting. Mounting first, he leaned over and picked her up as if she were a baby and placed her astraddle in front of him. He paid no attention to her terrified whimpering. Images of becoming a field nigger or, worse, life in a brothel flashed through her young mind. She didn't know then that Galloway had won her at cards and was not pleased at having to take a female slave instead of hard currency. Had he known Waite was putting up kind instead of cash, he would never have played the hand. What the hell was he going to do with a young female slave?

Strong arms went around her waist, steadying both of them as the mule moved uneasily with the extra weight. Her protruding belly got in the way. For a moment he hesitated, then his hand cupped against her front as he gently felt her abdomen.

"God almighty! You are with child, child!" he exclaimed angrily, taken aback by the discovery. "That's something else the bastard did not tell me—you are blown-up with child!" His hand felt her belly again to make sure his diagnosis was right.

"How long? Four months, six months?" Tears streamed down her cheeks, and she could not stop the sobbing. Having a strange man feel her and find the secret she had kept to herself was like the end of the world. Hysteria took over, and she lost all control.

She had wished to get rid of the horror inside of her—every night praying to God to take it away. No matter what she tried, it stayed there and grew and grew. She did not know who to turn to in Montego Bay for help. She was all alone. All she could do was adjust her Osnaburg smocks so as to hide her swelling belly. When the time came, and it came out, she had resolved to kill it. Standing beside the window, Lucy remembered it all, and tears quietly flowed down her cheeks.

"God almighty!" Galloway had said. "Get down! We not going have you bounce up and down and lose the child." Gently, this time, he handed her to the ground from the saddlebow. When she was safely down, Galloway dismounted and marched into the bar where he had been drinking and playing cards. Raised voices and harsh exclamations came through the open windows of the establishment into the hot night. One of the voices, slurring its curses, unmistakably was her last owner, Doctor Waite. A few minutes later, the doctor came out of the bar, swaying from drink. He looked at her huddled against Galloway's mule, sobbing.

"Bitch! You didn't tell me you are bred up. You think I would have let him win you from me if I had known? Is it mine, or some nigger you have taken up with? No, no, you little whore…" His voice dropped, then rose again as if in surprise. "You have been selling yourself to white sailors!" He moved menacingly toward her.

Newman Hall

"I should tear off your other ear to even you up. That would teach you—you little gripe!"

His shouting made her sob harder, and she fell on her knees by the mule, hanging onto a strap that dangled from the saddle. The animal moved away nervously, dragging her along. Waite moved forward again as if to hit her but thought better of it, as Galloway came back out to see what was going on.

"Never trust a mustee, Galloway!" Waite said. "The blackness under the white skin will cheat you every time." And he staggered away into the darkness of Water Lane.

In her near-hysterical state, Lucy didn't notice Galloway's return. He came over and pried her hands from the strap and helped her up. Putting his arms around her, he placed her head against his chest. She could smell the rum on his breath and feel the warmth of his body against hers. His voice lost its harshness, and she could hear him trying to sooth and quiet her. His voice rumbled through the chest wall. Gradually her sobbing lessened and finally subsided and, for the first time, she felt comfortably safe.

As he tried to move away from her, she desperately held on as if eternity depended on her efforts. Galloway relaxed and allowed her hopelessness to play itself down. Slowly the blood came back to where her fingers had dug into his flesh under the jacket. They stood, unmoving, together in that yard, with only the tropical stars as witnesses, until a donkey cart with a driver arrived.

Later she learned that he had hired them from the innkeeper to take her all the way back to Newman Hall, in consideration of her belly. She would never have made it walking behind his mule. Surely, if the weight of the pudding inside her had not dragged her to the ground that night, then a rolling calf would have taken her to the grave. Not even Massa could have saved her from that, no matter how brave he was.

It seemed to her a long trip through the darkness, with the moon showing the way to the estate. They finally arrived in the overseer's house just before dawn. Streaks of the first light outlined the earth's rim as the cart pulled up by the front steps. She was lifted out of the cart and put in the spare bedroom. From that moment, it became her room.

Until the baby came, she was given no duties, but she was told by Galloway to observe what went on in the household. After the birth of the child, Lucy would have to assume certain duties. For the three months remaining of her pregnancy, she tried to keep to herself and learn what went on at Newman Hall.

To the servants, it was obvious from the beginning that she eventually would be trained to take over the management of the overseer's place. Many resented the idea, viewing it as an approaching doom. Since Galloway had come as overseer, no one had been put in charge; it was unusual. All overseers had their housekeeper to run the servants in the day and received the master's desires at night. This was it, then; the girl had come. There would be change, they knew. She was a mustee and would bed with the master, taking the place of a white wife, establishing her and their status in household.

At first Lucy knew nothing of this plan. She was left on her own and looked over by Badalia, and in this, she was lucky. Badalia took a liking to her as only an older woman who had gone through the trial of motherhood could. Softly and cleverly, Badalia began her training. As a first step, the rank of mistress was conferred: She became Miss Lucy. And Badalia was established as her special maid. Other household slaves followed the precedent set. For once there was no bickering, and petty jealousies were put aside as they fell into place. Lucy became their charge and pupil. Each passed on to her their individual tricks of the trade. Some even took her into their confidence, and she learned all the scandals that circulated in and around the slave quarters on Newman Hall and other estates.

Almost unbeknownst to her, the establishment began to change, becoming less and less a bachelor's quarters. A child grew to womanhood, and her child enjoyed a father and mother's care. Meals were served hot and on time and with variety. Galloway's table became a favorite with visiting overseers. Yet, Lucy never dined with the master. A tray was brought to her room, where she would eat in isolation. It was her wish to do so at first and became the set pattern. Galloway never challenged her wishes. As time went by at Newman Hall, she watched her new owner come and go about his business and adopt her child as his. Gradually she came to regret her early need to be on her own.

They were mounted and rode away from the steps. Galloway, on his mule, led the jenny, with Tim astride her. His small hands clutched the saddlebow as he had been instructed. Now and then, Galloway turned to see how the youngster was faring as they slowly made their way toward the sugar works.

Mungo ambled behind his young master at a safe distance. Watching his lackadaisical gait and bearing, Lucy understood why Badalia had no time for the boy. She wondered what he would be like when Tim was old enough to ride a horse; Mungo would have to follow behind him as now. Like all gentlemen, Tim would have the slave run behind his horse wherever he rode. At a trot or a gallop, Mungo would grab onto the horse's tail and run to keep up. Lucy laughed at the idea of Mungo holding on to the tail of a donkey and running along for dear life. She knew the jenny would land him a swift kick at the indignity of having her tail used as a towrope. The mental image made her laugh loudly.

"What sweet you so, Miss Lucy?" asked Badalia, who had just finished on the floor and stood up to stretch, relieving the pain in her back.

"Nothing, Badalia, it's just Mungo."

"Lard! What *wotliss* boye dat. John should a get anodder boye who is a real elp."

Lucy had heard it all before, but Badalia loved to voice her disdain for those who did not measure up to her standards. She knew everything that went on at Newman Hall, and she knew everyone and had them pigeonholed. There were the very good people, the good, the not so good, and then the *wotliss* naygars. Young as he was, Mungo fell into the last group, in Badalia's mental nook.

Had Badalia had her way, Mungo would have been sold for a bushel of corn to feed the pigs, and she would have had the better of the deal. She hated lazy people. That was why she did the floors. Normally it was work for the young household servants being broken in, but Badalia said they were no good and did the drawing room and gallery herself. The young ones could do the floors that visitors did not see. Badalia loved to see her floors—as she thought of them—shine and smell fresh with the citrus she used to clean them.

At least, that was what Badalia said. But Lucy noticed that as Badalia buffed and polished with her cocoanut bristles, she mumbled and chatted to herself. Sometimes it seemed to be a quarrel and sometimes a conversation. She never really heard the words clearly, or understood what it was all about, but Lucy came to realize it was Badalia's way of coping with the burdens of her life. Lucy never inquired as to what these were. When Badalia gradually let her in on a few of her tribulations, Lucy realized that this signaled Badalia's approval and acceptance of her.

The small cavalcade turned the corner and out of sight. John she could still see, walking back to the stables to do his work, and Lucy thought it was time for her to do the same. There was marmalade and guava jelly to make today. She didn't like making it. Always hot work, standing over the stove, stirring the hot, bubbling mixture until it reached the right consistency. Her great fear was failure: it would burn or, worse, not set. Many times this had happened when the cook had taught her how to make the jams, and now every time she worried that it would happen again, although lately she had become quite the expert. Still, it was hot, miserable work. But the knowledge that it was for him and no one else made it worthwhile.

As she left the window to go about household business, Galloway's words about leaving Newman Hall pushed the problems of marmalade making from the forefront of her mind. In the pit of her stomach, she could feel that ball of apprehension beginning to form. Without thinking, she retied the flap strings of her little white crochet cap firmly under her chin. With her ears safely covered, she tossed her head from side to side and shook loose a river of soft, lustrous chestnut hair that flowed from under the cap, down her back, to stop just above the checkered apron waistband. She adjusted that, too, pulling it in further around an already small waist.

Her image in the mirror, standing alongside the grandfather clock in the hallway, made her pause. The round face with its small, soft mouth and big brown eyes looked back at her questioningly. Badalia, still standing behind in the drawing room, watched her and, as always, knew what she was thinking.

"Don't worry, Miss Lucy," Badalia reassured. "Anywhere but ere, not one going hask. Im tek you a foreign an you blen into white folk like one of dem."

Lucy's head dropped in embarrassment that anyone should be able to read her mind so easily. Her hands dug deep into the apron pockets as she hurried away to the kitchen. Yet, it was a comfort to know her secret was safe with Badalia. What would she have done without that woman, a second mother to a stranger in a strange place?

Galloway, Timothy, and Mungo moved toward the works. On arrival in the yard, Galloway lifted Tim off the donkey at the cut-stone archway to the boiler house. "This, Tim mi boy, is the gateway to hell," Galloway said, grinning. "You don't understand now, but one day you will appreciate the analogy." Like a faithful parishioner, the little boy looked up into Galloway's face, assured that whatever the God standing above him said must be true, even if he did not understand.

"Mungo, hold the animals and keep a close watch on Master Tim. I will soon be out," Galloway said, emphasizing his command with a flick of the riding switch to his boot. The gesture was not lost on the stable lad, who rushed forward to do what was ordered. Getting hold of the mule, he cautiously reached for the donkey. The jenny's ears laid back, her lips curled like a mischievous child's nasty, contemplative grin, and her neck began to stretch forward signaling an imminent attack on the outstretched arm.

"Im going bite me again, Busha!" wailed Mungo, jumping back out of harm's way while still holding on to the mule, who responded peevishly to the sudden tug at its bit.

"Don't be a fool, Mungo!" Galloway said. "If you show fright, the animal will know it and take advantage of your weakness. Grab the halter firmly, boy, and hold her. She is only playing with you. Go on, do as I say."

Nervously, Mungo reached for the halter again, trying to obey the order and stay safe. The jenny tossed her head upwards but did nothing more. Standing rigidly between them, Mungo held the mule's bridle with his left hand and the donkey's with his right. From his rigid posture, he was obviously expecting trouble and was ready to let go and run should either beast, especially the donkey, make a move that threatened his flesh.

"You should grow a third hand, so you could hold onto Master Tim as well. You are no good to me with only two hands, Mungo! I think I will have to sell you," Galloway said, his eyebrows coming gravely together, as if he were seriously considering the action.

"Lard Gad, Busha!" wailed Mungo. If he could have gone white, he would have; instead, his lower lip quivered as if he were a young girl about to burst into tears. He tried desperately to look contrite. Young as he was, Mungo was no fool. A life of ease and without injury was his first priority. One of the very few estates where he could indulge this fantasy, and perhaps make it come true, was Newman Hall. Gone from here would be a sentence of death; a life in the cane fields was all he could expect. The easy life of stable boy would be very hard to come by again.

"Massa, you wouldn't do dat to old Mungo!"

"Old Mungo! How suddenly you have aged. When did this happen?" Galloway said. The light of humor flickered in his eyes but was missed by the stable lad.

"Lard Gad, Massa!" Mungo let go both animals and threw his hands up in desperation, "What would appen to mi ol modder. She depend on mi for every ting, Massa!"

"Don't let go of the animals, fool!" Galloway said.

Mungo grabbed for the dangling bridles, agitating the already restive animals further. Minutes passed before they got them to settle down again.

This time, with the cold dampness of an Irish winter morning clouding his eyes, his overseer monotonically pointed out, "If your mother depended on you, Mungo, Newman Hall would be poorer by one. The old lady would be dead by now. Dead of starvation, most likely. On a second thought, Mungo, you hold the animals. I will take Master Tim with me. Come, mi boy, we will leave Mungo on guard while we inspect the boiler house of hell."

There wasn't much going on when they entered the boiler house. One slave stoked the fire under its boiler, while the other five boilers in the row were all dead cold. At times gushes of steam and smoke came up from around the active cauldron, obscuring its caretaker. He would be there and not there, then there again in the swirl.

Pointing to the scene, Galloway squeezed Tim's hand, saying, "You see, Tim, that must be like hell. Forever, the uncertainty of being." He gave a slight shudder at the thought, not missed by the small hand in his.

A young bookeeper came over to where Galloway and the child stood. All the signs of debauchery marred his youth. His eyes, red rimmed and glassed over as if with cataracts, were sunken in a blotchy face. Strands of unwashed, tawny hair stuck to his forehead, giving him the appearance of a damp, dirty rag doll.

"Morning, sir," the lad said bravely.

"Ah! McAfee. All functioning well, I hope? I want to see the repairs on the gutters. They have been done? He looked at the lad for the confirmation to his question.

"Yes, sir. I supervised the repairs myself."

Galloway stared at him full on. "You look terrible, lad; are you recovered?"

"Yes, sir!" McAfee showed a brave smile.

"You have recovered from Yellow Jack—have you?" More than a tinge of sarcasms came with the observation. "I suppose you celebrated your recovery last evening with them others?" Galloway's eyebrows lifted with his question.

McAfee looked down at the floor and shuffled his feet uneasily. "We went down to the Bay, sir."

"A-drinking and a-wenching, eh? How old are you, McAfee?"

"Nineteen, sir."

"Old enough to drink and wench, then?" Galloway's eyebrows rose again; he knew the boy to be lying. He was sixteen at the most and had only just come to Jamaica and Newman Hall from Sterling. Like a truant schoolboy facing the headmaster, McAfee shuffled his feet and dropped his chin to his chest. He was a good boy and worth keeping. Galloway had discovered he could read and write and do sums correctly, which was beyond most bookkeepers.

Britain's waste. White slaves sent out to the sugar colonies to fill positions demanded by arcane laws and greed. When they died, the gaps they left were refilled by more of the same. Humanity flushed away. Years of army service and his time in Jamaica had taught Galloway to understand it, but in his heart of hearts he refused to accept it as the inevitable.

As he took a deep breath, the heavy sugar smell that permeated the building almost blocked Galloway's nostrils. He surveyed McAfee from the top of his submissively bowed head down to his dirty boots, noticing the left boot was split at its side. One day he would write an epic poem about it all. Galloway smirked at the thought.

"Keep it up, boy, and they will have you in your grave before you reach twenty." Galloway did not give McAfee a chance to plead his case. "Supervised them yourself, you say? And all is well?"

"Yes, sir!" McAfee said, relieved the overseer had changed the subject from his drinking.

"It had better be so, or come harvest time and anything goes wrong, I will hold you personally responsible. We don't have much to do now, but in another six weeks, as you know..." Galloway wagged his index finger at McAfee to emphasize his point. "We really begin in earnest. I want every clarifier, boiler, and gutter in perfect condition come crop time January, February."

Picking Tim up, he walked over to the gutters that carried the hot cane juice from the clarifiers into the copper boilers. Putting the child down on the ground, he began to inspect the new gutter corking closely. His eyes searched for sloppy workmanship. Shortcuts and half-finished work were built into the slave system, and Galloway suspected it would be no different with the work done on the gutters.

From what he could tell, they seemed to have done a good job this time. But he wanted to see them working for himself. If they leaked badly, like last crop season, much of the cane juice would be lost on the ground, running from clarifier to boiler to the cooling tanks, reducing production. Galloway did not like his work, but he was still going to do the best job he could. After all, that was what he was paid for. A man's pride was at stake.

He pointed to the boiler room slaves. "Get some of them who are just shuffling their feet pretending to work to bring buckets of water and pour it down these gutters. I want to see if there are any leaks. Last year, I swear, half the juice sweetened the ground."

McAfee began yelling orders, and activity erupted in the boiler house.

"You, Billy and Moloch over there," he pointed at a fat, piglike man skulking behind a cauldron he had pretended to clean. "You heard the busha. Get four buckets of water and bring them at once."

Yes, sah, Massa, and *Coming, young Massa,* and *Right, Massa* followed by the inevitable screech of laughter impressed McAfee that some action was being taken. It wasn't the speediest action. Those he had called upon had verbalized subservience, and so, to them, that justified their near torpid movement. Eventually buckets with water slopping from them arrived.

"Pour what is left in there," Galloway said. He was not to be toyed with, the slaves knew, and they rushed to follow his instruction. In their haste, half of what was left in their buckets splashed on the ground before it got into the gutters. Galloway watched for the telltale drips that would signal cracks that would open wider with the constant flow of hot cane juice. He stood there, holding Tim's hand, saying nothing.

"Better than last year, but still poor," he said. He calculated how much the wastage would eventually cost the estate. There must be a better way of doing this. Wooden gutters were unsealable. Bad design and even worse workmanship.

"All right. Put them back on what you had them doing," Galloway said. New corrugated tin would be the answer. He had read about it. If they did not want to use it on its own, they could use it to line the old wooden gutters. It might not be perfect, but it would make a vast improvement on the present system.

Convincing the attorney to inveigle those far-off people who owned the estate into funding the new gutters was another matter. Never willing to invest in new technology, they preferred to milk the estate without a thought to refurbishment. It could only end in bankruptcy, and some Jewish merchant holding the notes on the estate would take over. What did they care? What a waste! So still was he in contemplation that Tim tugged at his hand to make sure that he would move again. Galloway smiled and ruffled the boy's hair by twirling its natural curl around with his index fingers. "That tickles!" the child said with delight.

"Come, Tim, time for us to continue inspecting." They walked across the cobblestone floor of the boiler house hand in hand, the child's short legs hurrying to keep pace with Galloway's strides. At the door the overseer paused and turned to the young bookkeeper watching their departure.

"McAfee, go over those gutters again and have them resealed; they leak like sieves. And, boy, ask Dr. Robertson when he comes for some cinchona bark. Follow his instructions on how to use it. You have got over Yellow Jack; the quinine will save you from Blackwater."

"Yes, sir."

"If I see him on his rounds, I will ask him for some for you."

"Thank you, sir."

"And, McAfee," Galloway said, turning back to the bookkeeper. "Do not mix it with rum or gin. You are not old enough for such foolishness, boy. Do you understand?"

"Yes, Mr. Galloway, sir," McAfee said.

Out into the fresh air again, they found Mungo where they had left him, frozen between the mule and the donkey. A little dampness left in the morning breeze refreshed them after the sticky heat of the boiler room. It soon passed as the heat of the rising sun burned it away.

"Tie up those animals over there, Mungo." Galloway pointed to a hitching post by the trash house. "When you have done that, Mungo, run to Miss Lucy and ask her to send a hat for Master Tim here; we forgot one this morning. Hurry up, now."

"Yes, sah, Massa, right away, Massa," Mungo said, his face split with a wide grin that displayed a mouthful of cane trash he had chewed the juice out of while awaiting their return. The mule followed his tug on its halter, but the jenny resisted, tossing her head back.

"Go wey, you wan bite me again?" Cane trash flew from Mungo's mouth as he defied the jenny, this time adding a little slap on her nose. Following Galloway's example earlier, he gave her an earnest look in the eye. Instead of capitulation, her ears flicked back for a second, drawing from Mungo another sharp flip on the nose with the back of his hand. Suffering the hurt and indignity, she surrendered this round to Mungo and followed along with the mule to be tied up.

Both Galloway and Tim watched the performance with some amusement. "We will be in the hospital when you get back, Mungo. Come there with the hat." Galloway indicated an imposing cut-stone building with many windows running along its facade. To the casual observer, the architect must have been a man of taste and imagination. Added to the elegance of the windows were fan-shaped cut-stone steps at the entrance, which looked like a cascading waterfall dropping from one level to the next. Situated differently on the estate, the building would have made a fine Great House. By far, it was grander than Newman Hall Great House and many a Great House on adjoining estates. "It is the grim irony of the slave and sugar business that hospitals should outshine the principal residence on the property," Galloway had noted in his journal. Weighed together, he realized they were just being practical. Few absentee owners ever came to the island to take up residence, but the hospitals safeguarded their investments, keeping them as healthy as possible. Doctors were not few and far between in the island, either. They were far more numerous on a population headcount than in England, even. Mostly it was a good living for doctors in the colonies, especially if they lacked the connections or money to get started at home.

"Let us go and inspect the lame and the lazy, Timothy." Galloway led the way, and again the youngster's short legs hurried to keep pace with the overseer. At the hospital entrance, Galloway picked up the boy and carried him inside.

Half the beds in the ward were occupied. Some bodies stretched out on the beds were groaning and moaning with real or imagined illness, and these utterances became louder when they realized the overseer was about. Others sat on the beds, obviously not ill. They were laughing and chatting—until tipped off by the rising cadence of pain and suffering. Magically, hands went to foreheads to wipe away the beads of fever, coughing began, and spit drooled from mouths. Those truly ill had family members sitting at their bedsides, tending to their needs. These did not even notice that their Busha was on morning inspection. To these bedsides, Galloway led Tim first.

From bed to bed, he and Tim heard it all. Galloway said nothing to the malingerers but noted who they were. Most of them did not surprise him. They worked harder at dodging work than actually doing work. At the bedside of one emaciated creature, he asked, "Quality, has Doctor Robertson been here today yet?"

"No, Busha," came the weak reply from the man, sweating in the bed from malaria.

"How do you feel?"

"It bad, Busha. Mi going die. Di black a come out of mi. Dem give me some bush tea las night, but it don't do no good! Di spirit man a come," he said with resignation.

"The obeah man?"

"Im going save mi, Busha."

"Dr. Robertson will do that, Quality. You are much too valuable to lose."

"No, sah! Mi see strange tings last night, and dat mean deat a come soon."

"You were delirious, Quality, and dreaming. Most likely the result of the bush tea you drank."

"No sah, it not what you sey, Massa Galloway. Di cold hand a deat touch mi last night. Lard Jesus, save mi soul!" Quality prayed aloud, grasping for any religion which promised salvation.

They moved to the next bed. Honed Irish logic could not answer the superstitions that encased the minds of these people. Africa lived in them from generation to generation. Its beliefs just intertwined with the local ones. He smiled at the comparison his mind made with the old saying about taking the farm boy from the farm but not the farm out of the boy. He had heard that one long ago in England, when his regiment was on duty in Yorkshire. What a damp and miserable time that was, billeted in the shadow of York Minster, he recalled.

Mungo brought the soft white hat Lucy sent along for her son. Mungo also brought along a new busha hat, as slaves called them, for Galloway.

"What is this?" he asked, when Mango presented it to him.

"Miss Lucy say you mus wear it. Di old one you ave on mash-hup, she say."

Galloway took the boy's hat and adjusted it on the child's head; he brushed aside the one Mungo offered him. "Carry that one," he said. "And when we return home, give it back to Miss Lucy and say I will wear it when this one good on mi head is *good-hen mash-hup*."

Checking again that the little cotton hat was firmly in place, they made their way out into the sunlight. It was none too soon. A queasy feeling had surfaced in Galloway's gut by the sixth bed. The smell of sickly sweet nosegays, putrefying flesh, and lye soap always made him feel uncomfortable. Long ago, he concluded that hospitals were distasteful places to visit. To him, the hospital smell was worse than the stench of a battlefield two days after the battle with all its rotting corpses crawling with carrion seekers. He even knew some soldiers who perversely enjoyed that stink, and he himself preferred it of the two noxious alternatives. Being a doctor would never be his profession.

They mounted up once again. Tim was safely strapped into his saddle once more, and Mungo took his position behind the donkey. This time, the jenny ignored him and made no move to dismember the slave with a bite or kick. Evidently, a truce had been called between them, as the day and its heat had progressed, adventurous attack and defense at this time being undesirable for both boy and beast.

As they rode between the building and back onto the road, coming toward them was a man with a boy, leading a mule. Galloway recognized Edward Lawrence, as the parties closed the gap between them. The boy with him was familiar, too. Galloway searched his memory for where and when he had come across the boy at the mule's head. Clarification came when he noticed a bamboo flute stuck in the boy's belt as both parties came to a stop alongside each other.

"Do you always carry that with you, Neddy?" Galloway said, pointing to the flute.

"You remember me den, sah?" Neddy said, with some pride in his voice.

"How could I forget the musician by the road who played his music with the zest of life?" Galloway chuckled when he said that. "Mass Edward, you know there is great musical talent living in your house?" He indicated Neddy with a nod of his head.

"Yes, sah. So mi wife tell me. An if she sey so, it so." Neddy looked away in embarrassment as both men laughed. He managed a small smile at the thought of his mam and wondered what her comeback would have been had she been there. It would have been sharp, Neddy knew.

"Haven't you heard him play, Edward?" asked Galloway.

"Yes, sah, all di time. An I got to say, im soun good. But you know, sah, it all dem hymn. Im don't play dance music or country song."

"You disapprove of hymns then, Edward?"

Edward did not get a chance to answer as a light trap bearing Doctor Robertson came up to them at a trot.

"Morning, Captain," called the doctor as he steadied his horse down. "Come to see how your crop of malingerers are doing. You know, a couple of good cuts from your driver's whip would do them more good than any physic I give them."

"No doubt, but I find that it is more economical to let them malinger than have to chase them from place to place, trying to get work out of them. And how are you this morning, Doctor? In a fine mood, I hear," Galloway said with a rueful smile.

The doctor ignored the comment and launched into his accustomed homily on sound planting methods.

"Well, if that's the case why do you not sell the brutes, Captain? Make use of the money elsewhere. Improve the place with the latest boilers and steam crushers. Look at my little place, Bracken; three servants for myself and five for the work outside. They are not overworked; they're well-fed and cared for. We have the latest machinery to do the work, and at crop I hire jobbers. My people retain their value. Pound for pound, we do better than even you here on these many acres with all your worthless miscreants. Still, I should not complain; you pay me well to doctor them." A look of satisfaction settled on his round face. Even the servant sitting beside him in the trap took on the look of an indulged cat.

"Sensible idea, and very canny of you to implement it," Galloway said. "But, of all people, Doctor, you should know we do not deal with sensible men. As only illegal slaves are coming into the island, they gamble their slaves will go up in value. Cash on the foot to their owners, you could say."

"Your employer, Captain, is lucky that Newman Hall is high up in the hills, where the juice boils at a lower temperature, and he gets a better quality and more sugar from the crop. If his estate were down by the sea, selling the lazy sods would be his only solution to raise money for new equipment, like the new vacuum pan that helps boil the juice at lower altitudes more effectively. Jamaica is being killed by new competition from the East."

"Yes, I know, Doctor. But I won't be long here."

"What do you mean, Captain?" the doctor said with a puzzled scowl on his face. "Are you planning on leaving the island, sir?"

"Thinking about it, Doctor."

"Where would you go, man?" There was disappointment in the doctor's voice, as he liked Galloway and looked on him as a good friend.

"A few of my old army friends in the Royal Engineers are building a canal in Upper Canada, and they are offering me a position."

"What do you know about engineering? You were an infantryman, weren't you?"

Galloway laughed at the hesitation in the doctor's queries. "Right you are, but they don't want me for mi engineering skills; they want me to oversee the Irish slaves digging the ditch." He laughed again. The left corner of his mouth twisted mockingly as he went on. "They think I have the necessary experience after being in Jamaica."

"Be serious, man! What are you talking about? There are no Irish slaves."

"Come, Doctor! The English made every Irishman a slave when they invaded us. Yes, sor! Since the days of Longbow, we have been cast down into slavery. Of all people, Robertson, as a Scotsman, you should know that. They did the same to you after Colloden. Turned clansmen against clansmen and sent the losers abroad like slaves. The Lairds who sided with that butcher, Cumberland, turned their own folk off their miserable crofts and sent them to foreign places like Jamaica, Canada, and many other rot holes in the British Empire. That is why we are here, man."

The doctor understood only too well. He, himself, would not have been so forthright. Long ago he had learned to adapt his bedside manner to everyday intercourse. Truth, he found, always made others uncomfortable.

"I'll be sorry to see you go," was all Robertson could say as Galloway's rasping conclusion hit home.

"Go, I must. This place palls on me. Besides, I want to be out of this accursed island before it burns to a cinder and sinks beneath the sea." He pointed to the Lawrences. "That's why Edward is here. He is going to build me some strong boxes to pack my books and stuff I take north with me. Aren't you, Edward?" Galloway turned and looked at the carpenter silently taking it all in.

"If dat is what you want, sah. I will build them for you," said Edward.

"What have you heard, Captain?" There was urgency in the doctor's question.

"Nothing. No more than anyone else. But it is to be expected, you know."

Neddy glanced at his father, looking for a reaction to the doctor's question and Galloway's answer. The elder Lawrence remained impassive; he was well-trained to efface himself when caught between whites' contentions, which his wife always berated him for.

"It is the cold hand crawling up mi back that is the warning." Galloway laughed at the expression on the doctor's face. He could not resist adding, "Mi hair rises on the nape of mi neck, Doctor, like a banshee is about to scream. It always comes before a battle."

"Ach, mon!" the doctor said with contempt. "You Irish are superstitious bairns; you are just like these black heathens here—with their accursed sorcery." The doctor's finger shook slightly as it pointed to the slave sitting beside him. Then he wriggled uneasily on the seat of the trap. The horse sensed the nervousness by the way the reins twitched. The bit jarred; the gelding's head went up as it sashayed to the side, jolting the two-wheeler uncomfortably. Robertson struggled for a minute to bring the animal back under control.

Galloway watched the tousle with a superior grin. "You Scots are more accustomed to walking than riding, one can see."

"Too young for a trap," the doctor said, as his horse settled down.

"Hmm." Galloway nodded and smiled.

"You will be taking this little one?" asked Robertson, pointing his whip at Tim.

"Of course! What would I do without him, now?"

"Finally!" the doctor said with passion in his voice this time. "They have replaced what you lost. Good, good, Galloway!" he joyfully exclaimed, and would have clapped his hands together as a seal of approval, if his horse had not been skittish. Then he lectured on as only a Scot could.

"It's never good for a man to be alone in this world. A wife and children he needs, to give him backbone and purpose in this world." The doctor gave his observation time to sink in. He did not get the expected response from the captain. Instead, Robertson observed Galloway's back straighten and his knees press his saddle.

"Well, I must go about my business. Can't spend the day gossiping." Robertson signaled his horse to resume its way toward the hospital.

"Oh, Doctor, before I forget," Galloway called after him, "there is that little ass of a bookkeeper of mine, McAfee, in the boiler house. He has just recovered from the Yellow Jack and still looks terrible. Malaria will probably be his next trial. Do, I beg you, give him some of that quinine bark." The doctor nodded and got the trap underway again. As it moved off, Galloway added, "Not telling you your business, Doctor, but Billy in the hospital could do with the same. The spirit-people are killing him with bush tea. Save them both for me—I need all my slaves." He chuckled as Robertson stopped the trap and turned in his seat to look at Galloway with a puzzled scowl.

He was about to get going when he turned back to Galloway and called, "Captain! Talking obeah, none of your people have started dirt eating, have they?"

"Not that I have heard. Why?"

"Not seen it for years, and then out of nowhere I got one down on Friendship. A young girl. Nothing I could do. By the time I got there, she was dead of dropsy. Nasty habit! For the life of me, I can't think why they do it."

"You know, anything can happen on Friendship."

Neddy's ears pricked up at the talk of Friendship, and he noticed Robertson's jaws clamped tightly together. Robertson nodded his head at the captain's observation while slapping his whip on the horse's rear with purpose.

"Let's hope it does not begin spreading around the estates. One does it, and then others follow—claim to be obeah," the doctor said, as the trap accelerated up the road.

"Edward, you must have thought we had forgotten you." Galloway smiled at the carpenter and his son, waiting patiently on the road. "I need boxes to pack my books and belongings. They have to be light and strong. Go up to the house, and Miss Lucy will show you what is to be taken. Make an estimate of how much it will cost and let her know."

"Yes, sah, Mister Galloway."

"And Edward, on your way, stop in at the boiler house and look over the gutters and all the woodwork for me, and let me know what is to be done. My people are less than good at carpentry work. Perhaps we can get you some extra work. With Christmas coming up, I am sure you could do with a little extra?"

The prospect pleased Edward, and it showed on his face. "It will be done, sah, as you wants," he said.

"Come, Tim, you have been a good boy, sitting there so quietly." The boy gladly slapped his small legs against the side of the donkey. He was getting to be quite expert. His elder followed, and both the jenny and mule responded. Mungo reluctantly dragged himself from the tree shade, where he had retired while the Backra Massas had their chat.

"Mass Edward," Galloway stopped and looked at the elder Lawrence and then at Neddy, "I would like to hire that young man for a day or two." Both Lawrences looked surprised at the offer.

"Tomorrow I am going up early to Lapland for bird shooting, and I want a reliable lad with me." Pointing his whip in the direction of Mungo, he went on, "Can't rely on this one here. I will pay Neddy a crown for his services. He will look after horse and mule and carry mi fowling pieces. Also, he can pick up the birds I shoot."

A fortune! Neddy was ever ready to earn the odd penny and was even more enthused upon hearing what the job was.

"Lard, sah! Half of dat is more than enough pay. Half a crown you can give im."

Neddy's face dropped slightly at his father's downgrading counteroffer. Whose side was he on, anyway? Galloway noticed Neddy's change of expression and pressed his lips firmly together, stifling a smile. Had he been the boy, he would have felt the same. Oh, how parents could undermine their children, thinking they were doing right.

"No, Edward, he is worth a crown. Besides, it could be two days' work, not just one. Rest easy; he would be only getting half a crown for each day."

"If it's all right wid di boy, den it is all right wid me."

"Neddy, what do you say?"

Neddy's teeth glittered in the sunlight. "Yes, sir, I would like that very, very much, sir." There was not a trace of patois in his answer. His first big job.

"Then it is set. Tomorrow, Neddy—early. You will have to stay the night. When you get up to the house, ask Miss Lucy to show you where you can sleep. Can you ride a mule?"

"Yes, sir," confirmed Neddy.

"Good! You will ride this one. I will ride my horse. We have to appear gentlemen up at Lapland. We will be guests of James Graham-Clarke, Esquire. Come, mi boyo," Galloway said, turning to Tim, who had begun to show signs of wear from heat and inactivity. The day was wearing on the child. Galloway could see beads of perspiration beginning to dribble from under the little hat his mother had sent. Tim should go back to the house, Galloway knew. But trusting Mungo to take him back was chancy. Much putout could happen on the way, and he was not willing to take that gamble. The captain decided to soldier on and, if worse came to worst, he would take the child back himself before finishing the morning rounds.

"Let's go and see how that new French cane is growing." This time they did not stop or look back.

Mungo's head drooped as he dragged his feet, very disappointed to hear that he would not be going to Lapland, and worse still, "Dat dutty pushup likkle black boye going get all dat money."

"What was that you said, Mungo?" Galloway said over his shoulder.

"Notting, sah. Notting hat all!" His bitterness came through clearly, and the overseer contemplated taking the opportunity to lecture Mungo on the virtues of honesty and hard work being rewarded; then he thought better of it. Mungo was the type of human who, from conception, was beyond redemption. The world needed all types to populate heaven and hell.

Neddy followed his father as they headed up the road toward the overseer's house. He was excited at the prospect of going bird shooting with the captain up on Lapland Estate and wondered what all that business of dirt eating was about on Friendship. Soon enough, he would find out from Watt. They would have plenty to talk about next Saturday.

Chapter 8

Bird Bush

All was settled. Edward knew he had to build some boxes for Massa Galloway, and Neddy knew he was to accompany Captain Galloway on the morn to a shooting party at Lapland Estate, up past Catadupa on the Great River. As they arrived at the back door of the overseer's residence, the greeting they received from a large woman, with a command still larger than her, was not the most cordial.

"What you back here for, Edward? No gal want you now, you know? You too old for dem. Dey would suck you in and blow you out like fan-fan!" A shriek of laughter followed her ribald warning.

"Hif mi too old for young gal, den no man or boye want a dry-up ting like you," Edward said and continued quickly before she could fire back. "You know some ting, when Backra Massa a name you as pickney, im was funning wid di name Badalia. Im should a pour di water pon your head an call you Madalia." He did not raise his voice but delivered the rebuff in a matter-of-fact style with an added look of pity.

She glared back; her mouth moved to answer, but Edward continued: "Mi no business with any *wotliss* little gal all hot up fi hood. Fi-mi business is to mek di Backra Massa some nice boxes, so he can pack up im tings and leave dis here place and all you lazy-no-good-bungo-naygars. Dat is why mi here."

The insult was too much for her. This time he had to be answered. Badalia was not going to let him get away with calling her a bungo-naygar. Naygar was one thing, but to throw in the bungo part—that she would not have.

"You tink you is bad na! Who you calling bungo? You want come in ya to do your business?" She pointed to the doorway over her shoulder and said, "Den it will be over mi dead body!" Both hands settled back at her waist with arms akimbo.

From Edward's perspective, she seemed to puff up like a bullfrog, standing at the top of the step. She was formidable; her eyes widened, then narrowed, flashing defiantly at him below her. He had gone too far. He had to make a verbal retreat to satisfy her dignity and save his own, especially in front of his son.

Dropping his voice and smiling, "Miss Badalia," he said. "I see you still boss around here." With the title *Miss*, he had thrown out the first pacifier. The acknowledgement of her household lordship was the next step. Perhaps he had gone too far calling her a no-good bungo. He knew she could cause a lot of trouble.

Still glaring down from her vantage point, Badalia would not be satisfied with the few sweet words he had come up with so far. Sugar and molasses would have to pour out with every word and sentence.

"Lordi! Lordi! Lordi!" His exclamations carried all the warmth of long-standing familiarity. "You know I was only funning? You is still a sweet woman. Any man would love to av you. Pity mi taken now, or I would be coming aroun." He was about to add *again* but remembered who stood just behind him and stopped. His verbal stroke seemed to let out some of her steam and reduce her to a more normal size. A flicker of a smile lit her face for a second; then the scowl returned, but the glow of hostility had left her eyes. Next, the corners of her mouth relaxed. One arm dropped from waist to her side. The other stayed akimbo like a coquette.

Listening to all this banter between his father and the woman defending the steps, Neddy realized there was more between them than just the usual back-and-forth jocularities. Maybe his father had known her in the past. He had grown accustomed to meeting these women as he traveled around the estates as his father's assistant. On occasion he even met some of his half sisters and brothers. He accepted it as normal. His father's business was his father's business, as his business was his business.

A great and pronounced sucking of the teeth came from her at the top of the back steps. "*Boss*! Mi *boss*! Man, where you get dat foolishness from? Mi here to look after di massa an Miss Lucy. Im is di boss, and she a learn to be di boss; mi, jus a help dem." Badalia's cackling laugh vibrated the eardrums.

"Badalia," Edward said taking a deep breath. "Beg you! Mi here to see Miss Lucy. Get her fi mi?" He smiled and added, "An don't give me any more of your back chat."

Badalia puffed up. "You is hackled up, eh? Auh!" She glowered down at him. Her bosom heaved like a man-o-war yawing to bring its broadside to bear on the enemy. She measured and fired; innuendo was the powder, and each word came like a measured shot: "What di matter, di African Quashiba a starve you again?" Her derisive laugh crossed the steps like chain shot shattering flesh, bone, mast, and sail. Before he could counter, she turned and flounced through the door to fetch her mistress.

They waited not more than two minutes before Lucy came out to the top of the steps. Behind her, Badalia stood like a sentry in the shadow of the doorway.

This was the first time Neddy had gotten a close look at Lucy. It surprised him to see that she was not much older than he. She must have been at least two years younger than he was now when she gave birth to the boy they had met on their way to the house. *Man! Captain Galloway like dem very young!* A sense of disappointment came with the thought. Then he remembered that when he had first met him, the captain had asked if he had gone a bush. His eyebrows crinkled together at this memory.

On that hot step, the complexity of people puzzled him greatly. There and then, Neddy decided that men and women masked their inner selves in shadow for protection against the harsh daylight of others, just as they hid their bodies from the heat of the day with clothes. As he mulled this over, the voices on the steps above him cut into his thoughts and brought him back to the moment.

His father stood halfway up the steps, explaining why they were there. Miss Lucy listened attentively. What he was saying reminded Neddy of his own instructions to ask her to show him where he would sleep that night. That was, if his father did not ask for him. He hoped he would.

Shifting his weight from leg to leg, Neddy tried to get more comfortable standing in front of her. The sun was up, between eleven and twelve. He wished they would hurry up and finish their chatter, so he could get out of the heat. Grown people never seemed to care about the young ones when they met together on the road or over business. Just babble, babble, babble, as if there were no tomorrow, as if the sun were not cooking their offspring. If the child tried to sneak off to the shade, the parent would bark, *Come back ya. Listen to what Mass, or Miss, so and so ave to say. Learn from dem, so you can be di de bes when you grow up.* He hated those moments and lectures. As a result, he had learned to wait patiently and pray silently that the babble would soon end.

To fill this fretful time, his eyes wandered up to the girl who stood at the top of the steps. He could see she had been called away from her den-hot work inside. Damp ringlets dangled under the front of her cap and stuck to her forehead. As she stood in the sunlight, glistening beads of perspiration formed on her skin as the rising heat of the day drew more moisture from her.

She was very pretty. Even from where he stood on the bottom step, Neddy could see long lashes shading big brown eyes. Under them, on her cheeks and small turned-up nose, the odd telltale freckle made it known she was no rich white lady who bathed in milk and exposed her face to no harsher light than that of the moon. Neddy thought the spots were like those on a banana skin, just as the fruit began to ripen, and that made him smile. They added a childlike quality to her face and banished the reality of her motherhood.

She dabbed her cheeks and forehead with a handkerchief from her apron pocket before asking Edward, in a subdued manner, "Yes, sah, what can I do for you?"

"Miss Lucy, di busha," began the elder Lawrence. His words trailed away as Neddy's gaze rested on Lucy's small mouth and the full bottom lip, which she nervously clamped and unclamped between her front teeth as his father explained the work he was to do. Every now and then, she would let the tip of her tongue moisten both lips. She would swallow, then bite again on the under lip.

Her breasts rose and fell as her chest expanded and contracted with each breath, as if she suffered from lack of air. A tiny pulse began to jump on the left side of her neck. Now and then she would dab nervously with the damp kerchief from her apron pocket at the ever-present droplets on her forehead. It made little difference, for as they were wiped away, more formed.

Above, the sun blazed, and, in retaliation, the earth and cut-stone steps threw their heat back at it. Neddy's toes wriggled uncomfortably in his sandals. For self-preservation, his mind forced this bodily discomfort out, allowing him to drift further into the dream space known only to boys close to manhood.

There arose in this quiescence a great desire to reach out and calm the lady's anxiety. It was a new and strange feeling, this desire to protect, and it excited him. Self-consciously, Neddy pulled his eyes away by half-turning around and shoved his hands deep in his trouser pockets, afraid others around would see his feelings and laugh. His apprehension subsided gradually with the realization no one was paying the slightest bit of attention to him, standing out of the way. He was a child, after all.

"Neddy, Neddy! What you dream about boye? You sleeping?"

Neddy jumped slightly at the sudden interruption. His father's voice brought him back to where he stood, baking in the sun on the back steps of the overseer's house on Newman Hall. He jerked a grubby rag from his pocket and wiped the sweat from his face. "No, sah!"

"What you expect when you keep di boye stan in di hot sun so?" Badalia said. "It no mus slow him down."

Edward ignored her. "Neddy, do as di busha tell you, boye. Mi not going to do it for you. You got to learn to take care of fi you business. Him a pay you for a job, an you got to make di arrangements to see it done good."

Badalia listened and silently approved.

"Miss Lucy," Neddy said, looking at her face. He hoped she could not read his recent thoughts. He feared his voice would crack or tremble. "Di busha wan me to go wid him to Lapland come a marning. Im tell me to ask you to show mi where I to sleep tonight."

"He is not taking Mungo, then?" The mistress looked surprised.

"Lard, Miss Lucy!" Badalia said. "Why would di busha take a lazy no-good like Mungo wid him up to Laplan, wid all di gentlemen dere? Him would bring disgrace pon de busha an us down on Newman Hall. No sah, Mam, di busha wan a sensible boye wid him. Dat's why im tek dis ya one."

Edward grinned, grateful that Badalia had taken a fancy to Neddy. From now on, the boy would do no wrong in her eyes. Nasty she could have been to the boy. Thank heavens she did not hold grudges and let them burn her insides out, like many others burdened by slavery.

His smile widened, remembering how Badalia loved well-set-up boys. Neddy certainly wouldn't have gone unnoticed by her, back in earlier years. These days she would just admire and sigh and go no further for decency's sake, of that he was certain. But the thought brought back those long gone times when he, too, had been young and fresh.

Although older than he, Badalia had been a good-looking woman and a wonderful teacher of the secret arts between man and woman. He remembered the first time Mistress Rachel sent him over to Newman Hall as an apprentice carpenter. Even then, when he was still the apprentice carpenter at Kensington, he was well on the way to being a lover of women and master cocksman. In those days she had really taken a fancy to him; and he, young and foolish, would seek every opportunity to go and see her. Then she got belly for him and lost it. Quashiba came by, and Badalia and many others got shunted off to the side.

Big and buxom, well into her middle years but still a strong woman, Badalia now stood one step behind her mistress, arms

Bird Bush

akimbo and ready to do battle with anyone who challenged. He had always been a little bit afraid of her but knew she hid a kind heart under that bossy exterior.

"Im can sleep over dere wid Mungo. I will get dem to put anoder cot in di room for im. It for two people anyway. Mungo a in dere all by imself." Badalia pointed to a small cottage beside three others where she and the house servants lived.

That settled, Edward, followed by Neddy, began to climb the steps to enter the house. As they reached halfway, Badalia pushed in front of Lucy, blocking their way.

"An where you tink you is going?" she demanded.

Edward stopped and shook his head from side to side in disbelief. Another battle in the making? He had no time for this.

"You na listen, woman, when mi tell Miss Lucy what mi here for? Mi have to see what needs to be put inside di boxes before mi start to mek dem. How mi to know what di busha man need?"

"A huh!" she responded. Her head stuck forward menacingly as her eyes narrowed and her mouth clamped shut. Edward made to continue up the steps and was blocked again. Her akimbo arms made passage around her even more difficult. "You na come across mi clean floor wid dem boots an fool-fool sandal." Badalia pointed at both their feet. "You nah go scratch hit up and drag di dut in ya!"

"Is dat all you fret bout! Notting easier." He turned to his son. "Neddy, tek off what pon you foot to please di ladies." Edward did the same and placed his boots side by side, just in the door shadow, out of the sun. He indicated a place for Neddy, who was very glad to slip off his sandals as he contemplated the cool floor under his feet.

"You don't mine if we put dem here, so dey don't get hot up in di sun?" Edward said, cocking his left eyebrow and grinning at Badalia.

"Hum," she said with a shrug and scowl.

At last! Neddy followed his father out of the sun and into the dark cool of the house. Miss Lucy led the way along the corridor across Badalia's shining floor into the piazza. The light was like dusk inside, and Neddy's eyes took their time adjusting to the half-light. Keeping the heat at bay, window coolers only allowed a minimum of daylight through their lattice shutters along with the refreshing air.

Seconds passed before the furniture around him took on shape and substance.

Although wider than normal, the piazza did not run the length of the house. On the right, where the dining table stood, a wall cut a good quarter off it. Against this wall was a large sideboard with glass tumblers, pewter mugs, and bottles of rum and brandy, along with a large silver bowl with a china cover. The silver handle of a large spoon protruded through the notch made for it in the bowl's lid. As Miss Lucy opened the door at the corner for them, Neddy looked closely at the flat part of the spoon handle and noticed an animal standing on its hind legs with a funny looking hat above its head. He had seen something like it before over at Mount Apfel when his mother had taken him to see Miss Appy, and there had been some silver spoons on a table.

Miss Lucy carefully put her bunch of keys back in her apron pocket and pushed the door open. She stood back, indicating they could enter.

"You not coming in, Miss Lucy?"

She shook her head. "I will wait here for you to finish, Mass Edward, and then lock it back." Neddy noticed that she gave his father respect by addressing him as *Mass*, and for some reason that pleased him. From her, it seemed to be genuine.

The windows had been left open in the room, and their eyes had to adjust to the sudden brightness. Neddy blinked twice to compensate. When the room took on discernible proportions, he could see two walls covered in bookshelves jammed with books. Neddy had never seen so many books before. Not even in the rectory had Parson Waldrich got that many books. How could anyone read them all? It would take him all his life and a half to get through a shelf. His eyes kept scanning the shelves in wonderment, and it struck him that even Watt would have been overwhelmed by the sight.

On the wall that cut the room off from the piazza hung a portrait of a young woman, seated on a bench in a garden. Jet-black hair came in a thick, lustrous roll around her long neck and ended curled just above her bosom. She had a small chin and mouth. A black mole on her left cheek contrasted with her white skin, giving it life. Spread around her on the bench was a white dress, embroidered on the hem with off-white lilies intertwined with each other. A little boy stood by her side. His hand rested on hers, holding a rose in her lap. He was dressed in deep red knee britches and a small jacket to match over a shirt open at the collar. Intensely blue eyes stared straight back at those who looked at him. Neddy speculated this must have been how Watt looked when he was four years old. He would have been blond, not black haired like this child in the picture. But it was the pink cheeks, oval face, and the honesty of the look in those very blue eyes that made him think them similar.

A single high-backed mahogany chair stood next to a large round table in the middle of the room. On the table, an open book lay alongside pens, an inkwell, and paper, ready for use. A sabre in its scabbard also lay across the table. Beside it, an open, velvet-lined case contained a pair of matching pistols in separate compartments. Across the room from the table, long guns stood in a rack in the corner, their barrels reflecting the sunlight that streamed through the open shutters. Edward walked over and looked at them. Not long ago, he had made the stand that now held the rifles upright. The case had doors that could be closed and locked for transportation. Obviously, nothing was needed for these guns.

"Is all dese mi have to make boxes for, Miss Lucy?" asked Edward, pointing a finger at the walls with the books. She just nodded in response.

"What him do wid di box dem come in?" he inquired.

"I don't know, Mass Edward. It was before mi get here."

"Well den, we ad better start from di beginning. Neddy," his father said as he turned to him. "You can use some of that learning your modder insist you have and count up all dem books, so we can know how many dere is and how many boxes needed, you understan?"

"Yes, sah," Neddy said, and set himself to work.

In the meantime his father sat in the big chair at the table and thought aloud what he was going to build.

"It would be better to build four box wid shelves in dem for di books. Den dey would be easier to carry dan fi dem in two big box," he said, as he stood in front of the shelves and let his mind's eye make the judgment. "How many book in dey?" he asked, without looking around at Neddy.

"Four hundred and fifteen mi count, da," Neddy said, after he had checked the shelves twice.

Edward continued his planning out loud, as if no one else were present. Occasionally, he would make passing reference to his son. "If we mek dem so dey become shelves to hold di books when dem stan straight up, now dat would be good! All we got to do, boye, is build di box like mi mek di gun case over dere." Edward pointed to the gun stand in the corner. "We can mek dem so di doors can slip off, an den you use di boxes like stan-up book shelves. Once in dey, di books never have to come out again, except when you tek one out to read."

Listening to his father's plan, Neddy agreed it made good sense. He began to understand why his father was in such great demand as a carpenter, and watching the pleasure spread across his father's face at the cleverness of his idea gave him pleasure, too.

Out came the folding yardstick from the work bag Edward carried on the job, and expertly he measured, marking down the measurements carefully on a slate he also produced from the bag.

Neddy had seen it all before, but still the mastery awed him. One day he, too, would be that good, and people would come all the way from Spanish Town for his work, and he would make them pay big time. He would be rich and famous.

"Four boxes, five feet high, tree feet wide," Edward mumbled, and scratched the calculation on the slate. "Wid one extra box for all dose tings dem going fin lef over when de job done." Nothing must be overlooked. Those who hired him never seemed to know what they wanted, and Edward had to anticipate their needs. He was taking no chances that his employer would be dissatisfied with his work. His pride was always at stake when he did a job.

Standing by, listening and watching, his son learned, as apprentices should.

When Edward had finished all his measuring and estimating, he turned to Lucy, who was watching the proceedings in the room from just outside the door. It was not that she did not trust Edward, but

Bird Bush

she had become fiercely protective of all that belonged to Galloway. This was his private room and, to her, a sacred place.

"You can lock de room back now, Miss Lucy. We finish in here." As man and boy left the room, they heard the latchkey turn in the lock, then the doorknob tried to ensure it had fastened securely.

At the steps they stopped to reboot. Badalia watched from the outside kitchen. Grinning, Edward gave her a flourishing bow, sweeping his hat from his head across his chest as a gentleman salutes a lady. They all laughed; even Lucy joined in.

Edward strode quickly across the back yard; Neddy had to jog to keep up. Once Edward's mind was set, there was no time to waste. They continued at this quick march up another hill to the Great House, which was about a half-mile away from the overseer's place.

The caretaker opened the storeroom under the house for them; it held lumber for furniture to be made on the estate. They spent the rest of that day in the storerooms, selecting the right pieces of wood for the boxes and setting up a temporary workshop.

Twice, they were interrupted as Badalia sent food for them. On each occasion a different maid carried the tray. Both were very young and pretty. When the second one turned up, Edward laughed loudly. The embarrassed girl left the food tray and ran back, holding up the front of her skirt. There was no doubt Badalia was tempting him with day and night food to see which way he would jump. The capricious nature of the female never ceased to fill Edward with wonder.

"What so funny, Da?" his son asked, as he helped himself to a hunk of yellow yam from the pot.

"When you get old enough, you will hunderstan. Dat is, if a man can ever hunderstan women. Lard! Dem twist dis way and dat, and a man never know which way dem going come out."

Finally, his father was satisfied with their progress and prepared to return home to Kensington. He tuned to Neddy. "I will tell your modder where you going tomorrow." Then he added, "I will miss your elp." He smiled and rested his hand on his son's head, as if giving a blessing, "You a good boye. You know dat?" he asked, expecting no response. "You won't let us down wid di busha, mi know."

Neddy felt good about the little speech. Till now, he had wondered if his father even noticed him beyond what was expected from the man who lived with his mother. They went outside to find that the short tropical dusk had fallen. There was just enough light for Neddy to get the mule ready for his father's return home.

It didn't take long, and Edward was soon on his way. Neddy watched him for a while, until the dusk melded with man and mule, and they were gone. Then, guided by flickering lights in windows, he wandered back down to the overseer's house to find Badalia and discover where he would sleep. He had to be shown Mungo's quarters.

"You come?" Badalia greeted him. "You fader gone back to Kensington? When Quashiba call, im better run." Laughing in her usual way, she turned away to move a kettle on the fire behind her. "An di busha wan you to come up to im when you get ya. You know di way. Where Miss Lucy tek you dis morning."

"Yes, Miss Badalia," he said politely. "I will go dere right now." He left the kitchen at a trot. Badalia turned round and waved the ladle in her hand at his retreating behind, as if threatening a spanking, "An remember, walk barefoot when you go in a di ouse. Mi floor is not for di likes of you to dutty up."

"Yes, Mam!" he shouted from halfway across the yard.

In a more kindly vein, she shouted back "An when you get back, mi will ave some ting for you to eat, an den mi will show you where to sleep."

She was gruff, but he knew he could hear kindness nestled under her bark. He had taken that in, listening to her set with his father, and concluded that most of it was just tek an show.

He found himself standing at the door of the room he'd been in that morning. Through the opening he could see Galloway sitting in the chair, cleaning one of the long guns. Another lay on the small rug by his feet.

"Come in, Neddy Lawrence, and learn what you have to do on the morrow." Galloway took a large swig from a rummer that sat on the table beside him and beckoned Neddy into the room. "Come in, come in, lad! Don't stand there like a rabbit."

214

Neddy did as the overseer ordered and came over to stand next to the table. The sabre and pistols must have been put away, for in their place was a glass and a nearly empty bottle of rum. On the table also was a box full of tiny little pellets and, beside it, a pile of little sacs with thread wound around their openings to keep their contents from spilling out. Neddy guessed that they held the little pellets.

Galloway looked at him with eyes slightly watery from the drink. "An invention of mine for quick loading and shooting," he said. "Takes time the night before, but saves you a great deal of fiddling around in the field the next morning, you see." He picked up a small square of flimsy cloth and pushed it into a small cup, just bigger than a thimble, so that the edges came over the top. Next, he took a measure of pellets and filled the cup. He brought together the edges of cloth hanging over the rim of the cup and wound thread around so as to seal the contents. "You see how it's done?" As he spoke, Neddy could smell the rum on his breath and flinched.

Noticing the reaction, Galloway laughed outright and, with exaggerated slur, teased the boy. "Yes, mi young Master Lawrence, as yous zee, I 'ave been in the claret, or is it rum? It's all the same after two glasses, you know? My boy," he went on, shaking his finger in Neddy's face like a schoolteacher, "as those damned Baptists preach, don't let demon rum get to you." He let out a peal of merry laughter.

Neddy fidgeted and said nothing.

Suddenly, like a neophyte drinker, Galloway tittered. He half expected a hiccup to follow and roared with delight, clapping his hands together in mock applause. "Yes, mi boyo, when older men in their waters speak to you, it is always best not to answer them. It only brings on an argument." Holding up the gun he had been cleaning, he abruptly changed the subject. "Ever seen one of these before?"

"No, sah."

"Didn't think you had. It is a fowling piece made by Henry Nock and given me by my late wife's father as a wedding present."

"You ave a wife?" Neddy's, eyes widened in astonishment. He had never thought of Galloway as a married man. But then again, there was not much he knew about this Backra Massa.

"Dead, boy. She and our child, dead. Both of them drowned coming out to this accursed island of yours." His voice sounded flat. For a moment after the pronouncement, there was silence between them. Inwardly, Neddy tightened up, waiting for what would come next. Galloway gazed at him for a moment; then, before the boy began to fidget as boys do under strain, he lifted the half-empty glass, indicated the portrait on the wall, and drank the rest of the rum. Just as suddenly as he had shared his loss with Neddy, he changed the subject: "If time allowed, I would teach you how to reload these pieces. As it is, in the butts tomorrow, you will watch me and learn.."

"Yes, sah," Needy said, feeling eager now that the tension was broken.

"Pick up that gun." Galloway indicated the one lying on the ground, as he refilled his glass.

The gun was surprisingly heavier than it looked, and the weight forced Neddy to hold it with both hands.

"Good." Galloway made sure the boy was turned away from him and the gun pointed to the outer wall of the room.

"Neddy." He took a sip from the refilled glass. "The first lesson you learn when handling any weapon is, never point it at another human unless you mean to kill him. Never point guns or draw swords unless you mean to do grievous bodily damage to your opponent. You understand?" He looked at the boy with a serious cast in his bleary eyes.

Neddy wanted to say that no, he didn't, but instead he nodded as if he understood perfectly. After all, this was a first. He had seen pistols carried by some overseers and bookkeepers, but he had never held a gun before, certainly not a long gun.

"I will load both guns. You will hold one and hand it to me when I have fired both barrels of my gun and I ask you for it. Not before, you understand? You will then hold the empty gun that I have fired."

"Yes, sah."

"Here is how we hold guns when we are around other people and do not want accidents to happen." Galloway stood up, holding his gun with both hands, one on the stock and one on the forearm as if presenting arms, with the barrel pointed at the rafters above them. To ease the position, you can rest the barrel against your shoulder, so." Neddy watched as Galloway, without moving his hands from where they were on the gun, allowed the barrels to rest on his shoulder. "That is when we are firing at flocks coming over our stand. When nothing is happening, you can rest the butt on the ground, with the barrels pointing up all the time," he explained. "We cannot afford accidents through careless handling of guns." Up went the rum glass, and he drained it this time.

Galloway walked out of the room to the sideboard and came back with a new bottle of rum. Neddy stood where he had left him, holding the gun tightly, afraid of dropping it. Looking at his rigid posture, Galloway was reminded of a soldier on guard duty and smiled. "You don't have to hold the piece as if you want to choke it to death, boyo. Not so tense! It is not loaded." He gave him a hard look: "But you never know." Neddy relaxed and rested the gun against his shoulder. "That's better," Galloway said.

"One more nicety, and then you can go to bed, because it is up early in the morn for us. Let me show you why you hold the gun that way." Galloway moved to stand behind Neddy. "No, do not turn around until I tell you," he said, as Neddy tried to face him. "When I tell you, turn quickly." With the gun barrels resting against his shoulder, Neddy pivoted around when given the instruction.

"Where is the gun pointing?" asked Galloway on the completion of the turn. Neddy's head went back as he looked up at the rafters to the slanting roof above. "Up dere, sah."

"If you had turned round quickly with that gun, it might have gone off. If it had," Galloway's forefinger pointed upward, "all that would have happened would be a hole in the roof, and rain water would come in. Better than life's blood soaking the ground. Now, give me that and go to bed, youth." He took the gun from Neddy.

"Yes, sah! Good night, sah."

As he headed out of the door, he heard a heavy, blurry Galloway voice say, "And good night to you, Neddy Lawrence, and thank you." Neddy wanted to ask, "For what?" but said nothing. Strange people, these grown-ups, when they were liquored up. Black or white, it did not matter. Rum changed a man; that was sure.

As he headed back across Badalia's floor, so polished it reflected the flickering of the two lamps in the piazza, the same quandary that foxed him on the back steps in the morning came again. *What trouble Massa Galloway?* he asked himself. *Im nice, but im strange. It like im bitter inside.* Not at all like his father's friend Monkey-man, when he knocked more than a few. *Like im sey, "it jus for di taste an flavor."*

Badalia was waiting for him in the kitchen. She pointed to a small table by the window as he came through the door.

"Sit down over deh." She indicated a stool on the side of the table opposite where she stood by the open fire.

As he settled down, an enamel plate filled with plantain, dumplings, and salt pork piled on top of each other was placed in front of him. Looking at the mountain of food, he knew of only one person who could finish that off, no trouble at all. Unfortunately, Watt was not with him, and he wondered how he was going to finish the pile without leaving some, risking insulting the cook.

Topping what was already on the plate, Badalia dolloped on a huge scoop of chopped calalu. "Eat dat, di greens is good for when unu growing."

He preferred it in a soup, especially when his mother made it, but he watched his manners. "Tanks, Miss Badalia."

She fussed around, watching him but saying very little. Neddy thought he may venture a question or two. His curiosity about Galloway was getting to him. He wondered about Miss Lucy and him and the little boy, and now that he knew Galloway had once been married, his curiosity got the better of him.

"Massa Galloway married?" he ventured tentatively.

"What your business wid dat?" she barked at him. There was no mistaking it. He was talking where no one was allowed.

"Oh, notting. Jus wonder, wid di picture pon di wall in di room, Miss Badalia," he said, with the most innocent look he could muster.

She turned from him to the big iron soup pot, boiling for the next day. With each turn of her spoon, the pot swayed on its suspension over the half-dead fire. Bending over to the embers, she methodically poked the ashes with the long metal spoon, stirring life back into the dying charcoal. She pondered the boy's question and whether to give him an explanation.

The coals stirred to life again, brightly throwing off heat that Neddy could feel at the kitchen table. Straightening, Badalia wiped ashes off the spoon with her apron before plunging it back into the soup to keep the yam, carrots, dumpling, and salt pork afloat in the thickening liquid.

"Urricane lick di ship dem was coming on from foreign. She an di child drown out dey so." Her eyes turned to stare through the window into the darkness, and she nodded in the direction of some unknown point beyond the hills and shores of the island deep in the Caribbean.

"Den im tek up wid Miss Lucy?" The speed at which he asked his question tipped Badalia off to his inner feelings. She let her head droop as if contemplating her ample bosom so he could not guess at her smile. "Lard! It nice to be young," she mumbled, gently swaying back and forth on her heels, remembering the pleasure, excitement, and disappointment of youth. But she could not let this go on. Wheeling around, she scowled at Neddy. "Boye, you facety and fass! What you wan meddle in older people business fa?"

The sudden assault stiffened him in the chair. "No, Mam!" he said, dropping his utensil onto the floor. "Just don't know what to say when dem around." It was a lame get-out. He knew it, and so did Badalia.

"Uhha!" She breathed emphatically, giving him a glare that could have kindled the fires of hell. Without a word or sound more, she turned back to agitating the soup. The pressure off, he bent to retrieve the spoon at his foot.

The ensuing silence was only disturbed by the occasional spitting of the coals as she spooned out unwanted black bits from the bottom of the pot and threw them into the fire. The other noise was Neddy's spoon occasionally scraping against the enamel plate, as he struggled manfully to consume a quantity fit to feed the host departing Egypt for the wilderness. It was imperative he do so in order to be reinstated in the good books of Badalia.

"Notting go on between dem," she said.

Her sudden words caught him by surprise, and he sat up and took notice, gladly ceasing his struggle with the pile of victuals still on the plate.

"Her pickney not for di busha. She come ya wid it in her belly. Mus be some odder white man, for Timoty can pass for white. Is di busha tek him on as hif him is his own." She banged the big spoon on the side of the pot as if signaling the end of her information. Neddy sensed she feared over-speaking to a little no-account boy.

"You finish yet?" She turned back to face him. He was glad to see that she did not look angry. "Too much for your belly?" Badalia smiled. Her expression transformed her from a virago to a kind, gentle woman moving on in years. "You eat like a young gal a watch er figure," she spat out contemptuously. "Mungo would a finish dat an hask for more. Im modder always complaining bout ow much he nyam."

"I know somebody like dat, Miss Badalia," Neddy said. "Don't know where it go. It don't show pon im. Funny, im is a white boy."

"What difference you tink dat mek? All boys got worms inside dem. Dat nyam up di food as soon as it swallows down. Don't you modder give you oil to clean you out?" Neddy knew only too well the oil of which she spoke and shuddered. Before he could reply, she went on, "You can leave what you can't manage and ave it before you leave wid di busha come marning. Maybe I give you too much." A broad smile puffed up her cheeks. "But," she said, "hit will mek tings big an strong when di right gal come fi you."

"Yes, Mam," he answered gratefully. His belly was more than full, and all he wanted was bed. Just then he twigged to her last words; his eyes opened wide, and he swallowed hard with embarrassment. Badalia let out a screech of laughter, watching his consternation.

"Leave di plate dere. Mi will look after it. Come, youth, follow me," she said. Thankfully, Neddy did as ordered and followed her out into the night toward a one-room cabin a few yards away.

"Mungo sleep in ya," she said, pushing the door open. It was empty but for two cots. "You tek dat one over dere. Mi know im sleep in dat one." She pointed to a cot in the corner, away from the lone window at the back of the cabin. She placed the lantern on a stool. "You will need di light." Badalia smiled at him. "Sleep tight and don't let di bug dem bite." Neddy watched her disappear into the night just as Mungo made his appearance through the evening gloom. Badalia said, "Where you a come from dis late, you *wotliss* ting?"

"Mi modder," he said, and emitted a strained laugh.

"You hexpect mi to believe dat, Mungo? Hmm! You tink me a fool na boye?"

When he entered the cabin, Mungo looked at Neddy as if he was an intruder rather than a guest. "You a go a Lapland wid di busha?" he asked grudgingly, knowing full well that was going to happen. Before he got an answer, he said, "Im giving you a monies?"

The contract between himself and the captain was none of Mungo's business. At close quarters for the first time, Neddy checked out Mungo. They were about the same size, he judged, and if a fight broke out, Neddy was sure he could hold his own, But a fight was the last thing he wanted, and he did not reply.

"Mi wan mi share. You tek mi job," Mungo said. Neddy remained silent. "You ave to give me a brawta," Mungo insisted.

"Mi will tink bout it," Neddy said, hoping the prospect of some money, which he had no intention of handing over, would shut Mungo up.

"You got somewhere I can wash mi face?" asked Neddy.

Mungo looked at him strangely. "You do dat at night? You not fraid you ketch head cold han dead?" From the astonished reaction, Neddy knew he had asked the wrong question of the wrong person.

"Don't matter," he said.

Mungo sat on his bed, watching Neddy take off his clothes and sandals. There was searching anticipation in the look. When Neddy climbed into bed, Mungo dropped his pants on the ground and threw his shirt on top of it. Their builds were similar, and Neddy, the unwelcome guest, realized Mungo would have been tough to beat in a tumble.

"Mi don't like sleep wid light on in di room," Mungo said, and walked over to blow out the lantern on the stool.

Apart from a small square of the night sky through the little window, the room was pitch black. Neddy's eyes fought to accustom themselves to the strange blackness in the uneasy room. Finally the far walls resolved out of the general gloom; then came a sound from the cabin floor, as if ghostly feet walked over it. Neddy shivered under the cover and recalled that dry old timber expanded at night. Damp invaded the cracks and crevices, extracting the heat of the day and swelling the wood. He gave up listening to the groan of the ancient planks. Sleep was more important. A rat scurried across the overhead rafters as he began to drift.

"You have gal yet?" Mungo's voice came from the dark corner of the room.

"Hu," grunted the half-awake Neddy.

Taking that for the affirmative, excitement rising in his voice with each syllable, Mungo questioned more: "Where you lick er, in a bush?"

"Aahu," Neddy said, hoping that would shut him up, but it only set Mungo to probing further.

"She tek it good, or she groan when di hood stick er?"

This time he got no answer. Silence fell between them. Steady breathing from Neddy's corner should have told Mungo that sleep was taking hold, and his questions would have to wait. But that didn't stop him.

"You want us do a little ting togeder?" Mungo's question jarred into Neddy's half-sleep. He opened his eyes again and tried for a second time to focus on his whereabouts. The window seemed brighter this time as starlight came through. He could see its frame clearly.

"You wan do it?" Mungo's voice trembled with urgency.

Neddy looked to the pitch-black corner of the cabin from whence the question came. Although he suspected, he wasn't sure what Mungo wanted. Whatever it was, he wasn't having any of it.

"Do what?" he said, wishing the other would shut up and let him sleep.

"You know," Mungo said. "Some ting? Any ting you want."

"Not wid you!" Neddy's answer came carelessly; he could have bitten his tongue as it shot out, and instantly it drew an angry reaction from across the room.

"Some ting wrong wid mi?" Mungo said, his voice aggressive now through the darkness. His cot made sounds as if he were about to get out of it.

"No, mi like you, but mi too tired and have to get up early," Neddy said. Making sure to pacify his roommate even further, he added, "A next time we can do any ting you wants."

"One night den?" the voice in the darkness growled. Neddy heard the side of the cot hit the wall as Mungo threw himself back on it in frustration.

"Yes," Neddy said. "It will be nice," he added to still Mungo further.

Nothing more was said between them, and the silence allowed Neddy to drift into the dream web of restless sleep.

He found himself in a place he did not know; the steady sound of a belly-drum, *dum, dum, dum, dum,* came to him. Thick mist swirled about a mountain peak, and the sound pulled him deeper: He strained to look into gaps as the clouds thinned and thickened, touching and leaving behind dampness as they moved. Far below on the mountainside, Mungo struggled toward him; he appeared and disappeared with kaleidoscopic symmetry as the vapors swirled open, only to close again. His eyes, now blue, became black, then blue, then black again; they bulged with hope in his naked struggle, sweating, clawing upward over bush and rocks, climbing, climbing, always climbing, his breathing heavy and labored. As the air grew thinner close to the top, each intake became short, sharp gulps. Exhausted, he flopped upon the ground at Neddy's feet and reached out, but he was still far, far away, beyond touch. Then Mungo faded to become Watt, and Neddy reached out into nothingness.

It seemed only a minute had passed when a rough hand shook him awake. Badalia held her lamp high and looked at his nakedness, grinning broadly.

"You be your father's son, all right. Im was good. Big an strong like you." Her grin dissolved into a kindly smile on noting his embarrassment as he quickly pulled the flour-bag covers up to his waist. Placing a finger in front of her lips, she indicated not to wake Mungo who lay on his belly on the next cot. His naked leg was drawn up as if in mid-stride. One arm lolled over the side, and the other stretched up to the head of the cot. In that posture he could have been swimming, running, or climbing.

Badalia looked down at him and grunted disapprovingly, "Even when im sleep, im all twis up." Turning to Neddy, she ordered, "Get up and dress yourself, and don't keep di busha waiting. Im trust an like you, so dat's why you go wid him. Now move, boye" She turned to leave as she reminded him, "You come and eat di food you lef from las night. It warm up for you. An I mek some bread an salt pork for you to carry wid you."

"Tank you, Mam," he answered politely, while pulling on his britches, now that her back was to him. "Miss Badalia," he added, as she was going down the two steps into the yard from the cabin, "is dere anywhere mi can wash mi face?"

Turning back and holding the lantern high to look at him again, standing there now half-dressed, Badalia said approvingly, "Lard Massa! Quashiba teach you good. Come, boye, mek mi show you where you can wash behind your ears."

Neddy followed her to the kitchen. Without his shirt on, the early morning damp touched his shoulders and made him shudder. He nearly put it on but decided to resist the temptation until he had washed his face and his armpits. It was going to be cold, and already his teeth clenched at the thought.

He need not have worried. Badalia would do for him what his mother would not have. She went into her little kitchen and brought out an enamel basin and put it down on the steps. "You can reach down de?" she asked.

"Yes, tank you, Miss Badalia." Neddy looked into the basin and wondered where the water was. Badalia returned with a kettle full of hot water in one hand and a bowl of cold water in the other.

"Mix dese together till you can wash," she commanded, handing him the kettle and the bowl. When he had taken them from her, his hands full, she looked into his eyes and smiled, "You did tink mi was going let anyone as pretty as you wash in cold water at dis time o marning?" Her familiar cackle followed while embarrassment swept his face once again. This time he was unable to cover up or turn away.

Bird Bush

Satisfied with her teasing, Badalia left him to mix the cold and hot water to his liking and went back into the kitchen to get the leftovers ready for breakfast.

Just as Neddy finished his breakfast, John entered the little kitchen. "Di massa wait pon you," he said. Downing the last of his coffee, Neddy immediately got up to follow John outside, but Badalia called him back.

"You tek dis wid you." She handed him a bundle, which he knew to be the food. "You a go to a strange place, you never know when dem going feed you next." She turned back into the kitchen before he could thank her properly.

"Come na," John insisted, and Neddy followed the stable hand to where Galloway, booted and dressed fashionably, stood waiting beside a big gray horse. His usual riding mule was there, too, along with a donkey that carried the baggage in hampers. Neddy could see the gun cases stowed in one hamper and a leather case in the other. Usually, slaves carried these things on their heads when their masters went abroad. Many a cavalcade Neddy had watched go by with the massa and mistress up front in a carriage, or mounted, and a dozen or more slaves with bundles and boxes on their heads, walking behind. If they were too young to ride ponies or donkeys, even the children of the massa and mistress were carried on the slaves' shoulders.

As he got to the mounting steps, Neddy wondered what others would say when they saw him riding a mule alongside a massa. If he were a big man, that could be all right. But a "boye" should walk behind, like Mungo did with the young massa.

When Galloway saw him, he said, "Brought your flute, Neddy?"

"Yes, sah." He indicated the instrument stuck in his belt. "Never go anywhere wid out it. Dat way mi can practice when mi get a chance, as you tell mi fi do, sah."

"I did?" Galloway said, surprised. "When did I do that?"

"Yes, sah. 'Play it for life,' you did tell mi on di road Sunday morning."

Galloway laughed outright when he heard that. "I must watch what I say to you, young man. Come, mount up. We have a ways to go and have to be in the stand before the first dove flies by this morning."

John held the mule's head while Neddy climbed aboard. "You can ride, boye?" he asked, casting a suspicious look at Neddy as he swung his leg across the mule's back. All John heard in response was a vulgar sucking of teeth, just loud enough for his ears only, as the boy settled in the saddle.

"You tink you is the only one who can ride? Course mi can ride, man." Neddy said. The stable man shrugged his shoulders and shook his head at the bravado of youth. He had heard it all before.

"Dem young ones know every ting, na sah," John said in the busha's direction.

Smiling, Galloway mounted the big gray and gave a, "Yoicks! And away!" as if on a fox hunt. Gently spurring the side of the horse, he set the pace toward the gates.

As they rode, a cold half-moon lit their way. Early morning damp seeped through Neddy's shirt, making him shudder, and he wished he had worn something heavy.

As if sensing his young companion's discomfort, Galloway looked back and said, "Chilly, are you?"

"A little cold ketch mi, sah."

"Surprising how cold it gets at night in Jamaica at this time of the year. Thinking about it, winter is in the north." He eyed the sky overhead. "Part of its chill must creep south, if only to get warm itself." Then he chuckled at his own twist of thought. Half turning in his saddle, Galloway reached behind with his left hand and began struggling with the straps holding the extra horse blanket he always carried on long trips. He got it free from the saddle and held it out to Neddy.

"Ride up here, youth. Take this and put it round you. It will keep you warm. The horse smell is a good healthy smell, much better than human."

Neddy urged the mule up so he could reach for the blanket. "Thank you, sah. The smell will not trouble me, sah."

When the blanket was wrapped around his shoulders, they set out again toward the gate. As he looked up at the sky, the stars did not seem so cold now to Neddy. Their blinking, flashing light had lost their icy aspect of only a few minutes before. They became friendlier as his body heat built up under the heavy blanket around his shoulders.

He looked again at the half-moon illuminating the countryside and watched wispy clouds hasten across its thin face, changing shape as they did; in the mystic light, they made him think of duppies appearing and disappearing. Despite the blanket's warmth, his back skin shivered at the thought. He glanced nervously behind as cloud shadows flitted across the moonlit field. He turned back quickly to make sure Galloway still rode in front of him. Reassured by the sight of the horseman, he was yet embarrassed at his own fright. Luckily, no one but he could see it. Eventually, they reached the property gates, which stood open to the road.

"Damn it to hell!" Galloway said. "I should flay the man alive who left these open."

Without waiting to be asked, Neddy jumped down from his mule to close the gates after they went through.

"Closing the barn door after the animals are gone, that's not going to help much. It will only keep the animals out. Leave it open, Neddy. They may wander back." The riding crop struck his boot in annoyance. "Half mi animals will be all over the place." He waved the crop around toward the hills. "Come, boy, that will have to wait until we get back."

Only the clattering of horse, mule, and donkey hooves on the gravel road disturbed the countryside as they moved on, up toward Lapland. From somewhere in the hills, the bark of a dog drifted to them, adding its voice to the sound of their movement. Although it was just past three in the morning, they had quite a few miles to go, and Galloway urged his mount into a gentle trot. Neddy's mule did its awkward best to follow, and he found himself holding tightly to the pommel of the saddle for safety sake. Bouncing up and down with the odd sway to the side confirmed for him that mules were not designed by God for trotting. That is, if God designed them in the first place. Many said the devil, most likely, did the work of creating them and even then got it all wrong.

Good mules moved comfortably at a walk, strong and sure-footed was their stock in trade, but speed was beyond them. They were not built like their horse fathers or mothers for any kind fast movement. An awkward jog was all they could manage, and their riders' bottoms and legs suffered the consequences at the end of the journey. Silently Neddy wished Galloway would slow down.

His discomfort was added to by the slowness of the donkey he led. It struggled to keep up, and it began to bray as the hampers it carried bounced around, slapping its sides with a confused urging. Its distress brought Galloway to a stop. He looked behind and saw the predicament he had caused by increasing their speed. The mule and donkey passed his stationary horse as Neddy tried to bring them under control. Knowing better than to interfere, Galloway watched as Neddy's struggles paid off when he was able to bring them down to a comfortable pace.

"Sorry," Galloway said. "For some reason I forgot you were leading that damned donkey. I must have been thinking about that open gate, which put the fact right out of mi mind."

"It all right, sah. They steady down now," Neddy said.

"You did that well, Neddy. Now let us move on at a slower pace. It won't matter if we get there after the first flights have passed. We can make up for them on the evening shoot, if they have one."

From then on they moved at a slower pace. They walked and sometimes half-trotted; and when he thought Neddy had had enough struggling with his mule and the donkey, Galloway slowed them back to a walk. In good time they passed by the Hampton court, Roxboro, and Brothers Union estates. Not until they got to Mount Apfel did any light show in the windows of the buildings. As lamps flickered in a window of the Great House of Mount Apfel, Neddy commented, "Miss Rachel or Mass Edward mus be up."

"You know them, Neddy?" Galloway said without looking behind him at the boy.

"Mi fader and modder know dem, sah," he said. "Miss Rachel and mi modder brought up togeder on Kensington."

Galloway said nothing for a moment. "Mass Edward is Mr. William Vernon, of Mount Vernon, son?"

"Yes, sah," Neddy said. "I see him over at Mount Vernon a directing tings, when mi go cross them lands."

"But I thought his name was William?"

"That's right, sah. I hear mi modder talking one day bout them, and she say his name is William Edward Vernon. But they call him Mass Edward so not to mix him up wid his fader. It don't matter now, for him is buried on Mount Vernon wid all the Vernons. Still, we call him son Mass Edward, like some do mi fader." Neddy felt proud to mention the respect people accorded his father.

They went on a bit further before Galloway asked, "You cross the plantation often, Neddy?"

"No too much, sah. Only when I go up to di Great River to fish. It a shortcut."

"You fish, Neddy? What a surprise! What for?"

"Mullet, sah, and crawfish, sah."

"What do you do with them?"

"Cook them same time, or tek dem home for mi modder, sah."

"Lord! How wonderful it is to be a boy," Galloway said, in a faraway voice, more to himself than his companion. They then rode on in silence until Galloway again spoke. "When I was a boy at home in Ireland, fishing was my favorite pastime. Our cook did them for me."

The fingers of dawn were just reaching to pull back night's shade, when they arrived at Jericho Pen. They could see from the road that much stirred there. Lamps glowed in the windows of all quarters. Voices barking orders drifted across the fields to them on the road. A conch blew, signaling the start of the workday. They could hear others on distant plantations doing the same. The slaves' day had begun with the rule of the conchi.

Had they been near enough, they would have heard the field hands curse the sound of the seashell. Then the commands issued by the overseers and bookkeepers who, like their charges, were none too happy being dragged from their beds at morning's light by that mournful sound.

As they rode by the pen's entrance gates, they heard again the deep boom of a conch vibrate loud enough to wake the dead. On cue, Galloway said, "So the Hebrews marched around Jericho, and Joshua blew the trumpet, and the walls came tumbling down."

His words were directed to no one in particular, but Neddy and the fading stars in the heavens above heard them. The biblical reference surprised Neddy, and yet it did not. The overseer was full of contradictions, the boy was discovering.

Neddy had heard the reverend refer to the fall of Jericho more than once, especially when he condemned the practice of slavery. Neddy paid it no mind until Galloway made bold with it that morning, when it struck him that it might be a telling of things to come.

On they went up to Lapland. The sun's appearance was imminent. Lapland, not that far from Jericho, could be seen perched on top of the hill overlooking the Great River, a mile or two along the road.

Galloway hoped they might yet make the early shoot. It had been a long time since he had been in the company of gentlemen, and he looked forward to the gathering. Polite society was rare in the high hills of St. James. It only happened when men like James Graham-Clark came out from England to inspect their estates. Clarke was a Galloway intimate. Their fathers had served in the same regiment, and thus had they met and been friends from a young age, although James was a few years Galloway's senior.

They had begun their climb up to Lapland and turned the corner from where the silhouette of the Great House could be seen on its hill against the morning sky. As if by witching, two black figures emerged from the ditch by the side of the road.

"Massa!" called one.

Galloway started at the unexpected appearance and greeting. Instinctively he reached for the pistol in his saddle holster. Many a traveler at this time of the morning on a lonely road in Jamaica heard such a greeting for the last time on this earth.

"Massa, Captain Galloway," called the other. "It all right, sah!"

Galloway pulled up his animal, and Neddy, behind him, did the same. The donkey he led naturally carried on, as if he only stopped when it suited it. Neddy hauled hard on the rope, and then the beast came to a grudging halt.

Bird Bush

The larger of the two figures approached them, his smaller companion following close behind. "Massa James sen us to you, sah. Im sure you is going be late for di shooting so we was to bring you up to di stan dey ave for you."

"That is nice of him, but we are not dressed for the bush. We had hoped to change before going in. I certainly don't want to have my clothes clawed off my back by macka and my boots cut to ribbons on honeycomb rocks."

"Lard a mussy, sah!" cried the smaller of the two. Throwing his arms wide, as if embracing the countryside, his laughter rang with honest humor. "Up ya so we don't hab honey rock, and di macka don't grow ere. Dat is for down below." He waved offhandedly in the direction from which they had come. "You will be all right, sa." He nodded knowingly. "Lapland is God's Kingdom."

"It is, is it?" Galloway said, looking hard at the two for a good long minute. If James Graham-Clarke sent them to guide him to the stands, then all would be well. Like his father, James flew straight as an arrow, and his servants would be the same. "Where do we go, then?"

"Follow us, Massa," said the larger of the two. "We got to go up dere." He pointed to a hill east of Lapland Great House. "Di bal-pate and di ringtail a come down ticker dan flies. You can lick di buds good from dere as dem fly over di hill come trough di gully, Massa." Pointing to the crest of the hill in front of them, his finger traced the flight path down to an unseen gully. "Billy will pick dem up as mi mark dem for you, and you lick dem wid di gun shot, sah. We very good at dat. Massa James train us imself," he said with pride.

Galloway cocked his left eyebrow at that. James only came out to view his holdings in the island about once every three years. Very doubtful he even knew this slave. Still, let them lie, for that was part of their nature, and they thought it sat well with Backra Massa.

"Shall we walk and lead the animals?" he asked, looking at the hillside.

"Lard! No, sah! You can ride all di way up. White man don walk on Lapland lan. Dat is only for black folks an naygar-man," said the shorter of the two, with his merry laugh of assurance.

"Lead on, then," Galloway said. "Let us have our shoot." They turned left and headed up a steep slope and then down a gully.

No longer fresh, the animals struggled, but they made good progress against the pitch of the landscape. Up again they went, through some newly planted hillside fields of cane. It was new land they had broken for cane growing. Pulling up for a moment, Galloway leaned over the horse's neck to inspect the shoots. It was the Frenchman's cane, the same type he was experimenting with on Newman Hall. Come crop time he would have to ask the Lapland overseer how it went. A smile crossed his lips as they rode on through the stalks when he remembered that he would be gone from the island just after this growth would be reaped and crushed. What it produced in the way of juice would be of little interest in the far north.

At the crest of the hill, the cane stopped. It was bush down the other side. If the new cane was successful, perhaps they would plant there in another year. That was how new cane lands were brought into production, if the overseer knew his business. Ratoons of first planting would be sprouting, freeing the slaves to break new ground. Good military planning was all it took to run a successful estate, thought Galloway. The only problem: unwilling soldiers to carry out the orders. You could not make slaves into willing soldiers. To the Irishman, the idea was humorous when he thought of the long history of England and Ireland.

His horse was struggling with the hillside, and he had to ride with care and long-learned skill. Every now and then, they would hit a patch of shale, and the horse would skid, almost going down on its haunches. Galloway had to hold its head up. Then the horse would brace itself. Occasionally he turned the horse back up the hill, like a sailing ship tacking against the wind; its hooves dug in and the powerful animal steadied, before heading down again. Neddy, coming behind him, had no such problem descending on the sure-footed mule, followed by the donkey. All he did was sit in the saddle and hang onto its pummel with his feet sticking forward in the rope stirrups.

They found themselves following a track into a heavy forest of cotton trees intermingled with guango, cedar, and mahogany. It was like walking unnoticed at the feet of giants on parade. The tree canopy blocked the early dawn, and they were pitched back into night. Galloway thought it best they dismount and lead the animals.

If they wanted to shoot at the first baldpate winging its way to breakfast, then stopping and waiting for light was not possible. Both man and boy followed the dim outlines picking their way along the path in front of them cautiously. Their guides knew the way and hurried along to catch the first flights they knew to be already on the wing higher up along the border of St. James and St. Elizabeth.

They broke through finally and came out on top of a hill. It had been a longer, steeper climb than they realized in that gloom. Man, boy, and animals were breathing hard, not only from the climb but also from the unaccustomed thin air. The altitude forced them to gulp oxygen by the mouthful as their lungs adjusted; white vapor issued from their nostrils as the reheated air mingled with the chill on the hillside. Only the two guides seemed unaffected. As normality returned, they could see the lights of Lapland far to the right and the clear outline of the buildings against the early touch of the morning sky.

"You want to stand ere or go up further, Massa Galloway?" As they used his name regularly, it seemed they confirmed he was their shooter-man and truly belonged to Lapland. The taller of the two pointed to another hill over the gully below the crest where they had stopped. Weary of the ride and thankful for a respite, Galloway, who had had not much sleep the night before, called a halt.

"This will do," he said. "Let them fly whichever way they choose." For a sporting man, he sounded disinterested at that moment. They tied up the animals, and Galloway loosened the girths of the saddles and hamper and took them off so that they could rest easier after so hard a march.

"Neddy, sorry about it, boy, but Challenger wants his blanket back. Don't worry, the sun will be on your back warming your blood soon." Galloway indicated where the sun would rise.

Surrendering the blanket with a smile, Neddy watched Galloway rub the horse down with it before throwing it across its back when he was done. There was no such luxury for the old mule or donkey.

Noticing the boy watching him closely, Galloway advised, "Always look after the animals that carry you through life, Neddy. Horse are especially delicate creatures. They will die for you, not like those two over there." He pointed to the donkey and mule. "Don't know why, but greys don't do well in this island. Too white, I suspect."

With the horse cared for, he took the cases that held his guns from the hamper and assembled and loaded the firearms. Neddy was fascinated by the care with which his mentor worked, as Galloway explained each step of the process.

"You see these little bags of shot I made up last night?" He tossed one at Neddy, who caught it expertly. "As I told you, mi own invention. Now, watch. First you load with powder, then you ram one of these little bags down the muzzle. You are putting shot and wad in at the same time." He looked at Neddy's puzzled expression and chuckled.

"I go too fast, eh, boy? Well, let me back up." He paused and held the gun and ramrod to demonstrate as he went along. "Normally you put in the powder, as I have done. Then you ram home a wad." He held one out to show Neddy. "Then you would put the shot in and again another wad. That is the normal way." He looked at the boy to make sure he had taken his lesson in. "My invention cuts all that out, and I ram home shot and wad in one stroke." A proud grin crossed his face. "Not only that, boy, but the little bag will hold the shot together for longer and I can shoot further out. Watch, you will see. They all wonder at it. Now you and you only know my secret." Neddy could see from his face that Galloway was enjoying himself. "We have not finished yet," he went on. Holding the gun up and half-cocking the hammer, he demonstrated the priming. "Here we put the cap in that will give the powder the spark, setting it off when I pull the trigger. All is clear now, see?" he said.

Lesson over. At last Neddy was handed one of the long guns to hold. With great care Neddy rested it against his shoulder like a soldier on guard. Soon the weight began to bear down on his collarbone, and he was forced to move it to the other shoulder. His excitement mounted as they waited for the first birds to fly within range.

"Mark in front!" The small guide excitedly pointed to a bird gliding toward their stand.

Bird Bush

"I see him," Galloway said, watching carefully as the bird came in range. Neddy could just see the white of the baldpate's head as it streaked across the brightening morning sky, going from roost to feeding grounds. It passed within range. Galloway's gun went to his shoulder, becoming part of him, and his whole body swung with the bird's flight. There was a loud report, the bird stopped in midair, shattered by pellets, folded, and crashed to the ground, dead. No sooner was it down than Galloway swung to his left, the left barrel went off, and a bigger bird balled and thudded to earth. "That one is a ringtail," he said, with some satisfaction.

Shrieking with joy, the guides raced in different directions down the hill to retrieve the birds. They were pleased with themselves, for they had guided a real shooter-man, not one of those who fired and missed, then cussed his bird-boys for not finding the birds he claimed to have downed.

As he reloaded, two quick shots rang out on a hill across from them as a double-barrel gun fired. Then another report from somewhere else. Quite suddenly, they seemed to be in a battlefield, as if trapped in an ambush. From behind, from their front, to the left and then the right, guns all about fired as birds came thick and fast. Flight after flight crossed the morning sky, not waiting around for those ones and twos of their number peeled off by the guns below them.

Big ringtails from way up in the hills flew high, and it took a first-class shot to bag them; speedy baldpates flashed by, and then great flocks of whitewing and pea doves that required no great skill to bring down. Rarely did Galloway miss. Neddy had no idea that anyone could be such a skillful shot. He counted only three misses all that morning. The shooter-man, as the guides kept calling him, made it all look so easy:

Up swung his double-barrel gun, tracking the bird; a flash at the muzzle, a *tha-rack* jarred the ears, and when the gun smoke cleared, a bird hung suspended in thin air for a breathless moment—shot-shattered, wings mangled, single feathers floating, the creature balled and spiraled down to thud upon the earth. The nearest bird boy retrieved the kill, expertly plucked its feathers, gouged out its innards with a finger, and hung it by the neck on a stringer.

Galloway would fire and reload when he could, or fire and take the gun Neddy held for him in exchange for the empty one. When both were empty, Galloway would reload them. This slowed his shooting. When one of the guides offered to reload for him, Galloway declined. Had Neddy been trained, he would have been reloading the empty gun while Galloway used the loaded one, so at no time he would be without a gun to fire. But it was Neddy's first time in the field. Galloway observed the excitement on Neddy's faced and promised to teach him reloading when they had more time.

During a lull, Galloway asked him, "Do you eat birds?"

"Yes, sah!" he exploded, beaming as if to say, doesn't everyone? He nearly licked his lips at the prospect. "Mi mam stews them down wid pimento leaves and bay leaves. Lard! They good, you see, sah!"

"I must try that. Badalia should know how to cook them with all those spices."

"Nu mus, if she barn here, sah," Neddy said more sedately.

"How do you get the birds?"

"We set trap, and lime the tree branch, sah."

"Lime the tree branch, Neddy?" Galloway's eyebrows came together in a puzzled manner.

"Yes, sah. You know the lime which mek them foot stick pon the tree branch? Once it stick, dey can't fly away. We grab them an twist di neck." He looked pleased after his explanation. It was his turn to enlighten the busha.

The sun had crawled halfway up the sky; morning had arrived at its midway mark. The birds had gone, but a few stragglers flew by. No one bothered firing at them. Ceasefire had been called, the war was over, and nature's sounds returned to dominate the hills and gullies. The boys had gathered more than a hundred birds shot by Galloway. The ground attested to the carnage; feathers and guts were thrown everywhere as the boys plucked and drew what they picked up. Galloway did not like the look of the mess but said nothing. They had done a good job picking up the downed birds; their diligence made sure very few had been missed and gone to waste, and he noticed that they had sensibly brought sacks to carry the bag of the day.

"Time to go," Galloway called out, ending his morning shoot. He unloaded his gun and checked the one Neddy held, to see that it was safe to disassemble and recase. When all was packed up, the horse and mule resaddled and the donkey rehampered, they began the return to the road.

This time Galloway made them walk, leading their animals for the first half over the hill with the shale patches. It was lucky he did, for they struggled, sliding backward on many occasions. He shook his head to think he had ridden down this in semidarkness. There had been no warning of the dangers from the guides. He could not fault them when all was considered. They were made ignoramuses by the nature of where they lived, and to them this was nothing for a white man and a horse to cross.

They walked among the giant trees again. The sun, powerful enough now, forced its way through their canopy to allow a little light to filter on the young shoots beginning to grow between their thick roots. They rode now out of the grove, up and through the Frenchy's cane. Looking at it in daylight, Galloway couldn't help wondering how Jamaican planters had managed to steal the plants and smuggle them out of Guadalupe and Martinique originally. He shrugged, for it was the pattern of the English to steal from their rivals' colonies any plant that gave them an advantage and take it to British holdings for replanting and distribution throughout the empire. Barbadians had stolen the first cane from Brazil and begun the whole plantation process in the islands a hundred or more years before. The Dutch East Indies had been raided for spice trees. Peru had the Cinchona tree filched from it for the curative bark that held malaria in check. There was no end to the perfidious tale.

The road finally came up, and they headed toward Lapland. On the far side of the valley, they could see the estate. It was a gentle ride; the road was well maintained as it wound its way around the mountainside, always going upward. They would arrive in time for the second breakfast; Neddy's stomach growled in anticipation. Long ago he had finished Badalia's leftovers. Silently he wished for wings to fly across the valley. A passing cramp made him think of Watt's perpetual hunger, which brought a snigger and eased the discomfort.

Chapter 9

The Shooting Party

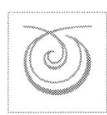

On they rode. Neddy relaxed in his saddle, letting the mule have its head. Galloway, in front, sat his mount with the ease of an accustomed horseman and soldier who wanted to conserve his energy for unexpected action. He moved along the road at a regular pace to allow the donkey and those who followed to keep up comfortably.

Standing tall on the highland, dark green, almost black, rainforests grew. Even at this time of the day, wet clouds swabbed the highest tops, clinging to the giant tree trunks and leaving only their crowns exposed to the sunlight. Down the hillsides, the thick growth of trees, vines, and tropical tangles gave way to patches of mountain pasture held in place by sheer walls of rock. Below them on lower hills eroded by wind, water, and the shaking of the earth, lighter green shoots of growing sugarcane took over and ran all the way down to the banks of the Great River, flowing in the valley on their right.

Looking down from the road rising to Lapland house, they could see the rushing water of the Great River like a rope carelessly thrown into a crevice of the earth, traveling along its twisted way. On Lapland, as with other estates on its course, the river had work to do. In the valley the sugar works, hospital, and slave quarters hard by its banks depended on it. The Great River did its duty on this plantation by supplying water for living things and turning millwheels crushing cane. And because of its largess and human direction, it was obvious that this estate was one of abundance.

From its spring the river ran inches by inch, feet by foot, yards by yard, miles by mile, down to sea level. Had it cut straight from the heights around Lapland to its eventual disappearance into the blue Caribbean, the Great River would have gone half that distance. But now it did what great rivers do—it carved its own way through the land before rejoining the watery universe from which all emerged.

Had there been sensibility in its waters, it would have conjured Britain to mind in its course and wondered at the incongruity of it all through a land where most who travailed on its banks were out of Africa. Yet, it too could have started there, for, like the Nile in Scipio's dream, over Catadupa the Great River cascaded. But then, a change in geography and time, and it was on to Cambridge, Chestercastle, and rushing down, across smoothed rocks alongside Forth's Shettlewood, and Montpelier estates, next it flowed rapidly past those named for Anchovy, Wiltshire, and Blairgowrie. Finally, on land, it settled to calmly meander by Unity Hall and on to the ocean, where all great rivers lost their discernibility to the senses of humans and beasts alike, its work for them done. No more waterwheels to turn or troughs to fill. Once again, it disappeared into the water womb.

With Galloway leading the way, followed by Neddy and then the two bird-boys who did the retrieving and cleaning of birds that morning, they passed through the monolithic pillars that braced the gate to Lapland. Along the newly pounded driveway of crushed stone the group rode and walked the two miles up to the house on the hill from the entrance gates. On their left they passed a small tarn bordered by flowering sedge.

A few cattle drank from it, and beyond them, on the gentle curve of the hillside, curly-horned Merino sheep pulled at the green tufts of mountain grass. Their lambs gamboled about, scattering small flocks of turkeys with their half-grown poults desperately trying to huddle around their mothers for protection. Off to the sides, five full-grown toms, their procreative duty at hand, marked off territory and strutted about, arrogantly displaying to the hens vestigial beards, reminders of their once-wild state, drooping from their chest. Occasionally they gobbled to the odd lowing of the cattle as they voiced contentment or irritability. The only other sounds were those of the hooves upon the gravel road as the procession went by.

Even at this late hour of the morning, with the sun almost at midday, it was cool and pleasant up here in the hills of St. James. A light breeze fluffed off the humidity of the flats, and breathing in the air filled the chest with the feeling of good health.

As they got closer, Galloway could see that the massive pile of Lapland Great House would have more suited a Scottish crag than a mountainside in Jamaica. But there it stood, imposing its dominance on all who saw it from far and near. Its cut-stone facade was unimpressive in its plainness, its one redeeming feature the large fan-shaped stone steps leading up to the thick wooden double doors that guarded the entrance like a castle gate. And like a castle gate, there was a smaller door, hinged within the left-facing door for everyday use when the main door remained closed against intruders. All that seemed to be missing was a portcullis. A careful examination of the entrance would have revealed there was place for it in the stonework, but it had not been installed. Whoever built the house was obviously a man of caution, interested in preservation for the generation to follow. The pile was intended to house and protect.

Today the main doors stood agape for the easy flow of all the shooting party guests and their attendants. They came and went from the lawns, into and out of the great hall on the ground floor, where food and drink in all its Jamaican abundance graced the sideboards and tables.

Lapland's liveried servants stood by to prepare plates for the guests; when ready, personal servants of the guests ported the loaded platters to their masters and mistresses gathered on the lawn under shelter of poinciana trees in full red bloom. To and fro across the close-cropped grass they went in answer to the petulant wants of their owners. Their fragility went unnoticed, as they balanced trays with cups, glasses, and plates, walking as if on tightropes in unaccustomed shoes. Even in the cool mountain air, some sweated with the effort, dreading the retribution that would descend should they falter and come crashing down in an unseemly display.

Under one tree gentlemen gathered; beneath another matriarchs; while still a third sheltered single ladies looking for husbands among those few males of their class who were as yet unmarried, dangling about them, thinking them beautiful and complimenting them on their whiteness.

In between these groups, children ran, playing tag in and around their elders, sometimes grasping the coattails of the gentlemen or the billowing skirts and sashes of the ladies, shrieking with laughter as they fled pursuers or ducked away from the swiping hands of their elders. Such was the liberty allowed the young of the island's masters.

Their nursemaids stood by, watching, waiting to rush forward, rescue, and coddle their charges when they fell and scraped a knee or ripped a dress. An abundance of hugs and kisses were showered on little faces, arms, legs, and rent garments; wherever and whatever was deemed necessary to kiss was kissed and fussed over in order to hush the child's inevitable bawling. Each howl, whether accompanied by eye water or not, gathered in the cherished warmth and security demanded by the little massa or miss.

Their mothers gave them not a second glance, their fathers not the first; their nursemaids were bought and paid to do that. So black proxy mothers catered to the meager minds of these children, giving in to all they demanded. When parents tired of them and censured their antics, the great sobbing that came with that rejection elicited from these black women even more love and adoration, the sort that could only be bestowed on the demigods and goddesses of folklore. It was the nature of things for the Creole child; and with these hugs and kisses came the black way to mix with the white way.

For every child there was at least one nurse and sometimes two, and then even they had their little slave boy helper, making three to watch and care for the little lordling. For each gentleman or lady at Lapland that day, there were at least another three servants waiting on their individual needs. One would be sent here, another there, and a third on secret missions with notes to solicit assignations—a pastime that would have better suited night hours rather than the glare of day. Into this conglomerate rode Galloway and escort.

As they approached, an elegantly dressed man in a blue tailcoat with a black collar and puffed shoulders called out, "Matthew, Matthew, Matthew!" He detached himself from a group under the poinciana tree with a nod and hurried across the lawn to greet Galloway. Behind him loped two huge black mastiffs.

His hails and moving figure made Galloway pull up and jump from his saddle. Neddy pulled up, too, but sat very still on his mule, as he watched the black dogs bounding alongside their master. Galloway handed him his reins to hold and went forward to meet the gentleman who hailed him.

"Matthew! So good to see you, Matthew!" the man cried enthusiastically again, almost out of breath as he arrived in front of Galloway. At close quarters they were about the same height, but the gentleman was easily Galloway's senior by ten years.

"Hello, James," Galloway said, as if he had seen him only yesterday. Steadying himself, taking a deep breath, the gentleman gave Galloway a quizzical look, and then they both began laughing like schoolboys. Their right hands came together in warm greeting with their left hands grasping at the other's right shoulder for assurance that each was truly there.

As they stood shaking hands, a young man who had been watching Galloway's arrival from across the lawn greeted them cautiously. His attire indicated that he had just come in from the bush and had yet to change. His right cheek was still soiled with burned powder and showed a half-hearted effort to wipe it off. Darker smudges on his fawn cravat and collar gave him the rakish look assiduously sought after by the young. He had all the petulance and certainty of youth about him.

"Ah! Sam, come here. Let me introduce you to a true friend." James Graham-Clarke beckoned the young man to come closer.

"My nephew, Sam Barrett. Samuel Moulton-Barrett, to give him his proper form. Sam, this gentleman is Captain Matthew Galloway, my oldest friend."

243

"A pleasure, sir." The young man held out his hand. "Uncle James has mentioned you to me more than once as someone to turn to for advice."

"He has, has he? Well I don't know that that there's much advice I can give you. Just arrived in the island, I take it?" Galloway said as they shook hands. He had looked him up and down and recognized that all about this young man smacked of England's finest tailors and bootmakers.

"How can you tell that, sir?"

"Your fashionable cut and lack of the browning given by the sun to all who reside here for any length of time. Your uncle is never here long enough to be so blessed by sol. The moment the golden orb reaches its zenith, he returns to the more temperate clime of England to preserve the lily whiteness of flesh and soul, which is his due."

"Not so!" Graham-Clark said with a laugh. "I stay as long as business at home allows. Can I help it if that is too short a time to get acclimatized to the island?"

"My God, sir!" the young man said with by an honest look of admiration, "You should set that to verse. If you don't mind, Captain, I'll mark it down and pass it over to one who pens such stuff in my family?"

"That is his sister Elizabeth, Matt. I sent you her little book over a year ago. Her first publication it was. Did you read it?" There was an urgency in the asking. and the smile that accompanied the question was a question itself. "As a literary man, what did you think? Be frank."

"How could I not have read your niece's work, James?" answered Galloway.

"Well?" Both uncle and nephew leaned forward awaiting his verdict.

"From what I remember of *An Essay on Mind and Other Poems…*" Galloway began cautiously. "That is the title of the work, isn't it?"

"Yes, that's it, Captain," young Sam said. "I hope you gave it a good review, so that I can tell her. It will encourage her much. She is sickly, you know. Can't get about, so she scribbles."

"No, I did not know—having never met the young lady. But I must say, it was an excellent first effort. You could see Pope's influence in it. She could not have chosen a better model for her work."

"*Pope?*" Graham-Clarke said. "You don't mean…"

"Not the pontiff! Capital *P*, James. Alexander Pope, the poet. *The Rape of the Lock*. Surely you know it?" Galloway looked across at the poinciana tree where the coquetting and gallanting was being played out and recited:

Say what strange Motive, Goddess! Cou'd compel
A well-bred Lord t'assault a gentle Belle?
Oh say what strange cause, yet unexplor'd
Cou'd make a gentle Belle reject a Lord?

Looking a bit uneasy, Sam said, "Don't think she does that, sir,"

"No, no," Galloway said. "That is perhaps Pope's most famous work, but he wrote on many aspects, especially as a Catholic caught in a Protestant world."

"You could always pull quotes from thin air to suit the moment, Matthew. How the dickens do you do that? Damned if I could—but ain't Pope dead?" Graham-Clarke said.

"You should read more, James; then you could impress us all with your literary prowess."

"Haven't got time for that, Matt. You know that. Back to Elizabeth, you didn't say—ain't Pope dead?"

"As a doornail, James. But she must have studied his works. His influence over her writing rings through clearly. That is why her effort is so good."

Uncle and nephew seemed satisfied with that praise. Obviously Galloway knew what he was talking about, and, as they themselves were only conversant with the generalities given off in literary circles, they did not venture further on the topic.

"How long have you been in Jamaica, Sam—and, more to the point, how long do you intend to stay?"

"Only a few months, sir. I came to keep Uncle Sam company at Cinnamon Hill. You know my aunt, his wife, died suddenly six months ago. Papa thought as I am named for my uncle and was doing nothing in England, I should come out to keep him company," Sam said. "And learn the plantation business at the same time," he added.

Galloway nodded. "Oh, please convey my condolences to your uncle. Although we have never met, the loss of a wife is a tragic loss at any time."

James Graham-Clark gave his friend a knowing look.

"I will, sir; it was a blow to him, as it was to all of us. Thank you. My uncle Sam will appreciate that." They were about to move toward the other guests when Sam changed the subject with a question more in keeping with the day and the enthusiasm of youth.

"Dare I ask, Captain, how many did you bag this morning?" From his eagerness, it was obvious he was hoping to be top gun for the day.

"Sam!" Graham-Clark said. "Gentlemen never ask about another's bag!"

Galloway chuckled, not only at his friend's protest but at the red face of the boy.

"A hundred and fourteen and tree miss, sah." The answer came from Neddy, forgotten in the enthusiasm of the meeting of two old friends.

"Neddy!" exclaimed Galloway, remembering the boy. He turned and looked at him still sitting bolt upright in his saddle, ready to spur his mule into a gallop. "You counted them?" he asked with some surprise and a grin on his face.

"Yes, sah!" Neddy said.

Both Graham-Clark and Sam stared at Neddy, the former with an amused yet perplexed look.

"Good God! An educated slave. Matthew, have you been teaching your slaves to read and write? You know they don't like that in the island." His eyebrow quivered slightly as he went on with a grin, "Planters are so damned backward here."

"Not a slave, James," Galloway said. "I have hired Master Neddy Lawrence, flute player *extraordinaire*, to be my gun carrier for the day."

Pride, embarrassment, and something else that goes along with those two rushed through Neddy's senses. Fidgeting was out of the question, so he just sat where he was, holding the halters of the three animals, waiting for the next word or movement to break the tension caused by the discovery of an educated black boy. The horse stamped his right back hoof on the gravel and shifted his weight. Young Sam Barrett took that as his cue.

"By God, sir! That is incredible shooting! What guns do you use, sir?" With the question came an eager look. His expression made it clear that he thought shooting ability must be somehow magically built into the guns one used.

To satisfy his curiosity and assure him that his skill would improve with the best from a top gunmaker, Galloway said, "I have two Nocks that I had changed over from flint to caps by his son-in-law, James Wilkinson. Had 'em done just before I came out here."

Sam Barrett seemed pleased when he heard that. "Wonderful gun, sir; wish I had a pair. Papa didn't allow me to bring a fowling piece. I don't think he approves of hunting and shooting. Uncle Sam found one for me to use at Cinnamon Hill. It's an old flintlock and probably belonged to my grandfather. Did adequate though, got me a few."

His uncle James looked at him with a good-natured smile. "You are straining to tell us, Samuel. I can see it in your eyes. Tell us then, young Sam, what was your bag?"

"Forty-six, I think, sir."

"What! Not the half-century! With Matthew's guns I suppose you would have scored a century."

"This was shooting, James, not a cricket game," Galloway said, laughing.

"Oh dear! I suppose it is, Matt. I must get my games in the right order when having a go at the young." He gave his nephew a friendly pat on the shoulder. "Yes, I believe you would be right there, mi-boy, about your father, I mean. He is a bit of a stickler. He wouldn't approve of this at all." His hand motioned toward his guests.

"Come, Matthew, let us go and join the others." Graham-Clarke turned to the two slaves standing by and ordered them to take the animals around to the stables and see that they were rubbed down and fed. They took the halters from Neddy, who was still mounted and wondering what he should do when his employer came to his rescue.

"Neddy, you had better stick by me. Dismount, lad." His reluctance to do so made Galloway urge him, "Come on."

"Di black dogs, sah," said Neddy, nervously looking at the great beasts by their master's legs.

"They won't hurt you, boy," said Graham-Clarke, but to be on the safe side he ordered the two slaves to take the dogs along with them.

"Thank you, James. You now the terror people have of black dogs in this island?"

"Heard about it but never did understand that, Matthew, but it is a good deterrent to any would be miscreant."

"Something to do with the Maroon uprising, and the soldiers hunting them down with imported Spanish hounds. They were black savage curs, evidently. Two broke away from their handlers, the tale goes, and tore a woman to shreds before they could stop them. Ever since then, black dogs have been considered devil dogs. You must know how Jamaicans embellish folk tales, James."

They sauntered toward the group of men under the poinciana tree. "By the by, James," Galloway said. "Much to my regret, we will be leaving early today. I have to get back to Newman Hall tonight."

"Good God, man!" exploded his friend. "I haven't seen you for all these years, and here you are galloping away on me before we have even broken bread. Deuced selfish of you, Matthew. You realize I leave the island shortly?" There was genuine distress in Graham-Clarke's voice.

"I am sorry about that, James, but being an owner, you have no idea of an overseer's responsibilities."

"Come and work for me, then." He meant the offer, too, and gave Galloway the intense look of a bargainer awaiting closing confirmation of a business deal.

"Thank you, James." Galloway gave a staccato laugh at his friend's offer. "But you know that would be impossible. I much prefer us to

The Shooting Party

remain friends. I fear working for you would put an end to that happy state of affairs."

"As you will." Graham-Clarke sounded disappointed but realized that was the only answer he could expect.

"This then, Matt, is the only opportunity we will be together for some time yet again. As I said, it is back to England next week for me. God only knows when I will return to Jamaica."

"You spend Christmas on the high seas, James? Why not stay in the island and go back after? Christmas in the island is well worth staying for."

Graham-Clarke shook his head. "Impossible, my friend; there is business I have to attend to at home. Shall we go inside or stay out here with the rest of these reprobates?" His right hand made an arch-like gesture toward his guests, including even the ladies sheltering from the sun in the shade of trees, parasols, and large decorative hats.

"I see you haven't lost the jaundiced view of your equals, James. Perhaps that is why we are friends."

"Well, what is it to be?"

"To the house, James. I have never been here before."

They began to walk in that direction when Galloway stopped and looked up at the Great House. "Good God! Lapland is a huge pile! Most unlike anything I have seen in the island. It is a madman's castle."

A peal of laughter came from his companion, and he too stopped to look at his house. "Madman, indeed! Yes, I have to agree. You know, Matt, it tickles me to think that Uncle Jacob must have intended to rebuild Claver House in this island. He lived here for seventy years. Came when he was twenty in 1746. When he died, they buried him down at Fustic Grove rather than here. I believe the old boy would have preferred to have been put under Lapland's earth. This plantation was his life's work."

"He left it to you?"

"No, no, he willed it to my father, and my father to me. It became just another of our Jamaican holdings, along with Bamboo and the rest," Graham-Clarke explained, in the off-handed manner of someone who took great wealth for granted.

Galloway nodded and said nothing more. It would have been impolite. Strange how these wealthy owners thought it improper to mention or discuss their great wealth. No, they had to hide behind the pretense that their possessions and the power they wielded were inconsequential.

They stood there, staring at the edifice. Eventually Graham-Clarke broke the silence. "Come, let us go to the gentlemen over there, instead of the house. You can see the interior later. They can bring refreshments to us." They changed directions and headed for the gathering under the poinciana tree.

Some of the guests clustered there Galloway recognized. Richard Breary and his friend Forbes-Dunbar were both lounging in easy chairs, their booted legs up over the extended armrests. Obviously they were all discussing the morning shoot. Some, who were not seated, were demonstrating by arm and hand movements how they shot or did not shoot the bird that now lived or died in their imagination.

Breary turned from his discourse and looked at the two approaching. Recognizing Galloway walking arm in arm with his host brought Breary out of his chair and onto his feet at the unexpected meeting.

"By God!" he said. "By God! Galloway, by God!" Since coming in from the shoot, he had obviously drunk more than one tumbler of rum and water. Glasses of Madeira and Canary wine were also going around. The drinks had not mixed well in Breary. Unsteadily he came forward and proffered his hand.

"Don't call on God too much, Richard. He has a nasty way of not answering when he is overused. How are you, Richard?" Galloway said, giving him a sideways glance to see if the man was too tipsy to carry on a sensible conversation.

"Changed, my friend. A changed man since we last met on that bleak road. Married the fairest lady in the land," Breary said, with the titter of a man unsure of himself.

"Yes, I had heard of the event. Miss Mary Vernon finally succumbed to your charm. My congratulations, Richard."

"We finalized it on the twenty-sixth of this month. You should have been there, Galloway."

"Did you invite me, Richard? I do forget." Graham-Clarke laughed at the thrust. He knew what his friend was getting at. Social distance was more important here than at home in England. No one in the planter class would have invited a lowly overseer to a family function like a wedding. As an old friend of the Vernon family, Graham-Clarke had been a guest at the wedding himself and noted with humor the elevation of an estate sugar-boiler engineer to the status of esquire. But such was island society. It was either that or allow white women to have clandestine affiliations with black men—a situation not unheard of, but one to be avoided if there was land to pass on. Ownership, namely, who owned what and where, was the defining force of these people.

"Well, now," Galloway said. "You were married on the twenty-sixth, and we are now the third of December, so you have been a gentleman for exactly a week, thanks to Miss Vernon."

"Matthew!" Graham-Clarke said. "You are much too hard on poor Richard. Mary has got a good man there." He patted Breary on his padded shoulder in friendly fashion. He hoped with the gesture to have softened Galloway's rather pointed barb—richly deserved, he knew, but Breary was, after all, his guest.

"Yes, yes, so she did," Breary said with a tipsy laugh, obviously pleased at his host's show toward him. "We are off to England next week to meet my lady wife's relatives in Warwickshire and get their approval." Flopping back into the chair he had occupied earlier, he gave another embarrassed cackle. He looked up. "Then it is to Yorkshire we go, to kiss my relatives."

"Always got to kiss relatives; good policy—damn good policy—especially if they have the wherewithal. Plenty tin is always the life-saver," Major Forbes-Dunbar said, slurring his words. Bloodshot eyes, surrounded by the dark rings of dissipation, inhabited what was once quite a handsome face—but one without any sign of strength. There was no structure to the bones or mouth, nothing that would have set him apart as a leader. It was a puffy, lethargic, selfish visage.

Graham-Clarke glanced at the speaker, annoyed by the remark. From his reaction it was clear that under other circumstances, the major would not be one of his guests.

"Matthew, Major Forbes-Dunbar. Do you know each other?" Graham-Clarke indicated the drunk in the chair, his head drooping toward the middle of his chest, signaling the unconscious state was near at hand. The cigar between his fingers had burned halfway down, the ash holding precariously onto its butt. Any movement, the slightest shock, would send it crumbling into his lap. The chances of this happening increased with each second as, on his knees in front of the major, a young slave knelt, polishing his wellington boots furiously.

"Get those damned scuffs out, boy," the major said in a mumble.

Forbes-Dunbar looked up at Galloway. "Damned if I know what the world is coming to; useless niggers and overseers out of their class."

His remark caused a stir from the others listening. Bad manners were one thing not tolerated at Lapland. Young Sam looked at his uncle, waiting for the reaction he knew would come.

"You forget yourself, sir!" Graham-Clarke's face had gone livid with anger, and he struggled to contain himself in front of his guests. "Captain Galloway is a friend of mine and an invited guest." He did not have to say more. Forbes-Dunbar knew what the host was getting at. He had not been invited but had accompanied Richard Breary, who had been on the official guest list.

The major jerked upright in the chair. Cigar ash cascaded into his lap. The slave stopped polishing and tried to brush it away with the cloth he had been using on his master's boots.

"What the hell do you think you're doing, you damned black bastard?" Forbes-Dunbar shouted at him.

Almost simultaneously there came a scream of pain, as the lighted stub of the cigar between Forbes-Dunbar's fingers was jabbed and ground into the slave's face. The man reeled backward from the assault, his right hand instinctively covering the burn on his cheek. Suffering excruciating pain, on his knees, he managed to bob his head up and down, signaling utter contrition, adding all the time in a rhythmic recitation, as if saying a rosary, "Sorry Massa, mi so sorry, beg you, Backra Massa, don't beat me, beg you. Beg you, sah. Mi so

The Shooting Party

sorry, sorry, sorry, sorry, you hear, Massa. Hit accident, Massa. Beg you Massa, no beat mi. Mi love you, Massa."

With the sorrowful begging came huge sobs along with tears of terror trickling down his cheek; on the right side of his face, the weeping ran between the fingers of his cupped hand protecting the burn from further savagery. The man's whole body shook with fright as he crouched at his master's feet.

"I'll have them skin you alive and nail it to a tree, you damned nigger," hissed Forbes-Dunbar, through bared yellowing teeth behind splayed lips, his facial aspect quite revolting. Still pressing his hand against the side of his face, the slave looked skyward and wailed for Jesus to save him.

"You will do nothing of the sort, Major," ordered Graham-Clarke. He turned to Richard Breary. "I think, Richard, you had better see that your friend is taken home. He is not fit company."

There was no mistaking the host's intent. As he had brought the major, Breary knew what was expected of him.

"Don't worry." Forbes-Dunbar held up a hand. "You want me gone? I shall oblige you, Clarke." Richard Breary tried to help the drunk to his feet and was brushed away. "When I need help, I will ask a gentleman, not some jumped-up mechanic." He heaved himself out of the chair and staggered a step or two.

Normally the host would have had him put to bed. Instead, Graham-Clarke said, "See the major to his carriage or horse and escort him off the estate."

His last words raised a few eyebrows among the group. None of them had ever heard a white man of their class put out like a dog. It just wasn't done in a land where they had to impress their superiority on what they owned and all other underlings.

"I will get his servants," volunteered Breary. "You there." He pointed at the slave still nursing the cigar burn on his cheek. "Get whoever else came with you, and take the major home."

"Yes, Massa," the man said, and ran off in the direction of the back of the house. Minutes later he returned with an older man. It was he who said to Breary, "It all right, Massa. Wi will see di major-massa safe back home. Leave im to us. Mi know what to do. Hit not di fus time dis ya appen."

Breary looked hard at the man, as if carving his face on memory. "What is your name?" he demanded, pointing a finger at the man to indicate that he was marked down mentally.

"Dem name me Abel, Massa." His head nodded twice.

"Well, see that the major gets home safely, Abel," Breary said.

"Yes, sah." He reached for his master, who staggered and almost fell flat. The slaves got hold from behind and guided him away toward the back of the house where his horse waited, already saddled.

"Don't trust those two," observed Breary, as he watched them handle their owner. "Think I will go and see him right."

"Well," said Galloway, "Better he be Abel than Cain."

Many who heard him were puzzled by the remark, which they knew should be picked up on, but they only recognized it to be waggish when Graham-Clarke and Sam Barrett chuckled. Then they all laughed to cover their ignorance and settled back comfortably in their chairs. A few had their glasses refilled, while others picked at the food still in the plates beside them.

"You know," began one, not older than twenty, with a distinct flat Jamaican sound to his words. "Dese damn naygars deserve a lesson now and den. Keeps dem in check."

"Oh?" queried Galloway giving the youth a particular look, meant to remind him of his youth.

"Well, sir, dem is getting out of hand dese days," the young planter said.

"I agree," said a rotund type whose modish jacket looked too small for him as he leaned against the trunk of the tree, giving some watching him the impression that any minute the seams could give way. "Have you heard all this talk about a freedom paper? If it comes, I am damned if they will get any freedom from me without mi proper compensation."

"Here, here," said someone, and a few laughed.

"And who is going to pay you that?" asked an older man, in a manner that suggested he had heard all these vexations before. The laughter stopped at the question, and all waited for a knowledgeable type to give an answer. "The government in England won't come through, and our legislature cannot raise that kind of currency to buy all their freedom," the older man said, since no one had taken up his question.

His listeners fidgeted like schoolboys. Some gave surreptitious glances at the old hand dressed in a light cotton short-coat and baggy pants well suited to the climate. His family had been in the island longer than any there and garnered the respect that was due. For this alone, they did not want to go up against him; plus, what he said made sense.

"What do you suggest then, Mr. Blagrove?" asked Sam finally. "My father will be most put out if they free the slaves and don't compensate. We stand to lose very heavily. At last count it was well over two thousand slaves on our estates."

"So will we all lose heavily," added a little man with a face crisp and cracked by years in the sun. Unlike the others, he sat bolt upright in a straight-back chair like a judge on the bench overlooking his court. "Damned ruinous if they free the Negroes and don't come through!" His voice rose as if issuing the precursor to a death sentence. "Can you not see it, gentlemen?" He paused and gestured toward the horizon. "Cane rotting, fields left to go fallow with no one to plow the dead ratoons under the sod." Then he held out his pewter goblet for a slave standing close by to squeeze more lemon, add a spoon full of sugar, and pour water plus rum to fill it.

There was an even longer pause while he took a long draught, and those listening waited for him to surface again. Finishing, he took a gulp of air like a man about to drown and exhaled loudly. "All lost, wasted, fields ruinate, houses tumbled down." His eyes stared at the ground as he murmured, "And family gone." A moment of silence followed.

"By God, Harry! What a gloomy prospect you do paint. Come out of your cups, man! It will never come to that; besides, we have half the lords in our pockets."

The little man bridled at this off-handed optimism. His head came back up, and he stiffened against the bracing chair back. "It's all right for you, Fitzgibbon. You can crawl back to your family places in England and live as if nothing happened out here, but this is all I have got, man!"

He was not the only one who felt this way. Many would lose all they had in the world if abolition came. All the bright prospects of their youth were fading before many had even reached middle age. All the wealth and power they believed to be their God-given rights were on the verge of vanishing if these rumors came true.

"Gentlemen, gentlemen," Augustus Roxburgh said with a drawl. "I think the home country learned its lesson in America when they imposed tax on them. We are too valuable for them to make that mistake again. Believe me, freeing the Negroes is not on. It would be the heaviest tax a man can bear."

"If parliament does that, we will just join America," said another, who till then had stood by listening and only now wandered into the conversation.

"They wouldn't have us!" interjected a pessimist in the group.

"Yes, they would. We are rich, remember. The Yank, like the Jew, loves money!" countered an optimist with a merry laugh.

"We had our chance to join them when they broke away, and we didn't. You think they will forget that?" fired back the pessimist, who knew his history.

"Trade is all the Yank cares about. They will take us," contended the optimist.

"Come hell or high water!" The straight-back chair teetered for a moment. "I am not going to give up Iron Shore, not for England, not for those damned Baptists, and certainly not for any slave."

"Come now, Irving," said Roxburgh, facing the little man. "Don't be a fool, man. No one is asking you to do that. They could never force us to give the slaves their freedom and give up our land. Blood would flow in Westminster."

"As it did in Haiti," said another man. "Give the blacks their freedom, and we will have chaos in St. Elizabeth."

"St. Elizabeth, George? Or do you mean Fonthill?" Fitzgibbon said, with a look of slight astonishment. George Beckford glowered at Fitzgibbon for a couple of seconds and, deciding against butting heads with him, turned back to his own argument. "They don't know how to keep civilization. It's not their way. Killing and brutality is theirs, not ours."

"Gentlemen! Enough of these gloomy pronouncements and speculation." Graham-Clarke clapped his hands to signal an end. "Let us have good fellowship! After all, Christmas is not far away. I expect all my guests to drink, eat, and be merry." He directed the servants, who instantly jumped at the signal, to go around to the guests and refill platters, mugs, glasses, and goblets.

But some of the men refused to let up.

"It's all those bloody nonconformists," grumbled one, as he was brought a plate piled with roast beef and ham. Lifting a large slice of roast beef on his fork toward his mouth, he announced, "We should never have allowed them in the island. I hear Richard Barrett has them preaching to his slaves down on Barrett Hall." He pointed the fork at Samuel Barrett, and waved it about. "Yes, young Sam's cousin, here." The roast beef on its prongs about to fall off, the speaker quickly transferred the meat to his mouth. "The damned fool," he said, in between chews, "thinks he will get more work out of the brutes if they are God-fearing. Did you hear our dearly beloved Custos has instituted the cat-o-nine to beat them with? He thinks that is more humane than the cow whip." Most laughed. "Isn't that so, Sam?"

But Sam had no chance to answer before Roxburgh interceded. "All that without choking, David." The group laughed. "At least Richard gave a good accounting for us in front of the committee at Westminster when he went to London."

"A mighty lot of good that did," a piping voice at Roxburgh's left declared. "Doubt if any of them listened to him."

"I hear your uncle has the Reverend Wardell living at Cinnamon Hill, Sam. Is that true?" someone said with concern.

"On Cornwall," corrected young Sam, beginning to go red in the face at the bombardment pointed at his family. But he would not let the present company bully him. He would face them all down if he had to.

"What's he doing there?"

Graham-Clarke came to his defense before Sam could answer: "Doing whatever Baptists do."

As his uncle spoke, a spaniel pup came bounding up, looked at her master, and bounced around his feet and yapped playfully.

"Does that belong to you, James?" Roxburgh pointed at the pup for confirmation.

"Yes, brought her out as a present for a little girl," Graham-Clarke said, as he bent down to pat the liver and white spaniel on the head.

"Good little gun dog, that. But not in this country; feet will get cut to shreds running over the rocks to retrieve."

"Well, she isn't meant for that, Augustus."

"Careful of her round those brutes of yours. My black bitch just had a bunch of white mongrels. If I had found the dog that did the dirty, I would have shot the beast. Spoiled a damned good bitch, that." As if sensing she was the center of attention the little spaniel trotted over to where Roxburgh sat and looked to have her ear scratched, and she got her wish.

"I wonder, Sir, if that is what they say about you?" intruded Fitzgibbon with a mischievous grin.

"What are you getting at, Fitzgibbon?" Roxburgh fixed him with a suspicious scowl, knowing his reputation for fun.

"You know, when you tup your black wenches, and they whelp white."

One man choked on his swig of rum and, along with the rest of the crowd, followed with a loud guffaw. Another stamped his foot on the grass, signaling his appreciation of the barb. Augustus Roxburgh had the reputation, from one tip of the island to the other, of fathering children filling the entire spectrum of the rainbow between black and white, mulatto to mustefino. So anecdotal was this reputation, it was a wonder he had the time to be at the shooting party that day.

Roxburgh took it in his stride with good humor. "Well they may, well they may—you know." He scratched his chin as though in thought and then boisterously joined in the laughter.

"You know, it is all our own fault? We could have solved this slave problem long ago, if we had a mind and the belly for it." The group turned to hear what Blagrove had to add on that subject. "We wouldn't have this dissension and the fear of constant rebellion every year, had we passed laws that children of black women and white

The Shooting Party

men were born free. In other words, they would have the same rights as children of white women and black men. We could have built a land with our progeny instead of scurrying them off to hide in England, never to return here."

"No! That would never do, Blagrove," Roxburgh said. "The half breeds would end up with all the land, and none would be left for white children. No! No! Can't have that!"

"Don't you see, Roxburgh? We would have one people. Not as it is now, split between black and white, slave and master. What is the difference between your white children and those that are tarred? Not a thing. Not a cursed thing, man! Except, some are free and others condemned to slavery. Back at home, the mixed ones walk as free men; why not here?"

"Not true!" protested Roxburgh. "I always see that they get their freedom—like the rest of you." His hand gestured lazily to make the point. There was a general murmur of agreement among those who had followed this tradition.

"Awful nuisance, not to mention the expense, having to get special laws passed for them. Got to be well in at Spanish Town to get it done," said a tub of a man at the edge of the group. Another murmur followed, along with nodding heads acknowledging the truth of the statement.

"And how would we bring about what you suggest, Blagrove? Are you suggesting we castrate all the black men, so we can have their women freely for our pleasure and progeny?" It was a bitter question from Irving in his straight-backed chair. "I can just see you taking the balls of that boy over there." He pointed directly at Neddy.

If his skin had been white, it would have gone scarlet at the suggestion; as it was, unnoticed, he turned darker with the rush of blood. They were all staring at him. Lord! Embarrassment forced him to drop his head and eyes; he shifted his weight from foot to foot. Being singled out as an object to be appraised was a new experience for him, and he did not like it at all.

Till then, he had stood in the background listening intently. This was the first time he had been around a group of white men, unaccounted and invisible. He had never thought that white men

259

could live in fear. As they talked, and argued, little by little, their own unease transferred to him. He wasn't sure what these pangs building up inside him meant. Was it caused by their fear, or his own, as the dice rolled out to settle the predicament of their future? His employer saved him from further degradation.

"I can assure you, gentlemen, free men, such as this boy, will keep what belongs to them for procreation. You would not be allowed to mutilate them."

"He is free!" exclaimed a man who until then had only listened, drinking and chewing his food with the precision of a guardsman marking time.

"Yes. I hired him for a day's labor."

They said nothing. A throat cleared, and another coughed with a deep rattle of a chest cold, as if in the last throes of blackwater flux.

"We are going to lose whichever way they turn, gentlemen. Let them go now. Let us begin to hire labor we pay for," Mr. Blagrove said, in all respects the *dominus* among the group.

From the outer circle, one who had listened and moved slowly from one to the other, testing the waters as the opinions came out, said, "Where do we get these from? Our niggers won't work for the lash. What makes you think, sir, they would work for money? They are damned lazy black bastards. This is a boy." He pointed a long forefinger in the direction of Neddy. "He is no example to toss in front of us!"

"As lazy and black you would be, Irving, if someone owned you," Galloway said, getting another shot into the verbal struggle.

Irving twisted to face him, his face contorted with rage and despair. He was about to say something to the overseer that he would have regretted but was saved from doing so by Mr. Blagrove in an attempt to counter the other's sally. "We will import the labor from India and China, as they do on the plantations in Ceylon and around those other islands in the Indian Ocean."

"The Seychelles, Mr. Blagrove." Galloway helped him out.

"It would be a disaster!" snapped one of the Tharpe clan, whose family seemed to own everything in Trelawny the Barretts didn't. "We would go back to the time when our ancestors first came here

The Shooting Party

and used indentured labor from England. They died like flies. Whites can rule, but they cannot labor. We all know that." There was loud acceptance of that law from the gathering. "Those who survived had to be compensated with land after their time was up. Damned stupid system, if you ask me!"

"Not I! Better the nigger you know than the nigger you don't know. We have enough trouble with the ones we have now. Bringing any more in as indentured labor will ruin everything." Again the little man in the high-back chair indicated that his mug needed refilling. The closest servant complied with water, rum, a squeeze of lemon, and a stirring of sugar.

"They are nothing but coolies anyway," someone to the right of their host added.

Graham-Clarke had tired of the conversation but, as a good host, did not interfere with its playing out. Quietly he turned to his friend. "Come, Matthew. Let us leave these gentlemen to chew on their dilemma. Most of them are heavily into their cups, and there will be no sense from them in a little while."

"There is no sense from them now, James," agreed Galloway.

Neddy followed, thankful to get away. They set off across the lawn toward the house. A light breeze came up as they walked, and Galloway found it refreshing after listening to the fear and bitterness he knew came with the end of an era. He could not wait until he set sail and watched the shoreline of the island drop below the horizon. For him, it would be salvation from the jungle where only jungle creatures dwelt. As he walked, Graham-Clarke said, "I confess, Matthew, as a businessman, my guess is, the end of slavery is inevitable." The left side of his mouth turned upward in a small smile "For the past two years, I have given instructions to sell my slaves." Then the smile broke into a merry chuckle. "I have replaced them with cattle and sheep on Lapland, far less dangerous and much more profitable."

"You are going out of the sugar and rum business, then, James?"

"Truthfully, it is inevitable. Not economic here anymore. Those fools can't see it. Blagrove is right. Plantations in Asia are killing us. For my coin, get out while you can."

261

"Is that how you see it, James?"

"Every day at home, I see the change coming. My agents give me the sugar and rum quotations, and we just cannot compete. Free labor is killing slavery. It is only out here no one will accept the change. You heard them, Matthew. They are damned."

"I can understand it."

"You can!" his friend said. "You, an intellectual, more the poet than the soldier—how can you conclude such a thing?"

"It is the power of one man over another, James; they can't give it up. It is the laudanum of waking moments. It's the father who cannot surrender his children to adulthood."

"Really, how interestingly you put it." Graham-Clarke gave him a look, not at him but through him—nay, beyond him, as if contemplating another situation.

"Why the strange look, James?" Galloway asked. But before an explanation was given him, their conversation was cut short. At the entrance of the house, a lady in her late thirties, wearing a simple white dress with broad green stripes—or maybe a green dress with broad white stripes, it was the beholder's choice—came up to them. On her head was a large brimmed hat of white silk with white lace trimmings and flowers in the latest French fashion. She raised the palm of her hand to stop them. Grasping on to her skirt was a little girl with a mass of curls tumbling about her head from under a small straw bonnet.

"Mary, my dear." Graham-Clarke extended both hands to her. "Allow me to present my very dear friend, Captain Matthew Galloway. Matt, Miss Mary Vernon."

She gave a merry little laugh, at the same time withdrawing her hands from his. "Captain Galloway, forgive James; as a man with so much on his mind, he forgets details such as attending my wedding last week. Mary Breary, Captain. I am so pleased to meet you at last," she said, as Galloway bowed to her.

"Oh, my dear! Forgive my oversight. Truth is, I cannot imagine you married." Graham-Clarke nearly added *to that man* but was stopped from making that slip by a little hand tugging at his leg.

"Mercy me!" he said when he looked down at the little girl, pulling his trouser leg like a bell cord.

"Another lady demands your attention, Matthew," he said, as he heaved the child up in his arms. "May I present Miss Eliza Stevenson." She paid no attention to Galloway, instead planting a loud, wet kiss on Graham-Clarke's cheek just below his left eye and saying, "Grandpa!"

He flushed slightly and returned the kiss. Galloway noted all. This was a time to let his friend explain, without prodding, if he wished. James was married and had children, but as far as Galloway knew, they were not married or, for that matter, old enough to have made him a grandfather on the wrong side of the blanket of a three- or four-year-old, as near as he could judge the little girl's age.

"Where did you come from?" Graham-Clarke asked her.

"Over there." She pointed to a man in his middle thirties, who was talking to another by a rose apple tree. Any observer could see from their arm movements that shooting was the topic of conversation.

"Have you escaped from Bekah, miss?"

She threw back her head, tossing off her hat to release a cascade of hair and ribbons. Laughing all the time, she leaned so far back that her grandfather struggled to keep her upright.

"Let me take her back, James," offered Mrs. Breary, just as her husband came to her side, forestalling the transfer of the little girl.

"Oh, there you are, dear," she said to her husband. "Captain Galloway." Her left hand gestured elegantly toward Breary. "Do you know my husband Richard?"

"As a matter of fact, Mrs. Breary, I do," he said politely.

"Then I do not have to make introductions. They are so tedious, don't you think? We should dispense with them in polite society. Everyone should know everyone else." A merry little laugh followed. "Richard, my dear." She turned to her husband. "I was about to send for you, dear. We ought to be getting back to Mount Vernon." Before he could answer her, she reached for the little girl in Graham-Clarke's arms and put her down on the ground. "Eliza," she said, bending over and looking steadily into the girl's eyes. "Where did you lose Bekah?" All she got for her inquiry was a shrug of the tiny shoulders.

"Ah, well!" Mrs. Breary shrugged her shoulders as well. "We will just have to find her, then."

"She lose," Eliza said, wiggling her head from side to side and shrugging her shoulders, indicating she had no knowledge where she had mislaid her nurse.

"No, no, my sweet, you would say, *Rebekah is lost*. You must learn to speak like a lady and not a servant. Just hold my hand, young lady, and we will wait until she is found." Mary Breary smiled and took the little girl's hand firmly in her own.

Turning back to Galloway, who had been entertained by the goings on between Eliza and her, she said, "Captain, my brother speaks very highly of you."

"And who might that be, Mrs. Breary?" Galloway said.

"William Vernon of Mount Apfel. Don't you know him?" She seemed somewhat astonished that he had not readily picked up on her reference.

As he was about to answer her, Richard Breary stiffened. "He is not really your brother, is he, dear?"

Galloway saw that the social bile of Jamaica had surged up in Breary's throat. This new arrival in the plantocracy was trying to lay down what was, and was not, proper for his lady to mention.

Mary Breary, nee Vernon, waited for those nasty seconds of silence that inevitably would follow when a husband corrected a wife in public. They were so necessary for emphasis; when they had passed, like a mother correcting an errant child, she turned, faced her husband, and placed her hand upon his arm. "Most assuredly, he is, my dear," she said emphatically but sweetly, her eyes never wavering from his.

Turning back to Galloway, she said, "Yes, William tells me that you run Newman Hall most efficiently. He admires how you do not use the whip on your people yet get the best out of them. He says you have them moving like soldiers on a battlefield."

He couldn't help himself; Galloway laughed heartily at that compliment. "He flatters me, ma'am. Truth is, I only know *of* Mr. Vernon." Continuing their polite conversation, Galloway asked, "Do tell me though, Mrs. Breary, is his name William or Edward? It was explained to me, but I am still a bit hazy on that point."

"It can be confusing, Captain." Mary Breary smiled. "The family calls him William, but the slaves call him Massa Edward, so as not to confuse him with our late parent. Even though our father is dead, they still persist with Edward. Custom dies hard with them. You could call him by either name, I suppose. They are both his, William in front and the Edward in the middle." Mrs. Breary placed a hand to her mouth and gave a little chuckle.

"It will be safer to call him what I have always called him— Mr. Vernon, don't you think, Mrs. Breary?" As he spoke, Galloway glanced at Breary and was tickled to see him flinch at his use of "Mister" in front of a colored man's name, as if he were an esquire. Breary was such a pretentious bastard; served him right that his new wife acknowledged her relatives of color. He would just have to accommodate it.

"He knows everyone around us and their methods," Mary Breary said. "He is a very keen observer of life." Again she laughed. "I know our father didn't want him to return to Jamaica. He is wasted here and would have been most successful at home." It was funny listening to her slight Creole accent referring to England as home.

"Well, it has been a delight, Captain Galloway, to meet you at last. I shall tell William Edward," she said with a smile, "of our meeting. We must be off. Again, Captain Galloway." Still smiling, she held out her hand.

"A pleasure, ma'am," he said, as he politely took her hand and bowed over it.

"Eliza, until Bekah is found, you, miss, will just have to stay with your grandfather and behave yourself."

"That is all right, Mary," Graham-Clarke said, as he bent down and lifted up the little girl. She threw her arms around his neck, planted another kiss on his cheek, and held on like a limpet.

They watched the newly married couple stroll away. Graham-Clarke waited until they were out of earshot before he explained, "Mary is the daughter of an old friend of my great-uncle Jacob— can't think why she married Breary. Suppose, out here, there is not much choice. We sail on the same ship from Falmouth next week." A scowl flitted across his face for a second. "The prospect of three months at sea with Breary is not pleasant to contemplate."

"Oh, I don't know, James; three months is nothing, when compared to a lifetime. Have pity for his new wife."

"You are right, of course, Matthew. Women seem able to put up with a lot from a man."

Galloway prudently did not break in; the subject was better left alone at this point. They began to head indoors, when they were stopped.

"Excuse me, Massa James." The voice made both turn around to see where it had come from. "Mi can take Miss Awa from you, sah."

"There you are, Bekah," Graham-Clarke said to a very pretty girl, fourteen or fifteen years old. She had a cool complexion and soft but finely defined features dominated by large, liquid eyes. Small nubile breasts showed through a cotton smock that covered a body forming to tantalize males.

"We were wondering where you were," Graham-Clarke said, now struggling to disentangle himself from the little girl who clung to his neck for all she was worth.

"Massa, sorry, Massa, she just pick up and run off before I can stop her."

"That is quite all right, Bekah, so long as her mama did not see her do that, or both of you will be severely lectured, I bet." He reached out and patted the young nursemaid on her shoulder in a fatherly manner.

"Miss Frances not come, sah. Is Massa Stevenson bring her, sah," Bekah said. She put out her arms to take Eliza, who reluctantly went over to her.

While all the explanation surrounding the little girl was going on, Neddy stood stiff, straight, staring; it was as if a biblical revelation had been given him directly by God. Transfixed by a bolt of lightning, rooted to the spot, he gawked. Gone from his mind were the Miss Lucys of this world; Bekah, as she was called, was the most enchanting girl he had ever seen. Perhaps fifteen, sixteen years old, if that. But his mind was oblivious to time's movement. He didn't notice her eyes, her small waist, her breasts. He didn't even notice that her hands and dress denoted a house servant, rather than a field slave. No, he noted not all those things that grown men notice in young girls. She walked, she breathed, she smiled, and that was all he noticed. She filled his world, and he felt like a baby emerging from the womb, taking his first breath of air in the living world.

"Then, take this mischievous miss back to her companions, and let us to our discourses go," James Graham-Clarke said. "And, Bekah, take Captain Galloway's young lad here with you. He has been forgotten and needs to be fed. Ask Nana to see he gets something to eat."

"Yes, sah, Massa." She dropped a curtsy and then, for the first time, looked over at Neddy.

"Thank you, James. I almost forgot the lad. Neddy, go with her, and I will send for you when I need you."

Neddy could not believe his luck. He was overjoyed to follow Bekah. Perhaps he could get to know her.

"Come, Miss Awa." She picked up the three-year-old with accustomed ease. Then, turning to Neddy, she looked him up and down to establish her superiority, as house servants do to field niggers. When satisfied that she had marked the social gap between them, she ordered, "Follow me, boye."

He could hear the contempt in her voice with the exaggerated *boye*. He flinched but did not set her straight and followed meekly. Miraculously, his huge hunger had almost disappeared in her presence. When his stomach rumbled to remind him of its emptiness, he prayed its quarrel would not carry to her ears.

As it rumbled again, that awful feeling began to swirl around in his gut, that inner state that brought on trembling and made it difficult to hold onto things. No matter how hard he tried to grip them, there was no strength in his hands. He was old and frail before his time, and, it seemed, the harder he tried, the weaker his hands became. He was tempted to scream at his impotence, for he knew not why it had overwhelmed him. Yet something stopped him. As he followed the girl, his knees trembled. He walked almost drunkenly. That was how he felt, even if others could not see it. It was how he felt!

His eyes were glued to her back and its graceful sway. Her lithe young body sent his mind wandering into the realms of wantonness that he knew the Reverend Waldrich would condemn, had he been there and known what Neddy was thinking. He was rescuing her from a cruel white master, and she had surrendered herself to him. He was on bended knee pleading, and she was granting him his every wish.

"What you staring at, boye?" she said; it shook him upright. "You wants to eat me?" How did she know what he was looking at? Her back was to him.

"That would be nice." The words came out, and he knew instantly he had made a great mistake. She spun around to face him.

"What you want, mi on a plate, wid banana and rice han peas?" The little Miss Awa clung to her nurse tighter when she spat out the last word. Neddy decided to be forward.

"Any ting, any ting would be nice." He smiled the smile many loved him for. She returned nothing but coldness, her face immobile, her body ramrod stiff. He knew it meant trouble. No winning smile could soften that stone face. He had gone too far with this girl.

If eyes could harden, become black granite, hers did, as she looked straight through him. Carefully she placed her charge upon the ground and said in a very grown up and proper manner, like his mother, "You insult me, little boy."

He could have died on the spot—he should have died on the spot—as her bolt passed through his very heart. He felt it strike there. If man or boy could feel like a jigger being picked out of a field naygar's yam foot, he did at that moment. His humiliation was complete. She turned and walked on with the little girl firmly in hand, without a glance behind to see if he followed.

"Lard Gad! Sorry, mi sorry, you hear!" He almost shouted in desperation and ran up beside her and put his hand on her arm. Without stopping she shook it off as one would brush a fly away. On she walked, still the little girl's hand in hers. Neddy stood flat-footed, watching her. He knew for the first time what humiliating loss felt like. Love, before it had begun, ended.

The Shooting Party

"Come, boye, let me get you di food yu massa order fi you," she said, her voice dripping with disdain.

They approached a bunch of children playing around another young nursemaid in the side garden. She looked up from her charges at Bekah and then at Neddy, then back to Bekah. "Who di pretty boye a come wid you?" She lifted her skirt and did a few dance steps. "You like mi set?" she asked them both, looking sideways at Neddy. "You capture im?" This time she looked knowingly at Bekah, then back to Neddy with a coquettish giggle.

"You fancy him, Nesta? You can ave im," Bekah said.

"Im nice." Nesta giggled again and added a flurry with her skirt. "Come set time a Christmas, im could dance wid me. I could be him Christmas pudding." Her teeth flashed behind a big, inviting grin.

"Mi tink you would ave to talk to di white man im belong to. Come Christmas or no Christmas, no white man going gives up im fancy boye to a no-good gal like you." To Bekah's mind, that should have placed both Nesta and Neddy in their respective places and ended the banter once and for all.

The blow was like a carpenter's mallet missing its mark and striking his forehead. Neddy's mouth dropped open like an idiot's. Mouth water almost drooled out. He stood there aghast. It was unbelievable, what he had just heard. He shook his head to clear his mind. How could she say such a thing about him? She did not know him. No one had ever spoken about him like that, and he did not like it one bit. It was cruel. His face darkened with anger. His hands began to tremble, and he knew that if he did not get control of himself, there would be a nasty scene, and he would be found wanting. Although his mind told him to remain calm, deep within himself, he heard a voice, not his, utter:

"I am no man's *boy*. I am a free man. I can buy you and sell you like any white Backra Massa—little black gal." As his ears made sense of the words, he was horrified they had come from him. Irrevocably, he had lost the battle and the war. The dream that had materialized in front of him became a girl, just another girl.

"Nesta, Bekah!" A small octoroon woman appeared through a side door of the house. "What you two wasting time bout?"

The question did not require an answer. But Nesta, ever forward, explained to the head nurse, "We got a black Backra Massa here who can buy an sell di likes of wi, Miss Nanna." She cut a curtsy in the direction of Neddy.

"What you talking bout, Nesta?" queried the head nurse sharply.

"Im come wid one of Massa James guest, and dem ask mi to show him where to go for food," Bekah said.

"Well, what you waiting for? Tek im," the head nurse said. "You can leave Miss Eliza wid me. Now get on wid it!" She took the child from Bekah, and with the back of her hand waved her off in an imperious way. "Sho-sho! What you waiting for, girl? Go-go, and don't hold up the progress of di day." She turned and marched back into the house, with the little girl struggling to keep up. Bekah stood looking at the retreating figures until the door closed behind them.

"You better come, boye," There was less hostility in her tone as she moved off quickly. Neddy followed obediently to the outside kitchens at the rear of the house.

There was a great bustle of servants coming and going. Some arrived with empty serving dishes to be refilled; others picked up serving dishes that had been replenished with turkey, lamb, ham, beef, and all manner of vegetables, and returned to the house. Among all this, too, were huge bowls, piled high with fresh fruit from mangoes to tangerines, and pitchers of juice and coconut water, as well as bottles of wine and rum.

There seemed to be a never-ending stream of servants. Some were decked out in colorful livery, but most wore clean cotton togs. There seemed to be much confusion. There were shouts to make way and curses for those who got in the way, and laughter in return. Most seemed to be enjoying themselves.

As they served the guests, they served themselves as well. Neddy noticed that, apart from the squeeze of unaccustomed shoes, a few swayed with the effects of rum or wine, or both. Many had splattered their fine jackets with food and drink. Others, too drunk to serve their owners, had staggered to sleep under a tree in the yard or flopped on the ground with their backs against the kitchen wall, store room, and servants' quarters.

The Shooting Party

Of the unconscious, heavily breathing bodies, Neddy counted eleven. If their example was followed throughout the afternoon, there was a good chance that by nightfall, few serving staff would be on their feet. For those who did not make the return journey with their masters, there could only be the retribution of the whip. Before that happened, however, the clever ones would sneak off to the hills or hide out on other estates, hoping that their mischief would be forgotten by the time they returned to their own places. By then their lies would be so well formulated they would become their own truth.

So it was with Kensington slaves when they were called by the new owners to account for absences. Few got away with it but protested louder and louder with each lash, as if each stroke transformed the lie into truth and etched it in their flesh.

Bekah pushed through the crowd, and Neddy followed. Standing in the middle of the large kitchen with her back to the cooking fires was a small, muscular, very black woman. Orders streamed from her. Any who ignored her instantly regretted it, as a massive wooden ladle came crashing down. Melvirah didn't mind where she hit her kitchen help. Many a pubescent male learned that very painfully, sometimes to the point of disgorging his insides. She took delight in watching them clutch their parts and double over in agony. Neddy arrived just in time to witness such an assault. She missed and struck the lad inside his left thigh. He yelped like a puppy and ran to do her bidding before she could renew the attack. Melvirah's kitchen was her kingdom. Everyone should mind their manners and do the work she assigned. Bekah approached the head cook with caution.

"Melvirah," she called.

The cook ignored her.

She tried again, this time in a louder voice: "Melvirah!"

Again she was ignored.

"MELVIRAH!"

'What you want, gal?" Melvirah said. "Who you shouting at?" The woman's arms went to her waist, ready for battle as she swung round. "An who you calling *Melvirah*? Who you tink you is? Ain't you got manners an respeck? Hits *Miss Melvirah*, to the likes of pickney gal like you." She glowered at Bekah, then turned back to lord it over her kitchen army.

Bekah's body stiffened; her eyes narrowed, her jaws clamped together in defiance, she let fly, "Massa James want you to feed dis ya boye, *now!*" she yelled.

That got her attention. Melvirah stopped what she was doing and turned back to look at the nursemaid. "What boye?" she asked in a more accommodating tone.

Bekah pointed at Neddy. "Dis one," she snapped.

"Im will get fed wid all di servant dem," the cook said, haughtily.

"Im not a servant." Bekah's lips formed in a superior half-smile as she imparted the information to all in the kitchen. She anticipated the effect the announcement would have on the cook and relished it.

Melvirah turned back to face her, some of her arrogance gone. She tilted her head to one side as if to say, *What you coming wid?* That gave Bekah her opening. The cook seemed less bloated with her own airs now.

"Him come wid a special fren of Massa James, an im no slave boye. If you don't wan trouble, you ad better treat im good." It was pleasing to watch the cook's face soften and her scowl give way to a subservient smile, as the ground beneath her feet grew less firm.

"All right, den, you can tek im outside and fine im somewhere wid a table to sit, and mi will sen out di food to im. But im can't stay in fi mi kitchen." She rounded on Bekah defiantly, who responded with a shrug of her right shoulder.

Melvirah gestured to Neddy that he go with Bekah. He did her bidding and followed the nursemaid outside. They went to one of the other outbuildings, looked inside, and found a small table and a chair.

"You can sit in here, an I will tell *Miss* Melvirah where you is. Your food will come," Bekah said.

She stood looking at him. Silence hung between them like a heavy hand clamped across the mouth, stifling breath. Neddy, shamefaced, stared at his feet. "Mi sorry, you know," he mumbled.

He did not see her face soften, but he heard his forgiveness: "It's all right, mi know you didn't mean any ting," she said.

He looked up as she turned to leave. "You live here?" he said.

"Why you want to know?" Her eyes squinted, waiting to see if he was going to be fass again.

"Do-know. Jus hasking."

"Mi live over at Stevenage."

"Where dat?"

"It run longside Laplan. Dat is where Miss Frances and Massa Stevenson live." She paused and smiled. "But when Massa James comes out from Hingland, mi spen more time over here wid Miss Eliza. He loves her so."

"Who?"

"Di little girl we call Miss Awa."

"Oh," Neddy said.

She had gone a few steps when he almost shouted another question, hoping to delay her: "You in a set?"

She wheeled around at him. "No! What you tink me is? You tink mi would be dancing in a set in all fancy red or blue dress a show off at Christmas time, like dat no-good Nesta?" There was that haughty bite to her voice again, and Neddy felt it cut like a knife up the middle of his belly.

"No, mi didn't mean it dat way!" He tried desperately to stave off her anger.

This time, she laughed, twirled round, did a couple of dance steps and, like Nesta, dropped a neat curtsy.

"Backra Massa boye, mi gone, you hear." She took off at a run. He watched her enter the kitchen and come back out. She looked over at him from the doorway, waved, and ran in the direction of the house. He could hear the jingle of her laugh all the way, till the back door closed on the sound, and she was gone from sight.

Melvirah brought the tray herself. She took the plates and carefully laid them on the table, but not before covering it with a cloth, as if the spread was for a white man. All the time she looked suspiciously at Neddy, not knowing what to make of him.

"Mi hope dis will be enough. Hif you wants more, you can send for it." He was too young for her to add, "sah," so she left it at that and waited for his acknowledgement.

His plates were full of all that had been sent to the guests. It was enough to feed himself and Watt, who suddenly popped to mind at the sight of the food. The image made him smile; he seemed to think about Watt whenever a meal was at hand, and he secretly wished for his company now. As not to antagonize the cook, for he had gathered what she was like in their brief meeting in the kitchen, he gave her the respect she demanded and complimented the food.

"Tank you very much, Miss Melvirah. Dis is plenty, an look sweet and very nice."

The cook seemed satisfied with that. She nodded. "Well, hif you wants any ting." He was left to finish the thought as she left through the door, heading back to her domain.

He sat and ate until there was no more room in his belly. There was much food left over. It was so good, leaving it would be a shame. He wondered if there was any way of taking it with him, but he did not have those carrying pots of his father's. He sighed at the thought that his friend would not be sharing with him this time.

Looking around the room, he noticed a paillasse rolled up in the corner. Neddy went over and gave it a kick and good shake to dislodge some of the grunge and insects that had made their home there. Laying it out on the floor, he flopped down on the straw mattress. Damp from it seeped through his shirt, and a musty smell came up to his nostrils, but soon he was breathing steadily, fast asleep at the behest of niggeritis.

It was the bigger of the two slaves who had been with them that morning who woke him. As he sat up, rubbing his eyes, he realized dusk was coming on quickly; then he remembered where he was, and how far he had to go to get home. He scrambled to his feet.

"Mass Captain a wait for you," the man told him.

"Where im deh?" The man led the way and Neddy followed, back the way he had come that morning, to the front of the house. He looked around to see if he could see Bekah to say good-bye, but she was nowhere in sight. He was disappointed.

The stragglers were still on the lawn, making merry. Other than them, and the few invited to stay at the house, most guests had left. Galloway and Graham-Clarke stood talking together. The smaller of

The Shooting Party

the two slaves who had met them was holding the horse, donkey, and mule ready. Galloway stopped talking to Graham-Clarke and glanced over at them.

"There you are, Neddy," he said. "It is time for us to go home." Turning back to his host, he continued, "Well, James, we won't be seeing each other for some time again."

"You are determined to go to Canada, then?"

"Yes. Ireland has no future for me, and neither does this island. It is time for new adventures and new opportunities, James."

"What about your uncle's estate here?" asked Graham-Clarke. "You may be giving up a very rich future." There was more than a little concern in his voice.

"That would be nice, if it were not for the burden of conscience that comes with it," Galloway said. "You know what I mean, James. It has never really sat well with your family, either. Look what responsibilities your father took on for his friends over here, when they sent him their mixed offspring to be looked after in England."

"They were family. You have to do your bit. You can't leave them as slaves. It's against nature."

"And civilization," Galloway said, smiling.

"That has always been your damned problem, Matthew. You are too damned good to live amongst us mortals."

"Nonsense, James. I have killed men."

"No doubt, justifiably." Graham-Clarke's head bowed slightly in resignation. "You know, we might never meet again."

"That may be, James, but as Alcock used to say in the mess, 'We will meet again, for I can feel it in my water.' We will, James, we will. Maybe not in this violent place, but we will meet again, my friend. How could we not?" They shook hands. Galloway took the bridle of the horse from the slave and mounted. He gave both slaves a shilling each for their help that day.

"Cook say she season an blanch di bud for you, so dem won't spoil. Dem pack in di hamper, sah," the smaller slave informed them.

"Thank her for me."

"Yes, sah."

"Get on, Neddy. Let us take our leave."

Neddy was given a leg up on the mule and handed the donkey's rope. Galloway saluted Graham-Clarke with his whip, then brought it down to the horse's flank, and they were off, heading back to the gates of Lapland. Graham-Clarke stood for a while on the lawn, watching them ride away before walking to the house.

As they passed through the gates, the mountains were solid black against the sky's mixture of gold, crimson, and a careless scattering of smoky gray clouds. In its sinking, between two peaks, the sun's fire burned itself out for the day and illuminated crowning clumps of trees on hilltops. Then it was gone, and they rode along into dusk. Behind them, lanterns, lamps, and candles flickered in the windows of Lapland Great House, and what was left of the half-moon from the night before showed white in the coming night sky to guide them along their homeward path.

"Neddy," Galloway said, "ride up beside me, and give me that blasted donkey's head."

Neddy could not think why, but he did what he was told.

"Now that you are relieved of the burdensome beast, you will cheer our way, lad. Take out your flute and play music."

At first it was difficult to play, sitting holding on to the mule with nothing but his knees. Every now and then, the mule's gait would throw him out of tune, as one hand would leave the flute to steady himself. He heard Galloway laugh when that happened, so he kept playing from the interruption. All manner of music floated from his piping: hymns, work songs, and even some airs he had picked up in the district from Scots. They all seemed to please Galloway. This way, time passed, and it didn't seem so long before they reached the still-open gates of Newman Hall.

Even at that hour, Miss Lucy had waited up for the massa. Within a minute of his arrival, she had servants bustling around, taking the pots with the birds to the kitchen and the animals to their stables and paddocks.

While the young mistress of the household looked after the needs of the master, Badalia took Neddy back to his quarters. Feeling very tired, he thankfully tagged behind her to the cabin without a word. She held up the lantern as they entered. On Mungo's bed, he and

The Shooting Party

another boy were pressed together, fast asleep. A third youth, mouth open, was softly snoring on what had been Neddy's bed. In no time, Badalia grabbed this boy by the wrist and dragged him off. She practically flung him on top of the sleeping pair. There were grunts and half-curses from the two; then, still half asleep, all three naked bodies entwined arms and legs together, and they went to sleep as one.

When Badalia wished him good night and left, Neddy looked at the sleeping trio locked in a ball like black snakes. They seemed comfortable with each other, and he hoped they would stay that way for the rest of the night. His shoes, pants, and shirt came off, and he lay down. The residual warmth of the previous occupant did not bother him. He leaned over and put out the lantern.

Chapter 10

Tangle River

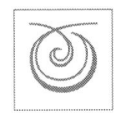

Neddy could hear the crunch of hooves coming on the gravel road. It was that nervous time of the morning, just before the sun comes up, when sound is crisp and clear, but objects remain indistinct to sight; there was nothing hurried about the sound as it came nearer in the darkness. Occasionally the beat of the clipping and clopping intermingled with rustling leaves and the groan of ancient branches resisting the diminishing puff of the night breeze. Neddy knew it to be the approach of a donkey. This was no heavy tread of more frightening night beasts, and a horse's gait would have been louder and more unsettled. But not a muscle twitched as he waited, gripping the edge of the bench; anticipation for the day to come was beginning to bubble in his belly.

Appearing as one, the donkey with rider rounded the corner and stopped at the edge of the square. At that distance, nothing distinctly marked them apart as a biped mounted on a quadruped. Only the vague outline of the big floppy hat told Neddy that Watt had arrived, mounted on his Rosinante.

Neddy chuckled with pleasure. Then the thought struck him, Watt probably imagined the hat shaded him from star burns come nighttime. Neddy started to laugh out loud, then stifled it. Anyway, he was very pleased to that see his friend had made it safely to Johns

Hall Square at that early hour. Good going for him, Neddy reckoned. As for himself, he was delighted his mother had allowed him to miss church that Sunday so he could be with Watt. It was going to be a good day, he assured himself.

He did not move from the bench. Watt could not see him sitting at the front of Tinka's shop in the darkness. Black on black was invisible. If Watt had owl eyes, he would have seen the faint gleam of white teeth through Neddy's smile. Neddy was waiting for some tomfoolery to begin.

In his left hand, Watt held the long bamboo pole he called a lance. One end was somehow stuck with his foot in the stirrup, while from the other end fluttered what looked like a piece of cloth, perhaps a bandana, but Neddy couldn't be sure in the murk. He could only just make out the movement of the rag, as the overcast sky cleared with the morning breeze to let some light filter through and reflect off the square's white marl surface.

Watt had pulled up in the middle of the square and sat there on the donkey for a couple of minutes, a solitary figure. Had an enemy been waiting in the shadows of the buildings with a gun or a knife, he would soon have been a corpse. An attacker might have shot him, but to be silent would sooner have slipped through the gloom and chopped him with a cane sickle.

Shifting the reins to his left hand, holding the pole, Watt stood straight up in the stirrups, like a rider showing off his horsemanship. All it needed was the donkey to kick up its hind legs, and Watt would have gone flying arse over tit. Luckily Rosinante did not move. Watt's right hand came up to his forehead, like an explorer looking to distant horizons. Turning left, then right, his eyes searched for movement, first in black places, then in areas where the glimmer of dawn had begun to clear away the night. Satisfied that there was nothing, he sat back in the saddle and proceeded to raise his voice, proclaiming, "Oh, my trusted Sancho Pancho, come forth from darkness of Hades and light the way of this knight-errant, so that we may go forth once again and do battle with giants and dragons."

Neddy rolled his eyes up high, so high that the pupils disappeared somewhere behind the lids, leaving only the whites showing.

"Shut up you mout! What you trying do, wake up de place?" muttered Neddy, emerging from the shadow of Tinka's shop into the square. There was a yelp of joy, and in the next moment his arms were pinned to his side, and Watt was wrapped around him, again squeezing the breath from him.

"One day," said Neddy, gasping, "you going gets dis back." From his immobile position, he could see the outline of the donkey over Watt's right shoulder, standing where he had dismounted, and a shadow against the white marl of the square, which he knew to be the long bamboo pole carelessly tossed on the ground. He wondered how Watt had managed to get from there to him so quickly.

Finally Watt allowed Neddy to breathe again. Then, taking a step backward and throwing his arms wide, Watt said, "Aha! You are here, my trusty friend. For a moment, just for a moment—I wondered if you had forgotten me."

"Mi forget?"

"Well, you could have been dead, you know!" Watt said, a finger pointed toward the heavens.

"Mi duppy would a come meet you den. Sometime you just plain fool-fool, Watt." The boys stood for a moment facing each other, grinning widely, not quite sure each was truly there.

"Come over here, mi have some ting for you."

"Food!" Watt exploded.

"Mi modder," Neddy got no further.

"Oh, a blessed lady! The savior of body and soul!"

"Will you shut up, an stop di foolishness before you have all di people a come out to find out what a go on?"

His eyes darting around the square at the still houses, Watt quieted down and followed Neddy to where he had sat waiting for him. Neddy picked up a covered wooden pail, took a bottle from inside, and passed it to Watt. "Di coffee is cold," he said. "She tink, you is going want dis, too." Neddy unwrapped a towel with thick slices of bread, sandwiching salt pork and plantain.

"How right she is! What a lady you have for a mother—must meet her and thank her myself."

His benefactor grunted, "Ahu." A few seconds of silence followed. "Mi mam, she like to meet you too."

"She would!" A hunk of bread, salt pork and plantain came flying out of Watt's over full mouth. "Damn! Sorry, hope I did not splatter you. Blast! Good food gone to ground."

"Hif you want to come…" Neddy began, pausing with uncertainty. "She wants you to come back wid me tonight…hif you wants?"

"She really does?" Watt's voice rose with anticipation.

"Will you keeps it down? Di people wan sleep, you know."

"Yes, but, but your lady mother wants to meet me!" Watt couldn't contain himself.

"Lard! Get di donkey, and let's go, before all di people come out and start fling rock-stone."

Stuffing the half-eaten sandwich into his mouth, Watt got hold of the donkey by its halter and picked up his bamboo pole from where it had landed.

The half-light of dawn had crept in, and features were now distinguishable as the boys moved out of the square. Watt tugged at the donkey with one hand, held the pole in the other, and every now and again awkwardly stuffed the rest of the sandwich further into his mouth. It was a marvelous contortion to watch.

"What you bring dat ting for?" Neddy said, pointing to the pole. He was having a hard time controlling himself and every now and again gave a little giggle. There was a bit of a struggle as Watt managed to remove the tail end of the sandwich and hold it in the same hand as his pole.

"Oh, since we are going fishing, I thought we could use this to fish with."

"You going juk dem wid it?"

"No, silly, tie the line to the end and use it like a fly rod."

"A what?"

"A fly rod."

It was bright enough for Watt to see Neddy's eyebrows crinkle in puzzlement, so the need for clarification was obvious. Immediately, he launched into a long and seemingly knowledgeable explanation of fly fishing for salmon in Scotland, something he had never actually done. Listening to him, one would have thought he had been at it from the moment he saw the light of day outside his mother's womb.

"When I am rich and return home, I will have a lodge in Scotland for fishing and shooting grouse," he said.

"You shoot?" Neddy sounded astonished.

"Not really, but I followed the squire when I was but a lad as he went for a rough shoot across his lands." In truth, it was the squire's gamekeeper who took him about, rather than the lord of the manor, but Neddy would never know the difference, and the squire sounded better. The gamekeeper had taken a fancy to the parson's son and took Watt around with him on many outings, where Watt learned the difference between poachers' traps and traps for poachers. All that knowledge came in useful to impress his friend on the road to Tangle River.

Neddy listened attentively as they walked. He waited for Watt to take a breath before returning to something Watt had said at the outset. "You are not a lad now?" The left corner of Neddy's mouth tightened and destroyed his stone-faced look as he asked the question.

Watt stared, then said, "Oh, no! I am beyond that stage." His hand showed it was so with a flick of his wrist, as if brushing away a nuisance fly.

"Oh!" Neddy said. He then let a few seconds pass before mentioning, off-handedly, "I went shooting with Captain Galloway up at Laplan, Wednesday gone."

That stopped Watt in his tracks.

"You did!" His voice went up two or three decibels. He reached over and gave Neddy's arm an excited tug. "Tell me all about it!"

As they made their way up the road, Neddy began to relate the tale of his adventures that week at the shooting party. Here and there he embellished, setting off a torrent of questions from his companion. When told how many birds the captain had bagged, Watt's astonishment seemed to know no bounds.

"How did he do that?" he had to know. Next, Watt demanded a demonstration of the captain's shooting style. Neddy complied. He stood in the middle of the road, swinging an imaginary gun right and left at the birds on their way to the feeding ground with sunup. "Bang! Bang!" he barked as they flew overhead.

When Conchie Blows

The makers of Galloway's guns fascinated Watt. For once he admitted to having little knowledge about guns. But he swore he would buy himself a set just like the captain's on his return home. His pair, of course, would have silver inlays on the stock with his initials and crest. Not that he had a coat of arms, but surely a gentleman of his standing would be granted one on his return.

"They must be the best fowling pieces ever made!" Watt said in wonderment. He kept repeating the maker's name over and over again, trying to commit it to memory. "On my return to Friendship, I will mark it down in my diary."

"Diary?" Neddy said. "What dat?"

"A book where I set down my private thoughts and what happens to me daily," Watt said.

"You do dat?"

"Yes. My father taught me. It's a way of keeping track of your life, so you stay on the straight road."

"Dat's sensible," Neddy said. "Mi should keep a diary record."

Neddy's description of the house and gardens and the people at Lapland had Watt spellbound. He went into a dreamlike state, as if he were a guest there—an estate owner of great stature. Neddy continued to wax wonderful, enjoying the effect his telling was having on Watt. As the accounting escalated, Watt became more enraptured with the images conjured up by his own fevered imagination. Further stimulation by his friend led him to miraculously transform the turkeys into peacocks, like those that strutted and preened on the grounds of Mount Vernon.

Watt said dreamily, "You say there are peacocks in the Gardens? Like in the Rajas' palaces in India? Oh, it must be a beautiful place, Mount Olympus no less." Stopping suddenly, he asked, "Can we go there?"

"One day, I can tek you, but it too far today, Watt." Satisfied with that promise for the moment, they walked on, saying little more.

The description of the food and drink seemed to send Watt into an opiate state. His hands slackened on the donkey's lead, and the long bamboo pole dragged along the ground as they walked. Then came the dramatic moment Neddy expected: Watt could not stand it any longer. He let go. The dry bamboo pole clattered to the ground and rolled to the edge of the road. Both arms went up in his usual lyrical appeal to the sky.

"Oh, my God! Oh, my God!" He stood still and, at the appropriate moment of staged direction, tossed back his head and stared for a full minute at the blank early morning sky. The floppy hat floated off his head and circled gently to the ground. A shock of blond hair streamed down to the nape of his neck like a glistening waterfall with flashes of red highlights.

"What torture," he mouthed. "What exquisite torture," he yowled aloud. To all intents, he was alone on that road. There was no one else to hear his prayer to the god of sustenance. Slowly, he faced his fellow traveler, who struggled to contain his laughter.

"If you had not fed me this morning before we ventured forth…" His voice cracked with emotion, his arms still lifted skyward. "But instead you had just told me about all that scrumptious food of the angels you devoured at Lapland…" His arms flopped to his side and, now facing Neddy, he concluded in a hoarse whisper, "I would have fainted right away, like a simpering female." A most woeful look engulfed his face. He sighed.

That did it. A screaming laugh shattered the tranquility of the moment. The sound vibrated through the bones, cut across the landscape, ricocheting off the rocks. Had they still been in Johns Hall in the colorless hours of the morning, lanterns and candles would have been lit in the sleeping houses and hands put over ears to protect them. Neddy had fallen on his hands and knees with tears streaming down his face. Watt knew he had been had.

Watt stared in wonderment; how could his companion be so cold-hearted, so bloody-minded? And with the knowledge of how much he depended on him—loved and treasured him? It was a total disregard of how badly treated he was at Friendship. The exhibition forced Watt to close his eyes in disbelief. For once, he was speechless.

It took a good two minutes for Neddy to get ahold of himself. He was weak from laughter. With the back of his hand, he wiped away the tears rolling down his cheeks. This was small revenge for that torturous hug Watt inflicted upon him, but his ribs were now doubly sore from laughing. When he got back on his feet, Neddy put his arm around his astonished comrade and exclaimed, "Lard, man! You good!" With the back of his other hand, he wiped away the last of his tears. He choked back a half-chuckle as they walked on for a little while in silence. Then Neddy added, "You know, mi tink di stars sey we should meet." Without a word, Watt's arm came around Neddy's shoulder, and, with Rosinante following along on his own, they walked on toward Tangle River.

About two miles up the valley, past Newman Hall, they met their first early morning traveler in dress-up-go-to-church clothes. Neddy knew him to be a Moravian and wished him good morning. Looking straight past him, he ignored the black boy's greeting but lifted his hat to the white boy.

"Marning, Massa," the man intoned, and walked on without a second glance their way.

Watt was quite oblivious to the subtlety and touched the brim of his hat in return. "I have to admire Jamaicans," he said. "They are so respectful to each other. At home, it is not so. Depends on your class whether they greet you or not."

Neddy chose not to enlighten him. Probably the man had speculated as to why, at this time of the morning, the white boy walked beside the black boy with a saddled donkey trailing behind them. It would be a topic for wagging tongues after church. That was certain. It worried Neddy. He did not like being the object of gossip. He decided to steer them off the main road onto a shortcut through the walk-foot backra smallholdings.

At least with these hapless whites, there would be no uncomfortable questions. And even if there were, they wouldn't matter. Most likely they would regard the sight of a white boy walking with a black boy with mild curiosity. Most of them would assume the black boy was the white boy's slave, or a servant, and would envy Watt his property rights.

At the next corner, Neddy pointed to a path that led off the road. "Come dis way."

"Lead on, my trusty Pancho," Watt said, grabbing hold of the donkey halter to bring him around to their new direction. They walked up a twisted, rock-strewn track, skirting the hapless whites' smallholdings, many of which constituted the final reward for the indentured labor of grandparents in the years before the black man was brought into the island as a replacement.

"Never knew there were so many poor white people here," Watt said. He could see life for these people was too hard for them to worry about what happened outside their miserable selves; they could only look on the great plantations across stone walls and in the valleys and wish for a thousandth part of what they saw there. He imagined that some of these blistered-back-raw men, who had not been ground down too far by the sun and rock-stone plots of land from which they eked a miserly sustenance, fantasized that one day their trifling acres would grow into great pens and estates, which they would rule as master. In the meantime, Watt could see they were forced to compete against the slave on his provision ground; these common people labored, like the slave, to produce that little bit extra that was sold to the Jew, who resold it to the town dwellers for ten times what he paid for the sweat and pain of black and white backs.

The villagers watched them with suspicion, but no one challenged them. Some may have wondered why the black boy walked in front of the white boy, who led the donkey. Surely, that should have been the other way around. All the same, as they made their way toward Tangle River, neither Watt nor Neddy could tell what thoughts filled the minds of these hapless folk, staring blankly or glowering in their direction for a passing moment.

They walked past the McDonalds' and the Frasers' places and on by those owned by Fletcher, Mills, and to the Gabays. A lone slave, grizzled and graying but marking his owner as rich and enviable in this meager community, said to Watt, "Marning, young Massa," as they passed him leaning on a hoe. His eyes followed them with the hankering of a dog left behind. With the day's progress, there would be only he and his master to deform and twist the land into giving on that hillside field: corn in one corner, banana suckers in another, and, the hardest of all to cultivate, yam hills dug out of the center. Ownership papers said the black was the slave and the white the master, but none could tell the difference by looking at them, as their hoes arced up and down in unison like pistons. A row of rocks and tree roots stacked like tombstones marked years of effort spent clearing the miserly land. No wonder the man watched the two boys go by longingly.

From a distance the girl had seen them moving up the hill and dismissed them as just two going about early business. One was black and the other white-white. As she turned away, the realization struck her: Boys! That was unusual in the settlement, and she took another look.

"Wonder who dem is?" she mumbled to herself. Lazily, Millicent threw handfuls of corn to the peel-neck chickens scratching in the dry dusty yard. A few of the scrawny birds clucked expectantly around her bare feet. She kicked them away and looked up again, using her hand to shade her eyes from the morning glare. The black boy looked familiar from the way he walked and held himself. The white boy leading the donkey—not from around here, that was certain. If they were, she would have known them right away.

One, two, three handfuls of corn spewed like sporadic jets of water around the yard from her cupped hand; the seeds bouncing like tiny pieces of rubber as they hit the ground. The chickens scattered, their beaks hammering at each coveted grain, sending it to their craws for the gravel there to grind, then passing on down their gullets for further refinement, eventually to be deposited on the yard for Millicent or her mother to sweep away.

Paying little attention to what she was doing, Millicent stumbled over a rotting plank on the ground. A roach that must have crawled there during the night scurried out into the harsh daylight. Chicken after chicken took up the chase. Pecking order and grain forgotten, one fowl and then another tried to gullet it; while the insect dodged, weaving its way to escape beneath the water trough. Clucking in frustration, the hens returned to the hunt for corn. But when the roach emerged on the other side of the trough, a young black Minorca rooster was waiting. Striking with lightning precision, the cock attempted to spear the insect with its beak. It missed. Again and again the red cockscomb bobbed up and down. At last! The beak clamped upon the roach, lifting it up. Still struggling, legs working for a grip in the empty air, it was hoisted still higher and then was gone, bulging for a moment as it was choked down to the grinding craw. Flapping its wings and stretching its neck upward, the cock crowed triumphantly to the world.

Millicent looked over at the bird and heard its satisfied cluck-cluck. She answered it with, "You soon get your ead chop hoff, han into di pot you going go. You just wait, you black ting, you!" A handful of corn pelted the young rooster, sending it flapping away. Millicent swayed and hummed to herself, her tension rising as the cause of her excitement got nearer. She could not help herself. She fantasized about being with the boys and kept looking in their direction, wishing they would hurry and hoping they wouldn't, so she would have time to contemplate possible moves.

Chicken feeding done, she lackadaisically whisked the dirt around with coconut boughs tied together in a makeshift broom. Forgetting its last undignified retreat, the rooster, followed by two sensay-fowl cockerels, got in her way; its glossy black feathered neck stretched to its limit, the cock clucked for more grain. The peel-neck cockerels did the same. Millicent swished the makeshift broom to shoo them away, but the black one returned, and this time she kicked viciously, sending it lopsided into the air. The two followers scurried left and right of her in panic.

She hated the broom and cursed that her mother didn't buy a real one from Tinka's shop. Her bloody lazy, bullying, pestering father could have made a better one. She looked up to see where the boys were and then turned back to the sweeping. But, oh no, Dada was more interested in her than the household. She stamped her foot in annoyance at the thought of her father and looked to see if her mother was watching from the dwelling. When assured she was not, she shaded her eyes with her hand, looking to see how near the boys had come.

It was nice to watch for new boys. Her heart beat faster, and her belly butterflies fluttered with expectancy. In one way or another, she already knew all the boys around her. What else was there to do? Marry one of them and become a slave like her mother on three acres of land under the burning sun? The question reverberated inside her skull painfully. No, sah! Two goats and a sheep would be all the wealth she could expect if they were lucky, and any surplus dragged from the unresponsive soil, sold to the Jew for a penny here and a quattie there. And Jews gave not a farthing more for the years of sweat and the cracks that grew upon their faces like gullies in a rainstorm. No, sah! Not for her. Much better to have fun when you can, and big boys were fun.

With all her being, Millicent hated the Tangle River district of downtrodden settlers and wished day and night to escape to town. She had never been there. Montego Bay was the magic place they talked about, and she yearned for its enchantment. One day, she promised herself, she would go and never, ever come back to these rock-hard hills that killed people with unmerciful toil—where women, year after year, gave birth and watched those withered things come out, shrink, and die of lockjaw, just like the pickney. A pickney mumma she would never become for white or black. If she should catch a pickney from enjoying herself, the obeah woman would scrape it out of her belly.

Looking around at the house and yard to see if they were clear of watching eyes, she took off, scattering the chickens about the yard in her haste. One crossed her path, and she could not resist giving a kick to send it flying to squabble with the others. Tossing the coconut broom to the side of the open gate, she ran down the hill to the roadway.

On the road, she sneaked around the corner where the boys had to pass and where the opposite bank hid her from sight above. The road was extra narrow there, and bush grew on the rise, adding a screen. Selecting a position where the boys could have a full look at her, she undid the string ties at her neck so that her young breasts were obvious and gave them an extra heave to fill out the blouse. Next, Millicent pulled up her knees to support her breasts while wrapping both arms around her legs, lifting the skirt just enough to show her ankles and bare feet.

Glancing at her exposed upper bust, she grimaced at the sight of all those blotchy freckles. Corn seed her brother called them, suggesting cow-itch weed would get them out. He put it down her blouse once when she would not let him sex her. Lord! The itch made her suffer for days. Inspecting herself further, she sucked in her breath, touching the painful sunburned patches on her arms.

As if suddenly recollecting why she was at the roadside, Millicent tossed her head and ran her fingers through her hair, fluffing it out to let some fall suggestively to the side of her face. Boys loved touching it; that was her best feature. She brushed it until it shone, using the old brush she always carried in her apron pocket. It came to her after Grandma Dougal died.

She loosening the blouse a bit more; she hated the freckles, but luckily they never turned off the boys. Her lot was to perspire in the merciless sun all day and pleasure herself with the first taker under the stars of the night. The spots couldn't be seen when the boys grubbed about her tits. Today she would risk doing it under the sun. It would be so nice to have soft, white skin like the ladies she heard about in the Great Houses and in town, bathing in cow's milk and never coming out in daylight. "One day!" she told herself.

Millicent Dougal waited on the bank for the boys to pass. As they came closer, she recognized the black one. He was from Kensington. Neddy, they called him. She sighed and wished that she would know him better. Often she had seen him down at Johns Hall and sized him up. In her short years, she had learned quickly which one had what, by just looking at how they carried their bodies and what showed through their clothes. The other boy, a white boy, she didn't know. Perhaps he would be interesting, too, but it was Neddy who held her attention. He must be bigger than the rest of them, she was sure. *He is so pretty. Lord! When did man make man such?*

If she could not have the one she desired, then she would take both. Millicent giggled. At sixteen, there were never enough boys. White or black, it did not matter, but the black boys filled her up. There was never an end to them. She giggled again. She moaned at the thought of them inside of her and wondered that they could not sense her presence and need from a distance.

A shudder shook her body at the memory of her mother catching her with one of them in the banana patch two years past. Millicent's eyes closed at the recollection of the lash cutting into her backside and across her shoulders. But it was what they called her that hurt the most—not just a whore but a nigger-loving whore. She never understood that. The high and the mighty, the rich owners of many slaves could love blacks and take them onto themselves, pamper the children that came out, but not so for the poor white. What was the difference, she asked herself, was it the wealth and position?

No slave ever had such a beating, but it did not stop her. The pleasure was too great, and for the time the boys were there she was alone, untouched, committed only to herself, free. If anything, Millicent preferred the black to the white, and a whipping was a small price to pay for their sexing. But it did not matter what the color; none of them was satisfying. After the first time, her father turned out to be the best of them, but he was white. A silent bargain was struck between them. He got what he wanted so long as he shared her with the blacks.

Romantically, she yearned for love and dreamed of the right one coming and marrying her, then whisking her away to a great house with slaves to wait on her, hand and foot. Often she looked longingly at men who rode by with their slaves trotting behind, but they never, ever glanced in her direction. Thinking about the rich, and the not so rich but powerful, drove her to utter frustration; a stream of spit squeezed between her two front teeth and landed on the dirt in front of her. A walk-foot backra was the lowest in the island, and that was what she was. Only the Jew figured lower. Young as she was, Millicent understood her social trap, and she resolved to get what pleasure there was whenever and wherever possible.

Lordy! She needed to go. Would she have time before they walked by? Nature had to be answered. She ran across the road, scrambled up the bank, and squatted behind a bush. Closing her eyes, gritting her teeth, she let go; as the piss flowed, it burned like hot oil spitting from a frying pan onto her flesh. Damn her father! Silently she cursed him every time.

Branded on her mind was the first time, when he took his virgin daughter to cure him of the clap. He was furious at the discovery she wasn't a virgin. He about beat her silly. Then it dawned on him that he had fucked his own daughter, and there would be trouble with his wife if she found out. Millicent could see him thinking it. Her mother always spoke the Bible at him. Often they would hear her at mealtime, going on about Lot and his daughters, as if that would prevent what went on between father-daughter and mother-son among both blacks and whites. Millicent recalled the look Dada gave her and knew what he was thinking; her mother would have no rival, especially not a daughter. Before throwing the switch away, he slashed her twice across the shoulder. In the end, both ended with the pox, but she had a hold over her father, and she took in exercising it when she stopped him going for her younger sister. She wondered if he had given the pox to her mother. She hoped so. Then all three could suffer in silence.

At last, the burning ended. She fanned between her legs with the hem of her skirt, then ran back to her place opposite and took up position. Her eyes focused on the boys; in seconds, wanton thoughts drove away the memories of the cause of her discomfort. Closing her eyes tightly, she could see and feel boys dancing in her body, and the image almost made her sing out with pleasure.

Could she hook them for a few minutes down yonder among the banana suckers? She would try. There may never be another chance. Few boys could resist her invitation. This time she wouldn't waste time with back-and-forth chat to make it seem they were doing the choosing. Boys were such fools, sucked in by her desires and then cast off, finished and wrung out like a washrag. How they begged for a second go; how delightful it was to play with them, to lead them on and then refuse. Their baleful faces gave her so much pleasure, sometimes even more than when they were in her, because it could last much longer.

Watt saw her first. "There is a girl sitting on the bank up in front of us," he said, pointing at her with the bamboo pole. Neddy looked up the pathway and recognized Millicent. At that distance, she looking deceptively healthy, but he was not fooled.

"She a notting," he said. "Jus walk on by er."

"Do you know her, Neddy?" Watt got no answer at first. They must have moved a good few paces nearer to her before finally Neddy came out with confirmation.

"She a gal who hangs bout."

"So?"

"She is big trouble, mi hear," Neddy said, thinking he had settled the matter.

As they got closer, the girl looked really good in the morning light. The sun had browned her rich and dark on the face and around her neck and arms, like the white meat of a chicken basted on a spit. Her mousy brown hair flashed with reddish highlights, and then her full breasts caught Watt's eye—firm and prominent as the sun shone through the flimsy blouse. He googled, then squinted to get a better look. There followed a surge of excitement—he could have sworn her nipples stuck out.

"Magnificent titties!" he declared aloud. All he got was a sideways look from Neddy, who hoped Millicent had not heard.

"I never thought I'd see white girls sitting on road banks in Jamaica," Watt said. "Until today, I'd thought all white people in Jamaica were rich, or in charge." For a good ten paces, he got no answer from his companion.

"Not all of dem. Plenty are poor. Mi da says slaves ave it better."

As they closed in on her, Watt became aware he was being inspected. Her eyes went from feet to middle to head and down again. He felt naked and went a light shade of pink. In turn, the girl did the same to Neddy. Obviously she was an available slut; Watt's face flushed almost scarlet with excited anticipation. He gripped the donkey's lead tightly and shoved his other hand into his trouser pocket, clenching his fist hard. She was there to be had; he knew it from the way she looked at him and Neddy.

As they came alongside the girl, a warm, welcoming smile transformed her face to that of an innocent. "Marning, Neddy," she said. Her mouth was soft and moist as it gave them the welcome; her eyes crinkled at the corners, and the beckoning irises were large and hazel like a doe rabbit's.

Neddy stared back at her without blinking. "Marning, Miss. How you know mi name?" he said. Too late, he regretted asking. It was the wrong thing to say. He wanted no truck with the likes of her and turned his eyes, looking down along the road in the direction they were headed, making it obvious that he was moving on. No sooner did he step forward than she stopped him.

"Where you going? Every gal here bout know Neddy." She looked him up and down again. "Dem tells me—it big-big and sweet like ripe plantain." She measured a length with her hands, then let out a dirty laugh. She threw her head and shoulders back, placing her arms behind, with the palms of her hands flat on the bank so as to stretch her blouse and make her breasts more prominent. The front threatened to break open and let them tumble out. Watt's mouth dropped open like a thirsty puppy's, his eyes wide. In and up the valley that separated each breast, he wandered, and on the enticing nipples his eyes stopped.

Neddy did not answer. He was furious. No crab-louse, yaws-leg, jigger-foot, backra-walk-trash had ever spoken to him like that before. This was one dutty little gal! If she kept carrying on so, she would get one big brute box across her face. The thoughts rushed Neddy as he turned to face her, sitting calmly on the bank. Her eyes ran up and down, assessing him, just like the day in Johns Hall square when his mother was there. He thought he would die then; now, he felt the anger rising. He wanted to strike out, hit her where it would hurt her the most.

It was as if she knew what he was thinking. She laughed, daring him to lose his temper, for then he would be hers. No black boy could hit a white girl and get away with it, no matter what his or her station. Suppressing the urge to retaliate for the humiliation, not even waiting to see if Watt followed, Neddy turned and walked quickly away.

"Mi know you wants it!" she taunted his receding figure. "Mi will give it to di white boy, too. Tink you can both tek mi? Come on. Mi sweet, you know." Her harsh laugh sounded heavy with disappointment.

Neddy almost broke into a run. He felt sick. Behind him, Watt urged the donkey to keep up. They had just about got around the next corner when Millicent's cry caught up with him: "Next time, Neddy, mi will give it to you and see how it stanup!"

He was trotting by then. Getting away from this bitch was the most important thing in his life at that moment. Watt was shouting to slow down, but he paid no attention to him, breaking into a run for a short while, then back to a trot. He must have gone a good mile and a half before he eventually slowed to a walk and stopped to let

Watt catch up. He trembled with anger. This was a dyam provoke, even more now than when he made a fool of himself with Bekah at Lapland. There had been no dirt attached then, but it was he who now knew what it was like to feel small and almost irredeemably soiled. Sitting down on the bank, he covered his face with his hands and shook his head. In the last couple of days there had been shame, shame, shame. First, the white men, then Bekah, now this. He was hurt, confused, and ready to strike out at anyone.

"Wait for me!" Watt said, puffing and wailing, tugging at the donkey and urging it, "Come on, Rosinante! Rosinante! Don't be a silly jackass, come on!" Finally he caught up with Neddy. After catching his breath, pushing his hat up, and wiping the sweat from his forehead, he stared at Neddy. Watt pointed back down the road and exploded, "What's the matter with you? What did that girl want?" He had guessed, but he wanted to hear it from Neddy.

At that moment, Neddy wasn't quite sure how to take Watt. He was about to scream at him. His fist clenched to hit him. Did he really not understand what she was? Looking at the sweat trickling down his red face, the blond hair stuck to his forehead, and that wide blue, blue-eyed stare, Neddy realized his friend only half knew what it was all about.

"She wan go a bush wid you," he said, and forced out a laugh.

"Really! Must say, that's very forward of her."

But Neddy discerned the excitement in Watt's voice. His eyes opened wide and a silly grin of uncertainty appeared around his mouth. What came next was expected.

"Let's go back, then!" Watt's Adam's apple pumped up and down like a yo-yo as he swallowed hard. Again it repeated, then twice more, to be rid of the excessive saliva which had flushed into his mouth, as if he anticipated food.

"You mad!" Neddy said. Horrified, his mouth dropped half-open. "You wan go back to dat nasty ting! Dat dutty gal!" Before his friend could answer, Neddy shouted: "*Raatid!* You mad to *raatid*!" They faced each other squarely in the middle of the narrow roadway.

"What's the matter with her?" Watt demanded, with a silly look on his face.

"You go a bush wid dat nasty, stinking little gal, and you come out wid di sickness, dat's what is di matter!" Stock-still, they glared at each other in silence. As the tension subsided, Watt eventually asked, "You mean she will give me the clap, like Duar's got?"

"*Clap*, you calls it? You go a bush wid her, and she will give you one bitch-clap you won't forget!" His voice fell back to normal when he said, "Much worse dan any clap your modder hand can give you. Your modder han pon your batty sting, but it soon gone." He nodded in Millicent's direction down the road. "Hers last forever."

The seriousness of the warning began to sink in, "You mean…" Watt hesitated. "She is a poxy doxy, and I would come out of the bush sounding like Duar at night, going for a piss?"

"Wad dat?"

They walked on. "We can hear him groaning and moaning as it comes out," Watt said, then became silent for a few more steps. "Sometimes he just whimpers like a beaten cur. It is a pitiful sound. Shirley just laughs and says, 'Serves the bastard right.' Is that what you mean, Neddy?"

"Yes!" Neddy said and stopped, staring at Watt to drill in the point. He didn't really know, but that sounded right, from all he had heard during after Sunday school chats with boys who claimed to know these things. "Yes," he said more calmly. Someday his innocence, his unworldliness, would kill this friend who walked with him to fish in Tangle River.

"She would mek yu suck salt trough a wooden spoon forever." There was no mistaking Neddy's meaning.

"Never heard that one before."

"Well now you knows it!"

"I thought Duar had blackwater at first. Then Shirley set me right."

"If him got blackwater, den im feel no pain—him dead to Rass!" Neddy laughed without humor, and there was nothing more to be said on the matter.

The boys continued to Tangle River along the well-trodden path, which was neither a path nor a road but a way beaten into shape by unshod white feet, before bare black feet outnumbered them in the island. Occasionally they met these walk-foot white people going in the opposite direction; some on the way to hoe yam roots from their grounds, or to church because they could afford that luxury, or to church because they needed the assistance of the Lord to help them provide for their families.

There was a willingness in the faces of those who passed them on their way to worship. At least, in the cool of the church, with the drone of the parson's voice to lull them, the men could sleep, a respite from their daily life for which they would be eternally grateful. Their wives would indulge them. They said nothing and did not nudge them awake. Their husbands were with them and appeared to adhere to the parson and the ways of the Lord, and that was what pleased them. The outward seeming was all that mattered. They were assured in the knowledge that the bounty of the Lord awaited them in the hereafter.

They had gone some way without speaking when Watt said, "Halt!"

Neddy looked around at him. He still looked sweaty and was obviously not accustomed to these long hikes under the sun, which had begun to turn up the heat at the eleventh hour of the day. Every now and then, Watt would lift the big, floppy hat and mop his brow with what now looked like a dirty sodden rag. They would be at Tangle River before the sun reached its full blast at midday, and then they could cool off in the water, but would he last until they got there? Neddy almost smiled at the thought, but the back of his neck still rankled from the taunting of Millicent Dougal, so he waited to hear the rest from Watt.

"Why in the name of Hades are we walking while this beast of burden trots behind us unburdened, as if out on a Sunday walk?"

"Auh! Im is." Neddy shrugged his shoulders and began to walk.

"A Sunday walk, indeed!" Watt fired after him indignantly. "Time for him to earn his grass. Let us give him our burden to carry."

"Im can't tek di two of us," Neddy said, without breaking his stride or even looking back.

"Yes, he can. He is as strong as anything. You can ride up on his shoulders, and I will sit his haunches behind you."

"It not going to work, Watt." Neddy stopped a few yards away. "It would be better hif we take it in turns. You walk, mi ride, and den we switch."

"That's an idea. But, I tell you, I need a rest. We must have come ten miles since leaving Johns Hall."

"Bout four."

"There you are. We are exhausted."

Neddy smiled. "All right den, you fus."

"No, together, or not at all," insisted Watt.

"Yu want kill di donkey? Tell you what, let us spin a coin to see who goes fus."

"That's sensible. Have you got any money?" Watt turned out his jacket pockets to demonstrate his penury.

Neddy carefully took out some copper coins from a little bag he had tied to his belt. He chose the brightest of them. "Dis a new half-penny." He showed it to Watt. "You wan spin it?"

"No, you toss it up, and I will call."

Neddy flipped it with his thumb. Up it went, twisting over and over, flashing in the sunlight.

At its zenith, Watt called, "Heads!" The coin hung for a moment and then began its spiral to the ground.

Neddy was first on it. "You win," he said, before Watt could see which side was up. "It a head."

Watt looked at him, narrowing his eyes in disbelief. "Do it again," he said, those blue-blue eyes of his not wavering for an instant from Neddy's black-black eyes, which stared back unblinking.

"No, yu win." Neddy grinned.

"Then let me do it," Watt said, reaching for the coin, his face determined.

"What's di matter wid you, you don't believe you win?" Neddy said, exasperated. He clasping the coin in his hand so Watt could not pry it away from him, if he tried.

"Mek mi tell yu something. Hif me win, on dat damn donkey mi batty sit right now. You tink mi foot not tired? Yu win—you hear? An hif yu don't ride im, mi will." Neddy turned and walked on, making an end to the argument.

Watt couldn't understand why Neddy always seemed to get the better of him. After all, was he not Don Quixote and Neddy Sancho? Perhaps that had been Cervantes's intent in his book?

Watt struck a pose in the middle of the road; a frown screwed his eyebrows together, and his right hand stroked his chin, as if he were some great philosopher pondering the question. He looked up to see Neddy's back getting further and further away. Without giving it a second thought, he grabbed the donkey's halter and nimbly vaulted into the saddle. "Giddy up, Rosinante." He kicked the donkey into an uncomfortable trot. When he got alongside Neddy, he said, "Don't be silly. Rosinante is a big donkey, and I have seen two people riding one donkey many times."

They stopped and looked at each other squarely—Watt, with a pathetic countenance marked with dirt where the sweat ran down, and Neddy, his scowl duplicating the seriousness of a teacher about to deliver a lecture to a miscreant student. The sour face didn't last long. Watt's pathetic look was too funny.

"All right, den." Neddy gave in with a big grin. "We haven't far to go. You move back, and mi will sit front-side." The big jack hardly seemed to notice the added weight as they settled themselves on his back.

Not much farther along from where they mounted together, Neddy turned Rosinante right onto a path going up a hill. They could see that, over time, the beat of heavy rain had carved gutters in the land, aiding its water torrent downward. Rocks, dug up from the earth, were washed clean and smoothed by the rains hammering during the season; then, for the rest of the year, the sun baked them white until they resembled the vertebrae of gigantic animals long dead. A few smallholdings gave way to more unruly growth, with the odd hut and yam-patch of some free Negro or, more likely, slave who had just taken off from his master without as much as a *by your leave, Massa*. They were entering rougher country not far from dense bush, where escapees could hide and wait for their pursuers to give up.

Many in the district were there without freedom papers, overstaying their leave from their masters. As soon as their masters appeared, they gave themselves up quietly, knowing that they could and would flee again. The thirty-nine lashes they got would not deter them. If warned in time, they disappeared up into the hills around Mocho, returning when the all-clear sounded. It was a cat-and-mouse game they played with their massa and the maroons who hunted them for the bounty.

Head down, Rosinante labored, carrying the boys up the hill past a small, blue-washed house on their left. Patches of whitewash had been daubed here and there on the blue as an added touch, giving the walls a mottled appearance. In front of the cottage were the signs of many stamping feet, which, with the help of wind and rain, had kneaded the grassless yard dirt into clay on which the sun had later baked a hard crust with a smooth brown sheen.

Two wooden posts bound together in the shape of a *T* stood in the middle of circle of whitewashed stones. From each end of the crosspiece, a white chicken dangled by its claws. Both birds had their wings spread stiffly apart, as if they had gone into a headless dive. Blood had splattered the wooden posts and dripped to the dry, absorbing earth. An unruly hedge of croton bushes with yellow and scarlet leaves enclosed the yard. Overhead circled John Crow, waiting his turn to feed upon the dead, rotting carrion suspended from the cross.

"What's that?" Watt asked, pointing at the cottage, trying at the same time to grab the reins from Neddy in order to stop and take a closer look.

"Keep going," Neddy said, signaling the donkey to do the opposite with his heels.

Watt did not protest and let the animal continue on the way. "That's a strange color to paint a house. I have seen one like it before."

"It a duppy blue. It keep duppies away. Where you see one?"

"The place I went to. There were no dead chickens hanging upside down, though."

"When was dat?" Neddy said, pulling the donkey to a stop just past the dwelling. He half turned to look over his shoulder at Watt, eyebrows raised in astonishment. This was very strange. Neddy wanted to know when and where Watt had encountered obeah. After all, it wasn't long ago he had listened to him scoffing at the idea of obeah, duppies, and, worst of all, rolling calves.

"It was last Tuesday," Watt replied.

Neddy nudged Rosinante to move on as Watt spoke.

"The day was about to close; I had to take the bullocks back to their paddock. I collected Mount Joy and the rest of his company and started off to their pasture." Watt paused. "Hmmm," he said. "Don't understand it, really, but a girl had died on the day before from eating dirt. What a thing to do."

"Mi know bout dat." Neddy glanced over his shoulder.

"How could you?"

"Doctor Ferguson come by Newman Hall and tell the captain. I heard him."

"Oh."

"Go on wid what yu was telling me." The donkey kept moving forward, uninterested in the conversation being held on his back. If they could have read his thoughts, if he had any, he would have wanted only to get where they were going, so he could unload them and get to the grass.

"Bardolf appeared. Couldn't believe it. First time I had seen the slug outside the Great House since arriving at Friendship. There was this dray being pulled by two mules and driven by that one they call Marky. Bardolf sat in a chair placed in the middle of the platform, and beside him, lying flat out, that disgusting slave of his, Biblow. He was moaning and groaning, as if harpies were tearing his innards out. A young boy stood beside Bardolf's chair, holding a parasol over his master's head. The sun was nearly down, so I have no idea what the parasol was for, probably to keep the boy steady while Bardolf's arm was round his waist—for support I suppose?" Watt's shrug went unnoticed, as did Neddy's head movement as he rolled his eyes.

"You have never seen anything like that! The field slaves, who were just going back to their huts, set up a cheer and began to laugh when they saw the equipage. You could see them nudging each other and just hear what they were saying about the Zulu, as they call him, and the boy, and that lizard laid out on the dray. Bardolf, the slug, didn't care."

"What dat mean again?" asked Neddy, as if he had heard it before.

"What?"

"Equi... ting."

"Oh! Horse and carriage, but Bardolf's was mules and dray," Watt said, with a merry, tinkling laugh.

Neddy noted *equipage* for the future. There was no doubt, he was learning from Watt, just as Watt learned from him.

Rosinante plodded on. The grade of the hill grew steeper, slowing the donkey's pace as it struggled for the first time with their combined weight. The boys did not notice; they had all day together, and it was wonderful to be free from supervision, alone and adventuring. Watt carried on with his story.

"Bardolf saluted the slaves with a wave of his hand. They cheered again. Then he saw me on top of Mount Joy and signaled me to approach—he is the overseer, after all. I rode the bullock over. Never remembered he was so fat and awful; it had been weeks since Mr. Fray had taken me to meet him, and I had forgotten. Chalmers does all his work." Watt paused, took a deep breath, and continued.

"His hat was like a Chinese coolie hat. You know what I mean? It comes from a point at the center and spreads down in a circle like a cone. Its rim goes so far out, it even shaded his shoulders. It suited him. The boy with the parasol was obviously only for show. The sun was almost down, and he had the hat on anyway."

Neddy let him go on chatting without interruption until Rosinante began to noticeably labor with their weight. Neddy suggested it was time to dismount to give him a rest. But Watt ignored him and continued.

"The fat rolls his face up, and his eyes are chinked. You could not tell him from a Chinaman in China, except he is bigger. Just sat there, looking like the big fat yellow Buddha on my father's mantelpiece. Look at what I mean." Neddy turned to look over his shoulder to see Watt squish up his face to make his eyes squint. "That's what he looks like!"

"Yu going look like him if yu keep doing dat."

"Never! I will never be that fat, no matter how much I eat. Besides, they are starving me to death. I'll be a skeleton first." They both laughed at that idea.

WHEN CONCHIE BLOWS

"Come Christmas," Neddy said, "with a face like that, yu can join di Jonkunnu and dance bout an beat drum an blow whistle."

"Who are those?"

"Yu don't know? Lard a mussy! Boye! Next two weeks dey will be all bout, beating drum and frightening children." Neddy remembered how they scared him when he was a little boy. He would hide behind his mother, nuzzling in the folds of her dress and clinging tightly to her as they danced and cavorted about the roadway. Even now, they still brought a feeling of apprehension when he heard them beat their drums and watched those ugly, horrible animal masks on their heads, bobbing and weaving in and out of the ecstatic Christmas crowd. A donkey-headed man with its tongue hanging loosely from a mouth with red teeth; a bull head with its horns lit with torches; and, most frightening of all, black and white face masks with mirror eyes, flashing light everywhere they looked, like spirits freed upon the living world from the deepest, darkest pits. He disliked this aspect of Christmas. Juju and obeah were at hand, instead of Christ. Neddy's bottom tightened, and his back flesh crawled at his mind's pictures, even now in the hot sun. Nervously, he glanced back to where they had passed down the hill.

Unaware of this ball of fearfulness gripping his friend's innards, Watt calmly continued with what had happened, puckering his forehead as he tried to imitate all the voices. "Bardolf said to me, 'You ave to come wid us, Massa Cope. We a go somewhere to cure Biblow.'

"'What's the matter with him?' I asked the slug. He didn't answer, but that Marky did for him.

"'Duppy a sit pon im bed at night and suck out im soul.'

"'Cockamamie!' I exploded." Before Neddy could ask for an explanation, Watt was onto it. "Means *nonsense*. Heard an American sailor use it on the ship I came on. He had been pressed, you know? Wonderful word, don't you think?" Watt saw the back of Neddy's head move up and down in a nod, confirming the rightness of the word, and he continued.

"'Di young Master Watt Tyler-Copes come a Jamaica, and im don't believe in duppy, Marky?' the Zulu said in mock astonishment. 'We going ave to teach him different, Marky.' Bardolf chortled, and

304

that jellyroll of a stomach began to waddle up and down and sideways as well."

With a little hand-rub on the side of his neck to stop a kink, Neddy turned again, looking over his shoulder at Watt, this time with an eyebrow cocked in disbelief.

"I swear, up and down and sideways," insisted Watt.

Neddy turned back around. They were both so absorbed—one in the telling and the other in the listening—they did not notice their mount was taking smaller and smaller steps on that steep path.

"'All right, whose duppy is sucking out his soul? Does he have one?' I smirked. That got the slug going.

"'Course im got a soul, as good as any white boy,' Bardolf snapped at me. Quite put-out, he was, at my idea that the lizard-like creature lying moaning on the dray was a soulless reptile.

"'Di little gal who nyam di dut,' put in Marky. Biblow whimpered as if to confirm it was her.

"'Duppy doing him in.' Marky jerked his thumb in the direction of Biblow. 'She say, im tek er pussy wid out she give im, and dat's why she eats di dut an dead.' Biblow groaned again—Marky screeched with laughter. He was cut short when Bardolf cuffed him around the ears.

"'Shut you mout!' Bardolf rose unsteadily and turned to me. 'You come along wid us. Anoder white man won't urt,' he said. 'You can ride im.' He pointed to Mount Joy.

"'Mr. Bardolf,' said I, 'what about the rest of the cattle? We can't just leave them wandering about.' I had hardly finished when the slug turned and bellowed at the late stragglers from the fields: 'You come ya, now!' They stared at him without moving. 'Come now! Or I will strip your black hides wid di cow whip.' He meant it; they knew it and ran over to us. 'Tek de cow dem to where dey goes—now!' he shouted, pointing a fat finger in their direction and then turning away, paying no attention to their *Yes Massa, yes, sa, Massas.*

"'Young Mass Cope,' he turned to me. 'You follow behind us.' He cuffed Marky again. 'Move off an keep yu mout shut bout Biblow, you unnerstan!'

They got to the top of the hill, and Neddy called a halt. Rosinante obeyed, breathing heavily from his effort. "Let im rest a little. Di river just down di hill." All three breathed in the air for about a minute before Neddy guided their mount around to face the way they had come and pointed below, to the left of the settlements scattered on the hills. "Dat is Kensington, where mi live; an way below is Friendship, where you lives. Kensington is where we going wid di fish we catch."

"If we catch any."

"We going catch plenty. What di matter wid yu! Yu want to know where Laplan is? See dat house way over dere." He pointed to the left of Kensington much further up into the hills, again past the smallholdings. "Dat Mount Apfel, where mi mam's fren Miss Appy lives. Lapland is way past dat, right up in di hills. Yu can't see it from ere. Dat how far it is. I will tek yu some time, but we ave to go early—early."

"I will keep you to that promise, Neddy. Where is the river we are going to? I can't see any."

"Right down dere." He pointed to the valley below them, thick with clumps of bamboo.

"I can't see any water. You sure there is a river down there?" Watt frowned.

"Course I 'm sure. See it over dere." Neddy pointed to where a river meandered through the settlements. He turned in the opposite direction. "See it over dere as well." He pointed to a silver thread in the distance that disappeared into the jungle. "Tangle River twis and turn all bout. An down dey where we going, di bamboo hide it."

His geography lesson done, Neddy turned the donkey back and gave it a kick to descend to the river in the heavily forested valley below.

"Finish what yu was tellin mi appen to yu, Watt."

Rosinante began slowly and surefootedly to pick his way down the hillside, as Watt went on with his story.

"I don't know how far we traveled with me tagging along behind the dray on Mount Joy. Biblow moaned and groaned all the way. We got to a gully. One of them warned Bardolf not go down it. He argued it was the shortest way, and down we went. Quite hair-raising. We skidded most of the way down, because it was all limestone shale, and not even the mules could get their footing. Old Mount Joy managed, but he had trouble and went down on his haunches once or twice. I only stayed on by holding on to his hump. He is of the Brahman breed from India, you know.

"Coming out on the other side of the gully was impossible. Naturally we could not get up the side with the heavy dray on the shale. The mules could not get their footing and kept sliding back down. To make things worse, night had fallen, and the pitch black was even blacker, if that is possible, in that hellhole. We could not see where we were, or where we were going. All we had were two weak lanterns giving off very feeble light. Mark Antony panicked and began to scream:

"'Lard Gad! We lick batty gully! We neber gets up, we going bury ere. We goin dead an bury!' He kept repeating it hysterically, till Bardolf couldn't stand it anymore. Again he struggled out of his chair and let Marky have it about the ears, *whack, whack*. The cuffing turned his bawling to a whimper. That was a most pathetic sound to hear in the darkness. Like a lost spirit wondering about in nothingness for eternity."

"Yu soun like Captain Galloway."

"Really! Has he a poetic turn of phrase, as well?"

"Go on wid di story, Watt."

"We kept on trying to get up the bank. They whipped the mules without mercy. Bardolf began to blubber like a babe. It was sickening. Then Biblow began howling. Ever heard a dog howl in pain? Well, that was he. I did not know what to do. I just sat there, Neddy, atop Mount Joy, with not even a dim outline in front of me but all those strange sounds echoing in the cavernous night."

"Where were di lantern dem?"

"One had gone out and the other one might as well have, for all the use it was," Watt said.

"At last, along came two men out of the darkness. 'Lard Gad!' one said. 'Batty gully grab dem. Yes sah, massa! Dem stuck good.' You could hear in the man's voice that he was pleased. Don't know which estate they came from. Didn't matter to Bardolf. He ordered them to help us. That's when all hell broke out.

"'Oo you ordering, red man?' They must have known Bardolf. But it was so dark we could not see who they were or which one was speaking. The lantern did not illuminate to where they stood, and they were invisible in the starless night in that hollow. They kept well clear of being seen properly, let me assure you.

"'You damned nigger!' Bardolf said in a rage. 'If you don't elp us, I will kill you.' He ordered me, 'Massa Cope, shoot di rass where he stan.'

"'Can't do that, sir,' I said. 'The man's done nothing.' Neddy, I had hardly finished when a screaming laugh shattered the night. It gave me the willies, and even Mount Joy's hide shuddered. It was a cross between joy and the anguish of one whose flesh is burned from living bones.

"In between his horrible sounds, the man got out, 'White man understan black man. Black man understan white man. You know why, red man? White man got a country, and black man got fi im country, but red man got no country. When di white man free di black man, im gone im country, and di white man gone a his but where di red man goin go?' There was another burst of scoffing laughter, and you could hear the man slap his thigh, as do many Negroes when they laugh.

"I don't."

"Well, you are not—" Watt stopped. "You are different—you are my best friend."

Neddy laughed and slapped his thigh.

"Oh, stop being a jackass! And let me continue," Watt said, grinning.

"This denouncement came from somewhere in the darkness. You could not tell where exactly. They kept moving around so that Bardolf, who then had his pistols out, could not get a bead. He just kept waving them around dangerously at every sound of movement. I was worried he would blast Mount Joy or me. I sat not twitching a muscle, and the bullock stood stock-still, as if he knew there was a madman loose. Then the voice stopped, and all we heard was the occasional crunch of gravel underfoot as they slunk away.

"We were stuck. A deathly silence came over us down in that black pit. Only the puny flicker from the lantern gave any relief to that colorless place. Bardolf ordered it placed on the dray, and I could see their outlines.

"Biblow stopped his stupid noise, and Bardolf sat back in his chair, not moving. The boy squatted down beside him on one side, with Biblow lying still on the other. It was all very ghostly in the feeble lantern glow. A duppy sight if there ever was one." Watt laughed. "It looked as if we were going to be there all night. Then, I got a brilliant idea.

"'Mr. Roy, why don't we harness Mount Joy to help the mules pull the dray out of the gully?' It galvanized them into action. There was hope again; an extra rope was found, and we rigged the great bullock in front between the mules. I led the animals in the pull, and Marky and the boy pushed. Bardolf and Biblow stayed where they were on the dray. Exhausted, we finally got out over the crest of the gully.

"Once we were safe again, Bardolf, half weeping like a girl, declared, 'Mi will alway remembers you wid kindness, Massa Cope.' I suspect he always addressed me as Massa because he knew I had a special relationship with Mr. Fray and perhaps because of my color. Why are brown people disliked by black people, Neddy?"

"What appen next?" Neddy said, ignoring the question.

"We must have traveled another mile or so at a very slow pace. We went up a bush path, like the one Rosinante just brought us up, and there was a hut, just like the one we passed."

Neddy grunted, and Watt continued. "There were no dead chickens hanging from posts—well, none that I could see—but the walls were painted blue. You could see by the torchlight. It was quite a change from the silly lantern we had. You could see the place miles away. What did you call it, duppy blue?"

"Uh huh," Neddy said.

"There were torches stuck around the yard in a circle and a few Negroes sitting on stools, as if waiting for someone to appear. Some of them came out and helped Bardolf down to the ground and lifted Biblow off the dray. The boy and Marky stayed outside with me and Mount Joy."

Suddenly Watt pitched forward. He threw his arms around Neddy's waist to keep from toppling off. The donkey had arched its back, trying to steady itself on its descent.

"Whoa dere, whoaaaa!" Neddy said, and brought Rosinante to a stop. "We better walk down from here. It steep, an di bush get ticker down dey."

They slid off the donkey's back and continued carefully down the incline with Rosinante in front of them.

"Now!" Watt exclaimed, as if on a stage, his forefinger stabbing at the sky. "For the frightening part of my little adventure with Bardolf and his confederates."

"Dere is more frightening dan what yu tell bout in di gully?" Neddy looked wide-eyed. "Boye! Yu really go trough some ting den."

"There was I, still perched atop Mount Joy, when this decrepit crone came out the door of her hut. She looked up, and in the flickering torchlight saw me on good old Mount Joy. Immediately she placed the palms of her thin, clawlike hands over her eyes. At the same time she opened her mouth wide, not a tooth in her head, and she let out a scream that peeled your skin away, as if you were a banana."

Neddy looked across at Watt. "Yu mus a put yours back on den," he said, his white teeth flashing in the sunlight. Then he giggled, which brought a contentious look from Watt.

"Oh, really!" Watt said and sulked down the hill for a few minutes before continuing.

"Several minutes must have gone by before they silenced the old bitch. 'What di matter, Modder?' asked one woman, rubbing the claws with her hands. 'His all right, you ear?' Finally the old woman stopped trembling and pointed a boney, knurled, crooked finger at me."

"'Di white boy a ride a white rolling-calf. It di mark of deat! All di niggers goin dead!' She let out a moan like a sick cow and slumped onto the ground in a sort of trance. Then her body jerked as if stuck with needles, and she began to beat the earth with her palms. She thrashed about on the ground, like a chicken with its head cut off, until as suddenly as it began, so it stopped. There was silence. Still lying on her back, the gap in her face that some might call a mouth opened to expose an abyss of unspeakable depth. As if from the bowels of the earth, her voice rumbled: *'Deat rides on di lan. Im hooves crush di nigger. Im sward chops di nigger. Deat! Deat! Deat!'* She lay still, as if dead herself. Two men who came from inside the house picked her up between them. Her head hung back, nearly touching the ground. Her eyes were wide open, and she stared at me unblinking, as they transported her indoors.

Neddy looked at him with a serious cast on his face. "Yu not fooling, Watt?"

"Tell you, Neddy, I don't mind saying, it made me a bit nervous. Bardolf said something to Marky and the boy, then to me he said, 'Massa Cope, you got to go quickly, sah! Di boy ere will go back wid you and guide you.' I took the boy up in front of me on Mount Joy. He didn't mind, and off we went. I was glad to be gone from the place.

"At last! The sky seemed to brighten up; the clouds moved off so that the stars shone through and lit our way home. We skirted the gully. It took longer, but the boy knew which way to go. Don't know what happened to Biblow, and don't much care."

"Dem would give im a bush bart or some ting, to drive di duppy off a him," Neddy told him.

They had made it to the bottom of the hill, and Neddy guided them onto a little-used track meant for only one walker at a time. Bush had grown up in many places, hiding the way and making the going difficult. They had to push through the growth leading the donkey, who came along reluctantly. Neddy had to get behind and slap him a couple of times to move him forward. They ducked under low branches and avoided others that seemed to reach out and claw at them. Eventually they broke into a small clearing.

Rosinante was tied to a tree with enough rope to allow him a wide feeding area. With the donkey comfortably secured, Neddy grabbed his things and signaled Watt to follow him through a seemingly impenetrable wall of bamboo. With his guide in the lead, Watt managed to squeeze through this natural palisade to come out on the river. To his surprise they were suddenly standing on soft, buff-colored sand beside a crystal clear pool ringed by protective bamboo. A small waterfall cascaded over smooth rocks at one end, keeping the pool fresh and new; somehow at the other end, the pool transformed itself back into flowing water to rejoin the main river hidden beyond.

Dropping his voice, as if in church, Neddy said, "It a mi secret place." His hand swept around in an arch. "Dis come off di main river. Dat is over dere, behind di bamboo. If yu over dere, yu don't know dis is here." He pointed to the pool and the waterfall. "The bamboos keep it hidden." Watt placed his hands on his hips and turned slowly about; at the sight of the sparkling waterfall he took a deep breath as if, indeed, this were a holy cloister.

The last of the food was unpacked from the bucket. Neddy walked over to the pool and half-filled it with water. They would need the bucket to carry the fish they caught, he explained to Watt. And he added, "We can eat later. Wi going swim and fish fus."

Watt stared at him for a second with a hungry look, his mouth half-open as if to protest his starvation. Neddy waited for it, but this time no request for food came. Instead Watt exclaimed, "Great idea! A cooling swim after our hot march." In a flash, he was naked and in the water before Neddy could get his shirt off.

After sloshing around for a bit, they got down to the serious business of catching crawfish. Watt had to be shown the trick, and when successful, after a few tries, he threw out a challenge to see who could catch the most. The hunt began directly. In the excitement that followed, they waded from rock to rock, sticking their hands under to scoop out sand and sometimes a wriggling crawfish, which was thrown into the pail half filled with water.

A consequence of their chase was to churn up the bottom of the pool, obscuring its inhabitants. That put an end to their competition. Who had won, neither could say. Both had lost count of their captures. One claimed victory and the other denied it. This led to a rough and tumble in the water, churning it up even further. Eventually the even match came to a halt.

"We got nuff-nuff to cook ere and to tek for mi modder," Neddy said, pointing to the bucket on the bank.

"I thought you were going to catch a mullet. How are you going to do that without a line and hook?" asked Watt, with a superior look.

"Get out of di water, so yu don't fuss-fuss it up. Den, mi will show yu ow to catch di sweetest fish in a di world."

"Me! Fuss up the water!"

Ignoring his protest, Neddy pointed to a smooth rock at the top of the falls where Watt could watch the action. "Go stan up dere, Watt."

Watt looked up at the rock and obeyed without argument.

Neddy watched him gingerly climb up the falls from rock to rock until he was safely in position. He had to admire the effort and realized that physically, they were much alike. Neddy wondered what Millicent would do if she could see them now. He ducked his head under the water to wash away the thought. Surfacing, he shook his head like a dog, then banged the palm of his hand against his right ear to clear it of water.

Trying not to stir up any more of the river bottom, it was his turn to move watchfully through the shallow pool to the point just below the falls where they had found most of the crawfish. Watt stood, looking down. It was still murky, but the sand was settling, and the translucence of the water had begun to return.

Where the eddies swirled about, Neddy bent over, letting his hands dangle in the water by his feet. He must have stood like that for two to three minutes without moving, the waterfall crashing noisily behind him

To Watt, on his designated perch, it seemed everlasting. He kept very still, though, watching, waiting, straining to see through the water. Dark, idling shadows began to appear around Neddy's hands and feet. Were they fish, or a trick of light? Suddenly, with a flurry of water streaming from them, Neddy's arms came up, and something was sent flying through the air—flashing silver in the sunlight—to land flopping, gasping on the bank by the pail containing the crawfish they had caught earlier. A minute later, another one followed, landing not far from the first. After that, Neddy looked up at Watt and signaled to the fish on the bank.

"Get dem an put dem in wid di crawfish, to keep dem alive an fresh," he yelled over the sound of the falls. He watched as Watt scrambled down from his perch across the rocks back to the bank, then returned to his catching posture.

It was not long before the third fish narrowly missed Watt's head to land at his feet.

"Marvolouso!" Watt yelled, jumping into the air to avoid another flying fish. He bent and added it to the burgeoning contents of the bucket.

Neddy hooted with laughter, watching his antics.

"Let me try that!" Watt said. And before Neddy could stop him, Watt rushed into the water with legs going up and down like a prancing horse.

"Slow down, yu goin frightens dem away!" Sure enough, the waters became clouded with sand. The fish vanished. Neddy just laughed and shook his head.

He spent the next few minutes demonstrating the technique of catching fish without a line and hook. "Yu wait till dem cross yu hand, and den yu gently tickle dem on di belly. When dem steady now, and just lay dere, yu flip dem out." He left Watt to it and went over to the bank to get a breather and watch the fun.

Again and again Watt tried, sending much water flying but no fish. He was making too much noise, and the fish were fleeing. Neddy let him carry on. His head nodded into a doze, then a cry jerked him wide awake. A fish came flying through the air to plop on the bank not a foot away. Watt was rushing through the water, sending spray everywhere with each plunging step.

"I got one! I got one! A big one!" he shouted, unable to contain his excitement. He fell upon Neddy in his joy. The next thing they knew, they were locked in a wrestling match. Neither would give way; back and forth they rolled, arms and legs entwined, each trying to get above the other. Locked in battle, their breathing came in short, sharp gulps. So close was the combat that at times they looked like the fused black-and-white grain of polished mahoe. At last they broke apart, their passion abated, and lay still, trying to catch their breath, neither one a winner or a loser. Two, maybe three minutes passed. Half recovered, Watt rolled over to retrieve the fish that lay almost dead on the sand and place it with its kind in the bucket. He returned to lie beside his friend, who had not moved.

For some time nothing was said between them. Then Watt, with a slight tremor in his voice, broke the silence: "We will always be friends, Neddy?"

After a pause, Neddy rolled over on his side and looked at the white boy for a good few seconds. "Yes," he said, then rolled back to watch the clouds drifting over the waving crest of bamboo above.

As the wind passed through the alcove, the bamboo creaked and groaned at its joints, like those not far from the grave; the leaves added their hush and whistle to the mournful sound, like fearful crones whispering in unison about a boiling pot of skin of snake and leg of lizard. But the waterfall added a cheerier voice, as did the song of a joyous petchary on the wing. Lulled by these sounds, the exhausted boys slept as if in a nursery. Dusk's shadow began to fill in the space between the clumps of bamboo before either of them stirred. Neddy woke first, frightened at the lateness of the day, and shook his companion hard.

"Come on, Watt, we got to go. Lard Jesus! It late!" Hastily, they brushed the sand off themselves and got dressed.

"God! I am hungry," Watt said.

"It too late to cook up di fish now. Yu going to ave to wait till we get ome."

"I'll die by then. Can I eat it raw?"

"Yu mad, yu know!" Neddy grinned.

"No, just hungry," Watt said. They both laughed, and for some reason the laughter made them feel better.

"Mi got two dry Johnny cake lef in a di cloth and some plantain. Yu ave one and mi ave one." Neddy went over and got his bundle, and they sat down to eat the last of the food.

"Don't suppose you have anything to drink in that bundle of wonders?"

Neddy shook his head, and Watt shrugged.

They were about to go when Neddy stopped them. "Wait a minute. I want to tell yu some ting. Sid down back, Watt."

When Conchie Blows

Watt obeyed, a feeling of apprehension beginning to work its way around his gut.

"Mi don't want notting to appen to yu, so mi going tell yu. Three tings yu got to be frighten of in Jamaica." Neddy began the count. "Hurricane is one; when de foreign man invade his di secon one; an slave rising his tree. Dat is di worse one. Every year, we get one or di oder of dem."

Watt's dread began to diminish as his friend spoke, as it all sounded like the oncoming of a great adventure. He let Neddy continue.

"Jamaica black man bad, and mi tink dere is going to be one big some ting soon. Bunning, killing, and tiefing. Trouble always appen bout Christmas time. Mi want yu to be extra careful dis Christmas."

Watt looked at him from under his eyebrows, "You forgot there is something else to be frightened off."

"What dat?"

"Duppy and rolling-calf." No sooner had he said that than he went into a rollicking laugh.

Neddy got up, grabbed him by the shoulders, and shook him for all he was worth. "Mi serious! Lissen nu—mi serious!" he said, staring into the other's eyes. The laughter abated, and the smile closed.

"I have heard tings." Neddy said. "Yu have to be careful."

"When is this going to happen?" Watt said as he adjusted the floppy hat, the nervous feeling creeping back into the pit of his stomach.

"Mi don't know—but mi hear tings all di time."

Neddy picked up the bucket and began to lead the way out. On reaching the bamboo opening, Watt turned back to take a last look at the little waterfall and pool in the fading light. He took a deep breath, held it, and slowly exhaled. "You know, Neddy, this is a magical place," he said, with the calm assurance of its truth.

"Mi know."

Chapter 11

Saturnalia

With a mule and a donkey pulling, the higgler's cart made its way slowly up the driveway of Kensington Pen. Both animals struggled with their uneven size and gait to keep moving forward and upright as they passed the sugar works, trash houses, and fermenters, and rolled on in front of the Great House toward the slave quarters. On reaching these huts crowded together in no specific order, the cart trundled along more slowly between them. Miss Dodd was in good humor. When all was said and done, this was Christmas time! There was money to be made and enjoyment to be had. Thus she paid little attention to the mismatched animals in the traces of her cart.

Heads appeared through doorways and bodies from behind the dwellings: Hands waved in her direction, and in return she greeted these, her sometime customers and suppliers, with a cheerful wish for a Happy Christmas and freedom next year. It pleased her to hear them come back with, "Freedom! Yes sah, freedom! It come fi true."

Wishing a Happy Christmas was all right, but freedom was dangerous. She could be in trouble for inciting the slaves against their masters, but the risk was worthwhile if it filled her purse with Christmas cheer that jingled like the little silver bells the white people hung by the windows for the breeze to blow tinkle-tinkle.

When Conchie Blows

Freedom had to come, and she was for it because it would fatten her purse, or so she thought. With everyone expecting the freedom paper, to say nothing would have marked her as one of them, rather than one of us. She could not afford that. It would be bad for business, and Miss Dodd loved business and money too much to keep her mouth shut. Let the overseers and bookkeepers challenge her—damn them! Their days were numbered. She waved, she bowed, she smiled, and she laughed merrily.

Daddy Sharpe and the Baptists were working for it, and freedom would surely come. Only a matter of time. After Christmas the sitting-down strike and demand for wages would begin. Freedom and wages for work. She could almost hear the clink of coins going into their pockets and then into hers. She kept this part of the knowledge to herself and moved on, like a great lady in her carriage, bestowing her good wishes to the right to the left and down the middle.

A few of the girls, involved with different sets, came up to the side of her cart, begging her to look if there was any more ribbon for them in Montego Bay. She smiled, waved, nodded, and kept going, but stopped the cart when a few held out glistening coins. They would really like the new gold or silver ribbons, but they couldn't afford them, so the red and blue would have to do; would she bring what she could find?

Out came a little hard-covered ledger from the bulging pocket of her traveling apron over her voluminous skirt. From underneath the cart bench, a small box held tightly shut by a leather strap was produced; and from its innards she brought out two turkey-cock tail feathers cut to write with, a bottle of black ink, and one of blood red. Carefully, Miss Dodd noted who had a down payment and who did not. In black ink she wrote the names of those with money and in red those with payments to come. As her quill scratched and dipped for more ink, Miss Dodd thanked the Lord for the profit.

Rich young white men would look under their frills and feathers for prospects hidden there. Old white massa was a better catch yet. The girl's best chance for success came with the three days allowed for festivity at Christmas. They had to outdo their rivals, but, if worse came to worst, they did not mind sharing with each other or with the one who already held the housekeeping position. The white missus, if there was one, didn't matter. It was expected her husband would bed a girl elsewhere in town. Besides, there were ways for the missus to make up for her husband's absence.

To catch the eye of the right massa who would look after them as they had his children was a dream prospect for many pretty little gals. It was their door to freedom, with the added pleasure of having to do no work except sleep with him when he demanded. That was better by far than dreary labor on an estate. As the twenty-fifth of the month drew near, they were almost at fever pitch with expectation. It was so when Miss Dodd was young, and she suspected it had always been that way. Pretty girls, and those who thought themselves pretty, excitedly begged around her cart.

Miss Dodd promised to see what she could do by Christmas Eve morning, shrewdly pointing out it would cost them extra; at the same time, she mentally noted those who complained that it would be too late; other sets would steal the march on them in town and would get the best pick. These girls could cause her worries. It was the best she could do: It was "takes it or leaves it," Miss Dodd told them. Some, knowing full well that she was taking advantage, accepted and agreed to pay the extra; others said they would do with what they had and flounced away from the cart, sulking that they could not afford any more adornments to their dresses and themselves.

One tearful girl pleaded for Miss Dodd's help. She had bought cloth to make her dress from de Lazarus, and when she washed it, the color ran and spoiled the cloth. With eye water streaming down her face, she begged Miss Dodd to let her owe her for new cloth. But the higgler wisely told her it was too late for any help from her and added next year she should remember not to deal with the Jew. The girl's sobs became uncontrollable. A friend got her out of the way to a nearby hut. Girls had no money for ribbon, never mind a dress!

"Ha!" Miss Dodd said. "Di Jew man grab di pickney gal money and run wid it like Bra Anancy tief di cooking pot full a rice an peas." She laughed, knowing that the parable would be well noted by those listening. "She just a spit of a gal anyway. Di titty not come out yet.

Er time will come—don't bodder tink oderwise." That said, the girls would understand why Miss Dodd would not extend her credit.

A nicely shaped quadroon girl pushed forward. With hands placed on her hips, she shook above her waist from side to side and asked coyly, "Fi mi own sweet enough for a nice gentleman, Miss Dodd?" If she expected the affirmative, she was disappointed.

"How mi to know dat, mi dear? Mi not a nice *gentleman*," said the higgler woman. The most unladylike shrieks of laughter came from those who heard. From the other side of the cart, one girl muttered, "Masie tink she better dan us because she brown," followed by a sucking of teeth. Miss Dodd looked directly at the speaker and decided against making a rejoinder; she had refused the girl credit for a pair of shoes.

Returning each item to its proper place, the ledger to her pocket, and the writing implements to their box under the seat, Miss Dodd gave salutations and moved her beasts forward. As the cart left, the girls began laughing, giggling, and chatting among themselves as to what they were going to do with the ribbon when it came. Prettiness was all that mattered to them, and the more the merrier. Good taste did not cross their minds. A gaudy show could win the attention they sought. For this they needed to add to their already overdecorated dresses.

Finally, the mismatched pair in the harness pulled her lumbering cart past the throng toward Quashiba's house. That was where she was heading in the first place. Edward would be long gone to work, so she could have a sit-down chat with Quashiba before getting down to business.

Would Quashiba let her son come with her? That was the question in Miss Dodd's mind as the mule and donkey struggled to pull her cart up the hill. She needed extra help, and the boy struck her as just right. Few boys could be trusted, but Neddy was another matter. Miss Dodd reckoned he was like his mother, straight and true. His assistance at this time of the year would be just what she wanted. She did not like admitting it, but time was crippling her. The legs did not move as fast as they did once, and her back gave her pain with all the lifting of baskets.

At their last meeting, the boy had been willing and able and seemed trustful. Calculating two shillings currency for a day's labor at this time of the year seemed right. That would be enough money for a boy his age. More than most men could get. She would offer to pay him the two shillings for the day's work. Half a crown was the most she would go. Maybe, hif he was good, an extra six pence for Christmas brawta. That would be generous, and the thought gave her a nice feeling inside.

Her mind was awhirl with figures. Adding a halfpenny more to a quart of Jerusalem peas would cover his expense without troubling her profit. Many would complain, but they would pay. *Anoder quattie to di Christmas okra*; she nodded, doing the mental addition. "Yes, sa!" Miss Dodd said to herself and her animals. "Christmas time, we can mek a little ting, not just change fa change." The prospect pleased her as she looked up to see Quashiba waiting on her arrival.

Her hostess-to-be stood watching from the small verandah Edward had added to their house. Quashiba was glad to see the higgler coming up the hill. Miss Dodd would know all the latest about the freedom paper and would bring her the news. Observing the conveyance, she smiled. There had been some additions since last they traveled together to the bay. A new mule added to the donkey and a bigger cart. Miss Dodd must be doing well, thought Quashiba, as she called out her greeting when the cart drew up to the steps.

"Lard! It good to see you, Quashiba," called Miss Dodd in return, heaving herself off the cart seat. "It getting harder with each day to manage, you know." Her breath came in hard draughts as she lifted her voluminous skirts to mount the three steps leading to the verandah.

"Come tek a cup of tea with me, Miss Dodd. Sit yourself down, and I will get it. Di water a boil, so it won't be long." Quashiba left her guest to catch her breath in the rocking chair while she went through to the back where the meals were prepared for the family.

She reappeared on the verandah with a tray carrying a china teapot and two white bone china cups. She placed the tray on a small table beside her chair. As she picked up the teapot to pour, she looked up at her guest, "You tek sugar and milk, Miss Dodd?"

"Only milk, tank you, Quashiba." Her hostess poured the tea into the cup first and then the milk.

"Some tink it is better to pour di milk in fus and den di tea."

Without looking at her guest, Quashiba corrected gently but firmly. "Well, my teacher was Miss Rachel Fowler, who owned dis estate, and hif anyone knew her God and her manners, she did. Besides, milk in tea is only a new fashion. You know, Miss Dodd, dey used to drink it from saucers, an first time some even eat di tea leaves in England."

Miss Dodd knew she had been bested. Her attempt at creating social distance had not worked. It was better to say no more. How this countrywoman knew about fashion was another matter. It was unsafe to inquire into such mysteries. Better stick to what she knew about, and that would put them back on a balance.

"You hear bout the freedom paper?" Miss Dodd said.

"Not a ting."

"Dem say it in Jamaica, but di planters won't give it to di people."

"You don't believe that, Miss Dodd. If it in Jamaica, dem ave to give di freedom," Quashiba said.

"Mi don't know bout dat. Seems Daddy Sharpe knows some ting an im not saying." Miss Dodd gave Quashiba a knowing look after her pronouncement and heaved her large bosom from side to side to make the point, much as the young girl had done in front of her cart to show off. Miss Dodd's chair squeaked in protest, as her movements went contrary to their designated direction.

"Hif he does, den we would all know soon enough."

"Im always play tings close to im chess, you know." Quashiba was given that knowing look once more. Miss Dodd would not be outdone on this matter.

"If di paper is here, and de people don't get dem freedom, dere will be trouble. Dat will be di extra trouble."

"What extra trouble?" Miss Dodd looked a little surprised. She took a sip of her tea, making it look as delicate and ladylike as allowed by her once voluptuous lips.

"Christmas."

"What bout it?"

"What day it pon?"

"It drop pon Sunday dis year."

"Right den."

"Mi don't see, Quashiba, what you talk bout?"

"It a go round dat Christmas Eve pon Saturday, Christmas pon Sunday and Boxing Day pon Monday dis year; di slave dem only get di Monday off, and it's is back to work on Tuesday. You know di law say dey to get three days Christmas time, and dem always get Sunday off."

Miss Dodd nodded her understanding of the problem. "Dey should get Monday, Tuesday, and Wednesday off dis year an dem normal Sunday. Mi see what you mean. Yes, sa! Dem na get it, den trouble." Her voice dropped ominously with the last words.

"Take here," Quashiba said. "When old Miss Rachel live ere, no more dan fifty slave pon Kensington. Since she dead, an Massa Morris run it, dere is well over a hundred an fifty, an most of dem are bad naygar—lazy, tief, and drunk. Im buy an sell dem like cow. One time de Dutchman, what im name?"

"Lindorp," volunteered Miss Dodd.

"Yes, dat him."

"Im is a Jew, you know," Miss Dodd added, with obvious distaste.

"Im bring some slave from Cuba to sell Massa Morris, but im wouldn't buy. Im sell some of im own to di man. They mus a gone a Cuba or America by now. But what left pon Kensington…" Quashiba leaned forward in her chair. "Dem not barn pon this place. Dis is not dem home. Dem don't respect it!" She leaned back again. "When freedom paper not come—problems." She took a deep breath, folded her hands across her lap and exhaled, moving her head from side to side, as if anticipating sorrow. "Big problems, Miss Dodd, very big problems."

"It sound bad," Miss Dodd said. "But I tell you, Quashiba, if dem follow Sam Sharpe instruction to stop work, and work only if dem get pay, we will win. Lard Help us!" She threw her hands up. "If dem start trouble—dat's all di massa want. Di soldiers will shoot dem down like di backra shoot down bud up in a di hills."

As her friend ended, Quashiba remembered all those birds Neddy had brought back from Lapland that Massa Galloway had given him. She remembered, too, her son telling her how many Galloway and the other gentlemen had shot. He had seen hundreds being plucked and cooked at Lapland to keep them from spoiling. She didn't like Miss Dodd's comparison at all.

"God willing, none of that will happen," she said boldly, keeping her inner trepidations from her guest. There was a moment of silence as each contemplated the possible outcome of future events. Before Quashiba could continue, Miss Dodd opened up the real subject of her visit.

"Quashiba, mi come to beg you some ting," the higgler said, showing the big, kindly smile she kept for her best customers.

"What that, Miss Dodd?" A funny thought struck Quashiba as she replied. She never called Miss Dodd by her Christian name. That intimacy did not seem necessary between them. Come to think of it, she had never heard anyone call Miss Dodd's name. For the first time, sitting there looking at the higgler, waiting for her to continue, Quashiba wondered if she had a Christian name—or had they baptized her *Miss Dodd*? She stifled a chuckle, replacing it with a gracious smile.

"Mi want hire Neddy to help mi over di Christmas Eve." Miss Dodd anticipated a few *hums* and *ahas* and then, *yes*. How could his mother refuse her smiling offer?

Instead her hostess sat straighter in her chair with her hands firmly placed on its arms.

The posture worried Miss Dodd; it looked like a refusal was coming. Her smile became stuck in place.

Quashiba said nothing. She let the silence sit between them as she contemplated the asking. It was one thing for Massa Galloway to hire her son but quite another thing for a higgler to suggest employing him. She was not sure about this. He wasn't for anybody to take on like a common slave, even if it was for money. She was about to refuse, saying she was sorry, he was needed at home on Christmas Eve. That would have been an acceptable excuse, but Miss Dodd would probably have seen through it as a slight. The higgler drew out a big bandana and dabbed her face. To offend Miss Dodd was not wise or wanted, but Quashiba would have to establish what was what, regarding her boy.

"I will ask him." She did not return smile for smile. Just to make sure that Miss Dodd understood that this was a special time and not a request to be tolerated again. Quashiba articulated clearly, "As it is Christmas time, and I know you are in need of help, we will make this a special exception." She made the point without shifting in her chair, as she had seen done many years before. There could be no mistaking her intent. It was as if Miss Rachel Fowler were speaking through her, not on the small verandah of Lawrence's cottage but on the verandah of Kensington Great House.

"I will pay im well, Quashiba," Miss Dodd said, hoping that would settle her hostess. Money was everything to everyone, according to Miss Dodd.

"I know you will, Miss Dodd, but it's not the money. It's that you will take him to Montego Bay at this time, when all the looseness goes on, and thiefing, fighting, and may well be killing."

"Don't worry bout dat. I will make sure notting bad comes his way."

The higgler got a look she understood to mean, *you had better*, along with a mother's tentative reply. "I am sure you will."

Miss Dodd sat back in her chair, her big smile glued to her lips; she would get her helper and not have to pay him the extra shilling she was going to add to her ready-made calculation, if his mother had bargained.

"He is out back. I will call him, and you make the arrangements with him, Miss Dodd." Quashiba got up and went through the house. Miss Dodd could hear her calling to her son. There was a conversation between the two that she could not make out. A minute or two later, Quashiba returned to her guest. "He will soon be ere. Im just washing up before coming to see you."

Miss Dodd nodded, with the smile evident again. "Neddy come like a nice boy you can trus, dat's why I hask," she broke out. Not waiting for his mother's agreement, she continued, "Dem boye you can get to help you, huh! Dey help demselves before dem help you.

When Conchie Blows

Dem call *Helpers*. Dem is well named." She opened her mouth and cackled at her own play on words and rocked backward and forward in her chair with enjoyment. Its squeaks protested her weighty movements, threatening collapse, but the chair held together.

"Honesty is not big wid people anymore," Quashiba said. "Dem days gone. Sometimes I wonder hif it is because freedom is in di air, and dey tink dat when slavery over, dem can do any ting dey want." Her words lost their stricture as their talk returned to the state of Jamaican society.

Miss Dodd thought about what had been said and added, "You know, you right; freedom can cause problem we don't tink bout." They both fell silent. Neither wanted to say more. If they continued the conversation, both feared they would be in danger of discovering some flaw in their held beliefs.

"You want to see mi, Miss Dodd?" Neddy appeared around the corner of the house, tucking his shirt into his pants and retying the knot in the rope which held them up. It was the relief both ladies wanted.

"Yes, man," said Miss Dodd, cleverly adding status to his youth. "Mi need some elp. Mi is prepared to pay you well." She turned on her big smile for him, as if bestowing some great beneficence. "Mi will pay you two shillings to elp wid mi ting tomorrow, Friday. Mi will bring you back by Saturday, for Christmas Eve wi your modder and fader to celebrate di birt of our Lord Christ." She raised her hands and clapped joyously in Baptist fashion.

"Dat is two shillings for each day, Miss Dodd? Four shillings all togeder?"

The smile vanished from the higgler's face. What was this, a little boye bargaining wid di great Miss Dodd, di bes higgler woman in di land! She couldn't believe what she was hearing. As quickly as it had faded, her smile returned. Casting a look at his mother, Miss Dodd made her appeal. "Lard Gad, Quashiba, di boye fancy imself. Him will brok mi!" Her expected support did not come; she was left to dangle on a limb.

"Well, it is between di two a you, not fi mi business." Quashiba gave her son a smile of encouragement.

"Mass Galloway pay me half a crown for one day's wok, and im brawta it up to a crown in di end."

"Im a spoil you!" Miss Dodd almost screamed in shock.

"Mi couldn't do no wok for a day under two shillings an sixpence, Miss Dodd."

Hearing that, she thought she had got him. "All right, mi will pay you di half crown hif you come wid mi now."

"Mi mus come now, den tomorrow and come back ya on Saturday?" Neddy looked at the sky as if calculating what time it was and how many more hours he would spend with her on Saturday.

"Since di day nearly finish, it one shilling for today, half a crown tomorrow and two shillings for Saturday." He counted on his fingers, "Dat will be five shillings and sixpence, Miss Dodd." His face stretched with a wide grin.

"Mi brok! Mi brok! Mi brok! All my little Christmas monies gone to dis ya boye!" she loudly exclaimed, at the same time wondering where dis ya boye gets so much sense. There was no getting away from it—the price of the Jerusalem peas would have to double. Her mind was going like a Chinese counting machine. Abacus beads flew from one side to another, counting a farthing added there, a half penny more to this, and a penny more on the Christmas okra. The sorrel, now, was scarce this year. She could double their price, and they would still buy. About four beads flew from left to right. Ginger! She could tell them, *It bring all di way from Christiana, where di bes grow.* Charge more for that; more beads mentally joined the pile on the right of the frame. Yes, she could pay him and get more out of it for herself.

"All right den, five shillings his mi lass offer."

"Mi will take dat," said Neddy, in an off-handed manner.

"You got to come wid mi now, you unstan?"

"Yes, Miss Dodd, hif Mam let me go?" He looked across at Quashiba, who had taken it all in with wonderment, secretly relishing the realization that her son was no fool. She gave her consent with a nod and thus sealed the bargain between Neddy and Miss Dodd.

"Hum!" Miss Dodd said. "Tell you, Quashiba, when freedom papers come, hif dem all like dis boye—nobody going hire dem.

Coss too much!" Her hands spread wide, palms up to emphasize her point. It hadn't come to mind before that free labor, banded together, could ruin business. She understood well enough that everybody had to make a little money, and if one group demanded more than their share, everyone would suffer and business would dry up. She began to rethink freedom and its financial benefit. In her heart of hearts, she knew the boy was not asking too much. His was a fair bargain, but most of the slaves were ignorant and greedy. Let loose, who knows what would happen?

"Mi will feed im well, Quashiba, and im will ave a comfortable bed to sleep on tonight over at my place."

"I am not worried bout him, Miss Dodd." Turning to her son, Quashiba cautioned him, "Behave yourself, keep out of trouble, and do as Miss Dodd tell you."

"Yes, Mama," he said, making sure to look serious, rather than betraying his feelings of joy at being employed again—and this time going to Montego Bay to see all the Christmas fun.

From the back of the cart, he could see his mother standing on the verandah as they made their way past the buildings of Kensington. Neddy could tell she would not move until they were out of sight through the gate and on the roadway. It was reassuring that she was always there, watching over him. Sometimes she could be too much, but he knew how to get around that. He had learned not to take her on headfirst like his father did. Sweet her up and do as she said, then he got most things that suited him.

From the verandah, Quashiba watched the slow progress of the mule and donkey pulling the cart with the higgler and her son; it was a bit of an emotional jolt for Quashiba to realize her boy was growing up fast. *Too fast*, she thought. Soon he would be a man and want to take a wife. Her fingers tightened on the verandah railing. Then she shook the thought from her head. That fancy would be years from now, she reassured herself, and relaxed her grip on the wood. At least when the time came for him to take on regular paid work, to support a family, he would know how to manage. That thought pleased her. She smiled to herself thinking, about his performance with Miss Dodd. To hold his own, or even best her, at his age was quite something.

When the cart rolled out of sight, Quashiba's mind wandered back to the upcoming Christmas and the rumors circulating around the state of the freedom paper. Edward had even joked that the governor at Spanish Town used it for "Blood Clart." She shook the crudity from mind. What was Daddy Sharpe playing at? He knew that the paper was not in the island. Surely it would be better to come right out and say so, like the other preachers. That would keep the peace. Knowing how people stay, if the paper was not here, would they obey the call for them to stop work and demand pay? Perhaps that was it. Keep them guessing, then they would follow him. If that was it, then it was a good plan, but if anything went wrong…"Lord help us!" she said.

* * *

Galloway stood, checking himself in front of the long hall mirror. Timmy stood at attention like a good soldier, watching him.

"An how do I look, sor?" the captain asked the child.

His answer came in the form of a military salute and big smile.

"Soldiers are not supposed to smile on a parade, sor," Galloway said, as he picked up the four-year-old and held him aloft. Then he hugged the boy close and kissed him on the cheek before putting him back down.

"You look fine, Massa," the boy said with glee.

The expression on Galloway's face changed. He winced as if lashed when he heard the response. "Don't call me that, Tim," he said emphatically, but without rancor. The child's smile vanished, and a look of hurt came over his face. Galloway immediately bent down picked him up again.

"It is time…" He hesitated briefly as he looked straight into the boy's eyes. "You called me *Father*. No more of this *Massa*—do you understand, Tim?" He kissed the boy again, putting him back down.

Galloway had not heard Lucy come into the passageway. It would not have mattered anyway. He had reached the conclusion that his domestic affairs would be changing in the New Year, and there was no time like the present to begin the process, at least with the boy.

Normally the child called him *Sir*. His mother must have taught him that. But occasionally the *Massa* would come out, and Galloway hated that from someone to whom he had given his family name and the name of his father. It was time to move forward; official fatherhood would be his once again.

Lucy stood back in the corridor, not daring to move. Her heart and mind were racing. Christmas was upon them. Was this going to be the present she dreamed about? Galloway looked at himself in the mirror again and saw her reflection behind him.

"Ah! An unbiased opinion on mi turn-out, at last! This little one flatters me and says I look fine. If I had been in my true regiment's uniform, I could understand that." Galloway tugged at the front of his jacket with both hands and flicked an imaginary speck of dust off the red facings of his blue uniform coat. Half pivoting, he tried to see what he looked like at the back by standing sideways to the mirror. "Mi have doubts in this militia get up," he said. "How do I look?" he asked her firmly.

"You look fine, Massa."

"*Sir*," he corrected sharply. Noticing her wince with the rebuke, he explained in a more kindly manner, "I would prefer that from now on you address me as *Sir*. Leave the *Massa* for the rest, Lucy."

Further niceties would have to wait for some other time. Duty called him now, and he had to get on to Montego Bay. His post as captain in the militia cavalry, on duty in town, waited to be filled. Every Christmas time it was the same. The militia was called to the main centers of the island in case there was trouble. Not much had happened in the last couple of years, but this year there was an undercurrent of trouble, swelling and rising as the full moon tide ran. Rumor after rumor about freedom had hotted up the slave population.

They were always a volatile lot in Jamaica. Some quirk of the trade had landed slaves from the most warlike tribes in Africa, like the Fante and the Fang, and sometimes they even made the mistake of bringing on board an Ashanti to work the plantations. But the most belligerent were the Coromantees. Fierce people at the best of times, at the worst, they were like the Viking berserkers, whose lust for blood was insatiable. When in a frenzy, they had been known to lop heads off and play ball with them, rolling them from man to man to kick at.

In fear of this, some overseers refused to give meat to their people and kept them fed on vegetables. Galloway laughed when they tried to convince him that was the way to tame slaves. "Meat," they claimed, "stirs their blood to rebellion." Overseers would burn dead cattle before letting their people make use of them as food. Galloway, on hearing these stories, was never sure who was the greater savage— the overseer or those he oversaw.

It was getting late as he descended the front steps to John and his waiting mount. As he settled himself in the saddle, he touched his boots with the whip. "You did a good job on these, John," he said. "Thank you."

"Dat fine, Backra, always a pleasure for a gentleman, sah."

Galloway kicked the horse into a trot and set off down the drive. Halfway to the gate he saw a cart, with a mismatched pair drawing it, coming toward him. Dusk made it difficult for him to make out the occupants. It wasn't until he was practically on them that he recognized the local higgler and behind her his erstwhile employee, Neddy.

Pointing the riding whip at him, Galloway said, "Ah ha! Neddy! I take it you are working for Miss Dodd? Good man! I hope she is paying you well? She should be, at this time of the year."

"Christmas time, Massa, mi always give dem little extra," Miss Dodd said, with a show of dignity befitting a lady of position and wealth.

Galloway smiled, leaned forward in the saddle and touched her arm gently with his riding crop.

"It is not Christmas to which I refer, Miss Dodd. It is Saturnalia. The Winter Solstice is upon us; the Lord of Misrule roams the land, when masters become slaves, and slaves become masters. You should know that, Miss Dodd." His eyebrow arched upward as he gave her a hard look. If she could have turned pale at that moment, she would have. But, no more cream could be poured into her coffee half. Her color had been cast a long time ago. So she smiled the smile of stupidity; she only vaguely understood the captain's words, but their underlying meaning came through sharply. She stared over his shoulders at the hills behind, as if appealing to a higher authority, wondering what he knew.

The captain backed his horse away from the cart, giving Miss Dodd room to heave a sigh and breathe more easily. He knew she was the carrier of hearsay that flew from mouth to ear on the estates, and he would have loved to hear her latest half-whispered communications. They might have enlightened him about the coming events, he suspected.

"Lard! Look how di sky red like blood!" Miss Dodd said loudly while pointing a fat, beringed finger over Galloway's shoulder at the sunset. Cleverly, the higgler latched onto the opportune distraction to divert the conversation from the direction in which it was headed.

Caught off guard, Galloway turned in his saddle and looked behind him. "It is a winter sky come down upon us, Miss Dodd." He turned back to fix her eye-to-eye. "Not often seen in the tropics. Many souls are calling for entrance at heaven's portals. Yes, sor!" Galloway paused, his eyes half-closed, and smiled. "A good and safe Christmas to you, Miss Dodd—and to you, Neddy. May she triple the money she is paying you, boy."

Galloway chuckled, knowing full well the impact his words would have on her. It gave him a little pleasure, seeing her grimace before he rubbed more pepper on the wound. "Yes, mi boyo, a rich lady like Miss Dodd should pay you triple, or at least half a guinea and not currency, if for nothing else but to guard her goods. It is a strange time of the year. She could lose it all in a flash, for ruffians, rapscallions, and reprobates walk her way at night." With a mocking smile, he touched his hat's brim with the whip, then brought it down onto the withers of the horse, and off they trotted toward the gate.

Neddy watched Galloway post up and down rhythmically in the saddle until he was out of sight. Beside him, Miss Dodd grumbled.

"What im tink mi is? Give wey di little profit mi mek. What would be lef? Im want me to live in di poor house." Carefully she avoided looking at her helper.

For a moment, Neddy had thought maybe, just maybe, she would pay him at least the same as the captain. Her words dashed any expectations of that, when the horse cantered away. A bargain was a bargain, Neddy reassured himself, and settled back in the cart. He looked up at where the sun had set over the hills. Miss Dodd was right; the sky was red as blood. Long, dark clouds like plumes of smoke curled across it, and as he gazed at the crisscross pattern on the red backdrop, a slight evening breeze touched his flesh and made him shiver with its damp. He had never seen a sunset this red before. Strangely, he did not admire the sight, and the vision and the breeze made him shiver again.

"What di matter wid you?" With a worried look on her face, Miss Dodd studied him. "You not coming down wid night-air fever?"

"No Miss Dodd, jus di breeze ketch mi."

She gave him another side look as they trundled on toward the house. She had no wish to hear what his mother would say if he came down with a cold or a fever.

Mule and donkey pulled them on up the hill. This was Miss Dodd's last call to pick up some white yam and extra sorrel from one of her suppliers on the estate. She knew this one well. He made a special effort to have those extras, come Christmas, for her. He was a good farmer, farming all of his provision ground to provide for his family, with any extra produce to trade with her or de Lazarus. Time after time he complained to her that he worked for "de tief, di Jew man, you, den miself, and den again de tiefing-tief." Thinking about his words, forgetting Neddy would hear, she began talking to herself.

"Yes, sa, Massa! De naygar bad, bad. What de white attorney call it: *praedial larceny*?" She laughed at pronouncing the fancy phrase and then went on with her self-conversation.

"No sooner de crops came to fruit, den anoder come in the patch a tief-tief. Dem don't even wait pon it to ripe. Rooting and stripping just like a pig, dey destroys all di Sunday hard labour of anoder slave." She grunted her disgust. "Hif it wasn't the white massa crops dem steal, dem steal from anoder same like dem. It going be di same when freedom come," she said.

Sitting behind her in the cart, Neddy listened as Miss Dodd became more agitated.

"What mi going do when di freedom come? Dem na work. Dem tief! Wid slavery, now, mi know di sun come up and di sun go down. Freedom come now, which way tings turn?" She fell silent. Life, Neddy realized, had become uncertain for Miss Dodd.

It was late when they got back to Miss Dodd's house. It was small, but neat. One large room and two smaller rooms at the back. There was no porch or verandah, like his home—but then Miss Dodd wasn't, like his mother, married to the best carpenter in the world.

As compensation for this shortfall, she did own nearly ten acres planted out in crops. What she didn't use, she sold. Her holdings alone could keep her well, but she loved trading and higgling. For planting and clearing, she hired jobbing slaves. The end of slavery wouldn't mean much to her there. Paying people for work on her land was all she ever did.

In her house, well, that was different. She may have felt a Baptist shame, but she had bodily needs. Miss Dodd owned a young brown-skinned gal who did housework. She hadn't bought her. The girl came as repayment of a debt. De Lazarus and the other sons of Abraham were not the only moneylenders available to those who needed quick cash to indulge a fancy. Many thought the girl was Miss Dodd's own. She had acquired the girl in her younger days, when she began her higgling and wasn't all that particular about what she sold. She did not naysay those who held that they were mother and daughter. Her church people preferred that to the idea that one of them owned another human. There was even a resemblance—like the one they say a dog takes on from his master.

It was to this girl that Miss Dodd spoke when she asked that food be brought for Neddy and herself.

"An Janet, mi want you mek up di bed in dat room, where you sleep, for dis young gentleman." Neddy's eyes opened wide at that, making Miss Dodd chuckle. Her ample bosom heaved up and down with the sound. She really broke out into a merry peal of laughter when she caught the frightened look on the maid's face.

"Mercy me!" she said between her laughing. The big bandana came out to wipe her eyes. "You too young for dem games. Night food not fe you just yet." She looked over at Neddy. "You modder would a kill me. Gal, you going sleep in mi room, wid mi. Now, go get what fe eat."

Relieved, Neddy couldn't help but see the humor in it and laughed. Miss Dodd looked at him "You a grow up." She punctuated this assertion by shaking her forefinger in his direction.

They were up very early the next morning. The sun had not yet cast its glow on the eastern horizon when they departed for Montego Bay. Miss Dodd was up, and all were busy before Neddy had got the sleep out of his eyes. She had the animals together and harnessed them, while, to start their bellies off for the day, Janet prepared the coffee and turn-cornmeal with callaloo mixed in and salt herring on top. Wasn't often that Neddy got cornmeal other than as porridge. He remembered when he was about eight, at Christmas time, cornmeal was given out to the slaves along with their cloth, rum, and fish. His mother had bought some, making it into the nicest bread he had ever tasted.

By the time they had got past Barnett and Catherine Hall, it was eight o'clock. As they entered the outskirts of Montego Bay, Miss Dodd began calling on her customers and delivering their orders, always enticing them to buy more of her produce, insisting they did not have enough for all the guests who would be showing up at Christmas time. Most of them agreed. Those who owned slaves knew this only too well, for in addition to their friends who attended their dinner parties, their slaves came to dine as well. Masters and mistresses fed them at Christmas by tradition. In they came to dance and course, like any white person, in the halls of their owners, in town and on the plantation. Usually the town servants behaved well enough, but in the country, drunken naygars could get unruly, especially when they were let into the Great House to cavort with their massa.

It wasn't until well past nine o'clock that they reached the upper part of Union Street near the girls' school. They had drawn up at Miss Laird's place, right across from Miss Cope's school for young ladies with pretensions to gentility. Neddy had not really paid much attention to where he was. He had carried out Miss Dodd's orders as they came. Montego Bay was unfamiliar to him. Sure, he had been there a couple of times, but the side streets were unknown, and the people were strangers. Miss Dodd gave the orders, and he carried them out to earn his shillings.

Both his hands carried baskets loaded with yams, sorrel, gungo peas, and a precious half-turned breadfruit. Where Miss Dodd acquired that at this time of year was a mystery. But Neddy could be sure it would cost Miss Laird double what she would pay ordinary times.

"Neddy! Neddy!" someone shouted, and to hear his name stopped him in his tracks. Instantly, he knew who it was, and a broad grin covered his face. He turned to see where it came from. "Up here! Up here!"

He looked for Watt, but saw no one. What was he doing in Montego Bay? "Up here, Neddy, look across the street." On the upper verandah of Miss Cope's school was Watt, waving both arms like windmills.

"Wait there, I will be down straight away. Don't move!" Watt said.

Miss Dodd looked at the shouter and back to Neddy.

"Who dat?" she asked, as the figure disappeared into the upper floor of the house before emerging again out of a side door into the garden. "Im somebody me know," Neddy explained. "Im a book-keeper over at Friendship." By the look Miss Dodd gave him, he knew that piece of information should have been kept to himself. It was too late now. Watt came charging across the road, but before he could do his usual embrace, Neddy prudently sidestepped him.

"What are you doing here?" Watt asked breathlessly.

Still smiling at their unexpected meeting, Neddy said, "Miss Dodd employ me for Christmas and is paying me to elp er."

"Wonderful! And who is this eminent employer?"

"She a stan right behind yu. Yu bline?"

Watt turned around to look at the woman, with her arms akimbo, staring at him with a disapproving look.

"Ah!" said Watt. "You are the redoubtable Miss Dodd, I presume?" He bowed to her. Neddy knew the move. He had seen it once before, when Watt was introduced to his mother after their trip to

Tangle River. She had been bowled over by his charm and total disregard for what was proper between white and black in the island. He could do no wrong from that moment on. Every Sunday from then on, Neddy had to carry the choicest food for Watt, from his mother.

This time Watt was up against a worldlier lady. Miss Dodd scoffed, cocked an eye, and asked brusquely, "Who you is, boye, a make like you is a gentleman?"

He bristled at her aggressive manners. "Watt Tyler-Cope, madam," came his haughty reply. "And you," he looked her up and down, "are a higgler, no doubt." This was new for Neddy. He had never seen or heard Watt behave like this before, and he looked askance at him. It was obvious they were sparking and not hitting it off. Quickly he interceded.

"He is Miss Cope's nephew, Miss Dodd." On hearing that news, her countenance changed. Immediately, she was all smiles.

"Oh! You Miss Hannah nephew come out from Hingland. Well, dat different. Im," she pointed at Neddy, "tell me you wok for di Zulu out at Friendship."

"I do, Miss Dodd. Yes, I do work for the slug at Friendship."

Her mouth dropped open, and her eyes almost bulged with surprise. "You call im di slug!" Her hands clapped the Baptist way, then settled on her hips. She threw back her head and cackled, then clapped her hands together once more, as if the spirit of the Lord had possessed her in chapel. It took her a while to stop. "Lard! Dat one good! Di slug! You all right, young Massa." Peace had been restored between them. "Mi coming right cross di street to your auntie. Mi got some Jerusalem peas and sorrel for her."

"What's that?" asked Watt, now feeling he was one with her.

"Dis here," replied Miss Dodd, pointing to the gungo peas and sorrel bush in the back of the cart.

Watt stared at them for a moment. "Don't know the red bush, but aren't those pigeon peas?" He pointed to a half-open hemp sack on the floor of the cart.

"Some people call dem dat, but Jamaican call dem gungo peas, and round Christmas time, dem get holy, an we call dem Jerusalem peas," she said, with the look of pleasure belonging to one steeped in the niceties of her trade.

"Oh!" Watt said, and quickly changed the subject. "Miss Dodd, wonderful! And a knowledgeable lady of the marketplace. May I borrow your helper for the rest of the day? Of course, when you have finished with his services. "Pointing to Neddy he made his case. "Look at him, he is overworked and ready to depart this world for the next. Now you wouldn't want that, Miss Dodd?" He went all soft and coy. "Think how you would have to answer to the Lord in the next world, Miss Dodd? The charge—killed Neddy by overwork. Slaved to death!"

When it seemed he would never end the babble, Miss Dodd put up both hands, palms facing him, as if in surrender. "Boye, you good! You can stop di nonsense right now. What mi gong do den hif him go wid you? Mi pay im to elp mi all day. Di day not done yet. You can have im hif you pays me."

A look of astonished anguish came over Watt's face. "Pay you, dear lady? Me, pay you for him?" His finger trembled pointing at Neddy, who was bursting to laugh. To contain his laughter he turned away from the scene.

"Are you selling him, like a common slave? Oh, no! Oh, no! I could never pay someone for my noble Sancho Pancho."

"What you talk bout?" Miss Dodd asked, with a perplexed expression on her face.

"It's all right, Miss Dodd, im chat foolishness all di time. Pay im no mind," Neddy said, as he turned back to face her.

"Well, im wants you to go wid im, dat is obvious," she said. "Tell you what. When shell blows, you can meet up. But Neddy, when me a go home, you ad better be behind di courthouse to come—you understan, boye?"

"Yes, Miss Dodd."

"All you boye want is go look pon di set gal as dem sashy bout. Tink mi don't know?" she laughed. And, as if by magic, the sound that ended the day for all the workers, both slaves and freemen, sounded over Montego Bay. The boys stood silently, like soldiers listening to the trumpet signaling campfires out. The low, mournful sound resonated through Montego Bay. With its dying tone, their release had come.

"Dere it is!" the higgler said, looking to see where the sun was in the sky. "Dem early tonight. Sun still up!" She looked at the boys about to scarper. "Before unu go, come elp me take dese tings in for Miss Hannah over at di school."

No sooner had she asked than Watt seized the sack of peas, and he and Neddy, with an armful of sorrel, were headed across the road to the school. The last they heard as they entered the garden gate was Miss Dodd warning Neddy once more to be at the back of the courthouse no later than eight o'clock. That left them a good three hours to enjoy the wonderful sights, sounds, and smells of Christmas in Montego Bay.

After depositing the peas and sorrel in the pantry and introducing Neddy to Watt's Aunt Hannah, they made it to the bottom of Union Street and into the crush of people who had begun to gather for the pre-Christmas Eve show. On their way down the street, Watt stopped at each street vendor, no matter what type of sweet he was selling. He made a point of questioning them on their wares, claiming that he had come to Jamaica especially to sample the local sweets. No one really believed him, but they gave out samples in good humor, which he piled one after another into his mouth. Always he demanded another sample for Neddy, and always he got it. Then there would be a big show of smacking his lips, licking the sugar off his fingers, and wonderful pronouncements on the desirability or nondesirability of the goods. They would move on, leaving the vendor poorer by one or two sweets but in fits of laughter. It was a fair exchange of sorts. The classic event happened with the tamarind balls covered with sugar. As the scene unfolded, it was all too familiar to Neddy: Watt held one of the tamarind balls between his forefinger and thumb to the sky, as if he were a great expert on tamarind balls, which, incidentally, he had learned about from Neddy not ten minutes before at another street hawker's stand.

"Yes, yes, it is round enough," he said. "Sugar enough, methinks." Gently he let his tongue touch the ball. "Not too big for a lady. Not too small for a gentleman to put into his mouth." He looked at the seller. "Is it pregnant with seed, or have you removed the offending pip?

Her mouth fell open, understanding nothing of what he had said. "What you sey, Massa?"

"Are you without sense, woman? Does this ball hold a seed or not? Is this sweet meat free of that encumbrance?"

She responded with a blank stare before going on the attack: "What unu coming wid?" She was obviously irritated and moved as if to snatch the tamarind ball from between his fingers. Watt jumped back, inadvertently crushing it.

"Control yourself, my good woman! Oh, dear! Look at what you made me do," he said, looking at the brown mess oozing between his fingers. "How much are you selling these for?" That she understood.

"Tree penny a dozen." Neddy was shocked at the price and was about to object but Watt got in before he could say anything.

"That is robbery! How dare you sell at that price? The law should take you up, madam. They probably have a seed in them, too."

"Dem don't ave seed, Massa," the street seller said in a more circumspect manner, sensing a buyer was at hand if she played her cards right.

"Tell you what," Watt said. "If I bite into this and find a seed, you give me a dozen. But if I find no seed, I will buy a dozen of them from you, three pence did you say? Theft, mind you, but being a great noble, I will pay you half your outrageous demand. Now, what say you, my good woman?"

"Mi tell you no seed dey," she said irritably, still unsure what he was saying.

With great delicacy, Watt's upper and lower front teeth bit into to the remains of the tamarind ball. Stopping halfway, leaving his teeth bared, he cried out, "A seed! A seed, it has broken my tooth! You owe me a dozen tamarind balls. A contract is a contract." That did it. The cussing began in earnest.

"Go wey! What you come wid?" the street seller screamed. "What you tink me is? A fool? You tink white man one ave sense? You tink brown people fool-fool. Go wey! Mi going call mi brodder dem. You tink we afraid of white boye? Freedom a come soon! Mi a free woman! Unu can't treat mi like fool-fool naygar woman a come down from Mocho!"

The time to go had come. Neddy tugged at Watt's sleeve. He worried the woman would bring down other street sellers on them to protect their livelihood. If that happened, they would have to make a run for it. Luckily, the crowd was intent on other things, as the fife and the drum of Jonkunnu could be heard coming down a side street. In the end, the seller flounced off with her tray balanced on her head, leaving them both staring after her.

"She hasking too much for dem balls. Dey should be penny-ha'penny and no more." Neddy knew that Miss Dodd had been overcharging, too; he did not approve but had said nothing. He learned that in business, taking what you could get at the time was the way it went. Something about that did not sit right with him, but thinking it out would have to wait for another time.

"Oh, well! It's Christmas. I would have given her the three pennies. It was worth a try for a dozen free." Watt licked the sugar off, one finger at a time. "They were not very good, anyway. Sour as hell. Need more sugar. I think my favorites are coconut drops. They have lots of sugar."

They could hear the fife and drums getting closer, and both of them pushed forward. Neddy could feel his Jonkunnu apprehension of Christmases past rising within him. Unconsciously he came closer and closer to Watt, till their shoulders were just brushing against each other. In the crush of people, the closeness went unnoticed. Neddy's hand trembled, and he fought off the temptation to reach out to hold onto Watt. Instead, he followed Watt as he pushed forward into the crowd, intent on getting up close to the macabre figures posturing to the throbbing drum and piping fife.

Led by their king, the masked horrors danced and posed. Flexing knees with torsos rigid, hopping forward and then back, twisting this way and that way, pausing statuesquely, and, after each movement, moving on. Dramatically they advanced on the crowd, as if about to attack, scattering it in fright; then the drums beat a crescendo, and the fife whistled, and the frightful group backed away to begin again.

Changing the action startlingly, a shipheaded monster wove in and out, around and about, rocking backward and forward, as if in the grip of a turbulent ocean. Flowing robes of blue and gold painted with skulls and corpse-like things ballooned around the figure like sails caught by a strong wind as it rushed in and out of the crowd. The ship whirled past them, deftly seized Watt's arm, and dragged him, shrieking with laughter, back into the circle. Neddy stood by helplessly and watched the horrible horned beast with two swords, dripping red with animals' blood, act out a ritualistic cutting of his throat. The rotting head of a goat was tossed into the crowd to loud cheers and orgiastic laughter.

The drums drummed louder and louder, till their beat became a numbing thud, and the fifes shrilled one note till the backbone shivered. Watt, the hapless victim, came running back to Neddy with a big grin: "I have been slaughtered, sacrificed to the African devil." Neddy saw nothing funny in this but grinned foolishly nonetheless. From all directions pennies hit the ground at the dancers' feet, and a small figure with a monkey's mask scrambled to collect the reward.

As they pushed back through the multicolored swarm, trying to get deeper into Charles Square, a hand fell on Watt's shoulder.

"Enjoying Montego Bay, Watt?" A good-looking young man dressed for riding had him firmly by the shoulder.

"Oh! How are you, sir?" Watt said, extracting himself with a little difficulty from the other's grip.

"Does my father-in-law know that you are not pon Friendship?" the stranger inquired, looking at Watt through half-closed eyes.

"Not yet, sir. Mean to call on him later."

"The ladies first, eh!" His eyes took on a faraway look. "Yes, I know how it is...but you know the law, young sir?"

"The law, sir?" A puzzled expression changed Watt's merry countenance. "What law?"

"You don't know? All estates must have the requirement of white men on them at this time of the year, in case of trouble."

"Didn't know that, sir. Just told the slug..."

The young man stiffened at that, his left eyebrow quivered.

Watt pulled back, uncertain if he had said something he oughtn't.

"You mean Bardolf Roy, Watt?" His hooded eyes and aquiline nose made him look like a hawk about to swoop. For a moment, it seemed as if Watt might be in trouble, but he went on decisively, "Yes, sir."

Like Miss Dodd, the young man laughed. When he had gathered himself together again, he said, "Must tell old man Fray that one. He will be most amused."

Relieved that retribution had not descended on his head, Watt took the cue to continue. "Yes, sir, told him that I was going to spend Christmas with Aunt Hannah. He seemed pleased to be rid of me. Besides, he has got those three with him."

"Suppose it is all right. I have to get back to Stonehenge tonight, and it's a long ride to Clarks Town from here. Merry Christmas, Watt." He turned and disappeared into the crowd, which had begun thinning out around them.

"Who dat?" Neddy said, having gone unnoticed during the discourse.

"Mr. James Vernon. I have only met him a couple of times before. Surprising, he remembered me. Married to Mr. Fray's daughter. That's how I know him."

"Mi know who dat is," Neddy said. "Im a Miss Mary an Massa William relative. Im live over at Stonehenge estate."

"Stonehenge, don't know where that is."

"It over so, in Trelawny." Neddy pointed down the road—as good directions as any he could give. He had only heard of the estate from his father.

They moved further across the square and came upon a white-faced creature in female warrior costume. Whip in hand, she snaked back and forth, cracking it now and again, keeping the crowd at bay. In her other hand, she wafted a fan in their direction, and, depending on how it was held, it seemed to change magically from fan to a menacing sword. Unbelievably, despite all the menacing movement, a crown with lit candles balanced on her head as she shrieked for money and demanded praise for her beauty. On either side of the spectacle, attendants held poles with lanterns and, with their free hands, neatly plucked from the air coins thrown in the creature's direction.

"Dat a actor boy," Neddy said.

"Great Babylon!" Watt said, astonished. "These are far better than the Morris dancers. Even better than those who dance in devil masks and black garb."

The crowd pushed around them again. Bodies against bodies, screams of laughter and outrage crashed into their ears. Watt grabbed a hand he thought was Neddy's hand creeping under his jacket to frighten him. The hand tugged to pull away. Instinctively Watt tightened his grip. There was a shriek of pain that went unnoticed in the hubbub, but it made Watt look to see what he had caught. At first it was a puzzle. Neddy stood to his right, and what he held was on his left. He looked down and was amazed to find he was holding onto a tiny boy of no more than ten years.

"Who are you?" Watt said, taken aback but gripping the strange paw even more firmly.

"Please Massa, please, please, let mi go," the urchin said. "Mi no mean it, sah."

"Who dat? What im a do?" Neddy said, looking at the boy wriggling like a fish on the end of a line.

"His hand was on my jacket pocket," Watt said indignantly. "The little rat!"

"Im try tief you! Give im one bitch lick and run im," Neddy said. The boy wriggled even more against Watt's grip. Neddy could have told him it would be no use. It would be better if he gave up the struggle.

"You little bastard! Steal from me, would you!" The boy's ears were set ringing as Watt showed him no mercy and cuffed him about them, once, twice, thrice. Feeling satisfied he had handed out just punishment Watt let him go. Instead of tears of contrition, both he and Neddy got dire threats screamed at them. Watt made as if he would give chase, only to see the wretch vanish behind an expansive female, who was pushing in their direction like a great Argos making way against a heavy sea.

"This is what he was after." A large handkerchief came out of his pocket. Carefully Watt undid it to display his hoard of coconut drops. Neddy let out a shriek of laughter.

"Is dat all you ave?" he said, between guffaws. "Im was looking for money."

"Oh! Well, he could have had a copper or two if he had asked."

"Im couldn't ave di sweetie, den?"

"Well," Watt made up his face. "*No*," he said. "They are for you and me. But he could have had a penny."

Neddy looked at his friend, smiled, and shook his head side to side.

The parish church clock began beating out its eight strokes of the evening hour. Because of all the noise in the square, they did not filter in on Neddy until the clock reached number four. He almost exploded.

"Lard Gad! Miss Dodd! She lef and gone." He began to run in and out, nearly crashing into people to get across the square and behind the courthouse. He prayed she had not left. Watt was right behind him as he turned the corner, racing from cart to cart, assembled to return to their respective homes. His heart began to fall at the thought of the long, long walk back home. He stopped and looked around desperately.

"Lard Gad!" he said. "She a gone an lef mi. Mi mam going kill mi."

"Good!" Watt said, "Now you can stay with me, and we can have much more fun." Neddy could feel his anger begin to rise. He was about to reply hotly but caught himself, realizing Watt only wanted to be with him.

"No, mi can't stay. Mi mam want me back for Christmas Eve and di Day." They stood for a moment, not daring to move.

"If you must go, you can borrow Rosinante. You can ride him back," Watt said.

"Maybe dat—" Neddy never finished the sentence, for he spotted Miss Dodd at the far corner in the cart, waiting. They took off at a run. She spotted them coming toward her and hailed, obviously relieved at their arrival.

"At lass! Where you bin? Mi a wait ere for you from di clock strike seven."

"Sorry, Miss Dodd, sorry. We get old up."

"Boye, get in. We got long ways to go tonight. Mercy!" she said, sucking in her breath. "Mi carn, dem bun me!" She exhaled. "Dat always mean trouble a come." She leaned down to take off her right shoe and began wriggling her fat toes in the evening air. Neddy looked at her foot and, even in the dim lantern light, could not help but compare her toes to the lumpy ginger root they had picked up in sacks earlier. Before he could jump into the back of the cart, he found himself pinned to Watt again.

"Happy Christmas and a wonderful New Year to you, Neddy, my friend. And to you, Miss Dodd," he added as an afterthought, releasing Neddy at the same time.

"Di same to you, Watt," Neddy said.

The cart moved off at Miss Dodd's urging. "Dat boye," she said, just loud enough for Neddy to hear, "love you." Watt stood and watched them around the corner before turning to go back to the center of the festivities. He was determined to take in all he could, this first Jamaican Christmas.

They had passed the outskirts of town, gone through Catherine Hall estate, and had just entered the road that cut the boundaries of Fairfield when Miss Dodd was hailed up by another higgler heading in their direction. *At last!* Neddy thought, pleased to get relief from Miss Dodd's constant chatter and complaining about corns.

"Get down, boye, an go in di back an let Miss Coney come up beside me." Neddy gladly did as he was told.

"Miss Coney, tie di animal on di back an come ere beside mi, so we can talk."

Quickly jumping down from the seat, Neddy took the donkey's lead from Miss Coney and led it to the back of the cart.

"Is Quashiba's boye dat?"

"Yes, mi tek im to elp mi wid di rush."

"Nice boye. Im got manners. Not like all dem young ones dat run bout di place."

He liked when people complimented him and set him apart from all the others. But thanking Miss Coney was not advisable at that moment, for it would only bring on more chat, which he could do without. He pretended not to hear as he climbed up into the back of the cart and stretched out among the empty sacks on the floor of the cart.

He could hear them on the seat above his head, going at it. Their chatter about the day's business droned on and made him feel sleepy. It had been a busy day. He was pleased he had run into Watt and met his aunt. He wouldn't have minded staying with him. But, he knew, his mam would never have approved. It was a pity; they could have enjoyed the Christmas Eve together and watched the set girl parade.

The stars glittered like chips of ice above him, as he lay on his back looking up. There was an iridescent blue tinge to the night sky that added to its cold aspect. Somewhere out of his sight, the moon lent its illumination to the far horizon. As he pulled a hemp bag up to cover himself, he thought it must be the winter sky the captain mentioned earlier. For a short time before his eyes closed in bumpy sleep, he watched small clouds whimsically change shape as they danced across the evening stage. One in particular formed and transformed, reminding him of the actor boy, whose fan turned into a sword and back again to a fan.

* * *

At the far end of the Queen of Spain Valley, twenty miles from where Miss Dodd's cart jolted on its homeward journey, strange white-faced things stood on the dark side of the bell tree in front of Castle Dunbar Great House. Hanging from a branch above them, the rusted iron bell that summoned slaves to and from their beds to eat, to work, to punishment, and sometimes tolled the death of a master, slowly swung with the night breeze. Its clapper scraped discordantly against the cracked housing whenever a wind came up to bend the branches.

Those things that stood outside the Great House could see in the cold moonlight that it had junjo growing upon it, dark splotches of what would be green mold to the eye in the daylight leached to the walls: The mold had spread down from above and eaten away the pointing cementing the cut stones together. On the roof, gaps had appeared where shingles had crumbled, leaving their supporting beams naked to the sky. From around these holes, other shingles had fallen inward or slid off, enlarging the openings for rain to enter the building unimpeded.

Many shingles lay decomposing on the ground where they fell. Two that had recently become dislodged from the eaves could just be made out in the dim light, lying by the steps to the main door to trip the unwary. At any time, night or day, climbing these steps demanded caution, as the soft limestone was worn and crumbly from years of use and neglect. The stench of decay permeated the structure and its environ and was all the more apparent on this crystal-like night before the Christ Child's birthday celebrations of 1831.

Each night the main door of the Great House was shut and barred against intruders. But for those who had purpose, this represented only a small obstacle to entering the dilapidated dwelling. At the back was the main bedroom. In it, on a raised platform, square in the middle, stood a huge canopied four-poster mahogany bed, similar in aspect to a high altar; faded mohair curtains with embroidered crosses draped all four sides of the bed, wishfully intended to keep the sleeper safely barracked against the unknown stalker of the night.

Many years back, the bed's designer and first user had considered its elevation an advantage to the sleeper and a disadvantage to any would-be assailant. It would, he had reckoned, give the occupant time to awaken and beat back any assault. None had come to him, however. After him, his descendants had traveled to the island and slept in the bed's mausoleum-like confinement as Massa.

One such scion now lay within, sleeping the unsleeping fog of drink. Through his torpor, he thought at first the girl he had kicked out earlier had returned to sneak up beside him in the bed. But there was no other body to feel; only he lay at the bed's center. "Damn it!" he mumbled, as he rolled over. "These blacks are darkness itself." He tried to focus his eyes in that seamless space he floated in. Light, any light, would bring sanity to that gap, but no glimmer appeared to define shapes.

The odor was stifling. He gasped for air. The stench of field nigger assailed his nose. That shouldn't be. He was imagining smells now. Even after these years in the island, he still gulped for air at the stink of the sweating nigger. He must be dreaming, but again he listened to the rustling sound made by trash dragged across the floor. There it was. He must be mistaken; it was the wind through crevices moving curtains and drapes. But there was no draft he could feel. He sat up, absolutely sure rustling trash was the noise that had awakened him in the first place. He was certain. It came again.

Instinctively, his hand reached for the pistols beneath his pillows, and he lay still, his heart beating rabidly, sweat on his palms. *Shuh-shuh-shuh-she-sheshe-shuh*, moved around the bed. One second it was on the right of the drapes, then in front, back on the right, behind, onto the left and in front, *She-shuh-she-shuh-she-shuh*. A nigger was there in the room with him. It went on again. *She-she-she-shu-sheee.*

"Nigger!" he screamed, as one of his pistols exploded in the direction of the rustling sound. The shot's sound crashed within his confines; for a second, the flash lit up the inside of the shrouded bed, and burned powder hung entrapped by the mohair drapes. Its acridity stung his eyes, nostrils, and mouth, as he sucked it in for fresh air. He choked. Belly acid hit the back of his throat and spewed onto the bedspread, adding the stench of stale rum to the surrounding pall.

She-shuh-she-shuh-she-she-she.

He had one shot left, and he knew his life depended on that one shot. He wanted to be outside the blanketing drapes. Sally forth like a true soldier, take on the enemy outside; that was the way to do it. Attack, not hide like a frightened rabbit. Attack, attack was what he would do in India. No nigger, whatever his caste, could stand a white man's determined blow. Yet, he still did not move as the *she-she-shee-shuh* continued spinning around his bastioned position. Although muffled by the drapes, a drum beat in the distant hills. Eerily it seemed to beat time for the *she-she-she-shuh*. He strained to distinguish between the sounds. Only then did he notice the likeness to the cadence of a funeral drum.

All went still. As if cut from life itself, the drumming and that soft sound of the *she-shuh* that danced around his room stopped. The smell of nigger sweat penetrated beneath the curtains to mingle with the tang of spent gunpowder that still hung within. It kept him taut and aware of the danger. A mosquito got through the bed's defensive shield and buzzed in his ear. He sat straight up, awaiting the next move, waved the pistol vigorously at the buzzing, farted—and did more from sheer fright.

"*Nigger!*" he screamed, like a desperate battle cry and plunged through the curtains, firing his last shot. As the pistol flashed, he saw three hideous white masks on naked black bodies. One groaned and fell over, shot through and through. Before they could recover from his onslaught, he rushed for the door, shouting for help. It was barred from outside, and his thumping on it went unnoticed. Black arms latched to his on either side and dragged him, struggling, back to be tied against the bed. A head butted him and sent the back of his skull crashing off the carved mahogany post. The canopy overhead shook with the force. Cord was twined and knotted about him. Tighter and tighter the cord bit with each struggle; blood began to trickle down his arms where it cut into the flesh, and breathing became difficult as it pulled around his neck. Reason told him to stay still, for life's sake.

The drum began again. He wasn't sure if it was in the hills or somewhere in his head, which throbbed mercilessly. Slowly opening his eyes, he faced the two. Given half a chance, he would fight for his life. No nigger was going to take it easily, not if he could help it.

"Untie me, you damned black bastards!" he said, his voice hoarse and defiant. But they made no move toward him. Their dim figures wavered before his drunken eyes. They began a strange whirling dance, and the *she-she-shuh* became clear in the dim light. Dried trash tied to their ankles and wrists, hiding both feet and hands, made the noise as they danced. They moved quickly round and round like dervishes over their dying mate, whose rattling breathing told of a lung wound. The blood frothed with every breath he took, giving him the satisfaction that the shot was fatal.

The drumming stopped. But in front of him and around the bed, the two whirled and danced to an unheard pulse.

No other sounds disturbed that macabre scene but the rattling breathing of the dying on the floor and the *she-she-shuh* of the dancing two. One would stop in front, twist, twirl, and move black arms in and out toward his chest. Whitened fingers would touch where his heart beat; a clenched fist would pull back, as if tearing it out to hold aloft in triumph, then lower it into a gaping mouth. As their mania built up, strangely he wished to hear again that distant drum beyond the walls. Frenzied, on and on they danced. Their sweat splattered him; their stench added to his struggle for air. White masks and whitened hands seemed to detach and float, spinning hypnotically in front of his hazed eyes. He wished for a finish. No longer fear but exhaustion invaded his body. He hated the island, oh, how he hated the people of the island, and most of all he hated the world that had brought him to this.

He did not notice the first cut. The second one across his belly made him grunt acknowledgement. With succeeding passes, flashing knives slashed at him. They appeared out of the gloom, held in whitened hands half-covered by the tendrils of trash that hung from their wrists. He tried to move forward and was seized by the knots. He remembered dimly how he had been propelled across the room and bound to a bedpost.

The drumbeat inside his head grew louder as the dancers became more frenetic. Magically, one danced with small, glowing brands in each hand. Sweeping by, *she-she-shu-she*, they stabbed it at his face, first at this eye and then the other, just missing contact. His head jerked back and hit the post behind, numbing him yet again He screamed in agony when the firebrand was finally stubbed into his right cheek. Life, he realized, was still in his being.

His tormentor danced away again behind the bed to reappear and match the first burn on his left cheek with one on his right, before dropping the lighted sticks on the ground and dancing away again. This time he did not scream. The nigger would not have that satisfaction twice. He noticed now that there was only one dancer; the other had vanished, and so had the wounded one. The lone dancer persisted; round and round he came. Again and again he slashed, each time tearing off some of his trash and leaving it on the ground, along with a piece of his victim's night shirt. Finally, both were stark naked, except for the white mask. Naked to naked now, no longer did he bother spinning around the bed but jumped and whirled and jumped in front of his massa, with cane-cutting sickles weaving wonderful patterns in the air, their keen edges catching the moonlight filtering through the window.

When Conchie Blows

Loss of blood, coupled with his drunken state, made him only dimly aware of these things. Through the haze, a familiar black face was nose to nose to his. He could feel his hot breath and smell the rancid stomach mingling with his nigger sweat. The black man had a scar on his cheek, like a rose branded there. He felt the knife enter just above his pelvic bone and twist; slowly it moved upward, twisting again, and then up again and twisting again to stop in his breastbone. He hiccupped blood and knew it splattered over the black face and chest in front of him. Then the nigger embraced and kissed him on the mouth, as if sucking his soul out. He did not feel the hand reach inside for his heart.

His intestines uncurled toward the ground. Rum acted as an anesthetic, but there was a dull agony for a few seconds left to him. Christmas Eve morning, his shell was dead.

* * *

After a large breakfast, Watt got into Charles Square early. He had added some of his aunt's pimento dram from a decanter on the sideboard to his coffee, and even now wished he had not. Its taste reminded him of medicine for coughs and colds. Even for him, the dram was too sweet and cloying. He had never tried it before and resolved not to again. Much more to his liking was the red sorrel drink flavored with ginger and jiggers of rum. Two tumblers of this gulped down removed some of the pimento taste from his mouth but not all, judging by the way it repeated. But between these disliked and liked drinks of the morning, Watt was in very high spirits when he pushed forward into the crowd to get a better view of the gaudy girls' parade.

One of the servants told him the parade would begin around eleven o'clock, but, aware that natives knew neither time nor how to keep it, he left earlier. After looking around the square, he was pleased to have gotten there at nine in the morning. All manner of people were already there to watch the set girl parade. Well-dressed young men of wealth and good family milled about. They greeted each other, chatted, laughed at ribald remarks, then parted to repeat the process with others of their kind. Time and again they would circle the square, only to find themselves yet again with those they had already met. It did not matter; there would be another scandal picked up on their walk to pass on. They were enjoying themselves, waiting to choose a fancy girl, if they could. Vying with each other as the parade passed would be half the sport and highlighted Christmas time for them.

One especially Watt noticed. He was in the latest fashion, high cravat, black broad coat and top hat; his slave followed him, carrying a bucket with cooled wine bottles. Every now and then he would require his glass be refilled. Elegantly he leaned on his walking cane as friends came up to join him. From the raised glasses his slave provided, obviously they were toasting the girls before they had arrived. Any bystander could see that, as the day progressed, this would degenerate into a riotous party. Watt wished he were part of them. Others, not so chic, were swigging rum punch and their loud bet-making drifted over to where he stood. A ginger beer seller came by; Watt settled for that.

Before the sun beat down, there was a hush of anticipation in the throng. The Parish Church clock struck ten, the music sounded, and the parade was on.

The four grand masters took the lead in the procession, followed by the flag bearer, hand drummer, tambourine, triangle, and violin, and all repeated again across the square. Then came the commodore and the jack-in-the-green and girls all in magnificent dresses, feathers, red brocade, blue damask; the army and the navy were represented, and then the French girls flaunted themselves. This estate and that estate rivaled each other. Clutch after clutch danced their steps, and the young men cheered loudly. Noise and music mingled indistinguishably, stimulating and deafening.

Watt's hand reached into his pocket and found nothing there. His hand fumbled in disbelief. His handkerchief with molasses candy carefully wrapped in it was gone. Across the street, his hand in another's pocket, was the urchin of last evening. Watt silently vowed to use his belt across the boy's bottom, if he ever laid hands on the little wretch again.

* * *

When Conchie Blows

On Christmas day, the overseer of Castle Dunbar had been called by the assembled slaves outside the Great House. They had arrived, demanding their right of entry and entertainment by their master on this day, as tradition dictated. But the doors had been barred against them, and even under this thoughtless massa, this had never happened before.

The overseer ordered the main door forced open, and they smelled the putrefaction of the dead. He entered the main bedroom of the Great House; there, the overseer found the body of his late employer, mutilated, tied to his bedpost. He gagged and withdrew to the dining hall, bumping into furniture as he went. There were shrieks and wails from slaves who saw it and smiles from others who heard of what they found. Despite the protests of *Im duppy a come fi sure!* the overseer had the body cut down and laid out on the great bed. It was a messy business, with great quantities of blood congealed on the sheeting and floor. It amazed him that so much blood could come from the human body. Among the splatter, he noticed the burn marks on the face of the victim and the cold brands cast aside, and he thought how lucky it was that the house had not gone up in flames. Perhaps that had been the intent. A trail of blood led to a window at the back of the house. One had been wounded, at least.

Catching his breath outside and regaining reason, the overseer was not surprised that Forbes-Dunbar had met such an end. A slave was dispatched to get the nearest justice of the peace and another for the local reverend. That was all he could do for the moment.

From the steps, the overseer watched the uninhibited carousal going on below, celebrating the birth of Christ or the death of Forbes-Dunbar—he knew not which—and he wondered if this was the beginning of the trouble they all expected. His hand rested on the butt of a pistol stuck in his belt as a powerfully built field slave reeled across the yard, yelling up at him.

"Busha man, mi hear dem mek duppy out of Backra Massa." He then convulsed into vulgar laughter, letting his bottle fall and shatter on the ground. Like blood, the dark red rum spread across the paving stones to remind the overseer of the horror within.

Chapter 12

The Beacon

Christmas had come and gone, yet three girls, all of about the same age, cavorted in magnificently gaudy blue dresses on the front lawn of Mount Vernon Great House. Their costumes had been made for the set competition in Montego Bay, three days earlier. Recalling the event, the most petite of the three tossed her head and eloquently demonstrated the hand motions and dance steps she had used to send out her signals among the young men. The quadroon girl watching joined in, followed by the tallest of the three. To the first girl's display, they added flourishing kicks, making their skirts flare provocatively, as an allure to those who had caught their attention. They joined hands and danced round and round in a ring, like children frisking along to the nursery rhyme, "A ring around a rosie, a pocket full of posies, hush, hush, hush, hush, all fall down." That they did, as if cued, ending their merry-go-round in disarray on the grass. The tinkle of their laughter drifted across the lawn on the soft day. When the laughter died down, they chatted about their hopes and dreams in animated fashion.

On this December morning, somehow, the shrill laughter and frolicking in the garden did not seem out of place; even though the performers were just as much chattels of the estate as the big black dog that joined in their play. It was, after all, the third day of the

Christmas season, which, by law, was theirs to enjoy at will. Their mistress and her new husband were off to England, so why not take advantage of the absence and make use of gardens that would normally be forbidden territory for servant girls?

With lithe agility, the tallest girl jumped up, brushed off the back of her dress, and did a dainty step this way and that way, adding a curtsy to a twirl in front of her companions, who applauded with delight. Then one who had not shown her own individual technique rose from the grass, with hand movements like a flower opening, to demonstrate three steps on tiptoe. Pivoting, she made a slow, gracious curtsy, which allowed her dress to spread outward, like a cloud unfolding in the sky; with much demur she held out her hand, keeping her head bowed and eyes averted in modesty.

Thus she indicated a potential beau had noticed her. Then, with right arm raised and left arm upon her hip, she whirled, as if in defiance. Gold brocade sewn on her dress caught the sunlight like the tinged eyes on the peacock's tail.

Not too distant from where she danced came a loud, defiant squawk. A peacock, unnoticed by the girls, stood watching, his own tail feathers fanned to full spread. Perhaps he saw these girls as new rivals in his garden, so gorgeous were they. One girl picked up a stick and threw it in the bird's direction. It missed, but the message was understood. Folding his fan, the peacock stalked off in a slow, dignified manner to another round of laughter.

They knew they should not be in the front garden of the Great House, but Miss Mary and her new husband were in England, or at least on their way there. Anyway, Miss Mary would have let them in the garden to do as they wished on this day. In past years, she would have even joined them and shown a step or two. Most likely, Miss Mary would have let them enjoy themselves any day of the week in the garden, so long as they caused no disturbance when society called. After all, the eldest child of old Massa William and Miss Ann Buchanan was one of them; she was born and raised here in Jamaica, just like they were. She was just luckier than they, because old Massa William was her father. All their gamboling in the garden that morning was to ensure, if possible, that their children would be as fortunate as Miss Mary in having a father like Massa William.

Through one of the large arched windows in the long drawing room, William Edward Vernon, Mary's half-brother, stood watching the girls at their play. His back was to the man who had just shuffled his bare feet to let him know of his presence. William did not move to acknowledge the man's presence or give any indication that he had even heard him. At least a minute passed before the barefoot man boldly cleared his throat. This time the massa had to hear the grating sound in the room, but he made no response. The man knew then to be still and not to address the massa. The slaves had charged him to thank Mass William for letting them have the day, as it should be. It was theirs by right. Mount Vernon slaves were given what was theirs, and there had been no trouble, as there had been on other plantations where overseers and owners demanded work because Christmas had fallen on Sunday. One more day should be theirs. The man couldn't help himself, he shuffled again. He wanted to carry out his charge, thank the massa, and get about his provision grounds and drink some rum before the day was done. For when morning came, he would become the driver of the gangs again to bring in the crops; the cane was ready for cutting, crushing, and sugar- and rum-making, a hard and beastly time of year.

"That little girl is very pretty," said William Vernon, continuing to look through the window. "She looks good in that blue dress she used in the set. It suits her."

"Mus a be Betsy you talk bout, Mass William."

"Is that her name?"

"It a di little gal dat Massa James fancy."

"Oh?"

"Yes, sah! Im tek to dat one, but mi na tink notting appen as yet." He gave a short, sharp laugh. "Lard, how many pickney im breed pon di place, an im a jus a pickney imself? Hu! Wat a boye im is!"

William looked over his shoulder at the speaker and pursed his lips but added nothing. He let the man continue.

"Since im marry Miss Jane, im settle down in di last few month. Mass William, ow many children you tink im got wid different women now, sah?"

"I don't know, John Leslie."

"Well, im got one ya so. Dem say im got tree over on Stonehenge."

"Forget Massa James, John." It was time to put an end to the gossip about his cousin. "What did you want to see me about?"

"Lard, sah! Di people hask me to tank you for di day."

"That's all right. It was Miss Mary's wish. She said so before leaving for England." As he said that, he thought of the protest let out by Breary on hearing her orders. A smile played on his lips at the way she ignored him. William knew that a Vernon ruled the Breary family.

"She a good lady, just like her an your own fader, old Mass William. Dat was good man."

"John, there is tell going about that trouble is coming soon. Have you heard what people are saying?"

"Well, mi hear little bit, but mi don't tink it will amount."

"Maybe, and maybe not. John, I want you to keep a good watch and let me know if there is any trouble brewing. I cannot be here and at Mount Apfel at the same time. I will be depending on you."

"Mass William, you know mi will protect di place when you not here. Di Mount Vernon people won't cause trouble. Dem know freedom a come, but nutting going appen till di paper is read, and dem is declared free persons."

"It's not the Mount Vernon people I am worried about, John. It's the outsiders. I notice many strange faces roaming about. More than usual—even for this time of the year. Have you noticed them? What estates do they belong to?"

"Yes, sah. Dere are some nayga-man mi never see before."

"Keep a keen watch, then."

"Mi hear tell…" He stopped and looked at the busha facing him, framed by the arched widow; the sunlight, silhouetting his outline, obscured his features, hiding any readable message that may appear there. John Leslie looked at the floor. His stance transmitted unease to the Master.

"What?" William asked.

"Mi ear tell," John Leslie began, uncertainty still quivering his voice. "Dem ave an army ready fi di waar."

"Army! Who is 'them'? Come on John, out with it." There was an impatient edge to the order.

"Dem ave five undred men up at Lapland, and Colonel Lawrence ave more over by Kensington."

"Colonel Lawrence! At Kensington? Are you mad? Do you mean Edward Lawrence the carpenter?"

"No, Mass William, not im! Anoder Lawrence. Mi don't know where im come from. But im a colonel, dem say.

"Who is the general?"

"Di Baptist preacher man, sah. Di one name a Sam Sharpe. Im is di general."

"What do they intend to do?"

"Don't know, sah. He hexpect dem na work unless dem get pay fi it. Dat is what mi hear."

"Do you think they intend trouble, I mean real trouble?"

"Can't say, sah. Some of dem got gun, and all of dem got machete or sickle."

William Vernon looked around the room. He loved this house and hoped that someday, as it wasn't passed down to him, he would be able to buy it. Rightfully it should have had been his share by birth, but he was neither white nor legitimate. Still, he could not complain. At least he had been acknowledged by his father, accepted into the Vernon fold, educated in England, and left two hundred acres of the best land of the Mount Vernon estate. That they couldn't destroy. The crops, maybe, but not the land itself.

The house and works were another matter. If trouble came, there was no one there to defend the house and works, never mind the fields. Slaves would rampage unstopped through the place, torching everything as they went. Fire was their weapon; it had been in the past, why should there be any difference this time? If a volcanic rebellion erupted, absentee landowners would learn the lesson again, to their pecuniary sorrow, that any undefended property attracted the full rage of fire in the hands of slaves.

Should he bring his family to stay over here, and leave his own home? Leaving Mount Apfel unattended would be a difficult decision for him to make. Rachel would never stand for that. She was more likely to worry about Kensington, where she was born, than Mount Vernon. No, he would have to leave this place unattended and hope for the best. It was a five-mile ride between the two estates. If worse came to worst, maybe he could patrol both? These thoughts beat about in his head. He turned back to look through the window at the girls in the garden, but they had already left. William Vernon sighed audibly.

"Some ting wrong, Massa?"

He nearly laughed at the question from behind him but didn't. What was the use of explaining that everything was wrong, wrong because he could not get a clear picture of what was out there?

"Go get my horse. I am going to leave you in charge when I am not here. After all, you are the head driver, and there are no white men about."

"Yes, sah!"

"John." William stopped, then turned and look at him earnestly. "You are a free man, aren't you?"

"Yes, sah. Your fader leaves me mi freedom when im dead. Di paper say John Leslie is a free man."

"Why are you still at Mount Vernon, then?"

"Where mi a go, sah? Mi barn ya. Dis is mi home."

William's face registered little surprise at the explanation before he turned once more to stare through the window into the garden. How pretty it was, with all the blood-red and orange royal poinciana trees. How wonderfully they had contrasted with the girls' blue frocks. A minute must have passed in silence before he gave instructions to the driver.

"Tomorrow, first thing, they are to begin work like normal. This is crop season. I will ride over and see how they are going. Do you understand, John?"

"Yes, Massa."

"Good. Now go get the horse," William added in a gentler tone.

John Leslie's bare feet made no sound on the floor as he padded out of the room. William turned to watch him go. *A trusty man, that,* he thought. His kind were few and far between. He belonged to the estate from birth and was one with it and with the family, come freedom or no freedom.

The idea of slave regiments made him smile sardonically. They couldn't stand up to the militia, never mind the regular army. With the Maroons thrown into the affray, they didn't stand a chance in hell. That had never stopped them before. Slave rebellion in Jamaica was as common a hazard as malaria fever. Usually it was a spontaneous uprising that spread to other estates but could be put down quickly. This time there were regiments and armies; that meant organization and planning.

Haiti jumped to his mind. Although he was only a child then, he could remember the great fear, thirty years before, in Jamaica; branded onto his mind was the conflagration when the blacks of Santo Domingo burned and slaughtered indiscriminately. As he had grown to the state of understanding, that uprising was constantly refreshed in conversation, its details becoming enlarged with each account. Even in the nursery, nannies used the Haitian terror to threaten their young charges, as the French ogre had been used by English nannies to bring their charges to heel.

The best that Napoleon could send against them, the ex-slaves had defeated. Half-trained black men mangled the whitest of Europe led by General Leclerc, one of their youngest and brightest leaders. Leclerc's promise was such that Napoleon, then first consul, had him as a brother-in-law. As it turned out, his wife became a problem for the general as the *noir* burned, raped, and pillaged the beautiful productive land he had been sent to recover for France. While Leclerc battled in earnest with yellow fever and against the blacks that Satan had sent to face him with the fires of hell, his wife embraced and engaged in sexual combat with most of his staff officers. It must have been most galling, thought William. In the end, yellow fever got Leclerc, and the blacks got the rest of his army. She, the wife with the small, deformed ears, returned to Paris, not any the worse for the experience.

He smiled at the perfidy of the French women. Jamaicans were loose by necessity, but the French female seemed to come on her sexual proclivity naturally. That was how it had seemed to him when he visited France. Even at that late stage, when they heard he was from Jamaica, they had brought up the Haiti expedition and, of course, the part played by the general's wife. It always caused great amusement in the salons, especially when they speculated it was not the thin Vin Blanc she desired but the robust Pinot Noir.

Looking at the carefully tended garden with its flowerbeds and clumps of colorful annatto bushes with their full red blooms, William wondered if the carnage of Haiti was to be visited now on Jamaica, thirty years later. Luckily Sharpe, the Baptist preacher, was no Toussaint, and thank God he was no monster like Dessalines. He shuddered at the thought of that brutal black Beelzebub. The stories of babies torn apart by his bare hands and left for the John Crow to clean up made William shiver a second time, as the image of his own children in pieces strewn on the roadside flooded his imagination.

Had he been in charge, instead of a Baptist preacher, how would he have gone about planning the rebellion, he wondered? One thing for certain, they would have been drilled and disciplined into units. All that would have been done in secret, on Sundays. For their sakes, he hoped they had done this at least. But, he speculated, Sharpe had just given out titles to his most favored men and hoped the spirit of the Lord would give them Gideon's prowess in battle. Still, whatever their training, he knew their one weapon would make many a man poor in St. James, if the slaves decided to consume the parish with fire.

His thoughts drifted to the report of the Forbes-Dunbar murder. From all they told of it, had Dessalines been around, he would have approved its brutality. His dismemberment filled William with horror, the same nauseating fear felt by those who faced the ancient Assyrians who skinned their foes and hung their hides and carcasses from the battlements of conquered cities as a message to all who opposed them.

"Your harse his ready, Mass William." John Leslie had returned unheard, and his words startled William Vernon.

"Thank you, John," he said, without turning round. "Is it in the front or around the back?"

"Mi bring im roun by di front step, sah. Mi knows you always like leave by di front. Di back de is for bungo an red man. Hit not for a massa like you."

The attempted flattery William graciously accepted in silence; for the truth be told, that was how he saw himself. His father had never let him forget that he was a Vernon; color didn't matter—name and heritage did.

"Nurse send dis for you, sah."

William turned to look and recognized the opaque liquid in an extra-large tumbler offered him on a tray. Beads of liquid, like sweat, ran down the sides of the glass, showing that the liquid had been taken from a cooling clay yabba to the shock of the hot day. William sighed.

"Let me guess, John, that is a glass of barley-lemonade, which is good for me?" He pointed to the tumbler on the tray.

"Ow you know she sey dat, sah?"

"She has been making me drink that from as long as I can remember, John. Nurse has the notion that it guards against evil. The truth is, the only evil involved in that…" he nodded toward the glass, "is the taste. Thank you, John." He took the glass, sipped, and grimaced. "Thank her for me." He sipped again and placed the glass on a small side table close at hand. "I had better be getting back, or Miss Rachel will be sending out people to search for me. She has been edgy with all the rumors," he said, bringing the man into a family confidence.

"Mi don't know bout Miss Rachel, but fi mi woman, she is nervous like." He paused, then cleared his throat as if going to add further clarification, only he hesitated again, before finally coming out with, "She sey, trouble a come—because she can smell di blood."

He spoke so quickly that William nearly missed it. His forehead crinkled into a frown, showing perplexity rather than anger.

"It all chat-chat she a come wid, Mass William," John Leslie said quickly, to forestall any cross outburst. "Tell you di truth, sah, is er African feelings a come through." John sucked his teeth, forgetting where he was.

William could swear he saw the left eyebrow of his father's portrait on the far wall quiver and his lip curl in haughty distaste. He, himself, smiled.

"Go. I will be along shortly."

Once more he was left alone in that long room with the well-worn, high-backed, wide-armed, black and deep brown leather chairs. Their hides, cracked and polished from constant use, reflected the light in the room and matched their sheen to the gloss of the mahogany tables and sideboards. William gazed at the sideboard closest to his father's chair. It was different from the other two in the room. Standing about the same height from the floor, it was not as long as its companion pieces. Made from Spanish elm, rather than mahogany, it was inlaid with a variety of hardwoods of contrasting hues and was beautifully carved.

It was surprising that such a fine piece of furniture was made right here on the estate. Any manor in England, or townhouse in London, for that matter, would have considered it an adornment. The look of it proved that which was utilitarian did not have to be plain and uninteresting to the aesthetic sense. Jamaica was fast coming of age, William realized.

Prince of Wales feathers decorated the back panel and seemed appropriate as a backdrop for the full and half-full decanters of Madeira, deep ruby port, brandy, and the estate's rum. Around all these decanters, appropriate glasses were carefully arranged to comply with the latest fashion. Just any drinking glass was not good enough anymore. Long stemmed glasses for wine and squat, big-bellied ones for brandy were now the acceptable way to serve the drink. Many were gifts from the Irish branch of the family and were Waterford crystal.

Appropriately, the portrait on the wall above the sideboard was of his father. When he was alive and came in from his daily rounds on the estate, he made straight for the sideboard to pour himself a drink. Sometimes he would bring William with him and measure how tall he had grown against one of its legs, with its carved vines twining round and round till they reached the sideboard's skirt.

The Beacon

"When your shoulder reaches this," he would say, slapping the top of the sideboard with the palm of his hand, "you can have a drink with me." He would then gently rub his head with his knuckles and release a hearty but breathy wheezing laugh, as if he were gasping for air. It must have been a family trait, for his grandfather James laughed the same way. William's eyes drifted over to his portrait and then to the picture of his wife Hannah. Uncle Joseph, he remembered, favored her, while Aunt Mary, their daughter, looked like her father.

He stared at them, staring back at him from their frames. The artist had managed to capture them well enough. His grandmother Hannah, her round, honest face with the unwavering eyes that bespoke loving thoughtfulness, was the best portrait of any on the wall. The artist had captured William's dim memory of her.

He was her grandson, and there was no question of that relationship where she was concerned. "Gran Tannah," his young tongue would stumble out, as she tried to teach him to speak properly. She would smile and say, "That is a start. We will try again tomorrow, Billy." Off he would go with some sweetie or slice of cake, to play in the garden until his father or nurse came to take him home, if he was not spending the night at Mount Vernon.

Although he did not live with them, there was no question he was part of the Mount Vernon household. That was the way it was. Some Vernons lived at Mount Vernon; he and his mother, being the other Vernons, lived at Keith Hall. Every day his father would come over, and many times William would stay at Mt Vernon overnight or for weeks on end. He never gave it a second thought. Ironically, not until he was packed off to school in England at age ten did he realize there was a difference between his status and that of his cousins. It was this that propelled his father to send him to England. "I will not have my son treated as second-class because his mother is not white. What the hell is the difference between a Campeche Bay Indian and some doxy parading in her white bosom in a London carriage? The carriage!" he shouted defiantly to those who happened to be listening in the room at that moment.

When Conchie Blows

Looking from one to the other of those framed generational faces hanging on the wall, he decided they gave a feeling of permanence to the room, which was not often felt in the great houses of Jamaica. This was more home to him than any of the family residences in England that some relatives called home. His father never went back there and made it clear that Jamaica was his home. This was unusual. The blacks wanted Africa, at least they said so, and most of the whites wanted to return to England, even if they were not born there.

When he thought of it, Jamaica was left to the brown man. He supposed that idea had always been buried deep inside of him and compelled him to defy his father and return to the island. In the end, they were all buried here on the estate. And today, he felt a great need to stop at their graves before returning to Mount Apfel.

Once again his thoughts returned to what John had said, and to Haiti, where black, white, and brown tore each other apart. It was far worse than a civil war and far worse than any religious war could have got. As wars go, it was unique; it was a war of color. Black killed white, white killed black, both killed brown and were killed by brown. One's color decided which side one fought and died for.

Strangest thing of all, in Haiti, the French laws were the most liberal when it came to racial mixtures. If you were the son of a Frenchman, then you were a Frenchman, with all his rights and privileges. Nobles were born there with the tar well and truly encrusted in their spine, and they were counted nobles of the sword or robe, whichever degree their father belonged to. The republican general Dumas came to William's mind; he was the son of a marquis born of a slave mother in Haiti.

Le petit blanc was the downfall of Santo Domingo—jealous little men, who envied the power and wealth of the Creoles of color who had wealth and position. It was the small man there, as it would be the small man here in Jamaica, who would bring hell upon their heads. Ironically, the Baptists were the little people of Jamaica's torment. "There was never so right a man, as a righteous man," William said to the spirits in that room.

Standing there, with the morning nearly gone, he asked the question again of himself: was that to be Jamaica's fate? No answer

The Beacon

came back to him. Eleven o'clock issued from the big clock in the hallway before it resumed its tick-tock as its pendulum swung from left to right, wiping out the seconds, minutes, and hours. The clock brought him back from speculation on what was and what might be. For him, it was time to depart homeward.

It was difficult to leave, but there was business to be about. He had been at Mount Vernon since dawn, seeing to this plantation; now his own business at Mount Apfel needed his attention. When he arrived that morning at Mount Vernon, he had been surprised not to find the overseer on duty—also the two bookkeepers were nowhere to be found. Still drunk and carousing with their friends on other plantations, no doubt. Then he remembered Brooks, the overseer, was in the militia and therefore still in Montego Bay, but the bookkeepers should have been here. Because of their absence, he had been forced to remain on the plantation longer than had been his original intent.

As William Edward Vernon mounted his horse and rode away from the graves of his father, grandparents, and his uncles Thomas and Joseph, and then through the gates of Mount Vernon, Neddy, five miles away, sat on the cut-stone wall by Kensington gate, sulking. He was most dissatisfied with his current state of inactivity.

There was nothing much for him to do but stay out of the way. Everyone seemed to be miserable. The slaves were wretched because they had not been given the day off and felt cheated. Jim, his little friend, had to join his cleanup gang in the fields. At the thought of Jim, even with his current boredom, Neddy was glad he wasn't a slave.

His parents seemed jumpy and kept telling him to *go and do something*. That was his dilemma—what was the *thing* he should go and do? Fishing would be nice. If only he could get ahold of Watt, then they could both go to Tangle River, and that would be a very nice *thing* to do. Sitting on the wall, he tried to play the flute. That didn't work, so back into his belt it went. "Boye, what a day!" he mumbled grumpily to himself.

Should he go and see what Watt was doing? Problem was, he did not know if Watt was still with his aunt in the Bay or if he had returned to Friendship. Even then, if he was at Friendship, could he get away from his duties? That was doubtful. Neddy shook his head and sighed, shifted his bottom from the jagged stone edge that cut into it and mumbled, "Batty!"

Crop season had begun in earnest. Long, sweaty hours with bad food carried to the fields would be Watt's sentence for the next few months. From dark morning to midnight, he would have to be supervising cane cutting, loading, and carting to the crusher, if he was lucky. If unlucky, he would spend the time in the boiling house, where the heat would drain him, and sweat would sodden his clothes. There would be no difference between him and the black men stoking the fires, skimming the cauldrons, and ladling the juice from boiler to boiler.

Watt would watch, and they would work, coming and going in shifts while he continued to watch. Hunger would grip his gut, and his parched throat would demand liquid—any cooling liquid, and most likely that would be coarse rum and water with lemon squeezed and sugar stirred in the mug. By the time he made it to bed, the world would spin through his eyes into his head, and his steps would be staggered.

Too tired to eat, he would flop on his bed for what would seem minutes before the slave came with the coffee and cold, greasy plantain, if he had paid the beggar beforehand to bring him food. If no, then he would stumble to the fields and wait for dawn to break with an empty belly. Work would have begun before the first rays hit the earth, and the sun would cast its 10:00 a.m. shadow before they came with cold, half-cooked, stale food for him to choke down.

One thing for sure, by the end of the season, he would be a starved, miserable shadow of what he had been. Probably he would have taken to drink to keep going. Neddy had seen this happen to bookkeepers on Kensington and thought nothing of it. Perhaps, till now, he had been too young to worry about such circumstances. The hanging boy whom they cut down from high in the mango tree two years before had meant nothing to him. But the idea of Watt stringing himself up sent a shudder down Neddy's back. No, he would not let that happen to his friend.

While in his miserable thoughts, Neddy became aware that a remarkably ugly, half-naked slave had come through the gates and passed in front of him. Other than a tattered loincloth barely clinging to his waist, he was unclothed. Thick lips flapped like clappers in the center of a round peel-head, which matched the nude bang-belly protruding in front of him, with its hillock-like navel jutting out even further. Neddy would not have paid him any mind had he not been talking to himself vociferously as he walked. Nothing strange about that in Jamaica, where many people walked and talked with themselves. It was common. But it was the loudness of this human mound of flesh's conversation with self that attracted Neddy's attention. The man was very angry and was on the edge of shouting his discontent to world.

"Wat dem tink mi is? Some black African *naygar* slave for dem to sen an carry *dem* message on fi mi Christmas day? Mi is a *Christian*! Dem owes mi! Di law sey me fi get today. Mi got to carry letters a Backra Massa on fi mi day, now! *Raaass,* man!" he bellowed, fat, banana-like fingers slapping his flabby thighs for emphasis. The flesh where they clapped quivered like cow-foot jelly. "Mi should *chop* dem! Yes, sah, *chop dem to rass*!" he yelled.

On his back the flesh was blotched and crisscrossed like a tortoise shell, where his owner, or owners, had repeatedly penned the tale of slavery with the whip. The lash was meaningless to him now; the feeling had all gone. Sensitive flesh had been transformed into dead leather. Neither cold nor heat, wet nor dry, could he feel.

Between the wrapping around his waist and under his crotch, his seed bag had squeezed and dangled freely. He seemed oblivious to its nakedness and feel. With each pace the man took, his huge, balloon-shaped buttocks plunged up and down with a swaying motion, and his nuts banged against each leg like parangles on an overdressed woman. As they swung left, then right, Neddy noted they were as big as bull's balls that got nailed to the killing gate after one had been butchered in the field. That was the best thing he had seen all day, and the sight made him laugh out loud.

When Conchie Blows

The slave took no notice. Thick legs and bare feet carried him forward. As they did so, the sound of his anger faded, and Neddy went back to his thoughts on things to do. Sliding off the wall, he made for the bush to check on his calabans. He hadn't checked them for two days. That was the *thing to do*.

Drunken shouts came clearly from the cane fields as he walked across the pasture, avoiding the grazing cattle. Christmas never seemed to be done for some. Tomorrow many would still be drunk, and the drivers would use the whip, and the overseers would order them to lash harder. Instead of drunken shouts and challenges, there would be wails of pain that would only add to the misery rum had left them in after three days of drunkenness. He could hear his mother disapproving of it all and his father accepting the situation with the statement, *It what man do at dis time of year.*

Neddy began jogging toward the hill. Gathering speed, he vaulted a low stone wall into the next piece of open land, and as his feet touched down, he threw his arms aloft in victory. Eventually, almost out of breath, he reached the woods; they enclosed him, and the sounds of the estate disappeared, to be replaced by those of the birds in the trees and the scurry of lizards and other small animals darting out of his way to hide under roots or rotting logs.

Above him the trees groaned and rustled, as they resisted or gave with the push of the ever-changing breeze coming up from sea level; younger growth bent and let the moving air pass through their branches, issuing a soothing hush to soften the painful creaks of their elders' conflict. This wooded hillside tapestry closed in and incorporated Neddy as he began the search for his calabans.

Down at Kensington Great House, Richard Morris was given a note as he and his family were at their second breakfast on the verandah. His wife insisted they eat there rather than the dining room. Most peculiar, thought her husband, but in truth it was cooler than the house. Besides, from there, he could see what was going on in the vicinity. Many a time his overseer and bookkeepers were surprised that he had seen some event that was unacceptable in his eyes, or in the eyes of his uncle and partner in the business of cattle, slaves, sugar, and rum.

His only interest was extracting every penny from Kensington. It wasn't even his, but he and his uncle had leased it while the provisions of old Mrs. Fowler's will were sorted out. This added urgency to their plan. There was no time to waste. Quick money was uncle and nephew's aim. They had transformed the property from a pen into a sugar estate and packed it with slaves that they, with the Jews, bought and sold to anyone with the right amount of sterling. Very rarely did they accept local currency. They thought local currency not worth accepting for good black flesh, which had become the commodity in great demand since the abolition of the slave trade from Africa to the Indies and other British possessions.

Morris choked, and his left hand trembled as his eyes scanned the note and scanned again and then read it word for word. Instinctively he raised the serviette to his lips, covering his distress, but his wife noticed that he trembled.

"Is there anything wrong, my dear?" she said, while pouring herself a cup of coffee from the pot on the table at her right, even though a slave for that purpose stood behind her chair. Her husband looked up from behind his serviette mask, which hid the lower portion of his face.

"No, my dear; a friend has warned me that slave prices are dropping, and we have a few too many, perhaps. But it is nothing to worry about. We will weather the storm."

The serviette muffled his voice but it didn't matter. His wife was not even slightly interested in slave prices, so long as they brought in enough money to get them out of this dreadful island and back to England with a standard of living that suited a lady of her quality. She only cared about discarding, upon her return home, the mantle of poor relative. Using one hand to raise the demitasse to her lips, Mrs. Morris delicately sipped the tepid coffee, as if it was just the right temperature.

"You know best, my dear," she said, while taking a tiny bite of the toast and marmalade between sips of coffee with the fashionable lump of cream floating in it. As if practicing for things to come, she replaced the demitasse in its saucer and took up a lump of sugar; holding it elegantly between forefinger and thumb over the half-sized cup, she scraped it delicately with a small knife. First one, then a second chip of sugar plopped into the coffee, gently disturbing the surface and starting tiny ripples, which moved the slowly melting lump of cream to the side of the cup, where her next sip could take in coffee, cream, and sugar as one. Across the table from her, sweat broke from the pores on her husband's forehead. It was a most unseemly sight at the breakfast table, and she was relieved to see him dab at the beads and trickle with a handkerchief drawn from his pocket. Mrs. Morris made a mental note of his distress but dismissed it as the result of the rising heat of the morning inflaming the flesh.

"Would you like a cooling drink, rather than the hot coffee?" she asked her husband. "It would be refreshing." He ignored her and continued to study the note placed on his side plate. To the servant who stood behind his chair, he signaled with a wave of his hand to come around and face him. "Go and get my trap harnessed up right now. And I want that big nigger we put in the stables to come with me."

"Yes, sah."

"Get on with it," he ordered, signaling hurry-hurry by waving his right hand in an agitated manner twice then thrice.

"Yes, sah," parroted the man with that conniving smile, as he backed out of the room like a courtier bowing and scraping to a monarch.

"I have some business over at Maroon Town, mi dear. I think I should call on the young lieutenant in charge of the company there. We should invite him and his subordinate to dine with us some time, don't you think? It will be nice to entertain a couple of English officers for a change."

"Yes, my dear," she answered in her usual way.

"Laura might be able to meet someone acceptable?"

"Yes, dear."

"She is fifteen and rounding out."

His wife raised her cup and looked at her husband over its rim. "Yes, dear, but I was hoping we would be back in England before we had those considerations for her." She placed the cup with a slight rattle back in its saucer. He wasn't sure she was signaling he should end the matter of their daughter now, so he continued to explore possibilities for her.

"True, true, mi dear, but she could get some practice in first, don't you think?" There was the slightest quiver of amusement in his voice as the nervousness brought on by the arrival of the note began to abate.

He did not want any vapors. His wife was prone to dramatics. She was bored, he knew. In the island she had little to do, with all the servants at beck and call. Not even on the children did she need to expend her energy; caring for them was the duty of others. She had no regrets, being by nature lazy. In the years she had been in the island, her three children had become strangers, even the daughter she had given birth to at home in Hampshire. As a result, to compensate for her household helplessness, she had developed what he thought of as the domestic dramatics.

Clearing his throat nervously, he continued, as if he were a father faced with a delicate matter to convey to a virginal daughter. "Mi dear," he said, "would you see to the packing of trunks with clothes for you and the children and have them readied for my return? It would be advisable to pack the valuables as well. Would you see that is done?"

She stared at him. Her mouth became loose, and her tongue moistened her lips in a most common way. "Are we going somewhere, my dear?" she inquired, her eyes never leaving his face, like a doe staring at a wolf intent on her as its prey "You have not mentioned this before!"

"Circumstances, my dear, may force us into Montego Bay for a week or two. Business of the slaves, my dear, and I would rather have you and the children with me than left out here on your own."

"Is your uncle coming with us?"

"Yes! Of course he is coming with us, Ann."

Her husband was so adamant that she began to wonder. The old man was very much his own man. Why would he come with them to

Montego Bay when, whatever business there was, her husband could look after it for both of them?

Her husband saw the suspicion on her face and moved to allay her fears. "If he were staying here, I would leave you and the children in his charge, but we have to do the business together. The sooner we do it, the sooner we return home, mi dear."

That did it. She nodded and smiled at the thought of the sailing ship heading back to England. Then there would be parties for the girls and the theater to attend in Montego Bay. Although not the slightest bit interested in books, she would put in an appearance and chat with friends at the literary society. All very acceptable, for apart from the discussion of the latest novel, there would be talk of home. She almost cried out with joy at the prospect. Anywhere was better than being stuck out on Kensington.

"I will see to it as soon as you are on your way to Maroon Town, dear. What a nice outing it will be for all of us. A wonderful break from this dull place."

Morris did not wait. He seized the opportunity and got up, leaving his half-finished breakfast on the table.

The trap was waiting outside, a large, muscular man standing behind it. Morris didn't even notice him. He got into the driver's seat and started off at a trot. The man behind did the same, keeping up with the cart and holding his stride by holding on to a strap nailed to the back of the trap for that purpose.

Morris stopped at the overseer's house where his uncle Samuel lived. The slave ran around from behind the trap to hold the horse's head, while his master got down and puffed his way up the steps to the door. It was open, and he walked through the hallway and back to the piazza, where his uncle was breakfasting.

"Morning, Richard," said the older man at the table. "Splud, sir! What are you doing here, interrupting a man's food? You should be at your own. What's the matter, your cook spoiled it? Well, you can't take mi cook, you know." Richard ignored his uncle's attempt at humor. It was always bad, but Richard pleased him on occasion with the odd laugh. This time there was no laugh or banter, just a serious expression clouding his face.

"This morning, I got this." He threw the crumpled note on the table. His uncle picked it up and carefully smoothed it with his hand like someone pressing cloth with an iron. He read it, then read it again carefully. "Where did this come from?"

"An overseer I know."

"Where would he have got this information from?"

"His niggers! How the hell should I know!"

"He says they are planning to burn Kensington. Do you believe him?"

"Whether it is true or not, I am not taking chances. Their souls are as black as their hides. They are likely to do anything. They are savages! They are already disobeying the drivers and refusing to work. I am off to Maroon Town and the Kings Barracks to see the officer responsible there. I have told Ann to get packed in case we have to go quickly—evacuate to Montego Bay. I suggest you do the same."

"Leave here!" Samuel looked at his nephew incredulously. "You must be mad! My life's work and savings are tied up with this bunch of slaves and in our property. Do you think I am going to run away and let any damned nigger destroy what I have worked for?" The two stared at each other. Richard Morris knew his uncle's stubborn streak and said nothing to further entrench it at this time, when it could mean life or death.

"Very well; I am off to persuade them to send at least a squad to keep order. At least it will put the fear of God into the blacks. If they refuse, I am taking off to Montego Bay with Ann and the children. You, uncle, can do as you like. Come with us, or you can damned well stay here and do battle with the niggers if they rise up." He turned and stalked out of the room.

His uncle calmly went on with his breakfast and began mental preparation for the coming trouble. It would not be the first time he had faced rebellion in the island. His first had been ten years before, and there had been two others since then. He had survived all three. What could be different this time? Shoot a few and write them off? Double the price on those left, and he would not be out of pocket when all was over. A large piece of salt pork along with a mound of sweet potatoes squashed onto his fork made their way into his mouth, followed by a slurp of coffee. Following that, he took a swig of watered rum to keep back any fever that might come on.

Richard Morris laid the whip to the haunches of his horse, and as a result it began the six miles to Maroon Town with a jolt, nearly pulling the slave's shoulders out of joint and forcing him to let go the strap behind the conveyance. He caught up again after the horse settled into a trot as they cleared Kensington gate. Forgetting about the man following, Morris, in his near-panic state, varied the pace of the horse on some stretches of the road. The slave behind was almost dragged along these sections. Falling a couple of times, the man had to pick himself up and run full out to catch up with his master. After about three miles of this helter-skelter progress, Morris settled the horse down into a trot, making it easier for his slave. But in doing so, he thought more about the horse than the man behind.

They got to where Colonel Sandford had been killed in 1795. Morris had passed the spot many times and never paid it the respect of a thought. Why should he? That was thirty-seven years before. Today he looked nervously over his shoulder at the slave struggling to keep up near the spot where the colonel fell. He was glad to see the sweat running down the man's face and soaking his shirt with dark patches around the armpits and chest. To make sure he was still in charge, he felt for the pistol under his coat. Then his right hand gripped the buggy whip tighter, and that too added assurance.

On they trotted to Hunter's estate. Morris noticed inactivity in the fields. Slaves should have been working, but the gangs were sitting down or standing about; scythes and machetes were idle in their hands, and the cane remained standing uncut, while drays stood by empty. Drivers had gathered in knots at the edge of the fields and obviously were at a loss as to what they should do. That was a very bad sign. Morris laid the whip to the horse's hindquarters, setting it to move at a canter, forcing his slave to let go his dragging strap. Morris was not waiting around. His man would just have to catch up with him as best he could.

At last, the first huts on the outskirts of Maroon Town came into view. Horse and trap continued at a fast pace, cantering down the main street of the small town to the other end where the barracks was situated.

As Morris drew rein and half-skidded to a stop, two curs sheltering in the shadow of the guardhouse slunk away around the corner. The soldier on duty came up to attention in slovenly fashion as Morris got down from the trap and walked into the guardhouse. Ignoring the guard, he went straight up to the duty sergeant sitting at a table in the center of the small, hot, stuffy room.

"I want to see your officer immediately," he said.

"On what business, sir?"

"That is none of your business, sergeant. Just take me to him, and don't waste time with all your foolish military protocol."

"Can't do that, just so, sir." The duty sergeant tried to reassert his small authority.

"Can't do what? Don't waste my time, man! Take me to your commanding officer this instant! Or I will go to the colonel of this regiment and have you tarred like a common felon. Do you understand, sergeant?"

"Follow me, sir." The sergeant had lost, and he was not about to risk his rank for some jumped-up planter.

As they crossed the square, the sergeant marched quickly, making Morris half run to keep up with him. There was no stopping the pace, and Morris was panting by the time they reached the other side of the small parade ground. They came to a halt outside a small wooden building that served as the company office.

"Wait here, sir. I will see if the lieutenant will see you." He pointed his duty stick to a spot where he expected Morris to stand while he went in to seek an audience for him with his officer. Morris ignored the instructions and brushed past the sergeant into the room.

The lieutenant looked up at the intrusion. Noticing that his sergeant was accompanied by a planter, he restrained his impulse to yell. He had just taken over the post and did not, as yet, know the local planters. He thought it wise to be calm and hear the man out.

"What can I do for you, sir?" he said.

For the second time that day, Morris threw down the crumpled note on a table. The lieutenant looked at it as if it was some untouchable reptile. Morris did not move and did not offer an explanation, which forced the officer to smooth the paper much in the same way as it had been done before, then pick it up to read.

"What do you expect from me?" the officer said, tossing the piece of paper on the table toward its owner.

"I and my family expect your protection, sir!"

"Protection from what, sir? This is rumor. You do not really expect your slaves to get up and put you and your family to the sword and burn your house down, now, do you? They wouldn't dare! Certainly not with us just six miles away. That would be madness on their part."

"Of course I do, you young idiot!" Morris screamed. "How long have you been in this island? You do not know what these Negroes are capable of doing. Stop judging them as if they are white. Down the road they murdered one of your colonels. Lieutenants will be mincemeat for them. They will eat your flesh and hang your bowels from the trees for the crows to pick at. I want protection! At the very least, send a squad of soldiers to Kensington at once, sir!" Morris thumped the table with the whip handle.

The lieutenant remained unmoved, poured himself a glass of water on his desk, and took a sip. "Can't do that sir. There is no evidence that this will happen. I cannot spare any men. If there is an uprising, I cannot split my force, not good soldiering to do that," the lieutenant said. "You are out of luck. Must keep them together, sir. Divided we fall, united we stand." He repeated the cliché he had heard some time back in the mess from an old major who had fought against Napoleon at Leipzig.

"You can't be serious, young man," Morris said in a more subdued tone.

"Sorry, sir, that is the way it is. I suggest you return to your plantation and batten down the hatches, as they say when at sea, if you suspect there will be trouble. If there is, then you can stand them off until we come to rout them with full battle cry." He chuckled at that.

Morris's grip tightened on the whip in his hand. He exerted immense self-control to resist bringing it down across the lieutenant's shoulder; at least it would have taken the smug look of authority off his pimpled, pasty face. On the verge of apoplectic rage, Morris stormed out of the office, pushing the sergeant violently out of his way. Crossing the square at a half-run, half-walk, his portly frame showed distress with the exertion. Twice the back of his hand came up to mop his brow.

Both the sergeant and his superior watched the planter disappear through the back door of the guardroom and emerge from the front and heave himself with an effort up into the driver's position on his conveyance. He lashed the horse, sending it into a gallop with the trap careering forward, his unfortunate slave left to find his own way back. At first he tried to run after his master as a dog would, but gave up and stood watching the trap rock and bounce down the road with crushed white limestone flying from under its wheels.

Morris was only interested in getting himself first and his family second well away from Kensington before nightfall. He was taking the warning seriously. If his uncle decided to stay, then that would be on his own head. As the horse galloped along, and the trap bounced around the road, he hoped that Ann had obeyed his instructions and had ready all the baggage they would need.

It took Morris less time to retrace the road than when he went forward that morning to Maroon Town. He brought the trap to a skidding stop in front of the Great House, sending gravel flying in all directions. The horse, lathered with sweat and heaving for air, stood shuddering after its mad run.

"Ann! Ann!" Morris shouted, as he ran into the ground floor of the house.

"Yes, my dear. What is the matter?"

"Get the children and our bags. We are leaving right away."

"What is the matter, dear?"

"Don't ask. Just do as I say, damn you!" There was clear panic in his voice.

Under normal circumstances, the violent response she got from her husband would have sent her into the vapors, but this time she cut out the dramatics and got busy ordering the servants to bring down the bags she had packed that morning at her husband's insistence.

When Conchie Blows

Seeing the state of readiness she had prepared pleased and calmed him down.

Their carriage was brought around, along with a cart piled high with boxes full of clothing and whatever valuables his wife had time to cram into them. No matter what, it was better that they should carry all possible material needs in case her husband's fear, whatever it was, came true.

From her small front veranda, Quashiba watched the Morris family carriage and cart jolting down the road and through the gates. There was too much baggage for a day trip, and the urgency of their departure indicated that it was not just a trip to visit a friend or spend a few days in Montego Bay or even Falmouth. She frowned. The overloaded wagon with the excessive luggage threatening to tumble into the road signaled trouble. Morris must know something she had not yet heard about. Also, there was no slave running behind the carriage, and she knew that the new Massa of Kensington liked having one do that, if for nothing else but show.

Her eyes wandered around the estate, looking for the trouble she felt must be boiling under the surface. Drunken shouts and bold threats came up the hill to her from the slave cabins. This she did not like at all, for that was not part of Daddy Sharpe's plan. The damned bad niggers were going to get out of hand and ruin all their efforts to gain freedom for all of them. Where was Edward? She looked around for her husband and was relieved to see him hurrying up the hill toward her. It did not take him long to reach her, panting, out of breath.

"Mi wan you an di boy out of here, now!" he said vehemently. "Dere is going to be big trouble. Where Neddy?"

They both looked around, and his mother called for him, but there was no answer. They looked at each other and knew neither was going to move until he turned up.

The Morris family was well on the way to Montego Bay when Neddy pulled the first of his two catches from its trap. He was about to wring the bird's neck when the smell of smoke drifted through the bush to him. Still holding the white-headed baldpate that had followed the seed trail into his cleverly constructed calaban, Neddy stood up, sniffing the air. The strong acrid smell meant there was a big fire somewhere close by. Turning around and looking through the trees, he could see the black smoke against the late afternoon sky. From the direction of the plumes, he knew Kensington buildings were afire. Panic gripped his stomach, and his hands relaxed on the bird, which instinctively forced itself to freedom and sailed up into the nearest tree branch, fluffed its feathers, and flew off.

Neddy took the cue and set off at a run back down the hill, through the tangle, when he remembered his second captured quarry. Turning back, he quickly scrambled to where it was and kicked the trap over, freeing the white wing. Then he began his descent again. By the time he cleared the woods, his legs and arms were scratched, scraped, and bleeding. But that did not slow him down.

The trash house was ablaze, and the fire had spread to the works. People were dancing, shouting, and making no effort to put out the blaze. Their things were going up in smoke along with the massa's. That did not matter; they were enjoying themselves. Some were stoking the fire by throwing working implements into it, and Neddy even saw men pushing carts of cane into the blazing buildings with the intent of fueling the fire even further. Neddy tried to skirt the scene and ran around by the overseer's house, where Massa Samuel lived. Another crowd had gathered there, and, as he slowed down to a half jog, he could hear the old man berating them from a front window. Next, two pistol shots rang out. There was a groan from the crowd and then silence.

"Im kill Zekie!" someone yelled. "Lard Gad! Ezekiel dead. Oh!" another sang out.

"Mek we kill im! Mek mi chop im," voices shouted from the mob. A musket shot rang out again. A moan, and a body fell, leaving a hole in the crowd. Instead of melting away with their tails between their legs, beaten by superior firepower, they melded into an enraged mass of moving arms and legs with one voice that alternated in pitch from the piping female to the guttural male.

"Duppy time come," a female screamed. "We going mek a duppy out of you, Mass Samuel." Another shot and another, and two more slaves were peeled out of the conglomerate and lay groaning on the ground. Twenty, thirty—maybe more, maybe less; Neddy could not tell, they were packed so closely together as they rushed up the narrow steps to the barred front door. It collapsed inwards from the sheer pressure of their bodies.

His own terror matched the man's inside the house, but Neddy was lucky to be on the outside of those walls. His breathing hurt as he ran for dear life along the path between the slave huts, now ablaze, up the hill to his house.

His father saw him first and grabbed him up to stop his headlong rush. Holding him by one arm and his mother by hers, he ordered them to be gone from Kensington. Quashiba rested herself away from her husband's grip.

"And where you going?" she said. Her eyes blazed with defiance.

"Woman," he began, slowly but firmly. "Don't give mi trouble now. Tek di boy an go. Mi staying here to save our place."

"Edward, we married dis long time, you don't understan mi yet. Where you go, mi go. Dat is why we married in di church. Mi is you an you is mi." She settled for herself and husband, but not for their son. While he stood watching them argue, Neddy's breathing became easier, and the pain in his chest began to diminish. His mother turned to him now.

"You to go to Miss Rachel over at Mount Apfel. Tell her what as happened here. She will mind you for mi."

"Mi not going wid out you," Neddy said boldly, and was about to say something similar to what his mother had said to his father but was stopped by a stinging blow across his face by the flat of his mother's hand. For the first and only time in his life, he felt her rage and desperation. She did not even give him a chance to recover, her forefinger pointed right under his nose.

"When mi tell you to do some ting, boy, mi don't want back chat. I give you life, an no drunken nigger going tek it." As quickly as it was said, she hugged him to herself and kissed the top of his head.

The Beacon

"Now run!" she screamed at him. Neddy leaped off the small veranda with tears streaming down his face. He ran to the back of the house and up the hill. At the top, he looked back, tears blurring his sight of Kensington Great House. The overseer's house, the trash house, the works, the hot house, and all the slave huts were burning out of control. Thatch-roof huts, one after another, flared up like torches and then burned like a bonfire. They did not last long. In a few minutes, only row upon row of piled ashes remained.

A crowd was moving up the hill to his own small house, where his mam and his da were. Drumbeats and screams of laughter, shouts of *Bun dem, kill dem!* came up to where he stood. A great loneliness engulfed him, and he was tempted to go back to join his parents, but the left side of his face still smarted from his mother's slap, and that made him turn and head for Mount Apfel as she had ordered.

* * *

"Massa Sam! Massa Sam! Massa Sam! Come quick! Lard Jesus! It a start!"

Young Sam Barrett ran out into the backyard, wondering what the commotion was about. Old Martha, with her uncombed white hair standing straight up like a thick crown of feathers, was looking at the darkening landscape above Cinnamon Hill. Pointing her crooked, gnarled, trembling fingers at a huge blaze, way-away up, she declared, "It di sign for all to see." Sam saw the flicker where she pointed, and as he watched, it got larger.

"It start," she said again.

"What start?"

"Di freedom, Massa. Di freedom!"

"What are you talking about, Martha? Where is that, anyway?"

"Dat look like it. A Kensington give di signal, sah! It flames write *freedom* in the sky."

"What the hell are you talking about, woman?" demanded young Barrett.

"Freedom! Dats what mi talk bout, Massa. Freedom signal. Can't you no see it up dere in di hills?" As if welcoming God's last trumpet call to judgment for the quick and the dead, she raised both her hands with their palms up, crooked fingers spread wide against the oncoming night sky, indicated the blazing plantation in the hills. Then on the right, another blaze shot up. And again another; within minutes, it seemed, estate after estate became exploding infernos. They were all being put to the torch.

"Halleluiah!" sang out old Martha. "Halleluiah!"

Young Sam turned and went back into the house to get ready for the uprising. He would, at all costs, defend Cinnamon Hill. A shiver ran through his body as he fought back the blackness of terror that tried to surface and overwhelm him. St. James was ablaze, and Kensington had been the beacon that unleashed the inferno on the parish.

Chapter 13

Conflagration

Neddy made it to the top of the hill and took a last look back at his house before he began his descent along the path that led off Kensington in the direction of Mount Apfel. When he reached the wall next to the road, he sat on the ground with his back to it. It was time to catch his breath and settle his mind.

His hand came to his face where his mother had slapped him, and once more tears sprouted from his eyes and ran down his cheeks. A huge sob shook his body. There was no sting left, but the hurt he felt was deep inside. Confusion clouded his thoughts. Nothing seemed to come straight. It was all churned up, like a pond after cows had been driven through it to wash them down. Why did she slap him? He would have obeyed her—or maybe not, he wondered? Perhaps that was why she slapped him? Strange, though; the slap made him realize how much she loved him. Ultimately, that realization stemmed the flow of tears.

His world was coming undone; how was it happening? One minute all was as usual and boring, and in the next minute, his world was aflame with shots and hatred. From everything that had gone on in the last few weeks and what he had known about it, this should not be happening.

He stayed where he was, contemplating the day's events; these led back to the chats he had overheard during the past weeks. Slowly they began falling into place, one after another, as they trickled to the forefront of his mind. There were gaps in the puzzle, but only now did he begin to truly understand what all the Daddy Sharpe talk was about.

What was happening on Kensington was not meant to happen. They were not supposed to burn the place and kill people! He remembered the Montego Bay church meeting agreement. No work was to be done until they got paid for it, and the signal for the no work was to be when conchi blew for work to begin after Christmas. But all their plans had gone wrong, terribly wrong. The awful feeling surged up in his belly and made him want to throw up in terror.

Voices coming down the road interrupted his thoughts. Neddy brought his knees up to his chest and hugged them, trying to make himself very small against the wall. He sat very still, breathing slowly in and out, hoping they wouldn't hear him, at the same time fighting to hold back his vomit. Closing his eyes he began to count, imagining the numbers as his mouth moved, as if saying them aloud. He wished they would pass quickly, but there seemed to be a never-ending river of drunks going by on the road.

At least fifty men, with one or two women in a bunch, came by first, and then came groups of fives and sixes, then down to twos and threes, followed by the odd straggler. They were singing and yelling about freedom. Many were almost falling-down drunk but kept demanding more rum from the others. One man stopped, leaned on the wall, and began to retch. This made Neddy's predicament even worse and his struggle to contain himself more intense. The man disgorged finally, mumbled some curse, and moved on. Another added his pee to the other side of the wall, just down from the boy's hiding place, before he too continued on his way. The air stank. Oh, how Neddy wished them gone, so that he, too, could move and be on his way to Mount Apfel and safety.

Adding to his olfactory misery, the soft evening breeze brought the acrid smell of burned sugar mixed with sweat. It hung in the air, long after they had all passed. Neddy knew there must be more fires

Conflagration

than just Kensington for that to reach him, sheltering behind the wall. Those were not Kensington slaves, of that he was sure. Their direction was all wrong for them to have come from his place. They must be from other estates they had set on fire.

Finally, all went quiet. For a time he did not move. Gritting his teeth, he finally edged upward and peeked over the wall to see if the coast was clear. In either direction there were no strange shadows lurking about that he could not account for, so Neddy scrambled over the wall and stood in the middle of the road, taking a good look around. Close by at the top the hill on his right, the Mount Pleasant estate house and works blazed against the early evening sky; black billowing smoke of burning molasses and sugar curled slowly upward, folding into the sky of oncoming night. Standing on one spot, slowly, Neddy turned round and round. It was as if huge torches had been lit on all the surrounding hills. One after another, they blazed in the night sky. To him the world was a fire, and he remembered the Reverend Waldrich preaching about the cauldrons of hell.

He had to make a decision. Which way should he go to Mount Apfel? He wondered if that had been torched as well. He dearly hoped not. Going through the smallholdings would be the safer way, Neddy decided. No slave would be burning those. It would be longer but the best path to take.

Turning to his right, walking quickly, he headed down the road. It was not long before he came to the path that led him up through the settlements. Jumping over the half-gap in the wall, he headed up the familiar way that led him past Brothers Union, also owned by the Morris uncle and nephew. If the slaves there had heard what had happened down at Kensington, he suspected that property would have been set ablaze as well. They would have seen the fires anyway and guessed what was going on down there. It would take only that to set them off on a rampage. There was a bunch of bad niggers there, according to his father, who on occasion went to do some carpentering on that place.

Thankfully, the moon had come out and lit his way better than any lantern could have done. It was friendlier light than the fires burning in the hills around him. Neddy felt safer, and fright began to fall away as hunger took its place. Not since morning breakfast had he eaten. Once at Mount Apfel, he would be fed, but that was at least three miles further on. His belly rumbled its needs as he walked. He thanked God that Watt was not with him; just imagine the fuss he would be kicking up about food and starvation. Neddy wondered, as he walked past darkened cottages, if Watt suffered from worms. He remembered how his own mama physicked him with castor oil every now and then, in case he carried a belly full of worms. That ordeal was much worse than anything he had suffered in his sixteen years of life. She mixed it with orange juice, and if he did not vomit it all up, he spent the day getting rid of his innards at the other end. He hoped he was past that stage, but he suspected his mam would dose him yet again. He would take it happily, if all was well after this day.

Just off the path, on the edge of the Fraser place, there was a custard apple tree. It had to be investigated, if the coast was clear. The last time he and some friends tried to help themselves, old man Fraser chased them off, limping along on his wooden leg, vowing to nail their hides to his shed door. As they ran, one of his fellow fruit raiders screamed back at the old man chasing them, "We going tief you tonight."

That enraged him even further, and he threatened to roast them first before skinning them. They believed him and did not venture back. Because of his infirmity, all the children around thought old man Fraser a bogeyman who would eat them at night if he ever caught them.

The memory of the chase made him nervous, but he was still hungry. At this time of the year, custard apples should be bending the tree with fruit, and even at night he could feel for a fit one to eat. His pace quickened at the thought of the luscious custard apples waiting to be picked. The idea of their sweetness made him drool. He thought of other fruit trees in the area to raid; unfortunately, there were no star apple trees close by that he could recall. They were coming into fruit as well. In December only a few would be ready. But he might be lucky. He scratched his chin like a wise man and tried again to think of one close by, but none came to mind. They were all Worcester and Retirement way. Besides, they would be too tall to climb at night and especially dangerous with some man looking out to catch him.

There were no lights in the small Fraser house that he could see. All was still. Neddy hesitated before he scrambled over the rustic log fence and made his way cautiously toward the custard apple tree standing apart in the field. A dog barked, stopped, then began barking persistently. It would not shut up. Neddy did not like that. The thought of being chased by the old man two years before surfaced again. He could almost hear the lopsided flip-clop of his one good foot followed by his wooden spike chasing him. Boye! Did he run that day. He sniggered to himself. "Damned dog!" he whispered.

Crouching low, chancing it anyway, he moved quickly across the open space hoping no one was watching. A door squeaked open. As it opened, he stopped dead in his tracks just before reaching the custard apple tree. Cold sweat sprang to his forehead; someone was standing at the entrance of the cottage, framed by the open door. A faint light flickered in the room behind, outlining the man holding a gun. Neddy did not move but squatted down. The dog had boldly come forward to the edge of the yard, barking. How he wished for a stick to wallop it into silence.

"Who out dere?"

The dog stopped barking, as if waiting for an answer to his master's question.

"Who dere? Show yourself, or I will shoot. Anyone out dere?" The voice sounded as jittery as Neddy felt. Neither of them moved. Again the damned dog barked. Then he heard another man's voice say, "Be silent." This voice, he recognized as belonging to old man Fraser.

"You better come out, or mi going shoot unu." That definitely was the old man Fraser. It sounded miserable enough. The first voice must have been his son Fred, thought Neddy.

Cold sweat soaked his shirt, and his hands and knees trembled. He was tempted to get up and make a break for it, but common sense told him to hold still where he was. When the opportunity presented itself, then he would creep under the tree and put the trunk between him and the house. That would ensure his immediate safety.

Obviously they could not see him, or the old ogre would have fired by now.

Out there in the darkness, new dangers lurked, liquored-up slaves with cutting knives. They knew that, Neddy knew that. If they walked out, a flashing blade in the moonlight would probably be the last thing they would see on earth. It was safer to stand by the door and be able to retreat behind their house walls. Wandering into their yard to find what walked abroad was not an option for the Frasers. They would hug to the hearth this night.

"Meee sees you!" shouted the old man. "Mi goin shoot you. You black burning bastard!" He fired. The flash of the gun clearly showed two men in the doorway. They were not looking in his direction at all. The old man had fired his gun straight down in front of his house rather than to his left and the field where Neddy was crouching. Slowly, he moved forward to the tree. It would be safer to cross the field and go round behind than try to make the road again and pass by the front of the house. No sooner was he crawling forward than the dog started barking again in his direction. Neddy swore aloud.

"Gimmi de gun," Fraser demanded of his son, and for a moment Neddy thought the old man had heard him curse. There was another shot. This time it was in his direction; the ball whistled overhead, cutting through the branches of the tree. Neddy lay flat on the ground behind the trunk, not daring to move. It seemed an interminable time. He prayed hard they would not harm him when they came down to the field and found him there. But nothing happened. No footsteps approached. Eventually the dog stopped its noise, and he heard the door slam shut. A few more minutes must have passed before enough courage returned to have him crawling forward again. The dog barked, but the door remained closed. Old Fraser must have decided it was better to hole up than wander into the dark, vaporous night air.

He made it to the far fence and over it into a coffee and banana piece. At least the thick bushes would hide him if slowing his progress. As he walked, the moonlight helped him pick his way between the rows of banana and coffee. From their sweet smell, he could tell there were ripe berries on the bushes. He picked a few and chewed.

Conflagration

Better than nothing; at least their slightly sweet flesh moistened his throat somewhat, but he wished the Frasers had not spoiled his chances for a custard apple. That would have done both jobs, filling his belly and cutting his thirst.

No sooner was he back on the path than he could hear voices coming up from behind, and from the sound, they were closing in on him. Quickly he dodged back to where he had come from and lay down among the coffee bushes to let them go by. Better they be in front than behind him; then there would be less chance of them spotting him on the road. Neddy had no idea whether the voices belonged to black or white men. Whoever owned them, on this night, they were equally dangerous. Wisely, Neddy was not about to take the chance that they were friendly just two miles away from the safety of Mount Apfel.

As they came closer, the loudest voice sounded familiar. He could see they were carrying a lantern from the way the small light swung close to the ground.

"When mi ketch mi a white gal, mi going split er. She never tek any ting like dis one. She going remembers dis ya one, mek mi tell unu dat." A familiar voice boasted. "She going tek me too, Mungo." A nasty high-pitched cackle followed.

"She going tek all of us," confirmed a third voice.

"Hif mi can't tek it, ow a white gal going tek it? Mungo not going leave us any ting," said the one with the lantern. All three screeched with laughter.

"Mi tell you, some of di white gal good-good, but not dat good."

Neddy lay still as they passed on by, pumping each other up. The lantern light was enough for Neddy to recognize the boy who was sleeping with Mungo the night he had returned from the bird shooting at Lapland. The other boy was somewhat of a surprise: Neddy recognised him as Coco from Kensington. For some time after they passed him by, their voices drifted back with their intentions.

"Di firs white gal we can grab get licks by tree of us tonight."

"Dem white gal tink dem is special. Mek er a baby modder, mek er drops a black pickney."

"What you talk bout? A brown mulatto pickney it would come out a her." There was another shriek of laughter at that. Their chatter faded round the next corner on the path.

At last Neddy felt safe enough to emerge from his hiding place. He could not help thinking that if those three were looking to make trouble, then all sense must be gone in the world. "Dis is very bad," he whispered to himself.

Neddy stood on the path for a while to let them get well ahead before continuing on. The moon showed the way clearly for him. It was almost bright enough for him to read what was written in the Bible that was always open on its stand in his church. Why his thoughts ran there at that moment, he did not know, and it was not the time to question them. Instead he continued with caution, staying close to the fence, so that escape was close at hand. Bucking his toe on a stone made him curse and put his sandals back on his feet. Captain Galloway's warning came to mind. Sandals slowed him; that was why they were not constantly on his feet, despite the captain's warning. He had taken them off and hung them around his neck to cross the field. They had stayed there when making his escape from the Frasers.

Neddy realized that any other night but this one would have been perfect for night fishing or even raiding fruit trees in the provision grounds. Bright starlight combined with moonlight made day of night and chased all duppies and rolling calves away from his path. Instead, this night's brightness put him in danger at every step, not from dead things but from live ones intent on making dead things out of people not with them.

As he looked around, the landscape stood out clearly. He smiled, remembering the complaints coming into his parents about provision ground raids. They could never prove their suspicions, but he still got sent to bed early with only bread and water for supper. Standing in the backyard in front of his father the next day, without letting a single muscle twitch, he listened to a lecture on bad behavior. Not a flicker, not a smile confessing guilt, showed on his face. He thought at the time he had heard it all before, but this was his father's way of trying to get a confession out of him. The attempt was not very clever. He wasn't about to be shamed into admitting guilt.

When his mother explained later how important those provision grounds were to the slaves, there was sense to the lecture; after that, his raids stopped. Walking along and thinking about it all, he admitted to himself that he missed the nighttime adventure with his friends. It was boring, asking and getting permission to help himself to the mangoes and the other fruit as they came in season. He even helped to pick them for market and earned the odd penny for his assistance. But he yearned to sneak in, pick the fruit, and sneak off to eat it. Lord! Those mangoes, oranges, star apples, and custard apples always tasted sweeter when they had been gotten that way.

All that happened before Watt. Now, there was a quandary. Up to this moment, he had accepted Watt as just another boy who was out of his depth in this island and needed to be taught to swim. Apart from that, he had not thought much further.

Watt had proved to be a very good friend, more than a friend. Now, for the first time, with the acrid smell of smoke burning his nostrils, color crossed his mind, and he began to wonder about white against black. Was this a war between them? Until now, there had been no question of color. But if color made a difference, then where did he and Watt stand? How intimate could friendship be?

Regardless—black, brown, white—he knew that by this time, Watt would have got himself into trouble and be in need of his help. Somehow, in the morning, he would have to get himself down to Friendship and find out what was going on there.

Mount Apfel wasn't much further. He stopped for a moment and looked about. Then quickened his pace. Hunger spurred him on. Instead of sticking into his rump like spurs, its sharpness jabbed his stomach. Food, any food, tantalized his thoughts. Instinctively he sucked to bring saliva in and around his mouth, letting tongue moisten his lips. On he pushed, now and then breaking into a jog to reach Mount Apfel sooner.

About a mile from his goal, someone shouting in front of him on the path brought his progress to a halt. Neddy cursed. Instantly, he ducked off the track and into a cornfield. The voices were not much further ahead. The sound told him that much.

God almighty! That was Mungo and his friends. They sounded like a pack of mangy dogs worrying a cow or a horse. Any minute, Neddy expected to hear one yelp as a dog was butted or kicked.

Instead, he heard a shot. Carefully he worked his way forward to see what they were at. The shot worried him. Were they doing the shooting, or was someone shooting at them, as had happened to him? Then he heard a female scream, and the order from Mungo.

"Leave dat one. Er pussy too small. Dat one! Grab er!"

He rounded the corner, crouching low. The two were chasing a girl around a small pasture. Another girl was fleeing down the road. One of the boys was standing watching her run, and it was obvious he had fired the shot. He was pointing the empty pistol at the fleeing girl. It was Coco; he must have stolen the pistol from Kensington Great House or the overseer's place.

The running girl was soon out of sight, and Coco turned and walked into the field, setting himself up behind the other girl with his friends circling on both sides of her. She was trapped. They surrounded her effectively. One moved in to grab her and was surprised when she struck him hard across the face. He reeled backward, clutching at where the blow fell, yelping like a dog. From his reaction it was obvious the girl had something in her hand and had laced her attacker with it.

"She cut me!" he cried out. "She got a rock-stone in er and."

It wasn't Mungo that had been struck but his bedmate. Like hunting dogs, they moved in at her again. One ripped her blouse from behind and she swung round to strike. Another collared her round the waist; this time she managed to bring her hand with the stone down on top of his head. Stunned, he let her go. "Bumba!" he uttered, as his hand rose to the crown of his head, and he wisely backed off from her. They continued to circle her, but for a while they did not dare approach. Mungo was the only one who had not yet suffered a wound from this animal that he and his fellow curs held at bay. He had let the others take their knocks for him. But the time had come; as leader, he had to show the way. There was no hurry; he awaited his opening.

One of them lunged at her; he backed away quickly before her stone could do him any more damage, but he'd thrown her off balance. Mungo moved in quickly and tore at her breasts, shredding her blouse. After that maneuver, her full white breasts were exposed clearly in the moonlight. Watching from his concealment, Neddy found himself strangely excited.

Mungo made another grab for her right breast and at the same time put his other arm around her waist, clamping his mouth on her nipple like a hungry puppy. She put both hands against his chest and gave a mighty shove, breaking his hold. Repulsed but undaunted, Mungo moved forward eagerly to resume the onslaught while the other two watched. His manhood was at stake. Defiantly the girl stood her ground. Neddy recognized her. It was Millicent Dougal. They had taken on more than they knew, he thought. His instinct to go and help a girl in distress subsided with the discovery of who she was. She would have them, and for a long time afterward her gift would be with them. They deserved her.

"Grab her, man, an give it to er. She wants it bad," the yellow one of the trio shouted.

At that, Millicent screamed back at them, "You want it? Den come and tek it, if you feels you can!"

She lay down on the ground, pulled her skirt up around her waist, and exposed what they all wanted to see and enter. Not one moved; instead, they stared at what all had dreamed about—a white gal. It was Mungo who took her on first. Quickly he shucked his pants and was on top of her, trying to mount. After much grunting and struggling that showed his inexperience, he eventually rooted, with some help from her. She wrapped her legs and arms around him, as one holding dearly to a tree trunk in the fury of a hurricane, and they began their animal mating.

The other two, in their own excitement at their own prospects, urged him on. They did not notice Neddy sneaking by on the path behind them. Keeping low, he left them waiting to close in on her and seek their own individual pleasure.

At a safe distance, he stood up straight. From the shouts he could tell the second one was now having his way with Millicent. If what he remembered Miss Dodd had said about her was true, they would regret what they had done for a very long time, hopefully all their lives. He felt sorry for Millicent, even if she was a "dutty, nasty little gal." The thought of them receiving this gift from her pleased him. She would have her nightly pleasure and revenge for months, even years, to come.

As he walked, he thought of how the sight of them had excited him. The realization made him feel embarrassed and ashamed. For a moment he stopped and took deep breaths, hoping that all would subside. There was great relief, thankfulness, that it was nighttime, and that he was alone.

Not long after, Mount Apfel appeared on its low hill. Neddy breathed a sigh of thankfulness that it was still standing. Mount Apfel was not a big estate but a very productive, well-run plantation. The few slaves on Mount Apfel were all treated as if they were free anyway. His mother always used them as an example of a stepping-stone to complete freedom—not in front of Miss Rachel, however. He had heard his mother talking about the way Massa William and Miss Rachel ran their holdings. Mass William hired slave jobbers when he needed extra labor during cropping or planting seasons. Miss Rachel had learned that from her mother. He did not fear that any would cause trouble for the owners.

Neddy began to run toward food and safety. Panting from the exertion, he slowed when he got to the outbuildings. Faint lights and voices came from within the slave huts as he passed them. People were up, and they were nervous. Neddy could feel the apprehension and expectation exuding from indoors, and he moved quickly by at a trot.

On entering the front yard, Neddy walked carefully toward the main house, noticing as he did so that there were no lights showing. Yet, he did not get the impression that the people within had retired for the night. There was that odd feeling of being watched.

A dog barked, making him look around with a jerk. There were some big, nasty black dogs called Imp and Bess at Mount Apfel that always made him nervous when he came with his mother. Were they loose and about? He looked in all the dark spots to see if shadows moved. Not that he would be able to tell if they lurked there, for their coats were as black as the devil's heart.

Mama would tell him not to be foolish when they came barking down the hill, terrifying him. Once, when they had reached the veranda, he jumped up on the rail when they rushed out at them as they reached the top of the steps. Quashiba laughed and called him a baby. He did not care if they were supposed to be just large, friendly dogs; they looked like killers. When they licked his face, he closed his eyes, expecting at any minute to feel the flesh being torn from his head. Another deep bark from indoors told him where they were, and he breathed a sigh of relief. Nevertheless, he moved cautiously across the yard. Then a man's voice called out, "Who is that? Don't move any further, or I will shoot you." It sounded like Mass William.

"It's me," he shouted back fearfully. "Mi modder send me to Miss Rachel." He hoped that would get him a welcome.

"Me who?"

"Neddy, Mass William. Neddy Lawrence. Quashiba's son."

There was silence for a while; he fidgeted nervously. Another bark followed by a slightly higher bark from inside told him both his scourges had not yet been let out.

"Come forward into the middle of the yard, by the steps, so I can see you."

He did as he was told, knowing that a gun pointed right at him. He stopped by the first steps, took a deep breath, held it, closed his eyes, and waited, praying silently that Mass William would not shoot him. A minute or two passed, and in them another lifetime passed by Neddy. He heard the door open, then a bark, followed by the sound of dogs rushing down the steps toward him, their claws scrabbling on the steps. He did not move. Sweat flowed from his pores down his neck under his shirt and along the crevice of his backbone. Two large dogs were snuffling around him. His eyelids tightened hard against one another. One dog began licking his hand and gently mouthing it, as if getting ready to chomp down. The other jumped up on him, its front paws on his shoulders to lick his face. He heard a laugh and then an order to the mastiffs, but they did not obey their master, continuing to lick him as if he were a block of salt.

"Imp, Bess, get back up here." They ignored their master again and continued to lick Neddy. "Nothing for it; come up, boy."

Neddy struggled to push the dogs off. The one with his hand in its mouth growled at the rejection.

"Imp, Bess, up here!" This time there was no softness in Mass William's voice. That did it, thankfully. At last they left him, racing back up the steps and through the door.

As Neddy followed the dogs through the front door, a dimmed lantern just illuminated Miss Rachel standing by the dining table. Mass William behind him slammed the door shut, pushing the great beam of wood through slots to hold it in place.

"Come over here, Neddy," said Miss Rachel, with a warm smile. "Where is your mother?"

"She still at Kensington, Miss Rachel. She wouldn't leave mi da. She made me come. I did not want to leave dem, but she mek mi," he said. She held out her arms, and he went to her. An age seemed to have passed since he felt that safe.

"It's all right, Neddy. She will be all right, I am sure."

He choked back a sob to answer, "Yes, Miss."

"You must be hungry. Have you had anything to eat?" she asked, and then added, "That first. Then you can tell us what has happened. We know there has been trouble at Kensington. We could see the smoke all around from here, but we are not sure what is going on."

She led him through the dining room to a twisting stairway at the back and down to the dining room on the ground floor. There was another low light that allowed them to see their way across the flagstones to the pantry at the back. It was not a time for bright lights. A woman was half asleep in the pantry, sitting with her head resting on a table. She lifted up when they came in.

"Hmm! Miss Rachel, just getting little res, Mam," she said apologetically.

"That's all right, Ruth. Have you got any food ready to eat?"

"Yes, Mam, we got plenty, but it cold. You wants me to hot it up?"

"No, we can't risk that. No fires tonight."

"Mi can do it in di little pot belly, Miss Rachel."

"No, Ruth, don't risk it. Perhaps for breakfast, but not now." The cook did not answer her mistress, but instead went over to a cupboard and brought down some bread, freshly churned butter, and ham.

"It for im?" she asked, nodding her head toward Neddy.

"Yes," said Miss Rachel.

"Im is growing boye an look ungry. Mi will feed im, Miss Rachel."

"When you are done, Neddy, come back upstairs to us."

"Yes, Miss," he answered.

Rachel smiled at him. "Eat your supper and don't worry about your mother. Your father is with her and knows what to do."

"Yes, Miss Rachel. But I wish mi mam didn't send me away."

She leaned forward bending to him as if to tell a confidence. "Neddy," she said, with a serious expression. She stared steadily at the boy sitting at the table. "Mothers always know what is best for their children."

He lifted his eyes and stared back at her, cocking an eyebrow suggesting disbelief. Understanding the look, Miss Rachel gave a merry little laugh before turning and going back up the stairs.

From the table, Neddy looked at the food being cut and carved for him. Ruth was more than generous. She cut four thick slices of bread and spread freshly churned butter over each piece generously, and she wasn't stingy with the ham. He loved ham. At Christmas it was his favorite food. That, along with sorrel drink, made Christmas time special. Expertly, she sliced the ham thinly; slice after slice stacked higher and higher on the plate. Neddy's eye bulged in anticipation, and his stomach added its voice. The rumble made the cook comment, "You mus be real ungry. When las you eats?"

"Dis marning."

She sliced some more ham and asked, "You like mustard?"

"Yes, Miss," he answered politely, not sure what mustard was, but figuring it must be food.

She walked back to the cupboard and brought out a small earthenware jar. "Dis come from Hingland, but it saff. Hit needs pepper to make it nice. Massa put it on di ham," she explained. "You can ave cold tea, sugar water, or lemonade. Hif you want dat, mi can throw little rum in it to warm you hup."

"Mi don't care for di belly wash, Miss. Di lemonade would be nice." A large rummer was filled and placed beside his plate and a touch of rum added. At last, Neddy took his first bite of real food. His teeth sank into the bread, ham, and butter. A great weight fell upon his thigh. He knew it was a paw placed there to tell him there was another mouth to feed. Out of the corner of his eye, he saw a black head nearly level with his. Big, floppy ears and baleful eyes stared at him and the food. One of the four-legged tyrants, which he felt always saw him as a meal, was demanding some of his. He could not tell if it was Imp or Bess. For some reason, he felt it was Imp. He always seemed to be the more persistent of the two. Now the dog pawed his leg, scratching his skin with its rough pads and nails, telling him share and share alike. It was insistent. Neddy had not even truly tasted the food, and this beast from the darkest of reaches of the underworld was demanding its brawta. He felt like slapping it, but those begging, baleful eyes pleading made him feel kindly.

Hunger ruled at that moment, and Neddy decided it was time to make a stand. The dog didn't share its food, so why should he? Taking the bread from his mouth and placing it back on the plate, Neddy looked the beast straight in the eye and ordered, "Get out of here. Go on. Go upstairs." His hand pointed the way empathically. To his astonishment the dog turned with its tail down and walked across to the stairs, stopped, and looked back, its ears half perked as if to say *please*.

"Go on!" Neddy said, again pointing the direction for the dog to take, slapping his other hand on the table for emphasis. Its begging unsuccessful, the dog bounded up the stairs two at a time in full retreat. Neddy went back to his meal, taking an extra-huge bite out of the sandwich in celebration. As he chewed hard with his mouth full, the taste was doubly sweet. He had won. No longer would those two big black dogs terrify him.

"Dat Bess, hum! Always begging food," said Martha. "Di massa won't ave dem roun di table when im eating. Di children spoil dem in di nursery. Dem give di dog what dem doesn't eat. Nurse always complain but don't stop it. "

She grunted and went on shuffling things around in the cupboard. Neddy got down to the eating, cutting out the conversation. He had nearly finished when Ruth came over with another plate and put it down beside him.

"When you finish, dis will sweet your mout." She looked at him intently. "You like corn pone?"

"Yes, Miss Ruth, best of all," Neddy assured her. She poured some coconut milk over the pone in the dish. "You likes it with coconut milk?"

"Di ticker di better," Neddy replied with a large grin.

When he had finished, he felt like the slave he had seen earlier with the bang belly. Every inch was stretched, and he was weighed down with food like a pregnant woman eight months with child. Niggeritis had begun to set in. All he wanted was to lie down and go to sleep, but he rose from the table, thanked Ruth for her ministrations, and made his way up the stairs to where Massa William and Miss Rachel were in the drawing room, waiting for him.

As he entered the room, Miss Rachel looked at him and said, "Neddy, you must be tired. You think you can tell us what happened today at Kensington?"

"Yes, Miss Rachel. If mi can keep mi eye dem open."

"We won't keep you up," Mass William said.

A large leather armchair was indicated for Neddy to sit in. Obviously, it was the one normally used by the master of the house. Tonight the master sat beside his wife at the table, and both looked at the boy expectantly, waiting for his story.

As he began, a big black head rested itself on his hand on the arm of the chair. Neddy looked down and to the side. Once again he could not tell whether it was Imp or Bess until Mass William said, "She likes you." He nodded his approval.

Neddy put out his hand and patted her head. He was surprised at how silky it was. The sensation was pleasing. As he began his tale, and while speaking, without being aware of it, his hand stroked the dog's head, keeping time with what he had to say. When he had finished, his hand came up to cover a yawn. In reaction, as if it was the natural rule, the dog lay down at his feet.

"That settles it. Rachel, tomorrow we move to Samaria. It is only us and the children. I cannot defend here, Mount Vernon, and Samaria. Of all three, Samaria is the easier to stand off an attack, if one comes."

"They wouldn't dare attack us!" his wife declared emphatically.

"Yes, they would. Samaria it is for us. Samaria is insignificant, out of the way; they may miss it all together. Boy, go to sleep on the couch over there. It is quite comfortable, you will find. It is where I catch a nap on many a day. Tomorrow we have to move and do so fast. Rachel, go and get some rest, my dear. I will come in shortly."

No one argued with Mass William. Neddy was grateful to curl up on the big couch in the corner. Miss Rachel came over with a cover for him. Bess moved from beside the chair to lie down on the floor alongside the couch. Looking at the black shape there on the floor, Neddy felt safe. How strange, when only a short while ago her proximity would have had him trembling with fright. Even in his current state of exhaustion, he wondered at the peculiarity of the situation when friends become enemies and enemies become friends; his eyes began to close with sleep.

It was still very dark when Mass William woke him. It seemed he had only just gone to sleep. His fists rubbed his eyes, which smarted from lack of rest and the residue of burned sugar that had gritted to his face and eyelids as it permeated the air all the way from Kensington. He had been too tired to wash the night before and regretted not following his mother's rules. It took a minute of rubbing before one recognizable object after another settled into place. Miss Rachel was standing beside the couch with a plate of food in one hand and a bundle in the other.

"Eat, Neddy," she said, "and take this with you. Mass William is going to tell you what to do. We have to leave here, now. There are fires over at McDonald's and some of the other smallholdings."

"Neddy," said Mass William, "I am going to ask you to risk yourself. While I take Miss Rachel and the children over to Samaria, would you take a message to John Leslie at Mount Vernon for me? A lot depends on it."

"Yes, sah," Neddy said a little hesitantly, somewhat puzzled, but willing to help. Such a mission would give him a sense of being needed and important in this time of crisis.

"After you give Leslie the message, you must ride for Samaria and us, you understand? Do not come back here. My reckoning, when they find it empty, they will burn Mount Apfel, as they have everywhere else. They are attacking the small white farmers. Empty, Mount Apfel will be a big target for them."

"Yes, sah."

"Ced him
"Tell John Leslie not to take the gangs to the fields. Tell him to go into the Great House and take anyone whom he trusts with him. If people are in the house, they won't attack and consume the place with fire, as they seem to be doing everywhere else. Have you got that, Neddy?"

"Yes, sah. I will tell him what you say. Don't worry bout that, Mass William. Then I will come back to you and Miss Rachel at Samaria."

"Come boy, sit here. Eat, and then we will get going." Massa William pointed to a chair at the table.

"I got some coffee from Ruth. There is nothing like something hot in the morning," Miss Rachel said, pouring the steaming coffee into a cup beside him.

It tasted good after he scraped lumps of sugar into it. Although his belly still bulged from all he had eaten not two hours before, Neddy chomped into what he was offered. What he could not eat he sneaked to Bess, who sat beside him at the table. He thought Mass William had not noticed until he said, "Normally I do not allow my dogs to be fed at the table. Today is different. As she likes you, she goes with you. Bess is a good dog, and you may be thankful for her company.

Somewhat embarrassed at being caught feeding the dog, he nodded with a sheepish grin, as a thank you to the master of the house; at the same time, he was strangely pleased to hear Bess would be coming with him.

They all finished and went outside. There was a cart piled with trunks and boxes. A small carriage was drawn up behind. In it a nursemaid was taking care of three sleepy children, who were whining at being up and uncomfortable. Their mother got in beside them, and with a few stern words to quiet down, they settled. One boy persisted with his complaints and earned himself a smart slap. He yelped and then shut up. The lesson was not lost on the other two children. All of them fell silent.

"Neddy," said Mass William. "I have saddled my riding mule for you. He is an old boy but reliable and can move along quickly with a little urging. You can ride?"

"Yes, Mass William."

The mule was tied up to step railings, along with a horse. Neddy moved to untie the mule. He led it away from the horse to mount easily. Massa William watched. Satisfied the boy was no slouch in the saddle, he nodded acknowledgement.

"Bess here will go with you." Mass William pointed to the dog. "I'll take Imp with us. Do you know where Samaria is?"

"Mi will find it," Neddy assured him. "Don't worry, Mass William, mi will take care."

"It is two miles from Lapland, just before you cross into Westmoreland."

"Mi been dere once with mi mam, sah."

"When you have given John Leslie the message, get out of there and come straight over. If there is any trouble, let him take care of it. You…" he pointed his finger at Neddy, "do nothing. You understand me?" With that, he mounted and led the way out of Mount Apfel, followed by the carriage and cart. Neddy watched them go before spurring the old mule into action.

At the gate the family turned left toward Lapland and beyond. Once more, to make sure his orders would be followed, the master rode back to him. "You remember: do as I say. Take care, you understand, boy?"

"Yes, sah."

"Here you are." He handed Neddy a stick with a large knob at the end of it. "I would give you a pistol, but somebody is likely to

Conflagration

take that away from you. This is better. They gave it to me when I visited Ireland. They call it a shillelagh. Anyone near you looking dangerous, give them a whack with it. They won't come back."

"Thank you, sah." Neddy took the stick and hefted it. Sure enough, one lick with it would speak a whole lot of pain. He let it dangle from his wrist by the leather loop attached to its handle.

They parted company. Mount Vernon was closer for Neddy than Samaria was to the Vernons heading there. He would deliver his message and be at Samaria before they got there. A mule would be faster than the cart and carriage. He watched the lantern on the back of the cart disappear around the corner of the road before turning toward Mount Vernon.

Bess moved easily beside him. Every now and then, the big black dog looked up at him in the saddle as if checking on her charge, remembering what Mass William had instructed her to do with the boy. She cleverly stayed off the stone road and on the grass verge.

She had been trained well to move with a horseman or carriage. Neddy looked at the dog and wondered where Mass William had got the two. Many estates had big black dogs on them. You always had to look out as you approached. Some were just for show, but others would have you for dinner if given half the chance. He was happy Bess was on his side. She made him feel important. He giggled at the thought of being a gentleman who owned a big black dog that could *nyam your batty*.

Obscuring even the usual early morning gray, a dark, gloomy sky hung overhead, clouded thick by the smoke from sugar works that still burned on every side, their flames flickering and glowing through the pall.

As he rode along, the smell of burning sugar in the air was thicker now than ever before. On his face and exposed arms, he could feel the stickiness of caramelized sugar particles in the atmosphere, piling up atop those that already coated his skin. He would have given anything for a good wash at that time; a wash in cold water would be so refreshing. Adding to his general discomfort were the heady fumes of raw rum, making his head swim and his mouth dry.

To Neddy, alone on that road, St. James reeked as if a catastrophe had happened in the kitchen and the cook had lost control of Christmas dinner. The world smelled as if the sweetmeats and pudding had burned to a cinder, and the house along with them. Dotted all over the hills were the fires that brought this impression. As he surveyed the scene from the back of his mule, some blazed away, while others belched heavy smoke that deepened the already gray morning light. It was a depressing sight.

Occasionally, a distant shot echoed across the landscape. The shots seemed to come from different directions, telling how widespread the rebellion had become. Neddy was sure the militia did not fire them, for they did not come all at once, like when they practiced the drill, but singly. That made him edgy. Quite a few came from the direction of Kensington, but many were closer to him. If they had been fired at Kensington, he doubted that the sound would have carried this far to him. Other estates must be under attack.

As shot after shot went off, he realized that the rebellious slaves had quite a few guns between them and must be randomly shooting at whatever moved; either that or they were just letting the long guns and pistols off for the enjoyment of the bang. They couldn't be shooting at white people, because from the sounds of it, they would have killed all in the district by now. They must be shooting at anything from dog to cow.

With the fate of his parents unknown, he pushed the mule into its characteristic and uncomfortable jog-trot. He prayed they would be all right, at the same time reassuring himself that his father would know what to do. If not him, then his mam would know what to do; she always seemed to understand what was right. He remembered what Miss Rachel told him the night before and smiled with the comfort of the thought.

Halfway between Mount Apfel and Mount Vernon, he was still contemplating the fate of his world; looking about, his imagination painted the worst pictures. As sunlight struggled through the winding sheet of smoke, striving to flood the landscape with light and push night back into its alcove, the fate of Watt and Friendship furrowed his brow. Perhaps, he thought, after Mount Vernon, when his business was done there, he would go down to Friendship and see if Watt was all right and then sneak back up to Kensington before going to Samaria. It would be a long day. He looked down at Bess panting beside him and wondered if she would be able to keep up. Already her tongue was hanging out, suggesting the need for water; in response, he slowed the mule to a walk. Mass William's idea to send her with him did not fit well with his tentative plans.

They had gone about another half-mile when the men jumped him. He did not see them until it was too late. Up they came, one from either side of the road. One grabbed at his leg, while on his right-hand side, the other held the mule's bridle. There was a scream of pain on his left, and the hand let go his leg. Spontaneously, Neddy swung with the stick he had been given with all his might. The shillelagh handle slipped from his grasp, but, fastened to his wrist by a leather strap, it whirred in a great arch, multiplying the blow's force. The knob struck and bounced from collarbone to arm bone. There was a sickening crack as it landed squarely at each point. A curdling screech of pain ensued, which made the mule shy backward, dragging the bridle out of the useless hand on the limp, broken arm that owned it. His attacker did not wait to be hit again but took off down the road in a lopsided run, his arm dangling uselessly by his side.

Bess had dragged the other to the ground and sat on him, fangs bared inches from the throat. His sobbing, bleating voice was muffled by her weight on his chest. It had all happened so quickly that a few seconds passed before Neddy paid any attention to the entreaties directed his way.

"Silence!" Neddy said.

"Please, sah, call di dog," the voice begged.

"Shut up you mout. Sit on im, Bess," Neddy said. The dog looked up for a second and back at the man beneath her and snarled nastily. There was no doubt the dog was doing what she was bred and trained for and relishing every growl.

"Im going kill me," the man wailed. "Please, Massa, beg you, Massa, mi didn't mean nothing." The words sounded so strange to Neddy that he looked about to see if a white man had come up to them and stood where he could not see. The realization that it was he

When Conchie Blows

the man addressed made him swallow hard. This wasn't another boy but a man at his mercy—begging for it. He held life or death at his say. A word to the dog could decide the outcome either way. Having such power was a new threshold for Neddy, and he loved the feeling.

"Hif you don't stop, mi will order di dog to draw your throat," Neddy said. That did it; the man shut up. Bess licked her chops, slobbering over her victim, which made him whimper like a frightened child. Neddy felt sorry for the man, recalling what it was like to be in close contact to that dog. But he was not about to show mercy or weakness. They wouldn't have shown mercy, had their attack been successful.

"Where you come from?" asked Neddy, looking down from the mule and swinging his cudgel menacingly.

"Roxboro estate jus down di way, sah."

"What you doing up ere, den?" Neddy asked, trying to be as stern as he imagined a man in charge would sound like.

"Dem bun it down, Massa, an free we."

"When dat appen?"

"Dis marnin early."

"Where di white men."

"Dem run wey, Massa."

Roxboro wasn't far from Mount Vernon. There was just St. James Park between them. He wanted to ask about that but was afraid of the answer. Still, he had to know.

"What else dem bun?"

"Mi don't know sah. Mi an Lewis run off soon as di fire start. Beg you, sah, call di dog."

"Tell mi what else you know, an mi will call di dog."

The man whimpered again, which made Bess growl. "Lard, mi don't know notting, Massa. Dem going a Mount Vernon, mi ear. Please, Massa, call di dog, it a squeeze mi to deat."

He could see the man was struggling to breathe with the mastiff on his chest. For the first time he noticed, as well, the torn pants and blood coming from his thigh where Bess had grabbed to pull him down.

Conflagration

"Bess. Come, Bess, back ya." He ordered the dog to heel, pointing behind the mule as he had seen Mass William do. She growled and made a snapping motion toward the man's face. For a moment, Neddy thought she had disobeyed him and mauled her victim. Relief swept over him when the dog got up, allowing the man to air. Quickly, on all fours like a dog himself, the man scrambled away from her. In an instant he was on his feet, sprinting down the road as if Bess were at his heels. He did not even bother looking at his wound first. Bess growled and gave one last long bay, as if she were on the hunt, that put the spur in his hide. He was over the fence and into the bushes like a man pursued by fiends.

"Good dog," said Neddy, half to himself as well as to Bess. All had happened with such speed that he wasn't sure what had happened and what he had done. The mule stood waiting for its orders, and the dog looked up, awaiting hers. A slap with the bridle had the trio moving again.

On the next hill, Neddy looked back toward Mount Apfel. There was no doubt, three plumes of smoke rose from that direction. They were about four miles back. About the right distance. But they may not come from Mount Apfel; it could be Prosper going up in flames. They were close enough at this distance for one to be the other. Or could it be both plantations? Neddy knew this was possible and kicked the old mule back into its uncomfortable jog. Bess trotted alongside, staying on the grass. Her tongue lolled out as a reminder she needed water.

Halfway down the hill, Neddy turned off onto one of his secret pathways that led to a stream that ran into the Worcester River. Stopping there to refresh the dog and the mule before moving on would be a good idea, he thought. It would also give him time to think. His worry was Mount Vernon; he hoped he would get there and deliver his message before they set it afire. All estates were the rebels' targets, it seemed. Very few would escape the flames. He wondered if the plan was now to burn them and make sure the slaves could not go back to work, and their leaders could negotiate for pay? Neddy shook his head in doubt; young as he was, he realized that would be too sensible for the slaves. They would burn *for bun sake*.

409

When Conchie Blows

Both animals seemed thankful when he stopped on the bank of the little stream. Neddy dismounted and went above them to drink in his turn. He wished he had a bottle to fill, but all he had was the bundle of food Miss Rachel had given him. That would be kept for later. Things were not going well, and he may have need later on. There was no telling when food would be plentiful again. Besides, he knew that Bess would need her share. And after today, she deserved all there was to give her.

There was an otaheite apple tree just on the other side of the stream. He could see the scarlet blossoms with their delicate tendrils like balls of fur clinging to the branches, but no fruit as yet. They were not ready. Another two months, and then all the apples he could eat. Beside it was a mango tree with fruit on it. He wasted no time going up and along the thick branches to find the fit ones. There were a few ripe enough to eat. A couple dropped from their stems as he touched them. To his amazement, when he climbed down, he found Bess chomping on a windfall. A dog that would eat fruit was something new to him. Since this one obviously did, Neddy nodded approval as her teeth cracked the seed as if it were an eggshell. Feeding her had gotten a whole lot easier all of a sudden. Neddy knelt down and patted her neck. She in turn licked his hand and gently put it in her mouth, testing it with her teeth and licking it again before returning it to her owner. He made a face and went over to wash the mangoed saliva off in the stream. Quickly he stripped down and splashed water all over his body and dressed again. His clothes would dry him, and the moisture they absorbed would evaporate in the sun as he rode. In the process it would refresh him, as long as he did not catch his death of cold, as he remembered the warning in normal times. It was already time to set off again.

Sucking a mango, Neddy steered their way on to a little-used path that led through St. James Park to Mount Vernon. It was unlikely he would meet people on the path. If he did, and they were nasty, Neddy felt confident enough now to bash them with the knobbly stick, and Bess would take care of the rest. He laughed out loud, "Boye, mi tell you!" Bess looked up at him and yelped appreciatively.

Conflagration

There was no one working the fields along which the path ran. Then they came to a spot where he could see the house and works of St. James Park through the trees. All the buildings were still intact. They had escaped the fire so far. But, again, not a soul was in the yard or by the slave huts. Smoke, he noticed, came from the outside kitchen of the Great House. That must mean the white people were still there—perhaps holed up inside, waiting for something to happen. Neddy moved on, more hopeful that Mount Vernon was, like here, still untouched.

Down the gully through the stream and up the other side the mule plodded. Soon he would know if Mass William's message could be delivered. His heart beat faster as they approached the crest of the ridge, from where he could look down and see the situation without himself being seen. At the top, for a second, Neddy closed his eyes, not daring to look. When he did look, to his delight, the house was still standing. They had not burned it; he exhaled with relief.

However, from his position on the gentle slope east of the house, he could see people milling around on the front lawn. They had kicked over the large pots with their blooming abelia shrubs and, in their trampling about, mashed down the flowerbeds. Some drunken youths were running amok, rooting up or chopping at tree trunks just for the hell of it. The mob's intent to destroy was clear. Shouting came up to them, and Bess pricked up her ears and uttered a growl and a yap. "Shuh!" Neddy quieted her quickly.

A man standing at the top of the welcoming arm steps shouted back at them in the garden. Flanking him on either side was a younger man and a woman. The older man standing between them was berating those below the steps, but what he was saying was unclear, as his words were caught up with all the yelling coming from the mob in the yard.

From his position on the hill it seemed to be a very tense stand-off in the garden below. Clearly it was not the time to be noticed. Neddy decided not to ride in. They might be Mount Vernon slaves, and again they might not. He couldn't imagine that they belonged to the plantation, but after all, the world had gone mad. Off to the side, at the edge of the pasture, was a small clump of trees. There he tethered the mule, making sure it was out of sight. He gave Bess her orders to stay on guard; the mule was too valuable to be stolen now. With Bess there, they would have to kill her before taking the mule, and that was unlikely. Feeling he had them hidden safely, Neddy set out toward the house. On foot, no one would suspect him; he would just blend in.

Feeling a bit nervous, he jogged across the pasture, climbed over the wall, and took the road up to the gates. No one paid any attention to him as he hung at the back of the gathering in the garden.

"Bun di place!" yelled a woman at the front, jumping up and down as if on springs. "Bring di trash!" she yelled again.

Others joined her yelling for trash to burn the house. The voices began to rise in a screaming rage. Some were banging sticks together and others metal pots. The noise was deafening. Bottles of rum were being passed from one to the other. A man would take a long draft, and then a woman would swig an equal amount. One bottle came in Neddy's direction, and he noticed the Mount Vernon markings on its side as he took a sip to keep in with the throng. In their rampage, they must have raided the works storehouse to get the rum. Many, with too much in their bellies, poured the spirit over their heads to cool down. In all the hubbub, a nasty thought struck Neddy; he wished to put a match to those wetting themselves with the rum, and instead of stinking of the alcohol they would become the flaming attraction, diverting attention from the house. But he dared not attempt such a thing and only wished for more courage.

Out of sight of the garden, black smoke began to rise in the direction of the works. From the smell, Neddy's guessed it was the still house. Then he heard another female scream at the top of her lungs, "Dem light di ut dem!" She was ecstatic. To hear her, Neddy knew there was little hope of saving Mount Vernon. They were destroying everything, and if they had set fire to the slave dwellings, that was the beginning of the end, for that had signaled the destruction of Kensington. He turned to look and saw people fleeing from inside the huts. For certain, these in the garden were not Mount Vernon people. Only a matter of time before the Great House went up.

Conflagration

A peacock trying to escape the milling about in the garden did not make it. As it ran by, flapping its clipped wings, trying to take off, a man swung his machete. Its crested head went one way, and its gorgeous body, still flapping wildly, went another. There was screeching laughter from those watching. As the headless bird struggled on the ground in its death throes, a scavenging urchin rushed in, grabbed the pulsating corpse and swung it around his head by the legs, blood splattering everywhere. The laughter made Neddy shudder and notice, for the first time, the vulgarity of the Negro laugh. For some reason he felt ashamed hearing its wild, cackling screech.

War-War-War-War, the mob shouted in waves. Neddy's heart raced with fright as the chant grew louder, but he held steady to see what would happen. A stone crashed through one of the large, arched windows, bringing glass shattering down like raindrops. A large shard hit and sliced into one man standing beneath the window. He tried to staunch the blood flow, but it oozed through his fingers onto his ragged shirt. Immediately he set up the howl, "Bun di ouse!"

A few began throwing cane trash though the first-floor windows. More trash was tied into bundles, which were lit and thrown up toward the gaping hole left by the broken window, but they hit the wall and fell back among those below. Another ran forward, picked up the torches, and tried again, but he, like his predecessor, failed.

The man on the steps began to point at men in the mob, singling them out by name. "Scipio, William Clark, and you, George Longman, as mi name is John Leslie, mi mark you hif Mount Vernon bun."

That got a murmur going. For a moment they backed off. The thought of the hanging rope and the lash must have made them hesitate.

"Mi know," he went on, "you don't belong to Mount Vernon." He pointed again at one. "You belong to Hampton, fi your name me calls already. Mi name you again, Scipio." The man didn't like being fingered and shifted quickly out of the center of the mob.

With his arm extended and finger pointing, John Leslie, standing where the welcoming arm steps met, searched for others. He knew his stand was intimidating all those milling about below him.

The man and woman standing at his side gave him moral support. From one to another, his accusing finger moved, then stopped as he shouted. The one identified would slink away, trying to lose himself in the mass that no longer pressed forward but had begun to give ground in the opposite direction.

He came again to George Longman. "You belong to Massa Clarke. Yes, sah, Massa William Clarke own your hide, and im going tek it off wid the whip when im find out you is the one that lead all of dem here." His arm swept over the crowd. "Is you leading dem astray, away from di path of goodness to the crooked way of the devil." He sounded like a preacher. Just for a moment, it seemed by sheer force of personality and the word of God, he was going to disperse the multitude.

Suddenly Longman screamed back in desperation and fear, "Who you going name? You is a dead man." He rushed up the right arm of the steps and pushed the woman to one side. There was a short struggle. John Leslie lost his footing and fell back along the wall and down the left side of the steps. Longman raced after him, and before the old man could rise from his knees, Longman's hand with a shining machete rose and fell. There was a nasty thud. John Leslie's head came away cleanly from the body, which began to jerk and gyrate on the ground, like the peacock's. Blood spewed from the decapitated trunk to form a large pool on the green grass. All watched, fascinated, waiting for the flow to end. Finally it did subside into a thick stream, then a trickle as his heart stopped pumping. Every now and then, there was a jerk and a short spurt of blood. Neddy stood transfixed, mouth agape in disbelief.

A curdling scream of lust went up from the rabble. They surged forward, some up the steps with lighted trash torches. The door gave, and in they went. Furniture, cloth and clothes, books, and chairs were thrown through the windows to be picked up by those who stood outside. Capturing what came out, they rushed off with their prizes. Greedy ones struggling with their loads became targets for those who had not been as fortunate in the initial grab.

Neddy turned and ran for all he was worth down the drive and vaulted over the fence into the field. He didn't even notice when

Conflagration

he hit and skinned his shin on the top rail. On he went, breathing hard, desperately trying to get away from that murderous scene. Up the grade he ran to the clump of the trees, where the mule and Bess awaited his return. Bess sensed his coming and barked a welcome. He was unaware of it as he sprawled on the ground, his breath coming in great gulping sobs of despair and fright.

With the sucking in of air, he managed, "Di lard is my Shepard, mi go through di valleys of the shadow of deat. Di evil." On and on he jumbled the words, with his eyelids crimped together, as if trying to force out the image they had allowed in. His hands sank into the grass, holding on tightly, as if trying to find what was real. More than ever, he prayed for his mam. "Oh, Lard," he entreated "Save dem all. Keep mi mama and mi da safe. Keep Watt safe, too."

The dog licking his face brought some comfort to him. He got up on all fours and stayed there. It took a few seconds for his eyes to focus as opened them again to see how much the world he knew had changed. Through the distortion, his hands on the ground seemed covered with blood. Quickly he got to his knees. As his eyes focused, the image cleared, and he realized he had gone down in a patch of red leaf of life weed. He sat back on his heels and took a deep breath. Before rising and mounting up, he looked around, expecting to see the changes that must have come about. As far as he could see, there was nothing new. But he felt there must be a change.

As they cleared the trees, he glanced down at Mount Vernon. The Great House was an inferno. The roof ablaze crashed in on the walls. Soon there would only be charred ruins. Years of hope gone.

Urging the mule on, Neddy tried desperately to put as much distance as possible between himself and the events of the morning. Bess followed obediently. Soon they were off Mount Vernon and onto Kempshot land. The mule continued on with its ungainly jog. Its gait went unnoticed by the rider. If anything, as one mile went by and then another, it jolted feeling back into his numb body.

At last, they were heading down to Worcester estate. Glancing over his shoulder, he saw heavy black smoke rising from behind. A breeze stirred up by the hot air of midday and burning fires bounced off the hills, blowing the smoke about and acting on the fires like a bellows. From every direction, smoke clouded the sky.

Despite the acrid air, Neddy breathed easier and brought the mule down to a walk. His hands had lost their strength holding the reins, and his knees felt weak trying to grip the sides of the saddle. Never before had he seen a man killed. The horror of it would stay with him forever. The image of the head separated from the body and the blood that seemed to come on and on made him shiver and feel like throwing up. He retched, but there was nothing in his stomach to come up; yet, the action gave him a sharp pain that for some unknown reason made him feel whole.

It came to his mind that there should have been a difference between a peacock and a man. Yet, both heads came off, and both died. Surely a man was better than a bird? He didn't think he would ever be able to chop off the head of a chicken again for his mother. There should be a difference! A man had a soul and went to heaven— or hell. A chicken didn't have a soul. Yet, why did they die the same?

Pulling the mule up, Neddy just sat, staring down the road in front of him as it ran between cane fields, where no slave sang out the work song giving regular rhythm to the gangs slashing and staking the tall sweet grass that produced such wealth. He had a choice: Samaria, where he was expected, or Friendship, where he was needed.

Chapter 14

The Siege

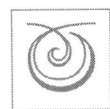

Shading his eyes with his hand, Neddy looked up at the sky. Through the smoke, he glanced to see where the sun stood in the day. It had just about passed its middle point; he gently rubbed his right eye with the back of his fist. It smarted even more from lack of sleep and from the ever-thickening smoke drifting across the landscape. Breathing had even become difficult; his chest felt as if the inside had been rubbed with sand. The shirt stuck to his skin uncomfortably, and he wished for another stream close by to wash in. But he did not move. Lethargy had overtaken his mind and body. Even when the mule shifted its stance, he hardly noticed.

The hot breeze coming from the fires seemed to move the unburned cane in the field on his left, waving ever so slowly in front of his blurry eyes. Bess sensed that things were not quite right and looked up at him as he just sat there in the saddle; she whined, licked her chops, groaned, then yapped, as if to say, *time to go*. Even with her urging, still he sat unmoved as the sun added its heat to the already scorched land.

Perhaps five minutes passed before the dog whined again, reminding him to make up his mind and get going in one direction or the other. This time he agreed to Bess's urging and kicked the mule into motion, heading toward the Worcester River. She barked approval and took the lead. "It all right, dog. We going get im," Neddy said to her. As if comprehending what was said, the big dog looked back at the rider and gave a deep growl of agreement.

Neddy, in turn, glanced furtively over his shoulder toward Kensington, seeing the mental image of his mother watching his every move with disapproval. He knew she would want him to head straight for Samaria, as Mass William had ordered him. She would just have to understand, Friendship came first. Knowing her as he did, in time she would agree with his actions. After all, it was not that he was going to disobey his orders, just that there would be a slight delay in carrying them out. They trotted on a bit further before he added aloud, "Mi bet im is in trouble."

At the river, Neddy dismounted, unsaddled the mule, and tied it to a tree. After making sure the animal could crop the grass, he undressed and got into the river for a second bath. This he needed more than anything at that moment. Washing the stickiness off his skin and out of his eyes would make him feel clean again—just like washing away sin, he imagined. It was important to feel clean, for only then could one face one's maker.

What had been happening all about the parish made him feel ashamed of people. Not till then had he thought of them as cruel and vicious. It took barefaced murder to make him realize that the Bible was right. As the reverend said, "Man is a sinner from the day he is born." Redemption came only at the end of the world.

The cold water was just what he needed. Washing away the accumulated residue of burned sugar along with some of his tiredness felt so good. Lying there, he closed his eyes and let the river rush over him, making him appreciate the healing powers of pure water. The Worcester River became the River Jordan, healing his body and bringing quiet to the confused hurt he felt.

Ten minutes went by before he crawled out onto the bank. His clothes smelled awful, making his nose curl in disgust. Dried sweat permeated the cotton shirt. The trousers were just as bad. The thought of what his mother would say made him shake his head. There was no way he could wash them out. There was no time for them to dry, and putting them on wet was unthinkable. He would just have to wear them and suffer their stink.

Under a tree on the bank, Neddy stretched out naked and in seconds was fast asleep. Again it was Bess who roused him by slapping her heavy paw on his chest and giving out a loud, groaning whimper. Jolted awake, he stared into a large black snout with surprisingly gentle eyes set in front of big floppy ears. For a moment, his heart skipped a beat. Her foreleg pressed down on his chest like a log. His body rocked slightly with the motion of her wagging tail as it translated to him through her paw. There was in it that action a reminder of his mother waking him every morning. Gently removing the dog's paw, he rolled over onto his side, then knelt and said a quick prayer before standing upright.

The stink of the shirt as he pulled it on over his head made him feel dirty again, bringing on the temptation to plunge back into the river for revivified deliverance. Instead he sniffed his armpit and grimaced. There was no time for cleanliness, and godliness would just have to wait. He had slept longer than he intended. Time had been lost that he could not afford to waste.

As he saddled the mule, he noticed the bundle of food carefully tied to it that had been given him that morning, and pangs of hunger seized his innards. Bess must have noticed the bundle too, for she cocked her head on one side, looking in its direction. She gave a little grunt, licked her chops, and began to pant with her mouth open. She licked her chops again and made a funny little sound like a baby on the verge of tears. It struck Neddy as so funny that he could not help but giggle and lean over to pat her. He was tempted to sit and share the food with her, but better sense prevailed. His senses told him there was a time coming when they would be more thankful for it. Instead, retrieving the two mangoes left in the saddlebag, he gave one to the dog.

She seemed satisfied with the mango and bit in, cracking the seed with a crunch. As Neddy made a small opening at the bottom of his mango with his teeth and began to squeeze, sucking the juice out of the hole, he marveled at how Bess devoured her mango, skin, seed, and all. Then, in a ladylike fashion, she licked the excess juice into her mouth with her tongue. After a few swipes, most of the yellow residue was gone from her black chops, and her final lapping in the river washed away the leftovers.

Neddy headed for Retirement, deciding it was better to stay on the Kempshot path leading behind Worcester. As they broke into the open, he noted that the sun had moved three quarters of the way across its day and was on the edge of its descent. Only a quarter of the day remained before they would be plunged into the dark hours. There was no time to waste. Friendship was still about three miles away; the realization spurred him into action. Banging both his legs against the mule's sides, he said, "Mule, move. *Move!*" He got the desired response; refreshed from the rest, the mule tossed its head up and began jog-trotting.

As they reached a hill overlooking the valley where the Worcester River ran down through the estate, he could just see the sugar works' water wheel. As he expected, the buildings were on fire. Heavy smoke drifted up to him on the hill. Details of the destruction were difficult to pick out while the mule jogged along the crest, but to stop and take a look was not worth the time. It would be the same as all the rest. Skirting Pitfour Pen in its steep hill and gully terrain, he kept on going, taking a right-hand fork that led onto Retirement land.

At a vantage point still fairly high up in the descent from Kempshot, Neddy stopped the mule. To his surprise, the Pitfour buildings looked still untouched by fire, but to the right, across Retirement River, that estate's buildings were blazing. Even now thick smoke and the stink of burning sugar curled up to him on the hill. The fires were freshly set, and the smell meant that the curing house, still, and storehouses were all going up. Before riding on, Neddy looked back at Pitfour to make sure that property, at least, was intact. He felt so tired, but it was time to go again, and he slapped the mule into a jog-walk heading in a direction that made sure to avoid the Retirement works' area. Running into more slaves, drunk with the power of fire and rum, would not be wise. If they did no more to him than hinder his way to Friendship, then luck was on his side. But he was not going to stick around to find which way luck fell.

The Siege

By his reckoning, if both Worcester and Retirement estates had burned, then Friendship must have gone up as well. All three were batty and bench to each other. Slaves in one would incite slaves in the other. They were so close that it would not need a mob of slaves moving from one to the other to hot them heads up.

The thought made him urge the mule forward. It sensed his urgency and surprised him with its uncomfortable jerking canter, and they began to make up time. For an animal with so poor a reputation, the mule gave its best. The ever-constant Bess kept up easily, loping along at their side. Her ears flapped up and down, and her tongue lolled outside of her mouth, drawing sustenance from the air. She seemed tireless, as if bred to run beside a carriage or run a quarry to earth. Looking at her beside him, Neddy not only approved but also wished she belonged to him. If she ever did have pups, he would beg one from Mass William. His terror of her and Imp now seemed like a memory of childhood.

From Mount Vernon, they had not run into a soul. Neddy could not be other than thankful for that, considering the murderers that morning, but soon after crossing the Retirement River, that changed. A boy in a great hurry appeared on the path approaching them. Neddy reined in the mule and waited till the individual came up, making sure there were no others with him. Bess moved in for a sniff. Until then the stranger had not seen her. On her appearance the boy backed away quickly, putting the mule and rider between the dog and himself.

"Di dag going bites mi, Massa?" youth said nervously. For a moment his expression changed, became furtive, as if he had said something he shouldn't. It happened so fast that Neddy almost missed it, but his brain unconsciously filed it for future reference.

Looking him over from head to toe, Neddy noted they were about the same age. But other than his age and new shoes tied together dangling around his neck, as he sometime carried his sandals, there the resemblance ended. Shuffling out of the way, the youth cringed up his toes on what was obviously unaccustomed rough ground beneath them. Obviously the shoes were being saved for future use or sale. The rest of his dress also suggested an easy life. As well, his color, fine features, and pale green eyes marked him as held apart from field hands. A quadroon at least, maybe even a free mustee, but his hair was red and kinky. That implied the former classification.

But it was his dress Neddy focused more on. Even for a house slave, this boy was very finely turned out. Such finery was a dead giveaway that someone held him in special reserve. New sheeting trousers fitted snugly to show his legs and thighs off to their best advantage. His jacket was York stripe fashion, the kind Neddy always liked and knew was beyond his meager hoard of wealth, and certainly his mother or father was not about to spend on that vanity for him. Under the jacket he could see what must be a new Holland shirt with thin stripes complimenting those on the jacket. Suspicious that anyone in such a turn-out should be wandering along a bush path in the back of Retirement, he asked, "Where yu from?"

"Mi live over at Friendship way," he said with a cocky, self-assured wave of the hand in the estate's direction.

"Wid who?" Neddy came back, his face blank, unreadable to all who looked there.

"Mi modder."

"What er name? Why yu not wid er?" Neddy said, his eyes narrowing, like an overseer who had just heard a lie.

"She over wid mi aunt up dere." The boy's finger pointed nonchalantly in the direction Neddy had come from. Stone-faced, Neddy stared at him. The boy looked up at him on the mule and shuffled uneasily, tightening up his toes in the dust till their joints were bloodless white against the brown earth. Neddy recognized the reaction.

Staring at the boy, Neddy remained motionless in the saddle. Even the mule stood still. Perhaps a minute passed. Bess, too, remained on guard, not a grunt, whine or yap coming from her. The revealing fidget of a liar caught out began in earnest. The lad's hands twitched. From beside his thighs they snuck into his pockets. When he realized that was not acceptable, out they came to disappear behind his back, in an attempt to hide the uneasiness they were betraying. Watching the movements, Neddy knew he was gripping them together out of sight, in the hope of a respite.

The Siege

His feet began to shuffle. Neddy could almost see the boy's mind trying desperately to find a way to squirm a way to freedom. As each silent second slipped by, the desire to run mounted in the boy. Backing away from the mule he half-turned but stopped dead in his tracks as Bess growled, reminding him she was faster. Had he been shod, he probably would have risked running. Shaking his head, a nervous half-grin flickered for a moment and died where it began; the black dog was the deterrent to any such attempted escape. She stood poised for the chase not two yards away, head forward, muscles tensed, eyes fixed on him. He may have been able to dodge across the fields away from the mule and rider, but he was sensible enough to know there was no way he could outrun Bess and survive.

"Mi modder run wey when di niggers began to bun every ting," he volunteered. Neddy sat unmoved on the mule, still staring at him, waiting for all to come out as he knew it would.

"We free people got to look out fi wi self," he continued. "You is free an a big massa, mi can see dat. You ride a mule and have a big dog a follow you."

After hearing that piece of flattery, Neddy knew the boy was a house slave. The smart talk and the way he was dressed confirmed that. "You know the overseer over at Friendship?" he asked.

"Di Zulu man! Lard, who don't know im?" He slapped his thigh and gestured suggestively as if he was an intimate of Bardolf's. He looked up at Neddy; seeing no reaction, he let out a forced laugh, hoping to break the tension.

"What im name?" Neddy said, pushing the youth.

"Massa Zulu."

"No, im real name."

The boy seemed less comfortable with the prying and probing. "Massa Zulu, "he repeated.

"You damn lie," Neddy snarled, and Bess joined him, reacting to his displeasure.

"Mi na no," the boy admitted, with a nervous look in the direction of the dog. "Lard, Massa," he pleaded. It was the *Massa* that made Neddy truly suspicious in the first place. No freeborn would have used that to him, a black boy. He sounded like the man who attacked him earlier that morning and was forced to grovel by Bess. All that seemed such a long time ago.

"What's you name?" demanded Neddy.

"James, sah." He bowed his head in the manner of one not daring to look a backra massa, in the eye.

"Where yu sey you come from again?"

"Friendship, sah."

"Who yu belong to?" Neddy dismissed any pretense that the boy was a freeborn or freed slave.

"A Dutchman bring me from Kingston an want fi sell mi to di one dem call Zulu. Im don't like me. Im sey mi too white, an mi have bad hair!" His lip curled at that indignantly. "You ever ear any ting like dat!" he said, his expression one of amazement and his hands gesturing in support. "How can mi be too white, sah? Who want to be black?" he mumbled almost imperceptibly, as if talking to himself.

It was loud enough for Neddy to hear, and his eyebrows shot up in surprise at the boy's musings. He had always been comfortable with his color. As a matter of fact, his mother had always rubbed it in—black was the color to be. The reality that his father wasn't fully black did not seem to bother her though, nor that he himself had been described on occasion as a cool-skinned brown boy. Without being prodded further, the runaway continued to volunteer information: "Mi get wey when di troubles start. Hif mi stay, and di Zulu man don't want mi, di Dutchman will sell mi in Cuba or America. No sah, dat not fi mi. His Kingston or Spanish Town mi a go."

"Dat more like it," Neddy said, calmly ignoring the travel plans. Kingston and Spanish town could have been on the moon at that moment for all he cared. "Tell mi about di trouble at Friendship."

"Dem bun some of di slave hut and di overseer's place."

"What about di bookkeepers?" asked Neddy anxiously.

"Dem don't bun dat, yet. One of dem white boye helping dem mek bullet and showing dem ow to shoot di pistols and long gun dem tief from di busha house dem bun."

"Which one?" It was a useless question, because Neddy already knew it would be Watt.

"Mi don't know im name. But di two of dem a help di naygar."

The Siege

"Two of dem?" Neddy asked cautiously, his eyes opening wide with surprise.

"Yes, one little one wid gold hair from foreign, and di odder one barn ya so." Neddy was sure that was not Duar. Watt disliked him, and he did not sound the type to be helping slaves. That must be the other one he had been told about, Shirley. Whatever and whoever, he knew Watt was in trouble, and he bet Watt didn't even know it.

"Tanks," Neddy said, riding off. He stopped the mule and turned back to the youth, still standing watching him, and shouted, "Dat is not the way to Kingston, unless you going over di hills to St. Elizabet first. Dat way to Falmouth," he pointed, "an along di coast. Bu watch yourself," he advised, before spurring the mule on.

There was no time to waste. The boy's information made Neddy almost forget his newly learned caution as he pushed the mule through old ways he knew and across unfamiliar ground to save time getting to Friendship. He made it onto Friendship land, having only to dodge behind a clump of trees to avoid a man and woman with children. They were loaded down with bundles of loot taken from burned homes. The woman had the biggest one, made out of a multicolored covering balanced on her head, as she held two large serving dishes under each arm. A trip or a sudden fright would have sent all crashing down. Her man carried similar packaging in each hand, with his machete tucked under his armpit. If they were stopped, he could drop his load and reach quickly for the weapon. Their three children each straggled along with smaller bundles. Other than those people, Neddy did not buck into any other stragglers or roving gangs before he reached Friendship's cane land.

When he reached the buildings—or, rather, what was left of them—the boy's information proved correct. It seemed that the slave huts had been the first to go. Blackened Spanish walls, still smoldering, were the testaments to the uprising. Most of the structures were completely gutted. A few, only half-burned, stood lopsided, like dry coconut husks tossed into a fire by some giant. The overseer's house had gone up in flames along with the slave quarters. At least that could be rebuilt on its cut-stone foundations up to the first floor—if anyone wanted. The roof had gone, and so had the floors. Just a shell was left to give the would-be rebuilder a start.

Neddy took in these details and ignored them, as they had become commonplace. On the other hand, both animals were reluctant to go by the smoldering places. They made it through the ruins with much snorting and shaking of heads when he forced the pace. Ash blowing about in the heat currents irritated the dog, mule, and rider. Neddy made directly for the wooden structure that he knew must be the bookkeepers' place. It was empty when he entered the main room. To make sure, he checked each room. There was no sign of Watt or the other two he had heard about.

With dread mounting, Neddy walked quickly through the front door, almost running into an old woman making her way across the yard, looking for things that had escaped the flames. Remembering his manners, he apologized and asked, "Modder, where Mass Watt?"

She looked at him through bleary eyes, not comprehending the question. Neddy repeated it. She took her time focusing on his face. "You not from ere," she said, her jaw set aggressively. "What your business?"

Obviously this was going to be awkward. There wasn't time for niceties, but he tried to soothe her. "Mi got to see di young massa, modder," Neddy said, in a consolatory manner she may have been accustomed to hearing.

"You not from ere," she repeated, pointing a gnarled finger in his direction. Time had come to change tactics. Manners thrown out, Neddy grabbed her shoulders and shook. He expected to hear her bones rattle. Instead, to his surprise, her left hand grabbed his right wrist and broke the hold.

"Let mi go! Who you tink you is a grab me up so!" There was a very angry woman staring him down. Neddy did as she demanded and took a step back.

"You tink mi is some jingy-pingy to fool wid, boye?" She shook herself, mumbled something he did not catch, rubbed her shoulder to stimulate circulation, then pointed to the boiler house. "Im is over dere. Im a show dem." With her assailant forgotten, she didn't bother finishing the sentence but turned away, head down, continuing the search for scattered leavings that might be of use to her.

He did not wait around on the chance of hearing more. Taking off at a run, with Bess close behind, Neddy headed in the direction the old woman had indicated. He was in such a hurry he left the mule where it was, loosely tethered to a hitching ring by the bookkeepers' door. The boiler house was packed with men as he entered. He forced his way through the crush to see what held their interest.

Not surprisingly, it was Watt. They were watching him intently as he demonstrated something over one of the boiler fires. Watt had a small copper pot on it. Neddy was in time to see him remove it and pour the contents into what looked like a funnel, going into another container on the floor. There was a distinct plop, then a hiss, as what looked like thick silvery molasses went from the copper through the funnel and dropped into the container below.

After decanting the molten stuff, he looked up at his watchers: "That is it, all very easy. Let them cool a bit, and you have lead balls to fire from pistol or musket. I have showed you how to load and fire. Now this is the way to make your own musket shot when you run out. Any lead will do. Take it off the roof, as I did with this. There are lots to be found about. Church roofs are the best."

Neddy could not believe his ears. Watt had gone mad. Did he not realize that he was getting himself into trouble that even Mr. Fray or his aunt couldn't get him out of? Before Neddy could make a move, Watt spotted him.

There was a yelp of joy. Unable to sidestep him in that crowd, Neddy was, as usual, seized in a Watt-type embrace. His arms and chest ached from the pressure, and he closed his eyes and waited, as if his face were being licked by the mastiffs. At last, the arms relaxed, and he found himself staring into those laughing blue eyes topped by blond hair, now stuck to Watt's forehead by sweat brought on by the boiler-house fires. A big grin spread across Watt's face; again he hugged him, letting go when he heard a deep unfamiliar growl close by and a shout of, "Watch di dog, Massa!"

For the first time, Watt noticed Bess. Without thinking he stretched out to pat her and found his arm firmly held in iron jaws.

Luckily his jacket protected the flesh from being punctured by her teeth. Tugging only irritated her, and she responded with a growl deep down in the throat.

"Let im go, Bess. Im all right sometime." She opened her jaws and freed him on Neddy's say so.

"Where did you get her? What a marvelous dog. German breed, ain't she?" Watt admiringly extended his hand to pat her large head again, only to withdraw it with the speed of a striking snake as his gesture was greeted by another snarl.

"Fi mi," Neddy fibbed. Then, relenting, he added with some pride: "Mass William tell her to guard mi when he sen me to do some business for him."

"Oh!" Watt exploded. "My faithful Sancho Panza, I knew you would come to join this great adventure." He was about to throw his arms around Neddy again but thought better of it, glancing down at the black mastiff watching his every move.

"What you doing? " Neddy said, narrowing his eyes as his mother did when she suspected that he had been up to no good.

"Can't you see? Teaching these people how to fight—and win their freedom from the oppressive master."

"You mad! Wha you know bout fight an make bullet an all?"

"Mad, no. It is as I have read, Neddy. It is my destiny to lead them into battle. Our rights must be won." His arm waved regally toward the crowd, which murmured in agreement.

Neddy grabbed his arm and tugged him along through the men, who gave way to let them pass. When outside, Neddy said, "You have to come wid me. Now! No fooling around. Dis is serious business. Dey will kill you for dis."

"No, they won't," Watt said stubbornly. "We will win our freedom."

"What di *rass* you talk bout? You are not a slave. What freedom you going win?"

"All our freedoms. The freedoms of an Englishman. Like the Americans. Like Watt Tyler."

"You did tell mi, di King kill dat one."

The Siege

There was a moment's pause. Watt had been caught out. Neddy had remembered things he should have forgotten, and there was no immediate comeback from Watt.

"Well, we will win," he said, sulking.

In exasperation, a mixture of English and patois poured out of Neddy: "Di army a come. When dem get here, the soldiers will shoot and hang every last one of dem." He pointed to the boiler house. "Mi know dis because mi hear bout di las time dem get up and bring down rebellion pon di country. Why you think they got soldiers all about di place?" His words tumbled out. "Why you tink dem got di militias? Why you tink dem got di police for? Di owner dem not going to let di slaves get away wid bunning up di place. You help dem, and you gone wid dem. If you lucky, dey shoot you rather than hang you. And I would not like to see anyone of dem happen to you. Now, stop you foolishness an come wid me, right *now*!" His speech done, Neddy dragged in a deep breath and stared at his friend, waiting for him to say one sensible word, at least. Instead, Watt's spirited rejoinder was not what Neddy wanted to hear.

"I know, but we are right. God is on the side of right."

"When you dead, nobody will care if you right or wrong, dead is dead." Neddy snapped, almost on the point of anger. "You are coming wid mi. We getting out of ere now, before it too late."

"No, I am not! That would be desertion. Shirley is with me, but he cannot lead these men. I must—it is my duty to God and the King."

"Is im worry mi, di King. He will get you." There was nothing more to say. Neddy stood back, fuming, to let events unfold. There was no chance of talking sense into Watt; he was determined to live or die in his war. Neddy would wait and watch and be there if all went wrong, which he suspected it would.

As Watt reentered the boiler house, Neddy realized his own position was becoming tenuous. Very easily he could be accused of aiding the cause. He had not considered that. Being free gave him the confidence of a free person. The idea that an authority would accuse him, mistakenly, did not enter his state of mind till then. It was his friend he had come for; anybody could see that.

When Conchie Blows

Calling Bess, who had followed them out of the boiling house, Neddy started back to where he had left the mule. Bess looked at him and gave a snappy bark that turned into a short howl, as if to say he dealt with a fool. With the stub of her tail sticking up, she retreated with Neddy, leaving Watt to his battle plans.

The mule cropped grass a few yards off from where he had been left. It had taken advantage of the slack hitch to extend its feeding range. Neddy got hold of the bridle and led the animal out of the yard past the burned-out huts and ruined overseer's house to a hillock across from the Great House. This offered the best viewpoint from which to watch events unfold.

After tethering the mule securely, he sat with his back against the trunk of a large, spreading poinciana tree. Above him in the branches, settling in for the night, black-feathered clings-clings had begun to gather like people in a public stand to watch a show. Their constant squabbling over perches was irritating, but if one listened carefully, it was quite easy to follow the dispute. It was as if they copied humans, or humans copied them.

Normally their squawking would have elicited a stone rattling through the branches, but Neddy shut them out of his hearing; it was the Great House that held his attention.

All the windows were shuttered tightly with thick wooden panels, leaving the shooting slots open. On either side of the door on the small porch at the top of the long narrow steps, were two small swivel cannons. Many great houses had these for defense, and Friendship was no exception. Neddy looked around for any more cannons. Usually there were some bigger ones on wheels that could be moved. There were none in sight, and he prayed that Friendship did not have any. He had never seen a cannon fired at people, but he could imagine the mess they would make of a crowd.

No sooner had these thoughts passed through his mind than Watt emerged from the boiler house with the mob at his heels and another white boy, whom Neddy had not noticed before. They stopped in the yard, and Watt began to give orders and wave directions. A bunch of men ran in the direction of the hospital and disappeared behind it. Six more followed them. A short while later, they were back, pulling two six-pounders on wheels, the very cannons that Neddy had wondered about. Their work done, the men were ordered back in line with the others now drawn up in ragged formation composed of three equal squads of about twenty men each. Seemingly, their commander knew what he was doing; as such, Watt stood at the head of the center formation.

Neddy could hear him ordering that the cannons were to be put on the outside of his men in between his left and right wing squads. After they were positioned to his liking, he went over to each one and checked them, paying particular attention to their touchholes. Satisfied with his inspection, he gave each a pat. Then Watt's arm went up, and his order, *Forward!* carried clearly to where Neddy was seated.

As the scene unfolded in front of the Great House, the cling-clings, like an expectant audience, went unusually silent. Had they listened intently, the only sound they would have heard beneath their poinciana treetop was Neddy's heart, racing with apprehension at the expected disaster. It thumped like a drum to marching feet. Thirty, forty, sixty slaves, he could not tell, moved forward in unison. Their leader urged them boldly toward the Great House. Along with them went the shadow of the evening as the sun set behind the hills, taking with it the light of day; its final red glow reflected off the cut-stone walls of the house under attack.

There was no way they could invade the house up those stairs. The men with Watt did not stand a chance, even if Bardolf had only a few loyal servants with him. Only one man at a time could go up, and a shooter, through the window slots, would pick him off, with time to reload for the next. One swivel gun could clear the yard in front while reserving the second for any mass attack, should that be tried. Even Neddy could see that Watt's only chance lay with the cannons he had managed to get hold of. The question was, did they really know how to load and shoot them? Perhaps they did, judging from Watt's inspection of them.

If they were sensible, they would wait until it was truly dark, in about half an hour. But that would not be Watt's way. Neddy glanced at the shadows to judge the time. They were moving quickly. Already the area that had housed the slaves was growing dim, along with the ruin of the overseer's house.

Someone fired a shot from the ranks behind Watt. The ball lodged in a shutter, and a few splinters flew from the wood. Neddy could not hear what he said, but Watt was not pleased. His finger was pointed at the one who fired, and his voice was raised, but the words were lost in the hubbub surrounding him. Behind Watt's battalions were the inevitable camp followers—women in fear for their men's lives and the scavengers, those who hoped to strip the fallen. All but the commander fell silent, and it seemed the gap between them shrank. Words became more distinct. Clearly, now, Neddy could hear Watt ordering this way and that and marveled at the presence he conveyed. He was no longer a sixteen-year-old boy; he was a general of a disparate army. Given enough time, he would probably have shaped them into a true fighting force.

"Stay in line. You there, get back. Over there, come up. Present a united front, damn you!"

Watching the ragged parade, Neddy wondered if their general was aware of the swivel guns pointing down at him and his troops. They would be loaded, he knew. If one fired now, bodies would be spattered all over by nails and lead balls.

Watching them continue on their foolish course, he could not stop the throbbing in his chest or quiet the thunder in his ears; his hands trembled, defying every effort to steady them. His palms were slippery with sweat. Rubbing his hands together or on his trouser legs made little difference; instead, it only encouraged more sweat to come. Where had all his manhood gone? He longed for the time of innocence, when manhood did not count, when nothing counted but friendship and stealing fruit. Fear took over. He began to feel sick. Images of Mount Vernon reappeared in his mind. Only this time, the fear surfaced before the event, not after, as it had that morning—all those years ago, it seemed.

They stopped at the steps when Watt called a halt. Chanting began, but not of the island's making. Feet stamped together, first forward and then backward, as an almost forgotten African ceremony came to Jamaica.

The Siege

"A hum!" And the right foot stamped forward. Then "A hum!" And the left followed. The rhythm built.

Watt, their leader, was no longer in control as the foreign war dance took over.

It was beyond Neddy's ken. Yet far from the dance, under the poinciana tree, deep within, what was he? A stirring vibrated through Neddy, an exhilarating feeling that urged him to join. But as the movement and chanting pumped them up in front of him, he resisted the compelling call by pressing his back ever more firmly against the tree trunk.

"*Zulu, Zulu, Zulu!*" the chant began, and kept going. Even the women behind began a strange dance, weaving in and out; bowing down, rising up; hands and arms moving subtly, like coconut boughs in a high wind—as if casting out sprits. They added their shrill voices to the call for *Zulu*.

The lone gunshot had drawn a reaction: Slowly the front door opened, and a white something was waved at the end of a stick. Over their heads he could see Watt's hand go up to call a halt. Silence fell. No one moved. Neddy held his breath, exhaling only when the door creaked open, reminding him, since he could hear it from this distance, always to goose-grease hinges.

Bardolf appeared. His belly came out first. With great care, as if walking on hot coals, he moved onto the small porch, leaving the door behind him open for a quick retreat. Each hand held a pistol. It was too far to see if they were cocked, but in all likelihood they were. With Bardolf standing on the small porch, covered by loose robes hanging like royal drapes, there was about him a sense of Nebuchadnezzar in decline. His huge belly heaved. When it settled back into its normal position, he began to speak.

"What you tink you is doing?" The words came out halfway between bass and falsetto.

"We arc here for our freedom," Watt the general said, standing at least six paces in front of his troops.

"You a joke, white boyc. What freedom you waaant?" Bardolf said, his voice rising.

"All these people," Watt said, his hand sweeping majestically in an arch to those stationed behind him, "demand their freedom, like all Englishmen."

From the top of the steps came the familiar high-pitched, false laugh, ending in a short, sharp cough as Bardolf's throat dried out in the effort.

"You rass! Hinglishmen! Dem is niggers. What Hinglishmen you talk bout, Massa Watt Tyler-Cope? Where di Hinglishmen dey? You bline nu? Look pon dem skin. Is out of Africa it come. It black. Boye, you his a joke, you hear. Now stop di foolishness before me shoot you rass," Bardolf hissed.

"Black they may be, but this…" Watt pointed downward, "is English soil, and that makes them Englishmen."

Bardolf let out another screech of laughter that sent a shiver down Neddy's back.

"Dem is Jamaican niggers, dem is." He waved a pistol at them. "Mi can shoot dem down like mongrel dog. You tink mi can't? You watch, you little white backra massa. Mi can shoot your white rass, too. You help dem in dis rebellion. Hif mi don't shoot you, mi will make sure you swing pon dat tree over dere." Bardolf pointed his pistol to a guinep tree in the yard.

"That will be after we slit that fat belly of yours, Bardolf, and spill your guts for the pigs to eat," Watt shouted.

"Is who going to do dat? You and dat put-put boy over dere?" Bardolf pointed the pistol in his right hand, leveling it at Shirley. "Im tink because we are related, im is safe? Mi goin ang is rass alongside yours. No, mi going ang you one way, an im di oder way."

His words had not even sunk into the crowd at the bottom of the steps, when a shot stopped the back and forth between Watt and the overseer. The ball struck Biblow, standing behind his master, full square in the chest. He pitched forward against Bardolf, who was unaware of his favorite's position, before slumping to the floor dead.

As he watched the lifeblood spread, staining the stone floor, the overseer became unhinged. All he had ever truly loved lay dying at his feet. In a screaming rage, Bardolf let loose, "You damned bastard white puss-mouth boye!" He fired the pistol in his right hand at Shirley. The shot missed Shirley and struck a slave standing beside him, who went down as if poleaxed. "You his responsible for dis, you little backra bastard. *Mi going kill you!*" His screamed open-mouthed as he fired the second shot. That one struck its target. Watt reeled with the impact of the pistol ball.

"Bumba!" Neddy shouted. Jumping up, he ran frantically out of the trees and into the crowd. Pushing his way through men milling about, he reached Watt, now lying on the ground, blood spewing from his left arm. Neddy knelt down behind his friend, lifting his head off the ground and onto his knees. Watt looked up at him. "He has killed us, Neddy," he said, and passed out.

Neddy did not know if he was dead or alive. All he knew was the bleeding had to be stopped, otherwise there would be no blood left in his body. Quickly he took off the rope holding his pants up and wound it around Watt's arm above the wound. Slowly the bleeding subsided. Then Neddy cut open Watt's jacket and shirtsleeves with his knife. Shattered bone poked through the flesh.

"Is he dead?" asked Shirley.

Neddy looked up. "Don't know. Mi don't tink so, but im need a doctor." Shirley turned away and walked forward to what had been Watt's position.

"Bardolf!" Shirley screamed, his face flushed with rage.

"What you want, puss-boye?" Bardolf said.

Shirley hurled the cane sickle in his right hand at Bardolf on the steps above him. It curved over and over again in the air, spinning upward to its target. What light there was, flashed off the honed blade. Strangely, it appeared to spin slowly on its way to the target, till it stopped dead center in Bardolf. They all heard it strike with a sickening flop.

Dazed, unbelieving, like an idiot child, Bardolf looked down at the sickle protruding from his body. Both his hands came up in a futile effort to extract it from his belly. It was firmly anchored, as a hook in a fish. A stain like a bull's-eye spread round the metal protruding from his center onto the white robes. Bardolf turned to retreat inside when the second one stuck into his back, just between the shoulder blades. Its force spun the bloated body back again to face the slaves below. In his struggle with these barbs, he slipped in Biblow's blood, missed the step, made a futile grab, for the rail and tumbled forward, bouncing down the long steps of the Great House like an inflated pig's bladder used by small boys to play ball. At the bottom, his body jerked spasmodically and released a sound like gas escaping, as Bardolf breathed his last. For a moment all of them watched, expecting him to rise and face them, whip in hand. Nothing happened. There was just a mound of flesh, unmoving, before them.

Suddenly, a cannon went off. Its bang brought them back to what they were there for. A cluster of men fell apart as the lead balls shattered them. Flesh, blood, and bone splattered everywhere. Neither Watt nor Neddy escaped the shower. Bad as it was, the blood that splashed them made Watt's wound look even more serious. A scream announced, "Im dead now!"

The swivel cannon had fired from the top of the steps. Shirley, who had watched the end of his cousin with some pleasure, responded immediately and ran to one of their cannons. With the aid of some men, heaving and pushing, he got the gun to move around, pointing in the direction of the upper story of the Great House. Grabbing a lighted torch, Shirley put fire to its touchhole. It hesitated, then the cannon heaved backward; with a deafening roar, a red flame flashed from its spout, followed by a white ring of smoke like a cigar puff billowing upward.

The front door blew apart almost at the same instant that the roof erupted, as the six-pound shot exited through rafters and shingles. Shattered wood showered the defenders. On the ground, hands went up to shield heads from the splinters raining down. Some found a mark with telling force, causing yelps of pain. As the last of the debris hit the ground, there came a moment of reverence, followed by a screaming battle yell. Shirley ran to the second cannon and fired, with much the same result. More roof fragments came down on them. Prudently, many of the attacking forces backed off this time.

One of the shutters was thrown open. A makeshift rope of blankets tied together was thrown out, and down it slipped Duar. Others followed his example. Many didn't bother with the rope that Duar had used to bail out of the house. They just jumped. Smoke had begun to rise from the interior of the house. Somehow a fire had started, perhaps at the hand of a house slave or the result of the cannon balls.

As the defenders hit the ground and took off, they fired pistols and long guns at the attackers. Bodies were hit and fell. Those slaves who had guns retaliated, but with less success.

Led by Shirley, jumping over Bardolf's body, they followed at a run after those deserting the Great House. Many were obviously rum-inspired, taking swigs from the jars and bottles that they carried, splashing the alcohol over their faces, necks, and chests as they ran. Their blood was up.

Neddy watched them go. This was his opportunity to get Watt out of there. He grabbed him under his armpit and began to pull. They didn't get far before there was a chilling screech of pain. Instantly Neddy let go. As Watt hit the ground, he screamed again.

"You alive den?" Neddy shouted with relief.

"Hell bent! Did you think I was dead?" groaned Watt.

"You look dead. You white like a duppy."

"Well, I am not your favorite duppy," Watt said weakly, with a grimace of pain.

Neddy leaned over him, examining where he had bound the rope around his arm, and gently probed the hole.

"Yu bone broke."

"Oh?"

"It a stick trough di flesh."

"I can't feel my fingers."

"Is because mi tie did rope to stop di blood. The flesh a turn black an frowzy where it tie."

"Quickly then, untie it and let the blood flow then tie it back."

"You got enough for dat?" inquired Neddy somewhat skeptical.

"Do as I say," Watt barked. Looking up at his friend bending over him, he could see hurt on his face at his abruptness. After all, he was helping. "It's all right. My uncle told me that's how they do it on the battlefield. If you don't, the flesh will abominate." That speech exhausted him and he fainted.

WHEN CONCHIE BLOWS

His instructions didn't sound too right, but he had never been in that situation before. Watt was a madman. Better try what he said. Resigning himself to losing his friend, holding back the tears, Neddy gently undid the knot. "If him dead, im dead an gone," he whispered huskily to himself.

Blood began to form a pool just under the wound. A sickly sweet smell hit his nostrils. He turned away, holding his breath. Exhaling, he turned back and once again tied the wound off to stop the bleeding. Miraculously, Watt groaned and came out of his faint.

"You wake up!" Neddy almost shouted in surprise. Greatly relieved at seeing a turn for the better, he said, "Stay dat way while me get di mule. Mi got to get you out of dis place." Watt raised his right hand in acknowledgement. Neddy ran to get the mule.

Watt entered a state of half-consciousness, drifting in and out of sense. He was just aware when Neddy returned with the mule and Bess. The big dog sniffed him, snuffled, and yapped; whether Bess uttered disgust or sympathy, Watt was too dazed to care.

"You can stan up?" asked Neddy hopefully.

"I can try. If you help me."

"Dat's what mi here for, boye, assured Neddy.

The problem was getting Watt to his feet. There was no way he could be lifted from under his arms. Kneeling behind Watt, Neddy ordered, "Try an sit up." Groaning and moaning with the effort, Watt sat up, with Neddy's hands helping him behind. "Don't go back now, Watt. Mi goin grab you roun your waist an lif."

"Let's go, Neddy."

They struggled together, with many a foul word out of Watt. Once on his feet, Watt had to be held in place as he swayed. With the yard lit by the burning Great House, Neddy looked around to call someone to help him get Watt mounted. To his amazement, they were all alone. Watt's army had run off. All that was left was Bardolf's corpse and five others, killed by the swivel canon. For a moment he watched two mangy mongrels sniff at the John Crows' meat left at the foot of the steps and those lying twisted in death on the field of battle. It would be nasty if they were left unburied for the vultures. Neddy shuddered at the thought of those birds, pecking out the staring eyes and tearing at the flesh. At least he was reassured Watt was still alive and would not lose his blue eyes down a John Crow's craw.

Getting him mounted was their next trial. To get his foot into the stirrup was the first move. With Watt swaying backward and forward, it took three tries before his foot found the position. Heaving him up and getting his other leg over the saddle came next. A spate of foul words screamed out of Watt's mouth into Neddy's ears. Bess barked, and the mule flicked its tail. But, thank God, the old animal sensed that being still was what was needed at that moment; it stood rock solid while the wounded warrior was pushed and shoved onto its back.

As Neddy began leading the mule, he looked to see Watt begin to slide off its back. Just in time he caught and held him from slipping to the ground. There was only one way for it. He knew the mule would be able to bear their weights. Neddy mounted on its haunches behind Watt in the saddle. The mule didn't seem to mind and set off at a brisk walk.

Soon they were through the gates and on their way to the shortcut he took to church on Sundays. The light was gone, but Neddy knew the way well. As they neared the spot, there was the glow of fire and the acrid stink of smoke. Some destructive fool had torched the fields on both sides of the path. Uncertain as to what the next move should be, Neddy halted. He could just see the church steeple over the tops of the burning cane against the evening sky. That gave him hope, for it meant the smoke was blowing away from them. If he could cut across, that would save a lot of time. A groan came from Watt.

"Hif mi push di mule to run, you can stan it?" Neddy said.

"Pancho, my true and trusty friend, I commend my body and soul to you."

"Don't sey dat! God don't like it when you fun so."

Watt did not reply but slumped forward into another half-faint. Neddy tightened his grip around Watt's waist and kicked his heels hard into the mule's sides. It took off at full gallop, pitching forward and back like a rocking horse. There was nothing else for him to do but hang on and pray to God that they would not fall off. If that happened, Watt would suffer greatly. Neddy even feared the tumble would kill him. As they pounded along, his broken arm dangled by his side, swung uncontrollably. At every stride of the mule, it seemed likely to drop off. Neddy wished he had tied it to his body. Too late now; he did not want to watch if it came off, so he turned his head to look right. There was the dim outline of good old Bess running with them all the way. Somehow he knew they would be all right. Bess was so like his mama—always reliable.

They made it out of the burning field through the gap in the stone wall that marked the boundary between church land and Friendship and rode up the knoll over the grave stones into the churchyard. Neddy tightened his arms around Watt to hold him secure as he yanked the reins. The bit crushed the mule's mouth, and its head went down. They pitched forward, and Neddy feared they would both going over the animal's head. He hung on with legs clamped to the mule's side and arms around Watt's middle, pressing the wind out of both mule and boy. Miraculously, the mule's back legs came forward to brake, and they skidded to a stop on its haunches.

With Neddy's arms still locked around Watt's waist, they slid to the ground from the mule's back. Neddy managed to keep his feet and hold Watt as he slumped forward, a dead weight. Taking a deep breath, Neddy, his arms locked around Watt's waist, dragged him backward to the vestry door, his heels leaving a trail behind them through the gravel.

The vestry was usually left open, and he hoped it would be so tonight. When he got to the door, he pressed his back against it, but there was no give. Still holding Watt with his left arm, he fiddled with his right to find the latch. Flipping it up he pressed against the door again, and it gave inward this time. It was pitch-black, but he knew the lay of the room and hoped that nothing had been moved that would trip him up. They entered. Just about in the center, Neddy lay Watt on the floor. Watt groaned. That was a good sign, Neddy thought.

For a moment he tried to let his eyes get accustomed to the blackness. The only relief was the open door. He went by memory and touch, feeling his way around the long refectory table, and made it to the cupboard. It was never locked, and he remembered the candles and lantern on the top shelf. They were there. Then it struck him, he had no way of lighting them. His hand slipped to the next shelf and found the next best thing in his hour of darkness, a Bible. With it in hand Neddy made his way back to Watt on the floor and placed the good book in his right hand.

"You still fainting?" he asked.

"Nearly; the stone floor feels nice and cool."

"Hold di book tight in you good han. Mi going to get di Reverend and Missus Waldrich. Dey will elp you. Don't move now—you hear? Guard him, Bess!" A faint chuckle came through the darkness from the floor, the sound made him feel better.

Neddy ran straight through the vestry door and fell flat on his face in the yard, tripped by an outstretched leg at the door. A boot drove into his side; the toe dug beneath him and expertly flipped him over onto his back. Cool metal pressed against his forehead, and a voice said, "Move an inch, boyo, and your head comes off wid the little piece of lead at this end of mi barrel." Neddy did not move. Once more fear enveloped him. He was almost getting used to the feeling. With each sickening reappearance, its terror had lessened. Unconsciously, he was learning to overcome its weakening effect. Nothing to do now but wait.

He remained perfectly still as the man ordered. At the same time, he desperately tried to focus his eyes and make out who held him down. Against the night sky, the silhouette of his hat marked him as a soldier. Regular or militia, Neddy could not tell.

Then another voice coming toward them asked, "What you got there, Taffy?"

"Get the sergeant. We got one of the burning, bloody, black rapscallions running out of church, no less. The captain will like this one, as well, Billy," his captor said in a singsong tone, the sole of his boot pressing Neddy's gut.

A man leaned over him, shading a candle he had just lit. It illuminated dull red and green facings of a uniform, and a dry, sallow face with matching yellow teeth grinned at him. Neddy could not get a clearer picture, as the muzzle of the other's musket wavered just above his right eye, blocking its sight.

"He is only a young one."

"Don't matter, Billy; they will kill you as soon as look at you."

"Wonder what white man's blood this is?" Yellow Teeth said, sticking his finger into one of the bloodstains on the jacket. "A coat of many colors, you would call it in chapel, Taffy." A nasty laugh followed.

"Go get the sergeant, or get back on point, Billy."

"Point it is. They are right behind me, Taffy." Blowing out the candle stub, he returned to his point duty.

With the soldier's departure, Neddy and his captor were plunged back into darkness. To make sure he didn't move, a boot sank even further into Neddy's stomach, just where his chest bone stopped and the soft belly began. There was a nasty pain, and he fought for breath. Even if he had wanted to move, he was pinned to the ground firmly. The soldier did not let up, even though he heard the rasping sound of struggled breathing below him. Relief came only when a lantern held by another man in uniform swung over his head.

"Take your boot out, man, before you kill him!" Instantly the pressure was gone. At first, breath was hard to pull in, but with gasps it came back to fill his lungs and belly. A strong hand grabbed the front of his jacket and heaved him to his feet. The lantern was pushed forward and moved up and down his front as the soldier looked him over.

"Aren't you a bloody one? Who you been killing?" There was nothing nasty in the question, just matter-of-fact, spoken by one who knew nothing else but killing. "You had better come and see the captain. He will want to ask you a thing or two. You," he barked at the soldier. "Get back on point."

"Yes, Sergeant." Boots scraped to attention on the gravel, and Neddy watched the soldier depart into the night.

"March!" the sergeant said, and whacked him with his stick across the bottom, putting him to a half-run. Resentment welled up in him for an instant, but he realized this was not a good time to try running. He was in enough trouble by helping Watt, who was dying in the church.

Within a hundred yards, the sergeant screamed, "Halt!"

Again he felt the whack of the cane across his backside. He winced and resented the soldier even more.

The Siege

"What have you got there, Sergeant?" a familiar voice asked from horseback.

"A murdering little wretch, sir!" Boots crashed into the gravel as the sergeant came smartly to attention behind Neddy.

"Hold up the lantern, and let me see this murdering little wretch," the officer mimicked. "Neddy?" the officer said, as the light flooded over him.

Relief flushed through Neddy. He couldn't believe his luck. He had imagined death would be his, swinging from the cotton tree up the road by Worcester. His only consolation had been that Watt would be dead, too, and they could go fishing together in heaven.

"Massa Galloway, tank God it is you, sah, Captain. Help us, please." Neddy's words tumbled out of his mouth. "Mi friend a dead inside there." Neddy pointed at the church.

"Steady, boyo. What are you talking about?" Galloway said.

"They shoot mi friend. He is in the church, where mi bring im. I was going for the parson when di soldier grab mi up, Captain."

"A likely story," mumbled the sergeant behind him.

"Bring up Dr. Robertson, he may be wanted here," Galloway said. "Also, send for the parson. At least one of them will be needed. Give me the lantern, man. Come, Neddy, lead the way."

No more encouragement was needed; Neddy ran in front of the captain to the vestry door.

Bess growled as they entered. "Hush, dog, he a fren," said Neddy. Galloway swung the lantern in the direction of the growl.

"Nice dog," he commented, then turned the light on Watt lying on the ground. Judging by his color, he should have been dead, but they could see slight chest movement demonstrating life remained in his hulk. Galloway bent over him and inspected more closely.

"Nasty wound. Don't think that will hang on there." He held the lamp over the left arm. "How did he get this in his other hand?" he asked, looking at the Bible. "You put it there?" Galloway looked at Neddy with an ironic smile twisting the left corner of his mouth.

"Yes, sah," Neddy confessed, fidgeting.

"You sent for me, Galloway?" Neddy recognized Doctor Robertson dressed in militia uniform, standing at the vestry door.

"Yes, we need your skills here to save this boy." Galloway pointed to the prostrate body.

"Looks too far gone to me. Ah, well, get him up onto the table, and we will see if there is any use trying. Arm looks like it has to come off," the doctor observed first.

That sent a shudder through Neddy. They lifted Watt onto the refectory table just as Reverend Waldrich and his wife appeared.

"Vot you doing in my church vith guns and boots?" the reverend demanded.

Mrs. Waldrich noticed Neddy and gasped at the sight of blood on his clothes. "Vot you do to Neddy?" she said, throwing her hands heavenward in anguish.

"Is his blood." Neddy pointed at Watt stretched out on the table.

"Come vid me and get cleaned up," she said.

"Not yet, madam," countered the doctor. "He stays to help me. A little more blood won't make any difference on his clothes. That is, if this man has any left." The Scotsman gave a little laugh at that. Neddy did not find it funny but kept silent.

"Doctor," the parson's wife said with an edge of indignation in her voice. "Is zat necessary?" She pointed to the door. "Surely one of dem soldiers can help you. Vy ze boy?"

"He looks capable," grunted the doctor. "Your husband can give us a hand, too. And madam, I would appreciate some hot water. We may need it and an extra bottle of rum." He turned away to stop any further argument from her. "By any chance, madam," he added, as he cut away Watt's shirtsleeve, "you wouldn't have any whiskey, would you?"

"Schnapps is better." Her alternative offer to the doctor's request sounded like a half-sneeze, half-spit to those in that dim room who had never heard of schnapps.

"I want to drink and enjoy it, madam, not cauterize my innards." Doctor Robertson didn't even bother to look at Mrs. Waldrich. "Oh well, rum will have to do."

"Doctor, how can I help zi poor boy?" the reverend said.

"Stand over here until I call for you." The hand with the scissors waved him around to the opposite side of the table.

"You," the doctor snapped at Neddy. "Stand at his head, and hold onto his shoulders. No fainting, now." He pointed the scissors at him and smiled. "I am sure you are man enough to watch the saw cut through flesh then bone, and, after it comes free from the body, clear the dead arm away, laddie? Mi self had to watch that every morning before breakfast in the hospital at your age."

Neddy gulped when he heard what was going to happen. Before the doctor started, Neddy's hands began to tremble, and that sick feeling invaded his stomach. "Lord," he prayed silently, "let this day end."

A ball of yellow, matted hair lay on the table in front of him. Some strands stuck together to make a crisscross pattern on a bloodless forehead. In the poor light the doctor had to work with, it was impossible for Neddy to see whether his friend's eyes were open. His face had gone pasty white and puffy, like dough that had been left on the kitchen table to rise overnight. Only the hesitant heaving of the chest told him Watt was still alive.

The doctor poked at the arm, grunted, and mumbled to himself. "Where is that wife of yours, sir?" he suddenly asked the reverend, looking up from the wound he had been probing.

"She vill be along, Doctor. Ah, here she is!" he said with relief. However, on turning to greet her, he found not his spouse but Captain Galloway, who had been outside with his company.

"Reverend, we will be camping here tonight. I have ordered that the soldiers stay outside your church. We will be in the yard."

"Thank you, Captain. Zat will be fine. We vill feel safer for your presence. The slaves deserve dere freedom, but zey ave gone vilde. Drink is ze devil's vay. And today he is giving zem plenty to drink."

"This boy's arm has to come off, Galloway. The flesh is torn to shreds, and the bone is broken. It will all turn bad by morning if it does not go. Get some men in here with lanterns. I need much more light, man."

Even with taking the arm off, the doctor did not sound too reassuring that Watt would survive the amputation. Furthermore, Neddy was beginning to doubt whether he, himself, would be able to last out the operation without fainting. "Oh, God," Neddy began a silent prayer again but was interrupted as a warm head rubbed against his leg and rested on his foot. It was Bess, looking up at him. To his shame, he had forgotten to relieve her of guard duty over Watt. He nodded approvingly at her. She grunted and closed her eyes, continuing to use his foot as a pillow.

Not long after the captain's return, another step on the gravel outside heralded the return of Mrs. Waldrich. She put on the floor a bucket of hot water with an enamel basin covering it and handed a bottle to the doctor.

"Your rum and vasser, Doctor."

"Thank you, madam. To your bonny face and very good health." An amused expression played on his face as he lifted the bottle, saluted her, and took a huge swig. Neddy wondered if the reverend saw that as more of the devil at work, or a small stimulant from God to steady the doctor's hand. He glanced from one to the other to Mrs. Waldrich, and then back to his friend's head, held between his hands. His reaction was not lost on Robertson.

"Here, boy." He handed Neddy the bottle, over the protests of Mrs. Waldrich. "Take a shot; you will need it yourself, laddie." The doctor picked up a glinting, sharp-edged knife from among those laid out neatly on a chair, brought up beside him in place of a table.

"Now, to work. Bring the bucket over here," he ordered one of the three soldiers who had come in, bearing lanterns at Galloway's orders. Expertly, the doctor washed the wound with a rag soaked in hot water. Once it was clean to his satisfaction, he loosened the crude tourniquet.

Blood began to ooze again. Doctor Robertson took another swig from the bottle and then poured some of its contents over the wound.

"That should clean out its ill humors. Whisky would have been better." Using the scissors, he quickly snipped away at the hanging bits of flesh. It was all quite neat. Many a seamstress would have approved. After the last strip was gone, his knife came slicing down through the flesh, as if he were carving ham at the dinner table. Then came the terrible part Neddy feared—the sawing and grating against the bone. But he held steady, turning his head away to forestall the blackest of black moments that threatened to invade his inner shell and overwhelm him.

The Siege

He did not even notice when the soldier grabbed him by the ankles and dragged him outside by the vestry door at the doctor's orders. He couldn't understand why his cheeks stung as if they had been slapped, while Mrs. Waldrich was rubbing his hands vigorously.

"Drink," she said poking a bottle between his lips, forcing his mouth open. He spluttered as the harsh liquor stung the back of his throat. It warmed his gut. The second huge swallow stunned his brain.

"Schnapps is goot, ya? You fainted," she said, helping him to his feet. With her arm supporting him she led the way through the churchyard where the soldiers were camping and down to the small rectory.

"Come," she said, opening the front door. She led him through into the kitchen at the back. There was one of those new iron stoves with pots boiling and a table with plates, all neatly arranged, on it.

"Sit," the pastor's wife said, touching a chair at the table with a spoon she had picked up from the table. After he had taken his place, she left the room. Soon she was back with a clean piece of cloth and shirt. "Come, Neddy, follow me," she said. They went outside to the well. "Draw some water and wash yourself." She handed him a small jar of homemade lye soap.

"This shirt is an old one of Reverend Waldrich zat you can have. Give me zat von, and I vill vash it vor you." She took the bloodstained shirt and held it up. White with dark splotches or dark with white splotches—one could not tell in the poor light what the true color was. Mrs. Waldrich threw it into a bucket of water to soak.

Neddy was filling a very empty belly when the front door was opened by Reverend Waldrich. Behind him came the refectory table, carried by four soldiers. On it lay Watt.

"In here. In here, men," he called. "My wife says he should go into the spare room." He led the way up the stairs. For a brief moment, there was an argument about taking him up while still on the table. All agreed that would not be practical. Finally, Mrs. Waldrich solved the question. Very gently two soldiers lifted him off the table and placed him sitting upright in a large wicker chair. With the chair at a tilt, so his head rested on its back, the men, one on either side, carefully carried him up the stairs. Bess followed, still on duty. Not until Watt was safely on the bed, with Mrs. Waldrich fussing around him, did Neddy call Bess downstairs to share his food.

Watching Neddy scrape the last of his dinner into an old bowl he had found for Bess, the reverend commented proudly, "A very good hound, zat; she comes from my country, ya." He served himself from the pots on the stove and added more food to her bowl.

"Yes, sah. She is dat." Neddy didn't know if she came from his country or not, but he willingly confirmed that Bess was indeed the best of dogs.

The Reverend nodded his head, taking it he was right on both counts.

They heard the front door close as Mrs. Waldrich showed the soldiers out and thanked them. She then came into the kitchen to take charge, fussing over her husband, and asking Neddy if he needed any more food. Without waiting for confirmation, she refilled his plate with dumplings, carrots, and meat.

"When you are finished, you can sleep upstairs in your friend's room. I had ze soldiers put a cot zere vor you." She looked over at Bess licking the bowl. "Ze hound can sleep up there, too. Call me if ze boy gets vorse."

With a full gut for the first time in what seemed like months, Neddy got up and headed for the door.

"Vere you go?" Rev. Waldrich said.

"Mi mule, reverend. It is still up in the churchyard. Mi going bring it down here."

"It's all right, Neddy," interrupted Mrs. Waldrich. "Ze officer in charge made a soldier bring it down when zey bring down ze boy. I had him unzaddled and tied outzide. He vill be nice vor tonight. Tomorrow you can look at him."

Dog and boy went up the stairs. A lamp dimly lit the room. In its light, Watt looked bloodless and dead, lying bandaged, half covered by a sheet, on the bed. Bess sniffed, grunted, and settled down across the doorway. On the cot alongside Watt's bed, Neddy stretched out; and during the rest of the night hours, both boys in their unconscious states forgot what had passed before in the day hours.

Chapter 15

The March South

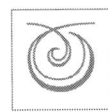

They were in the backyard of their house on Kensington. He watched as his three-year-old face was being washed. The rag was wet, warm, and rough and scraped his skin. Mama held him by one hand, as she always did while giving him a bath. Strange, it was stiff and white, but scabs of blood congealed to it; she was using her black hand to wipe away blood which dripped onto his skin from above. The red rag rubbed one cheek, then the other—once, twice, three times, as if polishing them. Neddy struggled to get away, but the rag was insistent. Watt was standing naked, grinning from under his big straw hat; he was whole again. Watt waved his right arm at Neddy, but it faded away. The sun was shining through a window. Something snuffled in his ear; something warm and wet slobbered on his neck.

Neddy sat bolt upright on the cot, colliding with Bess. He winced at the unexpected encounter. Startled, she backed off. Only half awake, he pushed her away from the cot and wiped his face with his hand and around to the nape of his neck, where her tongue had reached. Mrs. Waldrich, who had been watching the performance, giggled and confessed, "I told ze hound to vake you. Vunderbar! She gives you a bath as vell." Mrs. Waldrich laughed outright. "Ze captain," she went on, "vaunts to speak vid you. But first you vash properly, and den have breakfast." She nodded, indicating the direction he should go. Looking over at Watt, she checked to see if he was breathing comfortably and then left the room to allow Neddy to rise and get ready.

As he pulled on his pants, he realized it was all a dream, but just to make sure, Neddy turned to look at Watt. Mrs. Waldrich had been ministering to him. A basin with bloody water and rags were on the small table beside the bed. In the pale morning light that had crept onto the diaphanous mosquito netting shrouding the bed, he seemed to see Watt's skull stand out beneath the drawn, stretched facial skin. Gone was the round, smiling face. The sight frightened Neddy. It made him inhale sharply, and his head swam as a result. He realized that was how he would be, after a few hours in the grave under the crushing weight of earth piled on top of his coffin. Neddy shuddered. Burial was so awful. After death, there must be some other way of taking care of the body. That cold earth on top of one for eternity—until the final trumpet when the quick and the dead would rise and go forth to meet the Lord—was not a pleasant prospect to contemplate. He shook his head vigorously to be rid of the spinning images.

The giddy feeling lasted only a couple of seconds, and when he became focused again, his friend's face was more recognizable. It was hard to tell if he was alive, though. Driblets of sweat glistening on his forehead showed at least that he was still in the land of the quick. Neddy lifted the netting, and when he rested the back of his hand on Watt's cheek, it felt like a pot warming beside the kitchen fire. Reaching for a cloth left on the bed, he wiped the perspiration away and then swabbed his face with cool water from the jug on the dresser. A fever raged, but Neddy knew that so long as water came out of him, there was a chance for life. It was when the skin was dry and flaky that people died. He had heard that often enough, growing up.

Holding his own breath, Neddy listened to the unsteady breathing coming from the bed. Its unevenness suggested Watt was ebbing lower. That, Neddy did not like at all. Blood oozed from the bandages around the stub of his left arm. To stem the seepage and make him more comfortable, Neddy tried to place the cloth he had been using to wipe Watt's face under the stub. Then Mrs. Waldrich came back into the room and took over for him.

"You are a considerate boy. You vill be vell-loved by some-vone, vone day." Her head nodded up and down as if confirming this prediction. She took a clean cloth from the pile on the dresser to swab the sufferer. "Help me prop him upright, vid ze pillows. It vill try to keep the fever of infection back."

There was no response from her patient as they struggled on either side of the bed to prop him up with pillows behind his back. The lack of anything from Watt, even a groan, made Neddy fear that it would not be long before his only true friend went to meet his maker, and he prayed silently. Tears began to trickle down his cheeks, and he fought to stop their flow. Men did not cry. They hid their feelings. Women cried, but not men. That recognition did not help him, however. His sniffle made Mrs. Waldrich give an understanding half-smile. Her hand came round to pat his shoulder. And yet, there was no lecture on male behavior in such circumstances, as might have come from someone else. She understood that if David could weep for Jonathan, so could Neddy weep for Watt.

Thoughts of their first meeting, along with the promise he had made to himself at that time, crowded into his mind. As he looked at the semi-corpse that now was Watt, he felt as if he had let himself down. He should have dragged Watt from that boiler house and taken him away. All these thoughts congested together; none of it made much sense. For these thoughts supposed that Watt would have allowed himself to be dragged off obediently. There was nothing more that could have been done, insisted a logical corner of his mind. Still, regret threatened to overwhelm him. Astutely, Mrs. Waldrich recognized the inner struggle and came to the rescue.

"Go downstairs, vash yourself, and ave some breakfast. Cornmeal porridge and plantain vid salt fish is zere vor you. Coffee in ze pot. Ven you finish, remember di captain vait in the vestry vor you. Now, hurry, Neddy!"

He did as he was told. Out of that room, he breathed easier. He was glad that Mrs. Waldrich had left the windows open all night and not turned the room into a hothouse, as they did in the estate hospitals. They were always stifling hot on his occasional visits.

Downstairs in the kitchen, he was glad to see that food had been provided for Bess as well. Both of them gobbled their breakfast down. She licked her plate before he had finished, then looked up at him expectantly. Luck was on her side: She won the last scrapings from his plate, as Neddy did not want to annoy the captain by keeping him waiting in the vestry.

As he and the dog left the parsonage and walked up the slight gradient to the church, Neddy could see the soldiers already breaking camp. One or two stared; others didn't even give him a glance as he and Bess passed by. Neddy furtively looked for the ones who had captured him the night before but could not distinguish any, as all men in uniform looked alike to him.

At the door he could hear voices he recognized. One was Dr. Robertson, while the other was unmistakably the Reverend Waldrich. There was another he wasn't quite sure of. Although the door was ajar, the men were out of sight. There was no response to his knock. Again he tried and still the voices continued in the room, ignoring his efforts to attract their attention. Neddy stood there listening and realized that the other voice was the sergeant from the night before, the Kaka who had hit him with the stick. He smarted with indignation at the memory. No damned stranger had ever done that to him before. Evidently the sergeant was giving a report, as every other sentence ended with *Sha*.

"There is nary a white man or a dog left at Friendship, Sha. All the buildings are burned. I had the men bury the white man and the blacks, Sha. Most slaves have run off. Only a few old ones left, Sha."

"Thank you, Sergeant. Get the men ready to move. We will stop at Newman Hall and then camp tonight at Maroon Town. Tomorrow we will reach Lapland, if we haven't picked up too much baggage on the way. You can go, Sergeant."

"Sha." There was stamping of a foot on the ground as the warrant officer came to attention and about faced. As he opened the door, Neddy was standing there with a pebble in his hand, about to knock again. The Sergeant stared at him for a second, without turning, then shouted, "Sha. That black person we captured last night is here, about to assault the reverend's door with a stone, Sha!" The last *Sha* assailed Neddy in the face, making him instinctively back away. His eyes widened and he looked from the Sergeant to the pebble in his hand. He had only picked it up to knock louder so that they could hear him.

"Should I drill some sense into him, Sha?" snapped the Sergeant, a bit calmer now, but with a glint of malevolent anticipation in his eyes.

"Bring him here!" Galloway barked the order. He sounded cranky. "Oh! It's you, Neddy, mi boyo." His voice came to a more reasonable level when he realized whom the sergeant meant. "It's all right, Sergeant. Carry on."

The subordinate snapped to attention, saluted, and marched away.

"Never mind the sergeant, Neddy. He would love to have you on his square and torture you! He believes all young men should be in the army, especially in Jamaica. There is no harm in the man, really."

A second or two passed, as Neddy's eyes adjusted to the light filtering through the two narrow windows into the room. Galloway half sat on the refectory table facing the door. His right buttock rested on the edge of the table, supported by his left leg planted on the floor. He looked in control, compared to the doctor and Reverend Waldrich, standing on the far side of the table as if waiting to receive his orders.

"Neddy," Galloway said with a very serious expression. "That boy, the bookkeeper, the one you saved last night, where is he from?" A grilling was coming. Neddy could feel it. The walls of the room began to close in on him like a trap. Automatically his head bowed. Galloway's riding boots reflected the light creeping across the floor. The right one swung just above the ground like the pendulum of a clock, while the left, stock-still on the ground, supported his weight, its spur flashing like a silver fish in the light.

He mustn't fidget, he told himself. Yet, it was as if a giant hand, from some dark and unknown place came out and moved him like a puppet. His weight shifted from leg to leg, and his toes wriggled in their sandals. Those in the vestry observed his nervous movements. He could feel their eyes on him, penetrating right through his flesh to the bone marrow.

"Friendship, sah," he said, swallowing hard. The spit going down his throat popped his ears, and he knew they heard it. Galloway said nothing but shifted his weight on the table slightly; one leg continued its support on the ground, and the other, swinging with deliberation to and fro, ticked away the seconds. He dragged a chair round for his left arm to rest on its high back. Obviously he was waiting for Neddy to fill in more information.

No one moved. Then Galloway said very quietly, "We captured about three of the miscreants from Friendship last night, and they had a lot to say, mi boyo." His right forefinger gave a little flick in Neddy's direction with the last words. His leg went back to swinging. Both the parson and the doctor watched but said nothing. Robertson put his hand in his pocket and came out with a small cigar case. Realizing he had no way of lighting one, he returned it to his coat.

"They told me that a certain white man taught them how to make pistol balls and to shoot a gun. It was he who led them against the overseer's house. They told me that Bardolf shot at him, and that he killed Bardolf." Galloway sounded most matter-of-fact. Neddy was not sure of where he stood. Again the invisible hand made him shift his weight about and wriggle his toes.

"Dat not right, sah!" Neddy burst out. "Mi don't know bout making bullets," he lied. "But di Zulu Bardolf shot im." He paused a good second before thoughtfully adding, "Massa." That brought an unexpected response.

"Don't grovel to me, boy," Galloway snapped. "I neither expect nor want that from you, Neddy."

"Sorry, sah. But Watt never mean nothing; it was di other white boye who fling di sickle dat stick into Bardolf. Then someone else fling anoder one dat get im in his back. Im shoot Watt before dem get im, sah."

Neddy paused to catch his breath, then went on, "Watt is a fool-fool youth, who like play im is cre to lead di people to freedom, like dem do long time ago in Hingland." The words came fast as if Watt's life depended on their speed, and they had all three men looking very puzzled. Before any could interject, Neddy raced on. "Im call me im faitful servant Pancho Sandwich or some ting, an im don't believe in duppy." That was the worst foolishness of all, it seemed to Neddy, as he caught his tongue wondering if he had gone too far.

Galloway's face relaxed as the doctor asked, "What are you talking aboot, laddie?"

"All di time, sah, im say im fader name im for some man dat got killed making trouble wi slave dem in Hingland." Neddy's speech verged on a nearly unintelligible patois.

"There are no slaves in England, Neddy. Never have been." Galloway corrected.

"How could he say such a thing about England? And ze only leaders ze slaves have here are zhe Baptists. Zere man Sam Sharpe, a lay preacher, he is ze leader, I hear," said the reverend, adding to what Galloway had just said.

"What's his name, Neddy?" Galloway asked.

"Watt, sah."

"Watt?" echoed Galloway, a puzzled frown returning to his face.

"Yes, sah, Watt Tyler-Cope, im name."

Galloway looked at the ceiling and hooted with laughter. It all made sense to him, if not to the doctor and the parson, who now looked at the captain in wonder.

"Gentlemen," he said, the palms of his hands turned up toward the ceiling "Watt Tyler. The boy is a dreamer, as they all are at that age. Somehow Watt Tyler has got mixed up with Cervantes." There was no recognition of the names on either the face of the protector of souls or the healer of flesh.

"Watt Tyler led the peasant revolt in England and got murdered for his pains," Galloway explained.

"Oh," said the doctor. "Murdered like William Wallace, no doubt. The English are good at murdering people who do not agree with their ways."

"Neddy," a serious look came over Galloway's face, "Your friend's actions have got him into a great deal of trouble. They are court-martial offenses. If found guilty, he will be hanged."

"Oh, no!" exclaimed the parson. "Zat poor boy! Zat is wrong! Zey can't do zat."

"They can, and they will," Galloway said. "As a matter of fact, I have to place him under arrest."

"Hardly worth that, he will most likely be dead by sunset," the doctor said.

"You think his days as a knight-errant tilting at windmills are over then, Robertson?"

"An what are you talking aboot now? Have both of you begun to speak in tongues." The doctor pointed first at Neddy and then his commanding officer. "Ireland is a good place for that, they tell me."

"You have never read Don Quixote, Doctor? I would have thought all educated Scotsmen would have him down pat."

"A man in my profession hasn't got time for frivolous readings, Galloway," snapped the doctor testily.

"It would do your soul a lot of good to join the poetic society of Montego Bay, Doctor," the captain said, wagging a finger in Robertson's direction.

"Ah! Utter nonsense, mon. All we Scots need is Rabbie Burns. Now there is a true poet fer you—in words and music!"

"To a mouse, To a mouse, To a weee mouse," exaggerated Galloway, mocking the doctor.

"Ach! Go away wid you, mon." Robertson said, dismissing the ridicule with a wave.

"To serious business gentleman. Now, what am I to do about our rebel?" Galloway looked from one to the other, getting back to his problem.

"Please, sah, let im go. Im not know what im doing," Neddy said.

Galloway contemplated the boy's face before proceeding to justify his position as a serving officer. "I have my duty, boy. A man swears an oath, and he has to keep it."

"Ach, man! Duty be damned!" exclaimed the doctor. "He is harlf-grown boy and three-quarters dead anyway. Move him, Conner, an he will be a fully dead boy." The doctor's use of first name to his military superior eased the situation. "What do you want, a death certificate now?" The doctor's sardonic question got him a surprising answer.

"That would help." It came out very casually, but Neddy noticed the captain's leg had stopped swinging.

There was a moment's silence as both men stared at each other. The parson had lost the thread of the exchange between the two men. Neddy stood listening, not sure if it was going good or bad for Watt. Just then, he was somehow more concerned about Watt reaching the end of the day still breathing than about his being hanged.

"Pass my bag over here, laddie." The doctor turned to Neddy, pointing to a medical bag that was never very far from his side but now was just by the door. Quickly Neddy did as he was told. The doctor took a sheath of paper from its innards, as if extracting a human organ. Unrolling it, he slid one onto the table.

"Have you got pen and ink, Reverend?" he asked, rolling his *Rs* excessively it seemed. "We may as well involve all in the conspiracy."

As he waited for the parson to rummage in a cupboard and return with an inkwell and a pen, the doctor turned to Neddy and asked,

"His name, this champion of yours?"

"Watt Tyler-Cope, Doctor."

"Good long name. Well," he took his watch from his vest pocket and flipped it open, "he died at eight o'clock in the morning, this day of our Lord, twenty-ninth day of December, in the year of eighteen-thirty-one. That is what the certificate will read."

"Let me have that when you have filled it out, Robertson." Galloway walked out of the vestry.

"In the meantime, Neddy, you can go outside, find a spade, and dig a hole to bury this, before it begins to stink beyond reason." The doctor pointed to a bloody bundle on the floor. For a moment Neddy looked lost. He had not noticed the unsightly wrapping on the ground before.

"It is his arm, boy. It won't grab you. Ask the parson where you can dig a hole "He didn't look up but continued writing.

"We can find space for it among ze graves, Neddy," the pastor said kindly. "I vill help you." He looked at the bundle and then at Neddy. "We should find a box or some zing to put it in." His eyes searched the vestry but saw nothing that would do.

Then Neddy suggested, "Di box we keep di prayer book in by the organ would be nice. Im han would fit in dat."

"No! No!" the pastor protested. Then he caught himself. "You are right, Neddy, ve can have another made. Yes, go get it. You are right."

Before Waldrich could change his mind, Neddy was through the door that led into the church. He pulled the box out from under the organist's small bench and piled the books neatly back under it. There would certainly be comments from Miss Foster when she saw it was missing. She would hold him responsible, and it gave him pleasure to think that, this time, she would be right.

"Don't shake the table," barked the doctor as Neddy placed the box beside the doctor's bag. He was writing in a ledger now. The death certificate, already written up, lay to one side of the book. Pointing at it with the butt end of the pen and then with the nib toward Watt's late arm, Robertson instructed Neddy, "When you are finished putting that piece of meat in the box, take that to Galloway. I mean the captain," he corrected himself.

"Yes, Doctor," Neddy said hesitantly, staring at the bundle on the floor.

"What's the matter, boy? It's only a dead part of your friend. Just lucky it isn't all of him. You may yet have to box that up later. Now, pick it up."

Neddy wavered.

"Lord God! I do not know what the youth is coming to in this age. You should have been at the battle of Culloden Moor, boy," the Doctor said. "Chopped arms and legs lay all aboot. Sassenach and good Scot mixed up in a slaughterhoose. Their kin couldna tell them apart. Not a modder could tell the ham from the pork." The chair scraped on the vestry floor as the doctor pushed it back to get up, very satisfied that his images had made the right impression. Even after Neddy's recent experiences, they made him shudder. Neddy closed his eyes briefly, trying to shut them out, at the same time doubting he would ever look at either the fresh or salted pig meat the same way again.

The doctor walked over, picked up the bundle containing the arm and handed it to Neddy. It was surprisingly stiff, heavy, and cold. The odor of decay stuck in his nostrils.

"You just going to stand there holding it for eternity, boy? Put it in the box," the doctor said, in a kindlier tone of voice.

Neddy was glad to do that. Once in the box, Neddy took a Bible from the cupboard shelf, as he had done the night before, and put it inside the arm coffin. Reverend Waldrich said nothing. He thought of objecting but stopped himself; if one of his parishioners thought it was necessary for a Bible to go into the box with the arm for burial, and that parishioner was more Christian for it, then God and Germany would provide more money for other Bibles. He and Neddy walked out to the graveyard with the box.

"Ask my vife to show you vhere ve keep ze gardening implements. Zose vill do for zis."

Leaving the reverend beside the small coffin, Neddy went to the parsonage to ask Mrs. Waldrich for pick and shovel. She pointed him to the shed at the back of the house, where he found the tools and hurriedly carried them back to the graveyard.

Galloway watched Neddy pile stones atop the little mound where he'd buried Watt's arm.

"Neddy," he called, "What are you doing?"

"Mi don't want dag to dig it up, sah."

"Do you think they will?"

"Don't know, sah. Me nah go chance it. Bess wouldn't, but dem nasty maaga dog that run about—mi don't trus dem. "He patted the big dog as she sat by him, watching the digging to bury that part of Watt that would never again aid in squeezing the breath out of her temporary master.

He went back to carefully placing one rock atop another, then built the tomb outward with the rocks side by side. You would have thought a whole body was under the pile, not just a boy's arm. That was a good impression to give. Galloway approved. "You are doing a good job, but don't overdo it, Neddy."

Knowing the Negro mentality and penchant for exaggeration, Watt Tyler-Cope's death would soon be spread far and wide, and his duppy would walk at night, for his death was violent, and he would be seeking revenge. Given time, he might even evolve into an eater of pickney. Galloway watched for a minute longer and then called to Neddy, "You don't have to worry. That's enough. Nothing will dig that out."

"Mi don't know bout dat, sah."

"I do," said Galloway. "England's left hand shaped this island and is buried deep inside her soul; nothing can dig that out. Unlike Ireland, now." His own hand went to the back of his neck to scratch. "England's hand," he went on, "had no deal in shaping it, and still we can't dig it out." He gave a snort.

"Don't understand you, Galloway," said Dr. Robertson, who had just come up and overheard the last part of the conversation. "You dislike the English, yet you faithfully serve them."

Galloway turned to look at the doctor and laughed. "Might have known you would sneak up like my conscience to remind me of that." His grin broadened. "But of all people, you should know, like the Scots, we love and hate our English mother at the same time. That is the strangeness of it." He his thumb in the direction of Neddy, still on his knees piling stone upon stone. "Now, this boy would like to know about his friend. Will he live?"

"He is a strong lad," was all the doctor said.

Galloway shook his head as if resigning himself to the noncommittal answer of the Scot. "Is that all we are going to get out of Scotland today?" he said, looking at Robertson. "She continues to weave her devious path among the universal scheme of things."

"Did you give the captain the death certificate, Neddy?" the doctor said, ignoring Galloway's last barb.

"No, sah."

"Well, give it to him now, and be done with it."

"Go on, Neddy," urged the reverend. He had done his bit at the graveside, saying a prayer over Watt's arm at the request of Neddy. It was highly inappropriate, but these were highly inappropriate times, and it seemed to him at the time an appropriate human action.

460

The March South

Taking the slightly crumpled certificate from his pocket, Neddy stopped his tomb building and walked over to the captain and handed it to him. Galloway took the sheet of paper and glanced at the doctor's indistinct writing and the signature. "Good," he said. Stuffing the certificate into his inner coat pocket, he walked toward the sergeant awaiting his orders. He stopped and looked back after a few yards. "Neddy," he called, "we have to go. Get your mule and ride behind the column." He pointed to where the soldiers were being drawn up into formation. "We have to rescue all the good-good white folk all the way up to Lapland from the savage beast let loose on the land. Isn't that right, Doctor?"

Robertson looked at his superior officer over the rims of his eyeglasses, not answering. Methodically, he took them from his nose and held them up to the light, studying their cleanliness. With a large bandana taken from his inner coat pocket, he carefully wiped each lens before returning them to his face. When they were comfortably positioned, he followed Galloway, who had left him completing his task.

"We march south up the hills to St. Elizabeth border, Doctor. They are mi orders," Galloway said.

Taking one last look at his effort, Neddy wondered if more of Watt would be under there by the time he got back. Then Neddy did as he was told. Calling to Bess, he went to say good-bye to Mrs. Waldrich and have one last look at his friend.

The patient looked about the same. His bandages had been changed again. More bloody bandages waited to be taken away for washing. Mrs. Waldrich was taking good care of him; Neddy could see she was Watt's best chance of survival. He wished he could talk to him, but that was impossible. The labored breathing and the occasional rattle of air fighting its way past the accumulated scum deep in Watt's throat made that obvious. Then Watt began to cough and splutter. Neddy rushed to support him. Stuff came out of his mouth and dribbled down his chin. Taking a small rag from beside the basin, Neddy wet it and wiped the mucus away. For a moment, the blue eyes flickered open and stared at him blankly, then they closed

When Conchie Blows

again. Making sure he was propped securely by three pillows, Neddy left the room, taking one last look at Watt on the bed.

Mrs. Waldrich gave him a bundle of food for himself and a larger one for Bess. "Ze hund vill need more zan you. She does not ride on ze mule." It was her fun. She tittered in a girlish manner while walking over to the table to pick up a third package, which she handed to Neddy. It was neatly rolled in paper, tied with red ribbon. It was soft to his finger's pressure.

"You vill never be able to wear dis again, unless your mudder can get out zee stains," she said. "But you should keep it as a reminder." Her head bobbed up and down with her conclusion. "Ze von you vear is yours to keep. It is old, and my husband vill never use it again." To Neddy's surprise Mrs. Waldrich hugged him. It was a gentle, affectionate squeeze, then she pushed him away and, with both hands resting on his shoulders, looked sternly into his eyes and gave her orders. "You travel safely and get right back to your mudder. She vill vant to know you are safe." Just then her husband came in and added his stricture to his wife's: "You obey her now, Neddy. I have to!" There was a gentle smile on his face when he said that, and it got a nervous laugh from his wife.

Neddy stopped at the door and turned back to the couple. "Watt ave an auntie in Montego Bay, Miss Hannah Cope. She keeps a school."

"I know of ze lady," Reverend Waldrich said, nodding at the same time. "Ve vill tell her. Zank you, Neddy."

All done, Neddy, followed by the ever-faithful Bess, went out to saddle the mule. Then they were on their way. Not long after leaving the church precinct, he caught up with the slow-moving column and pulled the mule in, to avoid overrunning the back ranks. As the mule dropped into a slow walk, Neddy wished they were headed in the other direction, toward Montego Bay and the coast. Sadness filled him. But his apprehension soon passed, and a certain amount of resignation to their slow pace and direction set in.

Passing the shortcut across Worcester bottom to Retirement tempted him to sneak off that way. Johns Hall and all those turns in the road to Kensington would be cut out. At least two miles would be saved. Bess, he thought, would be better going that way. She had moved off the road now, and was sticking to the grass at the side. He searched for an excuse to desert the column and actually pulled the reins over in the right direction toward the pathway. The mule moved to obey and then found the order countermanded by its bit. It straightened, continuing as before, following the slow beat of the marching feet in front. Neddy realized the captain would not be pleased if he took off without permission. That action could jeopardize Watt, if he survived.

On the corner down from Worcester gate, they passed under the duppy tree on the left. At that time of the day the big cotton, with its old man beard moss stuck to its heavy branches, didn't look so frightening. Yet his eyes roamed around its canopy, looking for what he didn't know. There was no strange fruit to see. Under it, without a glance upward, the regular soldiers marched, paying no attention, not even to admire its size and vast spread of branches. A tree was a tree to them. But the local militia men paid it mind. Neddy noticed some of them did as he had, looking up and around, a sign that sensible men were in the column.

Soon they crossed the bridge over the river and halted by Worcester gate. A detail was sent in to check on conditions there. It soon returned, and the corporal reported, "Burned-out buildings and no white people there, sir." Galloway returned the man's salute. His acknowledgement set the sergeant off screaming orders, at which the men fell back in to column, and off they marched. They could have saved time had they asked him, thought Neddy, as he jerked into motion behind the troops.

Four men took point duty. Their captain was taking no chances of an ambush. Galloway on horseback headed the column. His lieutenant fell to the rear to take over should they fall into a trap and find themselves attacked from behind.

As they moved higher into the hills, extra precautions had to be taken. They may as well begin now. Each step moved them further away from support stationed on the coast and in Montego Bay. Reinforcements would take some time to bring up, if they became cut off. No one had any idea what lay ahead—what forces opposed them? Talk of how strong the slaves were came with every wave of panicking white planters coming into the relative safety of Montego Bay with their families. Most sensible men thought them exaggerated, but their talk added to the confusion.

It was amazing how many proprietors deserted their estates and plantations. Before, in other rebellions, they would have stayed, defending what they had. No damned Negro was going to take away their chance to enjoy wealth and power at home in England. But not this time. Fear ruled. Fermented in their imagination was thirty years of the telling—over and over again—of the tale of Santo Domingo. Reality and mythology had become mingled; all they knew was that a gem of the Indies had become a black debacle.

To calm the crowd, General Cotton, the officer on his way from Kingston station to take charge of the situation, had requested reinforcements be sent. In the meantime, he ordered troops to sweep south up to Lapland and bring any whites found alive back to the Bay area. At the same time, Cotton ordered troops to march east along the coast toward Falmouth and west to Lucea. Those moving west were ordered to turn south at the Hanover border and move inland, parallel to the Great River. Strategically, these were to give Galloway's company support, should it be required.

One major problem with this plan was the countryside between Galloway's route and the troops ordered west and then south for his support. Hills and dense bush interspersed with plantation stood between them. Knowing the terrain well, Galloway was well aware he was, for all intents and purposes, cut off and on his own. He would move slowly, with points out and rear guard watching their back. At Maroon Town he would pick up the soldiers stationed at that post, assuming they had not been wiped out, and move on. To hear tell, they were up against a huge slave army. Against those odds a platoon of men stood no chance, even if they were regulars.

Not far back in the collective memory of Jamaica, along with Santo Domingo, were the Maroon Wars. A few blacks had put even British regulars in desperate situations for much of that show. They gave up only when their food grounds were found and ordered burned. In the end, any armed slave became, in the white imagination, a regiment of ferocious warriors intent on slaughter. Most of this mythology was nonsense in Galloway's book, but he knew many a "dashing" officer had thrown his and the lives of his men away when he had tossed caution out the military haversack. He was not about to make such a mistake.

They moved up from Worcester to Johns Hall. Just outside the square, the column halted. Six regulars went in to check if there was any danger. That did not take long; soon they were back, reporting all was clear. Galloway gave the order, and the column moved forward into the village square.

As the men fell out, Galloway pointed to Tinka's shop and ordered the sergeant to have a man check the building. The bench outside where drinkers sat, the captain noticed, was broken. Alongside its shattered pieces were a couple of enamel mugs dashed down on the ground. Those, he knew, would not have been carelessly tossed away by the owner of the establishment.

A soldier moved forward and began banging on the door with the butt of his musket. The assault brought nothing out, other than a whining yelp from Tinka's mongrel. He banged again, and still there was no human response. He looked for further orders to the sergeant, who looked to the captain with an inquiring expression on his face.

"Again, Sergeant." Not waiting for confirmation from the sergeant, the soldier set to with more vigor. A couple of good hits, and the wood cracked in the center.

"What you buss mi door down for?" came a desperate cry from behind the now mutilated wood panel. "Leave mi tings alone. Go bout your business." There was fright and desperation in the voice, which was enough to stop the soldier from completely shattering the wood.

"That's enough, Mathews. Fall out," the sergeant said.

"Tinka, come out here," Galloway said. Nothing happened. "Get out here Tinka, or I will have the men tear it down." That threat was enough to move Tinka. Opening the door was a problem at first, as it had become wedged in the frame.

"Mathews, push from this side," the sergeant said. Eventually they were able to move it enough for Tinka to emerge.

Like an animal chased from its den, he seemed bemused. The sudden light made his eyes blink, and he rubbed them to help them adjust. His face was sour, but as he became accustomed to the daylight his eyes shifted back and forth under their brows with suspicion. He looked over his shoulders to see if the soldiers were behind him as well.

"Why you buss down mi door, Massa Galloway? Mi na do notting to you."

"We know that, Tinka." There was a tinge of exasperation in Galloway's voice. "I noticed you had unwelcome visitors. We were just making sure you hadn't gone the same way." Galloway pointed to the broken bench.

"No, sah. Some rude boye come drunk—but mi chase dem," Tinka said, brightening up.

"When?"

"After dem bun down Worcester."

A door creaked open across the street, and a woman stuck her head out. On the upstairs floor of the next house, a window shutter half-opened, and more people looked down at them. They kept back behind the half-open shutter. A soldier quickly pointed his musket up, ready to fire, in case it was a hostile slave. "Lower your weapon, man," the sergeant said.

The woman at the door recognized Dr. Robertson and ran over to him. There was a brief exchange of words, and Robertson followed her into the house.

"Sergeant," called Galloway. "Send a corporal and a couple of men to find out if any of these people want to come with us." He indicated the houses with a sweep of his riding whip. For an instant the sergeant hesitated. Galloway realized that this was because they were not white. And from the look on his officer's face, it was clear to the NCO his thoughts were better kept unsaid.

"They are free people and deserve our protection Sergeant—now get on with it, man." At the order, the sergeant snapped to attention, responding with the usual, "Sha."

Galloway turned back to Tinka. "What have you heard from up top?"

"Notting, sah."

"Come on, Tinka, nothing happens within twenty miles of this place that you don't know about. Don't trifle with me," said

The March South

Galloway—the captain, not the overseer. Tinka understood the difference and promptly became compliant.

"Mi hear…" and he began listing all the places that had gone up in flames. Galloway listened unmoved, as if he knew already. Truth was, he expected all of it. There were no surprises. At the mention of Newman Hall, he stopped Tinka and began to probe for details. His face took on a strained look when the shopkeeper could tell him little other than that the buildings had been burned.

"You must be able to tell me more, Tinka?" Galloway said, as the riding whip tapped rapidly against his boot. He was leaning forward toward the shopkeeper, staring hard at the man.

"No, Massa Galloway!" the pathetic shopkeeper said. "Only… it not fi your people dat bun down di buildings. Dem is still on di estate a wait for you to come back." It was the good news Galloway wanted to hear. He stepped back from Tinka. With the pressure off, Tinka added, "Most of di troublemakers come from Kensington, wid a man dem call Colonel Lawrence."

"Edward Lawrence, the carpenter?" gasped the astonished Captain in disbelief. At hearing his father's name, Neddy, who had been listening, felt his heart jump into his mouth and pound in his ears.

The shopkeeper almost shouted at the captain, "No, sah! No, no, sah! Not im! Di colonel one his anodder Lawrence. Not Mass Edward di carpenter. Di one dem call di colonel come from Providence estate, mi hear." Even after letting his breath out with relief at Tinka's denial, Neddy was still trembling with fear. Tinka paused before starting to add, "Now, dat is sad ting—"

"Was anyone hurt or killed at Newman Hall?" Galloway cut him off. Those listening could hear the anxiety his voice.

"Mi don't know dat, Massa. Not like on Kensington—"

"Well, I suppose if you don't know, that is a good sign," Galloway cut him off again. "Is there other news I should know about?"

Tinka smirked. "Mi hear dem grab two bad boye dat a rape and tief in a di settlement an ang dem up. Dem chop dem ting off fus, an mek dem eat it before dey ang." Tinka screeched with glee.

When Conchie Blows

"Who did that?" demanded Galloway, revulsion clearly marring his features.

"Don't know dat one, Busha. Mus a some of di nasty white niggers who lives up dey so."

Standing by, listening to all that went on, Neddy could guess who did the hanging. He secretly hoped it was Mungo and his friends who swung. Almost as the thought passed, he had a second one. He didn't want them dead. Hanging meant death, and he regretted wishing it was them. He shuddered at the realization of their last meal.

"Mi hear also dat plenty men gather back a Mocho, an more coming all di time. Dat Lawrence man giving di orders, wid anoder one dem call Colonel Gardener, mi tink. Mi na know where dat one come from."

"My, my, they seem to have a regiment of colonels," Galloway said, still able to find humor in the situation. He thanked Tinka for the information before walking to where he had left a soldier holding his mount.

Tinka's news was far from good. If it was true, and the slave officers knew their business, Galloway and his company could find themselves outnumbered and perhaps outgunned, trapped between Lapland and Montego Bay. He began to think he might be forced to cross into St. Elizabeth or Westmoreland and join up with the militia there. That would put him further away from the main force in Montego Bay and supplies. Privation, his men could take, but women and children—especially these pampered Creoles—were questionable. Their lackadaisical, high-pitched whining always irritated him. What a spoiled crew they were: black, brown, or white, it made no difference; all of them were cast in the same mold. A slight shudder passed over him as he mounted. It disappeared by the time his foot found the stirrup on the other side of the saddle.

He didn't like the prospects at all. As he weighed his alternatives, his left hand resting on the saddlebow, Galloway twisted to scan the little square. Was he obeying his orders and gathering the planter families in, or seeking out the enemy and attacking them? Without even pausing, he dismissed the latter possibility. Half his troops were regulars, and the other half militia made up of rich planter and

The March South

merchant types who thought their militia duty a sporting affair. He smiled when he remembered the fool who appeared on parade without flint in the lock of his musket. When berated and threatened with a fine by his lieutenant, he had answered, "Fine away, fine away, my good chap. I can pay it. "With that attitude in the ranks, attack would not be his first option.

Obeying his orders was Galloway's only choice. He knew by the time they reached Lapland, his column would have grown to two or three times what it was at that moment. All the extras would be civilians, amounting to nothing more than baggage. Many armies were defeated because their camp followers weighed them down. They had to divert troops to defend it. The battle of Tours was an example, and it changed the course of history. We would all be Muslims now, had the Arabs let the Franks take their loot. Here, his force would be doing only that—defending the camp followers.

His thoughts were interrupted by the sergeant reporting, "These people in the village, Sha, don't wants to join us, Sha. They are afraid of thieves, Sha."

Next, Doctor Robertson returned. "Her daughter has a fever. Nothing much to be done for her. Gave the mother some cinchona bark physic to use, in case it is malaria. Pretty little girl," he said while climbing aboard his horse. Anyone watching his awkward effort at getting into the saddle would have known the doctor was more at home in a trap than on the back of a horse. Finally, he settled in with a grunt, after Tinka gave him a helping shove from his rear. Seeing that he was ready, Galloway mounted and gave the order to move forward.

As he rode contemplating the prospects, Galloway's thoughts turned to Shakespeare. Henry V and the battle of Agincourt. The horse's hooves on the gravel recalled the French knights charging to slaughter the English boys. Henry had left them vulnerable by not defending his baggage train. Instead, he slit his prisoners' throats to forestall trouble at his rear and concentrated on defeating an army ten times larger than his own. A glorious or inglorious moment in English history, depending on which troubadour sang the tale. Common French prisoners and English lads did not matter; only chivalry mattered.

Galloway resolved to defend his baggage train. Those were his orders anyway. As an attacking force, his men would be compromised by some of the militia who were already out of step at the rear, judging from the orders screamed by the sergeant. Threats of dire retribution rang in their ears. Not for one instant would he turn to look at the local rabble in the ranks. If he did, some sort of discipline would have to be handed out. This was not the time to be a martinet.

The chance of defeating a larger force, even if they were an undisciplined rabble, would be nigh on impossible. Should there be an attack, his only hope would be if there were enough men among the women in the column to bolster his numbers. *Women, children, and their belongings.* His head went back and his eyebrows lifted and fell. The sky was blue and cloudless, and he wished to be out of uniform and into cooler cotton clothing. *Why do women put so much stock in things?* he wondered, and gave his horse a gentle touch with the spurs, setting a snappy pace for the column.

Soldiers on point duty were ordered out to the rear and front as the company marched out of the village. As they rounded each corner of the winding road, the tempo quickened. Militiamen grumbled at the pace, the heat, and the steepness of the road. Regulars marched on, accustomed to the measure. From their faces sweat trickled under the stiff uniform collars. Dark patches soon widened around the armpits of the red wool tunics they wore as their body water soaked through. Those who had served in India understood this to be a good cooling agent and learned not to remove their jackets until they had dried out. Their women would wash away the white salt marks it left, making them ready for the next march.

Neddy, mounted on his mule, suffered none of this. Bess just kept going beside him. Every now and then she would stop at one of the streams that tumbled out of the hillside, refresh herself, then catch up to her charge. Neddy guessed the reason for the quick march. Newman Hall was the next stop, and Galloway was in a hurry to get there.

Even a few large boulders in the road, placed just around corners, did not slow them. Rather than have them removed and rolled into the gully, Galloway ordered the troops to skirt them. At one large tree lying across the road the foot soldiers were made to climb over, while

The March South

mounted men rode into the bush and around the log. Luckily there were no snipers hiding there. Only the civilians who had begun to follow the soldiers from just past Johns Hall complained. The military quick-marched on, ignoring them.

After those encounters, Neddy heard Galloway instruct the sergeant that at these barriers a point man was to stay and watch, while the other came back to warn the main force. They should not just carry on. Obviously these obstacles were meant to slow them. Even more obvious, those who laid them knew they were coming. All they had to do was wait for the soldiers on point to pass, kill them silently, and then let the main troop march into an ambush. So far it had not happened.

"The luck of the Irish," the doctor pointed out to Galloway, as if he were diagnosing an illness. Galloway just laughed.

At last Newman Hall entrance came up on the left. Galloway ordered that the gateway be righted up, as if it had been purposely left open. At least it looked less derelict as they marched through. He could see that some had tried to save the sugar works and still house. Half the roof was gone, and the smell of wet ashes filled the air. On the hill the Great House was in shambles. Windows were broken, and shutters hung from their hinges, much as they had found the gate. Stuff from inside was strewn about in the yard. It had been well picked over. What was left was of no use to the raiders.

The house had mostly survived. It had been torched, but the fire must have gone out by itself, for there was no sign of an attempted rescue. It was an ugly building anyway, rarely used by its absentee owners. All the slave huts were intact, and to Galloway's evident relief, so was the overseer's place. He called a halt and ordered the sergeant to fall the men out.

No sooner had he gotten to the bottom of the steps leading to the front door than it opened. There was a shriek of joy from just inside. Before his mother could stop him, Timmy came hurtling down the stairs to be picked up and held high by Galloway.

On entering his room, an unfamiliar sight met him. His bookshelves and his other belongings were gone. On the floor of the main piazza, the special bookcases he'd had made lay on their backs, locked. Alongside them stood his traveling trunks. They must hold his clothes, plate, and objects he was accustomed to seeing on display. An amused look transformed the puzzled expression when he noticed both fowling pieces and pistols laid out side by side on the table, pointing at the door.

"What were you going to do with those, Lucy?" he asked. Before she could answer, Badalia butted in, "Shoot any of dem dat dare come trough di door. What you tink we going do wid dem, Massa?" she said defiantly. A smile lit up his features when he turned on the ever-watchful Badalia and asked skeptically, "I suppose you loaded them?" Her neck arched and both eyebrows shot upward as if to say, *dat is man's work*. But Badalia explained, "Mi, sah, no, sah. Mi don't know ow to do dat, but ol John knows, an im do it for us. Den im show us how to do it."

That surprised Galloway. "Where is he?"

"Im downstairs, waiting for dem nasty niggers to a come; den im shoot fus and we shoot dem second."

"Good Lord!" thought Galloway out aloud. "You had it all planned out like a military operation."

"Dem naygar man know dem is in trouble hif en dem come ya so. Dem know better dan to try." There was a distinct note of pride in her voice. Her mistress stood silently by and let the ever-faithful Badalia explain their plan of action.

"What is all this, then?" Galloway pointed to the bookcases and the trunks.

"You tink Miss Lucy going let any ting appen to your tings?" Badalia said.

"Miss Lucy and me an John pack up all your tings, so we can get dem out of ya quick-quick hif dem set di place a fire. But dem know better an leave us alone."

Galloway walked over to Lucy, still holding the boy, and put his free arm around her, kissing her on the forehead: "You are a true woman," he said. "No longer a girl, but full grown. That's what a man wants and I need. Lucy, we will marry and be gone from this place." It was a statement without passion, only certainty.

The March South

It had come at last and at an unexpected time. Lucy could hardly breathe. Her arms came around his waist, and she rested her trembling head against his chest, half expecting to be eased away. Instead, he put Tim on the ground and hugged her to him. Badalia watched, well pleased that all her predictions were coming true.

The striking of the clock brought them all back from the interlude. Galloway looked around and became all orders and business.

"Badalia, get John up here. Lucy, pack your and the boy's things. We are leaving here. Hurry now, we have not much time. We have to be at Maroon Town before night falls."

Lucy said proudly, "But we are all packed, ready to go."

Galloway smiled and nodded his approval. He was aware she had caught herself before ending the sentence with the traditional abasement.

"We cannot take all this now. They are too heavy. We will come back for them when all this is over," he assured her. "Pack a box with a few things for yourself and the boy. Quick now, hurry, my dear."

"What bout mi, sah? Where Miss Lucy goes, mi fi go." It was Badalia standing right behind him, and the tone of her voice wasn't asking, it was telling. Galloway had no option but to acquiesce.

"All right come, come, come. But get John first," he insisted. While the women began to bustle about, Galloway knelt and opened the bookcases. His finger ran over the titles, searching. At Shakespeare, he extracted the volume. Dean Swift was next to come out. Edmund Spencer and Alexander Pope followed. He was about to close the case back up when Timmy, standing beside his kneeling figure, pointed at the books on the floor and asked, "Is *My Man Friday* there, too?"

Slowly Galloway's head turned to face the boy, a smile of satisfaction on his lips. "No, sor, but he soon will be." He opened up the other case and began to search for Defoe. "Aha! Here is your *Man Friday*." Handing the book to Tim, he said, "Since this is your book, keep it safely till we get a chance to read together. Now, go and ask your mother to pack it for you." The youngster scampered off, holding the treasure with both hands to his chest.

Next Galloway picked up the guns, carefully inspecting each in turn. As he unloaded them, he couldn't help chuckling. One of the fowling pieces had too much powder stuffed down its barrels and the other too little. They couldn't have been fired anyway, because the caps had not been inserted for the hammers to hit. But it was a brave effort, and he approved. He remembered his first wife would have been the same way. Only she would have known about the caps. Lucy would be taught, just as *herself* had been.

Looking at the portrait still on the wall, he said softly, "There will never be another like you, but you will understand, my dear, there are others who need me, as I need them." As he talked to his late wife, he thought it strange they had not attempted to take the portrait down and pack it. Then he remembered Lucy's trepidation at coming into the room. Badalia, who protected her at every corner, would leave the portrait where it was. In all likelihood, she hoped it would burn if the house caught fire. That would forever cut his connection with the past.

Unloading the pistols was quite different. They were flints and could have been fired. Each one had been carefully loaded and primed. Whoever got them ready knew what was what. It could only have been John. If his stable man knew how to load pistols this expertly, then the same skill must be out there among his opposition in the hills. Some plantations had a slave regularly hunting birds with a fowling piece for the dinner table of the Great House. All it would take was one man to teach them about firearms, and, even undisciplined, their numbers and firepower could overwhelm his force.

Galloway only hoped that, if push came to shove, those damned militiamen would stand and obey orders. If he could hold them in a square to fire and load, rank by rank, then they would do well enough. They were brave, but he suspected they would treat it like a sporting event and shoot as if firing at birds. Their fusillade would be ragged and ineffectual. His regulars would stand and fire when ordered, but part-time soldiers? "Questionable, questionable," he muttered under his breath.

John interrupted by tapping gently on the doorpost and coughing. "You sen for mi, Massa?"

"Yes, John. Get the big trap ready for Miss Lucy, Massa Tim, and Badalia."

"Yes, sah."

"Do you know someone you can trust to stay in here and watch the place while we are gone?"

"Yes, Busha. Mi wife, di cook, an mi can do it. Billy di cook-man, im good too."

"Right, get them, and get a few men to move these boxes into the cellar. They should be safe there if the house gets burned down. It is all cut stone."

"Dem not going bun di house, sah. Not wid mi an di others in ya. Anyhow, Busha, dem gone to di ills. Dem na come back."

"That's good to hear; now go."

As he reached the door to carry out his orders, Galloway called, "John, who taught you to load pistols?" A broad grin spread all over John's face. The gap between his front teeth was clearly visible, and two halfway back in the lower jaw were missing.

"You, Massa," he answered proudly.

"Me!"

"Yes, sah, Mi na watch you load dem up one day."

"Oh!" Galloway said. He watched John's back disappear through the door. It was only a matter of time before these people, or their descendants, took over and ruled Jamaica. He sighed, hoping that in their freedom the island would not degenerate into barbarism, but he was skeptical. Too often, it seemed, humanity took that path. It was freedom's easy way. Inevitably it ended in servitude all over again.

The men formed up again in the front yard. Badalia heaved her body onto the driver's seat of the trap. Miss Lucy and Tim sat on the other seat across from her. When they were settled, and Badalia had grumbled at the few things they brought with them, she turned and looked at Neddy standing beside them.

"Ow come you not wid your modder an fader, boye?"

"Mi modder sen me to Mass William, Miss Badalia."

"Which one dat?" Badalia asked.

"Mass William Vernon an Miss Rachel—at Mount Apfel," Neddy said, with a frown that said *Is there any other?*

"Don't mek up your face at mi, boye. Mi will give you one lick. Why you not wid dem now?" Badalia said.

Her interrogation made him defensive. "Mi had business to do for Mass William."

Badalia detected the defiance in his voice. "An I suppose some ting fi yoself? What it was? Mine you modder don box you—you know?" She went into a loud cackle. Blood rushed to his cheeks with that reminder of his mother's slap. In the corner of his eye, a tear squeezed out. The back of his hand quickly wiped it dry.

During their banter, Galloway rode up. Only Miss Lucy and Timmy noticed him.

"Don't be too hard on the boy, Badalia, he is a good soldier," Galloway said, laughing.

"No, sah. Mi jus keeping im straight," Badalia said, with a heave of her bosom.

"Are you people settled? Follow behind."

Just as Galloway turned to ride back to the head of the column, Neddy stopped him. "Sah, sah." The captain looked at him. "When we get to di road split, can mi go to Kensington? Mi will come back to Maroon Town after mi fine out bout mi mam and da?"

"Yes, Neddy. We will not wait on you tomorrow, if you are not back by then. You understand, boy?" Neddy nodded his agreement, and Galloway rode off.

As they passed through the gates, they were met by an old couple in a wagon piled high with their most precious belongings. They had come over from Spring Mount and declared they felt much safer with the soldiers about them. They seemed genuinely grateful to be in the column. The old man complained loudly about losing his life's work because of damned Baptists. His wife put up with it for a while and then ordered he be silent. They would return and rebuild. It would not be the first time. He fell silent for a little, but by the time they had covered a mile, he was back to muttering.

As they closed in on Kensington, they had transformed into a cavalcade. Neddy had never realized that so many white people lived so close about! Never before had they been gathered in like this. To him, seeing them one-one among slaves, they appeared like the occasional white bean soaking along with black beans in a bowl to be cooked later.

The March South

Each mile from Friendship, more joined the procession. They seemed to materialize from thin air. Carriages, wagons, mounted horsemen, mules, and donkeys with hampers full of worldly possessions merged together to form an ever-longer procession. Many he knew by sight. Some even recognized him and asked that he tell his father that they had work for him the moment the troubles were over. One or two of the poor young ones came across to talk fishing and catching birds. The way they carried on about his recreation, it dawned on him that this was an important activity to feed them and help out their families; it meant the difference between eating and not eating meat—another distinction between poor and rich whites. As they moved along, he amused himself by observing them more closely.

First, there was a clear divide between the white people. Those who walked barefooted, wearing patched, threadbare clothes, hung back, almost avoiding contact with the lowly bookkeepers and their overseers. These in turn followed behind the proprietors of estates and pens, with a few faithful slaves carrying boxes on their heads or children perched on their shoulders.

Even among the rich and powerful, he detected slight differences. Massa Pournelle was standoffish to Massa Grant, who was a nice man to his father. It didn't make sense, now that they were all in the same predicament, burned out and running for their lives. Yet, seemed to make no difference; they still had time for the niceties of difference. Massa Pournelle, Neddy knew, owned two and three estates, while the others had more modest properties.

It was like a new world opening up in front of him. Only once before, when he and the captain went to Lapland, had he seen so many white people together. What made the difference was that this time, these whites weren't like each other. Just looking at them, you could tell. Women with their sweetsop complexions traveled next to the brown, cracked, scrawny ones who toiled for husbands who savaged them, like bulls kept to service cows.

Neddy next studied those of color in the group. To his astonishment, he saw the same pattern in them as among the whites. Although not certain, their dividing lines seemed based on skin tone and general looks rather than wealth. The whiter they were, the more prestige they took onto themselves and separated away from the mulattoes and quadroons. Oddly, many coloreds seemed able to mingle with the whites freely. Some he knew must have a family connection, because they were called by the same last names.

They behaved just like his own free people, he realized. There were the same distinctions between them. His mother always insisted that he not play with this child or that child. He even remembered her scolding him severely for disobeying her orders. Only now did he truly understand. All his life his mother made sure he mixed only with whom she defined as the right people. Just like the white people did in front of him. It was very fascinating and kept his thoughts occupied and away from boredom. At Kensington, he came back to his business.

"Miss Lucy," he called. "Mi going leave you here. Mi will ketch up wid you."

"You tek care now," Badalia said, slapping the reins on the mule's haunches to continue up the road. As they moved, the stubborn little jenny tied at the back of the trap resisted. Her hooves dug in, and her neck stretched trying to break away. Her halter was about to slip over her floppy ears when Timmy called to her, "Come on! Stop that, Betsy!" At the sound of her master's voice, she gave up the struggle and trotted behind the trap.

By what was left standing of Kensington gateposts, Neddy watched the long tail of civilians pass him by. When the last one turned the corner and disappeared, he called to Bess and continued into Kensington. All was not well with his home. From as far down as the gate, the telltale remnants of loot were tossed about. Empty rum bottles and broken casks were strewn by the way. There was even a bolt of cloth that must have fallen from a thief's bundle. Above, John Crow circled. Cows trapped in the field next to the Kensington entrance lowed for water. No one had been there to let them out to drink at the pond. Neddy moved his mule to the fence, where he got down and slid the bars of the gate, one by one, across to leave an opening. The cows would find their way to water.

The March South

Mounting again, he moved on up the driveway. Nothing seemed right. That was confirmed by the now-familiar sight of burned buildings. As he rounded the corner, he saw that the overseer's house, where Massa Morris lived, and the Great House, where the other Morris and his family lived, were both gone. Their charred walls were the only reminders of their recent existence. Wisps of smoke rose from the smoldering Great House ruins.

Neddy continued through the yard. Bloated carcasses of two dead donkeys and a mule were being stripped by John Crow. They had already picked clean two sheep. It was the gathering of the harbingers of death. There must have been over a hundred in that yard. Their stink, along with that of their meal, made him turn away, holding his breath. Bess made a run at the nearest feast, barking, sending some vultures into flight, but they were soon back again to gorge. More stayed than flew. Not even the great dog was going to drive them off so tasty a meal.

He moved on through the ashes of the slave quarters, not daring to look up to where his house should be. Instinctively he knew it could not have survived, but fear and hope drove him to kick the sides of the mule into its uncomfortable fastest gait. At the end of the burned-out quarters, he pulled the mule to a stop. Taking a deep breath of that stinking air, he looked at the hill and saw his worst fears had been realized. A charred, unrecognizable ruin occupied the space where once stood the house his father built for Quashiba his wife, and where Neddy first drew breath. Tears streamed down his face as he urged the mule up the small hill.

Leaping off the mule, he ran onto the little verandah. As he stepped on what was left, his foot crashed through the half-burned boards. The accident brought him up sharply. He extracted himself with care but still managed to scrape his shin as he crawled back out of the ruin. He stood staring at the burned walls and rafters that had somehow stayed in place as the flames took all others around them. Ten, twenty minutes must have passed. Time was meaningless. When his tears had stopped, he felt lost and empty, adrift in unknown water. His safe harbor was gone and, with it, his parents.

"Mama, Dada…" he screamed. "Where you dey?"

God must have heard his fright, for a voice to his right said, "You modder over wid Miss Dodd, an you fader buried over by di Massa Fowler grave yard."

At first, the voice came to him distantly and unreal. A woman holding a small child in the crook of her arm was standing beside him. He did not recognize her, but she must belong to Kensington if he knew his mother and father. She wasn't making sense, so he asked, "What you sey again?"

"You modder over wid Miss Dodd," she repeated. Then, after looking at him for a good long moment, she said, "She bury you fader over dere, after di soldiers come an shoot im den bun di house."

"Di soldier shoot mi fader!" Neddy cried out in disbelief, holding an outburst in check. He was not going to scream or yell at this foolish woman. She must be wrong. Why would the soldiers do such a thing?

Watching his face, the woman knew he needed more explanation from her. Shifting the child in her arms, she said, "Dem come here an bun what was left of di hut dem, den dem shoots up di place. One off dem no-good liars tell dem, fi yu fader is Colonel Lawrence. An before you know what appen, dem shoot im, bun down di house, an den find out dem wrong, after Massa David, di little half-dead bookkeeper, tell dem dey wrong."

The woman was still talking when Neddy leapt on to the mule's back. They headed down the hill at full gallop, forcing some of the feeding vultures to take off again as he rode through them to the back of the Great House; the old mule continued to respond to his urging across the kitchen garden, then an open stretch to the walled plot where the Fowlers were buried. Bess was with him all the way in his mad chase and stopped panting when he pulled the mule to a violent stop.

As he stood staring at the new mound of earth, just outside the iron railings of the family burial patch, Bess rubbed her nose against his dangling hand. This gave him some reassuring comfort, and he walked over and looked at the new grave. Standing there, even with this evidence, it was difficult to believe what the woman had said. There must be some mistake. This grave had to be a Morris. This could not be his father. Convinced that this was so, Neddy set off at a jogging pace for Miss Dodd, where all would be set right.

She didn't move from the chair when he entered the room but sat staring at him. It was as if Quashiba were unsure her son was really there, standing in front of her. To confirm what her eyes were telling her, her hands reached out and held him by the shoulders and brought him closer in so she could get a better look. The palm of her open hand rested on the cheek that it had slapped, and her thumb wiped away an imaginary speck of dirt lodged just under his eye. Then both her arms enveloped him, pressing his body to hers, as if trying to make it part of her again. And for the first time in his life, with her head pressed on his chest, Neddy heard his mother sob. She began trembling gently as the tears flowed. Then cries of anguish shook her body like waves pounding the shore. They subsided, her body rocked with grief against him. In this way she related all her love and loss to her son, and he knew his father was dead.

Chapter 16

Bekah

Neddy's head drooped toward his chest, full in the knowledge that they were in the depth of night, the darkest hour of their day. Morning was on its way, he told himself, but there was no glimmer of it yet in the eastern sky. Every now and again, he looked up for its flash, only to look down again. Anything! Oh, anything to relieve the melancholy weighing down upon his soul. But nothing brightened the gloom, above or inside him. Only a starless void overhead, and around them nameless sounds as they trudged through the early hours toward Maroon Town.

Day would come again, he was sure of that. His mind told him so. Always something compensated for the feeling and foulness occupying his mouth and stomach. It had to! Never before, he hoped never again, would he taste such despondency. He felt empty, as if purged by the devil's mixture of sulfur. Compared to how he felt, even a dreaded dose of castor oil would have been welcome at that time—if its nasty taste would take away this bitterness. Then he could try and relieve the thick oiliness and smell with an orange.

If only it could have been that easy. His mother always gave him an orange to eat after she had spooned the oil down his throat while at the same time holding his nose. He would gag. At that, she would squeeze his nose even harder, and the hurt would temporarily take away the taste of that awful, inhumane ooze she had boiled out of that evil castor oil pod. Had he been allowed, along with all the other children who suffered the dreaded dose, all castor oil trees would have been destroyed, just as the planters had wiped out the poisonous manchineel tree, which blistered flesh with the touch of its sap, and slaves used as a poison to be rid of their masters.

Till now, Neddy had never thought there could have been a taste, a revulsion, to surpass the horror of the purgative oil. Even now his stomach surged at the thought of it. Bravely he fought it back, determined not to disgorge what little was left in him onto the road.

Ahead of him, the hunched shape of his mother sat on the mule. As he walked behind, leading his father's mule along, carrying what little she had saved from their home, he wondered if his mother was aware of him. Certainly, if she looked back to check, he would be part of that gloom. Picking him out would be as difficult to her as it was to see her riding up in front. Even the mule was only vaguely there and, like Bess, running beside him, told of itself by sound rather than sight. Occasionally though, with Bess, there would be a slight relief to the blackness as the white canvas boots his mother had made and tied so carefully on the dog's feet showed through the negritude.

She had spent most of the evening making them for the dog: "Dem is to protect her feet," she said. "Mass William doesn't want any lame dog in im yard."

The task kept her occupied and brought her a small relief. It helped her keep a balance. Neddy realized, in the night, that she fought hard against being drawn down into the void that opens when that to which life and love are pinioned falls away and is lost to the active world.

Using Miss Dodd's scissors, she clipped and snipped the canvas into oblong strips. Each movement, each snip and clip, was deliberate. Carefully the edges were evened off. When satisfied with her efforts, she placed one on top of the other to see if they were exact. The ones for the back paws were slightly wider than those for Bess's front paws. Then began the sewing together. Occasionally her face twitched with pain when the needle juked her, repelled by the thick doubled canvas. She refused the offer from Miss Dodd of a thimble to protect her finger. She seemed to need physical pain as a signal that life continued.

When they were all sewn, she called Bess over to her and, for a minute, just stroked the great head resting in her lap. It was as though the dog sensed her need. After a while, Bess set a paw where her head had lain in Quashiba's lap. The dog looked at the woman in the chair, cocking her head to one side as if to say, *It will be all right.* One by one Quashiba took up the dog's feet, inspected them, and grunted with displeasure but said nothing aloud about the state they were in. Each boot was tried on carefully. Satisfied that they would work, the final touch was added. They were all edged around the tops with drawstrings, so they secured snugly to the dog's feet.

At first Bess resisted, trying to remove the one on her right front paw. Quashiba lectured her that it was meant for her own good. "You will get used to them," she admonished, wagging her finger at the dog much in the same way she did her offspring. The animal perked her ears forward, cocked her head to the side, and gave up. She knew an old friend was trying to be of help.

Neddy learned much that night. His mother was a woman who loved only once and deeply. He understood for the first time she was not invincible. She was vulnerable! It had never struck him before that his mam was like other people. His mother had always been strong, a giant to hide behind—but now, she seemed to have shrunk and become like everyone else. Inside him, the weakening effect of fright came and went, leaving doubt where once stood certainty alone.

His heart filled for her and himself at their great loss. He saw her, during and after making the dog's boots, stopping and looking to the door or to the window, as if expecting to hear someone call out before entering the room. When nothing happened, her head would shake from side to side, as if to clear it. Her shoulders would straighten and press against the back of the chair. Budding tears would be choked back, and the back of her hand would wipe their residue away. Sometimes she would turn and stare at Neddy. When she did that, there was distance in her eyes. He was thankful for the dimmed lamp. Anything was preferable to seeing her hurt.

Mentally, Neddy thanked God for Miss Dodd. She and she alone had saved his mam. Forever he would owe her a debt, and he swore that whenever Miss Dodd needed help, it would be hers free of charge. That would be a start. He looked over at his mother. Her shawl was pulled tight around her shoulders, as if protecting them from an unexpected storm.

He had slept fitfully on a cot in Miss Dodd's little room. The sound of his mother rocking back and forth in the next room kept him awake and aware of her agony. Then he would begin to go over what Miss Dodd told him. It seemed he must have done this mental exercise a thousand times. Yet, still he could not comprehend. Like his mother eyeing the door and windows, he could not believe that his father was dead.

Miss Dodd had heard that there was a ruckus over at Kensington. Next, someone shouted, "The soldiers coming!" Straightaway Miss Dodd went to see if her friends were safe. It did not occur to her then that she was risking her own property by leaving it. Ravaging slaves or vengeful soldiers would have delighted in setting fire to her home, which would have left her devastated. As she talked, Neddy's admiration for her grew. She was very brave to have risked so much for them.

After harnessing up the mule to the cart, she made it to Kensington quickly. There were dead and wounded on the ground. Some were helping, while others ran when they saw her coming, thinking her the soldiers returning. Ignoring cries for help, when they realized who she was, Miss Dodd made her way through the yard up the hill to the Lawrence place. There she found his mother, sitting on the ground, cradling the dead body of his father to her. Behind her, their house was a smoldering ruin.

The soldiers had come into Kensington, shooting and killing anyone they could see. They torched the slave huts that had survived the first burning. When the people ran out, they shot them down. Then came the mistake that had taken his father's life. When he had tried to stop the killing, one young soldier heard his father's name called, and he yelled, "There is the Colonel Lawrence leading these rebels!" No one was sure which soldier fired, but a musket ball ripped through his father's chest, and he fell dead. Quashiba ran forward and hung onto his body as if to keep her husband in this world.

It took some time for Miss Dodd to persuade her to let go. As she eventually relinquished her grip, Quashiba insisted on burying her dead husband herself. She was not going to wait for any parson. Later they could come and read words, if they wished. There was nothing the parson could do that she and her traditions could not. Miss Dodd offered to help her. They got a coffin from behind the hot house, where a number were always kept ready for the dead. Miss Dodd had turned away in modesty when Quashiba stripped the body of her husband to wash it. The ritual took time. Then she wrapped him in a sheet from a clothesline in the yard that had escaped the fire. When all was ready, Miss Dodd helped her lift the mortal remains of her husband into the dead people box, as she called the coffin.

Then, after they had rested for a few minutes, came the next big struggle: getting the coffin up onto the cart. It was a fight, but somehow the two women managed it. Slowly they went down the hill past the ruins of the Great House, over to where all the Fowlers were buried. Quashiba chose the spot just outside the Fowler family enclosure, right in line with Miss Rachel's grave. She felt Edward would be safe there, with old Mrs. Fowler to look after him.

It was only right. "He born ya, belonging to Miss Rachel. He dead here, he still belong to her. No damned Morris can claim him." Quashiba was adamant about that.

Digging the grave was the next major undertaking. Luck was with them on that, for Jacob, who had been hiding among the graves, came out when he saw who they were. He had known Edward from boyhood and said he would help them. From somewhere he got two hoes and two shovels, and they began digging.

It took them two hours of hard work before Quashiba was satisfied. With ropes, which Jacob produced, tied around the coffin, they managed awkwardly to get it into the hole. In the effort, the lid slid off, and Edward's corpse nearly tumbled out. Jacob was forced to get in and straighten it out, replacing the lid. None of them had thought to check for nails to secure the lid beforehand. Had the occupant been alive, he would have joshed them for their oversight. "Mi can't tek know-nothing people in mi business," he would probably have said.

Jacob climbed out of the grave and had his say: "Mi wouldn't do dat for anyone but it a Edward. No, sa, mi don't get in wid jus any dead man. Mi hope you know dat?" They filled in the grave. Quashiba left the mound without a cross. That would come later when the tomb was made, when they would have a proper burial service.

After that, Miss Dodd and his mother returned to what had been their home to collect all that she could save. Without emotion, as if it was her everyday chore, she took down her washing from the clothesline, shook it out, and murmured about washing it over again to remove the soot. From Edward's shed at the back, which had also escaped the flames, she retrieved his tools. These, her son would use and treasure, Miss Dodd was assured. A few pots and pieces of her precious crockery that had somehow survived, Quashiba carefully added to her pile. When all that could be had been collected and packed into two hampers on the back of Edward's mule, they left. It was that mule carrying the last of their possessions that Neddy now led behind his mother as they headed for Maroon Town.

As he walked, his mind wandered back to when it all began. Years seemed to have passed since it started. Neddy remembered sitting on the wall, watching bang-belly go by, talking to himself, then his going up the hill to check the traps. After that it came by in a blur. Burning, slaughter, people getting chopped, people getting shot, people getting dead. All this for freedom! What was that, anyway? As his father said, "When dey get it, what dem going do den?"

Slaves, apart from when they were in the fields and the driver lashed the laziness out of them, came and went just like freemen. What differences would freedom make? They had more freedom than he did. He couldn't walk off just so. Lord! If he tried that, his mam would lick him with the tamarind switch she kept specially for him.

Two years before, she had given him one crack with it for being late. He let out a cuss at her, just as his father came around the corner of the house. It all happened too suddenly to get a clear picture. Somehow a hand grabbed at the back of his neck, and the tamarind switch was coming down again and again and again and again across his bottom, across the back of his legs, across anywhere it could land. He was screaming with pain, and his mother was screaming for it to stop. Finally it stopped, and then he heard his father say, "No damn man, no damn pickney, and *no damn pickney of mine*, going talk to mi woman like dat!"

Never before in his then-fourteen years had he seen his father so angry. Never again would he see such rage in him. It taught him that, although he was their child, there was a bond between his father and mother where even he could not trespass. For a week he was reminded of that lashing each time he tried to sit. More weeks went by before welts on his calf muscles disappeared. Was he free? He got lashed just like any slave.

Slaves were bought and sold like sheep and goats, but he was stuck to his mother and father. They couldn't sell him, but that didn't make him any freer than those traded. As matter of fact, those who got sold saw new people and new places. He never did. Always the same people and places, except when he went to Montego Bay. But he hadn't been further than that. Falmouth, Lucea, Sav—those were just names. As for Kingston, the moon was nearer.

The thought struck him: his father was a slave. For the first time, Neddy realized his master could have sold his father. That would not have been kindly to him or his mam. They would have been separated! There was nothing they could have done about it other than buy his freedom.

For a brief moment, he paused and let his mother continue on the way as he considered this revelation. Before following on, he filled his lungs with the heavy, dew-laden morning air and exhaled slowly, watching the hot breath turn to steam as it hit the colder air outside. There were so many edges to the coin of freedom, he realized, and he would have to reconsider its shape.

Looking up, he could see his mother's figure more distinctly. She was still hunched over, but the pattern on the coat she had drawn about her began to show its colors. Its red and blue flowers became distinguishable in the approaching light. For some reason, at that moment he decided all children were slaves to their parents—just like in the Bible.

Without his noticing it, objects had begun to cast faint shadows. Day had snuck up. That meant they were not too far from Maroon Town. Looking again at the pattern on his mother's coat, he concluded that the death of his father had canceled any freedom he had ever had. From now on, his mother had become his responsibility, whether she agreed or not. For a moment he wished he could remember what freedom felt like, so he could understand it better. Looking at Bess jogging by his side, with her booties still on, Neddy wondered if she were free. The speculation did not go much further, for Maroon Town was already in sight.

As they approached the first building of Maroon Town, his mother straightened up in the saddle. Her head went up, pushing her chin forward. No one was going to see Quashiba carrying herself like some downcast slave. Neddy pulled his mule alongside hers and then went on in front to find where his party had spent the night. The crowd of refugees had expanded. Some of the small settler men were standing around in knots, chatting in subdued voices, afraid, most likely, of disturbing their betters at that early hour. Occasionally one would look up as mother and son passed them by. Neddy could feel what some of them thought as their eyes narrowed, but not one spoke out. At last he saw the trap over by the guardhouse being got ready by Badalia. He hurried on forward, with Quashiba close behind.

"Miss Badalia, Miss Badalia!"

She looked over her shoulder to see who hailed her like the wake-up call of a crowing cock. The instant she saw Quashiba riding toward her, she knew something was very wrong, and the admonishing words about to speed from her mouth toward Neddy were clamped off. Instead she stood waiting for boy and mother to come up to her.

Quashiba dismounted and came forward to this woman, whom she knew held some place with her husband. She was never sure, but she sensed it; and whenever they met, a strained politeness existed between them.

"They killed him," was all she said. Badalia's arms opened, and the two women became one. If a rivalry existed before, it no longer did from that moment on. There was nothing left to contend for. They rocked together, and Neddy could hear both of them sniffle and the *Never minds* coming over and over again from Badalia. At last they parted, and Badalia did what all women do under such circumstances—offered food. Quashiba shook her head in refusal, but Neddy nodded his head up and down emphatically, indicating his acceptance. Hunger had overridden his images of castor oil, and his mouth salivated for the taste of plantain, salt fish, any food at all, on its way down to an empty belly.

While he spooned up yam, ackee, and salt fish, his mother sat beside him, sipping from a large mug of hot coffee. Badalia fussed about in the outside kitchen by the guardroom, getting other dishes ready for Miss Lucy, the captain, and young Tim. She asked no questions, biding her time until she could hear the full story of how Edward died. If Quashiba did not tell her, then Neddy would. There would be time for that.

At last, they were on their way again, but even more slowly than before. The train of wagons and riders had doubled the size of the column of soldiers marching in front and slowed it considerably. The captain's frustration at their slow pace was obvious to his subordinates, but there was little he could do about their progress. Galloway only hoped they would reach safety before disaster struck.

His party members rearranged themselves for the leg up to Lapland. Quashiba had been found a place up in the trap, along with Badalia and Miss Lucy. Young Tim sat in Badalia's lap up front as she drove. Neddy's mother and Miss Lucy sat in the back. All of them seemed quite comfortable with this grouping.

Neddy was glad of the arrangement. He did not have to walk anymore and had taken back his place on Mass William's mule. His father's mule was tied to the trap, along with Tim's jenny. Once more, it was just Bess and himself on the road. It was a relief to Neddy, as he felt that family constraints had been lifted from him.

The column reached about where he and the captain had gone off the road and into the Lapland bird-bush, when Galloway brought them to a halt. Ahead was a stark reminder that war was in progress. A tree had been felled across the road. Fixed horrifically against it were the half-naked bodies of a mulatto woman and a young quadroon boy, who was obviously her son. Both had been used and then brutally hacked to death. A revenge killing, supposed Galloway. In all probability she was the housekeeper of some white planter. From what he could see of her face, a beautiful woman, and her son took after her. No one seemed to know who she was or where they came from.

After ordering their bodies to be buried, Galloway hurried back to check on his own people. For the first time he saw Quashiba. It was Miss Lucy who explained who she was. Neddy added that they had killed his father. Galloway said nothing at first, then, "Edward was amongst the best of men, Mam. You have my heartfelt sympathy." He saluted her and turned the horse back to head the column.

Just as he got to his position, shots were heard from the bush where his point men had gone to investigate. Shouts drifted to them, and Galloway ordered four others to follow up and give support. Between fifteen and twenty minutes went by. There were no more shots. A soldier emerged from the bush and made his way to the officers waiting to hear the report.

"About four or five black bastards in there, sir. We got one, but the others made it away. Do you want us to follow, sir?"

"No; bring your men back, corporal, and have those on point go on forward. We have not the time for wild-goose chases."

"Yes, sir." The corporal came smartly to attention and wheeled about. Then he stopped and about-faced again. "What shall we do with the man we got, sir? Bury im?"

Galloway looked over at the soldiers filling in the double grave they had dug, then back to the corporal. "No, not that dog. Drag it out here and hang him upside down from that tree over yonder." He pointed to a handy cotton tree, its branches spread across the road. "Strip him naked and cut his balls and thing off. Stuff them in his mouth. They want to send us a message. We will send back our answer."

The corporal's eyes widened to their full extent. Never before in his military life had he been given such an order, and he had served on the North West Frontier with the Honourable East India Company, where many stranger-than-strange incidents took place.

"Did you hear me, corporal?" Galloway shouted.

"Sa." He wheeled, slammed his right foot down onto the road and marched smartly off. They moved on, leaving the soldiers to carry out their grisly orders. Only those at the back of the human snake saw the results.

"That will tell them," one man said to his wife as they passed the swinging corpse. She grunted in response and looked away, not sure whether a white man should sink to such depths. That was the realm of the uncivilized nigger.

Sometime between two and three o'clock they passed through Lapland's gates. Neddy noticed there were no turkeys gobbling about or curly-horned sheep to be seen. Bullocks and heifers also were missing from the scene, except the bloated remains of two polluting the pond. Neddy looked up at the Great House. Even from this distance, he could see that the roof was half-gone, and the rafters stood out like the ribs of a rotting hulk on a beach. As they got closer, the char on the cut-stone walls became visible. Lapland had only just held back the siege for which it had been built.

Galloway halted the soldiers just on the edge of the garden and rode forward to the great door. As he got to it, the door opened just far enough to let a large woman out. She looked right and left, as if expecting to be attacked from either side before coming forward to the captain cautiously. When she realized all was safe, she broke into a jog across the lawn. As she closed the gap, her face became cheered on recognizing the captain.

"Oh, Lard, sah!" she exclaimed with obvious joy. "You are di special friend of Massa James, sah, that was here at the party when them shoot?" she asked breathlessly.

"Yes, why?"

"I am Nanna, sah. You remember the little girl Miss Eliza, sah? Di one we all call Miss Awa?"

For a moment Galloway's face scowled in an attempt to follow her question. "Not sure," he said with caution.

"She is Massa James gran-daughter, sah. Miss Frances's child. They live over at Stevenage. Massa Stevenson is her father." The last part of her explanation came hurriedly as she tried to jog his memory.

"You mean the pretty little girl he brought the spaniel for?"

"That is she, sah."

"Well, what about her?"

"She gone, sah."

"What do you mean, gone?" Galloway said. "Do you mean walked off, kidnapped? Why is she here and not with her parents?" His questions came rapidly.

"Miss Frances gone to Hingland with Massa James, and Massa Stevenson somewhere about, sah. Mi na know where. Miss Awa left, wid her nurse, in my charge. Now di chile pick up and gone." There was great distress in her voice.

"Calm down, nurse," Galloway said as he dismounted from his horse. "A three-year-old cannot have gone far."

"You don't understan, sah!"

"No, I don't. Explain, then." Galloway was getting irritated at the round and round of the talk.

Nanna took a deep breath, as if deciding to tell all. Galloway waited.

"Is her young nurse, sah, Bekah."

"What about her?"

"Is she tek di chile."

"What do you mean, she has the child to do her harm?"

"Oh no, sah!" she said.

"Oh, for God's sake, woman! Then *what?*" he shouted back at her.

"She gone to Montego Bay with her, sah."

"Then she is safe?"

"No, sah. She tek off widout my permission not an hour ago. She leave a message saying dis place too dangerous for Miss Eliza, an she taking her to Montego Bay for safety."

At last it had come out, and Galloway understood the problem, "Why haven't you sent someone to bring her back?"

"None of dem going. wid slaves bunning places and killing people, sah."

"I cannot spare any soldiers. We will have to find another to go fetch her."

"Who going do dat, sah?"

"Never mind," Galloway said. "I will find someone reliable." There was one person at hand whom he could trust and rely on. He mounted again and rode back to where his people were settling under one of the poinciana trees.

"Neddy," Galloway said.

The boy looked up at him from where he was helping his mother and the other ladies with the necessary trappings to cook food and settle down, for it seemed they would be camping there for the night.

"Sir," Neddy answered, like one of the soldiers.

"Do you remember a little girl with a spaniel pup when we came here to shoot?"

Before he could add more clarification, Neddy's face beamed for the first time in days. "Di one wid di nursemaid named Bekah, sah? The little facety gal, sah?" His words put a brave face to his memory of their first meeting, when he had been bested.

"You know who I mean, then," Galloway said with an understanding smile.

Neddy nodded without committing himself. Something was wrong, and he was going to be involved. He waited for Galloway to continue.

"The stupid girl has gone off and taken the child with her to Montego Bay through all this." He pointed to the refugees. "I want you to go get her and bring her back."

"Yes, sah!" Excitement at the prospect of meeting Bekah again made his reply less soldierly this time.

Nanna, who had come up and overheard what was said, added, "She tek a donkey wid the chile in a hamper."

"You better get started now, if you want to catch her before dark, young man," Galloway said. "Get going."

Neddy went to his mother. "If mi don't get back tonight, tomorrow you tek Bess and di mules and go over to Samaria to Mass William and tell dem what happened."

She stared back at him, her face registering her disbelief not only that her son was giving her instructions but also that he proposed to leave her side and ride out onto the road alone. She was about to refuse him when she saw, over his shoulder, Badalia vigorously nodding her approval. Exhausted with grief, Quashiba decided Badalia was probably more fit at that moment to make such decisions than she was. She relented.

Neddy ran forward and retrieved the stick he had been lent, which was hanging from a thong on the saddle. Galloway recognized the shillelagh immediately.

"Where did you get that knobby-knob, Neddy?"

"Massa William lend it for mi protection, sah."

Galloway took the shillelagh from him and hefted it before slapping it twice into the palm of his left hand.

"A good weapon, that. A real man's cudgel," he said, handing it back to the boy. "It will stand with you well. Now, come with me, and I will write you out a pass in case you get stopped by soldiers." They walked over to where his horse stood. Galloway called for pen and paper, which was brought by an orderly. Five minutes later Neddy was on his way, armed with a pass, the shillelagh, and a warning to trust no one in his hurry to catch up with that silly girl.

He didn't think Bekah silly. As he glanced over his shoulder at the captain, he felt a slight resentment at his remark. Wisely he said nothing and took off at a trot to carry out his orders. Halfway down the road to Lapland's gates, he began to feel the relief of being on his own again. Grown-ups gone. Independence was his again. And best of all, freedom from the gloom of his mother. That was the greatest reprieve of all. A twinge of guilt mocked him, but he shook that off in a few strides. Past the gate, he stopped and took a deep breath. Then he began to think what Bekah would have done. Which way did she go? How would she have gone? All these questions moved about his thoughts.

As his breath came easier, he decided the road would be the easier way. It was his fastest way. If she were on a path, off the road, then they were heading in the same direction. Sticking to the known road would make overtaking her simpler. Sooner or later they would be abreast if he stayed on the faster path. Risky, but what else was he to do? Gripping the cudgel, he swung it left and right, as if chopping with a sword. It cut through the air, making a whooshing sound. That reassured him it retained its power. He set off at a fast walk in the direction of Montego Bay. The one wish he had was that Bess had come with him. But then, he thought, she was better guarding his mother. He had the stick, and again he swung left and right to hear the reassuring whoosh as it cut through the air.

He must have jog-walked for about two miles along the main road heading down to Catadupa. There were people wandering around; some seemed lost, others intent on getting what they could out of this time of chaos. No one paid him much attention. For that, he was thankful; on occasion he waved acknowledgement and hurried on when they hailed him up. By the time he had gone four miles and had begun to flag, he realized Bekah couldn't have taken the straight road. No matter how fast she had tried to travel, the little girl would have slowed the two of them down. By now he should have spotted her.

Stopping to rest for a little and think about his next move made him realize it was also time to use a tree. He looked up, then down to see if it was all clear before going across the road to a red budge-gummy tree trunk by the side of the road. At his beginning, as is the habit of men and boys, he looked around again, then up to the sky, just to make sure no one was watching. Next, he looked into the river valley below and was satisfied it was all clear. When at full release, no longer able to contain or hold the flow, he caught a glimpse of movement between the trees, way down in the valley. He couldn't say who or what it was, but there was definite movement between the trees on the path that followed the Great River down to the seashore. He had used it many times fishing. At last, the mover broke into a clearing—it was a donkey led by a girl. He almost wet himself in the hurry to finish his business and hurry after her. He was sure they were his quarry.

He jumped over the stone wall and nearly went head-over-arse down the ravine but managed to stick the shillelagh into the ground and briefly steady himself. In quick time, he was sliding and scrabbling toward the path as miniature landslides followed his helter-skelter descent down the hill. At the bottom, he shook the stones and dirt from his sandals and began to run hard.

Each breath dragged into his lungs in gulps. Sweat poured down his face and back with the effort and the heat of the day; it soaked into his clothes and made them soggy against his skin. Paying no attention, he hurdled any obstacle in his path, hurtling along at breakneck speed. In no time he was in the clearing where the donkey and the girl had first appeared clearly. They were long gone.

Slowing for a bit to get his breath and give the cramp in his side time to abate, Neddy wondered if they were still ahead on the path. They could have turned off into the bush. He decided otherwise and pushed across the clearing back under the tree cover again. On his left, out of the corner of his eye, he could see the sparkle of the Great River below the path, rushing over rocks, keeping pace with him effortlessly. As he rounded a corner, between two large trees flanking the way, he was tripped by an exposed tree root and fell flat on his face.

Badly shaken, the wind knocked out of his chest, he lay without moving for a few seconds. Then slowly he rolled onto his back to look up into the branches of the overhanging trees. He groaned more out of self-pity than hurt. To his surprise a merry laugh came from just behind one of the trees. From his helpless position he saw no one, but he guessed who had laughed. In a sense he was glad, and in another he knew he had been caught in a fool's position again.

"You wants help?" asked a voice he had heard before.

Gritting his teeth, he righted himself onto his knees before standing up to face the girl.

"Mi can elp miself," he answered grumpily.

Bekah stood just off the path, half-hidden behind a tree. Neddy started to move forward but stopped dead in his tracks. His mouth fell open in astonishment. He was staring at the barrel of a pistol pointing at his chest.

"Don't come any closer," she said. The pistol, clutched in both her hands, wavered slightly, but he could see the set of her jaw. With that look he had sense enough to obey her. She was not to be fooled with, he recalled. There was no telling what she would do at any sudden movement. No, he was not Watt, and not about to foolishly challenge her. She would not hesitate to fire the pistol.

"You going shoot mi?" he said tentatively.

She ignored that and snapped back, "What you following me for?"

"Dem send me to get you and bring you and di pickney back." It was only then he realized there was no donkey or child in sight.

"Who sen you?" she snapped again.

"Di lady dem call Nanna and di captain." She seemed to relax at that. The pistol came down to her side. Neddy breathed a sigh of relief, and then he noticed that the hammer was still in place; the pistol had not been cocked. It made him wonder if she knew how to use the weapon. Wisely, he did not ask and find out one way or the other.

"Mi not taking Miss Awa back to be killed by dem. Miss Frances left me in charge of her before she go away. We going to Montego Bay and di church, where she will be safe."

"Church?" Neddy said, his eyes wide and mouth half-open with curiosity.

"Where Massa Stevenson go. Di parson man is a friend of theirs. Im always come an see dem," she explained.

"Which church, di Baptist?"

"Not dem!" The contempt in her voice was obvious. With her head angled proudly to one side, her chin up, she said, "Di church from Scotland."

Neddy did not know the distinction, but she seemed to.

"The one Revered McAlister preaches at on East Street across from di Baptist dem." Again with the word *Baptist*, there was no mistaking her dislike for them. She and her owners were one on that. He wondered what they had done to her for such opposition to come out.

From what she said, Neddy had a vague idea of her intended destination. "Well, it is better you come back to Lapland wid mi. It is safer, now di army is dere."

"We nah go back." Her hands went akimbo, and she stamped her foot resolutely. "Too many bad people around. It is safer to go down to Shettlewood and Montpellier, where di army is also. That just about two miles from here, and Lapland is far back."

"I know where it is," Neddy almost snapped at her. She was going to give him trouble. "Where is the child?" he said.

Bekah looked at him suspiciously, her eyes narrowing. "Why?"

"Because she is coming back wid mi," he said, his voice determined.

"She not going anywhere wid out mi. If you tink you is bad, jus try some ting." The uncocked pistol came up to point at Neddy's chest again. Before she knew what happened, he was quickly on her, grabbed her arm by the wrist, and with his other hand he wrenched the pistol away from her. She gave a little gasp of pain, drew back, and slapped him with all her might right across his face with her free hand. Neddy reeled, his blood rushed to the place of hurt, and his temper surged with it. About to strike her back, his fist clenched and raised when he froze like a statue, straining to contain his rage. Only his mother had ever dared to do that. He held the anger in with his eyes closed tight, with teeth gritted together hard. Slowly he lowered his arm as he fought to control himself.

Bekah retreated quickly behind the tree. This time, she felt the grip of fear and wished she had controlled her own temper.

When all fury had begun to subside, he opened his eyes again. On the ground lay the pistol. To make sure it would not be a danger again, Neddy picked it up and, holding it with both hands, cocked the hammer.

"What you going do? Kill mi?" asked Bekah from around the tree trunk. She sounded frightened and worried.

Neddy looked at her with a sneer. "You not worth it," he mumbled, and pointed the pistol in the direction of the river. Still holding it with both hands, he pulled the trigger. There was a click, some sparks flew when the hammer hit the firing pan, and nothing more, no big bang.

"*Raatid*! It not loaded!" Neddy looked at the girl with a puzzled frown. "It is not loaded," he said again, with emphasis. "What dis for den?" he asked, staring hard at her. Holding the pistol by the barrel with butt pointed in her direction he made as if to throw it at her.

"Frighten you, didn't it?" she snapped back. That froze his action. She could see from the puzzled frown on his face he was thinking about it.

They must have stood staring at each other for a minute before Neddy said, "We had better settle where we going, back to Lapland or down dey so." His thumb jerked in the Montpelier direction. He looked up at the sky, "We nah go much further tonight, darkness soon come."

"You coming wid us, den?" She sounded relieved.

"Di captain sen mi to protect you. Dem up at Lapland think that is important. It really Miss Awa dey worry bout," he added with a smirk.

"You protect mi! His you need protecting," Bekah said with a merry laugh. "Is who fall flat on him face, dey so?" She pointed to where he had sprawled.

Dis is one facety little gal, Neddy thought. Arguing with her was not going to get him anywhere. She was out of the same mold as his mother. With them there was no winning, only war—one battle after another.

They had to make a decision on the direction to take, or they would be stuck in the bush with nightfall. He thought about it and realized that Shettlewood, with the soldiers there, was the better option at this time of the day.

"All right den," he said. "Go on, mi will follow."

Bekah led him deeper into the bush where she had tied the donkey. In the right hamper on its back, the head of a small girl peeped over the rim.

"You leave di pickney here for anybody to find?" Neddy said, with a look of disbelief. He should have kept quiet, he knew from her next reaction.

"No one going fine her."

"What hif someone kill you?"

"You?" Again he felt the ground slipping. He was going to be on the losing end again. But he decided to give it a go.

"I could have."

"Boye, mi hear you a running back dere long before you fall down. You make so much noise coming down di hillside, for to break you neck. Lard, it look funny. Mi knew it was you."

His eyes moved from side to side, and his lips clamped together making sure he was not going to carry on the argument. How could she know it was him, when they had met only once before? Did she really know, or was she just saying that, to say that?

Bekah took the halter of the donkey, after explaining to the three-year-old in her charge that the "boye" was coming with them to Montego Bay. The put-down and her determination to go in the wrong direction made Neddy's jaws clamp tighter. Not a word of dispute came from him. The pistol he still held he dropped into the other hamper. It fell beside a powder horn and a canvas bag that Neddy assumed held shot.

"Mi see you have powder and di shot for di pistol?" he said.

"You tink mi going to tek di gun wid out dem tings?" Her superior attitude really jarred him, but he refused to be drawn in.

"Den how come you didn't load it?"

She made no answer. This time he had got her. He turned and led the way back to the path. They had gone a few paces on it when from behind him he heard her ask, "You know how to?"

He knew what she meant but decided to play her like a fish on a line. "How to what?"

"How to?" Her voice sounded thin and unsure.

"What you talking bout?" he said.

Exasperated, she burst out, "Di gun!"

"Oh, dat, you mean di *pistol*? Dat what you mean? Di *gun*," he smirked. He could just imagine how she wanted to stamp her foot and cuss him. Not a chance would he give her for that. She would just have to stare at his back as they walked.

"Sure, I know how to load di *gun*." It was his turn to rub salt into her wounded pride, and the opportunity was not to be lost. Maybe it would bring her down a peg or two from her high horse. His superior knowledge of firearms became his weapon. Glancing over his shoulder made him smile wider. Her pretty face with those big eyes was squished up; her jawline stuck out like the ass's jaw bone that Samson used to kill his enemies with.

Oh, how she wished to get at him and recover the high ground. "Well, you ad better load di pistol, den. We may need it."

Neddy had hoped she would not ask that. He thought fast to hide his boast. Holding up the shillelagh and waving it around in the air, he replied, "We don't need dat when mi got dis."

"What dat little piece of stick going do when five, six men grab mi?"

"Five, six men grab you! Dem would lose." He let out a raucous laugh, his back still turned to her. "One lick wid dis, and dem done."

"Fi you dat is all right. Mi want di gun loaded." She was adamant.

"Den load it yourself." There was silence from behind him again. It lasted so long that he thought he had won, and the awkward demand would not come up again.

But he was wrong. "Mi can't do it. I don't know how."

He was trapped. His eyes closed as he walked along, trying to picture what the captain showed him before they went shooting. He prayed he had it right before promising, "All right. Mi will load it when we stop. Just keep going; we got to get to Shettlewood before the sun goes down on us. An when mi do it," he said, "don't loose it off an kill mi."

"Is fraid, you fraid?" Then there was that merry little laugh of relief from her. At last they were moving onto better ground between them. But it made him no less afraid when it came to guns in the wrong hands. Recently there had been too many guns in the wrong hands.

"Yes, mi afraid."

She could tell he was not joking. For another hundred paces they went silent. Till then, the child had kept very still in her hamper basket, but the day and discomfort had begun to get to her. She had begun to whine, and her nurse tried to comfort her and keep up the pace at the same time. Suddenly Neddy stopped.

"You better take Miss Awa down an mek her do di business in di bush over dere." He pointed to a thicket. "While you gone, mi will see bout di pistol."

Bekah nodded and picked up the child. Neddy looked in the left hamper and retrieved the pistol, the powder horn, and a bag of shot.

He just prayed he would remember how to do this, and for the first time in a while he thought of Watt and wished he were there to rescue him and take over the pistol loading. Undoing the string around the neck of the bag of shot, he looked inside. The weight indicated it was lead shot, but it did not feel right in his hand. Opening the bag and putting his hand inside, he drew out fine pellets, not pistol balls. Letting them trickle back into the bag, he tied it back again.

"You do it?" came from behind him. Bekah had returned with the child who had stopped her whining, although she reminded them that they were all hungry when she asked her nurse for food.

"No, mi na do it. Di shot all wrong. You got bird shot, not ball for pistol."

"It matters which you use?" she asked, giving him a stare that said *try it anyway*.

"Women!" he smirked. "When you interfere with men bissness, you mess it hup."

She sucked her teeth at that and pointed at the barrel. "It don't matter what go in di hole. You put rock-stone down in de part, and shoot, it shoot same way. It come right out a di end." She was right, and Neddy knew it. Why had he antagonized her? Advantage was slipping away from him again. He said nothing but picked up the powder horn, unscrewing its cork, and let some down the barrel. He guessed at the quantity, praying all the time it was not too much or too little. He preferred it be the latter.

"I need a wad to hold di powder in."

"Wat dat?"

"Some ting to cork it wid. A piece of cloth."

"Dis do?" Bekah bent down and from beneath her skirt tore off a strip from her slip.

"It will ave to," said Neddy. Not once did her eyes waver as she watched him tear a small piece off the strip, using his teeth. Next he looked for the ramrod. It was not in its holder under the barrel.

"Where di rod?" he asked.

"What dat?"

"Di piece to push di powder an bullet down," he said, with a sigh tinged with superiority.

"Mi na know," she tossed back carelessly.

"Well, we nah go anywhere wid out it."

Once more they stared at each other. Neddy thought, if she wasn't such a pretty gal, he would stay well away from her. Why bother with her, he wondered? Nervously, with a smile and giggle of uncertainty, she asked, "Won't a stick do?"

He knew it! His mam would have said just that. Perhaps that was why he, lo…liked her. No, *sah*! Dat was not it. He sat there on the ground, pistol in hand, with bemusement written all over his face.

Looking at him Bekah thought his perplexity pertained to her question about the stick, for he had not answered her. She picked one up and offered it to him.

"Dis will poke it down?"

"Too thick," he said, without taking it from her. Without questioning, off she went soon to return with another stick. This time he accepted it. She watched him ram the makeshift wad down firmly. A small load of bird shot followed and yet another wad. These he rammed home as well.

" All right. It loaded now. You know how to shoot it?"

"Course mi do. You just point it an pull di ting dey." She pointed at the trigger guard.

"Fus you have to cock it," he told her.

Her eyebrows went up, and she drew back as if to tell him off, but caught herself. Neddy closed his eyes and bowed his head, shaking it from side to side in the manner of men resigned to teaching children and women about things beyond their understanding.

"Look," he began. "You cock it so." He spoke slowly, while pulling back the hammer to its firing position. "Then you point it and pull the trigger. That is what is called cocking and firing."

She didn't miss a thing.

"Now we can go," she said firmly. "We got to hurry."

Very carefully he let down the hammer, as he had seen the captain do with his fowling pieces when they were still loaded, and put the pistol back in its hamper. Bekah picked up Miss Awa and placed her in the other hamper, where she had ridden all day. She fussed again, but her ruffled feathers were soon smoothed by her nurse. Neddy was amazed at how loving and tender Bekah was to her charge and was surprised at the twinge of jealousy that electrified him.

As they were about to start off, Neddy turned to her and said, "Bekah, get up on di donkey and ride. We will mek better time so."

"Who you calling Bekah?" she snapped. "I am Miss Rebekah to you, boye."

That did it. He was not putting up with this any longer.

"Listen na, gal. Mi full of your facetiness. Hif you wants us to get along, you watch you mout." His voice had risen with each syllable and then dropped back." Or mi will—"

"You will do what?" She never gave up.

He looked her straight in the eyes and knew death would come first, but he said it anyway. "Mi will give you one bitch box across di face like you give me, wid dis." He held out the palm of his hand in her direction.

She believed him. There was no more backchat from her. She mounted the donkey. Like a market woman on her way to do business, she sat astraddle the animal's back, her two loaded hampers sticking out on either side. Her face was spoiled by a scowl at being bested. However, once more they were on their way.

Neddy led them across a fording he knew on to the back part of Shettlewood. It was safer and shorter than using the bridge. Bekah raised no objection. She just wanted to stop somewhere to comfort and feed the child, if she could find some food. That was the one thing she had forgotten in her haste to leave Lapland. Secretly, she was wondering if she had done the right thing. Her Montego Bay idea had seemed good at the time, but now she wondered.

They came through the fields into an empty pasture. Not far off, they could just see the buildings where they were headed. Halfway across, Neddy called a halt and leaned up against a pimento tree. A slight breeze rustled through its branches, and Neddy reached up to grab a couple of leaves. Crushing them in his hand he raised them to his face and drew in the refreshing perfume of the spice oil.

"Give me some of that for Miss Awa," Bekah demanded, remembering to add, "Please, Neddy."

That pleased him, and he did her bidding.

"You know, some ting funny here," he said, giving her the leaves.

Holding her hands to her face to enjoy the pimento fragrance, she looked at him between her fingers.

"What you mean?"

"Nobody in di yard. Mi don't see any soldiers." He pointed to the barrack buildings. Her hand moved to shade her eyes, which confirmed what he said.

They moved on. Both of them became watchful. Soldiers should be around, but none were in sight, and there weren't any slaves to be seen. To make matters even stranger, gates had been left open, and cattle roamed freely. Neddy noted that the mules and horses were also gone.

As they came to the backyard of the Great House, Neddy stopped them. Miss Awa began to fuss again. Bekah lifted her out of the hamper and held her in her lap for comfort. They stood there, taking in everything that moved—and that did not move. Chickens clucked about the yard, and a sow with piglets that had somehow got free from her pen rooted about, with the litter following her. Every move she made, ten or twelve piglets, pink with black patches, squealed as they desperately tried to latch onto a nipple and suckle from their mother. Otherwise, the yard was quiet. It was eerie. Furniture and household goods were scattered about the yard, as if waiting to be looted. One would expect to see some human scavengers at work. Yet, there was not a soul in sight.

"Mi don't like dis at all, at all, *at all*!" Neddy said, unwilling to move forward.

"We got to see. Wi need food, and dere is a kitchen over dat side." Bekah pointed to a small building beside the barracks with a little smoke coming out of the chimney. That tempted Neddy, and they moved forward cautiously. As they got nearer, his hand tightened around the shillelagh. Any moment he expected a confrontation, and he wanted to be ready for it. A mangy mongrel, after scavenging inside the kitchen, issued its challenge at the door with a snarl and a couple of yelps. Neddy swiped at it, but the cur was too fast for him, and the knob hammered into the half-open door, sending it swinging wider. The dog ducked under and scampered into the yard, tail between its legs but brave enough to look back and give a defiant, high-pitched yap.

Quickly Bekah dismounted, returning the child to the hamper, and tied the donkey to a post outside.

"Miss Awa," she said, looking meaningfully at the little girl staring up at her from the hamper, "You wait here and be extra quiet." She placed her finger to her lips. "I will soon be back. Mi going to try and fine some food for us. You understand now, shu-shu-shu."

She entered the kitchen, and Neddy went over to the barracks to have a look. Bekah was delighted to find half a ham and some bread in the pantry. There was some freshly made butter as well. Even more delightful were some large pieces of salt fish soaking in a bowl on the table, and in the grate a roasted breadfruit, still warm. On the floor were a couple of yampies and, better yet, there was a small wicker basket tossed down in the corner to carry them all in.

Bekah was about to step back into the yard with her prizes, but instead, she froze just inside the door's shadow. Men were in the yard. Her brain raced for a solution. One of them began yelling. Her heart thumped. His words brought terror.

"Look ya, sah! "An excited shout told of Miss Awa's discovery. Bekah trembled with fear for her charge. "Look pon di white pickney in a di hamper on di donkey over dere so. Someone bout ya!"

Bekah choked back the terror and held in a scream.

Another excited voice exhorted, "Mek we pick er up and dash er down. Buss er head open like a melon." A nasty laugh followed. Bekah screamed.

The laugh was cut short halfway to its crescendo. The one who had just spoken did not hear or see it coming. He did not feel a thing as the shillelagh hit the side of his head. To the others, there was a popping sound, like a large fruit dropping from a tree and busting open on a hard rock.

At the sound, Bekah guessed—rightly—that Neddy had snuck up and hit the man. He would need help against the others. This was the time for her entrance. Dropping the basket on the floor, she bolted out the door and straight toward the donkey, on the way vaulting over the prone figure on the ground without even noticing him; she got to the hamper with the pistol in it. Neddy was standing with his back to the donkey, stick raised, staring at the two attackers still facing him, ready to take them on.

Both had machetes and were walking boldly forward. They stopped dead when the girl came out of the kitchen, caught completely off guard by her surprise appearance. They started forward again, and again stopped in their tracks when they saw her reach the donkey and come back to stand beside the boy and point a pistol at them. One didn't even wait to be asked; he just turned and ran for dear life. The other hesitated, looked at the girl, then at the figure of his retreating friend, and then back at the two, and foolishly decided to be brave. That was his mistake.

The pistol pitched Bekah to the ground as she fired. Half the birdshot caught the man in the chest and right arm. He staggered, more from surprise than the force of the pellets. At the same time, Neddy charged forward, swinging the club about his head, ready to bring it down on his foe. The sight of the boy approaching and the shot burning in his body was enough for the man. Yelling blue murder, he took off after his friend. He wanted no more surprises. Another man, one whom they had not yet noticed, bolted out of the buildings he had been looting.

When they turned to the donkey, the little girl was standing in the hamper, gripping its rim and staring wide-eyed at them. Bekah leaned over and gave her a kiss, "You a good girl, Miss Liza," she cooed.

"We better get out of here," said Neddy. "Get on the donkey."

"Not wid out di food." Bekah rushed back to the kitchen for the basket. Once the food had been stowed along with the pistol, she mounted. Smiling, she said, "Told you we would need di gun."

Then she got the animal moving at quick time. Neddy ran behind, holding onto its tail. Unlike a horse, the donkey did not like this indignity and threatened to buck once or twice, so he let go and used his own power to keep up. At the bridge over the Great River, Bekah stopped the donkey. Neddy was breathing hard as he came up to her. It took him a little while before he could speak without gasping for breath. He looked up at the sky.

"It soon dark. We can stay ere," he said, when he had caught his breath.

"Mi tell you we would need di gun," Bekah repeated, very pleased with herself.

"You were right." Neddy was not about to question her use of it just then. Darkness was nearly upon them, and he was not familiar with this countryside.

"What you suggest?" she asked.

He thought a minute. There would be no use even proposing that they go back to Lapland. They were too far. He wondered about going back to Shettlewood to spend the night and looked back in that direction. Against the falling dusk, plumes of blacker smoke curled up. The familiar telltale signs scotched that idea. Then he recalled a hut close to Montpellier that belonged to a man who knew his father. Perhaps he would help them and let them stay with him until morning, at which time they would have to settle their rightful direction, which was back to Lapland. He would not take any more guff from this girl. They were on even ground now, and he was charged to bring them back to be guarded by the captain.

"Come," he directed, and led them off the bridge and onto a path leading into the bush. As the trees closed around them, he felt safer and hoped they were on the path to his father's friend. They came to a small provision ground that looked familiar even in the dark, and on the other side the path turned left and up a hill. That he recalled clearly. He was sure this was the right way and felt more confident. By the time they came out into a small clearing, the early stars had begun to give a little light. The outline of a thatched cottage was visible. There were no lights to be seen inside. No lantern or dish lamp, no fire glowed. They stood there wondering. Neddy moved forward once more, his hand tightening about his trusty bludgeon. This time, no dog or man rushed him as he looked through the open door into blackness. He waited for his eyes to adjust to the faint light coming through a little window in the far wall. The one room was empty.

"You can come in, it safe," he assured Bekah and her charge.

Chapter 17

The Battle

Bekah dismounted and lifted the child out of the hamper. She looked around at the humble establishment just outlined against the darker background and, as a good nurse, began to fuss about where she and her charge were to spend the night.

"You don't expect us to go in dey?" she sniffed with contempt. "Dis is a special child, you know; she Miss Eliza Stevenson, di sweetest little Miss Awa we got. She can't go on di dutty ground."

Neddy said nothing but listened to the cooing and cuddling and the happy gurgling that resulted. He walked back to the donkey, retrieved a blanket from a hamper, and handed it to Bekah.

"Here you are; tek dis an sleep pon di ground outside, den."

"Where you get dis from?" Her tone was suspicious.

"Find dem in a cupboard where di soldiers sleep. Dem mi was after, and come back with, when di man me lick with the stick come wid him wickedness."

Bekah held the blanket up to her face and sniffed. Her nose wrinkled with distaste as she held the offending covering away from her as if it was the most repulsive object that she had ever handled.

"Dem smell stale and musty. Long time since dey see sun. Lordy! White man nasty, eh!" she exclaimed, as if it were a universal fact. "Not even John Crow sit pon dis ya blanket." Neddy did not have a chance to answer her rhetorical exposé or her other comments, because they were both startled out of their wits by a voice from the corner of the hut.

"Who dere? What you want?" the voice demanded. Neddy spun round with his shillelagh raised, ready to strike again in defense.

"You can put dat down, boye. Mi can see unu, and unu can't see mi. Hif mi fling dis here machete in my han, you will feel it in a your belly before you see hit." The sickle flying through the air to stick Bardolf flashed through his mind. Slowly Neddy lowered his weapon, still trying to look through the darkness for the speaker. From the sound of it, the man was to his right, but no human outline showed. His eye strained for the darker figure projecting from the blackness. He could see none in the seamless void. "What you doing ere?" the voice demanded.

Neddy thought quickly and answered, "Looking for mi fader's fren, Rabert Simit."

"Is who you fader?" asked the disembodied voice from somewhere out in the yard.

"Edward Lawrence from Kensington." Mentioning his father's name gave him a brief feeling of sadness, but it did not dull the edge of pride in his voice that seemed to jump out of his mouth. A pause between him and whoever was part of the outer darkness held the tension.

"You Mass Edward son? Lard Gad! How you big so? Mi know you when you was just a likkle boye. You is a grown hup yout now. Time fly by Patu." A figure emerged from the shadows by the corner of the house, where it had crouched.

"Is you, Mass Rabert!" Neddy said, relieved. It was odd how he could not recall what the man looked like.

"His mi. You can res easy, Boye. What you doing, coming ere?"

He was a small man, bent over with age. He walked with a stick in front of him with both hands cupped over the crook. There was no machete. "Who dat over dey?" He indicated Bekah. Before either could answer him, he noted by pointing his stick in her direction, "She got a pickney wid er? Is yours?" He could not see the child's face, as Bekah held Awa close into the folds of her skirt. White would

The Battle

show up in that gloom as black did not. That would have sparked his curiosity even more. All Bekah's precautions did not matter, as the old man shrewdly guessed from the way she took pains to shelter the child. "Is not fi you den." He cackled. "Is white pickney you got dere?" There was no use hiding that fact any longer, and Bekah pulled the three-year-old to her side to pick her up.

"Yes," she said.

"She somebody important pickney?" the householder asked.

"*Yes*," she said again, making it clear he was not to inquire further.

"Hmmm! Careful she doesn't get killed along wid unu. Dem a kill all di white people dat dem come cross. Even when dem dead, dem kill dem."

At that statement, Neddy shook his head in confusion. "What you mean, when dem dead, dem still kill dem? You can only be dead once."

The question was ignored as the old man continued, "Mi is not ere, you know?"

If he could have seen the expression this statement engendered on Neddy's face, he would have read it to mean, "If you are not here, why are we talking to you?" It was doubtful the old man would have given an explanation for that statement, either. He couldn't see Neddy's expression anyway, so he went on, "Yes, sah! Mi is in Accompong."

As Neddy listened, an unease began to creep through his bones like early morning damp. He began to wonder if the old man was mad and deadly dangerous. What had he brought Bekah and the child to? Had the recent events turned Mr. Simit's mind, and was he now a crazy man?

"No, sah, mi na stay aroun here waiting for di soldiers to come back. Mi a go further up into to di hills. You had better do likewise."

Neddy breathed a sigh of relief. He understood what the old man was getting at now and remembered his father laughing and saying, after they had visited him one day, "Mass Rabert speaks round about, never straight. You never know what comes next." This was it, then.

"Di Maroon man will turn you back?"

513

"No, boye. Dem don't trouble an old man who look like Patu. Dem only interested in young slave dem get paid for. Mi too old for dem." He paused. "Dem colonel, Colonel Rowe—im is mi cousin. Dem na trouble mi."

"We was goin hask you hif we can spen di night here," Neddy tested him cautiously.

"You can spen di night, yes. But mi gone. Mi tek wing an flyway like Patu," said old Robert. With a flip of his stick, he pointed to the open door of his hut. "Come in." He led the way, and they followed inside. It was pitch black. As they stood still, the old man fumbled in familiar surroundings for a lamp and tinderbox.

He spoke from beside the wall. "Mi don't know hif it right to light lamp. Somebody could well see it an bring dem ere. Mi now, can see in di dark like Patu."

It was obvious that the owl was some kind of jumby bird for the old man. All Neddy knew was that, if seen in daylight, the owl was the harbinger of death. He smiled at the thought that night protected them from this Patu in the room with them.

Sparks flew as flint and steel came together over a small earthenware bowl. Then there was a little flame from the wick floating on some rendered fat in place of oil. The light was weak, but the smell it gave off was of burning flesh and hair. Bekah averted her nose. The old man saw and chuckled.

"Hif you wants to see, den cork you nose." He chuckled again. "Hif you got food, you can cook dey." He pointed to a three-legged copper pot siting over some dead ashes in a small grate. "Dere is some wood outside and some charcoal mi bun down in a di kiln."

Bekah walked over to the corner and spread the blanket on the floor and put her charge on it, telling her to stay and that she would get food for them all.

"Dere is some fresh water in dey." He pointed to a bucket on the ground by the door. "His mi bring it up di hill before di fighting start," the old man said, letting them know he was still capable of looking after himself.

"Tank you," said Bekah, looking at the old man for the first time in the dim light. To her wonder, he did look like a Patu of sorts.

The Battle

The skin around his eyes lacked pigmentation, giving them a strong owl-like appearance. Adding to the illusion, the back of his hands were mottled, as if they were covered with tiny feathers. The old man knew what she was thinking and chuckled. Obviously people looking at him were shy and backed off uneasily, preferring to leave well enough alone. This gave him protection from unwanted intrusion.

Robert Smith watched as Bekah began to busy herself with the tinderbox to light a fire with the wood she took from the bundle by the grate. He warned them again: "Careful now, plenty bad people bout ya, hif dem see di lamp and di fire."

Then he voiced his plans one more time. "Mi nah stay for dem, or when di soldiers come back to kill everyone. Lard! Watch na! Di gully going run red wid blood again!" There was a finality in his words that both Neddy and Bekah noted with a little trepidation.

"Come back?" Neddy said. "Dem na over at Montpelier? Where di soldiers gone?" A tinge of panic was in his voice.

"You don't ere what happen den! Bout di big battle dem have?"

"No," answered Neddy.

"While she a cook, come mek mi show you. Come," he said, and led the way outside. A step or two past the door, his hand grabbed Neddy's wrist firmly. Neddy flinched at the suddenness of it, and found he was unable to move his arm an inch. Struggling would have been futile, so he made no resistance.

They stood still. Neddy waited. His guide looked up at the sky. Stars had begun to show themselves and light the way, but the moon had yet to appear when the old man noted, "Di moon soon come out an mek di way bright for old Patu. Moonlight better dan sunlight; it cool, not hot an boddersome. Mek me feel good when mi fly pon di night air."

As abruptly as he had grasped Neddy's wrist, he let it go and took off, leading the way across the yard.

Mass Robert referred to his relationship with the owl so often as they walked that Neddy began to wonder whether he could really change from man to owl and back again. Many tales were told of obeah people who could change into animals. But he had never heard that Mass Robert was an obeah man. Normally that would have made him nervous, but this old man calmed him. But that still didn't stop Neddy from looking left and right before staring searchingly at the back of "Rabert Simit" in front of him, seeking some smidgen of confirmation one way or the other.

Nothing there, nothing he could find, either way, except the fancies of an old man's talk.

They crossed the open patch in front of the hut and passed into the trees opposite to the path Neddy had come by. The old man moved surprisingly quickly. Although there was no clear path, he kept his footing. Neddy struggled to keep close behind the little figure. Any minute, he feared, one more tree root could make him stumble and fall, crashing into the back of Mass Robert. They would both go down then, he thought. That would not be good. How much the old man could take was doubtful, and if he got hurt, Neddy would be obliged to look after him. That would delay their journey back to Lapland. He could not lug along a crippled person as well as Bekah and the child. Luckily his fears were not realized, and soon they were through the trees and on the edge of a hill overlooking Montpelier estate.

The moon had come up now. It was not the familiar warmth of the night light but rather the white moon of daytime. It cast a cold light over the landscape. There were no shadows, so that trees, rocks, and even the very blades of grass seemed to stand stark in the landscape. Neddy shivered in the cold, unfamiliar northern light. From their vantage point, the fields and buildings, or what was left of them, held their places on the checkerboard plan of the estate.

"You see dat building dey?" The old man pointed his stick at one with its roof burned off. "Hif you go down an look, you will fine di bun bones of di white man dey throw in a di flames. Black like any black man's bones. Like is hif de devil, his-self," he looked at Neddy, "throw you, in a him flames." He cackled. Neddy's lips twisted to the side. He was not very amused. His time would come, and he hoped not to meet the devil when it came. As if unaware of the youngster's discomfort at his foretelling, Robert Smith went on with the description.

"Yes, sah, Massa! Dem tek di man dey kill di night before in di great battle right out of him box and trow him in a di building

The Battle

dem set fire to. Den now, dem tek di coffin and put di body of dere man dat did get killed and put him in a di box. It a di one dem call Colonel Johnson from down Retrieve pen. Mi na know if it him, but di body get buried him like a Christian." He cackled again. "Dat, sah, his *justice*!" His voice screeched the last word, making Neddy jump at the intensity of its pitch. Nothing more passed between them for a moment, making Neddy glance over uneasily at the old man standing there, gazing down on Montpelier. Even in that light, he could see the old jowls working up and down, as if pumping water into his mouth so he could swallow or speak.

"Colonel Grignon, you know im?" The owl eyes stared at Neddy, waiting for confirmation. When it did not come, he went on. "Di one dem call likkle britches because dem too small fi im batty?" Neddy shook his head indicating his unfamiliarity with the man. "Im batty too big for im pantaloons, an im got notting to show in di front. You sure you don't know im?" Again Robert Smith watched his companion's head shake from side to side, denying knowledge of "little britches."

"Lard! Mi di tink everybody bout ya would a know dat man. Im is di one dem say want to kill every black man, so di white man can breed di women for demselves. Dat is how dem going keep slave bout. Freedom not for dem. Di women and di pickney slave forever. Well, you too young anyway, no matter." Once more, another laugh issued from him. As abruptly as it began, the cackle stopped dead in the middle of an ascending shrill screech, like an owl on the hunt.

They did not move. There was silence between them. There was silence everywhere. Neddy could not hear even a whistling frog or a cricket. He strained for sound in the stillness, and for a moment it seemed that only the worms crawling about their business underfoot thundered loudly in his ears. Finally, the stillness was broken by a prolonged and unusual hoot, a *cri de coeur* echoing across the landscape. The shadow of an owl flapped its way across the crystalline view below. Robert Smith plucked a small flask from his waist and thrust it at Neddy, exhorting him. "Drink dis, Drink dis and see what I saw!"

Neddy wanted to resist, but he felt compelled by the strange old man's insistence. The bitter concoction made him want to vomit, his head swam, his vision blurred and he felt as if transported above the trees, looking down on the great battle which had happened days ago.

* * *

Colonel Grignon was a small man in stature and, like many of his size, full of the gigantic image of himself. As he stared into the yard of his headquarters at Belvedere estate, his reflection in the broken glass of the window caught his eye, and he preened himself. His head cocked to one side, while the back of his hand gently patted the double chin in a vain effort to make it go away. His hand moved down to smooth his snugly fitting waist and went on to tap his belly before returning to its relaxed position by his side. Automatically he glanced down to see if his boots were up to snuff.

He had warned them about the Negroes gathering up around Lapland. They had paid attention to this, he hoped. There was nothing he could do about it now. With his little interior regiment, how was he supposed to look after the security of all, up and down the Great River? Already they had burned most places that bordered the river. It was only a matter of time until they would come after him and his men. He was sure the HQ was indefensible against the hoard of Negroes he expected to rush down from the hills. They were hiding everywhere. Even the bamboo clumps on the properties made perfect cover for ambush. That was what they did before and would do again. He knew them; yes, he knew them for what they were—deceiving, murdering black bastards.

As colonel of the Western Interior Regiment, he was responsible for the security of the estates all the way up the Great River valley. His men were part-time soldiers, really, but until the regulars came from Kingston, that was all they had. He was not going to risk them against thousands of niggers, no sir, not he. What if he lost? If he survived, his position as the representative for St. James in the legislature would be called into question. As a gentleman, he would be bound to resign. That would never do. His standard of living would decline. Worse, to maintain his position in society, he would have to sell at least half of his thirty slaves. Unthinkable! Worse still, being an attorney,

The Battle

his employers would snatch their estates away from his control. No, Grignon decided, staying at Belvedere was too risky. He would order withdrawal to the Kings Barracks at Shettlewood, down from here.

"Geddes!" he yelled "Geddes!" His voice bounced off the bare wooden walls of the overseer's house he used for HQ.

A young man in somewhat shabby uniform came bustling through the door at the summons.

"Yes, sir?"

"Ah, there you are, James. We have to move. This place is indefensible against these savages. Get the regiment ready to move out. We are going to withdraw to the Kings Barracks at Shettlewood. Move, man!"

The young ensign stared for a moment as he let the order sink in. He wasn't sure of it. Shettlewood was no better a position to be at than Belvedere. Seeing his hesitation, Grignon drew himself up, scowled, and barked, "What's the matter, man, didn't you hear the order?" He was not accustomed to hesitation suggesting a questionable action on his part. No, no, no. No one questioned William Stanford Grignon.

"Yes, sir," replied young Geddes, wheeling about to find the adjutant and give him the colonel's instructions. On his way, he was thoughtful enough to send in the colonel's black batman. At least that would stop him from yelling for his presence again.

Grignon had about one hundred forty men with him as they headed for Shettlewood. "These locals," he mumbled, forgetting he was one himself, "don't take their duties seriously." Even the mounted ones couldn't ride like cavalrymen. He watched them wandering over the place, completely out of formation, as if on a Sunday afternoon outing in the park. The foot soldiers straggled along as if they were in the great retreat from Moscow. This infuriated Grignon, and he ordered his adjutant to come forward to him, at the head of the straggling column.

"Ewart!" he snapped when the captain came up beside him. "Get these men into some type of military formation. Good God, man! What do you think would happen if the damned savages attacked us now?"

When Conchie Blows

"Do you mean the Negroes, sir?" asked the adjutant looking across the pasture of guinea grass they were traversing. "It would be their mistake in this open area. We would cut them down like cane stalks."

"That's as may be, man. I don't like to see sloppy soldiering."

As the adjutant rode away to carry out his orders, he couldn't help wonder whether Grignon had images of himself as Napoleon, or the Iron Duke? He himself always thought that being dragged away from his plantation for this march up and down the Great River area was a waste of time. After all, they had put down the Argyle estate rebellion six years before without all this. This time it was a bit more widespread, but nothing a few musket balls, whips, and rope could not cure. Still, he jogged over to the captain in charge of the foot company and instructed him to smarten his men up, then rode over to the young buck who had bought his commission in the cavalry company and delivered the same message.

When they got to Shettlewood, it was empty of all but a few old people. The men straggled in and sat down. One would have thought the two miles across pastures from Belvedere had exhausted them. The colonel looked around him and did not like what he saw. He shifted uncomfortably in his saddle and tried to remember what the best disposition of troops should be in this situation.

Desperately he tried to recall every detail of the terrain as far as he could. The more he thought about it, the farther away Montego Bay and safety seemed to get. He grew haunted by the prospect of being cut off from refuge. That was not good. Reinforcements were there, and more were coming in from Kingston, as he understood matters. They were not here in the interior. He had asked for them, but so far, nothing—neither man, woman, nor dog to augment his troops.

He sat his horse, waiting for his servant to come and help him down. Eventually the man did so. As his right leg came over the saddle, his britches stretched, threatening to separate at the seams, but miraculously the stitches held. There was a derisive laugh from some foot soldier, but for dignity's sake Grignon ignored it, not sure if it was directed at him.

The Battle

He walked over to the officers' quarters of the King's Barrack. The room was a mess. Obviously the niggers had been there and looted what they could take with them. He knew it would be the same over at the busha house and anywhere civilized company lived.

"Gentlemen," he began, when all his officers were assembled. "I have looked at the map, just to refresh my memory." There were some furtive glances, ensign to ensign, as they waited for the next pronouncement from their leader.

"We are on the wrong side of the river. We are cut off in Hanover." Grignon announced dramatically. "We can't afford to stay here with the damned Baptist-driven niggers running wild and burning us out of house and home, now, can we?" There was a murmur that could have been of assent or just wonderment. Grignon seized on it. "Right, then! We move from here and cross the river and take up our position on Montpelier. Get your men ready to move out," he ordered.

The troop moved slowly away from Shettlewood. They crossed back into St. James, fording the Great River without any trouble. That gave Grignon a sense of comfort. At last, the Great River was at his back rather than his front. It no longer presented a barrier to cross when they retreated to Montego Bay; he knew in his heart of hearts that course of action was inevitable, but damned if he would share his thoughts on the matter with his subordinates. He was their commander, after all.

Although the distances between Belvedere, Shettlewood, and New and Old Montpelier were nothing to speak of, there was more grumbling in the ranks. Many could not see the necessity for hopping from estate to estate within a four-mile radius. Quite a few resented the fact they were serving in the militia when they should be on their own places to defend against trouble, if it came. Not one of them had any idea where the hordes of slaves, as had been reported, were now. No great gathering had been seen. They must be there in the hills, for many plantations and estates were completely deserted, and those that had not already been burned waited undefended for the roving bands to loot and put the firebrand to them.

Still grumbling, but resigned to the whims of their colonel, Grignon's Western Interior Regiment began to settle in around the buildings of Old Montpelier Estate. By the morning, many of the men bet it would be "To hell with Lord Seaforth's estate!" And they would be moving again, this time to the safety of Montego Bay. Like Montpelier, all the other estates and everyone else along the Great River trench would have to look elsewhere for help. They knew Grignon. They sensed that Little Britches was most uncomfortable in his trousers and, as some said, needed to change into a bigger pair to accommodate his ever-piling residue. Vulgar laughter followed that conclusion, but if they did go to the Bay, it would be a better move than running around the place like headless chickens.

It was about three in the afternoon when the reinforcements that Grignon had requested over and over again arrived. As if on a parade, the Seventh Company of the St. James Regiment marched into Montpelier.

"They certainly look quite soldierly," the adjutant said to his colonel.

"Damn it to hell!" Grignon said. "They have sent me forty half-niggers. How the hell can you trust them in a situation like this?" He was glowering through the upper-story window of the Great House at his reinforcements coming to a halt, then doing the required movements before falling out as ordered.

"Sir, they are free men of color," his adjutant said in a subdued tone.

"That's the problem: you don't know which color is up—now do you, sir? We should never have given them and the damned Jews the same rights as white men a year ago. Voted agin it miself. The bloody blacks now think they should have them too. You see what trouble that has caused?" He snapped at the adjutant as if he were a member of the Whig party in England and should be reminded of how they had led people astray. "Go and see them settled in," Grignon added, as he turned away from the window in disgust.

"Bring me a cooling drink," he commanded. There was a shuffle and the soft pad of naked feet as the ever-present Negro servant went to do his bidding, and Grignon slumped into an armchair.

Night had come, and with it the sound of the conchi, signaling assembly. They could hear them gathering. Soldiers began to fidget

The Battle

and reach for their muskets and check the priming. From way across the river and into Hanover they could hear it; up into the hills, past Seven Rivers, all the way back toward Cambridge, came the resounding answers of shells blowing. West past Mafoota, down around Fustic Grove, below Montpelier, the conchi shell ordered blacks not to work but to do battle. No sharp clarion note, as from a trumpet, but a deep, mournful, agonizing baritone wail, as heard from a large beast of the fields moaning its last testament in this world.

They had all heard it on a daily basis. They had even ordered the blowing of the conchi shell to begin and end work on their respective plantations, but they had never heard it used thus, against them. Supporting that sad sound was the steady thunder of African drums. There were signals in the thumps, but the whites knew not what they said, only that it held no message of hope for them.

Grignon wiped his face with a cloth handed him by his man. His staff was awaiting orders, but their colonel seemed frozen with trepidation. Many wondered if his inaction would see them massacred where they stood.

The captain of the St. James boys was having none of it. On his own initiative, he assembled his men and marched the company out into the yard, facing the way he expected the slaves to come. It was pitch black, and seeing the enemy was going to be doubly difficult. Black skins in the black night was to their advantage. That worried him militarily. They would have no trouble picking up the white facings on their light-colored uniforms.

He knew many of them would be armed with a variety of stolen pistols, muskets, and fowling pieces. Many knew how to shoot them, he knew, but they had never used them in battle, and that could be to his advantage. In his reckoning, the captain of the St. James regiment knew that luck was with them; his enemy did not know how to use firearms the military way. Yes, some might know how to shoot birds and wild game, but as for battle weapons, they had no idea at all.

Then he began to think of the advantages they would have over his men and how to counter them. They would move silently, on bare feet. Stealth gave them an advantage, for certain. What disadvantages did they have? The inevitable drunk would be in their midst and would, perhaps, mark their position with drunken bravado—he hoped, anyway. While the conchi sounded, he knew, they were all right.

"You men!" His raised voice brought silence to the ranks. "You have to keep your eyes peeled and di wax out of your ears tonight, if the moon and stars don't come up soon. You understand?" That brought some light-hearted banter from the ranks, marking them as part-time soldiers. One asked, "Mi can tek di bayonet and scrape di dut out Jamie's ears, sah?"

Another whimsical rejoinder followed. "It all right, you know; mi modder wash fi mi ears before we come ya. What your modder do fi you? She wipe your batty?" There was a howl of laughter, which was cut short by their corporal. At least Captain Graham knew his men were in good spirits.

At last he could hear the Grignon Interiors coming to formation on his right. They weren't a bad lot, even though many of them still thought brown was inferior to white. Graham smirked at the thought. After all, he was descended from Claver House, and most of them, the bookkeepers and overseers in the Interior Regimental ranks, would have been at difficulty to find a mother who would acknowledge them.

"Remember your drill, men. Fall to formation on my orders. There aren't many of us, but we will make them pay dearly. I expect rapid fire when the time comes. It must be continuous. One line, then the next line. I expect you to load and fire three shots in a minute, as we practiced."

Conchi wailed up and down the countryside, signaling the closing-in had begun. The blowing and the drum beats carried across the Great River, deep into Hanover. From the accumulated sound, they would swear it came from as far away as Westmoreland and St. Beth. Grignon was glad he had got his men away from Shettlewood but was regretting not having given the order to march straight through to Montego Bay. From the sounds, he was trapped in a circle. There must be ten thousand of the brutes. There was no way he could get out. There was nothing for it but to stand and fight. Oh! He did hope that they had the edge with firepower. The blacks would have guns, too. He never did agree with the practice on estates of teaching black

The Battle

men to shoot, as some did. Silly idea that—that they would help defend against French and Spanish attacks. What was even worse was giving them fowling pieces to shoot for game. He recalled an argument about it that got him so angry in the mess. It began when he said, "Never did understand a white man training a nigger with a gun and then sending him out to get him game. Gentlemen should shoot their own game."

"I suppose it tastes better?" asked a wag.

"Taste better or not, you won't like it when they shoot and serve you up like a roast pig."

"My! I wonder how we taste? Do you think they will serve us with rum or Madeira?"

"That's enough!" barked the colonel at the time.

Thinking about it now made his blood boil. He was about to be peppered by a fowling piece and served with rum or Madeira.

The noise grew with each passing minute. Far up in the hills, fire blazed. They were coming for Montpelier. The colonel went into the main bedroom to relieve his bowels into the commode before rejoining his men on the grounds outside. As he came up and took over from his second in command, there were sniggers from the ranks again. Grignon wished he could order the lash for some of them. In a regular regiment, that was daily punishment, but this was the militia, quite a different kettle of fish. Some of the private soldiers could have bought Grignon many times over and not noticed the price. Perhaps, he thought, one of the bookkeepers would serve the purpose. No one ever cared what happened to them. An example should be made. He marked that down in his mental diary.

The drumming told them they were almost within firing range. Yet, nothing seemed to be moving out there. There was a conchi signal over to the left, and another down by the trash houses answered it. "Fall to formation!" Captain Graham of the St. James ordered. He was not waiting for the colonel. They must take their cue from him, not him from them. Deftly his men moved into position. One line stood up, the other line knelt. They would fire line by line, as ordered. Graham was pleased. Hours of drill had been put into his men. That was how it had been done in the Peninsula campaign

When Conchie Blows

against the French. He had been told all "aboot" it by his cousin, Major McCloud over in Westmoreland, who had served with Sir John Moore as a young man and been with the great man's body as they retreated back to Portugal, fighting a rearguard action all the way. Captain Graham looked to his right and felt proud of his men.

Graham couldn't believe their luck, but later he was to think it about par, where the slaves were concerned. A trash house went up in flames, followed by another and then a storehouse; the whole front was lit up, banishing night and the blacks' advantage. Truth was revealed; expelled from the fevered imagination of those waiting in the darkness were the thousands who came with the drumming and conchi blowing. Four columns of rebels were clearly visible in front of them. Possibly a hundred and fifty, at the most, advanced in each column.

"Fix bayonets!" Graham's men snapped to his order, as if they were truly Lord Wellesley's battle-hardened Peninsular campaigners.

In battles of this kind, no one is ever clear on who fired first. It did not matter to Graham. He barked orders with relish. "Front rank, kneel. Wait for it. Fire! Reload." Immediately the rear rank took one pace forward to become the front rank and were ordered, "Front rank, kneel. Fire! Load." The process repeated itself as Graham's orders rang over the blast of his men's muskets. *Front rank, kneel. Fire! Front rank, kneel. Fire!* And so it went, like a well-oiled machine. After each fusillade, he and his men had moved forward to the enemy. Graham was attacking. There was no standing still for the St. James regiment, unlike the Interiors.

The rebels advanced bravely and would have swarmed their foes, but not forty yards away from the St. James boys, the assault finally broke, and of the rebels fled their withering firepower, leaving behind dead and wounded. Gut-shot bodies kicked, groaned, and screamed for help from where they lay on the ground. Their voices fading with imploring words: *Beg you. Bring mi little water. Beg you!* came again and again. Their brethren, sheltering in safety behind stone walls, remained unmoved, confused, and terrified. Two of their leaders lay dead.

It had begun at about seven in the evening and was all over but for the flames in half an hour. The soldiers, with their one dead and four wounded, stood-to all night, waiting for the second attack, which

The Battle

never came. By daylight the flames had diminished, and the fires in the trash houses were all but out. The regiment was still intact; that was all that mattered to Grignon. Not a minute to lose, he thought. He would lead his men out of here and back to the safety of Montego Bay.

He left the men standing and marched back off to the Great House, followed by his adjutant and Ensign Ewart.

"Walker," he called to the adjutant. "You and Major Moncrieff get the men packed up; we march out of here." He pointed to Ewart. "You, sir, will ride with dispatches to Montego Bay." The prospect of going through rebel territory showed on the ensign's face. "What, man! You aren't afraid, are you? Get to it, man!"

"Yes, sir," the ensign said.

It did not take the colonel long to write the dispatch, describing in glowing terms the bravery of his men against overwhelming odds. Ten thousand slaves in rebellion were his opposition, he concluded. Carefully reading it over to see that no individual had been mentioned, Grignon sanded the paper, folded, and sealed it, then handed it to Ewart.

"Ride with this straightaway to headquarters. Tell them I am withdrawing, for there is no chance out here against this horde."

When Ewart was gone from the room and on his way, Grignon hurried down to mount his waiting horse and get away from Montpelier. As he gave the order to move, the adjutant asked, "Sir, should we not bury our dead man first?"

"Have you got him in a coffin?" the colonel said.

"Yes, sir."

"Well, he is safe enough there. He will be buried later. We haven't time for funerals and that sort of thing. Time is of the essence." For a moment the adjutant thought his commander was going to order him to leave the wounded as well. He was relieved when Grignon continued forward with the column.

* * *

"Massa! You hear di shell a blow. Yes, sah! Mi never hear conchi bawl so before in all mi life. Dem a wail all over di land. And drum beat and beat. Dat is how di great battle come an go. Di fool-fool black man light up di place like daytime an show di white men where to shoot. Lard Gad! Dem fool eh! All me know when mi stan-up ya and watch dem, mi tink dem lose. But when mi fly like Patu, den mi did know dem win. It not come now, but freedom come later. It coming just as sure as di hanging and di whipping a come fi dem now. Black man will be freed!"

Neddy blinked. He understood little of the last rambling about *lose* and *win*, but all had seemed to play out in front of him. He could still see it clearly in his mind's eye and hear the orders and the gunfire and the screams. That all came easily to him. He had seen it with his own eyes. No longer did he strain to imagine killings and burnings. When the old man Robert Smith spoke of the battle, mysteriously, Neddy too had watched with him from the hill.

They walked back to the hut much the same way they had left it, the old man taking the lead. When they got there, Neddy was delighted to see that Bekah had managed to get the fire going and prepared food for them. He was starving. The day had been exhausting, and no food had passed his lips since leaving Lapland.

To his astonishment, she ordered him to go and wash before eating. Old man Smith gave her a look that said, *Don't try that with me, young gal.* The bucket outside had water left in it, and once Neddy had satisfied her desire for cleanliness, he repaired inside the hut. All of them sat on the ground, and Bekah dished the food into an assortment of calabash shells she had found. Little talk passed between them as they ate. The old man must have been talked out. His jaws moved only to chew his food, and in the glow from the charcoals, the Adam's apple in his wizened neck bobbed as he swallowed.

"Missa Simit tell me bout the great battle dem have at Montpelier," Neddy informed Bekah. She looked up from feeding her charge and offhandedly commented, "Dat nice. Sometime you can tell me all bout it." Her tone made it clear: *sometime* meant *never*. Her attention was taken up with stuffing the little girl's mouth with food as the child tried bravely to stay awake.

The Battle

"Come, Miss Awa, jus tek a little more," Bekah said. The child's mouth opened obediently, and a small piece of yam went in, only to drop out again as her head nodded with sleep's onset, her little mouth agape.

"Leave di pickney to sleep," Robert said. "Den, you nyam fi you food and tek to sleep as well. Do unu all good. Mi going fly now an leave you." He rose and picked up his stick and a bundle. "You will be safe ere tonight." He looked about the small hut. "But me not sure dis will las long when di soldier come back. It a di New Year, and dere time fi bun down tings. Tank you fi di food." With that, he was through the door and into the night air.

What Smith said about the New Year made Neddy realize time had been passing quickly. He had forgotten the days and the date. Day and night came and went, and there seemed no difference between them. He tried hard to remember, to sort out the sequence of events as they happened from day to day. They all seemed to blend into one long day that faded and came back again.

Tomorrow would be 1832, and there would be no celebrations for the New Year. He looked across at Bekah, settling the child down in the corner for the night and making a place for herself beside her. Did she realize that a New Year was coming upon them—did she even care? He was about to mention it, but stopped when he thought about her reaction to his trying to interest her in the battle the old man had described to him. He laughed when he saw her place the pistol where she could reach it easily, above where her head would rest. She looked at him with a frown. "What sweet you so?" she asked. A soft smile reduced the furrows of suspicion on her face.

"Careful you don't shoot yourself in a di head wid dat. What you tink, somebody going grab you up in a di night?" Again he laughed.

"Careful!" she said. "You will wake up di child wid your laughing." With that, she settled down on her blanket and turned her back to him.

Midnight had come and gone when Bekah woke to stifled sobs. The charcoal had nearly burned out in the grate, and she could not see where the sounds came from. At first she thought it was the child,

529

but as she reached for her, she realized she was fast asleep. The sobs came from across the room, against the other wall. They could only have come from Neddy. Making sure not to wake the three-year-old, Bekah crept over to him on her hands and knees He became aware of her presence and turned away, trying to hide his weakness.

"What is wrong?" she whispered, afraid he had contracted some illness and was in pain. Through his sobs she could just make out what he said: "Mi have a bad dream." He choked again. She waited to hear more. Boys, men did not cry over dreams, she knew that much about them. Then he sobbed like a little boy afeared of the dark. "Dem shoot mi fader. Dem kills him. Dem shoots mi fren. All dat blood." With the last words came a heartfelt sob of despair.

For a moment she hesitated, and then her arm went around Neddy's shoulders and found he was shaking, as though burning with fever. She pulled him beside her, wrapping his blanket around both of them.

Ten minutes must have gone by before he settled down. She could feel his heat against her coolness. His body edged away from hers, but she gently moved herself close to him again. There was nothing deliberate, no mad tussle or wrestling match as she drew him in. As they joined, there was a sharp intake of breath and a gasp from Bekah. It wasn't pain so much that brought the reaction as the overwhelming feeling of being alone as she received him. It wasn't supposed to be like that.

Frightened by her cry, Neddy withdrew from her instantly.

"No—no," she whispered. "It a mi first time."

"Mi too," he whispered back.

It seemed hours, minutes, seconds, no time at all. Across from them the child whimpered and fussed, but they did not hear it. He wished it would end and not end, and then it did, with great gulps of air. They stayed like that until Neddy fell into a dreamless sleep.

A splotch of sunlight crept over the floor to wake him. Neddy sat up and looked around. Bekah and the child were gone. Quickly he pulled on his pants, which reminded him of what had gone by. For a second he felt embarrassed, then he smiled at the great pleasure it

The Battle

had been. He felt somehow there should be a change, but looking at himself he found nothing new to identify, at least on the surface.

Anxiety took over as he rushed outside, expecting to see the donkey gone. No, it was still there, pulling at what grass it could find within its tethered reach. Then he saw them. Bekah was washing Miss Awa with a bucket full of water. She looked up and smiled.

"You wake up? Bout time. We been up before di sun. Lard! You men get a little work, den you sleep night to night hif we women don't push you."

She was getting at him again, but he had learned it was better not to take her on directly. "Where you get dat?" He pointed at the bucket of water.

"Down di hill."

"Anybody see you?"

"What you tink?" She gave him a patronizing look.

He ignored it. "All right, den. We better not waste time because we going back now."

"Going back where? Hif it is Lapland you is referring to, you can go, Massa. Mi and Miss Awa going to Montego Bay dis ya day." Her eyes did not waver from his. "*Dat is what I know.*" She stood staring directly at him, holding the little girl firmly by the hand. Neddy stared back, not really knowing what to say or do with this stubborn gal. Bekah could see his dilemma and attempted to solve it for him with half an invitation.

"You can come wid us, or you can go back. You do what you want."

He had promised to bring her back, or at the very least protect her. Neddy stared back, contemplating making a swift grab and tying her up. Then he thought about strapping her to the donkey and leading it back. But he realized that was not very practical. With Bekah, it would not be a good idea at all. In the first place, he doubted he could get the better of her to that extent. She was much stronger than the little slip of a girl she looked. Their recent close contact had taught him that, at least. Without realizing it, he drifted off into that safe, wonderful never-never land of reverie. Her voice brought him back to the here and now.

"What you a dream bout?" He hadn't even noticed her approach.

"Mi don know," he lied. "Mi tink it would be nice to stay here." He threw that out nonchalantly.

She looked left and right and then back at him. "Di moon and old Patu mus a tek you mind last night."

"All right, all right, we a go," Neddy snapped.

He would be diplomatic: go with her and explain to the captain later. Galloway seemed far less fearsome than she, standing her ground in the morning light. "You win. We go to di Bay," he said, and watched the tenseness go out of her shoulders as she relaxed her hold on Miss Awa. Under the present circumstances, at least in Montego Bay, if they got there, she and her charge would be safer than at Lapland.

"Mi soon come back." Neddy pointed to the woods he had walked through the night before with the old man. "I going have a look down di hill, see what going on." She nodded agreement. "I will get di donkey ready den."

Neddy returned about ten minutes later. With Miss Awa safely stowed in the hamper, her head peeking out over the rim, Bekah stood by the donkey waiting. "See any ting?" she said.

"All di way to Falmouth," he joked.

"Hif yu see dat far, di Patu really bless you," she said, grinning. "Stop yu foolishness. What you see?" She was very serious.

"Mi don't like it. Men a wander all bout. If unu look closely, dem is wandering bout in di bush, in and out of di fields, along the road all di way down to Long Lane by Reading." Neddy could see from her expression that she did not like the report, either.

"Any road we can tek to get aroun dem?"

"No way mi know."

"What we going do?" she said. For the first time, she seemed lost and willing to rely on Neddy's judgment.

"Stay here?" Neddy said, grinning at her.

She stamped her foot. "Yu a joke too much, yu know?"

He laughed at her. "Di best ting," he said, "is for us to just walk down di road, like if we a go a market."

The Battle

It was simple, too simple. Bekah looked at him as if he had gone mad.

"Di moon really tek yu." She didn't finish what she had begun but scowled in deep thought and pointed her finger like a pistol at him. "Yu not so fool-fool as yu look after all. We going do dat. See what we can tek from here and put in di other hamper."

"But dey belong to Missa Simit!" Neddy protested.

"We can give im back later," she said, as she went inside the hut. A minute later she emerged with the copper kettle and pot. Neddy, in turn, went over and dug up a yam hill. Within a few minutes they had gathered enough provisions to convince anyone they were taking advantage of the chaos to make money. It was soon packed in one hamper, with the lighter stuff piled in such a way around the little girl in the other hamper, to hide her, should anyone poke in there. It took some wheedling from Bekah to get her to accept the cramped space and many a warning to keep very still if somebody came up to them. Bekah made sure her pistol was packed close to where she could reach it.

"Yu load it good?" she said, to make sure.

Neddy sighed and rolled his eyes.

Bekah shrugged her shoulders, mounted the big jack donkey, and settled down for the road to Montego Bay.

They had come off the hill and gone about a mile on the road without too much bother. Another couple with their donkey passed them, going in the opposite direction. From the bulge and weight of their hampers, Neddy guessed they contained goods that had belonged to others not long before. The greeted each other, bantered, and passed on. Other travelers passed on by. The males seemed glum, hanging aimlessly about, uncertain where to go and what to do. There were no white men about to give them direction. The countryside was theirs, and they were lost in it.

They began to relax. Long Lane was not that far off. Bekah imagined she could smell the sea air when, on rounding a corner, they came upon a bunch of men sitting by the roadside. Neddy saw two rum jugs by their feet and knew they had been drinking even at this early hour. His heart began to beat faster, for he knew Bekah and he would be put upon if the men were given half a chance. Instead of sea air, it was the stink of raw tobacco, jackass rope, that he smelled from a pipe stuck in the eldest's mouth. That was the one to watch. As they began to pass the group, he could see the man's bloodshot eyes following them. He wished he had the pistol. If he gave Bekah the order to fire at him, he would rush the others with the stick, and surprise would win the day, he reckoned.

It was a young one he had paid no attention to who forestalled his tactical move.

"Lard Gad! She pretty, eh? She prettier dan im!" exclaimed the young man, who could not have been twenty years. He began to fondle himself suggestively, which brought belly laughs and side-slapping from his mates.

"Mi wants er for mi prize, yes, sah!" He began to get up but sat right back down, too drunk to stand. That was Neddy's cue.

"Yu can av er, hif yu tink you is bad. She a mi sista, an mi dying to get rid of er." That brought more laughter, even to the dangerous face of the pipe smoker.

"Mi want er, man," the young one said. "She a sweet likkle gal, and mi can sweet er."

Neddy threw in a snigger. "Tek er den." His thumb jerked in Bekah's direction at the same time he kept on walking. He got the donkey half-jogging as they got alongside the men.

"One man tink im bad and try tek er. We bury im yesterday," Neddy sniggered again. He looked at the would-be suitor. "Yu too young to die. But hif you tink yu is bad an wan get you back brok, come tek her, na."

Adding emphasis to the warning, Bekah cut her eye at the man and tossed her head defiantly.

"Don't go near dat one, Sam," another one said. "She would a pop you in two soon as look at yu." The group laughed, and Neddy got the donkey jogging with a good slap on its hindquarters and jogged alongside. Bekah's admirer broke away from his fellows and staggered a few steps forward. Bekah kicked the donkey's sides, and the man stopped and waved drunkenly as if to say, *Go on yu way, mi can't be boddered.*

The Battle

Not far from the knot of men, Neddy said, breathing hard, "Yu can slow down, now. Let mi ketch mi breath." Bekah obliged, and they dropped to a comfortable walk.

They passed a half-mile in silence before she said, "Hum!"

A long pause followed.

Neddy waited, a feeling of apprehension hovering around the pit of his stomach. What would she come out with this time?

"How come las night mi like a wife, and today mi a yu sister?"

He knew better than answer her. His head bowed, his eyes watched the ground pass beneath his feet.

"Hum!" she said again.

Another pause followed.

"Boye!" she said, and another pause followed before finally she said, "A gal can't trus any man, can she? Dem tek advantage of yu an cast yu away."

Neddy began to feel the size of an ant. He hadn't meant to hurt her. He had only been trying to protect all of them.

He turned to her, his face contrite, ready to make his apology, when she let out a merry laugh.

Relief, and another wave of exasperation, broke over him.

Miss Awa's head popped up from the hamper basket. The little girl wanted something to drink. They stopped for a minute so Bekah could give her a few sips of water from a bottle she'd packed. When she was finished, Bekah cleaned the girl's face with a wet rag.

"Bekah, can I come out now an ride with you?" Miss Awa whined.

Bekah looked into the woods and up and down the road. "Soon, mi little darling. We not safe yet."

"The men won't hurt me, Bekah," Miss Awa said with spirit.

"We no trus dem till we are safe in Montego Bay, Miss Awa." She looked dead in Neddy's direction. "We woman can't trus any man. No sah, Miss Awa, no man can we trus." She threw her head back with a dry laugh. But something in her teasing and laughter didn't ring true. She was apprehensive.

"It won't be too long now, Miss Awa," Bekah said. "Mi can see Bogue Island, now. We will soon be down on the coast."

535

When Conchie Blows

Just as they started down Long Lane to go by Reading to the coast road, they spotted people hauling big rocks and trees to block the way.

"Miss Awa," Bekah whispered. "Keep very still now, yu hear? We passing some bad people. When we get pass dem, yu can come out." She had only just said that when someone called her name. Bekah looked up to see a young man about eighteen detach himself from a group piling stones to block the road against the expected soldiers. He approached them and grabbed the donkey's bridle to stop it.

"Where yu a go?" he said, smiling. But his smile faded when he noticed her companion. He looked back at her with the hungry longing that haunted youth.

"Where yu a go?" he said again. "An who dis?" he pointed at Neddy with a machete. Then he moved to look in the hampers.

Bekah lashed his hand with the switch she used on the donkey, "Why yu so nosy, Alfy?" she demanded. He drew back in pain. She then resettled herself on the donkey making sure that the folds of her skirt covered the hampers as much as possible. "Hif yu must know, his a few tings for me auntie in Montego Bay."

"Where you get dem?" he asked, an all-knowing smile spreading across his face.

"Dem trow dem wey in Lapland," she reassured him. "His me save dem. Dem doesn't want dem, but mi old auntie can use dem." Her patois had broadened to make this field hand feel more comfortable as he reached above his station to a house slave.

He let out a howl of laughter at her cleverness. She tried to guide the donkey on, but he held the bridle firmly. Neddy, watching, was considering cracking him with the trusty stick, but that was impossible, with so many watching. They would swarm him if he tried to get rough.

The young man turned and stared at Neddy, his laughter gone. His serious frown with narrowed eyes spoiled his pleasant features. "Is who dis den?" he said.

"What yu talk bout, Alfy?" Bekah said suggestively. "Yu jealous?" The boy looked at her, wide-eyed. He had never dared to think she

THE BATTLE

had noticed him gazing moon-struck at her. "Yu know is mi cousin from Kensington. Is im bun down di place."

Alfy released a silent but obvious sigh of relief, then laughed and slapped Neddy on the back.

"We can't waste time chatting all day wid yu, Alfy." Taking advantage of his relaxed posture, she ordered, "Giddy-up dey, donkey," and they were off again, with the youth looking after them. Out of earshot, Neddy growled, "Who dat?"

Bekah smiled to hear the heavy rasp of jealousy in the question, which she did not answer, pretending to be occupied getting Miss Awa into the fresh air.

They encountered no more trouble on Long Lane. A few of the rebels looked at them, and a few more good-humored comments were passed. Neddy guaranteed them all, "Freedom come!" with both hands raised to the heavens.

They passed Reading and reached the coast road; five more miles to go to the outskirts of Montego Bay.

Miss Awa, now released from her hiding place, sat in her nurse's lap on the donkey. The breeze from the sea brought a freshness for which all three were thankful. But just at the border of Fairfield estate, they were brought to a halt by a military picket.

A private advanced in their direction with a musket at his hip, its bayonet fixed. Neddy stopped and held on to the donkey's halter. He saw others with guns pointing in their direction from behind the wall. It would be stupid to take a chance here. Captain Galloway was too far away to come to their rescue. He stood still beside the head of the donkey, holding it firmly.

"Where are you going?" demanded the soldier. He had not noticed the little white girl being held by her nurse.

"We tek di chile to Montego Bay," Neddy said.

"What child?" Then looked up at Bekah. "Dat is a white child! What are you doing with her?" The soldier moved forward for a closer look and then shouted over his shoulder, "Sergeant, they have a white child ere!"

As he moved toward them, Bekah backed the donkey up. "Don't come ya," she snapped. Neddy was surprised to see that this stopped

537

the soldier. Before the situation could get away from them again, Neddy said, "We tek her to the Presbyterian Church in Montego Bay, where she will be looked after." Then he thought of a way to impress the soldier, "Captain Galloway sen us." That brought the soldier around to face him.

"You have proof of that, boy?" the soldier said. "Seargent, dis here slave says he has the permission of Captain Galloway."

"I am not a slave," Neddy snapped indignantly at the private.

That caught the man up. He scowled at him. "Then what are you, boy?"

"A free man," declared Neddy with dignity.

There was a howl of laughter from the soldier that was cut short when his superior shouted at him from behind the wall,

"Barker, what are you laughing at?"

"This here Negro says he is a free man, Sergeant."

"Well, that could be. Check him, man. Get on with your duty, or march him over here, and I will check to see where he comes from—our side or the rebel side."

Neddy pulled out his pass and handed it to the soldier.

"What is this?" he asked looking at it with suspicion.

"Captain Galloway give me di pass."

The man turned it over twice, stared at the writing, but did not move one way or the other. "Sergeant," he called.

"Yes, Barker, what is it now?"

"He says he has a pass, Sergeant."

"Well, does he?"

"Can't tell, Sergeant."

"Read it, man," ordered the sergeant, exasperated.

"Can't do that, Sergeant."

"Why not?'

"Can't read, Sergeant."

"Can't read! Can't *read*! Any Scotsman can read," the Sergeant said.

"I ain't no bloody Scotsman, Sergeant," the private replied indignantly.

"Where are you from, Baker?"

"Bristol, Sergeant."

"A Bristol man should be able to read as good as any Scotsman, Baker." By the time he had finished the sentence, the sergeant was alongside them and snatched the pass from the Baker's hand. It took him a minute or two to let his eyes focus. Neddy could see his lips moving slowly as he mouthed the written words on the paper. He understood by this that the sergeant could castigate his subordinate all he wanted, but he himself was not too well acquainted with writing.

When the sergeant was satisfied that all the words made sense, he announced proudly, "All seems to be in order. Move on, son." He waved Neddy and Bekah on toward Montego Bay.

Well out of earshot, Neddy said, "Lucky the captain give me di pass. It could have been bad for us."

"Hum!" Bekah said, and nothing more.

The picket was not long out of sight when a pair of gunshots rang behind them. Neddy looked at Bekah, whose eyes stayed fixed straight ahead. Someone else, perhaps, had not be so lucky. Neddy slapped the donkey's side to quicken their pace.

At last, their odyssey ended. They entered Montego Bay; they walked down Church Street to East Street and found the Church of Scotland. They tied the donkey and went inside. Bekah placed Miss Awa on the altar of the kirk and ran across to the manse to fetch the minister.

"Me lef her dere, sah, because her grandfather is Mr Graham and in time of danger Scottish kirk mus give her refuge, sah,' Bekah parrotted an obviously well-rehearsed line to the Rev Mr Robert Bruce.

"Graham of Claverhouse, eh? Well true enough, true enough. The wee lassie is welcome here." He beckoned to his wife. "Sarah, you have charge from now on.

Bekah and Neddy faced each other outside on the steps of the church.

"Tek di donkey back to Lapland and leave it dere. It belong to dem," instructed Bekah. Even if it was going to be slow, Neddy thought, at least he did not have to walk. On the way he would stop and see how Watt was doing—if he was still alive.

"Come here," Bekah said. Neddy obeyed, and she put her arms around his body and pulled him to her, kissing him full on the lips. A second must have passed, perhaps two before Neddy responded.

Passersby thought their display of affection in public vulgar. Especially on the church steps! But, they likely thought, Negroes knew no better.

Their kiss ended as quickly as it began when Bekah pushed him away.

"That was for all the help you give us," she said.

"Bekah—" Neddy said.

"Miss Rebekah to you, boye," she said. She gave a little laugh, then did those dance steps she had done the first time they met, turned, and scampered up the steps without looking back. As she entered the door, she heard her charge's small voice say, "Mi see you biting the boye and him biting you back. Mi going tell Nanna." Bekah picked her up, giving the little girl a big nuzzling and kiss on the cheek. She responded with shrieks of joy. Holding the child in her arms, Bekah walked up to the altar, where she quietly thanked the Lord for their safe deliverance.

Neddy turned the other way down Church Street, leading the donkey, heading for Charles Square to St. James Street. On the corner he checked the pack saddle holding the hampers. When the saddle was ready, he mounted and headed out into the country once more. He had no regrets, no longings. Strangely, his heart had given way to his head. Bekah was too much like his mam. He would always be "boye" to her, never a man. Both women needed to know he was no longer a boy.

Chapter 18

Deliverance

Bacchus had finished his carnage, which he celebrated with gusto. The huge, fat, ugly slave hanged all who had to be hanged, as ordered by Captain Gordon and the Courts Martial.

"Swing him," Gordon said coldly, without looking up from where he sat on the judge's bench. There was no need for him to look; he condemned on suspicion of taking part in the insurrection.

"Found where?" he would ask.

"In di bush, sah."

"Armed, was he?"

"Well, im av—"

"I asked if he was armed?" the captain said.

"Im av a hoe, Massa."

"Then he was armed."

It was enough. The black face of Bacchus glowed with the task. As their bodies jumped, jerked, and twitched, strangling at the end of his rope, their spirits on the way to heaven or hell—he did not care, for it gave him pleasure to send them on their journey—as he watched the death agony, a fat red tongue would moisten thick red lips, causing saliva to drool down a black chin. From the marketplace in Salter's Hill to Montego Bay, Bacchus hanged the condemned, cut them down, and hanged more in their place. It was the task he had waited for all his slave life, and he wished it no end. But it had to end; for owners were growing restless, watching their property turned into meat for John Crow.

Even the whistling sound of the flaying whip through the air to its final crack upon the flesh had fallen silent. Those who had survived its five hundred lashes now waited, condemned to the hulks offshore Portsmouth or in the Thames—where they would rot, until the end came and, with it, final deliverance. A few lucky ones, along with other miscreants from England, were to be transported to the prison colony of New South Wales, where what was left of their strong backs was needed to tame that unruly land.

The Baptist and Moravian preachers who had been clapped up and treated roughly, as the perpetrators of the holocaust, had been freed, mostly because of their color and influence, rather than their innocence in the destruction. Many planters thought they should have been made to pay dearly, especially since they themselves had paid so much, as evidenced by the blackened walls of burned estates and houses—and, after Bacchus, the remains of their human property flung unceremoniously into mass graves on the edge of town. More than a few of these proprietors would gladly have watched Bacchus do his work on these missionaries and seen their remains thrown in with their following. The stench of decomposing corpses would have been made that much sweeter.

Even the great Baptist protégé, Daddy Sharpe, the man they blamed for it all, had gone to his maker as he wished. "Better that than live a slave," he had said, and they accommodated him. However, his owner had taken pity and buried him with dignity.

Yet, those who remained did not realize that their time, too, had passed, that all that remained of it were the blackened ruins across the landscape. Slavery was over, although it would take a few more years for it to be officially expunged— and centuries to be purged from the soul of the people.

* * *

Deliverance

Driving the trap, Captain Galloway led the way with Miss Lucy and Tim beside him, while John drove the luggage wagon with Badalia stiffly upright beside him on the bench. The party moved slowly away from Miss Hannah Cope's school. Her nephew waved good-bye from the back of the cart, where he sat with his feet dangling over the backboard. Neddy sat beside him. Miss Hannah waved and wiped her eyes with a large handkerchief, while the little boy who followed her everywhere hung to her dress, half hidden, his little hand imitating the waving of the grownups. Watt waved back at him with his one arm and called, "Good-bye, David." And the child waved more enthusiastically at the sound of his name.

Watt's short stay at his aunt's place had given him an insight into the ways of the island, and he had realized that the boy was his relative. Crossing of stock, so to speak, was a daily occurrence, familiar in the land. Looking at how the boy's aspect favored his aunt, it became obvious he had a brown family member, and that was all right with him. It was a pity, though, now that his dreams of becoming a rich planter had come to ruin, that he would not be able to watch the child grow. Perhaps they would never meet again. If they ever did, it would not be in this island; there was certainty in that. For a moment, he wondered what his father and his uncle would have thought of their new nephew. His father would have accepted him; his uncle, too, after a few choice words. It would not have been the child's color that would have worried his father but the unmarried state of his sister. He would have taken to David and relished the task of teaching him, as he had taught his own son. He was quite a little devil, young David, with an adventurous spirit that would have captivated those in England, had they been fortunate enough to know him. He would have made them a good companion in their aging.

As little David fell out of sight, Watt looked to Neddy sitting beside him and felt a great sadness. More than everyone else, he would miss Neddy. Apart from rescuing him at every opportunity, Neddy had been at his sickbed, even with the burden of new responsibilities since his father's death. On occasion he had spooned some of Mrs. Waldrich's broth into his mouth after she had bustled into room, bearing a tray with steaming bowls for both of them, along with great slices of bread slathered with piles of freshly churned butter.

The cart rumbled over the cobblestones and headed down the hill from the school along Union Street. At East Street, they turned left and passed the Baptist and Presbyterian churches, then right onto Church Street toward the Parish Church. As the cart rounded the corner, Neddy could not help but look back at the steps in front of the kirk and remember the last time he was there. It seemed years had passed since Bekah had teased him and done her little dance. Since then, he had neither seen her nor heard what had happened to her and Miss Awa. Well, they were not dead, for that he would have heard. More than once he had thought of trying to see her, but each time, second thoughts stayed his effort. One day, perhaps, he would try again. She was such a puzzle.

As they turned through the church gates into the yard, Dr. Robertson and the Reverend Newcombe were waiting at the vestry door.

It was a fine day. The boys, bouncing along on the back of the cart, could see white clouds scudding across the sky and feel the sea breeze blowing up from the harbor through Charles Square to Church Street and across the yard. The air would enter the church through the open door to refresh the wedding party as the Reverend D'Arcy Newcombe asked the questions that tied male to female "till death do them part."

Watt leaned over to Neddy and whispered, "Have you been to one of these weddings before?"

"Yu forget, man, I play mi flute in mi church. Dis is notting new," Neddy said, putting Watt firmly back in his place.

"Better than funerals, don't you think?" whispered Watt, not giving him an inch.

"Mi don't know, yu know. Jamaicans love dere funerals. Some of dem better dan weddings. We always got funerals, but we don't always have weddings," explained Neddy, continuing in his role as mentor. "Boye! When dem dead, dem can trow party, yu see! Go on for tree days."

Watt gave him a quizzical look.

Deliverance

"It's true!" insisted Neddy.

Sitting up front, Badalia looked back and gave them a scowl just before the arrival of Reverend Newcombe. Neddy looked about the Parish Church and was impressed by its size and all the marble plaques and statues on its walls and in niches commemorating the dead of prominent families. At the rear, curved mahogany stairs climbed to the highly polished gallery, where the choir sat and sang. This was a far grander church than his simple Irwin church, but it took him only a second to decide he liked his own church better. His seemed friendlier.

Captain Galloway stood and went forward. The congregation began to shuffle into place. Then Dr. Robertson came up the aisle with Miss Lucy on his arm. Dr. Robertson had the unique privilege that day of both giving the bride away and standing up as Galloway's best man.

Badalia held young Tim, and John stood beside her. When all were in place and all was quiet, the reverend called, "Let us pray."

At that moment, a small bird flew in through the open door and fluttered round and round the candelabra hanging from the huge cedar rafters, eventually settling on it with a gentle tinkling of the crystal baubles.

"A witness from God," the Reverend said, looking up at the bird, before launching into a short prayer. "Who giveth this woman," he began, and continued until rings passed from hand to hand, kisses were given, and Captain Matthew Conner Galloway and Lucy Waite were pronounced man and wife, let no man put asunder.

Afterward, they all repaired to the vestry to sign registers and to partake of refreshments that D'Arcy Newcombe had put on for his friends.

After toasting the bride and wishing both long life and happiness, they all settled automatically into their natural knot of companions: Badalia with John at the back of the room; Miss Lucy, sitting with young Tim; Neddy with Watt, where the food was to be had; and the three gentlemen together, glasses in hand.

"As I said already, I am very sorry to see you leave, Conner. You are one of the few civilized people in this place."

"That is why I am taking myself out of here. You know, D'Arcy, you must be the only person in the world, except my sainted mother, who calls me *Conner*. Everyone else calls me *Matthew*. Why is that?"

The Reverend Newcombe looked puzzled and scratched his chin with a long forefinger while still holding onto his prayer book. "I don't know. Perhaps Conner suits you more than a saint's name," he said, laughing. "Yes, yes, that must be it. You are closer to the devil than God, but today you took a step in the right direction for your salvation. I am happy for you, Matthew." They both laughed, then Reverend Newcombe let his head fall back and looked into the sky, as if expecting to see some answer there. When none was apparent, he broke the silence.

"You will be sorely missed, you know, Conner." He paused again and then went on, "Those damned Baptists set all this off—an unholy conflagration. I can't believe this is how God wanted freedom to be forwarded. Death and destruction are never his will for man."

"You should be glad it was them, D'Arcy, and not some other," Galloway said, smiling at his friend.

"What do you mean, man?"

"If it had been a L'Ouverture, a Christophe, or, God help us, a Dessalines, instead of Brother Sharpe trained by the Baptists, it is doubtful we would be here having this conversation." Galloway patted his friend on the back. "Every day you pray, you should thank God for the Baptists, D'Arcy. As a matter of fact, the Church of England should write a special prayer for the Baptists and read it at every Sunday service." Galloway chuckled at the look he got in return from his friend.

"No hope of that, eh, D'Arcy?"

"I agree with Galloway, there," the doctor said. "It would have been much worse for us if just one of those were in command of our slaves."

"Robertson, after this, are you going to stay here?" Galloway said.

"Come on, Galloway, where else am I to go? Scotland? Never again. There is nothing there for a Scotsman, you know? Sassenachs, like Newcombe here, have taken it all. Jamaica, or where you are going, is all that is left for us, the dispossessed," he said, as dramatically as if he were on a stage.

"I suppose you are right, Robertson," Galloway said.

"They will still need doctors here. I will stay behind and try and salvage what I can from my place. If I cannot, then I may join you in Nova Scotia, man."

"Oh! I am not going there."

"Where then?"

"Upper Canada, they call it, and to the canal they have built or are building. They need military men. I will activate my old commission. So they have promised me."

"How far is that from Nova Scotia?" the parson asked.

"The other end of *quel ques arpents de neige*. Miles and miles and miles, D'Arcy."

"What do you mean by that?" the Reverend asked. "You are always speaking in riddles."

"Tongues, D'Arcy, tongues. You should read more. That is how Voltaire described the country after Wolf took it."

The refreshments over, they drifted outside. It was time to go. The ship was to sail with the offshore winds that afternoon. She was loaded with what had survived the destruction, and her captain hoped to make a swift passage north and sell his cargo at a good price. Prices had been rising with the disruption of shipments of rum and sugar from the Jamaican north coast.

"Once again, I will miss you, Conner. I will miss you greatly," Newcombe said. "I am honored that you asked me to perform the ceremony."

"Who else? One church is as good as another, D'Arcy. One day you will find that out. Besides, Lucy is one of your flock. You remember—you christened the boy, too."

They shook hands for the last time, and Galloway climbed onto the driver's seat of the big trap. Lucy sat beside him, with Badalia and the child behind them this time. After the trap came the wagon with their luggage boxes. John drove, and Neddy, with Watt beside him, sat by the tailgate. With a crack of the whip, they lumbered down Church Street for the seafront.

When Conchie Blows

The two boys did not speak. Both knew this would be the last time that they would be together. Watt's Aunt Hannah had decided that somewhere other than Jamaica would be better for him. Even her friend, Mr. Fray, had been most accommodating on that point. All were in agreement. Watt felt that Mr. Fray, in a roundabout way, thanked him for getting rid of Bardolf—although Mr. Fray had said nothing on that point. How else could Watt explain the small bonus he had not earned, which Mr. Fray had given him?

When the captain offered to take him to Upper Canada and seek a placement for him there, Hannah Cope gladly accepted on her nephew's behalf. It was a godsend. She could have wanted nothing better for him, and she was sure her brother would have approved. After all, his silly teachings got his son into trouble in the first place, thought the schoolmistress. Now, the final day had come. They were on their way to the harbor to embark for Nova Scotia.

They had passed through Charles Square, where the gibbets still stood as a stark reminder, but no bodies hung from them. Captain Galloway led the trap across the Strand behind the courthouse, heading to the harbor and Parish wharf, when, from the right of the street, came an unexpected and unwelcome shout.

"Galloway! Where are you taking that little nigger wench you cheated me out of at cards?" Anger mounting in his face, Galloway looked over at the man. Lucy put her hand on his arm as if to say *It does not matter*, but she felt his arm trembling through his coat sleeve. "I hear you married the little bitch. Yes, Galloway, news travels fast around the Bay. Here in Jamaica, we don't marry tar-brushed wenches, no matter how lightly tarred they are, you know? We just use them—unless they are rich." He spat a half-smoked cigar onto the ground and moved toward them.

Doctor Waite stood in front of the cart, caught the reins, and stopped them dead in the middle of the street. For a fat man, he moved with much agility. Galloway tried to move the horse back. Waite hung firm. John, not paying much attention to what was happening in front of him, drove the cart alongside the trap, blocking the road completely. When he realized what he had done, he stopped the cart to apologize. Before he could utter a word, Galloway leaned

Deliverance

over and grabbed the cart whip from the bench where John sat. He unfurled it to full length, snaked it through the air, and brought the lash down expertly onto Waite's head. The doctor reeled backward. The horses shied, Galloway's hand quickly bringing the pair under control.

"What the hell!" the doctor said, staggering.

A second blow of the plaited cowhide struck and wrapped around his face two, three, four times, like the coils of a constrictor. Then Galloway jerked the whip back, as if spinning a top. The doctor's ear and a piece of his cheek tore away as he twisted with the whip's action. Blood and saliva spattered the ground, and his scream could be heard across Charles Square. He was lucky his neck was not broken.

Lucy sat stiff with fright, in the recesses of her mind hearing her own screams again, when he on the ground had forced his body into hers. She had screamed, frightened and in pain from his thrusting and ever-tightening grip on her breasts. The more she screamed the more excited he had become, until, at last, his rage ended. When she continued to sob on the bed beside him, he slapped her and shouted at her to be silent. She could not stop. Enraged by her sobbing, the doctor dragged her outside and nailed her by the ear to the doorpost. The next morning they found her fainted in a pool of blood on the ground, with half her ear stuck to the doorpost. That night with that foul thing now writhing on the ground in front of her was burned forever into her mind. It was her Jamaican legacy. With one arm around Timothy, she held her child tightly against her breasts to shield him from the sight. As she watched, she wished Galloway would stop, and yet wished him to continue at the same time.

People were in the street, pleading with Galloway to stop. A man approached the cart and shouted, "You can't beat a white man!" To his horror he learned that some white men *did* beat white men, as he reeled away, gasping, to nurse his own wound from Galloway's lash.

That seemed to enrage Galloway even more. He continued to count as each lash cut into the now unconscious Waite on the ground. It was Lucy who stayed his hand.

"That is slaves' punishment, and those who inflict it should also feel it. No man insults my wife and gets away with it!" he shouted at the crowd watching.

With that, he dropped the whip to the ground.

"Come on, John, let us go," he said, walking the horse on. But the cart did not follow. He stopped and looked back. "What is the matter?" he said, the anger still heard in his voice. Then he saw Neddy standing by the cart, looking at the unconscious Waite in the gutter. He was shaking, unable to comprehend more horror. Watt was trying to persuade him to get back into the cart.

"Come, boy," Galloway called to him in a calmer voice. "It will be all right. Evil deserves evil. That is all you have seen here." Neddy looked up at him and then climbed back onto the tail of the wagon to sit beside his friend. They moved on and watched as bystanders carried Waite toward a house on the side of the street.

"Reverend Waldrich always say, 'Revenge is mine, sayeth the Lord, let no man take it,'" muttered Neddy. However, as they bumped along, he had an uneasy feeling that the Lord had just taken his revenge.

Time had come for final good-byes. The ship rocked and swayed, and the rigging squealed with the offshore wind building to push her out to sea. Neddy's stomach felt each roll, each pitch, each toss of the ship. Watt stood in front of him, for once unable to speak. His blue-blue eyes filled with eye water as he looked for the last time on his one true friend. Finally he blurted out, "Come with us, I beg you." His eyes pleaded above the half-open mouth, an expectant cry of joy just waiting to come out if Neddy accepted his appeal.

Neddy smiled and shook his head. "Who would look after mi modder? Mi can't go. Beside, Jamaica his fi mi country. What mi going do up dey?" His eyes filled too, to the brim. One tear from the left eye and then another from the right raced each other down his cheeks. The back of his hand came up to wipe them away. Watt rushed forward and threw his one arm around him desperately trying to give one last bear hug, but it wasn't the same. Neddy laughed, and it was he who put both his arms around Watt and tugged him close.

Deliverance

He thought of paying him back for all the pain and suffering Watt had inflicted with his hugs, but didn't. He was still too frail from the loss of his arm. Neddy could tell this from the one-armed hug he gave. There was no strength to it.

When they parted, Neddy said, "What Watt going to do?"

Straightaway he got his answer: "Become a one-armed Nelson and fight Frenchies, what else?" Watt said, with a not too convincing grin.

"Good," said Neddy, "But you got both eye. You can do better dan him did. "

"I will try, my true and trusted Pancho. Oh, how I do…" Watt trailed off there. There was nothing more to say.

Neddy nodded.

"I got something for you to remember me by," Neddy said.

"I do not need anything to remember you by. I have you here, and here." Watt pointed to his head and chest.

Neddy took from his belt the flute he always carried there. "It for you. Maybe yu can learn to play it one-handed."

"I can't take this!" Watt said.

"Yes, you can. It all I got to give to bring you luck and keep you steady, Watt," Neddy said.

Watt did not answer; he couldn't. He held the bamboo flute tightly and pressed it to his chest.

"I got to go. Di boatman waiting." Neddy nodded again and walked to the side of the ship. Galloway was there.

"God keep you an Miss Lucy, sah," he said.

"And he you, Neddy. May you always play the flute for life."

"Yes, sah. I will do that."

"How you going to do that? You just gave it away," said Galloway with a smile.

"Mi will mek anoder one, sah; dis time from rosewood. You forget, mi is now a carpenter, sah."

"Good luck, boy."

Galloway patted him on the back as the boy threw his leg over the rail. Neddy went over the side and down the rope ladder like an expert before Galloway could say more. As the lighter pulled away

551

from the Northern Lady, he stood unsteadily, looking at Watt, who stood by the railing unmoved. Just as they reached the shore, Watt's right arm waved his last farewell.

Neddy took over the trap to follow John in the cart. He looked out at the Northern Lady. Sailors were in the rigging, and sails dropped down and began to billow. Watt still stood at the railings. Neddy stood up in the trap and waved his hat back and forth and was delighted to see the answering signal from the rail. The ship tacked with the wind, her stern coming round to Montego Bay as she headed out to sea.

Afterword

"When Conchi Blows" takes place during the so-called "Baptist War", the last slave rebellion in the British colony of Jamaica. Enslaved Africans blew the conchi or conch shell, as well as the abeng or cow horn, as a signal. Sam Sharpe, a Baptist deacon and a slave, led the uprising over the Christmas/New Year period of 1831-32. It was brutally put down by the authorities, but slavery only survived another two years until August 1, 1834.

Jamaican society in the early nineteenth century had slavery as its bedrock, and was divided along color and racial lines. But it was rife with ambiguities. Although most blacks were enslaved and most whites were free, many blacks were free and several whites were not. There were strict laws about black and mixed race people owning and inheriting property. People were classified as mulatto, quadroon, octoroon and mustee according to the amount of "white blood" they had. In practice, these categories were ignored or conflated, and the laws were flouted with wealthy land owners deciding that they had the right to leave their property to their children as they chose, regardless of color. Indeed, most people privately surmised that anyone claiming to be white in Jamaica probably had at least "a touch of the tarbrush".

Life was brutal and the most appalling abuses were unthinkingly carried out. Despite arguments that it was uneconomic to treat slaves badly, many slave owners treated slaves and those with less power in the society abominably, sometimes simply because they could, and sometimes because they felt that this would act as a deterrent to slave insurrections. History bears witness to the fact that this strategy clearly did not work.

"When Conchi Blows" relates the views and experiences of sixteen year old Neddy as he struggles to understand his place in this complex society, his new-found friendship with Watt Tyler-Cope, the dreamer and the equally complex relationship with the overseer Galloway, who takes young Neddy under his wing. Bekah, his first love also causes him to examine his concept of himself. Their intricate web of relationships demonstrate that in a slave society, no-one is entirely free, yet despite differences of age, status and race, strong bonds can be formed.

Emancipation may have come, but in many ways, twenty-first century Jamaica is as complex, ambiguous and violent as its nineteenth century predecessor. People still struggle with the privations of color, race, and class. A society founded in horror continues to be brutal. Trickery (Jinnalship), crime and cruelty continue to be commonplace, with the result that from an early age many are desensitized and made casual towards brutality.

Yet through all these difficulties Jamaicans still join together to dream into being a newer world.

Rachele Evelyn Vernon.Ph.D

Glossary

Jamaicans developed a common language so that Europeans and kidnapped Africans from many tribes could speak with each other. In 'When Conchi Blows' several people are fluent in both Patwa (Jamaican) and English and change from one to the other even in the same sentence.

Patwa speakers often pronounce 'th' as 'd' or 't', so words like 'there' and 'them' become 'dere' and 'dem', while 'thank' and 'think' become 'tank' and 'tink'. The 'h' sound may be added to an English word or left off, so 'happen' may become 'appen', but 'own' may become 'hown'.

There are several terms in 'When Conchi Blows' which may not be easily worked out. For instance there are several words referring to people of mixed race. Mulatto meant a person was half black and half white , a quadroon was one quarter black and three-quarters white, an octoroon or mustee was one eighths black and seven eighths white, while a mustifino was one sixteenth black and legally counted as white. A sambo, on the other hand usually had a mulatto parent and a black parent. Of course, none of this was in any way logical. How would one classify the child of a mustee and a sambo, for instance?

Black water fever, dengue, jiggers, yellow fever, lockjaw and yaws were all diseases found in nineteenth century Jamaica. Baldpate, chicken hawk, jabbering crow, John crow, pea-dove, pitcherie, ring-tail, white-belly and white-wing are Jamaican birds.

Robert Vernon

Other Terms
Aks: Ask
Annatto: Plant whose seeds are used for food colouring
Annie Palmer: Known as the White Witch of Rose Hall, Mrs Palmer was a white Jamaican proprietor who was widely believed to have dabbled in obeah and to have murdered three of her husbands.
Backra: White person. Sometimes used with Massa to emphasize their dominance
Batty: Buttocks
Bawl: Weep.
Bline: Blind.
Blood Clart: Blood cloth- Sanitary towel for feminine hygiene
Brawta: Extra given by a seller for luck
Bout: About.
Boye: Boy
Buck up:Meet
Bucky Massa: Same as Backra Massa.
Bud: Bird
Bungo: Extremely stupid, foolish person- Very derogatory & insulting.
Buss: Burst
Calaban: Bird trap
Chile: Child.
Conchi: The conch shell. This and the abeng or cow horn was used by Jamaicans to signal meetings and often revolts.
Dawg: Dog
Do-Do: Have bowel movement.
Don Quixote: Spanish character in Cervantes novel, famed for noble deeds
Duppy: Ghost, Spirit .

Glossary

Dut: Dirt.
Dutty: Dirty.
Fader: Father.
Facety: Impudent, rude, bold.
Fass: Meddlesome, Nosy.
Fi: For.
Freedom papers: A freed slave was given 'freedom papers'.
Fus: First.
Gad: God
Go a bush, Gone a bush: Have or had sexual intercourse
Gravalicious: Greedy
Jinnal: Underhanded, sneaky, tricky person
Jonkunnu: Christmas masquerade characters in African attire- often ghoulish.
Juk: To poke or stick.
Lard: Lord
Likkle: Little.
Loss: Lost
Massa: Master.
Mek: Make.
Mi: Me.
Mocho: A place in rural Jamaica seen as "the back of beyond" location- Backward person.
Modder: Mother.
Mussy: Mercy (Lard a mussy) Lord have mercy.
Mustee: Person reckoned to be one eighth black
Mulatto: Person reckoned to be half black and half white
Nah: Not
Naygar: Black person (Negro) – Derogatory term
Niggeritis: Laziness
Nyam: To eat voraciously.
Obeah: Witchcraft practiced in Jamaica.
Patu: Night owl, usually associated with duppies (ghosts)
Peenywally: Firefly
Pickney: Child.

Picaninny (Pickney) Gang: Group of slave children who worked on the plantation usually from the age of five or six.
Pum-Pum: Female genitalia.
Quadroon: Person reckoned to be one quarter black
Raatid: Expression of surprise.
Ratoon: New sugar-cane plant which grows from the stubble of the old crop
Rass: The buttocks.
Rolling calf: Type of spirit which makes the sound of a calf dragging along a chain.
Rosinante: Don Quixote's horse
Sah: Sir.
Sancho Panza: Don Quixote's squire
Sambo: Person reckoned to be the child of a mulatto parent and a black parent
Tief: Thief (Used as a verb-to steal)
Titty: Breast
Unu: You - Often interchanged with **Yu** and **You** in the same sentence.
Wat: What.
Watt Tyler: Leader of the Peasants' Revolt in England in 1381.
Wey: Away.
Wid: With.
Wotliss: Worthless, worse than no-good; extremely derogatory.
Yu: You.
Ya: Here.

Made in the USA
Charleston, SC
25 November 2014